# CULTURAL
## *Anthropology*

# CULTURAL
# *Anthropology*

## A Perspective on the Human Condition

**EMILY A. SCHULTZ**
**ROBERT H. LAVENDA**
**ROBERTA ROBIN DODS**

OXFORD
UNIVERSITY PRESS

# OXFORD
## UNIVERSITY PRESS

Oxford University Press is a department of the University of Oxford.
It furthers the University's objective of excellence in research, scholarship,
and education by publishing worldwide. Oxford is a registered trade mark of
Oxford University Press in the UK and in certain other countries.

Published in Canada by
Oxford University Press
8 Sampson Mews, Suite 204
Don Mills, Ontario, M3C 0H5 Canada

www.oupcanada.com

**Library and Archives Canada Cataloguing in Publication**

Schultz, Emily A. (Emily Ann), 1949–
Cultural anthropology : a perspective on the human condition / Emily A. Schultz,
Robert H. Lavenda & Roberta R. Dods.—2nd Canadian ed.

Includes bibliographical references and index.
ISBN 978-0-19-544278-6

1. Ethnology–Textbooks. 2. Ethnology–Canada–Textbooks.
I. Lavenda, Robert H. II. Dods, Roberta R. III. Title.

GN316.S38 2012          306          C2012-900066-3

Cover image: Masaaki Toyoura/Getty Images

This book is printed on permanent acid-free paper ∞
which contains 10% post-consumer waste.

Printed and bound in the United States of America.

2 3 4 — 15 14 13 12

# BRIEF CONTENTS

# CONTENTS

9

37

## Part II | The Resources of Culture   77

### 4 | Language   78

### 5 | Culture, the Individual, and Identity   97

### 6 | Social Relationships: Marriage, Family, Kinship, and Friendship   129

103

131

248

282

309

# MAPS

Dakhleh 9

Ju/'hoansi 142

Utkuhikhalingmiut 41

Bolivian Tin Miners 281

# FOREWORD ···············································································································

## Emily A. Schultz and Robert H. Lavenda

We are pleased to see the second Canadian edition of our *Cultural Anthropology: A Perspective on the Human Condition*. Roberta Dods has done a very fine job in adapting our book for Canadian students. While we wrote a book that has had success internationally, we recognize the advantages of tuning a book for a particular academic environment; the Canadian educational system is sufficiently different from that of the United States to justify differences in textbooks at the university level. But it is also the case that Canada has long had its own anthropological history and set of problematics, not reducible to the Anglo-American narrative that has dominated English-language anthropology.

Our original book aimed not only to show beginning anthropology students something of the varieties of human culture around the world, but also to draw their attention to the intensifying flows of people and culture from many parts of the world on unpredictable journeys, producing sometimes surprising encounters. When we began, we did not realize the journeys our book would take outside the United States, and even outside the English-speaking world, as translations allowed it to encounter audiences we never anticipated being able to address. The Canadian edition of our book has undergone a somewhat different kind of customization process, since it is still in English, but has, thanks to Roberta Dods, been more fully customized for Canadian readers, thus enriching our original efforts with a wealth of new ethnographic examples by a wide range of Canadian anthropologists. It is a pleasure to learn from our own book!

While we have taken an explicitly global perspective in the book, we recognize that what anthropology does best when it looks at the global is to concentrate on the local in order to grasp the effects of the global. So making our anthropology text more Canadian paradoxically makes it more global as well.

Dr Dods is correct in commenting that we take students seriously. We believe that when students are challenged, they rise to the challenge. Anthropology is a vibrant, challenging discipline, perhaps the earliest discipline to take the diversity of human culture seriously. We have tried to capture that in the text we wrote in a clear, straightforward, and uncluttered manner, and we are delighted that Dr Dods has also taken these same challenges seriously and has presented all of us with a successful hybrid text for a hybrid discipline!

# PREFACE TO THE CANADIAN EDITION ·······················

**Roberta Robin Dods**

This second Canadian edition of *Cultural Anthropology: A Perspective on the Human Condition* continues to situate students in a world view informed by a concern for social justice within a discussion of the discipline of anthropology, specifically cultural anthropology. In this edition, we have added a new chapter—Chapter 9—that focusses on the growing field of medical anthropology. Some chapters have been restructured to make room for this new material but, as with the first Canadian edition, we have preserved the conceptual integrity of previous editions. Additionally, we have retained the 14-chapter structure designed to fit with the semester system of most Canadian universities. Each chapter begins with an outline and a set of learning objectives and concludes with a list of key terms, a chapter summary, critical thinking questions, and lists of suggested readings and related websites. These framing materials challenge students to integrate learned concepts while providing them with a window to a wider world of inquiry.

In Chapter 1, we begin with a discussion of anthropology and its four traditional subfields—biological anthropology, archaeology, linguistic anthropology, and cultural anthropology—as well as what could effectively be considered its fifth subfield: applied anthropology. The theme of applied anthropology in its various forms echoes throughout this text. We continue with an introduction to cultural anthropology—its scope and its goals. Further, we explain the concept of culture and examine the recent critique of its use within a wider historical perspective, and we emerge with an understanding of the efficacy of a holistic approach to anthropological study. We also introduce the methodology of fieldwork and its resulting reportage—ethnography—and conclude with a discussion of ethnocentrism.

We examine ethnographic fieldwork in detail in Chapter 2, offering insight into forms of data collection, ways to prepare for 'the field', professional ethics, and culture shock. We also compare three principal modes of ethnographic research—positivist, reflexive, and multi-sited. Our explanation of the dialectic of fieldwork considers the roles people play when acting as an anthropologist's guide in the field, the effects of fieldwork on all involved, and the value and open-ended nature of anthropological knowledge.

Our focus in Chapter 3 is on colonialism, capitalism, and modernity. Viewing historical developments through a critical lens, we examine the rise of political economies and place anthropology as a 'player' in the colonial encounter. We then critique the development and use of various classification systems including the culture areas classifications that evolved in North America. In conclusion, we reflect on post-colonial realities as a counterpoint and a challenge.

In Chapter 4, our objective is to understand the theoretical and practical aspects of language and its use. Here, we discuss the relationship between language and culture and the importance of symbolic representation. We introduce some of Charles Hockett's design features of language, and we overview the components of language (phonology, morphology, syntax, semantics, pragmatics, and ethnopragmatics). We also consider linguistic inequality and areas of negotiated meaning exemplified by pidgin languages. The chapter concludes with a brief statement on the dialectic between experience and language and the creation of ambiguity in symbolic systems.

Beginning from the observation that every individual views the world from a unique position, we investigate the nature of identity and the individual in Chapter 5. First, we explore how individual psychology is situated in the context of a symbolic, cultural world and how cultural schemas and prototypes shape the ways we perceive our experiences. We then outline interpretations of intelligence, cognitive (learning) styles, reasoning, and logic. Next, we examine emotion as the product of the dialectic between bodily arousal and cognitive interpretation mediated by, and embedded within, a cultural matrix. In addition, we discuss ranges of sexual and gender identities and how those identities are culturally informed. Finally, we consider the self and how this 'entity' interprets the world and, specifically, how the self survives in the face of violence and trauma.

In Chapter 6, we analyze the complexities of human social relationships, focussing on different interpretations of marriage, family, kinship, and friendship. Throughout the chapter, we investigate what determines relatedness and group membership, with an awareness of the role of sex and gender in systems of social organization. We discuss marriage as a social process in the context of economic exchange and family alliance. As we explore the dimensions of family life, we outline various family structures and note how families change over time and in response to new global circumstances. We also compare kin-based versus non-kin-based societies and conclude with an appreciation for the nuances of the dimensions of group life.

Making a living is our central focus in Chapter 7. We begin with a consideration of subsistence strategies before moving on to discuss the relationship between production, distribution, and consumption. Additionally, we note the differences between internal (needs) and external (resources) explanations of consumption patterns. We also explore the cultural and symbolic nature of consumption and then elucidate distribution and exchange at local and global levels by examining various forms of exchange—from reciprocity to redistribution to market exchange.

In Chapter 8, we discuss play, art, myth, and ritual. We begin with play, which is an open system that allows us to communicate about communicating (metacommunication) and provides an entrée to meaningful reflexivity. From play, we move on to discuss first sport as embedded in the prevailing social order and then art as play that produces significant transformation-representation. We also explore the relationships between myths, as charters for social action and providers of stories of truth, and ritual, a culturally defined schema that brings text and performance together and that can function as a powerful form of metacommunication.

Chapter 9 focusses on an applied discipline that has been gaining attention in recent years: medical anthropology. While a chapter is not enough to cover all the diverse topics of study that medical anthropologists investigate, we discuss many themes at the heart of the discipline and offer examples of how researchers have applied these themes to real-world situations. We emphasize holism, particularly in our discussion of the impact of physical, social, and cultural environments on the well-being of individuals. We also consider various culturally informed approaches to health-care and ways of labelling and defining illness and disease. In addition, we revisit some ethical considerations as we explore the challenges involved in studying human health. Above all, we emphasize the importance of being open to traditional knowledge and non-Western ways of healing.

In Chapter 10, we consider the seemingly simple—yet actually very complex—subject of world view in the context of key metaphors. We explore the role of metaphor, metonymy, and symbolic thought and comment on the anthropological analysis of religion and secularism within the context of world view. As we come to understand world views as instruments of power, we also come to understand how key metaphors and world views are maintained and modified in a world of change.

We turn to social organization and patterns of human interdependence in Chapter 11, noting that no single cause can explain the complexities of human social relations. We consider the human power to act, various forms of social power, and explanations of why human beings submit to institutionalized power. As we investigate how humans invest the world with meaning, we also discuss how people bargain for reality as they negotiate the meaning of history and tradition.

In Chapter 12, we delve into social inequality and explore the multi-dimensional nature of inequality in terms of class, caste, race, and ethnic divisions. We begin by considering the implications of class-stratified societies and class mobility. Next, we present examples of caste, focussing in particular on how divisions of caste impact peoples' way of living in India. We then survey the discredited concept of race and its manifestation in today's world, keeping in mind the ethical implications that often arise when race is perceived as a social division. Finally, we reflect upon definitions of *ethnicity* before concluding with an examination of what constitutes a *nation*, what a national identity is, and how national identity may manifest in *nationalism*.

We explore the emergence of the *global world* in Chapter 13. In the context of the history of the development of political economies, we consider globalization and the pressures on nation-states as new cultural processes emerged and continue to emerge. A key issue is the challenge of human rights in a 'globalized' world, and we discuss cultural imperialism, cultural hybridization, and cosmopolitanism as responses to this challenge.

In the concluding chapter, we present the idea that anthropology encompasses so much more than what students will learn in a classroom. Anthropology is about the lives and worlds of the people who gift us with their world views. It is a portal to effective global citizenship in a world of uncertainty. Finally, it offers perspective and a way to develop awareness (reflexivity) in order to confront issues and challenge views on freedom and constraint.

## A Final Note

Each new edition of *Cultural Anthropology* has moved forward in some small and/or large way to illuminate the trends of the discipline. This time we have added a discussion of some key themes in medical anthropology. Nonetheless, what has been constant is the book's core value: a respect for students. Like Schultz and Lavenda, I, too, take students seriously. I believe that students have the capacity to read and think as involved adults. It has been my experience using this book over the years that students are happy to be seen as capable of the reflexivity the book espouses. They may sometimes complain about or struggle with the content and the concepts, but I have found they are charmed into learning as they come to appreciate that the text grounds them in an intellectual, emotional, and practical perspective that finds resonance in their—quite substantial—understanding of the world. What we offer are the tools for analysis. Inevitably, students appreciate how this book, and anthropology as a subject, situates them in a world of change and challenges them to be concerned citizens of that world.

# Acknowledgements

At the outset, I want to thank the people I met and worked with in the field who gifted me with their friendship and insights into their lives. They have been my true teachers, and their kind involvement has been a sacred gift. As this book has always inferred, such generosity helps us face the world with humility, while the study of anthropology situates us in a world of analysis that fosters the development of humble concern and deep hope. None of this could be possible without the kindness of others.

I would like to thank Schultz and Lavenda for providing the foundation upon which the Canadian editions of *Cultural Anthropology* have been built.

The work would not have proceeded without the exceedingly positive relationship that I developed with my editors at Oxford University Press. Here, I note three people specifically: Peter Chambers, developmental editor, Higher Education Division; Amanda Maurice, assistant editor, Higher Education Division; and Janice Evans, editor, Higher Education Division. Peter worked with me on both Canadian editions. Without his input and the work of Amanda, I could not have worked through the difficult process of making this book 'Canadian' while keeping the tone of the original authors. The second edition is what it is because of Janice Evans. To her fell the monumental task of smoothing out the tone of three voices, setting a better order for the material while reconciling the reorganization of chapters, and adding new material. Big job, well done!

All the people thanked in previous editions have their place in this edition as well. And to this list, I add a special thanks to my immediate colleagues at the University of British Columbia Okanagan, several of whom provided their insights here.

I would also like to join the publisher in thanking the following reviewers, as well as those who wish to remain anonymous, whose thoughtful comments and suggestions helped shape the first and second Canadian editions of this text.

Hugo De Burgos, University of British Columbia Okanagan
Steven Ferzacca, Lethbridge University
Diana French, University of British Columbia Okanagan
Dawn Grimes-MacLellan, St Mary's University
Magdalena Kazubowski-Houston, Wilfrid Laurier University
Chris Holdsworth, University of Calgary
David Howes, Concordia University
Carlota McAllister, York University
Laurie Milne, Medicine Hat College
Charles R. Menzies, University of British Columbia
Timothy Panas, University of Saskatchewan
David Ryniker, University of British Columbia
Alan Smart, University of Calgary
Douglas St.Christian, University of Western Ontario
Susan Walter, St Mary's University
Terry Webb, University of Western Ontario

*Roberta Robin Dods*

# What does it mean to be human? How do we define ourselves and others? Which of our qualities remain fixed across time and space, and which are subject to change?

These questions are at the very heart of anthropology. Of course, some of what makes us human is biological—our physiology is distinctively human, we possess a complex brain that is capable of high-level thinking, and so on. Yet much of our humanity comes from how we choose to interact with our fellow human beings and the world around us—the relationships we nurture, the traditions we learn and pass on, the ways in which we adapt to and transform our surroundings. In many ways, it is our capacity for *culture*, in all its forms, that makes us human.

Building on the solid foundation of past editions, this second Canadian edition of *Cultural Anthropology: A Perspective on the Human Condition* invites students to embark on a journey of cross-cultural comparison. Some of what they will encounter may be surprisingly familiar; some of it will be startlingly new. Everything will be thoroughly human.

## Key Features

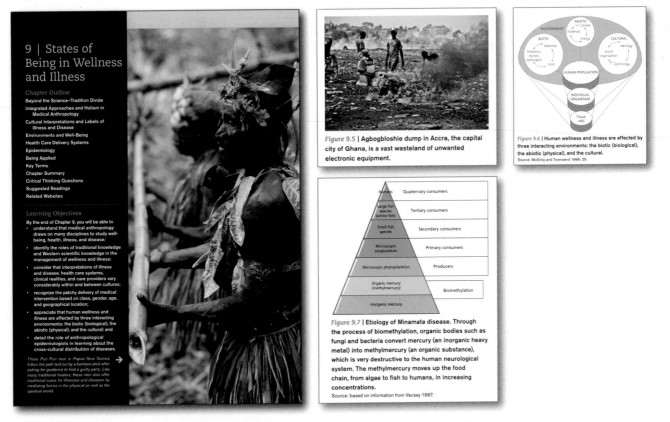

Figure 9.5 | Agbogbloshie dump in Accra, the capital city of Ghana, is a vast wasteland of unwanted electronic equipment.

Figure 9.6 | Human wellness and illness are affected by three interacting environments: the biotic (biological), the abiotic (physical), and the cultural.
Source: McElroy and Townsend 1996: 25.

Figure 9.7 | Etiology of Minamata disease. Through the process of biomethylation, organic bodies such as fungi and bacteria convert mercury (an inorganic heavy metal) into methylmercury (an organic substance), which is very destructive to the human neurological system. The methylmercury moves up the food chain, from algae to fish to humans, in increasing concentrations.
Source: based on information from Vecsey 1987.

*A new chapter on medical anthropology.* Chapter 9 gives students solid grounding in the fundamental principles of one of the fastest-growing subdisciplines of cultural anthropology. Numerous examples from the field demonstrate how medical anthropologists can contribute to the resolution of some of our most pressing global health concerns.

Figure 3.6 | Beverley Jacobs, head of the Native Women's Association of Canada from 2004–9, and Phil Fontaine, national chief of the Assembly of First Nations from 1997–2000 and 2003–9, stand alongside former residential school students in the House of Commons on 11 June 2008, awaiting Prime Minister Stephen Harper's official apology.

Figure 5.1 | Today, many Canadians are passionate about their anti-war stance. The points of view we develop depend greatly on what we have learned to pay attention to in the past.

*Canadian focus.* An array of Canadian examples, points of view, and issues offer insight into the many ways in which Canadians have contributed to the field. Students will also enjoy learning about the breadth and depth of anthropological research being carried out in this country today.

*Broad theoretical coverage.* The authors bring together traditional anthropological perspectives and cutting-edge theories that reflect the most recent trends in the discipline. The result is a comprehensive, holistic approach that sheds new light on standard topics.

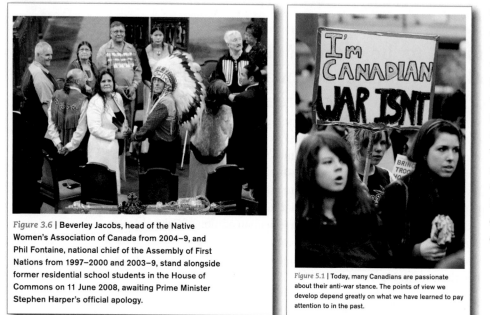

1 | The Anthropological Perspective on the Human Condition     7

Figure 1.4 | In North America, anthropology is traditionally divided into four specialties: biological anthropology, archaeology, linguistic anthropology, and cultural anthropology. Applied anthropology draws on information provided by the other four specialties.

**Biological Anthropology**

**Biological (or physical) anthropology** focusses on human beings as living organisms and what makes us different from or similar to other living things. This speciality of anthropology has its roots in the nineteenth-century interest in human physical variation, which was a by-product of centuries of exploration and encounters between geographically distant societies. At the time, variation in the physical appearance of peoples around the world was a matter of interest, and early physical anthropologists invented elaborate techniques to measure observable features of human populations including skin colour, hair, and body type. This 'scientific' evidence facilitated the classification of all peoples into supposedly unambiguous categories based on distinct sets of biological attributes. Such categories were called **races**, and many nineteenth- and early twentieth-century physical anthropologists were convinced that clear-cut criteria for racial classification would be discovered if careful measurements were made on enough people from around the world.

The peoples whom these early physical anthropologists were trying to assign to racial categories were, in most cases, non-European peoples, peoples coming under increasing political and economic domination by colonizing European and European-ancestry capitalist societies (a sobering discussion of Europeans' violent impact on the inhabitants of the 'new world' can be found in Mann 2005). These peoples differed from 'white' Europeans in ways other than physical appearance—they had their own languages and customs, and they possessed technologies that were, in most cases, no match for the might of the industrialized West. As a result, racial categorization not only noted individuals' physical characteristics but also made judgments on their mental and moral attributes, and races were ranked

**biological (or physical) anthropology** The specialty of anthropology that looks at humans as a biological organisms and tries to discover what characteristics make us different from and/or similar to other living things.

**races** Social groupings that allegedly reflected biological differences.

244     Part II | The Resources of Culture

**Symbol**

As people increase their understanding of themselves and the wider world by creating apt metaphors, they devise *symbols* to remind themselves of their significant insights and the connections between those insights. As noted at the beginning of this book, a symbol is something that stands for something else—be it a word, an image, or an action. Symbols signal the presence and importance of given domains of experience. They are special cases of metonymy. Some symbols—what Sherry Ortner (1973) calls *summarizing symbols*—represent a whole semantic domain and invite us to consider the various elements within it. Others—what Ortner calls *elaborating symbols*—represent only one element of a domain and invite us to place that element in its wider semantic context.

**Key Metaphors**

World views are attempts to answer the following question: What must the world be like for my experiences to be what they are? Over the ages, thoughtful people in all cultural traditions have drawn on different metaphors to suggest various answers to this question. Those suggestions that have become entrenched in any particular tradition are based on especially apt metaphors—**key metaphors** that make sense of experience in a variety of circumstances. Over time, as circumstances change and the established metaphors become less apt, new key metaphors replace the old, forming the basis for new world views.

Anthropologist Robin Horton suggests that people who construct a world view are 'concerned above all to show order, regularity, and predictability where primary theory [i.e., commonsense experience] has failed to show them'. As they search for key metaphors, therefore, they look at those areas of everyday experience that are most associated with order, regularity, and predictability (1982: 237). Cross-culturally, key metaphors typically relate to three such realms of experience: the societal, the organic, and the technological.

**Societal Metaphors**

In societies where human social relations provide great order, regularity, and predictability, the central model for the world is the social order. People within these societies

**key metaphors** Metaphors that serve as the foundation of a world view.

**societal metaphor** A world-view metaphor whose model for the world is the social order.

tend to use **societal metaphors** as they try to explain various aspects of their reality. For example, geneticist Richard Lewontin (1984) and his colleagues point out that biologists studying cells have used a societal metaphor almost from the very beginning. These biologists liken cells to a factory assembling the biochemical products needed to support the body's economy. This metaphor recurs in the twentieth-century work of Francis Crick, one of the discoverers of the structure of DNA (deoxyribonucleic acid). Lewontin and colleagues suggest: 'Read any introductory textbook to the new molecular biology and you will find these metaphors as a central part of the cellular description. Even the drawings of the protein synthesis sequence are often deliberately laid out in "assembly-line" style' (1984: 59) (Figure 10.2).

Similarly, contemporary sociobiologists have borrowed certain concepts from modern economic thought and used them to describe the behaviour of genes or of living organisms. Sociobiologists describe the nurturing behaviour of parents toward their offspring as 'parental investment'. They talk about the cost–benefit analyses that people make before deciding whether or not to sacrifice themselves for others and even describe genes as 'selfish'. To some sociobiologists, the natural world is just the capitalist market on a larger scale. Indeed, anthropologist Marshall Sahlins (1976a) and others have argued that, from its inception in the late eighteenth century, modern biology has taken its key metaphors from the social

Figure 10.2 | An example of a protein synthesis diagram laid out in 'assembly-line' style.

**'EthnoProfiles' boxes.** Brief overviews of relevant geographic, linguistic, demographic, and organizational information offer students contextual information on various societies discussed in the text.

## EthnoProfile

**'In Their Own Words' boxes.** Short commentaries from experts in the field provide students with alternative perspectives on key issues and also furnish insight into what it means to be an anthropologist.

## In Their Own Words

*Vibrant four-colour design.* A wide array of photos, illustrations, tables, and graphs helps bring anthropology alive!

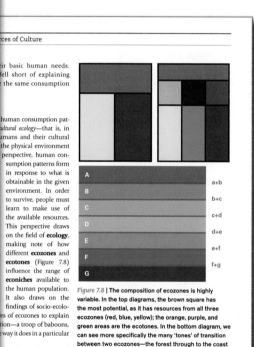

*Figure 7.8* | The composition of ecozones is highly variable. In the top diagrams, the brown square has the most potential, as it has resources from all three ecozones (red, blue, yellow); the orange, purple, and green areas are the ecotones. In the bottom diagram, we can see more specifically the many 'tones' of transition between two ecozones—the forest through to the coast line into the depths of the a river, lake, or the ocean.

*Engaging learning tools.*   Learning objectives, marginal definitions of key terms, critical thinking questions, annotated suggestions for further reading, and lists of related websites encourage students to actively engage with what they are reading and explore resources beyond the text to enhance their learning experience.

*Extensive ancillary package.*

The second Canadian edition of *Cultural Anthropology* is supported by an array of supplementary resources for the student and the instructor, all designed to enhance and complete the learning experience. The companion websites for *Cultural Anthropology* are found at:

**www.oupcanada.com/Schultz2e**

*For the student.*

**Student Study Guide.** An updated and expanded package of review material—including a list of relevant films, self-testing quizzes of multiple choice and true/false questions, essay topics, kinship diagrams, and weblinks to resources such as online ethnographies—is designed to reinforce student understanding of each chapter and provide direction for further research.

*For the instructor.*

The following instructors' resources are available online to qualifying adopters. Please contact your OUP Canada sales representative for more information.

- **Instructor's Manual.** This comprehensive package features chapter outlines, suggestions for discussion and debate, suggested teaching resources, and a sample syllabus for each chapter.

- **PowerPoint Slides.** These dynamic lecture slides summarize key points from each chapter and incorporate figures and tables from the text.

- **Image Bank.** This expansive resource contains hundreds of full-colour figures, photographs, and tables that will make classroom lectures more engaging and relevant for students.

- **Test Generator.** This comprehensive bank of test questions provides hundreds of multiple choice, true/false, short answer, and mini essay questions along with suggested answers and page references guiding students to related in-text discussions.

# Part I | The Tools of Cultural Anthropology

**In Part I we introduce anthropology—specifically cultural anthropology—as a way of exploring and gaining knowledge about our world and ourselves.** We also consider the possibilities made available by fieldwork, the principal method of data collection used by cultural anthropologists. Finally, we discuss the historical context for how anthropologists have attempted to make sense of human cultural diversity.

# 1 | The Anthropological Perspective on the Human Condition

## Chapter Outline

Explanations of the Human Condition

The Anthropological Perspective:
   The Cross-disciplinary Discipline

Anthropology and the Concept of Culture

The Challenge of Cultural Differences

Culture, History, and Human Agency

The Promise of the Anthropological Perspective

......................................................................................

## Learning Objectives

By the end of Chapter 1, you will be able to

- define anthropology's aims and scope of study,

- explain culture as a concept within anthropology,

- distinguish cultural anthropology as a subfield of
  anthropology,

- articulate connections and relationships between the four
  major subfields of anthropology in North America,

- explain the world views of dualism and holism and
  show ways that the conflict between them has shaped
  anthropology, and

- explain the relationship between cultural relativism and
  ethnocentrism and give examples of both.

← *A nomadic herder goes looking for his yaks in Mongolia, where
horses and horse handling have been cultural cornerstones for
thousands of years. His particular cultural experience is only one
of a vast array of such experiences that shape human behaviours
and beliefs in different ways across the globe.*

# Explanations of the Human Condition

## Dualistic, Idealistic, and Materialistic Explanations of Our World

What is the world like? And what is the human condition within the world? Indeed, does it make sense to speak of a *single* 'condition' shared by all human beings? Members of all societies pose questions such as these. And all societies develop their own answers. If asked what they believe about human nature, for example, many North Americans would answer that human nature has two parts: *mind* and *matter, soul* and *body,* or *spirit* and *flesh*. The belief that human nature, or reality as a whole, is made up of two radically different yet equal forces is called **dualism**. For millennia, from the time of the Greek philosopher Plato (428–347 BCE) onward, people of the Western tradition have debated the importance of each half of human nature. They have understood each person as made up of a material body inhabited by an ethereal mind. According to Plato, the drama of human existence consists of the internal struggle between the body (drawn naturally to base, corruptible matter) and the mind or soul (drawn naturally to pure, unchanging forms). Christian theology later incorporated the view that each human being consists of a soul that seeks God and a physical body that is tempted by the material world. This view of earthly life as a struggle between spirit and flesh is sometimes called *conflict dualism*.

Subsequently, Platonic and Christian theories of human nature came to emphasize that although human beings are equipped with physical bodies, their true nature is spiritual, not material; the body is a material impediment that frustrates the full development of the mind or spirit. This view is known as **idealism**. Conversely, others have argued that the activities of our physical bodies in the material world make us who we are. From this perspective, human existence becomes the struggle to exercise our physicality as fully as we can; to put spiritual values above

bodily needs would 'go against human nature'. This view is known as **materialism**. In their most extreme forms, idealism and materialism propose competing forms of **determinism**: idealists claim that human nature is *determined by* the causal force of mind or spirit; materialists argue that human nature is *determined by* the causal force of physical matter.

Many idealists and materialists have sought to strip away our seemingly extraneous or unnecessary attributes in order to reveal an unchanging core or **essence** of human nature. Indeed, across the history of Western philosophy, various philosophers have assumed that our species has an essence but have disagreed about just what that essence is. Yet other thinkers have argued that human beings come into the world with *no fixed essence*. For them, we are shaped by various forces we encounter throughout our lives. But what those forces might be, how many there are, and which of them is the most powerful remain part of the debate. Some nineteenth-century thinkers argued that the most powerful material forces that shape human nature were to be found in the surrounding *natural environment*. Rich soil, a temperate climate, drought, and the absence of animals amenable to domestication are examples of the environmental factors understood to shape past and present societies and, ultimately, their inhabitants' sense of who they were, indeed are. Karl Marx and his followers, by contrast, argued that forces shaping human beings' self-understanding were rooted in social relations shaped by the mode of economic production (from the German *Produktionsweise* meaning 'the way we produce things') that sustained a society (Figure 1.1). Because different groups, or *classes*, played different

---

**dualism**
The philosophical view that reality consists of two equal and irreducible forces.

**idealism**
The philosophical view (dating back as far as Plato in Western thought) that ideas—or the mind that produces such ideas—constitute the essence of human nature.

**materialism**
The philosophical view that the activities of our physical bodies in the material world constitute the essence of human nature.

**determinism**
The philosophical view that one simple force (or a few simple forces) causes (or determines) complex events.

**essence**
An unchanging core of features that is unique to things of the same kind (whether they are chairs, cows, ideas, or people) and makes them what they are.

Figure 1.1 | **Factory workers in Woodstock, Ontario, collectively toil to support war efforts during World War I. Karl Marx believed that modes of production shape social relations and, in turn, individuals' perceptions of themselves and their place in society.**

roles in that production process, members of each group would develop a different sense of what life was all about. An extreme idealist reaction against such materialist thinking, influential in cultural anthropology, has argued that human beings have no fixed essence when they come into the world, but they become different kinds of human beings as a result of the particular ideas, meanings, beliefs, and values that they absorb as members of particular societies (see Benedict 1934).

As liberating as the proposition of being born without a fixed essence may sound, such accounts are not always optimistic. A number of scholars have adapted this basic assumption to portray humans as passive, pliable creatures who are *wholly* moulded by environmental, socio-historical, cultural, or other forces beyond their control. According to

**holism**
A perspective on the human condition that assumes that mind and body, individual and society, and individual and environment interpenetrate and even define one another.

**co-evolution**
The relationship between biological processes and symbolic cultural processes in which each makes up an important part of the environment to which the other must adapt.

these scholars, the open possibilities with which we begin are inevitably closed down tight as human possibilities are overwhelmed by environmental determinism, socio-historical determinism, or cultural determinism.

## Holistic Explanations

Yet there is another approach to the human condition that is less distorting than dualism, less simplistic than idealism or materialism, and does not reduce human beings to passive lumps of clay: **holism** (see Figure 1.2). Holism assumes that no sharp boundaries separate mind from body, body from environment, individual from society, my ideas from your ideas, or their traditions from our traditions; rather, it proposes that mind and body, body and environment, and so on, interpenetrate and even define each other. Holism holds great appeal for those who seek a theory of human nature that is rich enough to do justice to its complex subject matter. Thus the whole (i.e., a human being, a society, a cultural tradition) is greater than the sum of its parts, and human beings are what they are because the mutual shaping of genes and culture and experience has produced something new, something that cannot be reduced to the materials used to construct it. Similarly, a society is not just the sum of the behaviours of its individual members but a unique entity, and human beings living in groups are so deeply affected by shared cultural experiences that they become different from what they would have been had they matured in isolation. Geertz notes that human beings raised in isolation would be neither failed apes nor 'natural' people stripped of their veneer of culture; they would be 'mental basket cases' (1973: 40). Social living and cultural sharing are necessary for individual human beings to develop what we recognize as a *human* nature.

Holism as a perspective allows us to consider human nature as the result of a **co-evolution**: Human beings are creatures whose bodies, brains, actions, and thoughts are equally involved in learning, co-determining, and co-evolving. Thus, we can view human nature as embedded in a wider world and profoundly shaped by culture. We can also infer that human beings are open to becoming something more than what has gone into making them what they are at a given point in time. This belief in the human potential can be a challenge, especially when we find ourselves in difficult times or confronted by confusing cultural messages. But consider this: our ability to cope in such circumstances relies in no small part on our capacity to try to make sense

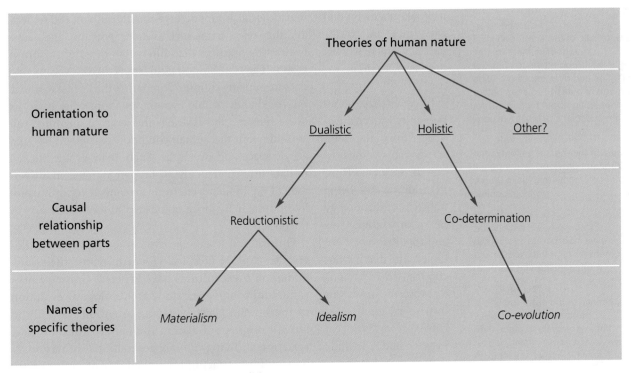

*Figure 1.2* | **Perspectives on the human condition.**

of these experiences, an effort in which the symbolic, meaning-making resources of culture play a critical role.

# The Anthropological Perspective: The Cross-disciplinary Discipline

From the optimistic promise of holism we can engage with the subject matter of **anthropology**, a scholarly discipline that aims to describe, in the broadest possible sense, what it means to be human. Anthropologists want to learn about different human ways of life. Essentially, the anthropological experience is a gift from mentors—teachers who live or lived in different social, economic, geographical, or temporal circumstances. Thus, anthropologists are often treated to the sweet discovery of familiarity and the joy of making the unfamiliar familiar. They often face, as well, the experience of the familiar becoming unfamiliar; as frightening as this discovery can be, it is also a source of great insight and immense pleasure.

Anthropologists are not alone in focussing their attention on human beings and their creations. Human biology, literature, art, history, linguistics, sociology, political science, economics—all these disciplines and many more—concentrate on one aspect of human life or another. Life and its origins is a topic for those in 'hard' sciences as they investigate the dynamics of the universe as seen, for example, in the work of Shapiro (2007). Yet, as Darnell notes, anything can be anthropology if only one views it from the anthropological perspective (2001: 24). The anthropological perspective, unique in the social sciences, draws on the findings of these other disciplines and attempts to fit them together with its own findings in order to understand how these data collectively shape human life. Anthropologists are convinced that explanations of human activities will inevitably be superficial unless they acknowledge that human lives are always entangled in complex and fluid patterns of work and family, power and meaning. Nevertheless, because unanticipated constraints and opportunities emerge out of these entanglements, the 'whole' of human life is always greater than the sum of its 'parts'. This holistic point of view recognizes that so long as they are alive, individuals and societies always remain open to influences and opportunities that

**anthropology**
The integrated study of human nature, human society, and human history.

**comparative**
A characteristic of the anthropological perspective that requires anthropologists to consider similarities and differences in a wide a range of human societies before generalizing about human nature, human society, or human history.

**biological evolution**
Evolution of the resources for human development provided by our genes and other elements that make up our physical bodies.

**cultural evolution**
Evolution of the beliefs and behaviours we incorporate into human development through the experiences of teaching and learning.

**evolutionary**
A characteristic of the anthropological perspective that requires anthropologists to place their observations about human nature, human society, or human history in a temporal framework that takes into consideration change over time.

may take them beyond what they are at the present moment or what they have been in the past.

To generalize about humanity requires evidence from the widest possible range of human societies. Thus, in addition to being holistic, anthropology is **comparative**. As anthropologists, we understand that it is not enough, for example, to observe only our own social group, discover that we do not eat insects, and conclude that human beings as a species do not eat insects (Figure 1.3). When we compare human diets in different societies, we discover that insect-eating is quite common and that our North American aversion to this practice is specific to our own society. In making such comparisons, anthropologists recognize that all social groups deserve equal treatment and respect, and they reject terms such as *exotic, primitive,* and *savage* to describe practices that differ from those of their own group. Thus anthropological study involves gathering data from many cultures, comparing those data to derive informed and testable hypotheses about what it means to be human, and investigating what, if anything, can be said about the human condition that might be valid across space and over time. Such analyses are situated in data from potentially all human societies in all periods of the human past, from the emergence of human-like primates in Africa some five million years ago to the present.

This interest in change over time leads anthropologists to explore how individual humans, their societies, and their cultures have evolved. Consequently, some anthropologists study the **biological evolution** of the human species, paying attention not only to human origins but also to the patterns of biological variation in living human populations; others study past cultures, tracing how elements of culture have changed over time. In general, one of anthropology's most important contributions to the study of human evolution has been to demonstrate the critical differences that separate biological evolution situated in environmental *circumstances*, as Darwin would term it, from **cultural evolution**. This distinction remains important as a way of demonstrating the fallacies and incoherence of arguments that assert that everything people do or think can be explained biologically— for example, in terms of 'race' or 'sex'. Because anthropologists are interested in documenting and explaining change, the anthropological perspective is **evolutionary** at its core. And today, as we move into an era in which even our biological being can be altered through technology, anthropologists' interest in human evolution has taken on additional cross-disciplinary implications.

The diverse ways we come to understand the meaning of being human through the anthropological perspective can be seen in Figure 1.4, which shows the connections among the four traditional specialties, or subdisciplines, of anthropology and their combined linkage to applied anthropology. As this figure illustrates, at the most inclusive level anthropology is the holistic study of human nature, human society, and human history.

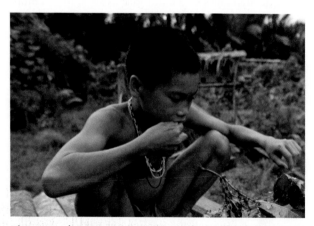

*Figure 1.3* | **A Mentawai boy in Sumatra, Indonesia, eats ants from their nest. While insects are not a staple in most Western diets, they are commonly eaten as a source of protein in many regions of the world.**

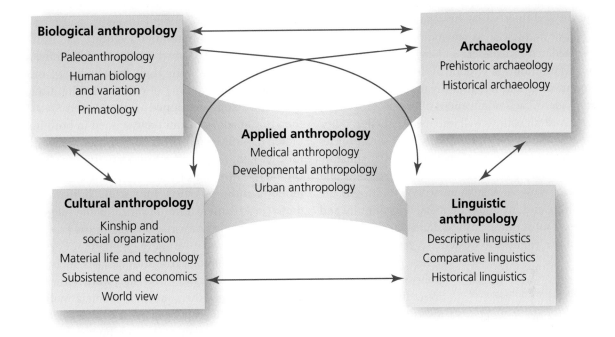

Figure 1.4 | In North America, anthropology is traditionally divided into four specialties: biological anthropology, archaeology, linguistic anthropology, and cultural anthropology. Applied anthropology draws on information provided by the other four specialties.

## Biological Anthropology

**Biological** (or **physical**) **anthropology** focusses on human beings as living organisms and what makes us different from or similar to other living things. This specialty of anthropology has its roots in the nineteenth-century interest in human physical variation, which was a by-product of centuries of exploration and encounters between geographically distant societies. At the time, variation in the physical appearance of peoples around the world was a matter of interest, and early physical anthropologists invented elaborate techniques to measure observable features of human populations including skin colour, hair, and body type. This 'scientific' evidence facilitated the classification of all peoples into supposedly unambiguous categories based on distinct sets of biological attributes. Such categories were called **races**, and many nineteenth- and early twentieth-century physical anthropologists were convinced that clear-cut criteria for racial classification would be discovered if careful measurements were made on enough people from around the world.

The peoples whom these early physical anthropologists were trying to assign to racial categories were, in most cases, non-European peoples, peoples coming under increasing political and economic domination by colonizing European and European-ancestry capitalist societies (a sobering discussion of Europeans' violent impact on the inhabitants of the 'new world' can be found in Mann 2005). These peoples differed from 'white' Europeans in ways other than physical appearance—they had their own languages and customs, and they possessed technologies that were, in most cases, no match for the might of the industrialized West. As a result, racial categorization not only noted individuals' physical characteristics but also made judgments on their mental and moral attributes, and races were ranked

**biological (or physical) anthropology**
The specialty of anthropology that looks at humans as a biological organisms and tries to discover what characteristics make us different from and/or similar to other living things.

**races**
Social groupings that allegedly reflected biological differences.

in terms of these attributes. Not surprisingly, 'white' Europeans and their 'white' descendants in power outside Europe were seen as superior, while other races were considered to represent varying grades of inferiority. In this way, the first physical anthropologists helped develop theories that would justify the social practice of **racism**. Indeed, racism influenced official social policies in many Western nations well into the twentieth century. In Canada, one of the most destructive of such policies was the government's implementation of mandatory residential schools for Native children. Chrisjohn and his colleagues wrote that these schools destroyed the circles of life and life-affirming metaphors of unity and wholeness, substituting instead Euro-Canadian 'circle games' of the 'empty non-existence of zero' (1997: 115).

**racism**
The systematic oppression of members of one or more socially defined 'races' by members of another socially defined 'race' that is justified within the ruling society by the rulers' faulty belief in their own biological superiority.

**primatology**
The study of non-human primates, the closest living relatives of human beings.

**paleoanthropology**
The study of the fossilized remains of human beings' earliest ancestors.

**archaeology**
The specialty of anthropology interested in what we can learn from material remains left behind by earlier human societies.

Yet even as racist policies continued to affect the lives of individuals, many physical anthropologists in the early twentieth century began realizing the fallacy of racial categorization. New theories, many based on principles of holism, led these anthropologists to question past assumptions, and new scientific advancements, such as the discovery of blood types, led them to add data on individuals' internal features to their calculations. The more they learned about the inner biological attributes of human populations, the more they realized that races with distinct and unique sets of such attributes simply did not exist. Thus they concluded that the concept of 'race' did not reflect a fact of nature but was instead a cultural label invented by human beings to sort people into groups.

Support for non-racial understandings of human populations has a long history among anthropologists in North America. Pioneering anthropologist Franz Boas, for example, who in the early 1900s founded the first department of anthropology in the United States at Columbia University, had long been uncomfortable with racial classifications. Boas and his students devoted much energy to debunking racist stereotypes, using both their knowledge of biology and their understanding of culture. As the discipline of anthropology developed in the United States and then in Canada, students were trained in both human biology and human culture to provide them with the tools to fight racial and ethnic stereotyping. Rejecting the racial thinking of the nineteenth century, many modern anthropologists who study human biology prefer to call themselves *biological anthropologists* and focus on patterns of variation within the human species as a whole.

Today, some biological anthropologists, such as Biruté Galdikas (Simon Fraser University) work in the subfield of **primatology**; others, such as Pamela Willoughby (University of Alberta), work in the field of **paleoanthropology**. Newer specialties focus on human adaptability in different ecological settings, on human growth and development, or on the connections between a population's evolutionary history and its susceptibility to disease. Forensic anthropologists, as noted below in the applied anthropology discussion, use their knowledge of human skeletal anatomy to aid law enforcement and human rights investigators. Molecular anthropologists trace chemical similarities and differences in cells, tissues, and organs; what they have learned about the immune system, for example, has enabled them to contribute actively to HIV/AIDS research. In recent years, new analytic techniques such as biostatistics, three-dimensional imaging, and electronic communication and publishing have revolutionized the field. In all these ways, biological anthropologists can illuminate what makes human beings similar to (and different from) one another, other primates, and other living organisms (Boaz and Wolfe 1995; Weinker 1995).

## Archaeology

**Archaeology**, another major specialty within anthropology, is the study of the human past through the analysis of material remains (Figure 1.5). Archaeologists must also be knowledgeable about the history of the sites they investigate—they must be familiar with past technologies and environmental as well as economic indicators (e.g., plant and animal remains)—so they can recognize valuable details and situate their findings within the greater scientific landscape. Archaeologists frequently work in teams with other scientists who specialize in specific areas of research. Their findings complement those of paleo-anthropologists and indeed sometimes become common interest. For example, archaeological information about successive stone-tool traditions in a particular region may correlate with fossil evidence of prehistoric human occupation.

One such example of an archaeological research project involving experts from various fields is the Dakhleh Oasis Project in Egypt (see EthnoProfile 1.1). Project director Anthony J. Mills, who initiated the project in 1978, describes it as

> a long-term regional study of the interaction between environmental changes and human activity in the closed area of the Dakhleh Oasis . . . since the first incursion of humans in the Middle Pleistocene, perhaps 400,000 years ago, down to the twenty-first century oasis farmers, and all the human activity and all the changing environmental conditions for which there is evidence within the time period. (Mills 2010)

Participants in the study include environmentalists, physical anthropologists, linguists, historians, and archaeologists specializing in various areas of study. The project has attracted researchers from around the

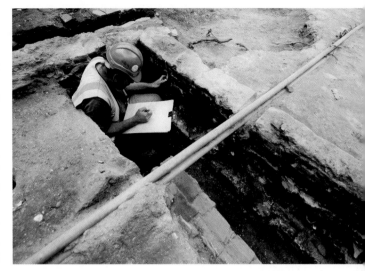

Figure 1.5 | Excavation work and analysis of material remains are central to archaeologists' study of the human past.

globe, and several Canadians—including anthropologist Maxine Kleindienst—have signed on to contribute to the massive undertaking.

Scientific dating techniques allow archaeologists to make hypotheses about the age, territorial ranges, and patterns of socio-cultural change in ancient societies, thus tracing the spread of cultural inventions over time and space. Sabloff tells us that archaeology is an 'action' science in the modern world, as it 'can play helpful roles in broad, critical issues facing the world today . . . [informing us] in general about lessons to

---

## EthnoProfile 1.1 | Dakhleh  · · · · · · · · · · · · · · · · · · · · · · · · · · · · · · · · · · · · · · · · · · · · · · · · · · · · · · · · · · · · · · · ·

**Region** Northeastern Africa

**Nation** Egypt

**Language** Nearly all of the 14 colonies that constitute the Dakhleh Oasis—including Mut, Al-Qasr, and Qalamoun—have their own dialect of Arabic

**Population** 75,000 (2002)

**Environment** Desert oasis

**Livelihood** Farming (dates, oranges, mangoes, wheat)

**Political organization** Region in a modern nation-state

**For more information** Chandler, Graham. 2006. 'Before the Mummies: The Desert Origins of the Pharaohs', *Saudi Aramco World* 57, 5: 2–11.

**language**
The system of arbitrary vocal symbols we use to encode our experiences of the world and of one another.

**linguistic anthropology**
The specialty of anthropology concerned with the study of human languages.

**cultural anthropology**
The specialty of anthropology that studies how variation in beliefs and behaviours is shaped by culture and learned by different members of human groups.

**culture**
Sets of learned behaviours and ideas that humans acquire as members of a society. We use culture to adapt to and transform the world in which we live.

be learned from the successes and failures of past cultures and [thus] provide policy-makers with useful contexts for decision-making in the world today. . .' (2008: 17). In such a context, archaeology becomes applied anthropology, as we will discuss later!

## Linguistic Anthropology

Perhaps the most striking cultural feature of our species is **language**. Anthropologists have long recognized the connections between language and human culture, and many early anthropologists were the first researchers to transcribe non-Western languages and to produce grammars and dictionaries of those languages. When investigating living cultures, linguistic anthropologists often connect with one or a few members of the culture who can act as guides to the language and customs of specific social groups (Figure 1.6). The loss of languages is also a concern (see Abley 2005), as each language is a unique way of understanding ourselves and our place in the universe. Contemporary linguistic anthropologists and their counterparts in sociology (called *sociolinguists*) study the way language differences frequently correlate with differences in gender, race, class, or ethnic identity.

**Linguistic anthropology** has become so highly specialized that modern linguistic anthropologists are deeply trained in both linguistics and cultural anthropology, and many cultural anthropologists receive linguistics training as part of their professional preparation. Linguistic anthropologists are applied anthropologists in some instances, working to maintain endangered languages, attempting to bring an understanding to all of us of the nature of language and our links to our cultural identity.

### Cultural Anthropology

Now we come to the central topic of this book: **cultural anthropology**. Sometimes called *socio-cultural anthropology*, *social anthropology*, or *ethnology*, cultural anthropology focusses on sets of learned behaviours and ideas that human beings acquire as members of a society. Recognizing that people ordinarily take their culturally shaped beliefs and behaviours for granted, anthropologist Michael Herzfeld has suggested that cultural anthropology might be usefully defined for us as 'the study of common sense', although 'sense' as a concept is neither common to all cultures nor particularly sensible to anyone unfamiliar with its specific cultural context (2001: 1).

Because people everywhere use **culture** to adapt to and transform everything in their wider world, the field of cultural anthropology is vast. Cultural anthropologists tend to specialize in one domain of human cultural activity or another. Many cultural anthropologists study language, music, dance, art, poetry, philosophy, religion, or ritual. Some study the ways particular groups of human beings organize themselves to carry out collective tasks, whether economic, political, or spiritual. This focus bears the closest resemblance to the

*Figure 1.6* | **On the road to Mouk territory in Papua New Guinea. William Thurston with his friend Avel, a Lusi speaker, who acted as guide and introduced Thurston and Rick Goulden to the community where they collected material on the Mouk language.**

discipline of sociology, and from it has come the identification of anthropology as one of the social sciences. In fact, sociology and anthropology developed during the same period of the late nineteenth and early twentieth centuries and thus share some similar interests in social organization. However, interest in *comparing* different forms of human social life sets anthropology apart from sociology.

Transcending the racism that permeated early anthropological studies, modern cultural anthropologists are concerned with studying *all* human societies, including their own, and they do research in urban and rural settings around the world. They reject, as do other anthropologists, labels such as *civilized* and *primitive* for the same reason they reject the term *race*. These concepts carry offensive connotations and do not help us make sense of the everyday realities of human life.

In recent years, many cultural anthropologists have studied contemporary issues of gender and sexuality, transnational labour migration, urbanization, globalization, and the resurgence of ethnicity and nationalism. Others have investigated the patterns of material life found in different human groups. Among the most striking are worldwide variations in clothing, housing, tools, and techniques for getting and preparing food and making material goods (Figure 1.7). Like archaeologists, cultural anthropologists interested in material life describe the natural setting for which technologies have been developed and analyze the way technologies and environments shape each other.

With the post-colonial and neo-colonial era upon us, cultural anthropologists have begun to investigate the ways non-Western peoples have responded to the political and economic challenges of colonialism and the capitalist industrial technology that came with it. For example, studies of the impact of Western technologies have shown the creative and unanticipated ways peoples use popular media and cybertechnology—including Internet communication tools such as e-mail and instant messaging—to make sense of their own local cultural context and situate it in a wider world.

As cultural anthropologists have become increasingly aware of the socio-cultural influences that stretch across space to affect local communities, they have also become sensitive to those that stretch across time. As a result, many contemporary cultural anthropologists make serious efforts to place their cultural analyses in detailed historical contexts. These anthropologists often work closely with archaeologists and historians who have related interests.

Cultural anthropologists, no matter what their area of specialization, ordinarily collect their data during an extended period of fieldwork (the topic of Chapter 2). Its central feature is the anthropologists' involvement in the everyday routine of those among whom they live. Fieldwork is a period when the anthropologist receives one of the most meaningful gifts that any human can receive— entry into the lives of others. This gift is part of an act of reciprocity. The researcher can enhance the reciprocal relationship by participating in social activities and negotiating the meaning of the observed with the people they work with. Fieldwork also requires that the anthropologist engage in what is termed *reflexivity*—thinking about why and how one thinks about specific things.

*Figure 1.7* | Cultural anthropologists investigate worldwide variations in clothing, housing, tools, and techniques for getting and preparing food and making material goods. Here, a Bedouin woman makes bread on the top of an oil drum, which she has bent and placed on three rocks; in the past, the process would have been similar, but she would have used more traditional materials.

**informants**
People in a particular culture who work with anthropologists and provide them with insights about their way of life; also called *respondents*, *teachers*, or *friends*.

**ethnography**
An anthropologist's written (or filmed) description of a particular culture.

**ethnology**
The comparative study of two or more cultures.

**applied anthropology**
The use of information gathered from the other anthropological specialties to solve practical problems within and between cultures.

People who share information about their lives have traditionally been called **informants**; however, some anthropologists object to the use of this term because it suggests a role that is limited to supplying information for the benefit of the researcher. Therefore, some contemporary anthropologists choose to describe the people they encounter in the field as *partners*, *participants*, *consultants*, or simply *the people I work with* because these terms emphasize a relationship of equality based on mutual respect. Others prefer the term *teachers*, which implies that fieldwork is an active dialogue between the researcher (the student) and the people who are the experts on their own lives (the teachers). Of course,

these experts, like all teachers, also learn and develop new perspectives as they interact with their students.

The recordings cultural anthropologists make in the field to document the lives of the people they work with are of prime importance. Often researchers make written notes, but sometimes they use videos or photographs as well (Figure 1.8). Indeed, the use of 'shadow catching' technologies—devices that capture a visual representation of life—in the discipline dates back to the earliest period of photography in the nineteenth century. Such photographs have been an invaluable record, even if some people have incorrectly assumed that these images represent a neutral stance (Ball and Smith 1992). In fact, visual records often say more about the photographer or videographer than about his or her subject, as illustrated by some of Franz Boas's pictures (e.g., Figure 1.9), taken for the US National Museum, and Edward Curtis's movie *In the Land of the War Canoes* (1914), which depicts a fictionalized account of the lives of the Kwakiutl peoples (Northern Vancouver Island).

At this point, it will be helpful for you to understand the distinction between the related terms *ethnography* and *ethnology*. **Ethnography** is a description of 'the customary social behaviours of an identifiable group of people' (Wolcott 1999: 252–3); **ethnology** is the comparative study of two or more such groups. Thus, cultural anthropologists who write ethnographies are sometimes called *ethnographers*, and cultural anthropologists who compare ethnographic information on many different cultural practices are sometimes called *ethnologists*.

## Applied Anthropology

**Applied anthropology** could be termed *action anthropology*. In applied anthropology, anthropological information is put to practical use to propose solutions to important social and cultural problems. You may be familiar with the practical applications of forensic anthropology—perhaps you've even encountered media coverage of forensic anthropologists such as Mark Skinner (Simon Fraser University) who have worked on highly publicized crime cases or genocide investigations. Although generally exposed to less public attention, other areas of application can also make important contributions to social life. For example, when working with a traditionally structured non-Western community, applied anthropologists could

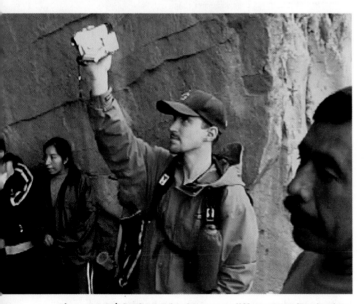

*Figure 1.8* | **Anthropologists use different technologies for different research purposes. Anthropologist Ryan Cook videotapes the spectators and ritual performers at the Popocatepetl volcano in Mexico.**

- use the culture's ideas about illness and health to introduce useful public health practices in a way that makes sense to, and will be accepted by, members of that culture;
- draw on the knowledge of traditional social organization to ease the problems for refugees trying to settle in a new land; and
- integrate traditional and Western methods of cultivation to help farmers increase their crop yields.

Because of the power of applied anthropology to solve problems and help those in need, many such anthropologists become advocates or activists for a cause. They use their professional skills to draw public attention to the plight of the people they study, to seek social justice, to fight discrimination, or to support human and cultural rights. In Canada, applied anthropologists have frequently acted to support First Nations land claims and resolve public policy issues (Hedican 2000).

While many anthropologists would argue that applied work can be done *within* any of the four traditional specialties, an increasing number of anthropologists have come to view applied anthropology as a separate field of professional specialization (see Figure 1.4). Thus more universities in Canada and the United States have begun to develop courses and programs specifically in applied anthropology.

*Figure 1.9* | **Franz Boas demonstrates a position in the Kwakiutl Hamatsa dance ritual, as he observed it at Fort Rupert, British Columbia, in 1894.**

## Anthropology and the Concept of Culture

Unquestionably, the emergence of culture has had a profound impact on the evolution of human nature and human society. Thus, it is not surprising that the idea of culture as a marker of our humanness has been central to anthropological thought since the early days of the discipline. Pioneering anthropologist Edward B. Tylor defined culture as 'that complex whole which includes knowledge, belief, art, morals, law, customs, and any other capabilities and habits acquired . . . as a member of society' (1958 [1871]: 1). Later definitions are more or less refinements or elaborations of this theme.

From the anthropological perspective, culture is central to explanations of why we are what we are and why we do what we do. Anthropologists have shown that members of a social group behave in a particular way *not* because the behaviour is an inevitable result of human biology but because it is *learned*—individuals observe and then copy certain actions performed by others. At the same time, no one would deny that biology plays a role in determining what we *can* learn. Thus, most anthropologists view human beings as **biocultural organisms**. Our biological makeup, formed by our genes and cellular chemistry, contributes to our capacity to create and use culture. Conversely, our survival as biological organisms depends upon learned ways of thinking and acting that help us find food, shelter, and mates and that teach us how to rear our children.

Of course, other living species learn, but our way of interacting with the wider world is distinct for two reasons: 1) our large, complex brains are capable of extremely intricate open symbolic thought and 2) our hands are capable of manipulating matter in both powerful and delicate ways. Being capable of open symbolic thought means that we are able to make sense of our world through **symbols**. We use symbols in many

**biocultural organisms**
Organisms (in this case, human beings) whose defining features are co-determined by biological and cultural factors.

**symbol**
Something that stands for something else.

ways. For example, we use alphabetic symbols (whether Latin, Cyrillic, Hebrew, Arabic, or Greek) to represent the sounds of spoken language. The sounds themselves are symbols, and they stand for meanings a speaker tries to express. The fact that we can translate from one language to another suggests that the same or similar meanings can be expressed by different symbols in different languages (or, as Shakespeare noted in *Romeo and Juliet*, 'a rose by any other name would smell as sweet'). However, we do not use symbols only to form language. Everything we do in society has a symbolic dimension, from how we conduct ourselves at the dinner table to how we bury the dead.

Culture's beginnings are deep in time and can perhaps be glimpsed among Japanese macaques who invented a custom of washing sweet potatoes and among wild chimpanzees who developed techniques to crack open nuts and to gain access to termites or water (Boesch-Achermann and Boesch 1994; Wolfe 1995: 162–3) (Figure 1.10). Our primate ancestors surely shared similar aptitudes when they started walking bipedally over five million years ago. Two and a half million years later, their descendants were making stone tools, and through human palaeontology and archaeology we can follow our cultural path to the silicon chip. Thus, as Potts puts it, 'an evolutionary bridge exists between the human and animal realms of behaviour' (1996: 197). Potts urges us to think of the modern human capacity for culture not as a uniform monolith but rather as a structure whose various pieces were added at different times in our evolutionary past (Figure 1.11). The foundation of culture, he proposes, contains five elements:

1) *transmission*, the ability to copy behaviour by observation and/or instruction;
2) *memory*, the ability to remember new behaviours, thus allowing traditions to develop;
3) *reiteration*, the ability to reproduce or imitate behaviour or information that has been learned;
4) *innovation*, the ability to invent and modify behaviours; and
5) *selection*, the ability to select which innovations to keep and which to discard.

To the five basic elements, Potts adds three elements that evolved later and made *human* culture possible:

6) *symbolic coding*, or *symbolic representation*, the ability to use symbols to represent elements of reality;

*Figure 1.10* | **A chimpanzee uses a piece of bamboo to get termites out of a hole in a large rock. Such innovative techniques, which are passed from one chimpanzee to the next, suggest the earliest stages of our own culture among our primate ancestors.**

7) *complex symbolic representation*, the ability to communicate freely about the past, the future, and the invisible or imaginary; and

8) *institutional development*, the ability to create complex and variable forms of social organizations unique to our species.

*Symbolic coding* is something we share with other species, in particular the great apes. *Complex symbolic representation* distinguishes human language, for example, from the vocal communication systems of apes, although we know that apes can remember complex symbolic structures and can hold information on remote things. But biological anthropologist Terrence Deacon argues that evolution produced in *Homo sapiens* a brain 'that has been significantly overbuilt for learning symbolic associations' such that 'we cannot help but see the world in symbolic categories' (1997: 413, 416). Moreover, the enormous adaptive value of complex symbolic representation for our ancestors appears to have led to genetic changes that improved our brain's symbolic capacities. Put another way, culture and the human brain *co-evolved*, each furnishing key features of the environment to which the other needed to adapt (Deacon 1997: 44; Odling-Smee 1994). Yet it is the final element given by Potts—*institutional development*—that made it possible for human culture to develop in such elaborate ways. As a result of our ability to create complex social organizations, culture has become 'the predominant manner in which human groups vary from one another . . . it *swamps* the biological differences among populations' (Marks 1995: 200). We are truly biocultural organisms.

Throughout our history, culture has helped humanity survive and prosper in often difficult situations. As cultural traditions are passed on to new generations, we can modify them to meet our changing needs. Many of the practical survival skills we learn, such as what is good to eat and where it is safe to sleep, are never explicitly taught but are nonetheless dependent on contact with other members of our social group. Such learning is sometimes called *habitus* since it is rooted in habitual behaviour. In addition, because cultural traditions encompass the varied situational knowledges and skills of many different individuals, they allow the group to adapt and accomplish beyond

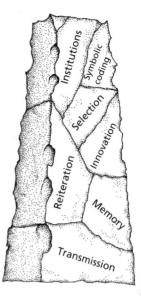

Figure 1.11 | The modern human capacity for culture did not appear all at once; rather, the various pieces that make it up were added at different times in our evolutionary past.

any individual's limitations. We participate as individuals, bringing our unique cultural skill sets to an encompassing cultural identity—effectively our collective, our culture.

Looking at human cultures across time and space, we can also note that they appear *patterned*; that is, related cultural beliefs and practices repeatedly show up in different areas of social life. Some such patterns are rooted in specific historical events: that English and French are widely spoken in Canada is connected to the colonial conquest and domination of Canada by speakers of English and French. Cultural patterns also vary across space: for example, the English of Newfoundland and Labrador differs from the English of southwestern Quebec, and from the various dialects used in different First Nations communities. It differs in rhythm and in vocabulary. Many factors contribute to such variation. In the case of First Nations communities in Canada, researchers have found that 'the heritage languages, language socialization, and cultures of Aboriginal peoples living in Canada influence the ways in which Aboriginal children and families use English' (Bernhardt, Ball, and Deby 2007).

Because of this patterned cultural variation, anthropologists frequently distinguish different 'cultural traditions' from one another. Although distinguishing such traditions can be useful as a kind of shorthand, we must remember that the boundaries between cultural traditions can be very fuzzy, ultimately resting on someone's judgment about how different one set of customs is from another. Indeed, customs in one area of a culture may contradict customs in another area, as when religion tells us to share with others and economics tells us to look out for ourselves. In addition, people have always borrowed cultural elements, so there may be much overlap between apparently distinct traditions. We must also remember not to assume conformity over time; cultures constantly change, and many people refuse to be limited by cultural practices of the past. Yet there is also the question of *traditional culture*—what of the past do specific peoples want to protect, maintain, or retrieve? (Note Regna Darnell's discussion in the 'In Their Own Words' box, below.) Worldwide this is a fundamental dilemma for peoples who have not fared well under colonization, and in the Canadian context this is of concern to First Nations peoples. Ron Ignace, a member of a First Nations band in British Columbia, expressed such concerns in an interview with anthropologist Noel Dyck:

> They [some anthropologists and museums] don't seem to understand that we still exist as a people, that we adapt and change and we have that right to adapt and change, while still maintaining some of our principles that were tried and true over the years. Particularly principles that are necessary for survival as a people. . . . [In a museum] you never get the social dynamism of the culture and how that culture has grown and changed and adapted over the years. (Ignace et al. 1993: 168–9)

As Ignace's comments suggest, the question of how anthropologists can best represent the cultures they study to an outside population is a matter that requires great consideration, sensitivity, and consultation.

## Anthropology and Culture/Cultures: Critique and Response

For many years, the culture concept anchored the anthropological perspective and illuminated the human condition in powerful ways. Yet, over time, the term

*culture* came to mean somewhat different things to different people, and culture has become the most contested concept of contemporary anthropology. What once was 'a shared discourse in anthropology . . . [a] common link among anthropology's subdisciplines' no longer exists, and there has emerged a 'growing intellectual fragmentation [that] has . . . led to greater specialization of each field . . .' (Yengoyan 1986: 368).

Essentially, the critique centres on the specific definition of *Culture* and of *cultures*. The former refers to the distinguishing human characteristic of being able to create and imitate patterned, symbolically mediated ideas and activities that promote the survival of the species, while the latter indicates a particular, learned way of life belonging to a specific group of human beings. Of the two definitions, the second has elicited the most objections. Those who 'write against culture' (Abu-Lughod 1991) continue to defend the validity of *Culture* as a concept, but they object to the use of the term *cultures* because it highlights the differences, rather than shared humanness, between groups of people, suggesting to some a lingering racism in the field of anthropology.

The controversy is heated because many anthropologists have viewed the plural use of *culture* as not only analytically helpful but as politically progressive. Their view reflects a struggle that developed in nineteenth-century Europe: supporters of the purportedly progressive, universal civilization of the Enlightenment, inaugurated by the French Revolution and spread by Napoleonic conquest, were challenged by inhabitants of other European nations who resisted both Napoleon and the Enlightenment in what has been called the Romantic Counter-Enlightenment. Romantic intellectuals in nations such as Germany rejected what they considered to be the imposition of 'artificial' Enlightenment *civilization* on the 'natural' spiritual traditions of their own distinct national *cultures* (Kuper 1999; Crehan 2002). This political dynamic, which pits a steamroller civilization against vulnerable local cultures, carried over into the usage that later developed in anthropology, particularly in North America.

The decades surrounding the turn of the twentieth century marked a period of expanding European colonial empires, as well as westward expansion and consolidation of control in North America. At that time, the social sciences were becoming established

## In Their Own Words | Invisible Genealogies

*Regna Darnell speaks to the concepts of 'tradition' and 'traditional' culture.*

'Traditional' culture is a moving target, always changing and adapting to new circumstances. It is located in the contemporary practices of the communities whose interests and concerns direct the work of anthropologists. The label 'traditional' is used with considerable rhetorical force in contemporary Native American communities and in their interactions with non-Native institutions and individuals. 'Tradition' does not imply returning to some idealized pure culture that existed before Columbus spearheaded the invasion of the 'new' world. Native Americans recognize that their societies, like those of white people, whether in Europe or America, have changed in 500 years; all peoples have a history in which living traditions are continuously invented and reinvented.

This discourse is, of course, very different from the non-Americanist one about 'invented traditions' that somehow lack authenticity because they are continually constructed by contemporary communities, often without attention to the scientific authority of the anthropologist to define their culture. In my view, anthropologists, in the field and in their writing alike, must respect both the cultural heritage and the contemporary practice of the peoples with whom they work. 'Tradition', in such a discourse, refers to that which is continuous with the past, in line with the practices and values of a moral community. Native people themselves can and should define what is traditional within their own communities. They do so in terms of innovations that serve to maintain the identity of the community and its members in relation to their collective histories and personal agencies. 'Tradition', in Native American terms, holds much of the meaning that 'culture' embodies for anthropologists. If it is invented, we must celebrate its creativity and adaptability under conditions of change. That anthropologists sometimes produce alternative interpretations for other purposes is, of course, another matter.

Source: Darnell, Regna. 2001. *Invisible Genealogies: A History of Americanist Anthropology* (Lincoln: University of Nebraska Press), 16–17.

in universities, and different fields were assigned different tasks. Anthropology was allocated what Trouillot (1991) has called 'the savage slot'—that is, the so-called primitive world that was the target of colonization. Anthropologists thus became the official academic experts on societies whose members suffered appalling racist denigration as 'primitives' and whose ways of life were being undermined by contact with Western colonial 'civilization'. And rightly, many anthropologists were determined to denounce such practices and to demonstrate that the 'primitive' stereotype was false.

Some found inspiration in the work of English anthropologist Edward B. Tylor who, as we noted earlier, presented a lasting definition of the term *culture*. His definition had the virtue of blurring the difference between 'culture' and 'civilization', and it encouraged the view that even 'primitives' possessed 'capabilities and habits' that merited respect. Thus, in response to stereotypes of 'primitives' as irrational, disorganized, insensitive, or promiscuous, anthropologists

such as Franz Boas and Bronislaw Malinowski were able to show that, on the contrary, so-called 'primitives' possessed 'cultures' that were reasonable, orderly, artistically developed, and morally disciplined. The plural use of *culture* allowed them to argue that, in their own ways, 'primitives' were as fully human as 'civilized' people.

By the end of the twentieth century, however, the plural use of *culture* began to appear pernicious rather than progressive. To some, the boundary that was once thought to protect vulnerability came to look more like a prison wall, condemning those within it to live according to 'their' culture just as their ancestors had done, like exhibits in a living museum, whether they wanted to or not (recall the quote above from Ignace and his colleagues [1993]). Contemporary critics argue that the plural concept of culture not only highlights the differences between groups of people but also assumes that group members uncritically accept those differences, want to preserve them, and naturally view cultural change as the loss of authenticity. Consequently, if group members disagree with one another publicly, import ideas or practices from other societies, or challenge traditional ways by, for example, protesting against social inequality, they may be condemned by insiders and outsiders alike as flirting with cultural treason. It is this 'totalitarian' concept of culture (Hann 2002: 260) that is the problem: it seems to endorse an oppressive kind of cultural determinism.

Anthropologists Michel-Rolph Trouillot and Adam Kuper have suggested that anthropologists who continue to use any form of the concepts of *Culture* or *cultures* as a part of their professional analytic vocabulary risk lending credibility to the way the concepts have been used to oppress rather than to liberate. This is a serious statement and we must, as anthropologists, be constantly vigilant that oppression is not the outcome of our work. Allowing or facilitating any outcomes of oppression from our research is a betrayal of the great gift of 'self' made to us, and through us to the world, by individuals and cultures in which we have conducted fieldwork.

In another take on the issue, anthropologist Sherry Ortner notes that the essence of the critique was that in the atmosphere of post-colonialism, 'many ethnic groups, and many contemporary post-colonial intellectuals, react very strongly against being studied as specimens of cultural differences and otherness' (1999: 8). Thus the critique of racism was not infrequent. However, Ortner also points out that it is not an issue of 'banishing' the culture concept, the 'Big C', but rather of thinking on the process of 'reconfiguring this enormously productive concept [*cultures*] for a changing world, . . . a changing landscape of theoretical possibilities' (8). What she calls for are three 'imperatives':

1) 'To the move to reduce difference, . . . add the move to exoticize and objectify the culture of the ethnographer, placing it in the same analytic framework. . . . In other words, maintain a strong presumption of cultural difference but make it do new kinds of work' (8).

2) 'Emphasize the issue of meaning-*making*', as it 'is central to questions of power and its effects. The idea that symbolic constructions of meaning are

actively made by real historical actors [is important to] . . . the fundamental assumption that people are always trying to make sense of their lives, always weaving fabrics of meaning, however fragile and fragmentary . . .' (8–9), however desperate their circumstances.

3) '[S]ituate cultural analysis within and, as it were, beneath larger analyses of social and political events and processes. Cultural analysis can no longer . . . be an end in itself' (9).

Attempts by anthropologists to deal with these complications will be a focus in future chapters, especially in our discussions of anthropological approaches to ethnicity and nationalism (Chapter 12), globalization (Chapter 13), and democracy and multiculturalism (Chapter 14).

# The Challenge of Cultural Differences

The same objects, actions, or events frequently mean different things to people within different cultures. In fact, what counts as an object or event in one culture may not be recognized as such in another. Even within a single cultural tradition, the meaning of an object or an action may differ depending on the context. Quoting philosopher Gilbert Ryle, anthropologist Clifford Geertz notes that 'there is a world of difference between a wink and a blink, as anyone who has ever mistaken one for the other has undoubtedly learned' (1973: 6).

Thus, human experience is inherently ambiguous. To resolve the ambiguity, experience must be interpreted. Human beings turn to their own cultural traditions in search of an interpretation that makes sense and is coherent. They do this daily as they go about life among others with whom they share traditions. But this interpretive activity does not cease at the boundary of their specific place in their culture, and serious misunderstandings may arise when two individuals are unaware that their cultural traditions or cultural ground rules differ. Noting the potential for misunderstanding in such encounters, anthropologists are careful to distinguish between two approaches: *ethnocentrism* and *cultural relativism*.

## Ethnocentrism

*Ethnocentrism* is the term anthropologists use to describe the opinion that one's own way of life is natural or correct, indeed the only way of being fully human. Ethnocentrism is one solution to the inevitable tension between individuals from different cultural backgrounds. Yet this 'solution' is problematic because it reduces other ways of life to distorted versions of one's own (see Miner 1956).

The greatest problems with ethnocentrism arise when the members of one society go beyond merely interpreting another way of life in ethnocentric terms and decide to do something about the discrepancies they observe. For example, if individuals from one group conclude that the other way of life is wrong, they might try to convert the members of the other group to their own way of doing things. If the others are unwilling to change their ways, the failed attempt at conversion may enlarge into an active dualism: we versus they, civilization versus savagery, good versus evil. The ultimate result may be war and *genocide*—'ethnic cleansing'—the deliberate attempt to exterminate an entire group based on race, religion, national origin, or other cultural features. Throughout history, such assumed differences have also been used as an excuse for economic and political gains by one faction over another. Indeed, ethnocentric justifications for war and genocide have been a problem in recent times, playing a large part in such conflicts as the Rwandan and Bosnian genocides in the 1990s and the continuing tragedy in Darfur.

Is it possible to avoid ethnocentric bias? A holistic approach to relationships between us and others, both across and within cultural traditions, holds promise. So too does our lifelong ability to learn—if we honour this potential in ourselves and others. People with a cultural background very different from your own may help you see possibilities for belief and action that are drastically at odds with everything your tradition considers possible. By becoming aware of these unsuspected possibilities, you become a different person. In effect you may be gifted with an 'Aha!' moment. In addition, when you share elements of your own culture with people from another cultural background, those individuals are likely to be affected in a similar way.

Learning about other cultures is at once enormously hopeful and immensely threatening. Once such learning occurs, we can no longer claim that any single culture has a monopoly on truth. Rather, we must recognize that the truth embodied in any cultural tradition is bound to be partial, approximate, and open to further insight and growth.

> **ethnocentrism**
> The opinion that one's own way of life is the most natural, correct, or fully human way of life.
>
> **cultural relativism**
> The perspective that all cultures are equally valid and can only be truly understood in their own terms.

## Cultural Relativism

Anthropologists must come to terms with the consequences of learning about cultural differences as they do their fieldwork. One result has been the formulation of the important, although now debated, methodological concept of **cultural relativism**. Boas taught that relativism was the considered response to racism and prejudice and the outcomes of such perspectives. One of his students, Ruth Benedict, commented that all cultures are 'equally valid patterns of life, which mankind has created for itself from the raw materials of existence' (1934: 279). Definitions of cultural relativism have varied over time as different anthropologists have tried to draw conclusions based on their own experiences with other ways of life. One definition that attempts a holistic approach states that cultural relativism involves 'understanding another culture in its own terms sympathetically enough so that the culture appears to be a coherent and meaningful design for living' (Greenwood and Stini 1977: 182).

Taking a relativistic approach can help us understand what at first might seem incomprehensible from an outsider's perspective. For example, cultural relativism can help us understand how genocide could develop in a society. Consider the example of the Holocaust in Europe. The Holocaust was intimately related to certain cultural patterns and historical processes that were, and perhaps are yet, deeply rooted in German and European society. Answering questions on the causes of the Holocaust involves investigating the historical roots of anti-Semitism and nationalism in Germany (Figure 1.12).

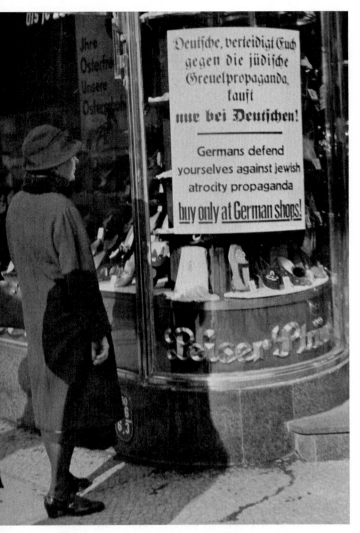

**Figure 1.12 | A sign posted in Berlin, Germany, in 1933 assaults passersby both in German and in English: 'Germans defend yourselves against jewish [sic] atrocity propaganda, buy only at German shops!' Such public displays of combined anti-Semitism and nationalism are evidence of the cultural preoccupations that led to the Holocaust.**

Some people might be inclined to take a deterministic approach to explaining such an event, arguing that the killers cannot be blamed for their own actions because they had no choice but to do what their culture dictated. These same people might also argue that all members of the culture committing the genocide are responsible because it was their collectively constructed culture that led to the genocide. Yet to accept

the argument that 'their' culture made them do it is to accept a pessimistic version of cultural determinism that can offer only a simplified account of any complex phenomenon. This sort of cultural determinism makes three fundamental assumptions about human nature and human society:

1) cultures have neat boundaries between them and are sealed off from one another;
2) every culture offers people only one way to interpret experience (cultures are monolithic and permit no variety, harbour no contradictions, and allow no dissent); and
3) people living in these closed cultural worlds are passively shaped by culture, helpless to resist indoctrination into a single world view, and incapable of inventing alternatives to that view.

Yet lived human experience undermines all three of these assumptions. To begin with, cultures are not sealed off from one another. Their boundaries are fuzzy, indeed porous, and people with different cultural backgrounds regularly exchange ideas and practices. Internally, they are not monolithic. Even without the alternatives introduced from the outside, every culture offers a variety of ways to interpret experience, although not all may be officially sanctioned. In addition, cultures are constantly being redefined by their members (Benhabib 2002). Finally, human beings are not passive lumps shaped unresistingly to fit a single cultural mould. There is no such thing as a single cultural mould in a society acquainted with variety, and in a society where options exist, choices must be made.

In contrast to the deterministic approach, a relativistic understanding of the Holocaust—and mass genocides in general—accomplishes several things. It makes the events more comprehensible, even coherent. It reveals, to our horror, how the persecution and murder of human beings can appear perfectly acceptable when placed in a particular context of meaning, thus challenging our own views on violence. The one thing that this relativistic understanding does not do, however, is allow us to excuse mass killers for what they have done on the grounds that it was all due to their culture.

Understanding something is not the same as approving or excusing it. When we grow to understand a cultural practice that we at first found repellent, we may arrive at a number of different conclusions. We may change our minds and decide that the practice is desirable, at least in some contexts. We may conclude that the practice in question is more suitable for the people who employ it than any of our own practices would be. We might even recommend that the practice be adopted in our own society. But the opposite may also be the case. We may understand perfectly the cultural rationales—for example, those behind such practices as slavery, infanticide, headhunting, or genocide—and still refuse our approval. We may not be persuaded by the reasons offered to justify the practice, or we may be aware of alternative arrangements that could achieve the desired outcome using less drastic methods. Indeed, it is likely that any cultural practice with far-reaching consequences for human life will have critics as well as supporters within the society where it is practised. This is certainly the case in North American societies where such sensitive topics as abortion, capital punishment, gun laws, and same-sex marriage have been and continue to be discussed in many contexts.

Cultural relativism makes moral reasoning more complex. It does not, however, require us to abandon every value our own society has taught us. Our culture, like every other culture, offers more than one way of evaluating experience. Exposure to the interpretations of an unfamiliar culture forces us to reconsider the possibilities our culture recognizes in light of new alternatives and to search for areas of intersection as well as areas of disagreement. What cultural relativism does discourage is the easy solution of refusing to consider alternatives from the outset. Also, it does not free us from sometimes facing difficult choices between alternatives whose rightness or wrongness is less than clear-cut. In this sense, 'cultural relativism is a "tough-minded" philosophy' (Herskovits 1973: 37). As Rosaldo (2008) comments,

Relativism . . . argues for engagement, for dialogue between cultures. This is not the kind of easy cosmopolitanism that implies enormous privilege—the capacity, for example, to spend three days in the Bali Hilton. It's a deeper form of knowing that entails some recognition that I am one among others. I'm not the centre of the universe.

Thus, at its core, cultural relativism is an argument against ethnocentrism.

## Culture, History, and Human Agency

The human condition is rooted in time and shaped by history. As part of the human condition, culture is also historical, worked out and reconstructed in every generation. As paleoanthropologists have shown, the human species is itself a product of millions of years of evolution. Hence, human history is an essential aspect of the human story.

Anthropologists sometimes disagree about how to approach human history. Nineteenth-century thinkers such as Herbert Spencer argued that an examination of the evolution of social structures over time was central to the study of the human condition. Other anthropologists, sensitive to the excesses of people like Herbert Spencer, were not interested in change over time. In the 1930s, A.R. Radcliffe-Brown justified this lack of interest by pointing out that in societies without written records, knowledge about past life is non-existent; any attempt to reconstruct such past life would be an unfounded attempt at 'conjectural history'.

Other anthropologists had no interest in history for a different reason. Western capitalist culture, with its eye on the future and its faith in progress—a theme from the Enlightenment—has had little use for the past. It is therefore no wonder that some anthropologists built clockwork models of social structures that could be trusted to run reliably without 'losing time'. In these models, human beings and societies are both likened to machines. If a living organism is used as the model of society, and if organisms are nothing but machines, then a machine model of society, with individuals as robot-like moving parts, is not at all far-fetched (Figure 1.13).

A holistic and dialectical approach—one that focusses on inclusive assessment of counter points of view—to human history, however, rejects these clockwork models. Our biocultural heritage has produced a living species that uses culture to surmount biological and individual limitations. The result has been the emergence of beings who are capable of studying themselves and their own biocultural evolution.

**Figure 1.13** | In the classic 1936 film *Modern Times*, Charlie Chaplin's tramp succumbs to the hectic pace of modern life and becomes trapped in a giant machine. This image offers a literal interpretation of the machine model of society, in which human beings are nothing more than moving parts caught in a mechanized system.

But just how free from limitations are humans? Opinion in Western societies often polarizes around one of two extremes: either we have *free will* and may do just as we please or our behaviour is *completely determined* by biology or society. Many social scientists, however, are convinced that a more realistic description of human freedom was offered by Karl Marx, who wrote, 'Men make their own history, but they do not make it just as they please; they do not make it under circumstances chosen by themselves but under circumstances directly encountered, given, and transmitted by the past' (1963: 15). As humans we regularly struggle, often against great odds, to exercise some control over our lives. We are *agents*, but agents who cannot escape from the cultural and historical contexts within which we act (Figure 1.14). We must frequently select a course of action when the 'correct' choice is unclear and the

> **human agency**
> Human beings' ability to exercise at least some control over their lives.

outcome uncertain. Some anthropologists even liken our existence to a minefield that we must painstakingly try to cross without blowing ourselves up. In such contexts, with their ragged edges and fuzzy boundaries, we human beings must make interpretations, formulate goals, and set out in pursuit of them. A holistic, dialectical approach to the human condition recognizes the existence and importance of **human agency**—the stuff of our dreams and the realm of our potential for growth.

# The Promise of the Anthropological Perspective

The anthropological perspective on the human condition is not easy to maintain. It forces us to question the common-sense assumptions with which we are most comfortable. It increases the difficulty we encounter when faced with moral and political decisions. It does not allow us an

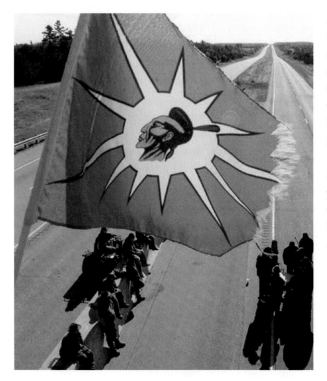

Figure 1.14 | People regularly struggle, often against great forces, to exercise some control over their lives. In 2007, Mohawk protesters from the Bay of Quinte successfully shut down Highway 401, one of Canada's busiest highways, as part of their protest of a housing development near Deseronto, Ontario.

easy retreat to ethnocentrism when the going gets rough. Once we are exposed to the kinds of experiences that the anthropological undertaking makes possible, we are changed—for better or worse. We cannot easily pretend that these new experiences never happened to us. Once we have had a genuine glimpse of the other as human beings equal to ourselves, there is no going back, except in bad faith.

So, anthropology is guaranteed to complicate your life. Nevertheless, the anthropological perspective can give you a broader understanding of human nature and the wider world—of society, culture, and history—and thus help you construct more realistic and authentic ways of coping with those complications.

## Key Terms

# Chapter Summary

1. The belief that human nature has two parts is known as *dualism*. Mind–matter dualism is deeply rooted in Western thought, dating back to figures such as Plato.

2. Idealism reduces human nature to ideas or the mind that produces them. Materialism reduces human nature to genes, hormones, or biology. Biological determinism, environmental determinism, and historical determinism are all forms of materialist determinism.

3. The most extreme position against the various forms of materialist reductionism—cultural determinism—argues that the ideas, meanings, beliefs, and values that people learn in society determine their behaviours. Optimistic versions of cultural determinism hold out the hope that we can change these determining agents and make ourselves whatever we want to be. Pessimistic versions conclude that we are what we are conditioned to be, something over which we have no control.

4. In preference to dualism, anthropologists have suggested holism, which assumes that objects and environments interpenetrate and even define each other. Thus, the whole is greater than the sum of its parts. Human beings and human societies are open systems that cannot be reduced to the parts that make them up. The parts and the whole mutually define or co-determine each other and co-evolve.

5. Anthropology is a scholarly discipline that aims to describe, in the broadest sense, what it means to be human. To achieve this aim, anthropologists have developed a perspective on the human condition that is holistic, comparative, and evolutionary. Because human beings lack instincts that automatically promote our survival, we must learn from other members of our society what we need to know to survive. For this reason, the concept of culture is central to the anthropological perspective.

6. In North America, anthropology is usually considered to have four major specialties: biological anthropology, archaeology, linguistic anthropology, and cultural anthropology. Some anthropologists consider applied anthropology to be a separate subdiscipline of professional specialization.

7. Biological anthropology began as an attempt to classify the world's populations into different races, an undertaking that some people used to justify the social practice of racism. By the early twentieth century, however, most anthropologists had rejected racial classifications as scientifically unjustifiable. Since the early twentieth century, anthropologists have used information about human biology and human culture to debunk racist stereotypes. Modern anthropologists who are interested in human biology include biological anthropologists, primatologists, and paleoanthropologists.

8. Archaeology is anthropology of the human past, but the material remains archaeologists recover can be of value to biological and cultural anthropologists.

9. Linguistic anthropologists try to understand language in relation to broader cultural, historical, and biological contexts. They study language acquisition, sign language, challenges to communication across linguistic barriers, and connections between language and social identity. Recent work focusses on the way political relationships influence language use.

10. Cultural anthropologists study human diversity by focussing on sets of learned behaviours and ideas that human beings acquire as members of different societies. Because cultural anthropology is comparative, research is done in various cultural settings, both Western and non-Western.

11. Through fieldwork, cultural anthropologists gain insight into another culture, both by participating with their informants in social activities and by observing those activities as outsiders. Ethnographies are published accounts of what was learned during fieldwork. Ethnology involves comparing ethnographic information from two or more different cultures. Because human experience is often ambiguous, adaptation requires cultural interpretation, which is a constant, necessary process, whether it is an attempt to understand people or symbols within one's own culture or those of another culture.

12. Applied anthropologists use information gathered from the other anthropological specialties to solve practical problems in areas such as health care and economic development.

13. Most anthropologists emphasize that human beings are biocultural organisms with a biological makeup that allows us to make and use culture. As a result, human

beings have produced a tremendous variety of distinct cultural traditions.

14. Many anthropologists have criticized the use of the term *cultures* to refer to particular, learned ways of life belonging to specific groups of human beings. Critics argue that the plural concept of culture seems to endorse an oppressive kind of cultural determinism, but many groups have incorporated the plural use of culture into their own self-definitions, which other anthropologists defend as valuable and progressive.

15. Ethnocentrism is a form of reductionism. Anthropologists believe it can be countered by a commitment to cultural relativism, an attempt to understand the cultural underpinnings of behaviour. Cultural relativism makes moral decisions more difficult because it requires us to take into account many things before we make up our minds. Cultural relativism does not require us to abandon every value our society has taught us; however, it does discourage the easy solution of refusing to consider alternatives from the outset.

16. Human history is an essential aspect of the human story, a dialectic between biology and culture. Culture is worked out over time and passed on from one generation to the next. Because human beings have the power to act in their own interests, the story of our species also involves human agency.

## Critical Thinking Questions

1. Using the concepts of idealism and materialism, how would you develop definitions of what it means to be human? How deterministic are your definitions?

2. Distinguish between *Culture* (singular) and *cultures* (plural). Why has this distinction become contentious in anthropology, and what is the suggested resolution to this problem?

3. Consider the concept of holism. How does anthropology use holism as a methodology as well as a concept?

Can holism succeed in anthropology without cultural relativism?

4. How do the four original subdisciplines of anthropology contribute to an understanding of humans? How does applied anthropology add to this anthropological perspective, and what would you consider its ethical position in anthropology?

## Suggested Readings

Ashmore, Wendy, and Robert J. Sharer. 2009. *Discovering Our Past: A Brief Introduction to Archaeology*, 5th edn (New York: McGraw-Hill). An engaging introduction to the techniques, assumptions, interests, and findings of modern archaeology.

Benhabib, Seyla. 2002. *The Claims of Culture: Equality and Diversity in the Global Era.* Princeton, NJ: Princeton University Press. This book discusses what we mean by political membership and what constitutes a political community. How do we bring immigrants, strangers, people we term aliens (immigrants, asylum seekers) into our political processes? What are the boundaries that must be negotiated?

Feder, Kenneth L. 2010. *Frauds, Myths, and Mysteries: Science and Pseudoscience in Archaeology*, 7th edn (New York: McGraw-Hill). An entertaining and informative exploration of fascinating frauds and genuine archaeological mysteries seen through an application of the scientific method.

Gamst, Frederick, and Edward Norbeck, eds. 1976. *Ideas of Culture: Sources and Uses* (New York: Holt, Rinehart, & Winston).

A useful collection of important articles about culture. The articles are arranged according to different basic approaches to culture.

Marks, Jonathan. 2002. *What It Means to Be 98% Chimpanzee: Apes, People, and Their Genes* (Berkeley: University of California Press). A lively and provocative text by a molecular anthropologist who explains what can and cannot be concluded from the fact that the genomes of chimpanzees and humans are nearly identical.

Ortner, Sherry. B. 2006. *Anthropology and Social Theory: Culture, Power, and the Acting Subject* (Durham, NC: Duke University Press). So you want to be an anthropologist? This is a must-read either now or when you are in an advanced theory course!

Relethford, John. 2009. *The Human Species: An Introduction to Biological Anthropology*, 8th edn (New York: McGraw-Hill). An excellent, clear introduction to biological anthropology.

Skinner, M., and K. Bowie. 2008. 'Forensic Anthropology: Canadian Content and Contributions', in *Handbook of Forensic*

*Anthropology and Archaeology*, eds S. Blau and D.H. Ubelaker (California: Left Coast Press). As the title indicates, this is a handbook for forensic anthropologists.

Voget, Fred. 1975. *A History of Ethnology* (New York: Holt, Rinehart & Winston). A massive, thorough, and detailed work. For the student seeking a challenging read.

Watson, Patty Jo. 1995. 'Archaeology, Anthropology, and the Culture Concept', *American Anthropologist*, New Series, 97, 4: 683–94. This article relates how an anthropologist/archaeologist evolved in her thinking about the nature of the subject of her discipline and her specialty within that discipline.

## Related Websites

**Applied Anthropology** www.thecanadianencyclopedia.com/index.cfm?PgNm=TCE&Params=A1ARTA0000237

**Archaeology at Parks Canada** www.pc.gc.ca/eng/progs/arch/index.aspx

**Canadian Archaeological Association** www.canadianarchaeology.com

**Hidden from History—The Canadian Holocaust** www.hiddenfromhistory.org

**Informant (Debated Terminology)** www.anthrobase.com/Dic/eng/def/informant.htm

**Residential Schools** http://archives.cbc.ca/society/education/topics/692/; www.cbc.ca/canada/north/story/2008/04/02/north-schools.html; www.cbc.ca/canada/story/2008/05/16/f-faqs-residential-schools.html

**Society for Applied Anthropology** www.sfaa.net

# 2 | Fieldwork: A Meeting of Cultural Traditions

## Chapter Outline

## Learning Objectives

By the end of Chapter 2, you will be able to

- understand the endeavour of ethnographic fieldwork,
- describe how fieldwork is used in cultural anthropology,
- outline forms of data collection,
- detail key stages in the process of preparing to do fieldwork,
- understand the importance of professional ethics,

- anticipate the difficulties of culture shock,
- compare and contrast three modes of ethnographic research: positivist, reflexive, and multi-sited,
- recognize the agency of both anthropologist and informant in the dialectic of fieldwork,
- consider the effects of fieldwork on all involved, and
- appreciate the utility of anthropological knowledge and its open-ended nature.

A researcher engages with locals in Colombia. Fieldwork offers anthropologists the opportunity to gain insight into new cultural worlds and to reflect on their own culture in a new way.

Many people around the world find something unusual about ethnographic fieldwork. Someone shows up in a community, plans to be there for a year or more, claims to be interested in the community's way of life, and then spends all of his or her time interacting with people, making observations, and taking notes! Yet by bringing people from different cultural backgrounds together, this process creates the space for serendipitous moments of deep learning. In this space, a great gift is given: people give of themselves and their resources, sharing their families and friendships, homes and food, as well as insights into their lives and their culture. Receiving such a gift can be a very humbling experience for the researcher. Through interaction—a process of *reciprocal* action and influence—all emerge changed in essential ways. Thus, **fieldwork** not only broadens anthropological understandings of cultural worlds but also transforms the self-understandings of anthropologists and the people with whom they work. However, it is important to remember that researchers get to go home, while the people they study *are* at home and have to live with what the researcher has transformed. There is, then, the incredible responsibility of behaving ethically in seeking and accepting the gift.

**fieldwork**
An extended period of close involvement with the people in whose way of life anthropologists are interested, during which anthropologists ordinarily collect most of their data.

**participant-observation**
The method anthropologists use to gather information by living and working with the people whose culture they are studying while participating in their lives as much as possible.

## Interaction in the Field

When conducting fieldwork, anthropologists use various methods to gather data. Both before and after they enter the field, researchers consult published literature and archives relevant to their research. Often, they conduct structured interviews. Sometimes they use questionnaires and psychological tests, but they never rely solely on such methods because, by itself, the information they produce cannot be contextualized and may be highly misleading. Therefore, anthropologists generally engage in methods of **participant-observation**.

Participant-observation involves direct, face-to-face interaction between the researcher and their local research partners, as they go about their daily lives. The method was pioneered by cultural anthropologists and remains characteristic of anthropological work. It allows anthropologists to comprehend what people say and do in the wider context of social interaction and cultural beliefs and values. As we will discover, participant-observation is the most productive method available to anthropologists who seek a holistic understanding of culture and the human condition.

## The Fieldwork Experience

For many cultural anthropologists, ethnographic fieldwork is the quintessential anthropological experience (Figure 2.1). Sometimes field experience begins in undergraduate or early graduate studies, when students work on research projects or in field schools run by established anthropologists. An extended period of fieldwork is the final phase of formal anthropological training, and many anthropologists incorporate additional periods of field research into their subsequent careers. Beginning

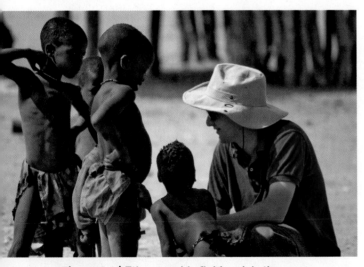

*Figure 2.1* | **Ethnographic fieldwork is the quintessential anthropological experience. Many students participate in fieldwork as the final phase of their formal anthropological training.**

anthropologists usually decide during graduate school where and on what topic they wish to do their research.

Students who have not yet been in the field often develop an idealized image of field experience: at first, the fieldworker is a bit disoriented and potential informants are suspicious, but uncertainty soon gives way to understanding and trust as the anthropologist's good intentions are made known and accepted. The fieldworker succeeds in establishing a rapport. In fact, the fieldworker becomes so well loved and trusted, so thoroughly accepted, that he or she is accepted as an equal and allowed access to the culture's secrets. Yet, as Karp and Kendall (1982) note, and as you will discover in this chapter, it is not just naive to think that the locals will accept you as one of them without any difficulty, it is also bad science.

Many novice researchers also do not anticipate the amount of preplanning that goes into a research project. Something as seemingly simple as finding a place to live may be challenging. Sometimes, a researcher will simply move into a pre-existing residence in the research locale; but other times, particularly when the researcher will be working among remote peoples in a rain forest, desert, or tundra area, he or she may need to bring along materials to establish adequate living quarters.

In addition, a project's success often depends on the researcher's ability to obtain authorization to work in a particular place—for example, permission from academic and government offices in the host country—and acceptance from the people who will be participants in the study. In the past, such acceptance was not always sought, and the people who were to be studied did not always know an anthropologist was on the way. Arriving in Pond Inlet, on Baffin Island, in 1963, Matthiasson noted, 'No one in the settlement knew of my impending arrival although I was equipped with an Explorer's and Scientist's licence properly signed by the appropriate officials in Ottawa—a bureaucratic prerequisite for research in the Northwest Territories' (1992: 13). Today this would never do! Researchers need to seek funds to support their studies, and funding agencies have strict codes of ethics for research involving human participants.

Getting grants from private or government agencies involves, among other things, persuading them that the work will focus on a topic of current interest within

anthropology and that it is connected to their funding priorities. As a result, 'field sites . . . end up being defined by the cross-hatched intersection of visa and clearance procedures, the interests of funding agencies, and intellectual debates within the discipline and its subfields' (Gupta and Ferguson 1997: 11). Since funds are finite, not all topics of current interest can be funded; to get around this limitation, some anthropologists pay for their research themselves by getting a job in the area where they want to do fieldwork or by supplementing small grants out of their own pockets.

Anthropologists who conduct field research must remember that they are accountable not only to the people who fund their projects but also to the individuals who allow them entry into their lives. To help researchers protect the rights and dignity of their informants, professional voluntary associations such as the Canadian Anthropology Society/Société canadienne d'anthropologie (CASCA) and the American Anthropological Association (AAA) provide networks through which researchers can connect with one another to discuss best practices in the field. Some associations also offer guidelines for conducting ethical research. The AAA's *Code of Ethics* states that 'Anthropological researchers have *primary ethical obligations* to the people, species, and materials they study and to the people with whom they work' and must 'ensure that they do not harm the safety, dignity, or privacy of the people with whom they work, conduct research, or perform other professional activities' (2009: III, A.1, A.2; italics added). In Canada, the *Tri-Council Policy Statement* (*TCPS*), first published in 1998 and revised in 2010, sets ethical guidelines for researchers and informs the research ethics boards (REBs) of all federally funded institutions. It explicitly states that 'researchers are expected, as a condition of funding, to adhere to the *TCPS*' (CIHR, NSERC, SSHRC 2010).

As you might expect, policies evolve from the problems, constraints, and considerations that arise from fieldwork, but no policy can suit every researcher or address every problem one might encounter in a research setting. Mike Evans, reflecting on his research into the Island Cache in British Columbia, has noted the problem of voice and representation within the constraints of confidentiality for informants as outlined in the 1998 *TCPS* (see Mike Evans's discussion in the 'In Their Own Words' box, below). Evans, like most anthropologists,

*In Their Own Words* | **Ethics, Anonymity, and Authorship in Community-Centred Research**

*Mike Evans is head of the School of Arts and Social Sci-encversiUniversity, Australia. Formerly he was at the University of British Columbia Okanagan as Head of Culture Community and Global Studies and Canada Research Chair (CRC) in World Indigenous Peoples*

Since its introduction in 1998, the Tri-Council Policy Statement on Ethical Conduct for Research Involving Humans (hereafter referred to as the 'Tri-Council policy' or just the 'policy') has had more and more impact on social science research in Canada. All across the country 'Research Ethics Boards' have been set up, and the eight central principles of the Tri-Council Guidelines now set the terms of reference for almost all university-associated research with people. . . . The eight central principles are:

1. *Respect for Human Dignity*
2. *Respect for Free and Informed Consent*
3. *Respect for Vulnerable Persons*
4. *Respect for Privacy and Confidentiality*
5. *Respect for Justice and Inclusiveness*
6. *Balancing Harms and Benefits*
7. *Minimizing Harm*
8. *Maximizing Benefit*

Respect, clearly a good thing, figures prominently. But, by way of example of why the uniform application of these principles is problematic, I would like to talk about . . . contemporary community-centred research and the way the Tri-Council policy is having some impacts that are, contrary to its central principles, not particularly respectful. . . . Community-centred research is just that, a research process that is both located at the community and one that centralizes community concerns and participation. The central question . . . is: Can community-centred research be respectfully undertaken while embracing the notion of anonymity of research participants?

\* \* \*

## Respect for Privacy and Confidentiality

. . . I will concentrate on some of the tensions between acknowledgement and anonymity in contemporary social science research—and especially community-centred research. . . .

Tri-Council policy enshrines 'Respect for Privacy and Confidentiality' as one of its eight central principles. In

the introduction of the ethics document, the following can be found:

> Respect for human dignity also implies the principles of respect for privacy and confidentiality. In many cultures, privacy and confidentiality are considered fundamental to human dignity. Thus, standards of privacy and confidentiality protect the access, control, and dissemination of personal information. In doing so, such standards help to protect mental or psychological integrity. They are thus consonant with the values underlying privacy, confidentiality, and anonymity respected. (CIHR, NSERC, SSHRC 1998)

On the surface, there is very little to disagree with here. However, I want to question the statement that confidentiality (anonymity) protects mental or psychological integrity. Confidentiality and anonymity can be quite valuable in protecting people in research involving psychological experiments or quantitative sociological surveys where there is absolutely no cost to the research, or it is essential to the validity of the research paradigm. In qualitative branches of sociology, history, anthropology, or Indigenous studies, and especially in the context of much community-centred research, anonymity can obscure community authority and voice, and the intent of the principle above is undone. In fact, misplaced confidentiality can 'disappear' people and communities. . . .

Section 3 of the Tri-Council policy deals specifically with issues of confidentiality and anonymity. Nowhere in this section, or for that matter anywhere else in the document, does a research participant's right to be recognized as the source of information get any ink. The document does deal very carefully with how to maintain confidentiality in the context of primary research and secondary data use. But except where information is collected individually and then aggregated (i.e., in quantitative research such as a demographic survey), confidentiality in a community is a much bigger problem than using pseudonyms or anonymity can accommodate. When talking about oral history and/or contemporary social issues, anonymity might protect people from outsiders, but less dependably from people within the community. This is especially a problem when there is an explicit commitment on the part of the researchers to make research results available to as wide a cross-section of the community as possible. . . . The same might be said of whole communities—i.e., the practice of assigning pseudonyms to communities only protects the community from people who don't care to do the little bit of digging required to figure out the real community identity. As researchers struggle to make research community centred—increasing the participation of community in setting research questions, undertaking the research itself, and producing community-accessible research products—confidentiality becomes more and more difficult to maintain and more and more costly (in terms of other values like representation, authority, and voice) to the communities.

Are confidentiality and privacy moot? No. Contemporary community-centred research agendas must recognize that anonymity is not a panacea for maintaining ethics and must not (to make a hybrid of two metaphors of common anatomical reference) become a Band-Aid that protects institutional butts while leaving community ones exposed. This may be an especially poignant issue when it comes to Indigenous communities who have suffered expropriation of various types. But if one goes to Section 6 of the Tri-Council policy, a section that deals directly with Aboriginal persons, you will find what is basically a call for participatory research without any reconsideration of the issues of anonymity.

What then? How does this affect 'science', as it surely does? I mean to imply that the content of research needs to be tested against the protection of (more positively, the benefit to) 'mental or psychological integrity', and I would add social integrity, of communities. For many people this might be heretical, tantamount to censorship—certainly and explicitly what I am saying means that some things might simply not be researchable in some contexts (of course the Tri-Council policy has the same implications). I do not mean to suggest that difficult issues should be avoided in, or by, any community (though I do mean to state plainly that some issues should be addressed in terms of intervention and community activism rather than as research problems). Against the loss of research results in the issue of benefits, the benefits to communities that come of effective participatory research, truly community-centred research projects, and research results that community members can interpret, own, and in which they see themselves reflected and named. Anonymity is not, at least not always, the best route to ethical research. The challenge is to do research and to produce research results that are ethical in content and structure rather than structure alone.

Source: Evans, Mike. 2004. 'Ethics, Anonymity, and Authorship in Community Centred Research, or Anonymity and the Island Cache', *Pimatisiwin: A Journal of Aboriginal and Indigenous Community Health* 2, 1: 60–75.

feels strongly that informants have the right to protect their identities. Indeed, the need for protection is paramount when informants belong to marginal or powerless groups that might suffer retaliation from more powerful agencies. However, Evans emphasizes that in certain situations, such as community-centred research when informants wish to express their identities and ideas, anthropologists need to record people's stories without depriving individuals of their right to be acknowledged. In such a form of ethnographic writing, the anthropologist serves primarily as translator and editor of the voices and opinions of individual informants (see also Keesing 1983; Shostak 1981).

Of course, before a researcher can look for funding or contemplate any specific ethical issues, she or he must choose a focus and a setting for the research. Classic anthropological fieldwork emphasized working 'abroad'—that is, doing fieldwork in societies that were culturally and geographically distant from that of the ethnographer. This orientation bears undeniable traces of its origins under European colonialism, but it continues to be a valuable means of drawing attention to ways of life and parts of the world that elite groups in powerful Western nations have traditionally dismissed or marginalized. More recent discussions of anthropological fieldwork have noted the significance of working 'at home', particularly when the ethnographer focusses on the forms of social differentiation and marginalization present in the society to which he or she belongs. This orientation has the added benefit of providing insight from an insider's perspective; increasingly, anthropologists working in their own societies interpret and write about their experiences both as observers and as members of those societies (see, e.g., Foley 1989; Kumar 1992). Such an orientation also notably incorporates traditions of anthropological research that have developed in countries such as Mexico, Brazil, India, and Russia, where fieldwork at home has long been the norm. In the twenty-first century, these developments are helping create 'decolonized anthropology in a deterritorialized world' that will be enriched by the work of anthropologists trained in different traditions, working at home and abroad, who seek to forge 'links between *different* knowledges that are possible from different locations' (Gupta and Ferguson 1997: 35, 38).

# Modes of Ethnographic Fieldwork: A Short History

When anthropology began to take on its own identity as an intellectual discipline during the nineteenth century, it aspired to be scientific. Anthropology still aims to be scientific in its study of human nature, human society, and human history. For several decades, however, scientists, philosophers, historians, and increasing numbers of social scientists have been questioning and re-examining many deeply rooted assumptions about what science is and how it works. One outcome of this work has been the demonstration that the so-called hard sciences (such as physics, chemistry, and biology) and the so-called soft sciences (such as psychology, sociology, and anthropology)

have more in common with each other than previously recognized (e.g., Barad 1999; Pickering 1995). Another outcome has been the revelation that there is not just one but a *variety* of scientific methods, each developed in different disciplines and able to produce reliable knowledge about the world (e.g., Knorr Cetina 2000). Therefore we can study an infinite number of 'logically possible worlds' (Popper 1979: 39) using diverse methodologies. What is important, according to Cohen (1994: 6), is that each inquiry has its own integrity, internal coherence, and results that can be tested.

These developments intersect in important ways with anthropologists' efforts to understand the scientific status of the fieldwork tradition based on participant-observation (see Figure 2.2). This research strategy came into its own in the early decades of the twentieth century in the work of pioneer ethnographers such as Bronislaw Malinowski (who, it is often said, invented long-term participant-observation–based fieldwork); Franz Boas (who based much of his fieldwork on the Kwakiutl in British Columbia);

*Figure 2.2* | Participant-observation has long been a hallmark of research in cultural anthropology, whether in the 1920s with Margaret Mead on the island of Samoa (left) or in the 1980s with Naomi McPherson in Papua New Guinea (above).

Boas's best-known student, Margaret Mead (who, on her own admission, 'escaped' Boas's control by going on fieldwork in the South Pacific); and Frank G. Speck (who worked with the Algonquians of eastern Canada). Since that time, the conditions within which fieldwork has been carried out have changed, and anthropologists have been prompted to rethink and revise their basic views about fieldwork in terms of its scientific status and as a form of human interaction. Three modes of ethnographic fieldwork have developed over the last hundred years: positivist, reflexive, and multi-sited. In this section, we explore the first two of these modes; later in this chapter, we will discuss the third and most recent mode, multi-sited fieldwork.

## The Positivist Approach

The traditional method of the physical sciences, which early social scientists tried to imitate, is often called *positivistic science*. Its proponents based their view of science on a set of principles most fully set out in the writings of a group of influential thinkers known as *positivists*, who were active in the late nineteenth and early twentieth centuries, though this view also refers back to French philosopher Auguste Comte (1798–1857) and his 'positive philosophy'. Today, **positivism** has become a label for a particular way of looking at and studying the world scientifically.

First, positivists are committed to explaining how the material world works in terms of material causes and processes that we can detect using our senses. Second, to achieve this goal, positivists are also committed to a separation of facts from values as part of scientific methodology. They justify this separation on the grounds that facts relate to the nature of physical, material reality—what *is*—whereas, in their view, values are based on speculation about what *ought to be*. To the positivist, scientific research is concerned only with the former. As a result all valid scientific inquiry, no matter the focus, should be understood as different aspects of a single, disinterested quest for knowledge, a quest that cannot be compromised simply because it offends some people's moral or political sensibilities. The truth remains the truth whether people like it or not, whether it conforms to their idea of what is good and proper or not. These examples point to a third feature of positivists: they are convinced that a single scientific method can be used to investigate any domain of reality, from planetary motion to chemical reactions to human life. The most ambitious positivists are convinced that all scientific knowledge will ultimately be unified in a 'theory of everything'.

> **positivism**
> The view that there is a reality 'out there' that can be detected through the senses and that there is a single, appropriate scientific method for investigating that reality.
>
> **objective knowledge**
> Knowledge about reality that is absolute and true for all people, in all times and places.

The traditional goal of the positivist program has been to produce **objective knowledge**. Positivists believe that their approach is the route to such knowledge because it seeks to describe the way the material world actually is, unobscured by any human-applied values or webs of meaning.

### Applying Positivist Methods to Anthropology

For the positivist, the prototypical research scenario involves a physical scientist in a laboratory. This prototype creates obstacles for those who study human life by means of participant-observation in a natural setting. Early cultural anthropologists were aware of these obstacles, and they tried to devise ways to get around them. Their first step was to approximate lab conditions by testing hypotheses in different cultural settings. These settings were carefully selected to exhibit the same range of variation, naturally, that a laboratory scientist could create artificially. As a result, the field could be seen as a living laboratory. Each research setting would correspond to a separate experimental situation, a method called *controlled comparison*. Margaret Mead used this method in the 1930s when she studied four different societies in an attempt to discover the range and causes of gender roles.

Anthropologists such as Mead were encouraged by the enormous successes that the physical scientists had attained by following positivist principles. From the mid-nineteenth to the mid-twentieth century, positivistically inclined anthropologists recorded the ways of life of peoples their contemporaries had neither heard of nor cared to know. Rejecting the slipshod, impressionistic work of an earlier period, they attempted to produce accounts of other cultures that were systematic and accurate, and they more or less succeeded, although they were sometimes accused of insensitivity.

Anthropologists found themselves confronting a paradox. In order to remain true to positivism, they had to record objective facts from the perspective of an invisible observer; yet in order to get closer to the truth, they had to admit that they were personally involved in the situation. In fact, they regularly developed close ties to the people among whom they worked, often defending their full humanity to outsiders and, at times, even intervening on their behalf with the government. Yet none of these efforts showed up in their ethnographies. To resolve these apparent conflicts, they needed to find a new approach.

### Questioning the Positivist Approach

The 1960s and 1970s marked a turning point in anthropological understandings of fieldwork. Many assumptions about the way the world worked were called into question, as was the nature of scientific inquiry. Freeman's critique (1983; 1998) of Margaret Mead's early fieldwork in Samoa illustrates the tone of the debate (see Côté [2000] for a summary of the Mead–Freeman controversy). Anthropologists began to write ethnographies highlighting the ways their own involvement with others in the field had contributed to the growth of cross-cultural knowledge. They were able to show how different observers, working from different assumptions, often produce different knowledges about the same society. At the same time, they noted that differently situated fieldworkers also draw similar conclusions, and these conclusions allow them to link their work in productive ways.

Consider the case of Annette Weiner, who conducted fieldwork in the Trobriand Islands nearly sixty years after Bronislaw Malinowski carried out his classic study in the same region. Malinowski and Weiner were anthropologists of different nationalities and different genders working in different villages with different informants during different historical periods. Weiner made an important contribution to our understanding of Trobriand life by describing and explaining activities involving Trobriand women's 'wealth' that were absolutely central to the continued healthy functioning of Trobriand life—but about which Malinowski had written nothing. Weiner might have published her findings by declaring that Malinowski had got it wrong. But this

route did not appeal to her, primarily because, as she alluded, he got so very much right. Malinowski's own preoccupations led him to write about aspects of Trobriand life different from those that interested Weiner. As a result, he left behind a portrait of Trobriand society that Weiner later felt obliged to supplement. Nevertheless, much of Malinowski's work remained valid and insightful to Weiner. In tribute to him, she quoted long passages from his ethnographies (see Weiner 1976; 1988; see also the EthnoProfile on the Trobriand Islanders in Chapter 7).

Beginning in the 1960s, anthropologists also began to reconsider the ethics and politics of positivist science in general and of participant-observation in particular. They began to pay closer attention to the nature of the relationships they developed with their informants, and they re-examined the laboratory model of fieldwork, noting the differences between anthropology and other more traditionally scientific disciplines. In the physical sciences, for example, it is fairly easy to justify a hierarchy elevating the inquiring intelligence of scientists over their subject matter. Indeed, it seems difficult to imagine the ethical or political obligations that a geologist might have to a rock. Matters are otherwise when human beings are the subject of inquiry. To approach human beings as objects, lacking the same inquisitive intelligence as the scientists who study them, is to mischaracterize the subject matter of anthropology. Anthropologists *do* have ethical obligations to other human beings; political factors *can* complicate the relationships ethnographers develop during fieldwork. Further, there is a mutual inquisitiveness that needs to be acknowledged in the fieldwork experience. It is *human interaction* that is central to cross-cultural understanding. Thus, by extension, the anthropologist comes to learn that they are *human beings* in relationships, not impersonal recording machines. In doing so, they become aware that observation 'has a subjective component by virtue of the observer's taxonomic decision to recognize certain distinctions' (Allen and Hoekstra 1991: 49); in effect, anthropological observation cannot be entirely value free.

Questioning positivist science is not taken lightly. Those who do raise objections are often accused of abandoning scientific discipline entirely, allowing material facts to be obscured by the researcher's individual, *subjective* values and preferences. But does the rejection of positivism turn anthropological fieldwork into just one person's subjective impressions of other people? Most anthropologists would answer with a firm *no*, because fieldwork is a *dialogue*; ethnographers engage in real conversations with their local research partners in order to learn about their ways of life. Such dialogues are often characterized by mutual patience and painstaking collaborative attempts to sort things out and to piece things together in mutually coherent pictures of reality. When successful, the outcome is a new understanding of the world that both anthropologist and informant can share. This means that field data are not subjective but *intersubjective*: they are the product of long dialogues between researcher and informant. Through dialogue, **intersubjective meanings** are achieved.

## The Reflexive Approach

The intersubjective meanings on which informants rely are public, not private. Informants take them for granted, but they may not be obvious to an outsider. In order to make these meanings explicit, anthropologist and informants together must occasionally step back from the ordinary flow of daily life and examine them critically. They must think about the way members of the culture normally think about their lives. This thinking about thinking is known as **reflexivity**; thus, fieldwork in cultural anthropology is a reflexive experience.

Reflexive fieldwork retains a respect for detailed, accurate information-gathering, but it also takes into consideration a broader range of contextual information than does positivist fieldwork. It pays explicit attention to the ethical and political context of research, the background of researchers, the full partnership of informants (who are really our teachers), and the collaborative relationships that produce anthropological knowledge. Consideration of these factors is essential to producing knowledge about human beings that is scientifically valid. Ethnographic knowledge shaped by reflexivity becomes what Donna Haraway (1991) has called *situated knowledge*. Here, 'situating' involves making explicit exactly who you are as an ethnographer—that is, your gender, nationality, political preference, class/ethnic/educational backgrounds, and so forth. Once you have identified your own social location, you will be better able to understand your unique perspective—your *situated subjectivity*—that informs your research choices. You will also be better able to present

who you are to the people with whom you will be working. Both these distinctions inform you as an ethnographer and shape the relationships you have in the field.

> **intersubjective meanings**
> The shared, public symbolic systems of a culture.
>
> **reflexivity**
> Critically thinking about the way one thinks; reflecting on one's own experience.

Being *aware* of who you are will help you identify the limits of what you can discover. For example, in some societies, being a female ethnographer may bar you from studying certain social activities that are central to the local culture. In such a case, your ethnographic account is bound to be partial and could be seen as weak under the test of 'scientific objectivity'. Nevertheless, many would argue that a detailed, reflexive account of what you were able to learn is far more reliable than a strictly 'objective' account. First, a reflexive account explicitly acknowledges the fact that you did not talk to everybody or see everything. Second, it openly admits that your observations are not universal but *situated* and thus avoids suggesting sweeping generalizations about an entire social group on the basis of partial knowledge. Far from making ethnographic knowledge subjective, reflexivity generates what philosopher of science Sandra Harding calls *strong objectivity*, which she contrasts with *weak objectivity* produced by traditional positivistic approaches (1991: 149ff.).

The commitment to reflexivity means anthropologists are scientifically obligated to reveal to everyone involved the ways in which they gather data. Some anthropologists have argued that they must also share their conclusions with their informants and include their informants' reflections on those conclusions in their published ethnographies. For example, after conducting fieldwork in a poor neighbourhood in the US, Bettylou Valentine (1978), persuaded several of her informants to comment on her manuscript before publication. She visited them for lengthy discussions and found that, in general, they agreed with her conclusions. In the published volume, *Hustling and Other Hard Work: Life Styles in the Ghetto*, Valentine includes both her own conclusions and her informants' voices in the final chapter. Valentine's ethnography presents a vivid example of the open-endedness of the dialogue between anthropologist and informant: no single interpretation of human experience is final. This kind of mutual reflexivity is at the heart of anthropological knowledge and provides the dynamic that such situated knowledge may be positioned in new worlds of meaning in the future.

As a final note, you should know that while the reflexive approach is accepted by most contemporary anthropologists, it is not without its critics. Several assumptions embedded in this approach have been questioned over the last few decades. Most criticism centres on the reliability of self-reports as to positionality (research subjectivity/situated subjectivity) since 'consideration of the possibility of reliable self-reports leads to skepticism rather than confidence' (Salzman 2002: 805). Yet even though the critics note flaws in the reflexive approach, most would agree that it is far more useful to anthropological study than the positivist alternative. Indeed, we would argue that the best ethnographies have always been reflexive, whether or not the ethnographers realized it at the time.

# The Dialectic of Fieldwork: Interpretation and Translation

Fieldwork is a risky business. Fieldworkers not only risk offending their informants by misunderstanding their way of life, but they also face the shock of the unfamiliar and their own vulnerability. Indeed, they must embrace this shock and cultivate this vulnerability if they are to achieve any kind of meaningful understanding of their informants' culture. They resist ethnocentric impulses by recalling 'that if what we observe appears to be odd or irrational, it is probably because we do not understand it and not because it is a product of a "savage" culture in which such nonsense is to be expected' (Greenwood and Stini 1977: 185).

Anthropologist Michael Agar uses the expression 'rich points' for unexpected moments when problems in cross-cultural understanding emerge. The phrase is apt because it portrays these moments as opportunities for insight. Agar observes that rich points, which are triggered by words or actions that signal gaps between the anthropologist's assumptions about how the world works and those of the local people, are the raw material of ethnography. As he says, 'it is

this distance between two worlds of experience that is exactly the problem that ethnographic research is designed to locate and resolve' (1996: 31). That the anthropologist doesn't understand what's going on is the anthropologist's problem, not the local people's; therefore, it is up to the anthropologist to identify rich points, interpret the words or actions behind such moments, and investigate the accuracy of his or her interpretations in the world of the local people.

## Interpreting Actions and Ideas

How does one go about interpreting the actions and ideas of other human beings? As anthropologists, we need to find a form of interpretation based on reflexivity rather than objectivity. In *Reflections on Fieldwork in Morocco* (1977), Paul Rabinow addresses this problem. He suggests that what we require has already been set forth in the philosophy of French thinker Paul Ricoeur:

> Following Ricoeur, I define the problem of hermeneutics (which is simply Greek for 'interpretation') as 'the comprehension of the self by the detour of the comprehension of the other'. It is vital to stress that this is not psychology of any sort. . . . The self being discussed is perfectly public. . . . [It is] the culturally mediated and historically situated self which finds itself in a continuously changing world of meaning. (1977: 5–6)

In the field, then, interpretation becomes a task of coming to comprehend the *cultural self* by way of comprehending the *cultural other*. In other words, the anthropologist's understanding of the cultural other is intersubjectively constructed, using elements drawn from the cultural systems of anthropologist and informant alike. As we come to grasp the meaning of the other's cultural self, we simultaneously learn something of the meaning of our own cultural identity. While the gulf between self and other may seem unbridgeable at first, and absolute understanding between one who is 'apart from' and one who is 'a part of' the culture under study may never be possible, anthropologist and informant can work together to negotiate meanings and arrive at shared understandings.

In the field, anthropologist and informant find themselves in physical proximity, observing and discussing the same activities. At first, they may talk past one another, as each describes these activities from a different perspective using a different language. However, all cultures and languages are open enough to entertain a variety of viewpoints and a variety of ways to talk about them. Continued discussion allows anthropologist and informant to search for areas of intersection for understanding and describing the same behaviour. Any intersection, however small, can form the foundation on which they may then build a new intersubjective symbolic language. This process is what Rabinow refers to as 'the **dialectic of fieldwork**' (1977: 39). Both fieldworker and informant begin with little or nothing in the way of shared experience that could allow them to figure one another out with any accuracy. But if they are motivated to make sense of one another and willing to work together, they can take steps toward understanding and valid interpretation—steps toward mutual recognition.

Let's take a look at how this process might unfold in a typical fieldwork situation. Traditional fieldwork often begins with collecting data on kinship relations in the host society. A trained anthropologist comes to the field with certain ideas about kinship in mind. These ideas derive in part from the anthropologist's own experience of kinship and from his or her knowledge of other anthropologists' theories about kinship (all in all *situated knowledge*). As the fieldworker begins to ask informants questions on kinship, he or she may discover that they have no word in their language that accurately conveys the range of meaning carried by the term *kinship*. This does not mean that the anthropologist must give up. Rather, he or she must enter into the dialectic process of interpretation and translation (Figure 2.3). The process works something like this:

- The anthropologist poses a question about kinship using the term in the informants' language that seems to come closest in meaning to *kinship*.
- The informants do their best to interpret the anthropologist's question in a way that makes sense to them. That is, each informant has to be reflexive, thinking about how people in his or her society think about a certain domain of experience.
- Having formulated an answer, the informant responds to the anthropologist's question in terms he or she thinks the anthropologist will understand.

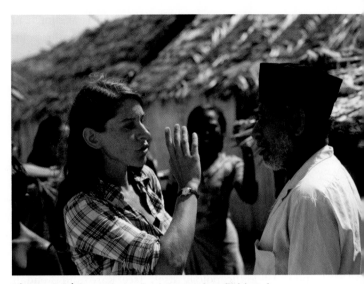

*Figure 2.3* | **An anthropologist uses her fieldwork skills to communicate with villagers of the Aru Island, Indonesia.**

- The anthropologist interprets this response, deciding whether it carries the kind of information he or she was looking for or whether it carries information that he or she can use to rephrase the initial question to get closer to an understanding.

In the dialectic of fieldwork, both anthropologist and informant are active agents. Each party tries to figure out what the other is trying to say. If there is goodwill on the part of both, each party also tries to provide responses that make sense to the other. As more than one anthropologist has remarked (see, e.g., Crick 1976; Rabinow 1977), anthropological fieldwork is *translation*. Translation is complicated and tricky, full of false starts and misunderstandings. As time passes and the partners in this effort learn from their mistakes and successes, their ability to communicate increases and they begin to learn about each other. Each participant learns more about the other: the anthropologist gains skill at asking questions that make sense to the informant, and the informant becomes more skilled at answering those questions in terms relevant to the anthropologist.

**dialectic of fieldwork**
The process of building a bridge of understanding between anthropologist and informant so that each can begin to understand the other.

The validity of this ongoing translation is anchored in the ongoing cultural activities in which both anthropologist and informant are participant-observers. These interactions also produce knowledge about the informant's culture—knowledge that is meaningful to both anthropologist and informant. This knowledge is *new* in as much as it is a *hybrid* that emerges from the collaboration of anthropologist and informant as they create a fragile world of common understandings and experiences.

While informants are equally involved in this dialogue and may end up learning much about the anthropologist, we must remember that the dialogue is initiated by the anthropologist. Anthropologists come to the field with their own sets of issues and concerns, which are determined not by the field situation but by the discipline of anthropology itself (see Karp and Kendall 1982: 254). This continues to be true even when anthropologists find that their research project is changing direction in response to developments at the field site. Furthermore, when anthropologists are finished with a particular research project, they are free to break off the dialogue with informants and resume discussions with fellow scholars. In many cases, the only link between these two sets of dialogues is the anthropologist who conducted the research itself.

Professional academics have traditionally relied on fieldworkers to interpret and speak for informants, often assuming that informants would not speak for themselves. In recent years, however, some scholars have begun to question this assumption, noting that many members of marginalized societies are perfectly willing and capable of discussing their cultures with the wider world. Although language and other barriers may prohibit informants from speaking directly to an audience of professional scholars, such difficulties are becoming less insurmountable in our increasingly globalized, wired world. In light of such changes, some anthropologists have suggested replacing the traditional dialect of fieldwork with a new, more inclusive model for generating anthropological knowledge. To do so, they argue, we must move beyond the Western-centric roots of the discipline and create a more global community of colleagues—both academic and non-academic—who can work together to generate and disseminate anthropological knowledge. Appadurai has called for just such a 'deparochialization of the research ethic' that would

allow global colleagues to become equal partners in 'a conversation about research' in which they can discuss their 'ideas of what counts as new knowledge' as well as their ideas of how to measure the researcher's accountability to those among whom they work (2002: 281).

An essential step toward creating a more inclusive approach to generating knowledge is identifying and moving beyond cultural biases that can distort a researcher's interpretation. Such biases can have a particularly enduring influence on anthropologists who study Indigenous cultures within their own country. Roberto da Matta, a Brazilian anthropologist who has studied Indigenous cultures in Brazil, has addressed problems associated with characterizing Indigenous peoples as 'others' (see 'In Their Own Words', below). The issues that da Matta suggests resonate with Canadian researchers who have examined our country's Indigenous cultures. As inheritors of the colonial concept of *terra nullius*, the 'empty land' (here substitute McGregor's 'view from the fort' [1985] for da Matta's 'empty Amazon and Central Brazil'), early Canadian anthropologists engaged with Indigenous peoples as the 'mythical other' or the 'noble savage'; even while approaching Indigenous cultures as 'new', these anthropologists essentially saw them as representative of an earlier stage of human evolution. While echoes of such interpretations persist today, more recent anthropologists have identified such views as extremely problematic with respect to professional and personal ethics (see Liebersohn 1994).

In light of such concerns, researchers have re-evaluated the responsibilities they have toward informants. Some have wondered whether it is enough to 'witness' the lives of others and discuss field observations in academic contexts. But should anthropologists go so far as to act as advocates for the people they study? Hastrup and Elsas (1990), who have explored issues of advocacy in relation to their fieldwork with the Arhuacos of the Sierra Nevada of northern Colombia, note that the question is not easy to answer:

There is a continuum of anthropological interest from the countering of Western, colonial ethnocentrism by providing systematic knowledge about other cultures to the active pleading of the cause of a particular ethnic group vis-à-vis a government (Van Esterik 1985). In principle this continuum

## In Their Own Words | Some Biased Remarks on Interpretism

*Roberto da Matta explores what it means for him to be a Brazilian anthropologist studying Indigenous cultures in Brazil.*

In order to grasp deep motivations in ethnographic styles, one has to deal with how Natives are represented as 'others'—as different, as distinct—in divergent national contexts. In Brazil, the 'other' is incarnated by a small Native population, scattered in the empty Amazon and Central Brazil, a population generically called by the name 'Índio' (Indian). But the 'Indian' is not alone, for with the category 'Negro' they form the basis of a singular and intriguing view of the immediate human diversity for Brazilians. The 'Negro' (who is fundamentally the ex-slave) is an intrinsic element of Brazilian social structure, haunting with his massive presence the 'whiteness' of a bourgeois lifestyle. The 'Indian' is an outsider, giving rise to the romantic fantasies of the noble savage who has to be either isolated and protected from the evils of civilization or eliminated from the national landscape for incapacity to take part in modern progress.

In this context, to be with 'Indians' is, for a Brazilian anthropologist, more than having the opportunity of living with another humanity. It is also to have the privilege of getting in touch with a mythical other. And by doing so, have the honour of being the one to overcome all manner of discomforts in order to describe a new way of life in the midst of Brazilian civilization. Thus, for Brazilian anthropologists, 'to be there' is also an opportunity of being a witness to the way of life of a different society. This is particularly true when that way of life runs the risk of succumbing to a contact situation that is brutally unequal in political terms.

Source: da Matta, Roberto. 1994. 'Some Biased Remarks on Interpretism: A View from Brazil', in *Assessing Cultural Anthropology*, ed. Robert Borofsky (New York: McGraw-Hill), 119–32.

leaves no anthropologist untouched by the problem of advocacy. . . . When anthropologists use their knowledge for a particular cause, they can be charged with furthering 'the colonial processes still at work by stealing crucial decisions and political initiatives from Indigenous peoples' (Henriksen 1985: 124–5). . . . There is . . . an inherent dilemma in anthropological advocacy. Anthropology is concerned with context rather than interest, while advocacy means making a choice among interests within the context. (1990: 302–7)

Our sense of ethics, as well as our concern for preserving human decency, leads us to understand that some things require our standing with others to achieve justice—choosing among interests within contexts.

### Examples from the Field

Fieldwork is, by definition, an active process that takes place out in the real world, in the middle of the action. Therefore, let's turn to two examples of researchers' experiences in the field to help illustrate some of the interests and concerns at the heart of the dialect of fieldwork.

Nita Kumar is an anthropologist from Delhi, India, who chose to do fieldwork in Banaras, a region very different from the one where she grew up:

Banaras was such a mystery to me when I arrived there in 1981, ironically *because* I was an Indian and expected to have a privileged insight into it. In fact, from Banaras I was *thrice* removed: through my education and upbringing, than which there is no greater moulder of attitudes; by language and linguistic culture; and by region and regional culture. (1992: 15)

Although her social connections smoothed the way for her in official circles, she had no special advantage when trying to make contact with the artisans whose way of life interested her (Figure 2.4).

Finding informants and establishing a rapport with them is an indispensable first step in fieldwork, but there are no foolproof procedures that guarantee success. In her fieldwork memoir, *Friends, Brothers, and Informants* (1992), Kumar shares her four failed attempts—and her final successful effort—to contact weavers. In her first

Figure 2.4 | **Prayer and worship on the Ganges, Banaras, India.**

Figure 2.5 | **Summer in the traditional lands of the Utku Inuit in Nunavut.**

attempt, the weavers she approached turned out to have well-established ties to rickshaw pullers and taxi drivers who regularly brought tourists to visit their shop and buy souvenirs. Not wishing to become just another business contact, she left. Her second attempt was with the Muslim owner of a weaving establishment whose suspicions of her motives caused her to turn elsewhere. Her third attempt was made through a sari salesman who took her to a market where silk weavers sold their wares. Unfortunately for her, he would periodically announce to all assembled who she was and invite weavers to come up and speak with her, a procedure she found deeply embarrassing. Her fourth attempt followed her accidental discovery that two members of a family selling firecrackers were also weavers. When she was invited to see one brother's loom, however, she grew 'uncomfortable with all the obvious evidence of bachelor existence and their readiness to welcome [her] into it. . . . [She] just went away and never came back' (99). On her fifth attempt, a silk-yarn merchant introduced her to weavers living in a government-subsidized housing project next to his house. In the home of a weaver named Shaukatullah, surrounded by members of his family, she finally found a setting in which she felt welcome and able to do her work, and 'in a matter of weeks [she] was given the status of a daughter of Shaukatullah' (105). That status was not only important to Kumar's research, but it was also a congenial status to her, one with which she was comfortable.

Jean Briggs is an anthropologist who was also adopted by a family of informants. Briggs worked among the Utkuhikhalingmiut (Utku, for short) in northern Canada (see Figure 2.5; see also EthnoProfile 2.1). There were several steps her informants took in order to figure her out once she assumed the role of daughter in the home of her new 'father', Inuttiaq, and 'mother', Allaq: 'From the moment that the adoption was settled, I was "Inuttiaq's daughter" in the camp. [They] drilled me in the use of kin terms appropriate to my position, just as they drilled [Inuttiaq's] three-year-old daughter, who was learning to speak' (1980: 46). The context of their interactions had clearly changed as a result of the adoption, and Briggs's family had new expectations both of Briggs and of themselves: 'Allaq, and especially Inuttiaq . . . more and more attempted to assimilate me into a proper adult parent–daughter relationship. I was expected to help with the household work . . . and I was expected to obey unquestioningly when Inuttiaq told me to do something. . . . Inevitably, conflicts, covert but pervasive, developed' (47).

Briggs found herself feeling increasingly uncomfortable and began to analyze her situation. She began to realize that part of the problem had to do with differences between her ideas of how parents ought to relate to their daughters and Utku beliefs on this matter. She

## EthnoProfile 2.1 | Utkuhikhalingmiut (Utku Inuit) ·····························

**Region** North America

**Nation** Canada (Nunavut); the area between Franklin Lake and Chantrey Inlet (Tariunnuaq) on the east side of Adelaide Peninsula

**Language** Utkuhikhalingmiut, or the Utku Inuit (*the people of the place where there is soapstone*), speak the dialect of Inuktitut called Utkuhiksalingmiutitut

**Population** 35 (1970)

**Environment** Tundra

**Livelihood** Seasonal fishing, hunting, and gathering

**Political organization** Communal, with hunting territories

**For more information** Briggs, Jean. 1970. *Never in Anger*: *Portrait of an Eskimo Family* (Cambridge, MA: Harvard University Press); 2000. 'Emotions Have Many Faces: Inuit Lessons', *Anthropologica* 42, 2.

also experienced contradictions between her role as daughter and her role as anthropologist. The dialectic of fieldwork aided her understanding of the meaning of those roles in her own culture. Moreover, Briggs was not the only person who had to be reflexive. Her Utku informants were forced to reconsider how they had been dealing with her since her arrival. As she was able to reconstruct it, their understanding of her went through three stages. At first, they thought she was strange, anomalous. After her adoption, they saw her as educable. But when a communication breakdown occurred, they concluded that she was 'uneducable in important ways . . . a defective person' (60–1). Unlike Kumar, Briggs found that assuming the role of daughter was uncomfortable. While it initially provided her with an opportunity to 'fit into' the community she was studying, it also posed challenges to the very continuation of her fieldwork.

Briggs's experience among the Utku illustrates how, despite strenuous efforts at mutual understanding and translation, the dialectic of fieldwork is not always smooth and how, despite one's best efforts, the ethnographer may fail to perceive how the same behaviour in different cultural circumstances can be interpreted differently. Briggs understood from her informants that anger was dangerous and must never be shown. She also became aware of the various ways her informants diverted or diffused angry feelings. Nevertheless, she remained ignorant of the full power of this value in Utku culture until she found herself having seriously violated it.

A few summers before Briggs's arrival, sportsmen from Canada and the United States began to fly into the inlet where her informants lived. Once there, they borrowed canoes belonging to the Utku. Although there had at one time been several usable canoes in the community, only two remained when Briggs arrived. That summer some sportsmen borrowed one canoe but ran it onto a rock. They then asked the Utkus if they could borrow the remaining canoe, which happened to belong to Inuttiaq.

Briggs was annoyed that their carelessness had led to the ruin of one of the last two good canoes. Because canoes are used for getting food and are not pleasure craft, the loss had serious economic consequences for her informants. When the outsiders asked to use the last canoe afloat, Briggs 'exploded'. She lectured the sportsmen about their carelessness and insensitivity and explained how important canoes were to the Utku. Then, remembering Inuttiaq's often-repeated admonition never to lend his canoe, she told the sportsmen that the owner of the remaining canoe did not want to lend it. When Inuttiaq insisted that the canoe be lent, she was shocked.

But this was only the beginning. Briggs discovered that following her outburst, her informants seemed to turn against *her* rather than the sportsmen. 'I had spoken unbidden and in anger. . . . Punishment was a subtle form of ostracism. . . . I was isolated. It was as though I were not there. . . . But . . . I was still treated with the most impeccable semblance of solicitude' (56–7). Briggs discovered just how much at odds her breaking point was with Utku cultural style. This breach might well have ended her fieldwork if a Westernized Utku friend, Ikayuqtuq, had not come to her rescue. 'I had written my version of the story to Ikayuqtuq, had told her about my attempt to protect the Utku from the impositions of the *kaplunas* [white men] and asked her if she could help to explain my behaviour' to the Utku (58). Ikayuqtuq wrote to Allaq and Inuttiaq, but the letter did not arrive until three months later. During that time, Briggs seemed to be frozen out of Utku society.

Once the letter arrived, everything changed. Briggs's friend had found a way to translate her intentions into terms that Allaq and Inuttiaq could understand. As Briggs recalls, 'the effect was magical'. Inuttiaq began to tell the others what a dangerous task Briggs had taken on to defend the Utkus against the white men. The ice melted. And Briggs knew that relationships had been restored (and perhaps deepened) when Inuttiaq called her *daughter* once again.

The struggle that ensued when Briggs tried to be a good Utku daughter stems in part from what happens when ethnographers struggle to keep the full expression of their own cultural selves in check, in an effort to avoid offending their informants. The situation is complicated by the fieldworker's imperfect awareness of the sort of behaviour that is likely to offend informants. As a result, fieldworkers have frequently felt that their motto ought to be 'The informant is always right.' Many fieldworkers therefore forbid themselves to express anger, disgust, or disagreement. But such self-imposed restrictions are likely to cause problems. After all, what sort of person is always smiling, never angry, without opinions? Anthropologists who refuse to challenge or be challenged by their informants dehumanize both themselves and their informants. Clearly, it takes a good deal of diplomacy to walk the fine line between ethnocentrism and depersonalization. Sometimes, as in Briggs's case, this may not be possible, and the fieldwork itself may be put in jeopardy.

These examples illustrate, each in its own way, how a researcher's reflexive awareness can affect the ways in which the dialect of fieldwork produces anthropological knowledge. They also illustrate how reflexivity can enhance the ethnographies anthropologists write. Unlike in earlier ethnographies committed to the positivist approach, in reflexive ethnographies the presence, personalities, and voices of ethnographers and informants alike become vivid elements. Finally, these accounts highlight the complications and misunderstandings that are a regular part of the dialectic of fieldwork. So these

two studies suggest the ways in which modern fieldwork has advanced beyond its positivistic roots.

In other ways, however, modern fieldwork is very much an inheritance from Malinowski and Boas. That is, most ethnographers engage in 'the intensively-focussed-upon single site of ethnographic observation and participation' (Marcus 1995: 96). Much valuable work of this kind continues to be done in anthropology. But changes in the world as a whole in recent decades have led many anthropologists to undertake fieldwork projects that include more than a single site.

# Multi-sited Fieldwork

Some of the factors pushing toward multi-sited fieldwork came from within anthropology and related social sciences as they responded to wider social and political changes. In 1974, sociologist Immanuel Wallerstein published a highly influential two-volume study called *The Modern World System* in which he argued that the rise and expansion of the European capitalist economy between 1450 and 1750 had incorporated vast regions of the globe into a world system held together by *the market*. This work had important implications for anthropologists, for Wallerstein argued that many parts of the world where anthropologists worked had been remade to occupy specialized niches within the capitalist world system (market economy). Thus, anthropological attempts to account for the current beliefs and practices of small-scale societies in these parts of the world could not ignore the historical impact upon them of world-system influences such as European colonialism.

Wallerstein's work was followed by anthropologist Eric Wolf's monumental *Europe and the People without History* (1982). Wolf's title is to be taken ironically: the non-European people about whom he wrote had their own histories—they had changed and adapted over time; in addition, they were very much involved in the history of European expansion. Tracing some of the same world-system interconnections discussed by Wallerstein, Wolf regularly abandoned the abstract view of the overall system in order to focus on the historical ethnographic details of specific societies affected by that system. Thus, in Wolf's discussion, Indigenous peoples of North America appear as actors creatively coping with the challenge of the fur trade and European settlement, developing some of their now characteristic forms of social organization.

Wallerstein's and Wolf's influence on ethnographers was profound. Marcus notes that single-site fieldwork continued, but it came to be conceived from the perspective of the world system (1995: 96). Anthropologists began to supplement their own data-gathering with archival research that allowed them to situate the society they encountered historically, and they began to rethink existing social arrangements and cultural understandings as the products of *active response* to outside pressures rather than as timeless practices. Such work reanimated their awareness of the *lack* of isolation of the societies they studied, both in the past and in the present, and reinforced their awareness of their informants' *agency* that had been emphasized in the reflexive approach. The result was that neat boundaries between particular societies and the larger world system, of which

they were parts, began to dissolve as ethnographers contextualized their own field data in relation to places and processes that stretched far beyond their original field site. By the early 1990s, after the break-up of the Soviet Union, the somewhat successful move of capitalism into China, and the extraordinary surge of migrants around the world because of war and economic dislocation, all traditional boundaries seemed on the verge of dissolution. This is more so the case today, as global processes increasingly link disparate groups of people. For example, think of the many ties between various fundamentalist activists—frequently described and actualized as terrorists—who are dedicated to promoting their individual causes by redefining political, ethnic, linguistic, economic, and religious boundaries and capitalists who promote continued economic growth at all costs, bringing the world together so they can gain access to dwindling resources and create markets for

## *In Their Own Words* | **Jihad vs McWorld**

*Political scientist Benjamin R. Barber describes the conflict between tribalism and globalism.*

Just beyond the horizon of current events lie two possible political futures—both bleak, neither democratic. The first is a retribalization of large swaths of humankind by war and bloodshed: a threatened Lebanonization of national states in which culture is pitted against culture, people against people, tribe against tribe—a Jihad in the name of a hundred narrowly conceived faiths against every kind of interdependence, every kind of artificial social co-operation and civic mutuality. The second is being borne in on us by the onrush of economic and ecological forces that demand integration and uniformity and that mesmerize the world with fast music, fast computers, and fast food—with MTV, Macintosh, and McDonald's pressing nations into one commercially homogenous global network: one McWorld tied together by technology, ecology, communications, and commerce. The planet is falling precipitantly apart AND coming reluctantly together at the very same moment.

These two tendencies are sometimes visible in the same countries at the same instant: thus Yugoslavia, clamouring just recently to join the New Europe, is exploding into fragments;

India is trying to live up to its reputation as the world's largest integral democracy while powerful new fundamentalist parties like the Hindu nationalist Bharatiya Janata Party, along with nationalist assassins, are imperilling its hard-won unity. States are breaking up or joining up: the Soviet Union has disappeared almost overnight, its parts forming new unions with one another or with like-minded nationalities in neighbouring states. The old interwar national state based on territory and political sovereignty looks to be a mere transitional development.

The tendencies of what I am here calling the forces of Jihad and the forces of McWorld operate with equal strength in opposite directions, the one driven by parochial hatreds, the other by universalizing markets, the one recreating ancient sub-national and ethnic borders from within, the other making national borders porous from without. They have one thing in common: neither offers much hope to citizens looking for practical ways to govern themselves democratically. If the global future is to pit Jihad's centrifugal whirlwind against McWorld's centripetal black hole, the outcome is unlikely to be democratic. . . .

Source: Barber, Benjamin R. 1992. 'Jihad vs McWorld', *Atlantic Monthly* 269, 3: 53–65, available at www.theatlantic.com/magazine/archive/1992/03/jihad-vs-mcworld/3882/.

their products. (Note Benjamin R. Barber's discussion in the 'In Their Own Words' box, below.)

How do you proceed with fieldwork, then, when the 'system' of Wallerstein's world system no longer seems so unified and the study of any cultural group demands the mapping of various disconnected, fragmentary processes in a disorganized, globalized world? For increasing numbers of anthropologists, the answer is **multi-sited ethnography**, which focusses on widespread cultural processes and leads the researcher from site to site, as new considerations present themselves. As Marcus describes it, 'Multi-sited research is designed around chains, paths, threads, conjunctions, or juxtapositions of locations' as ethnographers trace 'a complex cultural phenomenon . . . that turns out to be contingent and malleable as one traces it' (1995: 105–6). Like all good researchers working on complex issues, multi-sited ethnographers follow *people, things, metaphors, plots,* and *lives* (107).

Marcus (1995) admits that multi-sited fieldwork may present certain limitations. For example, compared to single-sited fieldwork, it appears to dilute the intensity of involvement, depth of understanding, and insight fieldworkers develop with their informants in each site studied. Further, some activist anthropologists who use their ethnography to draw public attention to the plight of those whose lives they study see multi-sited research as undercutting their political commitments to their primary informants.

Marcus recognizes these drawbacks but does not see them as fatal. After all, he notes, multi-sited fieldwork is usually *based* in one primary site; its major innovation involves doing fieldwork in additional sites and bringing information from all these sites together in a single study. Concerns about the way multi-sited ethnography may dilute the researcher's ability to adopt an unequivocal position as defender of a single group raise more complex issues. Multi-sited ethnography highlights the multi-centred, complex conflicts of the contemporary world in which clear-cut 'good guys' and 'bad guys' are increasingly hard to identify. When individuals legitimately claim, or are accorded, multiple

identities, some of which conflict, innocent 'identity politics' become impossible (Haraway 1991: 192). For example, to defend the views of working-class women in a single site is to downplay or ignore the points of view of unemployed women; it may gloss over differences *among* those women based on class, 'race', ethnicity, or religion; and it ignores entirely the points of view of men. Moreover, the spread of industrial capitalism across the globe means that the growth of an urban immigrant workforce in one place is probably connected to a lack of employment somewhere else. Multi-sited ethnography offers the possibility of juxtaposing more than one place, more than one time, and more than one point of view, thereby bringing to light connections among them that would otherwise remain unsuspected.

The multi-sited approach helps contemporary anthropologists meet the challenge of learning about human beings and their cultures in context. The nature of our world is changing, becoming increasingly complex, and today's anthropologists must continue their studies despite what Fischer has called our 'break in the ability to write about . . . traditional topics as if they were a stable source of values and social integration' (1999: 471). Of the modern world, Fischer notes:

> No longer is it possible to speak of modernity in the singular. . . . [The term] *alternative modernities* acknowledges the multiple, different configurations that modernities have taken and the recognition that modernization and globalization are not homogenizing processes. . . . It challenges old area studies frameworks, as well as old-style social theory, and requires re-studies of canonic anthropological societies, to provide a sense of the transformations of the past century, as well as new ways of doing fieldwork, engaging colleagues and interlocutors in new relationships. . . . (470–2)

So contemporary ethnographic practice must be part of reworking traditional notions of comparative work for a world that is increasingly aware of difference. It must also be able to contextualize human culture in light of widespread social forces. Fischer suggests the complexity of these social forces when he calls attention to three key overlapping arenas that should be of concern to anthropologists: the centrality of science and technology; decolonization, post-colonialism, and the re-construction of societies after social trauma; and the role of the new electronic and visual media (458). Each of these arenas is itself very complex, and each has had a complex relationship with contemporary cultures; multi-sited fieldwork encourages anthropologists to identify and explore these relationships.

# The Effects of Fieldwork

## The Effects of Fieldwork on Informants

Fieldwork changes both anthropologists and informants. What kinds of effects can the fieldwork experience have on informants? Anthropologists have not always been able to report on this, as the effects may take many years to manifest. Yet in some cases, it becomes clear in the course of fieldwork that the anthropologist's presence and questions have made the informants aware of their own cultural selves in new ways that are both surprising and uncomfortable.

Rabinow, who worked in Morocco, recalled some cases in which his informants' new reflexivity led to unanticipated consequences (Figure 2.6). One key informant, Malik, agreed to help Rabinow compile a list of landholdings and other possessions of the villagers of Sidi Lahcen Lyussi (see Map 2.2). As a first step in tracing the economic status of the middle stratum in society, Rabinow suggested that Malik list his own possessions. Initially, Malik appeared to be neither rich nor poor, and he considered himself 'not well-off'.

> As we began to make a detailed list of his possessions, he became touchy and defensive. . . . It was clear that he was not as impoverished as he had portrayed himself. . . . This was confusing and troubling for him. . . . Malik began to see that there was a disparity between his self-image and my classification system. The emergence of this 'hard' data before his eyes and through his own efforts was highly disconcerting for him. (1977: 117–18)

Malik's easy understanding of himself and his world had been disrupted, and he could not ignore the disruption. He would either have to change his self-image or find some way to assimilate this new information

Figure 2.6 | Paul Rabinow's reflections on his fieldwork experiences in a Moroccan village much like this one led him to reconceptualize the nature of anthropological fieldwork.

Map 2.2 | Sidi Lahcen Lyussi

about himself into his old self-image. In the end Malik managed to reaffirm his conclusion that he was not well-off by arguing that wealth lay not in material possessions alone. Although he might be rich in material goods, his son's health was bad, his own father was dead, he was responsible for his mother and unmarried brothers, and he had to be constantly vigilant in order to prevent his uncle from stealing his land (117–19).

## The Effects of Fieldwork on the Researcher

What are the consequences of the fieldwork experience for the fieldworker? While the experience is often exciting and enlightening, is not uncommon for field researchers to feel overwhelmed by the unfamiliarity of the situation. They need to adjust to local water, food, and climate, and many encounter plants, animals, insects, and diseases with which they have had no previous experience. In addition, the cultural differences a researcher faces—the very reason the researcher has entered the field in the first place—can be a source of added stress. As a result, many field researchers experience **culture shock**. In fact, many anthropologists feel very anxious and isolated in the field, at least in the early stages of a project, as they find they have nothing familiar to turn to, no common sense on which to rely, and no relationships that can be taken for granted.

> **culture shock**
> The feeling of physical and mental dislocation/discomfort a person experiences when in a new or strange cultural setting. It can manifest most deeply on returning 'home', with home seeming exceedingly strange after extended stays in the fieldwork situation.

*Figure 2.7* | **Elephants on a road in Botswana. Many anthropologists encounter plants, animals, insects, and diseases with which they have had no previous experience. The physical and mental dislocation and stress they may experience in the field is called *culture shock*.**

The researcher's sense of isolation may lead her or him to search for close contacts in the research setting. Interpersonal relationships can often help researchers adapt to local culture, but they can also make a researcher more vulnerable to feelings of hurt or betrayal. They might also re-emphasize the distance between researcher and informant. Rabinow provides an example of such a situation when he recalls the relationship he formed with his first Moroccan informant, a man called Ibrahim, whom he had hired to teach him Arabic. Rabinow and Ibrahim seemed to get along well together and, because of the language lessons, they saw each other a great deal, leading Rabinow to think of Ibrahim as a friend. When Rabinow planned a trip to another city, Ibrahim offered to go along as a guide and stay with relatives. This only confirmed Ibrahim's friendliness in Rabinow's eyes. But things changed once they arrived at their destination. Ibrahim told Rabinow that the relatives with whom he was to stay did not exist, that he had no money, and that he expected Rabinow to pay for his hotel room. When Rabinow was unable to do so, however, Ibrahim paid for it himself. Rabinow was shocked and hurt by this experience, and his relationship with Ibrahim was forever altered. Rabinow remarks: 'Basically I had been conceiving of him as a friend because of the seeming personal relationship we had established. But Ibrahim, a lot less confusedly, had basically conceptualized me as a resource. He was not unjustly situating me with the other Europeans with whom he had dealings' (1977: 29). Rabinow's experience illustrates what he calls the *shock of otherness*.

To some degree, researchers can prepare for the mental stress of entering an unfamiliar setting by anticipating as many potential circumstances as possible. Nancy Howell, a demographer involved with anthropological research in areas such as Botswana (Figure 2.7), has explored risk factors involved in fieldwork and has observed:

> Anthropologists need to be mentally prepared to cope with . . . risks (diseases, criminal and political threats, vehicle accidents, etc. . . .) to their health and safety and to the health and safety of . . . others who accompany them on field trips. We don't need to write the kind of guidebook

that systematically warns about sunburn, jet lag, and the inoculations needed in various countries. . . . What is needed for anthropology is the sensitizing to the hazards that are likely to be encountered, systematic sharing of experiences with hazards in the field, the best available advice on prevention and responses when they are encountered, and some mental rehearsals of what to do under those circumstances. (1988: 786–7)

Yet in most cases, the immensity of what they will encounter is difficult for researchers to fully anticipate. Initially, just getting through the day—finding a place to stay and food to eat—may seem an enormous accomplishment. With time, however, researchers adapt, become more confident in their position, and feel more comfortable in their new surroundings.

## The Humanizing Effects of Fieldwork

Anthropological knowledge is the fruit of reflexivity produced by the mutual attempts of anthropologist and informant to understand each other. As a result, it ought to be able to provide answers to questions about human nature, human society, and human history. Good ethnography offers readers the extraordinary opportunity to experience 'the others' as human beings while learning about their lives. As researchers, we must work to maintain a position from which we can relate such an experience. This privileged position comes neither easily nor automatically. It must be cultivated, and it requires cooperation between, and effort from, one's informants and oneself. We have made an important first step if we can come to recognize, as Rabinow did, that 'there is no primitive. There are other [people] living other lives' (1977: 151). Everyone lives in their own modernity—their own place—in this world we share (Figure 2.8).

Multi-sited ethnography can complicate the picture by simultaneously offering rich, fieldwork-based portraits of 'other people living other lives' and by demonstrating, moreover, that members of these groups share important cultural commitments. In the best ethnographic writing we can grasp the humanity—the greed, compassion, suffering,

pleasure, confusion, and ambivalence—of the people who have granted the anthropologist the privilege of living with them for an extended period of time. It may also become more natural for us to talk about cultural differences by saying 'not "they", not "we", not "you", but some of us are thus and so' (Smith 1982: 70).

*Figure 2.8* | Unlike most Western commercial fishers, these men in Tanji, Gambia, use small boats and nets to catch fish for local markets. Good ethnography helps us recognize that members of other cultures are not 'primitive' simply because their lives appear to be different from our lives; all people experience their own modernity.

*In Their Own Words* | **The Skills of the Anthropologist**

*Anthropologists cannot avoid taking their own cultural and theoretical frameworks into the field. However, as Stephen Gudeman observes, fieldwork draws their attention in unanticipated directions, making them aware of new phenomena that constantly challenge those frameworks.*

According to the accepted wisdom, poets should be especially facile with language and stretch our vision with freshly cut images. Historians, with their knowledge of past events, offer a wise and sweeping view of human change and continuities. Physical scientists, who have analytical yet creative minds, bring us discoveries and insights about the natural world.

What about anthropologists? Have we any finely honed talents and gifts for the world?

Because anthropology is the study of human life, the anthropologist needs to know a little something about everything—from psychology to legal history to ecology. Our field equipment is primitive, for we rely mainly on the eye, the ear, and the tongue. Because ethnographers carry few tools to the field and the tools they have can hardly capture the totality of the situation, the background and talents of the researcher strongly determine what is 'seen' and how it is understood. But the field experience itself has a special impact, too. I studied economic practices in Panama because I was trained to do so, but the field research forced me to alter all the notions I had been taught. Most of them were useless! Anthropologists try to open themselves up to every facet of their field situation and to allow its richness to envelop them. In this, the tasks of the anthropologist are very unlike those of the normal laboratory scientist: the anthropologist can have

no predefined hypothesis and testing procedures. The best equipment an ethnographer can possess is a 'good ear' and patience to let the 'data talk'.

This is not all. In the field, anthropologists carry out intense and internal conversations with themselves. Every observation, whether clearly seen or dimly realized, must be brought to consciousness, shuffled about, and questioned. Only by recognizing and acknowledging their own incomprehension can anthropologists generate new questions and lines of inquiry. In the solitude of the field, the anthropologist must try to understand the limits of her or his knowledge, have the courage to live with uncertainty, and retain the ambition to seize on openings to insight.

But field studies constitute only a part of the total research process. Once home, the field notes have to be read and reread, put aside, and then rearranged. The anthropologist is a pattern seeker, believing that within the data human designs are to be found. The task is like solving a puzzle, except that there is no fixed solution and the puzzle's pieces keep changing their shapes! With work and insight, however, a picture—an understanding or an explanation—begins to emerge.

Eventually, the results of all these efforts are conveyed to others, and so anthropologists also need to have expository skills and persuasive powers, for they have to convince others of their picture and their viewpoint about how cultures and social lives are put together.

Source: Gudeman, Stephen. 1990. 'The Skills of the Anthropologist', guest editorial in *Cultural Anthropology: A Perspective on the Human Condition*, 2nd edn, eds Emily Schultz and Robert Lavenda (St Paul: West), 458–9.

# The Production of Anthropological Knowledge

If anthropological knowledge is the intersubjective creation of fieldworker and informant together, so too are the facts that anthropologists collect. The dialectic of fieldwork, however, often involves extended discussions about just what counts as 'the facts'. We can follow anthropologist David Hess and define **fact** as a widely accepted observation, a taken-for-granted item of common knowledge (1997: 101–2). Ethnographers' field notebooks will be full of facts collected from different informants, as well as facts based on their own cultural experiences and professional training. But what happens when facts from these various sources contradict one another?

**fact**
A widely accepted observation, a taken-for-granted item of common knowledge, that becomes intelligible only when it is interpreted and placed in a context of meaning.

Facts turn out to be complex phenomena. On the one hand, they assert that a particular state of affairs about the world is true. On the other hand, reflexive analysis has taught us that *who* tells us that *x* is a fact is an extremely important thing to know. This is because facts do not speak for themselves. They speak only when they are interpreted and placed in a context of meaning that makes them intelligible. What constitutes a cultural fact is ambiguous. Anthropologists and informants can disagree; anthropologists can disagree among themselves; informants can disagree among themselves. The facts of anthropology exist neither in the culture of the anthropologist nor in the culture of the informant. 'Anthropological facts are cross-cultural because they are made across cultural boundaries' (Rabinow 1977: 152). In short, facts are not just out there waiting for someone to come along and pick them up. They are made and remade

Map 2.3 | **Komachi**

- in the field,
- when fieldworkers re-examine field notes and reflect on the field experience,
- when fieldworkers write about their experiences or discuss them with other anthropologists, and
- when fieldwork is redone to mark the changes that have occurred.

For Bradburd, fieldwork begins with 'being there'. But simply being there is not enough. As he puts it,

my experiences among the Komachi shaped my understanding of them, and that part of field experience consists of a constant process of being brought up short, of having expectations confounded, of being forced to think very hard about what is happening, right now, with me and them, let alone the thinking and rethinking about those experiences when they have—sometimes mercifully—passed. (1998: 161–2; see Map 2.3)

After all, fieldwork is field*work*—there are notes to be taken, interviews to be carried out, observations and interpretations to be made. There is also the transformation of the experience of being there into what Bradburd calls 'elements of an understanding that is at once incomplete and impossible to complete, but also wonderfully capable of being improved' (164). According

to Wolcott, it is what ethnographers do with data that makes fieldwork experience different from just experience and turns it into ethnography; ethnographers are concerned with

making considered generalizations about how members of a group tend to speak and act, warranted generalizations appropriate for collectivities of people rather than the usual shoot-from-the-hip stereotyping adequate for allowing us to achieve our individual purposes. (1999: 262)

Multi-sited fieldwork elaborates upon and further complicates this experience because it involves being 'here and there'. In the course of the movement from site to site, new facts come into view that would otherwise never be known, adding a further layer to the thinking and rethinking that all fieldwork sets in motion. What happens if you find that your activism in support of the urban poor at one site works against the interests of the Indigenous people you have supported at a different site? 'In conducting multi-sited research,' Marcus says, 'one finds oneself with all sorts of cross-cutting commitments' that are not easily resolved. Unlike positivists, however, who might have found 'refuge in being a detached anthropological scholar', Marcus suggests that the multi-sited journey will itself shape the 'circumstantial activism' of ethnographers doing fieldwork in a variety of sites. 'If that sounds contradictory or ambivalent, it is nevertheless faithful to key features of the contemporary world in which we all live' (1995).

# Anthropological Knowledge as Open-ended

We have suggested that there is no such thing as purely objective knowledge and that when human beings are both the subject and the object of study, we must speak in terms of reflexivity rather than objectivity. Cultivating reflexivity allows us to produce less distorted views of human nature and the human condition, and yet we remain human beings interpreting the lives of other human beings. We can never escape from our humanity to some point of view that would allow us to see human existence and human experience from the outside. Instead, we must rely on our common humanity and our interpretive powers to show us the parts of our nature that can be made visible.

Since there truly is 'no primitive', no subsection of humanity that is radically different in nature or in capacity from the anthropologists who study it, then the ethnographic record of anthropological knowledge is perhaps best understood as a vast commentary on human possibility. As with all commentaries, it depends on an original text—in this case, human experience. But that experience is ambiguous, speaking with many voices, capable of supporting more than one interpretation. Growth of anthropological knowledge is no different, then, from the growth of human self-understanding in general. It ought to contribute to the domain of human wisdom that concerns who we are as a species, where we have come from,

and where we may be going. And the ethnographic record is and must be unfinished: human beings are open systems, human history continues, and problems and their possible solutions change. There is no one true version of human life. For anthropologists, the true version of human life consists of all versions of human life.

This is a sobering possibility. It makes it appear that 'the anthropologist is condemned to a greater or lesser degree of failure' in even trying to understand another culture (Basham 1978: 299). It also suggests that informants are equally condemned to never fully know their own way of life. And the positivistic orientation resists any admission that the understanding of anything is impossible. But total pessimism does not seem warranted. We may never know everything, but it does not follow that our efforts can teach us nothing. 'Two of the fundamental qualities of humanity are the capacity to understand one another and the capacity to be understood. Not fully certainly. Yet not negligibly, certainly. . . . There is no person on earth that I can fully understand. There is and has been no person on earth that I cannot understand at all' (Smith 1982: 68–9).

Moreover, as our contact with the other is prolonged and as our efforts to communicate are rewarded by the construction of intersubjective understanding, we can always learn more. Human beings have a vast ability to learn new things; even if we can never know everything, it does not seem that our capacities for understanding ourselves and others is likely to be exhausted any time soon. This is not only because we are open to change but also because our culture and our wider environment can change and will continue to do so as long as human history continues. For these reasons, the ethnographic enterprise will never be finished.

# Key Terms

culture shock   46
dialectic of fieldwork   37
fact   48
fieldwork   28
intersubjective meanings   35

multi-sited ethnography   44
objective knowledge   33
participant-observation   28
positivism   33
reflexivity   35

# Chapter Summary

1.  Anthropological fieldwork traditionally involves extended periods of close contact with members of another society. This form of research is called *participant-observation*.

2.  The nineteenth century saw the birth of positivistic science in Western thought. Early anthropologists who wanted to be scientific attempted to adapt positivism to their needs. They adopted a view of controlled laboratory research as the prototype of scientific investigation and attempted to apply the prototype to the field situation. In this way, researchers systematically collected highly accurate data in many parts of the world.

3.  In modern anthropology, researchers understand that they must recognize that informants are human beings and relate to them as such. When human beings study other human beings, research is coloured by the context and cultural presuppositions of both the researcher and the people they study. Successful fieldwork involves anthropologists who are reflexive—who think about the way they think about other cultures. Informants must also reflect on the way they and others in their society think and try to convey their insights to the anthropologist.

4.  The dialectic of fieldwork is a reflexive interchange between anthropologist and informant. It is a collaborative undertaking involving dialogue about the meaning of experience in the informant's culture. Fieldworkers and informants working together construct an intersubjective world of meaning.

5.  The potential to learn about another culture is often greatest following a rupture of communication between anthropologist and informant. Ruptures occur when existing intersubjective understandings prove themselves inadequate to account for experience. A rupture always carries the possibility of bringing research to an end, but when the reasons for the rupture are explored, and explanations for it are constructed, great insights are possible.

6.  Multi-sited ethnography encourages ethnographers to acknowledge that societies are not isolated. It focusses on cultural processes that are not contained by social, ethnic, religious, or national boundaries, and the ethnographer follows the process from site to site.

7.  Because the world is changing and cultures are challenged by change, ethnographic practice must be part of reworking traditional notions of comparative work for a world that is increasingly aware of difference.

8.  Fieldwork has the potential to change informants and researchers in unpredictable ways. Some anthropologists work with their informants to effect social change; however, others argue that anthropologists' main task is to clarify how people in particular places, at particular moments, engage with the world.

9.  Because cultural meanings are intersubjectively constructed during fieldwork, cultural facts do not speak for themselves. They speak only when they are interpreted and placed in a context of meaning that makes them intelligible. Multi-sited fieldwork complicates this process because it involves the anthropologist in cross-cutting commitments in different contexts.

10. The ethnographic record of anthropological knowledge is perhaps best understood as a vast, unfinished commentary on human possibility. We may never learn all there is to know, but we can always learn more.

# Critical Thinking Questions

1.  Many anthropologists consider participant-observation to be the central methodology for ethnographic data collection. What alternative methods could they use? How are these alternative methods different from participant-observation in the type of data they are suited to?

2.  Have you considered how and why you think in a specific way about people and things? When your observations are challenged, do you try to analyze how you have reached your conclusions? How do these personal reflections inform your understanding of the reflexivity discussed in this chapter and its use to the anthropologist?

3.  Three modes of ethnographic fieldwork have been developed over the last hundred years: positivist, reflexive, and multi-sited. What are the benefits of each approach? Would you expect different results from each?

4.  Anthropological professional organizations and government-fund granting agencies have codes of conduct. Why are carefully designed moral and ethical obligations a critical part of fieldwork, specifically, and anthropology, generally?

# Suggested Readings

Bradburd, Daniel. 1998. Being There: The Necessity of Fieldwork (Washington, DC: Smithsonian Institution Press). An engaging personal study of how the many seemingly small details of experience during field research add up to anthropological understanding.

Kumar, Nita. 1992. *Friends, Brothers, and Informants: Fieldwork Memoirs of Banaras* (Berkeley: University of California Press). A moving and thought-provoking reflection on the experience of fieldwork in the author's own country but in a culture quite different from her own.

Lévi-Strauss, Claude. 1974. *Tristes Tropiques* (New York: Pocket Books). A multi-faceted work about voyaging, fieldwork, self-knowledge, philosophy, and much more. Originally published in French in 1955, this work is considered by some to be the greatest book ever written by an anthropologist (although not necessarily a great anthropology book).

Liebersohn, Harry. 1994. 'Discovering Indigenous Nobility: Tocqueville, Chamisso, and Romantic Travel Writing', *American Historical Review* 99, 3: 746–66. A discussion of the development of the construct of the noble savage.

Nurse, Andrew. 2008. '"Their Ancient Customs Are Gone": Anthropology as Cultural Process', in Around and about Marius Barbeau: Modelling Twentieth-Century Culture, eds L. Jessup, A. Nurse, and G.E. Smith (Seattle: University of Washington Press). Examines the cultural significance of Canadian anthropologist Marius Barbeau's representation of First Nations in his ethnographic research.

Rabinow, Paul. 1977. *Reflections on Fieldwork in Morocco* (Berkeley: University of California Press). An important, brief, powerfully written reflection on the nature of fieldwork. Very accessible and highly recommended.

Salamone, Frank A. 1979. 'Epistemological Implications of Fieldwork and Their Consequences', *American Anthropologist*, New Series, 81, 1: 46–60. How do we manage as both the social scientist based in specific 'approaches' and the active fieldworker where various unexpected things may arise, some seriously counter to our expectations?

Valentine, Bettylou. 1978. *Hustling and Other Hard Work: Life Styles in the Ghetto* (New York: Free Press). An innovative, provocative study of African American inner-city life. Reads like a good novel.

# Related Websites

American Anthropological Association (AAA) www.aaanet.org

Interagency Advisory Panel on Research Ethics www.pre.ethics.gc.ca

Canadian Anthropology Society/Société canadienne d'anthropologie (CASCA) www.cas-sca.ca

# 3 | Anthropology in History and the Explanation of Cultural Diversity

## Chapter Outline

The Roots of Canadian Anthropology
Capitalism, Colonialism, and 'Modernity'
Anthropology and the Colonial Encounter
Toward Classifying Forms of Human Society

## Learning Objectives

By the end of Chapter 3, you will be able to

- define anthropology's aims and scope of study,

- explain culture as a concept within anthropology,

- distinguish cultural anthropology as a subfield of anthropology,

- articulate connections and relationships between the four major subfields of anthropology in North America,

- explain the world views of dualism and holism and show ways that the conflict between them has shaped anthropology, and

- explain the relationship between cultural relativism and ethnocentrism and give examples of both.

→ *A curator adjusts the head of an original terracotta warrior on display at the Museum of Ethnology in Hamburg, Germany. Originally crafted for the first emperor of China in the third century BCE, the terracotta warrior artifacts give us a glimpse into a past culture.*

**Central to third-century BCE Chinese scientific thought was the Five Element theory.** Each element (wood, metal, fire, water, earth) fit into a circular relational structure in which it could 'conquer' the preceding element based on its physical properties: 'Wood conquers Earth because, presumably, when in the form of a spade, it can dig up earth; again, Metal conquers Wood since it can cut and carve it; Fire conquers Metal for it can melt or even vaporize it; Water conquers Fire because it can extinguish it; and, finally, Earth conquers Water because it can dam it and contain it' (Ronan and Needham 1978: 151). Over time, the Five Elements gradually took on greater significance and 'came to be associated with every conceivable category of things in the universe that it was possible to classify in fives' (153) such as the seasons, the points of the compass, tastes, smells, numbers, kinds of musical notes, heavenly bodies, planets, weather, colours, body parts, sense organs, affective states, and human psychological functions. This typology eventually was associated with periods of dynastic history, the ministries and styles of government, and social order in general; therefore, many saw the Five Elements typology as logical and thus useful for retrodiction (historical explanation) and for prediction (future planning). In effect it was what anthropologists call a *key metaphor*—a symbolic representation central to a world view. Ronan and Needham conclude that, as with any apt metaphor or good scientific theory,

> these correlations met with criticism, sometimes severe, because they led to many absurdities. . . . Yet in spite of such criticisms, it seems that in the beginning these correlations were helpful to scientific thought in China. . . . [I]t was only when they became over-elaborate and fanciful, too far removed from the observation of Nature, that they were positively harmful. (156–7)

In the end, these criticisms resulted in a paradigm shift (Kuhn 1962).

Like the Chinese sages, anthropologists in the nineteenth century first sorted human cultures into different categories based on what they believed to be their similarities and differences. Over time, the purposes and the categories have been modified in ways that reflect changes in the wider world, changing research interests among anthropologists, and critical analyses of disciplinary origins. This chapter looks at these developments. By situating the discipline of anthropology within the social and historical contexts that have shaped its development, we can gain a clearer understanding of the kinds of situated knowledge anthropologists have developed.

## The Roots of Canadian Anthropology

Before we delve into the history of anthropological study in general, you should understand a bit about the way anthropology became established in Canada. By examining the specific intellectual, social, and historical contexts that shaped the development of the discipline, we will gain a clearer picture of the kinds of situated knowledge Canadian anthropologists have developed. Canadian institutions were somewhat late to the game, although cultural research had been conducted in Canada since the nineteenth century. The work of Sir Daniel Wilson (Figure 3.1)

*Figure 3.1* | **Sir Daniel Wilson (1816–92) is considered by many the first professional scholar in Canadian archaeology and ethnography.**

is illustrative of this early period. Later, A.G. Bailey's research of French–Indian contact (1969 [1937]) shows the mettle of what Canadian anthropology was to become. Bailey was influenced by his association with Thomas McIlwraith (Figure 3.2), who founded the first department of anthropology in Canada at the University of Toronto in 1936. Bailey's research 'prefigures . . . the development of American Indian ethnohistory' (Trigger 1975) and was important to the University of Toronto—and the Canadian—setting, finding favour with the '[American] fieldwork-orientated Boasians and the [British] social anthropologists of the 1930s' (1975). Three major anthropological schools of thought came to influence the development of Canadian anthropology: American, British, and French. Thus our proximity to the United States and our historical ties to England and France helped to shape anthropological study in Canada. The result, a

happy happenstance of time and place, was an integrative, flexible approach that has been productive for Canadian researchers.

# Capitalism, Colonialism, and 'Modernity'

In *Europe and the People without History* (1982), Eric Wolf reflects on the ways in which **capitalism** and **colonialism** emerged as global forces. In his analysis, he finds the seeds of anthropology in imperialist Europeans' first meetings with other cultures as they 'reached out to seize the resources and populations of the other continents' (1982: 18). He also finds in this history the beginnings of the problematic, 'tacit anthropological supposition that [Indigenous] people . . . are people without history', which 'amounts to the erasure of 500 years of confrontation, killing, resurrection, and accommodation' (18). If, as Wolf contends, anthropologists are the children of an imperialist/capitalist parent, what is our legacy?

As we discussed in Chapter 1, in the division of labour between the new social sciences at the end of the nineteenth century, anthropology was assigned 'the savage slot' as its 'field' of inquiry. In North America, this meant that anthropology's primary task was to examine the Indigenous inhabitants of the continent. They occupied what was characterized by Europeans as emergent borderlands along the edge of the province of the 'civilized'. These borderlands held different properties for Euro-Americans and Euro-Canadians. For Americans they were a frontier, a battle line over which the Native 'other' was first transported and later met with armed, face-to-face confrontation while Euro-Americans lived out their 'manifest destiny'. For the developing Euro-Canadian world view, they were an edge as well, not to a new frontier but to a vast and frightening, essentially empty, wilderness. In this wilderness Native peoples became shadows in a land of liminality in the Canadian context. Posed by Northrop Frye as the 'riddle of unvisualized land . . .' (1971: 201),

**capitalism**
An economic system dominated by a supply and demand market designed to create capital and profit.

**colonialism**
The cultural domination of a people by larger, wealthier powers.

*Figure 3.2* | Thomas McIlwraith (1899–1964), like A.G. Bailey, was interested in ethnology and how Canadian Native peoples were affected by change.

this dangerous wilderness was a place of fact and fancy seen in written descriptions of explorers and discussed as a cardinal truth in our literary tradition. Indeed, Margaret Atwood remarked that the 'central symbol . . . is undoubtedly Survival, *la Survivance* . . .' (1972: 32), meaning survival of 'the land, the climate . . . [as well as a] spiritual survival . . .' (33). This wilderness is what McGregor has called the 'view from the fort' (1985: 5), the observance, without contemplative engagement, of the world beyond the safety of the Euro-Canadian enclave. This wilderness then became the 'field' of the emerging Canadian anthropology.

The genesis of ideas for westward expansion out of Europe dates to the reign of Elizabeth I, with Hakluyt the Younger's 1584 *Discourse of Western Planting* (see Rich 1961: 4), which presented America as a

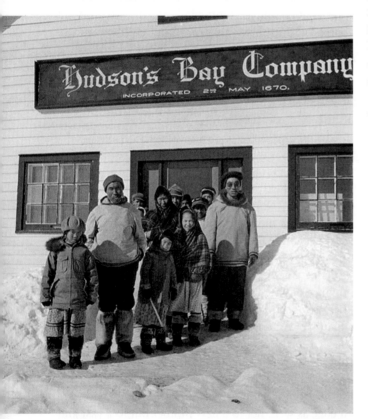

*Figure 3.3* | **The Hudson's Bay Company was an enduring presence in the lives of many Indigenous peoples in Canada. A group of Inuit from the Belcher Islands of James Bay stand in front of an HBC store in 1946.**

potential source of fresh resources and a distant place to effectively 'dump' redundant or troublesome populations. Of course in Tudor and Stuart times, and subsequently, population displacement became an issue as the structure of human–land relationships and the landscape itself were altered both literally and metaphorically in what has come to be called the Early Modern Period in Britain. In 1606 King James I of England granted a new warrant to the Virginia Company, essentially a cadre of gentlemen entrepreneurs, to establish a settlement in the New World. This settlement, known as 'Jamestown', would become the first permanent British settlement in what is now the United States of America. At the time, such ventures could be founded on royal letters patent under the assumption of *terra regis*—the belief that all newly discovered territories were the King's land by divine right; for example, it was a royal letters patent that gave the Hudson's Bay Company control of the area surrounding Hudson Bay, known as 'Rupert's Land', beginning in 1670 (Figure 3.3). The assumed objectives of the Hudson's Bay Company were the exploitation of Indigenous resources and continued exploration that included a search for the Northwest Passage through Arctic waters (56). Of course there were two vital differences between the Virginia and the Rupert's Land enterprises:

1) The Hudson's Bay Company was *all* about commerce, for although their Charter gave equal weight to trade and colonization, the Company, with a unified vision maintained over 200 years, was almost solely interested in trade (55). In contrast, the Virginia Company's Jamestown, in an effort to graft upon the wild the tame, included colonization along with commerce.
2) The Hudson's Bay Company endeavour required the participation, albeit manipulated, of Indigenous peoples, while the Jamestown enterprise dealt with Indigenous peoples as troublesome and mostly expendable threats to the safety of colony property and colonist life.

In these and other instances of colonization, early settlers 'knew virtually nothing of the Native languages of the Americas, even as they freely translated them' (Cheyfitz 1991: xv) with seeming accuracy that was a mere fiction of power. Language, as we will see in

Chapter 4, was a key element of the process of colonization. Indeed, on this topic Cheyfitz continues:

> What the English and Europeans could not achieve in actuality they achieved textually . . . [through] early narratives: the translation of the Indians into proper English. . . . [T]hese narratives became models of actuality, models for legal decisions in which the Indians were literally forced to speak proper English, to speak, that is, whether they could speak English or not, in the letter of a law that recognized only the terms of property. (10)

Thus the translation had commenced of North American Native peoples' oral kin-based societies into the English of the Early Modern Period, which was itself evolving to include a capitalist vocabulary. Translation errors abounded across the continent; too often, as was the case with Jamestown (and later Wounded Knee), the result was bloodshed. And of course translation errors were not unique to the Americas or to past centuries. We can find the same themes of unwarranted entitlement and misunderstanding that played out in North America in all colonial contexts—in South America, Africa, Australia, New Zealand, the South Pacific, and Asia—and in current land claims disputes across North America. The ramifications of European colonial aspirations and ideas of progress have been felt across time and space, even into what we consider our 'modern' era (see, e.g., Sahlins 1995).

## The Key Metaphor of Capitalism

Fundamental to these enterprises was and remains what has become a central component of capitalism—shareholder-owned company enterprises under government letters patent or warrants. On capitalism, Wolf comments that 'The guiding fiction . . . [and] one of the key tenets . . . is that land, labour, and wealth are commodities, that is, goods produced not for use but for sale' (1969: 277). The world is a market, and everything within the world has, or should have, its price. For early colonialists, capitalism very much became a key metaphor, Today, the metaphor persists, but it is no longer unambiguously aligned with a specific cultural tradition; it permeates the lives of everyone.

The genius of capitalism has been the thoroughgoing way in which its adherents have been able to convert anything that exists into a commodity. They turn land into real estate and material objects into inventory. They can attach price tags to ideas (e.g., patented inventions) and genetic materials (e.g., plant, animal, and even human DNA). At times, they have gone as far as promoting human beings themselves as merchandise (e.g., as enslaved labourers or sex-trade workers). In the Americas, the forced labour enslavement of Natives by the British was characterized in euphemistic terms of 'population recruitment' (Bailyn 1986), but we should note that regardless of their origin, Native or 'imported', all slaves shared one thing—they were considered 'first and foremost a commodity . . . chattel, totally in the possession of another person . . .' and they were used 'for private ends' (Kopytoff and Miers 1977: 3). Ultimately, capitalism reduces all workers, even those who are not slaves, to objects; their value is in their labour power, which is worth whatever price the laws of supply and demand determine. The market system also restricts the autonomy of the buyers, who are governed by capitalist dictates aimed at maximizing utility: buy cheap, sell dear, and do not be diverted from the bottom line by any personal or social considerations.

To be sure, complex commercial activity was not invented by Western capitalists. Stratified societies have always devised sophisticated socio-economic systems. In the early days of capitalism, therefore, elite members of such societies around the globe were prepared to take advantage of new economic opportunities offered by Western entrepreneurs. Thus these elites traded with Westerners, often helping to establish capitalist practices in their own societies and benefitting as a result. However, the consequences of capitalism were frequently negative for non-elite members of these societies, who lost many traditional socio-economic supports.

Capitalism was even more devastating in small-scale societies. Members of these societies saw their land turned into a commodity for sale on the capitalist market. They experienced the devaluation of their traditional social identities based on kinship, descent, alliance, and residence; they also witnessed the erosion of traditional obligations that protected them from destitution—they experienced colonialism.

European conquest of non-Western societies created colonial empires in two historical phases. In the first phase, which was led by Spain, Portugal, and Holland, colonies were required to pay tribute to the ruling empire through trading companies. In the second phase, which was driven by England and France, colonies were treated like 'plantations' and governed to meet the demands of industrial capitalism (Gledhill 1994: 74). To function intelligibly within the capitalist world order, colonized peoples had to begin seeing the world as a storehouse of potential commodities. Much of recent world history can be usefully viewed as a narrative of non-Western responses to this new world view and the practical actions it encouraged and justified. Some people responded with enthusiasm, others were resentful but accommodating, and still others were violent in repudiation or took action to protect themselves.

## Responses to European Colonialism: The Fur Trade in North America

Like other Native peoples across North America and beyond, the First Nations populations of northern boreal Canada have been through social, cultural, and environmental disruptions as a result of colonialism. It has been a journey of both immense tragedy and tremendous courage, and along the way they have made many compromises as they were forced to adapt to changed circumstances. The consequences of these disruptions can be seen in the modern circumstances of northern peoples today. The most invasive disturbances to northern life came from the fur trade.

The international fur trade had existed before Europeans first invaded the northern regions of North America, but its expansion into this new and untapped territory sent profits skyrocketing (see Wolf 1982: 158ff.). In North America, the 'winners' in all of this were the British—they outmanoeuvred and/or defeated both the Dutch and the French for control of resources, mostly beavers (*Castor canadensis*). Beavers were not only a keystone species—a species on which the balance of an entire ecosystem depends—but also a feature of the key metaphor of many Algonquian peoples (Dods 2003; 2007; Overholt and Callicott 1982: 74–5). At contact, beavers seemed to be an inexhaustible resource, as the estimate of the beaver population at sixty million to four hundred million suggests (Naiman et al. 1986:

1254). However, by the nineteenth century, the beaver populations in areas such as northern Ontario were reduced to the point of regional extinction.

The capitalist response to declining resources was to open new territory—they moved on. Yet this response was not viable for Native peoples who were deeply connected to the land. In many places such as northwestern Ontario, Native peoples were forced to change their food strategies. Rogers and Black (1976: 13–14) recount a notable example of such a forced shift that occurred in northern Ontario between 1880 and 1920. In what has been referred to as the 'fish and hare' period, the Anishinaabe (Ojibwe) of this region were forced by starvation to turn to fishing and trapping after the depletion of their primary food source, the caribou. Resource depletion also caused many social issues to develop among Native populations. For example, Bishop (1973) has identified the post-contact collapse of the food chain as the precipitating circumstance for the elaboration of the Wendigo complex, the fear of cannibals and cannibalism. This complex, documented in the early nineteenth century (Bishop 1970: 8), has been interpreted by modern psychologists as a psychosis. However, Bishop (1973) considers the condition to be the direct result of protein starvation, and his interpretation is somewhat supported by work done with Arctic peoples in Lapland, Siberia, and North America. In a similar case, Høygaard examined reports of 'hysterical fits' and 'periodical madness' among Arctic peoples and found the cause to be a lack of minerals or vitamins, in particular a low level of calcium 'which is essential for the nervous system' (Høygaard 1941: 72).

Additionally, disease played a significant role in the alteration of population patterns and social cohesion. The high mortality rate 'devastated and decimated some groups, modifying social organizational features and ecological relationships . . .' (Bishop 1981: 45). Further, Trigger notes that 'failure to cope with epidemic diseases led to a spiritual crisis . . .' (1981: 36). Often, settlements located close to active trade routes were most susceptible to infection in the nineteenth century (Ray 1976: 156). But the problem did not end with the turn of the century. During the Spanish flu pandemic in 1918–19, Norway House Cree Nation in northern Manitoba lost 18 per cent of their adult population (ages 20 to 64) in the span of six weeks; the average loss among other Indigenous populations in that year was closer to

3 per cent (Herring 1994: 96). 'Its key position in the fur trade network and frequent contact with locations to the west, northwest, northeast, and south left it particularly vulnerable to imported micro-organisms' (97).

## The Slave and Commodities Trades

While the fur trade unfolded in the north, the slave trade and the trade in commodities such as sugar and cotton accompanied the rise of capitalist industry in the south (Figure 3.4). Humans and crops as commodities were connected in world markets. The slave trade dominated commerce between Europeans and coastal Africans by the eighteenth century. The nature of the merchandise sought for this trade—people—had a devastating effect on the societies of the African hinterland, whose members were captured and sold to meet European demand. But the slave trade did not alter social relations in Africa alone. In the New World, it profoundly reshaped the lives of both local Indigenous peoples and European colonists. The growth of plantation economies in areas that had been used by hunters, gatherers, or small-scale farmers altered local ecologies as well as local societies. And the wealth produced in these economies transformed both the local gentry and the European nations who claimed sovereignty over the land. As a result, Africa, the Americas, and Europe became inextricably intertwined in one another's fate.

## Colonialism and 'Modernity'

What is 'modernity'? Its prototype was the European-style industrial city, which existed both in Europe and in foreign lands where Europeans settled. The colonial city was markedly different from the great Indigenous cities of pre-contact times. It was 'a conquered place' (Gilsenan 1982: 197). Colonial administrators, merchants, and local elites united in such places to defend their joint interests against those they perceived as 'outliers'—both the geographically removed 'others' of the resource-rich hinterland and the socially removed 'others' within the colonial cities. Colonial authorities set up elaborate systems for extracting raw materials, and they recruited labour for such enterprises, sometimes by force, from local populations. These and other capitalist-colonialist processes disrupted or destroyed existing Indigenous communities; at times, they also created new centres of population struggling to become

*Figure 3.4* | **A slave family works in a cotton field near Savannah, Georgia. The slave trade had a devastating effect on many Indigenous peoples around the world.**

communities, as was the case with the mining towns of South Africa. Thus, little by little, in an effort to streamline the system of exploitation, society was restructured.

To some, the term *modern* reflects the modernization—both of technologies and of ideas—that came about in the Enlightenment. The spirit of the Enlightenment was humanist, and its primary goal was to come to an understanding of the 'moral, genetic, and historical unity of mankind' (Mafeje 1976: 310). However, this intellectual environment also provided the rationale behind the notion of the 'civilizing mission' of Europeans, a notion that led to the 'rationalization of more mundane things such as economic plunder, political imposition, and other inhuman practices' (1976). Thus we can see at work the dual forces of modernity—progress and destruction.

In the colonial context, 'modernity' has often been understood as nothing more than adopting the practices and world view of Western capitalism. As a result, the so-called backward rural peoples often turned out to be either those who escaped capitalism's embrace or those who actively opposed it. For many of them, the colonial city and the life it represented symbolized everything that was wrong with the colonial order. This perception persists today among peoples who feel invaded by Western capitalism. At times of crisis in contemporary Muslim societies, for example,

> the modern city is itself called in question, taken to symbolize forces of oppression or a non-Islamic way of life. . . . For radical and millennial groups the city is a home of unbelief, not of sober, textual Islam. The true believer should, in an image that has great historical resonance, go out from the city, leave as the Prophet Muhammad did the hypocritical and unbelieving citizens of Mecca. (Gilsenan 1982: 214).

## The Colonial Political Economy

Because the colonial order focussed on the extraction of material wealth, and because it came to link communities around the globe in a diverse market system, it might be said that its reason for existence was economic. Yet this new economic order did not spring up painlessly by itself; it was imposed and maintained by force. For this reason, many anthropologists describe the colonial order as a **political economy**. The colonial political economy created three kinds of links:

1) connecting conquered communities with one another within a conquered territory,
2) connecting different conquered territories with one another, and
3) connecting all conquered territories with the country of the colonizers.

Wolf describes a particularly striking example of how some of these connections came together in the sixteenth century: silver mined in Spanish colonies in America was shipped to a Spanish colony in Asia—the Philippines— where it was used to buy

**political economy**
A holistic term that emphasizes the centrality of material interest (economy) in the organization of society and the use of power (politics) to protect and enhance that interest.

textiles from the Chinese (1982: 153). If we take Wolf's example one step further and suggest that the profits from the sale of the Chinese textiles in the European market were in turn used to fund colonialist endeavours in North America, we can see how the political economy might come full circle.

One way that colonial enterprises connected communities within a conquered territory was by drawing labour from neighbouring regions. For example, in Africa, mine owners recruited Indigenous Africans from some distance; money earned in one area was thus remitted for the economic support of families in another area. These linkages did not come about spontaneously, and the process of their emergence is very telling. In the beginning, Africans were still largely able to guarantee their own subsistence through traditional means, so they were unwilling to work for wages in the mines except on a short-term basis. Therefore, profitability in mining required that African self-sufficiency be eliminated so that Africans would have no choice but to work for whatever wages mine owners offered. The colonial government achieved this goal through two policies:

1) It imposed taxes on conquered African populations, and insisted that the taxes could only be paid in cash.
2) It deliberately prevented the growth of a cash economy in African areas. Thus, the only way Africans could obtain the cash to pay their taxes was by working for wages in the mines.

Of course, colonial administrators were generally convinced that the work of empire would benefit those they dominated—if not now, then in the future. However, as the misguided endeavours of past Canadian governments have taught us, policies that restrict the freedom of dominated people hold no benefits for those people.

As we noted in Chapter 1, one of the most devastating policies enacted upon Canada's native peoples was that which forced Native children to attend residential schools (Figure 3.5). Such schools, first introduced in the first half of the nineteenth century, are seen by First Nations peoples as factories of cultural genocide designed by the Government of Canada to eliminate the 'Indian Problem' one way or another, once and for all (Chrisjohn et al. 1997: 42). Like the colonial governments who

*Figure 3.5* | **Native parents camp by a residential school to visit their children in Birtle, Manitoba, in 1904.**

implemented pro-mining policies in Africa, the authorities who set up the residential school system suffered from the false belief that they were doing good work. Consider the widespread ideal espoused by Canadian politician Alexander Morris in 1877: 'let us have a wise and paternal Government . . . doing its utmost to help and elevate the Indian population who have been cast upon our care [doing] . . . our duty by the red man' (296–7); notice how Morris' sentiments echo the colonialist hubris of the 'white man's burden'! First Nations peoples have noted that the actual agenda was much more selfish:

> the 'problem' was (and is) that there were (and are) Aboriginal owners (and their legal descendants) inhabiting the land to which the Europeans wished to lay claim. . . . [The] genocide of Aboriginal peoples grew out of . . . [a] need to extinguish Aboriginal title to the land without

violating the letter and spirit of established British policy. (Chrisjohn et al. 1997: 51–2)

Others have likewise noted that the government's intent was cultural genocide; not the physical eradication of Native peoples, but their death 'spiritually, mentally, economically, and socially' (Waubageshig 1970: vi).

To help us make sense of the types of power that enter into such social relationships as those involved in colonialist domination, Wolf identifies 'four modalities in how power is . . . woven into social relations':

1) the individual's 'power of potency or capability', through which he or she can 'enter into a play of power';
2) interactional power that is 'manifested in interactions and transactions among people', through which an individual imposes his or her will on another through social action;

3) organizational power that 'controls the contexts' in which people act (such power is often enforced by laws, rules, etc.); and

4) structural power that 'not only operates within settings and domains but also organizes and orchestrates the settings themselves, and that specifies the direction and distribution of energy flows' (1999: 5).

Thus Wolf reveals power to be not 'a unitary and independent force' but 'an aspect of all relations among people' (4). As Wolf suggests, we can apply these modalities to understand the links between power and ideas—indeed, between power and ideologies that serve elite groups—in order to expand our understanding of the relationship between culture and power and realize that power is central in the reproduction of cultural coherency. In this view, ideas are originated through the first modality, actualized through second modality, instrumentalized through the third modality, and realized in the material world through the fourth modality. Wolf's ideas are not without criticism (see Barrett et al. 2001), but awareness of the interconnections among power, ideas, and culture is needed for historical analysis as much as it is needed to make sense of the power relationships that structure our world of today and push the shape of tomorrow.

## Women and Colonization

Ethnographic data show that colonial conquest did not affect all groups in the same ways. Notably, Indigenous women's experience with colonialism was different from that of Indigenous men. In addition, colonialism did not treat all groups of women in all conquered territories in the same way. We will see in Chapter 7 that Trobriand women of New Guinea (see EthnoProfile 7.1) were able to maintain status roles under colonial rule. Baule women of Ivory Coast in western Africa (see EthnoProfile 3.1) were less fortunate.

In pre-colonial Baule society, production centred on two products: yams and cloth (Etienne 1980). These products were indispensable for subsistence as well as for exchange in various traditional social contexts, and they played a particularly important role as gifts given to consolidate marriages. Both sexes worked together in the production of each, with men taking greater responsibility for yams and women taking greater responsibility

for cloth. These traditional realms of control grew out of the sexual division of labour: the men cleared and prepared farm plots for planting and the women tended the crops, while the women raised the cotton and spun it into thread and the men did the actual weaving. As a result, the balance of power between men and women was highly egalitarian.

France colonized the Ivory Coast in 1893. In 1923, in Baule territory, the French built a textile factory that sold factory-spun thread for cash. Baule men with cash could therefore buy their own thread, and they, not their wives, would control any cloth woven from it. French colonial administrators also encouraged Baule farmers to plant new varieties of cotton as a cash crop. Baule women had traditionally practised crop rotation with the yams and cotton. Now the fields were devoted to growing only the new cotton. This industrial crop required new farming techniques, which the French taught only to Baule men. Consequently, women's roles in cotton production were reduced considerably. Now women had to work in their husbands' cash-crop fields and the traditional yam plots. The agricultural work for women increased, and they had less time to spin traditional thread.

The colonial government required men to pay taxes in cash for themselves and for their wives, a move that seemed to justify the right of Baule men to control the production of crops that could be sold for cash. Under colonial rule, cash-cropping became increasingly important. As a result, Baule women found that their traditional autonomous rights to use their husbands' land for their own production gradually eroded, and they became increasingly dependent on their husbands' arbitrary generosity.

There is a final irony in this series of developments: by the 1970s, many Baule women had become wage labourers in the textile factory in order to earn cash to buy their own cloth, which they could then control. They were aware of the loss of status and power they had suffered over the years, and their discontent had undermined traditional Baule marriage. As Etienne reported in 1980,

The wife–husband production relationship has become a constant source of conflict. Because the production relationship has always been the foundation of marriage, and because cloth and cash now tend to be the measure of a husband's

## EthnoProfile 3.1 | Baule

**Region** Western Africa

**Nation** Ivory Coast; originally from the area where the Koussou Dam was built (1971), the project resulted in the relocation of many Baule to the forests in the southwestern area of the country

**Language** Baule are one of the Fante-Akan speaking peoples and make up approximately 20 per cent of the population of the Ivory Coast

**Population** 3,615,000 (2011 estimate)

**Environment** Savannah

**Livelihood** Farming (yams in particular); coffee, cocoa, and cloth production

**Political organization** In the pre-colonial period, no state and no clear stratification; today, part of a modern nation-state

**For more information** Vogel, Susan M. 1997. *Baule: African Art, Western Eyes* (New Haven: Yale University Press).

---

affection and respect, the whole personal relationship is also conflict-laden. Inevitably, many women prefer to remain unmarried and all seek to acquire their own cash. (1980: 231)

In this way, the traditional Baule mode of production was transformed by contact with the capitalist market. The previously egalitarian relations of production linking women and men (husbands and wives) were destroyed.

## Anthropology and the Colonial Encounter

This section's title has been borrowed from the title of a book edited by anthropologist Talal Asad. Published in 1973, Asad's book was the first high-profile work by anthropologists to consider the connections between anthropology and colonialism. Thus, the work constituted an important exercise in disciplinary self-scrutiny. Three decades after its publication, Asad (2002) revisited the questions raised in the earlier publication. In particular, he addressed the charge, made frequently from within and without the discipline, that anthropology was nothing more than a form of 'applied colonialism'. He concluded that the charge was false for two reasons:

1) anthropological findings were too specialized to be used by colonial administrators, especially compared to the enormous amount of information supplied to them by merchants, missionaries, and other government functionaries; and

2) colonial governments were preoccupied with day-to-day concerns of administration and, for them, social change involved the adjustment of conquered peoples to life under colonial rule; thus the research that would let them rule with as little difficulty as possible was of interest.

European anthropologists sometimes played an equivocal role in the colonial setting; colonial administrators valued them for the expert knowledge they could provide, but those same administrators also viewed them with suspicion because their expert knowledge might easily contradict or undermine administrative goals. For their part, anthropologists felt that they needed to navigate the colonial context with care in order to be allowed to access colonial settings and further their own goal of deflecting or mitigating the effects of colonial rule on subject peoples. Therefore, as Asad emphasizes, 'the process of European global power has been central to the anthropological task of recording and analyzing the way of life of subject populations' and therefore must be recognized as having been 'always part of the reality anthropologists sought to understand, and the way they sought to understand it' (2002: 134).

One way of coping with colonial power was to address it indirectly. For example, in the mid-twentieth century, a number of North American anthropologists tried to clarify what their role should be in the expanding world of capitalist colonialism. Two documents (Redfield et al. 1936 and Broom et al. 1954) bracket the period that Bohannan and Plog (1967: x) called the *high period of* the study of culture. The anthropologists involved promoted an impartial and scientific program of research that would, they hoped, discover the laws of culture change. They had a broad view of culture change. They considered situations encountered under colonialism, but they also considered situations where contact and change occurred in the absence of political conquest. The latter cases involved autonomous groups whose members could be freer about what they selected and rejected. The anthropologists did not see themselves supporting any particular political position in advocating that culture change be approached in this way;

## In Their Own Words | The Anthropological Voice

*Anthropologist Annette Weiner (1933–97) traces the history of anthropological challenges to colonialism and Western capitalism, pointing out why the perspective of anthropologists has so often been ignored.*

Colonialism brought foreign governments, missionaries, explorers, and exploiters face to face with cultures whose values and beliefs were vastly different. As the harbingers of Western progress, their actions were couched in the rhetoric of doing something to and for 'the Natives'—giving them souls, clothes, law—whatever was necessary to lift them out of their 'primitive' ways. Anthropologists were also part of the colonial scene, but what they came to 'do' made them different from those who were carrying out the expectations of missions, overseas trade, and government protectorates. Anthropologists arrived in the field determined to understand the cultural realities of an unfamiliar world. The knowledge of these worlds was to serve as a warning to those in positions of colonial power by charging that villagers' lives were not to be tampered with arbitrarily and that changing the lives of powerless people was insensitive and inhumane, unless one understood and took seriously the cultural meanings inherent in, for example, traditional land ownership, the technologies and rituals surrounding food cultivation, myths, magic, and gender relations.

   All too often, however, the anthropologist's voice went unnoticed by those in power, for it remained a voice committed to illuminating the cultural biases under which colonialists operated. Only recently have we witnessed the final demise of colonial governments and the rise of independent countries. Economically, however, independence has not brought these countries the freedom to pursue their own course of development. In many parts of the world, Western multinational corporations, often playing a role not too dissimilar from colonial enterprises, now determine the course of that freedom, changing people's lives in a way that all too often is harmful or destructive. At the same time, we know that the world's natural resources and human productive capabilities can no longer remain isolates. Developed and developing countries are now more dependent on one another than ever before in human history. Yet this interdependency, which should give protection to Indigenous peoples, is often worked out for political ends that ignore the moral issues. Racism and the practice of discrimination are difficult to destroy, as evidenced by the United States today, where we still are not completely emancipated from assumptions that relegate blacks, women, Asians, Hispanics, and other minorities to second-class status. If we cannot bridge these cultural differences intellectually within our own borders, then how can we begin to deal politically with Third World countries—those who were called *primitives* less than a century ago—in a fair, sensitive, and meaningful way?

   This is the legacy of anthropology that we must never forget. Because the work of anthropology takes us to the neighbourhoods, villages, and campsites—the local level—we can ourselves experience the results of how the world's economic and political systems affect those who have no voice. Yet once again our voices too are seldom heard by those who make such decisions. Anthropologists are often prevented from participating in the forums of economic and government planning. Unlike economists, political scientists, or engineers, we must stand on the periphery of such decision-making, primarily because our understanding of cultural patterns and beliefs forces on others an awareness that ultimately makes such decisions more formidable.

Source: Weiner, Annette. 1990. 'The Anthropological Voice', guest editorial in *Cultural Anthropology: A Perspective on the Human Condition*, 2nd edn, eds Emily Schultz and Robert Lavenda (St Paul: West), 392–3.

however, they were sympathetic to the plight of colonial subjects. One of the anthropologists involved, Melville Herskovits, was particularly outspoken in his defence of the right of Indigenous African peoples to control their own destinies.

In the years following World War II, European colonial powers were increasingly forced to come to terms with colonial subjects who rejected the role they had been forced to play as students of civilization. The colonial order was no longer a given, and its ultimate benevolence was sharply questioned. This critical attitude persisted after independence was granted to most European colonies in the 1950s and 1960s. It became clear that formal political independence could not easily undo the profound social and economic entanglements linking the former colonial territories to the countries that colonized them. The persistence of ties in the face of political sovereignty came to be called **neo-colonialism**.

The study of neo-colonialism led to a new awareness of just how strongly the fate of colonies and the fate of the colonizers continued to be interdependent. Recognizing the strength of this interdependence, scholars began to offer new explanations for the 'under-development' that characterized the new nations in what came to be known as the Third World. However, now we have what is termed the 'Fourth World'—subjugated original peoples struggling in ex-colonial or neo-colonial settings—to add to the analysis. In Canada, we cannot deny the realities of the remains of colonialism. We have only to read the newspaper or watch the evening news to know that the aspirations of the First Nations peoples of Canada have yet to be addressed in an adequate way. Today, through the efforts of organizations such as the Assembly of First Nations (AFN), Native peoples have a greater voice than they did in the past, but there is much work to be done. And the residential school ramifications continue to be a central problem, both of reconciliation and redress, regardless of the latest apology in Parliament (Figure 3.6).

## Toward Classifying Forms of Human Society

From our discussion thus far, we can identify several conclusions that have informed the modern anthropological approach.

First, all peoples live in their own modernity. Therefore, the peoples studied by anthropologists are not now—nor were they at the time of colonialism—leading timeless, unchanging ways of life unaffected by the presence of others. Cultural patterns have been affected everywhere by the arrival of Europeans and/or the transformations of the world set in motion by the spread of European capitalism and colonialism.

**neo-colonialism**
The persistence of profound social and economic entanglements linking former colonial territories to their former colonial rulers despite political sovereignty.

Second, many groups have shaped new identities and devised new social forms to deal with the effects of contact and conquest. These new social forms sometimes draw on very ancient traditions, reworked to meet the demands of new experiences. Additionally, ways of life that were invented long ago continue to prove their worth, and many ways that were lost as a result of colonialism are being reintroduced today—at times

*Figure 3.6* | Beverley Jacobs, head of the Native Women's Association of Canada from 2004–9, and Phil Fontaine, national chief of the Assembly of First Nations from 1997–2000 and 2003–9, stand alongside former residential school students in the House of Commons on 11 June 2008, awaiting Prime Minister Stephen Harper's official apology.

with the help of information gathered by anthropologists. Yet some ancient modes of living continue to fall before the advance of Western technology and the rigours of market capitalism (see, e.g., Lee 2002; 1992a; 1992b). Far from being static survivors of a timeless past, Indigenous peoples are actively coping with contemporary problems and opportunities.

Third, colonial empires have been replaced by the empires of transnational corporations. The reach of these corporations is vast, and their actions affect peoples in all regions of the world. As anthropologists, we must work to understand how these corporations influence everyday life and social relations; we must also devise new forms of recourse to challenge the agents of such change.

## Evolutionary Typologies: The Nineteenth Century

Early anthropologists, like all children of the Age of Enlightenment, liked to devise **typologies**. They believed that such classification systems would facilitate their study of similarities and differences in cultural and social responses. Of course, every system of classification reflects the attributes believed to be most significant by its creator. Therefore, different assessments can lead to different classifications. In the pervasive nineteenth-century Western view, Europeans described the differences they noticed between themselves and the various peoples they conquered in terms of *deficiencies*: lack of a state, lack of sophisticated technology, lack of organized religion, and so forth, much along the lines of discussion in Thomas Hobbes's *Leviathan* (1651). These terms reflected the cross-cultural experience that representatives of Western capitalist nations were having with non-Western peoples. For example, a colonial functionary eager to establish a smoothly working trading post and anxious to maximize profits in the fur trade would be most aware of the facets of a people's life that kept him from reaching his goals. How do you 'pay' for beaver pelts when the 'sellers' are not interested in money? Europeans faced with such practical problems were bound to see life outside Europe in terms of a series of deficiencies compared with what they could count on in their home country.

**typologies**
Classification systems based on systematic organization into *types* on the basis of shared attributes.

**unilineal cultural evolutionism**
A nineteenth-century theory that proposed a series of stages through which all societies must go (or had gone) in order to reach civilization.

More contemplative nineteenth-century observers pondered why there should be such deficiencies in the first place. As they sat in their libraries studying the reports of travellers and missionaries, as well as history, they learned that many of the social and technological patterns they took for granted had not always existed, even in Europe. So they came to believe that they might, by going back beyond the Middle Ages, discover that their more distant ancestors had lived much the same way as many peoples of America or Africa. Indeed, they found evidence to support their theories in the written accounts of Julius Caesar, who had painted a picture of Indigenous life in early Europe that resembled what Europeans were discovering in America and Africa, and in archaeological discoveries of ancient artifacts on European soil.

Thus, the experience of social change, together with historical and archaeological evidence of past social change, led these thinkers to a new idea: perhaps the ways of life of the non-Western peoples they were reading about were not only similar to but repeats of the ways of life of European generations long past. That is, perhaps the West had already moved through *stages* of history in which ways of life had been the same as those of contemporary non-Western societies. According to these scholars, if non-Western societies were left to themselves and given enough time, they would make the same discoveries and social changes that European societies had made in the past.

This way of thinking about social and cultural change has been called **unilineal cultural evolutionism** (Figure 3.7). It reached its most elaborate development in the nineteenth century, when ideas of social Darwinism were generally popular. Unilineal cultural evolutionism was used to explain the widespread cultural diversity that Europeans had been finding since the Age of Exploration. The theory accounted for this diversity by arguing that different kinds of societies represented different stages of societal evolution through which every human society either had passed or would pass if it survived. Proponents of the theory viewed their own late nineteenth-century European capitalist industrial society as the most advanced stage of cultural evolution. Living societies that had not already reached this level were seen as primitive relics of the stages the West had already left behind.

To understand how the stages involved in unilineal cultural evolutionism were conceptualized in the nineteenth century, we consider two popular schemes:

*Figure 3.7* | **E.B. Tylor (1832–1917), one of the founders of anthropology in Great Britain, was convinced that societies moved through a series of unilineal stages.**

1) the 'three-age system' (from European archaeology), and
2) the 'ethnical stages' of the American Lewis Henry Morgan.

C.J. Thomsen's systematic, 1836 study of artifacts in the Danish National Museum led to his development of the three-age system and popularized ideas on social evolution not long before Darwin published his first book on biological evolution, *On the Origin of Species* (1859). Based on the raw materials from which tools had been made, Thomsen proposed that Europeans had passed through three technological stages or 'ages': the Stone Age, the Bronze Age, and the Iron Age. Later the Stone Age was subdivided into the Paleolithic (Old Stone Age—itself divided into Lower, Middle, and Upper divisions), Mesolithic (Middle Stone Age), and Neolithic (New Stone Age).

Even more influential than Thomsen's typology was that proposed by Lewis Henry Morgan in *Ancient Society: Researches in the Lines of Human Progress from Savagery through Barbarism to Civilization* (1877). Morgan proposed three 'ethnical stages': 'Savagery', 'Barbarism', and 'Civilization'. The first two were also subdivided into Lower, Middle, and Upper categories and were defined by technological attributes, in particular food-acquisition technologies. One striking feature, however, effectively kept 'Civilization' for Europeans alone—the use of the phonetic alphabet. *Ancient Society* was based in equal parts on Morgan's mid-nineteenth-century in-field observations of the Iroquois of the Finger Lakes District of New York, the emerging concepts of evolution (biological and cultural), and the ideas of progress from the Age of Enlightenment. In effect it was an attempt at 'anthropological' synthesis of the evolutionary stages of human society. Morgan's typology was immensely influential in its time, and its popularity spread as other writers and thinkers expanded on and disseminated his ideas. Notably, Friedrich Engels, in writing *Origin of the Family, Private Property and the State* (1884), was greatly influenced by, and drew upon, Morgan's work. Well into the twentieth century, Morgan's classification, because of its link through Engels to Marxism, was *au courant* in some sectors of the academic world. For example, Morgan was the main—and, indeed, sometimes the only—authority cited in the cultural analysis found in Chinese archaeological reports well into the 1970s. In the Americas, Morgan gained renewed immediacy in the 1940s and 1950s with the unilineal evolutionary perspective of anthropologist Leslie White, whose approach differed markedly from that of his teacher, Franz Boas.

In various social and intellectual realms, such stages were used to justify racist ideas. Equally distinguished were those who had 'stagnated', in effect the cultural 'back-sliders', as well as those who were 'eminently gifted' (de Gobineau 1967 [1915]: 27). Racial inferiority, de Gobineau opines, 'is shown, not only by defeat, but also by the lack of the attributes that may be seen in the conquerors' (31). He asks: if all men are brothers and the brain of the 'Huron Indian' is the same as that of an Englishman or a Frenchman, 'Why then, in the course of the ages, has [the Huron] not invented printing or steam power?' (37). Of course, when he proposed the question, de Gobineau neglected to note that printing was actually the invention of a group classified by Europeans as Upper Barbarians—namely, the Chinese! Such omissions are indicative of the ways in which Europeans assumed credit for all social and technological 'advancements'. Europeans saw themselves, their technologies, and their social constructs as unique, unmatched in other civilizations, which were understood to be declining. That decline seemed proven when representatives of Western civilization found they could conquer the rulers of other civilizations, as the English had done in India or the Dutch in Bali.

The labels of unilineal evolutionism remained part of the vocabulary of anthropology for many years. Malinowski, for example, was quite comfortable referring to the inhabitants of the Trobriand Islands as *savages*. Today, anthropologists find such labels to be inadequate—indeed, misleading—and they reject the classification of human beings into different 'types'. Indeed, in 2007 the British-based Association of Social Anthropologists and the activist group Survival International initiated a campaign to 'challenge racist descriptions' in the press, citing the CBC, among others, for using 'Stone Age' in their coverage (Kesterton 2007). But both Thomsen's and Morgan's schemes continue to resonate, and their continued popularity among ordinary members of Western societies is neither surprising nor difficult to understand: they offer seemingly coherent frameworks for classifying all societies.

## Social Structural Typologies: The British Emphasis

Although unilineal cultural evolutionism may have justified the global ambitions of Europe and made colonial rule appear inevitable and just, it was inadequate for meeting the practical needs of colonials once they were in power. By the end of the nineteenth century, most of Africa and much of Asia had been divided up among European powers. At the same time, the United States and Canada assumed a similarly powerful and dominating role in their relationships with the Indigenous peoples of North America.

In order to effectively oversee their subject peoples, administrators required accurate information about those people. For example, one goal of a colonial administrator in Africa was to keep peace among the various contending groups. To achieve this goal, the administrator needed to know how those people were accustomed to handling

disputes. Most colonies included several societies with various customs for dispute resolution, and administrators had to be aware of their similarities and differences in order to develop successful government policies. Colonial officials also planned to introduce certain elements of European law and political economy uniformly throughout the colony. Common examples were commercial laws permitting the buying and selling of land on the open market. They also tried to eliminate practices like witchcraft accusations or local punishment for capital crimes. Reaching these goals without totally disrupting life in the colony required first-hand understanding of local practices. The earlier 'armchair anthropology' approaches, based on reading reports from distant places, were wholly incapable of providing that understanding.

These changes in the relationships between the West and the rest of the world fostered the development of a new anthropological research paradigm—one that grew out of a dissatisfaction with grand generalizations and a desire to gather detailed information on more societies. Unsettled conditions had made such work difficult in earlier times. But under the colonial 'peace', anthropologists found that they could carry out long-term fieldwork, with colonial governments supporting their research when it was seen as 'scientific' and contributing to effective colonial rule. This did not mean that anthropologists who carried out fieldwork under colonial conditions supported colonialism. To the contrary, their sympathies often lay with the colonized peoples with whom they worked. For example, Evans-Pritchard, who worked in central Africa for the British government in the 1920s and 1930s, saw himself as an educator of colonial administrators. He tried to convey to them the humanity and rationality of Africans. His goal was to combat the racism and oppression that seemed an inevitable consequence of colonial rule. Not surprisingly, such criticisms of colonialism often caused colonial officials to be wary of anthropologists and distrustful of their motives.

Colonial officials quickly learned that administering their rule would be easier if they could rely on traditional leaders as intermediaries to keep the peace among their people (Figure 3.8). Thus the British policy of *indirect rule* was developed. To help officials discover the best way to adapt indirect rule to each group, anthropologists were charged with the task of uncovering information on the traditional political structures of different

*Figure 3.8* | Colonial officers often relied on traditional rulers to keep the peace among their subjects through traditional means. This 1895 photograph shows the British governor of the Gold Coast (seated on the right) together with a contingent of Native police.

groups. As a result, British anthropologists developed a new way of classifying forms of human society. Their focus was on the **social structure**, especially the political structure, of groups under colonial rule. That British anthropologists came to call themselves *social anthropologists* reflects these developments. This focus on social structure influenced many anthropologists in the early twentieth century. For example, in 1940, in a classic work on African political systems, Fortes and Evans-Pritchard distinguished between *state* and *stateless* societies. This distinction had some similarity to Morgan's ethnical stages, and it described stateless societies in negative terms (i.e., in terms of what they lacked as compared to state societies), but it notably did not refer to 'progress' in relation to either system.

Thus the productive emphasis on contemporary social structures emerged and questions of evolution and social change were superseded by concerns about the enduring traditional structures of the societies in which anthropologists worked. Anthropologists came to believe that having a detailed knowledge of social structures would allow them to identify the social type of any particular society. They compared the similarities and differences of these types, and out of this comparison emerged a new classification of social forms.

> **social structure**
> The enduring aspects of the social forms in a society, including its political and kinship systems.

### The Classification of Political Structures

An example of a typical social structural classification is shown in Figure 3.9. In this system, outlined by Lewellen in 1983, the major distinction is between *centralized* and *uncentralized* (*egalitarian*) political systems. Lewellen's system is similar to that established by Fortes and Evans-Pritchard in 1940; however, we can note that uncentralized societies are now distinguished in positive terms. Whereas in centralized systems there is a distinct, permanent institution exclusively concerned with public decision-making, in uncentralized systems groups (and perhaps even individuals) enjoy relative autonomy and equal status.

**Figure 3.9 | A typical classification of forms of human society.**
Source: Lewellen 1983: 16.

In this typology, uncentralized political systems can be divided into two types:

1) **Band**: a small social group whose members neither farm nor herd but depend on wild food sources. Lewellen refers to three subtypes of a band, including the *family band*.
2) **Tribe**: a group that lies somewhere between a band and a centralized political system. A tribe is generally larger than a band and has domesticated plants and animals, but its political organization remains largely egalitarian. Lewellen identifies five subtypes of a tribe but comments that these subtypes hardly exhaust the variety of social arrangements that tribes display (1983: 26).

Centralized political systems differ from uncentralized systems because they have a central, institutionalized focus of authority such as a chief or a king. Some members of centralized societies have greater wealth, power, or prestige than other members. Thus hierarchy is an evident characteristic. Centralized systems are divided into two types:

1) **Chiefdom**: usually only the chief and the chief's family are set above the rest of society, which remains fairly egalitarian.
2) **State**: different groups suffer permanent inequality of access to wealth, power, and prestige, which signals the presence of social stratification.

Lewellen's typology does not attempt to make any hypotheses about evolutionary relationships. Tracing change over time is not its purpose. Instead, the focus is on structural similarities and differences observed at one point in time. This is not accidental—it reveals the lasting influence of colonialism on anthropology toward the end of the twentieth century. Remember that classifications of this kind were made in response to practical

**band**
The characteristic form of social organization found among foragers; a small group of people, usually with less than fifty members. Labour is divided according to age and sex, and social relations are highly egalitarian.

**tribe**
A form of social organization generally larger than a band; members usually farm or herd for a living. Social relations in a tribe are relatively egalitarian, although there may be a chief who speaks for the group or organizes group activities.

needs in European colonies. Colonial rulers assumed that they were *civilized* and that their colonial subjects were *primitive*, but they cared little about matters such as the origin of political systems. The pressing questions for them were more likely 'How do African political forms work today?' and 'What do we need to know about them to make them work for us?'

### Structural-Functional Theory

The theories of British social anthropologists dealt with how particular social forms function from day-to-day in order to reproduce their traditional structures. Such **structural-functional theory** was perhaps most highly developed by A.R. Radcliffe-Brown in the 1930s and 1940s. Social anthropologists began to question why things remain the same rather than change. For example, they asked:

- Why do some social structures last for centuries (e.g., the Roman Catholic Church) and others disappear quickly (e.g., the Shakers and other utopian communities of nineteenth-century America)?
- Why did some societies abandon foraging for agriculture thousands of years ago, while others are still hunting and gathering today?

Both kinds of questions are needed for a balanced approach, since the emphasis on social stability tends to downplay or ignore questions of change, and the emphasis on social change tends to downplay or ignore questions of stability.

In the first half of the twentieth century, the structural-functional focus in British social anthropology produced a succession of non-evolutionary classifications of human social forms. As data on more and more varieties of social structure grew, however, these typologies seemed to overflow with more and more subtypes. It is not surprising that most contemporary anthropologists question the point of developing such typologies at all.

## Attempting to Do without Typologies: Culture Area Studies in North America

Similarly, American anthropologists became dissatisfied with unilineal evolutionism. The most significant figure in the North American attempt to move away from this approach was Franz Boas. Boas and his students worked primarily among the Indigenous peoples of North America, including the First Nations peoples of Canada's west coast. The researchers worked to collect more and better data about these societies, especially data relating to the histories of individual groups. They found that these societies did not pass through uniform, shared stages as they changed over time. For example, they found that two societies with similar forms of social organization might have arrived at their current positions through different historical routes: one through a process of simplification, the other through a process of elaboration. To account for such situations, Boas determined that *historical particularism*—the study of cultures in their own historical contexts—was the appropriate approach.

Boas emphasized that many seemingly new cultural forms were actually borrowed from neighbouring societies (Figure 3.10). He and his followers were quick to note that if cultural borrowing, rather than independent invention, played an important role in culture change, then any unilineal evolutionary scheme was doomed. In addition, their focus on cultural borrowing emphasized the porous boundaries around different societies that made such borrowing possible.

The view of society that developed in North America was, consequently, quite different from the one that developed in Great Britain. Boas and his followers rejected the unilineal cultural evolutionists' view of societies as isolated representatives of universal stages, closed to outside influences, responsible for progressing or failing to progress. Critical of the structural-functional view of societies as bounded, *atemporal* social types, they saw social groups as fundamentally open to the outside world. Change was considered more a result of idiosyncratic borrowing from neighbours than of inevitable, law-governed *progress*. Therefore, the Boasians focussed their

**chiefdom**
A form of social organization in which the leader (a chief) and the leader's close relatives are set apart from the rest of the society and allowed privileged access to wealth, power, and prestige.

**state**
A stratified society that possesses a territory that is defended from outside enemies with an army and from internal disorder with police. A state, which has a separate set of governmental institutions designed to enforce laws and collect taxes and tribute, is run by an elite that possesses a monopoly on the use of force.

**structural-functional theory**
A position that explores how particular social forms function from day-to-day in order to reproduce the traditional structure of the society.

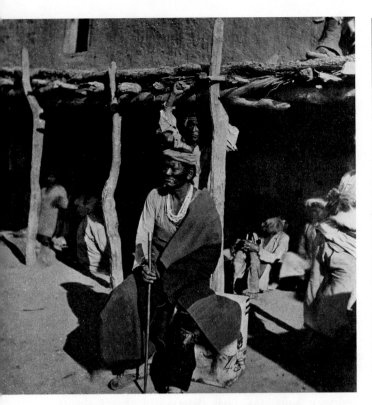

Figure 3.10 | As part of his study of historical particularism, Franz Boas cites the Zuni people of New Mexico. Boas rejected the notion that Zuni culture developed solely on the basis of the communities' geographical environments; instead, he supported the hypothesis that Spanish ideas had a deep impact on Zuni culture.

Map 3.2 | The Native American culture areas for North America, north of Mexico.

**culture traits**
Particular features or parts of a cultural tradition such as a dance, ritual, or style of pottery.

**culture area**
A geographical region in which cultural traditions share similar culture traits.

attention on patterns of cultural borrowing, a form of research called *cultural area studies*. They developed lists of **culture traits**, or features characteristic of a particular group: a ritual, for example, or a house style. They then determined how widely those cultural traits had spread into neighbouring societies. A **culture area** was defined by the limits of borrowing, or the *diffusion*, of a particular trait or set of traits (see Map 3.2).

Thus North American anthropologists, most famously Kroeber (1939), were able to discuss social groups without evoking 'timeless' classificatory schemes, like those of social anthropologists, or suggesting that societies were clear-cut entities with internally consistent social structures. Yet they ran into new difficulties, as they found that it is impossible to discuss in unambiguous terms societies perpetually open to cultural borrowing. Area studies created cultural classifications that were either broader than an individual society (culture areas) or narrower than an individual society (culture traits). The end product was a list of traits and a map of cultural areas in which the traits could be found. Rather than finding a typology-free method of analysis, these anthropologists had simply arrived at a new system of classification, albeit one in which societal boundaries were ignored.

## Post-colonial Realities

Then the world changed again. World War II was closely followed by the break-up of European colonial empires in Africa and Asia. Former colonies were now independent states, and their citizens rejected the traditional Western view of them as savages or barbarians. In these and other areas of the world, there was also a growing awareness of the need to promote human rights and principles of equality. Changing realities thus created for Westerners new views of the 'other' that made the pretensions of unilineal evolutionism beyond plausible.

Additionally, in many new states, leaders began to frame a national consciousness, pulling together supposedly disparate peoples within their borders. These efforts made the structural focus of pre-independence social anthropologists seem increasingly misguided, as it revealed that the traditional societies anthropologists had been studying had not, in fact, been structurally separate even under colonialism. Decolonization forced anthropologists to pay direct attention to colonialism as a form of political domination that eliminated the autonomy of Indigenous social groups and forcibly restructured them into subordinate positions within a larger entity.

At the same time, anthropologists with roots in the non-Western world began to add their voices to those of Western anthropologists (Figure 3.11). They have been highly critical of the cultural stereotypes institutionalized by unilineal evolutionism and structural-functionalism, noting that 'ranking' typologies have not disappeared altogether in contemporary cultural and social anthropology.

## Studying Forms of Human Society Today

Some contemporary anthropologists, especially those interested in political and economic issues, continue to find typologies useful; others reject typologies altogether, arguing that such categorizations are too limited to be of any use. Still, most would agree that an emphasis on cross-cultural similarities or differences is intimately related to the type of questions anthropologists are framing and the theoretical approaches they apply.

For example, let us turn again to Lewellen's classification of social types. Lewellen argues that his system is designed to reflect structural, organizational similarities and differences among various societies. To defend such criteria, he employs an analogy:

Two houses built of different materials but to the same floor plan will obviously be much more alike than two houses of the same materials but very different designs (say, a townhouse and a ranch house). . . . In short, a house is defined in terms of its organization, not its components, and that organization will be influenced by its physical environment and the level of technology of the people who designed it. (1983: 17)

Lewellen assumes that structural similarities and differences are both *significant* and *obvious*, seemingly affiliating him with the British social anthropology tradition. Thus, for Lewellen, the materials out of which the houses are made can safely be ignored. Sometimes this approach may work. Yet Lewellen's analogy raises other questions: Is a house's organization manifested in the floor plan of the builder or in the way the various rooms are *used* regardless of floor plan? Is a bedroom still a bedroom, whether in a townhouse or a ranch house, when the people living in that house use it to cook in? Does a family's ideas about how living space should be used change when the family moves from a thatched hut to an apartment with wooden floors and plaster walls?

Thus, not everyone would agree on what is significant and obvious in every case, and not everyone would choose to employ the same categories of classification. For example, the similarities and differences that seemed obvious to many political anthropologists

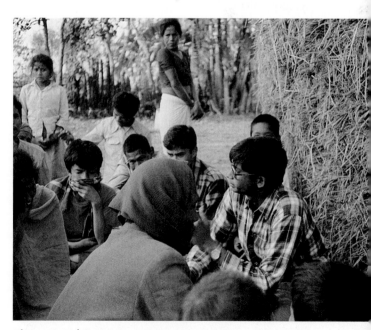

*Figure 3.11* | Sri Lankan anthropologist Arjun Guneratne converses with some of his informants in Nepal.

in the British tradition would not seem so sharp to an anthropologist interested in classifying the ways different societies make a living. Indeed, as we shall see in Chapter 7, anthropologists interested in how societies make a living employ concepts such as *subsistence strategy* or *mode of production* to order their typologies, focussing on the strategies and technologies for organizing the production, distribution, and consumption of food, clothing, housing, tools, and other material goods. Defining different domains of relevance always results in different typologies.

Since the end of colonialism, anthropologists have had to contend with new forms of classification. During the Cold War (1948–89), a new set of categories came into existence that classified states into the First ('developed') World, the Second ('communist') World, the Third ('underdeveloped') World, or the Fourth ('neo-colonial') World. Anthropologists adjusted to this transmuted context; many of them eventually became highly critical of the way 'development' and 'underdevelopment' were understood and addressed by scholars and government officials alike. These distinctions have become even more problematic in recent decades, as we leave behind the capitalist–communist conflict of the Cold War and face new divisions between capitalist and fundamentalist-religious ideologies.

Sometimes it is easy to emphasize the shortcomings of past classificatory approaches in anthropology, but we must also acknowledge the lasting contributions they have made. Despite its excesses, unilineal cultural evolutionism highlights the fact that cultures change over time and that our species has experienced a broad sequence of cultural developments. Structural-functionalist typologies may seem overly rigid and static, but the structural-functionalist ethnographies show just how intricate the social institutions and practices of so-called simple societies can be. The cultural distinctions of Boasian culture area studies may be at times too narrow or too broad to apply to individual societies, but they successfully de-emphasize societal boundaries and demonstrate that there are no distinct lines that separate one culture from the next. A focus on 'developed' and 'underdeveloped' societies may have raised more problems than it solved, but it was in the very attempt to explain why problems of equality existed that new anthropological understandings were achieved.

Today, virtually all of the familiar anthropological classifications are dropping away as anthropologists explore the continuing cultural creativity of all human beings in all societies, particularly as these societies face the effects of globalization. Thus, as we will discover in the following chapters, contemporary anthropologists have had to develop new and innovative approaches as they continue their studies of human nature, human society, and the human past.

# Key Terms

band   70

capitalism   55

chiefdom   71

colonialism   55

culture area   72

culture traits   72

neo-colonialism   65

political economy   60

social structure   69

state   71

structural-functional theory   71

tribe   70

typologies   66

unilineal cultural evolutionism   66

# Chapter Summary

1. Modern Western history has been characterized by the rise of capitalism. The key metaphor of capitalism is the world as a market in which everything—including land, objects, ideas, and human beings—can be bought and sold. Such a view was unknown in non-capitalist societies before Western contact. To function intelligibly within the capitalist world order, colonized peoples had to begin seeing the world as a storehouse of potential commodities.

2. Non-Western societies have not escaped the influence of historical forces. Many of the groups early anthropologists studied were relatively recent creations, forged in the course of commercial and political contacts between Indigenous populations and Europeans. The societies that survive today show that conquered peoples can actively cope with the challenges and opportunities offered by such contacts to reshape their social identities.

3. The European capitalist penetration of non-Western societies was frequently followed by political conquest, which then reshaped those societies in ways that promoted economic exploitation. Colonial empires drew together economically and politically vast and previously unconnected areas of the world. Indigenous peoples lost their autonomy and were reintegrated as component groups within a larger colonial political economy.

4. The context of European colonialism was an ever-present reality within which anthropologists were obliged to manoeuvre. Many hoped that the dismantling of colonial empires after World War II would restore sovereignty and dignity to colonized peoples. However, independence did not free former colonies from deeply entangling economic ties with their former rulers. These entanglements have, in some cases, persisted for over a hundred years and are called *neo-colonialism*.

5. A survey of the forms of human society identified by anthropologists over the past century and a half can illuminate the historical circumstances surrounding contact between anthropologists and their informants. Each classification depends on identifying those societies that are most distinct from one another based on certain criteria and then sorting known societies by their resemblance to these exemplars. The same social forms can be classified in different ways by anthropologists who have different analytical purposes.

6. The earliest important anthropological typology of forms of human society was proposed by unilineal cultural evolutionists in the nineteenth century. These individuals tried to explain contemporary cultural diversity by arguing that different kinds of societies represented different stages of societal evolution, and they believed that every human society either had passed or would pass through the same stages.

7. Anthropologists doing research in colonial settings in the first half of the twentieth century collected a vast amount of detailed, accurate information about aspects of Indigenous life, which colonial administrators hoped would help them to be more effective rulers. Their research focussed on social structural similarities and differences observed at a single point in time.

8. Following Boas, North American anthropologists rejected unilineal cultural evolutionism on the grounds that societies could easily borrow cultural forms from one another, thus skipping supposedly universal evolutionary stages. Consequently, the aim of much research shifted to making lists of culture traits and mapping the culture areas through which they had spread as a result of cultural borrowing.

9. Since the end of colonialism, new classifications have appeared, such as the Cold War division of nation-states into First, Second, Third, and Fourth worlds and the contrast between 'developed' First World societies and 'underdeveloped' Third World societies. While some anthropologists were dissatisfied with these distinctions all along, they have become increasingly problematic since the end of the Cold War.

10. Although some anthropologists still find some typologies useful for investigating particular kinds of issues, classifying forms of human society is not an ultimate goal for most anthropologists today. The fuzziness of category boundaries reminds us that taxonomies are human constructions, not pure reflections of objective reality. With the increasing importance of anthropological studies of globalization today, many kinds of traditional classifications are dropping away.

# Critical Thinking Questions

1. What were the three major schools of anthropological thought that influenced the development of anthropology in Canada? Why do you suppose these schools were so influential in Canada? How might historical and/or political factors associated with these schools have influenced later anthropologists' relations with Native peoples in Canada?

2. What were the crucial differences between the British colonial enterprise in Virginia and that in Rupert's Land?

How might these early encounters have affected later relationships between Native peoples and Europeans?

3. What are some of the criticisms anthropologists faced for the roles they played under colonial rule? How could they contribute to the effectiveness of indirect rule? How could their efforts help to improve the situation for colonized peoples?

4. How would you distinguish between *centralized* and *uncentralized* (*egalitarian*) political systems?

# Suggested Readings

Barnard, Alan. 2000. History and Theory in Anthropology (Cambridge: Cambridge University Press). A recent, concise overview of the history of anthropological ideas, tying together developments on both sides of the Atlantic.

Barrett, Stanley R., Sean Stokholm, and Jeanette Burke. 2001. 'The Idea of Power and the Power of Ideas: A Review Essay', *American Anthropologist*, New Series, 103, 2: 468–80. *A critique of Eric Wolf's* Envisioning Power: Ideologies of Dominance and Crisis (1999). The authors argue that the concept of structural power is redundant and expendable as it is presented by Wolf.

Driver, Harold E. 1961. *Indians of North America* (Chicago: University of Chicago Press). A comprehensive overview of Indigenous traditional life in North America.

Kroeber, Alfred. 1939. 'Cultural and Natural Areas of Native North America', *University of California Publications in American Archaeology and Ethnology* 38: xii (Berkeley: University of California Press). Also issued in hard cover as a separate book, this popular work explores the relationship between environment and culture. It has influenced work in cultural diffusion, cultural sharing, and analysis of cultural responses to environmental settings.

Kuhn, Thomas. 1962. *The Structure of Scientific Revolutions* (Chicago: University of Chicago Press). A seminal work on the way paradigms are called into question, challenged, and then changed.

Lewellen, Ted C. 2003. *Political Anthropology*, 3rd edn (Westport, CT: Praeger Publishers). Contains much useful information about the different kinds of societies that scholars have identified.

Quimby, G.I. 1954. 'Cultural and Natural Areas before Kroeber', *American Antiquity* XIX, 4: 317–31. An overview of the development of the culture area concept.

Weatherford, Jack. 1988. Indian Givers: How the Indians of the Americas Transformed the World (New York: Fawcett Columbine).

———. 1991. Native Roots: How the Indians Enriched America (New York: Fawcett Columbine).

———. 1994. *Savages and Civilization* (New York: Random House). All three of these books by Jack Weatherford are engaging accounts of the consequences of contact between the Old World and the New World in the past and in the present.

Wolf, Eric. 1982. *Europe and the People without History* (Berkeley: University of California Press). A classic text about European expansion and the impact this expansion had on European societies and the rest of the world. This work also discusses the effect of European contact on Indigenous societies.

———.v 1999. *Envisioning Power: Ideologies of Dominance and Crisis* (Berkeley: University of California Press). This is an analysis of the historical relationship of ideas, power, and culture in which Wolf argues that power is central to shaping the circumstances and form of cultural production.

# Related Websites

**A Brief History of Anthropology at the University of Toronto** http://anthropology.utoronto.ca/about/history

**Assembly of First Nations (AFN)** www.afn.ca

**Association of Social Anthropologists of the UK and Commonwealth** www.theasa.org

**Survival, the Movement for Tribal Peoples** www.survival-international.org

# Part II | The Resources of Culture

**The chapters in this section focus on a range of human capacities that lie at the centre of human cultural creativity, flexibility, and diversity.** We all survive, regardless our cultural identity, in a material world by means of open, flexible symbolic patterns that assign meanings to various aspects of that world and our place in it. As a result, we confront the material through a web of meanings of our own creation. Cultural meaning is perhaps most directly encountered in language, but it is also revealed in habitual patterns of thought and action as well as in social relationships, and is at its most elaborate in those creations that Westerners traditionally call art, myth, ritual, and world view. Through created meaning, we come to have our individual and group identities. Because our dependence on culture for survival is so total, a proper awareness of the depth, breadth, and complexity of human culture is, from the anthropological perspective, indispensable for an adequate understanding of the human condition in all its guises.

# 4 | Language

## Chapter Outline

## Learning Objectives

By the end of Chapter 4, you will be able to

- consider the relationship between language and culture,
- outline the design features of language,
- situate language in a context,
- understand the importance of linguistic relativity,

- identify the components of language,
- think about linguistic inequality,
- consider negotiated meaning using Pidgin languages as an example, and
- explore the linkages between language and truth.

↓ *The famous Love Wall in Paris, France, is covered with 'I love you' in over three hundred languages. Although language can create barriers between individuals, it is also the best tool we have to communicate with one another.*

Language as a system of arbitrary vocal symbols is a unique faculty that sets human beings apart from other living species. It provides basic tools for human creativity, making the cultural achievements that we view as monuments to our species' genius possible. And yet, despite all that **language** makes possible, its tools are double-edged. Language allows people to communicate with one another, but it also creates barriers to communication. One major barrier is linguistic diversity (Figure 4.1). There are some 3,000 mutually unintelligible languages spoken in the world today. Why should there be such barriers to communication? This chapter explores the ambiguity, limitations, and power of human language.

## Language and Culture

Human language is a biocultural phenomenon. Our brain and the anatomy of our mouth and throat make spoken language a biological possibility for us. At the same time, every human language is clearly a cultural product. It is shared by a group of speakers, encoded in symbols, patterned, and transmitted through teaching and learning, thus making communication possible.

### Anthropological Interest in Language

Language is of primary interest to anthropologists for at least three reasons:

1) Fieldwork proceeds through oral communication. Often, anthropologists must learn a new language to do fieldwork among people whose language is different from their own.
2) Language involves grammatical and conceptual intricacies that anthropologists can analyze to gain insight into a culture. Indeed, some schools of anthropological theory have based their theories of culture explicitly on ideas taken from **linguistics**.
3) All people use language to encode their experiences, to structure their understanding of the world and of themselves, and to engage with one another. Therefore, language is the best tool anthropologists have to access informants' perceptions and interpretations.

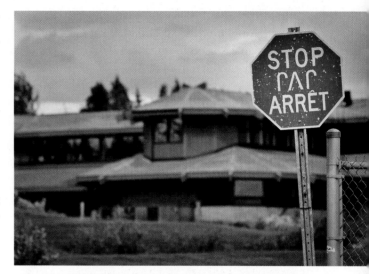

*Figure 4.1* | **Language, like universal symbols, allows people to communicate with one another, but language can also create barriers to communication.**

By learning another society's language, we learn something about its culture as well. In fact, learning another language inevitably provides unsuspected insights into the nature of our own language and culture, often making it impossible to take language of any kind for granted.

As with the culture concept, discussions of the concept of language have regularly involved a distinction between *Language* and *languages*. *Language* with a capital *L* (like *Culture* with a capital *C*) was viewed as an abstract property belonging to the human species as a whole, not to be confused with the specific *languages* of actual groups of people. This distinction initially enabled anthropologists to recognize that all human groups possess fully developed *languages* rather than 'primitive', 'broken', or otherwise defective forms of vocal communication. Indeed, just as there is no such thing as a 'primitive' human culture, there is no such thing as a 'primitive' human language. Today, linguistic anthropologists realize that totalitarian views of 'languages' can be as problematic as totalitarian views of 'cultures'. The difficulties associated with demarcating the boundaries between one language and another, or with distinguishing between dialects and languages, become particularly obvious in studies of pidgins and creoles, as we will see.

**language**
The system of arbitrary vocal symbols we use to encode our experiences of the world.

**linguistics**
The scientific study of language.

It remains useful, however, to distinguish *language* from *speech* and from *communication*. We usually think of spoken language (speech) when we use the term *language*, but language can be transmitted by various non-spoken media, such as written words, Morse code, or gestures (as is the case in sign languages such as Canadian or American Sign Language [CSL/ASL]). *Human communication* can be defined as the transfer of information from one person to another, which can take place without the use of words, spoken or otherwise. People communicate with one another non-verbally all the time, sending messages with facial expressions and body language, the clothes they wear, or even how long they keep others waiting.

In fact, even linguistic communication depends on more than words alone. Native speakers of a language share not just vocabulary and grammar but also a number of assumptions about how to speak. These assumptions may not be shared by speakers of a different language. Students learning a new language discover early on that word-for-word translation from one language to another does not work. Sometimes there are no equivalent words in the second language; even when there are, a word-for-word translation may not carry over the original meaning. For example, an English speaker who has eaten enough might say 'I'm full.' This may be translated directly into French as *Je suis plein*. To French speakers, this sentence has the nonsensical meaning 'I am a pregnant [male] animal.' Alternatively, if uttered by a man who has just consumed a lot of alcohol, it means 'I'm drunk.'

Learning to speak a second language is often frustrating and even unsettling; someone who once found the world simple to talk about suddenly turns into a babbling fool. The experience can result in a sense of culture shock that is as disorienting as being physically immersed in another culture! Often, it is less a matter of learning new labels for old objects than it is of learning how to identify new objects that go with new labels. The student must also learn the appropriate contexts in which different linguistic forms may be used. Therefore, in order to attain a holistic comprehension of a language, the student must move beyond abstract understandings and situate that language in its cultural context.

## Talking about Experience

Language, like the rest of culture, is a product of our attempt to come to terms with experience. Each language, having the ability to change and adapt, is adequate for its speakers' needs, given their particular way of life. Naturally, people tend to develop larger vocabularies to discuss those aspects of life that are important to them. For this reason, it may be easier to talk about the Polynesian concept of *mana* in Hawaiian than in English. In addition, different languages have developed to be more or less complex in different ways. Canadian anthropological linguist William Thurston notes that some languages such as Salish, San, and Kartvelian are phonetically much more complex than other languages such as Cree, Swahili, or Turkish; European and Australian languages are morphologically more complex than Mandarin; English is lexically more complex than most other languages; and Javanese and Malagasy are socio-linguistically more complex than Cree or Lusi. Yet despite their many differences, all languages are equal in their open potential to communicate experiences.

Traditionally, languages are associated with actual groups of people called *speech communities*. Nevertheless, members of particular speech communities do not all possess identical knowledge about the language they share nor do they all speak the same way. Consequently, there is a tension between diversity and commonality in all such communities. Individuals and subgroups within a speech community make use of linguistic resources in different ways as they attempt to create unique, personal voices. These efforts are countered by the pressure to negotiate a common code for communication within the larger social group. In this way, language is produced and reproduced through the activity of its speakers. Any particular language that we may identify at a given moment is a snapshot of a continuing process.

There are many ways to communicate our experiences, and there is no absolute standard favouring one way over another. Some things that are easy to say in language A may be difficult to say in language B, yet other aspects of language B may appear much simpler than equivalent aspects of language A. For example, English ordinarily requires the use of determiners (*a*, *an*, *the*) before nouns, but this rule is not found in all languages. Likewise, the verb *to be*, called the *copula* by linguists, is not found in all languages, although the relationships it conveys may still be communicated. In English, we might say 'There *are* many people in the market.' Translating this sentence into Fulfulde, the language of the Fulbe of northern Cameroon, we get *Him'be boi 'don nder luumo*, which, word-for-word, reads something like 'people-many-there-in-market' (Figure 4.2). No single Fulfulde word corresponds to the English *are* or *the*.

## Design Features of Human Language

In 1966, anthropological linguist Charles Hockett listed 16 different **design features** of human language that in his estimation set it apart from other forms of animal communication. Six of these design features seem especially useful for our discussion: openness, displacement, prevarication, arbitrariness, duality of patterning, and semanticity.

*Openness*, probably the most important feature, is the ability to talk about the same experiences from different perspectives, using different words and various grammatical constructions. This feature allows people to conceptualize, label, and discuss the same experience in different ways. Thus no single human interpretation of an experience is necessarily more correct in every respect than all others. To understand how truly significant the feature of openness is to communication, compare our spoken language to the vocal communication systems (or *call systems*) of monkeys and apes. Whereas our language allows us to endlessly combine and recombine elements of our experiences in new and various ways, the possibilities of meaning are much more limited when it comes to call systems. Primates have several calls, all of which are appropriate to specific situations: when the animal is in the presence of food; when it is in danger or pain; when it wants to show friendly interest or the desire for company; when it wants to mark its location; and so on. Each call is appropriate in only one situation, and primates cannot combine one call with another to express more complex messages. For these reasons, the call systems of primates are said to be *closed* when compared to *open* human languages.

Anthropologist Terrence Deacon (1997) points out that modern human beings still possess a set of six calls: laughing, sobbing, screaming, crying, groaning, and sighing. These calls, together with gestures and the changes in speech rhythm, volume, and tonality that linguists call *speech prosody*, all appear to have co-evolved alongside our use of language, which is probably why they integrate with one another so smoothly when we speak. Deacon

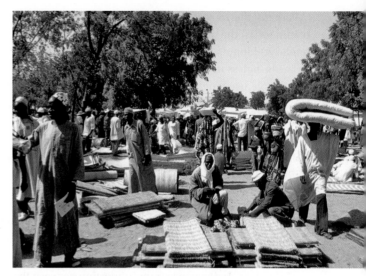

*Figure 4.2* | **Him'be boi 'don nder luumo.**

emphasizes, however, that closed primate call systems—which contain between 15 and 40 calls, depending on species—do *not* map onto any of the elements of human language and are even controlled by different parts of the brain.

Closed call systems also lack *displacement*, our ability to talk about absent or non-existent objects and past or future events as easily as we discuss our immediate situations. As Thurston noted in a recent conversation,

> **design features**
> Those characteristics of language that, when taken together, differentiate it from other known animal communication systems.

> displacement allows us to communicate about things that are not here and now; it also allows us to talk with great precision about things that do not exist, like unicorns. The important thing here is that it permits the extension of linguistic creativity to such phenomena as narrative, religion, rhetoric, politics, poetry, history, and science itself.

Although non-human primates have good memories, and some species such as chimpanzees seem to be able to plan social action in advance (as when hunting for meat), they cannot use their call systems to this extent. In a later extension to Hockett's discussion of displacement, Thurston notes that language also allows a person to 'refer to an entity without necessarily being emotionally involved with it'. In effect, language allows for the displacement of affect.

Perhaps the most striking consequence of linguistic openness is the design feature *prevarication*. Hockett remarks: 'Linguistic messages can be false, and they can be meaningless in the logician's sense' (1966). Not only can people use language to lie, but they can also use it to form statements that are grammatically correct but semantically nonsensical. For example, Noam Chomsky's 'Colourless green ideas sleep furiously' (1957: 15). This is a grammatical sentence on one level—the right kinds of words are used in the right places—but on another level it contains multiple contradictions in meaning. The ability of language users to prevaricate—to make statements or ask questions that violate convention—is a major consequence of open symbolic systems.

Also notably absent from closed call systems is *arbitrariness*, the lack of a transparent connection between the form (features of expression) of a symbol and its function or meaning. As Shakespeare's Juliet says: 'What's in a name? That which we call a rose by any other name would smell as sweet.'

Arbitrariness is evident in *duality of patterning*. Language, Hockett claimed, is patterned on two different levels: *sound* and *meaning*. On the first level, each language has a discrete set of sounds called **phonemes** (form/signal/ signifier). In combination, phonemes compose **morphemes** (expression), the shortest meaningful units of speech. Phonemes, in themselves, have no 'meaning' but morphemes do. On the second level, morphemes combine in grammatical ways to form meaningful clusters and ultimately sentences. There is an organizing principle to each language but the essentials remain the same: units at one level, patterned in one way (sounds/phonemes), can be patterned in a different way to create units at a different, more complex, level (morphemes,

or units of meaning). Under another set of rules these units of meaning become sentences and thus discourse.

With *semanticity* we have a very simple concept: language *means* things, or as Ferdinand de Saussure (1993), the 'father' of twentieth-century linguistics, would say, 'the signifier stands for the signified'. Even though the connection between the two may be arbitrary, and even though a word's meaning is never absolute, a word *is* connected to that which it represents when people perceive a connection. A word's meaning becomes certain in a specified context (Pike 1943; 1967). The association of linguistic signals with aspects of the social, cultural, and physical world of a speech community becomes significant because people use language to refer to and make sense of objects and processes in the world. Nevertheless, we need to remember that linguistic descriptions of reality are always selective, highlighting some features of the world and downplaying others. For example, a trained primatologist would distinguish apes (such as chimpanzees) from monkeys (such as baboons). In contrast, a person with no special knowledge of primates might use the words *monkey* and *ape* interchangeably to refer to chimpanzees or baboons. Each speaker links the same words to the world in different ways.

## Language and Context

Anthropologists are powerfully aware of the influence of context on what people choose to say. Linguists have noted that social and cultural context has a strong impact on how children develop **linguistic** as well as **communicative competence** (Figure 4.3).

> From an early age they appear to communicate very fluently, producing utterances which are not just remarkably well-formed according to the linguist's standards but also appropriate to the social context in which the speakers find themselves. Children are thus learning far more about language than rules of grammar. [They are] acquiring communicative competence. (Elliot 1981: 13)

The term *communicative competence* was coined by American anthropological linguist Dell Hymes (1972). As an anthropologist, Hymes objected to Chomsky's (1965) suggestion that competent language use consists only of being able to make correct judgments of

---

**phonemes**
Basic units of distinct sound that are characteristic of a language and that come together to form words (e.g., /b/ and /ɔɪ/ in boy). On their own, phonemes carry no referential or lexical meaning

**morphemes**
The smallest meaning-bearing units in any language (e.g., /bɔɪ/ refers to a young male). The change to plural form has the morpheme for plural added (in this case /z/, which we write as boys /bɔɪz/).

**linguistic competence**
A term coined by linguist Noam Chomsky to refer to the mastery of adult grammar.

**communicative competence**
A term coined by anthropological linguist Dell Hymes to refer to the mastery of adult rules for socially and culturally appropriate speech.

**Figure 4.3 | The contexts in which a child learns to communicate impact the ways in which she or he masters the rules of grammar as well as the rules of social and cultural appropriateness in speech.**

sentence grammaticality. Hymes observed that competent adult speakers do more than follow grammatical rules when they speak. They are also able to choose words and topics of conversation appropriate to their social position, the social position of the person they are addressing, and the social context of interaction.

For example, consider the issue of using personal pronouns appropriately when addressing another person. For native English speakers, the matter is clear, as we address all people as 'you'. But any English speaker who has ever tried to learn French has worried about when to address an individual using the second-person plural (*vous*) and when to use the second-person singular (*tu*). To be safe, most students use *vous* for all individuals because it is more formal and they want to avoid appearing too familiar with native speakers whom they do not know well. But if you are dating a French person, at which point in the relationship does the change from *vous* to *tu* occur, and who decides? Moreover, sometimes—for example, among university students—the normal term of address is *tu* (even among strangers); it is used to indicate social solidarity. Native English speakers who are learning French wrestle with these and other linguistic dilemmas. Rules for the appropriate use of *tu* and *vous* seem to have nothing to do with grammar, yet the choice between one form and the other indicates whether the speaker is someone who does or does not know how to speak French.

# Linguistic Relativity

During the first half of the twentieth century, two American anthropological linguists noted that the grammars of different languages often described the same situation in different ways. Edward Sapir and Benjamin Whorf concluded that language has the power to shape the way people see the world. This claim has been called the **linguistic relativity principle**, or the Sapir–Whorf hypothesis. This hypothesis has been highly controversial because it is difficult to test and the results of testing have been ambiguous.

> **linguistic relativity principle** The assertion, also known as the Sapir–Whorf hypothesis, that language has the power to shape the way people see the world.

The so-called strong version of the Sapir–Whorf hypothesis is also known as *linguistic determinism*. It is a rather dogmatic view of language that holds that the patterns of our thoughts and our culture are determined by the patterns of the language we speak. If a grammar classifies nouns and/or pronouns in gender categories, for example, linguistic determinism concludes that speakers of that language are *forced* to think of males and females as radically different kinds of beings. In contrast, a language that makes no grammatical distinctions on the basis of gender presumably trains its speakers to think of males and females as exactly the same. If linguistic determinism is correct, then a change in grammar should change thought patterns: if English speakers replaced *he* and *she* with a new, gender-neutral, third-person singular pronoun such as *te*, then, linguistic determinists predict, English speakers would begin to treat men and women as equals.

There are a number of problems with linguistic determinism. First, there are languages such as Fulfulde in which only one third-person pronoun is used for males and females, (*o*); however, male-dominant social patterns are quite evident among Fulfulde speakers. Second, if language determined thought in such an absolute way, it would be impossible to translate from one language to another or even to learn another language with a different grammatical structure. Yet human beings *do* learn foreign languages and translate from one language to another. Third, even if it were possible to draw firm boundaries around speech communities (which it isn't), every language provides its native speakers with alternative ways of describing the world. Finally, in most of the world's

**grammar**
A set of rules that aims to describe the patterns of linguistic usage observed by members of a particular speech community.

**phonology**
The study of the sounds of language.

societies, monolingualism is the exception rather than the rule, yet people who grow up bilingual do not also grow up schizophrenic, as if trying to reconcile two contradictory views of reality (Figure 4.4). Indeed, bilingual children ordinarily benefit from knowing two languages; they do not confuse them, they can switch readily between them, and they even appear to demonstrate greater cognitive flexibility on psychological tests than monolinguals (Elliot 1981: 56).

In the face of these objections, other researchers offer a 'weak' version of the Sapir–Whorf hypothesis that rejects linguistic determinism but continues to claim that language shapes thought and culture. In this view, grammatical gender might not determine a male-dominant social order, but it might facilitate the acceptance of such a social order because the grammatical distinction between *he* and *she* might make separate and unequal gender roles seem 'natural'. Because many native speakers of English are strong promoters of gender equality, however, the shaping power of grammar would seem far too weak to merit any scientific attention.

Neither Sapir nor Whorf favoured linguistic determinism. Sapir argued that language's importance lies in the way it directs attention to some aspects of experience rather than others. He was impressed by the fact that 'it is generally difficult to make a complete divorce between objective reality and our linguistic symbols of reference to it' (1966 [1933]: 9, 15). Whorf's discussions of the linguistic relativity principle are more complex and ambiguous, and his views have been more sharply criticized by later scholars. At least part of the problem arises from Whorf's attempt to view grammar as the linguistic pattern that shapes culture and thought. Whorf's contemporaries understood grammar to refer to rules for combining sounds into words and words into sentences. Whorf believed that grammar needed to be thought of in broader terms (Schultz 1990), but he died before working out the theoretical language to describe such a level.

## Components of Language

Linguistic study involves a search for patterns in the way speakers use language; linguists aim to describe these patterns by reducing them to a set of rules called a **grammar**. Over time linguists came to recognize a growing number of components that form part of the grammar of any language. The most widely acknowledged components of language are phonology, morphology, syntax, semantics, and pragmatics.

### Phonology: Sounds

The study of the sounds of language is called **phonology**. The sounds of language are special because they are produced by a set of organs, the speech organs (Figure 4.5), that belong only to the human species. The actual sounds that come out of our mouths are called *phones*, and they vary continuously in acoustic properties. As speakers of a

*Figure 4.4* | **Bilingual children can easily switch from one language to another without confusing the two.**

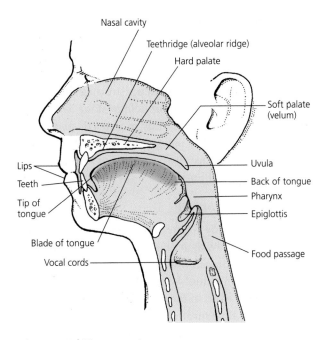

Figure 4.5 | **The speech organs.**

particular language, we come to specifically distinguish all the phones uttered by fellow speakers within a particular range of variation as functionally equivalent forms (called *allophones*) of the same *phoneme*, or characteristic speech sound in the language.

Part of the phonologist's job is to map out how speech sounds are produced and interpreted. Another part is to examine individual languages to discover the particular sound combinations they contain and the patterns into which those sound combinations are organized. Phonologists have found that no language makes use of all the many sounds the human speech organs can produce, and no two languages use exactly the same set. Canadian English uses only 38 sounds (more or less depending on the dialect). Researchers have also found that no two languages use exactly the same set of phonemes.

Speakers of the same language often differ from one another in the way their phonemes are patterned,

producing 'accents', which constitute one kind of variety within a language. This variety is not random; the speech sounds characteristic of any particular accent follow a pattern. Speakers with different accents are usually able to understand one another, but their distinctive articulation is a clue to their ethnic, regional, or social class origins.

## Morphology: Word Structure

**Morphology** is the study of how words are put together. What is a word? English speakers tend to think of words as the building blocks of sentences. But words are not all alike. Some words cannot be broken down

> **morphology**
> The study of the minimal units of meaning in a language.

into smaller elements. Consider the word *book*: even though we might think that *boo* is a word, the remaining *k* is not. The word *bookworm*, however, can be broken down into two recognizable words: *book* and *worm*, each a morpheme on its own. The puzzle deepens when we try to translate words from one language into another. Sometimes expressions that require only one word in one language (*préciser* in French) require more than one word in another (*to make precise* in English). Other times, we must deal with languages whose utterances cannot be broken down into words at all. Consider the utterance *nikookitepeena* from Shawnee (an Indigenous North American language), which translates into English as 'I dipped his head in the water' (Whorf 1956: 172). Although the Shawnee utterance is composed of parts, the parts do not possess the characteristics we attribute to words in, say, English or French (Table 4.1).

The study of the Indigenous languages of North America by linguistic anthropologists such as Sapir and Whorf revealed many kinds of word structures that were not found in European languages. To make sense of the structure of languages such as Shawnee, anthropological linguists needed a concept that could refer to both words

Table 4.1 | **Morphemes of Shawnee Utterance and Their Glosses**

| ni | kooki | tepe | en | a |
|---|---|---|---|---|
| I | immersed in water | point of action at head | by hand action | cause to him |

(such as those in the English sentence above) and the parts of an utterance that could not be broken down into words. This led to the development of the concept of *morphemes*, traditionally defined as the smallest meaning-bearing units in any language. The various parts of a Shawnee utterance can be identified as morphemes, and so can many English words (remember the example of *boys* above). Describing minimal units of meaning as morphemes and not as words allows us to compare the morphology of different languages.

Morphemic patterning in languages such as Shawnee may seem hopelessly complicated to native English speakers, yet the patterning of morphemes in English is also complex. Why is it that some morphemes can stand alone as words (*sing, red*) and others cannot (*-ing, -ed*)? So we return to our initial question, what is a word? Words, or the morphemes they are composed from, are the minimal units of meaning in a language. Thus, they represent the fundamental point at which the arbitrary pairing of sound and meaning occurs.

## Syntax: Sentence Structure

A third component of language is **syntax**, or sentence structure. In languages such as English, for example, rules governing word order cannot explain what is puzzling about the following English sentence: 'Smoking grass means trouble'. For many native speakers of Canadian English, this sentence exhibits what linguists call *structural ambiguity*. In our example, we must ask ourselves what kind of *trouble* is involved: the consequences of smoking an illegal substance or the danger of a prairie fire? In the first reading, *smoking* is a gerund, a noun derived from a verb (the act of smoking); in the second, it is a participle, an adjective derived from a verb (grass that is smoking).

We can explain the existence of structurally ambiguous sentences if we assume that the role a word plays in a sentence depends on the overall structure of the sentence in which the word is found and not on the structure of the word itself. Thus, sentences can be defined as ordered strings of words, and those words can be classified as parts of speech in terms of the function they fulfill in a sentence. But these two assumptions cannot account for the ambiguity in a sentence such as 'The father of the girl and the boy fell into the lake'. How many people fell into the lake? Just the father or the father and the boy? Each interpretation depends on how the reader groups the words of the sentence together. Linguists have discovered numerous other features of sentence structure that cannot be explained in terms of morphology alone, leading to a growth of interest in the study of syntactic patterns in different languages. The recognition that syntax is a key component of language structure remains central to contemporary studies of linguistics.

## Semantics: Meaning

**Semantics**, the study of meaning, can be a particularly tricky area of study, as *meaning* is a highly ambiguous term. What do we mean when we say that a word or a sentence means something? We may be asking about what each individual word in the sentence means, or what the sentence as a whole means, or what I mean when I utter the sentence, which may differ from what someone else would mean if he or she uttered the same sentence.

In the 1960s, a formal analysis of semantics was prompted by Chomsky's argument that grammars needed to represent all of a speaker's linguistic knowledge, including word meanings, as sets of abstract rules. Formal semanticists began by examining how words link to each other within a language, exploring relations such as *synonymy*, or 'same meaning' (*old* and *aged*); *homophony*, or 'same sound, different meaning' (*would* and *wood*); and *antonymy*, or 'opposite meaning' (*tall* and *short*). They came to define words in terms of *denotation*, or what the words refer to in the 'real world'. The denotations of words such as *table* or *chair* seem fairly straightforward, but this is not the case with words such as *truth* or *and*. Moreover, even if we believe a word can be linked to a concrete object in the world, it may still be difficult to agree on exactly what the term should refer to.

You should note that the formal study of semantics is related to but not synonymous with Hockett's design feature of *semanticity* (discussed above). Formal semantics studies the meaning relations among the words of a language as they might appear in a dictionary, whereas semanticity refers to the way actual speakers use those words to talk about things in the world. And, as Hockett stressed, the link made between the vocabulary items in a dictionary and objects in the world is open, never determined once and for all.

**syntax**
The study of sentence structure.

**semantics**
The study of meaning.

This openness suggests that we must construct meaning in the face of ambiguity. Formal semantics, however, tries to deal with ambiguity by eliminating it, by 'disambiguating' ambiguous utterances. To find a word's 'unambiguous' denotation, we might consult a dictionary. The *Oxford English Dictionary* (OED), for example, defines a pig as follows:

> An omnivorous, domesticated even-toed ungulate derived from the wild boar *Sus scrofa*, with a stout body, sparse bristly hair, and a broad flat snout for rooting in the soil, kept as a source of bacon, ham, pork, etc. Also with distinguishing word to specify the breed.

A formal definition of this sort does indeed relate the word *pig* to other English words, such as *cow* and *chicken*, and these meaning relations would hold even if all real pigs, cows, and chickens were wiped off the face of the earth. But words also have *connotations*, additional meanings that derive from the typical contexts in which they are used in everyday speech. In the context of anti-war demonstrations in the 1960s, for example, a 'pig' was a police officer.

From a denotative point of view, to call police officers *pigs* is to create ambiguity deliberately, to muddle rather than to clarify. It is an example of **metaphor**, a form of figurative or non-literal language that violates the formal rules of semantic denotation by linking expressions from unrelated domains of meaning called semantic domains (e.g., law enforcement and livestock). Metaphors are used all the time in everyday speech, however. Does this mean, therefore, that people who use metaphors are talking nonsense? What can it possibly mean to call police officers *pigs* (Figure 4.6)?

We cannot know until we place the statement into some kind of context. If we know, for example, that protesters in the 1960s viewed the police as the paid enforcers of racist elites responsible for violence against the poor, and that pigs are domesticated animals that are often viewed as fat, greedy, and dirty, then the metaphor 'police are pigs' begins to make sense. This interpretation, however, does not reveal the true meaning of the metaphor for all time. In a different context, the same phrase might mean something else. Our ability to use the same words in different ways (and different words in the same way) is the hallmark of openness, and formal

*Figure 4.6* | **The phrase 'police are pigs' is a metaphor; it does not suggest that police officers are literally domesticated farm animals.**

semantics is powerless to contain it. Thus, to understand what words or sentences mean, we must always be aware of the context in which they are used.

## Pragmatics: Language in Contexts of Use

**Pragmatics** can be defined as the study of language in the context of its use. Each context offers limitations and opportunities concerning what we may say and how we may say it. Everyday language use is thus often characterized by a struggle between speakers and listeners over definitions of context and appropriate word use.

> **metaphor**
> A form of thought and language that asserts a meaningful link between two expressions from different semantic domains.
>
> **pragmatics**
> The study of language in the context of its use.

Formal linguistic pragmatics, which developed during the 1970s and 1980s, has been described as the 'last stand' of formal linguists who wanted to explain speech entirely in terms of invariant grammatical rules (Hanks 1996: 94). Indeed, both language use and context are narrowly defined in formal pragmatics, and the arguments of formal pragmatics often closely resemble those of formal logic.

Michael Silverstein (1976; 1985) was one of the first linguistic anthropologists to argue that the referential meaning of certain expressions in language cannot be determined unless we go beyond the boundaries of a sentence and place the expressions in a wider context of use.

We must consider two kinds of context here: linguistic and non-linguistic. *Linguistic context* refers to the other words, expressions, and sentences that surround the expression whose meaning we are trying to determine. The meaning of *it* in the sentence 'I really enjoyed it' cannot be determined if the sentence is considered on its own. However, if we know that the previous sentence was 'My aunt gave me this book for my birthday', we have a linguistic context that allows us to deduce that *it* refers to 'this book'. *Non-linguistic context* consists of objects and activities that are present in the situation of speech at the same time we are speaking. Consider the sentence, 'What is that on the door?' To give referential meaning to the word *that*, we need to inspect the actual door and whatever is on it. Furthermore, even if we know what a door is in a formal sense, we need the non-linguistic context to clarify what counts as a door in this instance (e.g., it could be a rough opening in the wall).

By forcing analysts to go beyond syntax and semantics, pragmatics directs our attention to **discourse**. Linguistic discourse includes a spoken one-word greeting, a series of sentences uttered by a single individual, a conversation among two or more speakers, or an extended narrative. Many linguistic anthropologists accept the arguments of Mikhail Bakhtin and Valentin Voloshinov (see, e.g., Voloshinov 1986 [1929]) that the series of rejoinders in conversation are the primary form of discourse. In this view, the speech of any single individual, whether a simple 'yes' or a book-length dissertation, is only one rejoinder in an ongoing dialogue.

## Ethnopragmatics

Linguistic anthropologists analyze the way discourse is produced when people talk to one another. But they go far beyond formal pragmatics, paying attention not only to the immediate context of speech but also to broader cultural contexts that are shaped by unequal social relationships and rooted in history (Brenneis and Macauley 1996; Hill and Irvine 1992). Duranti calls this **ethnopragmatics**, 'a study of language use that relies on ethnography to illuminate the ways in which speech is both constituted by and

**discourse**
In speech, a meaningful utterance or series of utterances united by a common theme.

**ethnopragmatics**
The study of language use in a specific culture, grounded in an ethnographic approach, with close attention to the relationships among language, communication, and social interaction.

constitutive of social interaction' (1994: 11). Such a study focusses on *practice*, human activity in which the rules of grammar, cultural values, and physical action are all conjoined (Hanks 1996: 11). This perspective locates the source of meaning in everyday, routine social activity, or *habitus*, rather than in grammar. As a result, phonemes, morphemes, syntax, and semantics are viewed as linguistic resources people can make use of, rather than rigid determinants of what people can and cannot think or say.

If mutual understanding is shaped by shared routine activity and not by grammar, then communication is possible even if the people interacting with one another speak mutually unintelligible languages. All they need is a shared sense of 'what is going on here' and the ability to negotiate successfully who will do what (234). Such mutually co-engaged people shape *communicative practices* that involve spoken language but also include values and shared habitual knowledge that may never be put into words.

Most people regularly engage in a wide range of practical activities with different subgroups within a population, each with distinctive communication practices and the linguistic habits that go with them. For example, a university student might eat dinner with her family, go to class with other students, live in an apartment with her friends, attend religious services with her fellow worshippers, and work at a part-time job with other employees. In each situation, the student can successfully interact with others because she knows the communicative practices and linguistic habits particular to each subgroup. Each set of linguistic habits she knows is called a *discourse genre*. Because our student simultaneously knows several different discourse genres she can use in speech, her linguistic knowledge is characterized by what Bakhtin (1981) called *heteroglossia*.

For Bakhtin, heteroglossia is the normal condition of linguistic knowledge in any society with internal divisions. Heteroglossia describes a co-existing multiplicity of linguistic norms and forms, many of which are anchored in more than one social subgroup. Because we all participate in more than one of these subgroups, our language use is complex, even when we only know one language! Our capacity for heteroglossia is another example of what Hockett called linguistic openness: it means that our thoughts and speech are not imprisoned in a single set of grammatical forms and definitions. Indeed, if our university student reflects on the overlap as well as the contrasts between the language habits she uses at the dinner table and those she uses in class, she might well find herself raising questions about what words really mean. Here we can see that heteroglossia stands as evidence against absolute linguistic determinism. To the extent, however, that our student's habitual ways of speaking are deeply rooted in everyday routine activity, they may guide the way she typically thinks, perceives, and acts. And to that extent, linguistic relativity may be seen to operate on the level of discourse (Hanks 1996: 176, 246; Schultz 1990).

A practice-based approach to language use aims to show how linguistic components, human action, and human values are all inextricably intertwined. But this does not mean that we can ignore formal grammar. As Hanks puts it, 'The system of language does have unique properties, and we do better to recognize this than to try to pretend it isn't so' (1996: 232). Each language, as a system, has a particular set of formal possibilities that people can mobilize as resources when they talk to one another. At the same time, 'context saturates linguistic forms, right down to the semantic bones' (142). Thus the contextual situation has an influence on the words a speaker chooses. And not all aspects of the context are obvious—a complete comprehension of context includes understandings about social relationships and previous history that may never be put into words.

To understand the degree to which context influences the words a speaker chooses, consider how speakers tailor their words for a particular audience. Advertising agencies, for example, are notorious for slanting their messages to appeal to the people they want to buy their clients' products or services. In his work in a small Samoan village, Duranti (1994) learned that a sense of audience is highly cultivated among the professional orators who argue cases before the titled people, called *matai*, in the village council, or *fono* (Figure 4.7) (see EthnoProfile 4.1). Orators make use of a discourse genre midway in formality between everyday speech and ceremonial speech. Because the *fono* renders judgments that assign praise and blame, the main struggle between orators for different sides is 'often centred on the ability to frame the reason for the meeting as involving or not involving certain key social actors' (Duranti 1994: 3). Of all the grammatical resources used by orators, the form called the *ergative agent* most attracted Duranti's attention.

An ergative agent can be understood as a 'wilful initiator of an event that may be depicted as having consequences' for either an object or a passive recipient of the event (125). In Samoan, ergative agents are marked by the preposition *e*, to distinguish them grammatically. Other forms of agency are marked by different prepositions: for example, *i* or *ia* frames the human agent as the source of the transaction rather than as its wilful initiator; the possessive marker *o* or *a* attached to an agent focusses attention not on the possessor but on the object possessed, that is, on John's *food* rather than on *John's* food. These ways of framing agency in grammatical terms are common in the *fono*, as disputants argue over who should be held accountable for some act. Possible agents include God, particular individuals, or groups. It is perhaps not surprising that the speaker who produced the highest number of ergative agents in his speech was the senior

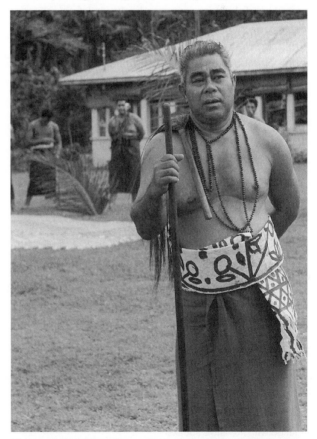

*Figure 4.7* | Although nominal power rests with Samoan chiefs, when village elders meet in the *fono*, titled orators such as this man from the island of Tutuila tend to direct its proceedings.

---

**EthnoProfile 4.1 | Samoa** ·······························································································································

**Region** Oceania

**Nation** Independent State of Samoa (known as Western Samoa 1914–97)

**Language** Samoan people are one-half of the Samoan speakers of the world; this language is of the Malayo-Polynesian family, part of the Austronesian languages

**Population** 214,265 (92.6 per cent Samoan), with 75 per cent living on the main island of Upolu

**Environment** Tropical

**Livelihood** Farming (tropical and subtropical crops), fishing, wage labour

**Political organization** Ranked, with linguistic markers for high- and low-status people; now part of a modern nation-state

**For more information** Duranti, Alessandro. 1994. *From Grammar to Politics: Linguistic Anthropology in a Western Samoan Village* (Berkeley: University of California Press); Mead, Margaret. 1928. *Coming of Age in Samoa* (New York: Morrow); Freeman, Derick. 1983. *Margaret Mead and Samoa* (Cambridge: Harvard University Press)

---

orator who ran the meetings and often served as prosecutor. 'Powerful actors are more likely to define others as ergative agents when they want to accuse them of something. Less powerful actors can try to resist such accusations by suggesting alternative linguistic definitions of events and people's roles in them' (133). In all cases, final judgments are the outcome of talk—talk that is saturated with socio-political awareness and deeply rooted in local historical context.

# Pidgin Languages: Negotiated Meaning

The Samoan village *fono* is a setting in which speakers and listeners are able, for the most part, to draw upon knowledge of overlapping language habits in order to communicate with each other about moral and political issues. But what happens when members of communities with radically different language traditions and no history of previous contact with one another come face to face and are forced to communicate? There is no way to predict the outcome of such contact on either speech community, yet from these new shared experiences, new forms of communication, including a new form of language—**pidgin**—may develop.

**pidgin**
A language with no native speakers that develops in a single generation between members of communities that possess distinct native languages.

'When the chips are down, meaning is negotiated' (Lakoff and Johnson 1980: 231). The study of pidgin languages is the study of the radical negotiation of new meaning. A pidgin language is different from and reducible to neither of the languages that gave birth to it, and its shape reflects the context in which it arises—generally one of colonial conquest or commercial domination. Vocabulary is usually taken from the language of the dominant group, making it easy for that group to learn. Syntax and phonology may be similar to the subordinate language (or languages), however, making it easier for subordinated speakers to learn. Morphemes that mark the gender or number of nouns or the tenses of verbs tend to disappear (Holm 1988).

Pidgins are traditionally defined as reduced languages that develop in a single generation between groups of speakers of distinct native languages. When speakers of a pidgin language pass that language on to a new generation, linguists usually refer to the language of the new generation as a *creole*. The creolization of pidgins involves increased complexity in phonology, morphology, syntax, semantics, and pragmatics, such that the pidgin comes to resemble a conventional language.

This traditional view suggested to Bickerton (1981) that the way in which pidgins form could shed light on the universal biological bases of language. He found that Hawaiian Pidgin English differed in many ways from Hawaiian Creole, which descended from it. Because, in his view, none of these differences could be connected to any of the languages available to those who invented Hawaiian Creole, he concluded that they were produced by the innate linguistic 'bio-program' of the creole creators, and he claimed that these same forms could be found in other unrelated creoles as well.

Other students of pidgins and creoles have tried to test his hypothesis. While their work has not confirmed his views, it has revealed that the distinction between pidgins and creoles is more complex than previously thought. In the Pacific, for example, linguists have discovered pidgin dialects, pidgin languages used as main languages of permanently settled groups, and pidgins that have become native languages. Moreover, creolization can take place at any time after a pidgin forms, creoles can exist without having been preceded by pidgins, pidgins can remain pidgins for long periods and undergo linguistic change without acquiring native speakers, and pidgin and creole varieties of the same language can coexist in the same society (Jourdan 1991: 192ff.). In fact, it looks as if heteroglossia is as widespread among speakers of pidgins and creoles as among speakers of other languages.

Awareness of heteroglossia in pidgin/creole speech communities has led to the redefinition of a pidgin as a *shared secondary language* in a speech community, where speakers also use some other main language in smaller groups, and a creole as *a main language* in a speech community, whether or not it has native speakers. According to the new view, creolization is likely when pidgin speakers find themselves in new social contexts requiring a new language for *all* the practical activities of everyday life; without such a context, it is unlikely that creoles will emerge (196).

Contemporary linguistic anthropologists view pidgin creation as a form of communicative practice, and they have explored the role of pidgin creators as agents in the process. It appears that as people negotiate meaning across language barriers, they have intuitions about which parts of their speech carry the most meaning and which parts can be safely dropped. Neither party to the negotiation, moreover, may be trying to learn the other's language; rather, 'speakers in the course of negotiating communication use whatever linguistic and socio-linguistic resources they have at their disposal until the shared meaning is established and conventionalized' (200).

# Linguistic Inequality and Oppression

Pidgins and creoles are far more complex—and the result of far more active human input—than previously thought, which is why they are so attractive to linguists and linguistic anthropologists as objects of study. Where they coexist, however, alongside the language of the dominant group (e.g., Hawaiian Pidgin English and English), they are ordinarily viewed by members of society as defective and inferior languages. Such views frequently stem from the situation that led to the formation of most of the pidgins we know about: European colonial domination.

In a colonial or post-colonial setting, the colonizer's language is often considered to be superior to all others. Colonizers generally look down on Indigenous languages as lesser forms of communication, and they characterize pidgins and creoles as broken, imperfect versions of their own language. The situation only worsens for dominated populations when formal education is carried out in the colonial language. Consider the lasting impact of the residential school system in Canada, where administrators firmly and sometimes violently discouraged children from using their original languages. In addition, speakers of a pidgin or creole or Indigenous language who do not master the colonial tongue may find themselves effectively barred from participation in the civic life of their societies.

To take one language variety as the standard against which all others are measured is linguistic ethnocentrism, and such a standard may be applied to any language, not just pidgins and creoles. This is one kind of linguistic inequality: making value judgments about other people's speech in a context of dominance and subordination.

A powerful example of the effects of linguistic inequality is found in the history and controversies surrounding African American English (AAE) in the United States. In the 1960s, some psychologists claimed that African American children living in urban areas of the northern United States suffered from linguistic deprivation. They argued that these children started school with a limited vocabulary and no grammar and thus could not perform as well as Euro-American children in the classroom—that their language was unequal to the challenges of communication. Sociolinguist William Labov and his colleagues found such claims incredible and undertook research of their own (Labov 1972). In their investigation, they proved that the form of English spoken in the inner city was not a defective pseudo-language, and they showed how a change in research context permitted inner-city African American children to display a level of linguistic sophistication that the psychologists had never dreamed they possessed.

When African American children were in the classroom (a Euro-American dominated context) being interrogated by Euro-American adults about topics of no interest to them, they said little. This did not necessarily mean, Labov argued, that they had no language. Rather, their minimal responses were better understood as defensive attempts to keep threatening Euro-American questioners from learning anything about them. For the African American children, the classroom was part of a broader racist culture. The psychologists, due to their ethnocentrism, had been oblivious to the effect this context might have on their research. Reasoning that reliable samples of African American speech had to be collected in contexts where the racist threat was lessened, Labov and his colleagues conducted fieldwork in the children's homes and on the streets of the inner city. They recorded enormous amounts of speech in African American English produced by the same children who had had nothing to say when questioned in the classroom.

Labov's analysis demonstrated that AAE was a variety of English that had certain rules not found in Standard English. Yet these rules do not make the language 'defective'; they simply make it distinct. Linguistic differences exist between most social subgroups in a society that is characterized by heteroglossia, and they mark a speaker's membership in a particular speech community. Since Labov's time, AAE has gone through stages of invention, borrowing, and evolution—stages common to all 'living' languages. Indeed, many elements from AAE have entered into more mainstream usage, both in North America and in other English-speaking regions of the world.

The situation is quite different for Native peoples in Canada. Today, many communities are struggling to retain original languages that have been pushed to extinction or near extinction by the consequences of colonialism (Figure 4.8). In many communities, English continues to be thought of as the language of domination and the medium of remembrance of the residential school experience. In contrast,

**language ideology**
A system of beliefs about how language features relate to social features and what they reveal about the people who use them.

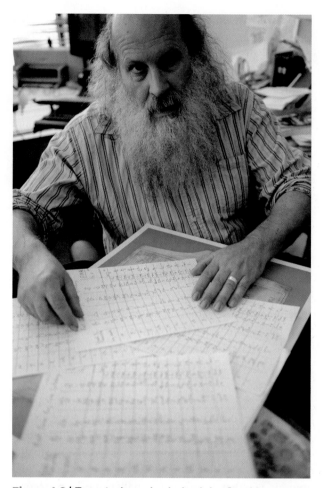

*Figure 4.8* | **Toronto-based scholar John Steckley, a native English speaker, is the world's last known Huron-language speaker. Huron language and history has been his academic focus for more than thirty years.**

Indigenous languages are thought of as tools that can recall and preserve the collective memories of the culture: 'Memory needs a place, a context. Its place, if it finds one that lives beyond a single generation, is to be found in the stories that we tell' (Kenny 1999: 421). Further, language learning becomes one route to healing the injured individual and group who have suffered loss through the colonial process. Thus, many First Nations communities are engaged in programs to retain and/or recall and teach their languages (see the 'In Their Own Words' box, below).

The various perceptions of languages and of their speakers we have discussed in this section lead us to consider the study of **language ideology**: the intersection 'between social forms and forms of talk' (Woolard 1998: 3). While

## In Their Own Words | The Round Robin Healing Circle

*Christine Schreyer writes on her initial field experience and one of the programs to retain the Tlingit language.*

On 25 June 2005, I arrived in Whitehorse, Yukon, for the very first time. I had come to begin my doctoral research with the Taku River Tlingit First Nation, located in Atlin, British Columbia, and the following morning I set out on the two-hour drive down the Alaska Highway to Jake's Corner, Yukon, and then turned down the windy gravel mountain road to Atlin. When I arrived in town, I managed to get a hold of someone who could give me directions to the Five Mile reserve where the majority of the Taku River Tlingit community members currently live, five miles south of town, and to the Round Robin Healing Circle family camp [Figure 4.9]. I would be spending two weeks living there on my own whilst getting to know the community and working on a volunteer project. When I finally managed to find my way to the camp, I was warmly welcomed by Louise Gordon, her family, and friends and promptly set up in one of the wall tents at the camp. The camp is used by Louise and her family for sustainable activities such as fishing, nature walks, and berry picking, as well as for community events such as culture camps. The volunteer project I would be working on with Louise and the Taku River Tlingit First Nation community was a Tlingit-language board game for language revitalization. The Tlingit language is an endangered language, and within their community there are less than five elders who are fluent in the language, and no children learn Tlingit as their mother tongue. The game, now titled Haa shagóon ítx yaa ntoo.aat (or 'Travelling Our Ancestors' Paths') incorporates knowledge about subsistence practices, such as those practised at the Round Robin Healing Circle family camp, including words for resources and place names in the Tlingit language. The game was created with the help of Louise's grandmother, Antonia Jack, who had travelled Atlin Lake in 1999 to record the Tlingit place names so that her children, grandchildren, and great-grandchildren could learn the names of the places that are part of their heritage. The game is used in language revitalization programs within the community and allows for children and adults to learn the language while having fun and interacting together.

Source: Schreyer, Christine. 2009. 'The Round Robin Healing Circle', guest editorial.

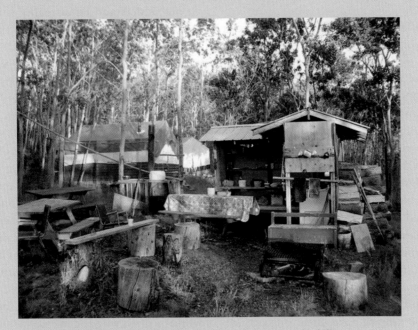

*Figure 4.9* | Round Robin Healing Circle family camp in Atlin, British Columbia, 26 June 2005.

the study of language ideology discloses speakers' sense of beauty, morality, or basic understandings of the world, it also provides evidence of the ways in which our speech is always embedded in a social world of power differences. Language ideologies are markers of struggles between social groups with different interests, revealed in what people say and how they say it. The way people monitor their speech to bring it into line with a particular language ideology illustrates that language ideologies are 'active and effective . . . they transform the material reality they comment on' (11). In settings with a history of colonization, where groups with different power and different languages co-exist in tension, the study of language ideologies has long been significant (16). The skills of linguistic anthropologists especially suit them to study language ideologies because their linguistic training allows them to describe precisely the linguistic features (e.g., phonological, morphological, or syntactic) that become the focus of ideological attention, and their training in cultural analysis allows them to explain how those linguistic features come to stand symbolically for a particular social group.

## Language Habits of Women and Men

Language habits differ not only among ethnic groups but also between women and men. Indeed, one of the early objections to work on African American English was that it focussed on the discourse genres of men only. Since the 1970s, the language habits of African American women and girls have figured in numerous studies (see, e.g., Morgan 1995: 336ff.).

Sociolinguist Deborah Tannen (1990) has gained much popular attention in the media with her study of speech patterns of men and women in the United States. Tannen focusses on typical male and female styles of discourse, arguing that men and women use language for different reasons: men tend to use language as a competitive weapon in public settings, whereas women tend to use language as a way of building closeness in private settings. Tannen shows what happens when men and women each assume that their rules are the only rules without realizing that the other gender may be defining appropriate language use from a different perspective. For example, when a husband and wife get home from work at the end of the day, she may be eager to talk while he is just as eager to remain silent. She may interpret his silence as a sign of distance or coldness and be hurt. He, in contrast, may be weary of the day's verbal combat and resent his wife's attempts at conversation, not because he is rejecting her personally but because he believes he has a right to remain silent.

## Language and Truth

For Thomas Kuhn, a philosopher of science, metaphor lies at the heart of science, and changes in scientific theories are 'accompanied by a change in some of the relevant metaphors and in corresponding parts of the network of similarities through which terms attach to nature' (1979: 416). Kuhn argues that these changes in the way scientific terms link to nature are irreducible to logic or grammar. 'They come about in response to pressures generated by observation or experiment'—that is, by experience and context. And there is no neutral language into which rival theories can be translated and subsequently evaluated as unambiguously right or wrong. Kuhn asks the question 'Is what we refer to as "the world" perhaps a product of mutual accommodation between experience and language?' (416).

If our understanding of reality is the product of a dialectic between experience and language (or, more broadly, culture), then ambiguity will never be permanently removed from any of the symbolic systems that human beings invent. Reflexive consciousness makes humans aware of alternatives. The experience of doubt, of not being sure what to believe, is never far behind.

This is not merely the experience of people in Western societies. Evans-Pritchard (1963) describes the same sort of disorientation among the Azande of central Africa (see EthnoProfile 10.1). The Azande people are well aware of the ambiguity inherent in language, and they exploit it by using metaphor (what they call *sanza*) to disguise speech that might be received badly if uttered directly. For example, 'A man says in the presence of his wife to his friend, "Friend, those swallows, how they flit about in there." He is speaking about the flightiness of his wife and in case she should understand the allusion, he covers himself by looking up at the swallows as he makes his seemingly innocent remark' (1963: 211). Evans-Pritchard later observes that *sanza*

adds greatly to the difficulties of anthropological inquiry. Eventually the anthropologist's sense of security is undermined and his confidence shaken. He learns the language, can say what he wants to say in it, and can understand what he hears, but then he begins to wonder whether he has really understood .... [H]e

cannot be sure, and even they [the Azande] cannot be sure, whether the words do have a nuance or someone imagines that they do. (228)

However much we learn about language, we will never be able to exhaust its meanings or circumscribe its rules once and for all. Human language is an open system, and as long as human history continues, new forms will be created and old forms will continue to be put to new uses.

## Key Terms

communicative competence   82

design features   81

discourse   88

ethnopragmatics   88

grammar   84

language   79

language ideology   92

linguistic competence   82

linguistic relativity principle   83

linguistics   79

metaphor   87

morpheme   82

morphology   85

phoneme   82

phonology   84

pidgin   90

pragmatics   87

semantics   86

syntax   86

## Chapter Summary

1. Language is a uniquely human faculty that both permits us to communicate and sets up barriers to communication. It is a part of culture that people use to encode their experiences, to structure their understanding of the world and of themselves, and to engage with one another. The study of different languages reveals the shared nature of language and culture and the contextual assumptions that speakers make and use.

2. There are many ways to communicate our experiences, and there is no absolute standard favouring one way over another. Individual efforts to create a unique voice are countered by pressures to negotiate a common code within the larger social group.

3. Of Charles Hockett's 16 design features of language, 6 are particularly important to an anthropological investigation of language: openness, displacement, prevarication, arbitrariness, duality of patterning, and semanticity.

4. Early linguistic anthropologists Edward Sapir and Benjamin Whorf suggested that language has the power to shape the way people see the world. This hypothesis is called the *linguistic relativity principle*.

5. Today, formal linguistic analysis is usually divided into five specialties: phonology, the study of the sounds of language; morphology, the study of the minimal units of meaning in a language; syntax, the study of sentence structure; semantics, the study of meaning; and pragmatics, the study of language in the context of its use. Formal analyses of language, however, often more closely resemble formal logic than patterns of everyday language use.

6. Ethnopragmatics pays attention both to the immediate context of speech and to the broader contexts that are shaped by social relationships and rooted in history. It locates meaning in routine practical activities, which turn grammatical features of language into resources people can use in their interactions with others.

7. Because linguistic meaning is rooted in practical activity, the activity and the linguistic usage together shape communicative practices. Different social groups generate

different communicative practices. The linguistic habits that are part of each set of communicative practices constitute discourse genres. People normally command a range of discourse genres, which means that their linguistic knowledge is characterized by heteroglossia.

8. The study of pidgin languages is the study of the radical negotiation of new meaning. In pidgins, two groups of language speakers who come in contact (often as a result of colonization or commercial domination) invent a new language different from either parent language.

Pidgin languages exhibit many of the same linguistic features as non-pidgin languages.

9. Colonialism is the main historical circumstances that has given rise to pidgins and creoles. Colonists' oppression of Indigenous peoples' languages provides evidence of some ways in which language use is embedded in a social world of power differences.

10. Linguists and anthropologists have described differences in the gender-based communicative practices of women and men.

## Critical Thinking Questions

1. Distinguish between phonemes and morphemes. How does the use of phonemes and morphemes distinguish regional and socio-economic accents in Canada? What social factors—historical and contemporary—might contribute to the variety of accents across Canada today?

2. Are all aspects of the design features of language used only by humans?

3. What are the processes of language change? How has language evolved in your lifetime?

4. Discuss the loss of languages and the struggle for language retention/learning in First Nations communities. Can programs for language retention play a role in reconciliation?

5. What makes Canadian English Canadian? Is it the Standard English of all of Canada, and is it stable or subject to change?

6. Consider words for various colours and shades of colour. How would you classify the colours of a rainbow? Is such a system of classification a cross-cultural phenomenon? Is it even consistent within your own linguistic community?

## Suggested Readings

Akmajian, A., et al. 2010. *Linguistics: An Introduction to Language and Communication*, 6th edn (Cambridge, MA: mit Press). A fine introduction to the study of language as a formal system.

Brenneis, Donald, and Ronald K.S. Macauley, eds. 1996. *The Matrix of Language: Contemporary Linguistic Anthropology* (Boulder, CO: Westview Press). A wide-ranging collection of essays by anthropologists studying linguistic habits in their socio-cultural contexts.

Lakoff, George, and Mark Johnson. 1980. *Metaphors We Live By* (Berkeley: University of California Press). An important, clear, and very accessible book that presents a radical and persuasive view of metaphor.

Salzmann, Zdenek, James Stanlaw, and Nobuko Adachi. 2011. *Language, Culture, and Society: An Introduction to Linguistic Anthropology*, 5th edn (Boulder, CO: Westview Press). An up-to-date and thorough text on linguistic anthropology.

Smitherman, Geneva. 1977. *Talkin and Testifyin: The Language of Black America* (Detroit: Wayne State University Press). An engaging introduction to Black English vernacular, for native and non-native speakers alike.

## Related Websites

Franglais www.yrad.com/franglais/

Language and Gender www.kichu.com/elp/gender.html

Logic www.philosophypages.com/lg/

Newfoundland Word Game www.nfld.com/nfld/other/words/word.html

Semiotics for Beginners www.aber.ac.uk/media/Documents/S4B/sem07.html

The Sounds of English www.antimoon.com/how/pronunc-soundsipa.htm

Terms at Grammar Bytes! www.chompchomp.com/terms.htm

Tok Pisin–English Dictionary www.tok-pisin.com/

## Chapter Outline

Perception

Cognition

Emotion

Motivation

Personality/Self/Subjectivity

Subject Positions of Sexuality and Gender

Structural Violence and Social Trauma

Individual Psychology and Context

## Learning Objectives

By the end of Chapter 4, you will be able to

- understand how perception organizes information,

- recognize that prototypes are central to the way meaning is organized,

- appreciate that cognition is 'a nexus of relations between the mind at work and the world in which it works',

- understand emotion as the product of a dialectic between bodily arousal and cognitive interpretation,

- consider that the sources of motivation are embedded within a cultural matrix,

- recognize the roles that socialization and enculturation play in shaping cognitive development,

- consider what sort of entity a self is,

- understand ranges of sexual and gender identities,

- identify how violence and trauma affect and are interpreted by the self, and

- realize that individual psychology is situated in the context of culture.

A father and son practice archery in Mongolia. As they explore the world around them, children learn how to act, think, feel, speak, and participate in cultural life from more experienced members of their societies.

**We do not all learn the same things, even if we live in the same society. Our learning is socially and culturally shaped by differences in status and experience.** Anthropologists are interested in the patterns and variations in patterns of how individuals engage in cultural learning—how individuals learn from one another within a culture. Historically, anthropology addressed this phenomenon by seeking answers for a series of persistent questions: 'What characteristics of our species are found in all times and places? What features are limited to specific groups of humans? How can we best take account of individual uniqueness?' (Bock 1994: ix).

Anthropologists who want to understand how individuals perceive and make sense of their world have incorporated psychological theories into their studies. This process has traditionally involved anthropological adoption and cross-cultural evaluation of different theoretical orientations in psychology. For example, some of the first twentieth-century anthropologists to take an interest in psychological matters, such as Margaret Mead and Bronislaw Malinowski, were influenced by the psychology of Sigmund Freud and attempted to test in non-Western settings certain Freudian ideas about personality development based on social relations in late nineteenth-century Viennese society.

These early studies initiated a pattern of analysis that has remained central to much psychological anthropology: that of critically examining universal statements about human nature produced by Western researchers, especially those based on assumptions about how people in Western societies are supposed to be. This critical role is especially important in those situations where researchers make extreme claims about all members of the human species. Such claims frequently get publicity and tend to generate controversy. Early tests of Freudian theory are a good example. Is the pattern of early childhood development described by Freud universal in all human groups—found in all times and places? Or, conversely, is it an example of individual uniqueness, characteristic perhaps of individuals with disturbed childhoods but not of everyone else?

In North American Euro-ancestry societies, claims about universal human psychology compete with assertions of individual uniqueness. One of the most deeply entrenched forms involves opposing 'biology' (nature) to 'culture' (nurture) as alternative, mutually exclusive explanations for some particular aspect of human psychological functioning. Such extreme claims and counterclaims never seem to be resolved, perhaps because they are too crude to illuminate much lasting interest. As we discussed in Chapter 1, most anthropologists view human beings as biocultural organisms. Thus, psychological anthropologists have typically concentrated on 'the intermediate zone of group differences' where it becomes possible to identify relationships between specific features of a given culture and specific individuals (Bock 1994: ix). This sort of demonstration has done a great deal to undermine ethnocentric prejudices, such as the assumption that all people are (or ought to be) 'just like us' or that some of us are 'rational' while others are 'irrational'.

One of the more promising approaches recognized by Bock, and taken by various psychological anthropologists in recent years (e.g., Ingold 2000), has been influenced by the work of developmental psychologist Oyama (1985). Frequently known as Developmental Systems Theory (DST), this approach has forced researchers to rethink the relationship between evolving species and the development of individual members of those species. DST recognizes that a developing organism is subject to many environments, identifiable at different levels of analysis, as it lives out its life cycle. Socially constructed environments—along with their social, economic, and political resources—get passed on to subsequent generations as faithfully as genes. This social transmission influences the developmental trajectory of future life cycles and, potentially, evolutionary selection pressures that impinge on the species itself. Together, biological and cultural forces shape the directions of our lives in decisive ways.

In this chapter, we will consider the basic areas of human experience: perception, cognition, emotion, and motivation. As we will discover, what results from experience is a personal position, called a *subject position*, from which one views the world. 'Once having taken up a particular position as one's own, a person inevitably sees the world from the vantage point of that position and in terms of [its] particular images, metaphors, story-lines, and concepts' (Davies and Harré 1990: 46). In turn, these images, metaphors, storylines, and concepts become a conceptual repertoire from which position can be further composed. As with language, this repertoire is an 'open system'. Thus any particular way of thinking or feeling is shaped by factors encountered in the course of development. Human psychology routinely develops in the context of culturally shaped activities that draw our attention to some parts of the world while leading us to ignore others. What we think or feel about something depends greatly on what we have learned to pay attention to in the past and the values we have learned to associate with it (Figure 5.1). As a result, different groups in a society—with different histories

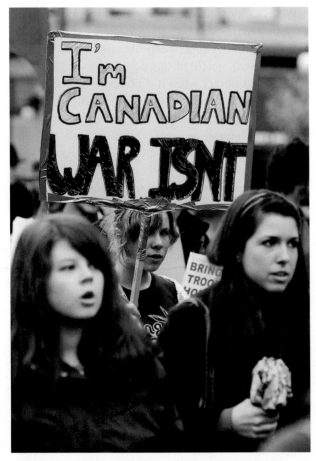

*Figure 5.1* | **Today, many Canadians are passionate about their anti-war stance. The points of view we develop depend greatly on what we have learned to pay attention to in the past.**

and experiences—are likely to develop unique points of view, pay attention to different things, and feel differently about those things.

As we discuss human psychological processes, you may find it useful to keep in mind the design features of language we discussed in Chapter 4. Besides openness (mentioned above), the features of displacement and prevarication can inform your understanding of these processes. Consider that when we learn from culturally shaped experience, we can use pre-existing categories to help us interpret new experiences. This is a version of *displacement*. Moreover, all our senses can play tricks on us, and we can mistakenly perceive something that 'does not exist'. Thus, *prevarication* is a built-in feature of human psychological processes.

Human psychological processes are heavily influenced by symbols, and the meaning of what we see, touch, smell, taste, or hear depends on context. As with language, two contexts are normally invoked: the *immediate* context of the perception itself and the *displaced* context stored in memory and shaped by culture. The 'same' object (or symbol) can mean different things in different contexts. Consider what seeing a butcher knife means (1) lying on a cutting board in your kitchen next to a pile of mushrooms or (2) wielded by an intruder who has cornered you in your kitchen.

## Perception

**Perception** can be defined as the 'processes by which people organize and experience information that is primarily of sensory origin' (Cole and Scribner 1974: 61). Traditionally, people have tried to deal with perspectives in two principal ways: through intellect and through emotion. On the one side there is rationality and logic (think of Spock); on the other side there is passion and intuition (Kirk). Most often, one side has been overvalued at the expense of the other. Anthropologists and some psychologists suggest that this approach is highly problematic. Also troubling is any assumption that perception occurs in a culture-free vacuum. In opposition to this assumption, anthropologists have always insisted that 'culture enters

**perception**
The 'processes by which people organize and experience information that is primarily of sensory origin'.

**schemas**
Patterned, repetitive experiences.

**prototypes**
Examples of a typical instance, element, relation, or experience within a culturally relevant semantic domain.

into every step of the perceptual process, initially by providing patterned material for perception . . . and later, through verbal and non-verbal means, by suggesting (or insisting on) the proper labelling of and responses to perceived patterns' (Bock 1994: xi).

Chunks of perceptual experience that appear to hang together as wholes, exhibiting the same properties in the same configuration whenever they recur, are called **schemas**. As human beings grow up, they gradually become aware of the schemas that their culture (or subculture) recognizes. Such schemas are often embedded in practical activities and labelled linguistically, and they may serve as a focus for discourse. People living in North America, for example, cannot avoid a schema called *Christmas*, a chunk of experience that recurs once every year. The Christmas schema can include features such as snowy weather and activities such as baking cookies, singing carols, going to church, putting up a Christmas tree, and exchanging gifts. In the experience of a child, all these elements may appear to be equally relevant parts of a seamless whole. At the same time, not

everyone will interpret a schema in the same way. For example, devout Christians may struggle to accept the secularization of what was originally a religious holiday, while non-Christian North Americans might question why they must be subjected to the Christmas schema every year when they have no affiliation with the religious tradition behind the schema (Figure 5.2).

People take for granted most of the schemas that their culture recognizes, using them as simplified interpretive frameworks for judging new experiences as typical or not, human or not (D'Andrade 1992: 48). Schemas thus become **prototypes**. Prototypes appear to be central to the way meaning is organized in human language. Words refer to typical instances elements, or relations and are embedded in genres of discourse associated with routine cultural practices.

When we organize sensory information on the basis of prototypes, however, the categories we use have fuzzy boundaries (openness) because our experiences do not always neatly fit our prototypes. Is a library a prototypical library when it contains fewer books than DVDs, videotapes, and electronic databases? In a case such as this, suggests the linguist Hudson (1980), a person must simply recognize the openness of language and apply linguistic labels creatively. Similarly, when confronted with novel perceptions, experiences for which no ready-made cultural interpretation is at hand, thinking and feeling human beings must extrapolate creatively to make sense of what is going on around them.

Inevitably, observers situated in different social and/or cultural positions will draw on different background knowledge and different prototypes; as a result they will often interpret the same sensory information in different ways. Classic research on variations in perception has related people's interpretations of their experiences to their understandings of *context*. For example, Cole and Scribner (1974) recount a study in which researchers tested non-literate South African miners using two-dimensional line drawings of three-dimensional objects (Figure 5.3). The test results indicated that the miners consistently interpreted the drawings in two dimensions. When asked at which animal the man was pointing his spear on Card 1, subjects would usually respond 'the elephant'. The elephant is, in fact, directly in line with and closest to the spear point

*Figure 5.2* | In North America, the Christmas schema involves public events in secular spaces—such as the annual rush to complete holiday shopping in the last days before Christmas—that non-Christians cannot avoid.

*Figure 5.3* | Line drawings used to elicit verbal responses in the depth-perception test in Africa.

in the drawing. However, the researchers thought that the subjects should interpret the elephant as standing on top of the distant hill. Did the subjects' responses mean that they could not perceive in three dimensions?

Deregowski devised the following test. First, he presented different African subjects with the same drawings and asked them to describe what they saw. Again they responded with two-dimensional verbal reports. Next, he presented the same subjects with the line drawings in Figure 5.4. This time, he asked his subjects to construct models based on the drawings using materials he provided. His subjects had no difficulty producing three-dimensional models.

In these tests, the 'correct' solution depended on the subject's mastery of a Western convention for interpreting two-dimensional images. For the drawings in Figure 5.3, the Western convention includes assumptions about perspective that relate the size of objects to their

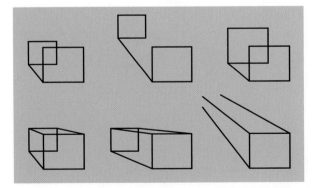

*Figure 5.4* | Line drawings used for the construction of models in the depth-perception test in Africa.

distance from the observer. Without such a convention in mind, it is not obvious that the size of an object has any connection with distance. Thus, far from providing us with new insights about African perceptual abilities, the tests highlight the assumptions behind Western perceptual conventions. As Cole and Scribner point out, the images make sense to us only once we accept certain rules for interpreting them (Cole and Scribner 1974). And we need to remember that *perspective* in Western drawing is a relatively recent 'invention' (fifteenth-century Italian Renaissance)—through our capacity for openness, our conventions changed.

## Illusion

If you examine Figure 5.5, you will see that marks on a piece of paper can be ambiguous. The signals we receive from the outside world tend to be open to more than one interpretation, be they patterns of light and dark, smells, tastes, shapes, or words. The contrast between literal and metaphorical language is not unlike the contrast between reality and illusion as it relates to perception. In both cases, knowledge of context permits us to distinguish between the literal and the metaphorical, the real and the illusory.

Gregory (1983), a cognitive psychologist, thinks that visual illusions are produced by *misplaced procedures* perfectly normal, ordinary cognitive processes that have somehow been inappropriately selected and applied to a particular set of visual signals. Thus perceptions are symbolic representations of reality, not direct samples

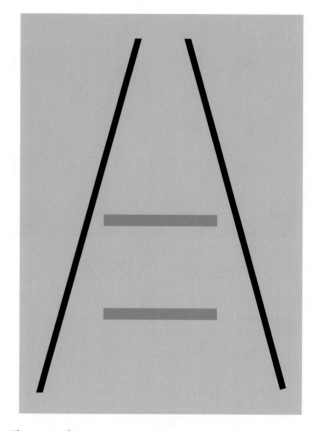

*Figure 5.6* | **An example of distortion: the Ponzo illusion.**

of reality. Perceivers must often work very hard to make sense of the visual signals they receive. When they are wrong, they are subject to illusion.

Consider the visual illusion Gregory calls *distortion*, in which what you see appears larger or smaller, longer or shorter, and so on, than it really is. Look at the Ponzo illusion in Figure 5.6. Typically, the upper parallel line appears to be longer than the lower one when in fact they are equal. The illusion occurs because we interpret the two-dimensional drawing as if it were in three dimensions. The shapes trick us because they are very similar to what we perceive when we stand on a railroad track and look toward its vanishing point on the horizon. The Africans in Deregowski's test did not attempt to interpret the Ponzo-like lines on Card 2 of Figure 5.3 as representations of three-dimensional reality. On the contrary, they seemed to work very hard to keep the relationships between objects in two dimensions, even if this meant that the sizes of the objects themselves appeared distorted. When

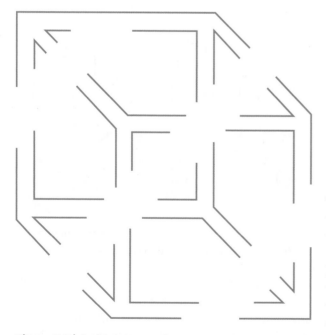

*Figure 5.5* | **Ambiguous marks.**

*Figure 5.7* | **A Mbuti pygmy mother paints her daughter's face with a black juice from the gardenia fruit called *kangay*, used for staining the body or for drawing patterns on bark cloth. About every three months the clan moves to a new site where the women erect sapling and leaf huts.**

we compare the Western interpretation of the Ponzo illusion with the African interpretation of the pictures in Figure 5.3, we discover something important: both sets of drawings are ambiguous, and both are potentially open to distortion; how people interpret them depends on pre-existing experiences and cultural conventions.

Turnbull worked among the Mbuti of the northeastern Democratic Republic of the Congo (formerly Zaire) for many years (see Figure 5.7; see also EthnoProfile 5.1). He discovered that these people, who live all their lives in a dense forest, have no experience of distance greater than a few feet and are therefore not accustomed to taking

distance into consideration when estimating the size of an object in the visual field. Turnbull took one of his informants, Kenge, on a trip that brought them out of the forest and into a game park. For the first time in his life, Kenge faced vast, rolling grasslands. Kenge's response to this experience was dramatic: 'When Kenge topped the rise, he stopped dead. Every smallest sign of mirth suddenly left his face. He opened his mouth but could say nothing. He moved his head and eyes slowly and unbelievingly' (Turnbull 1961: 251). When Kenge finally saw the far-off animals grazing on the plain, he asked Turnbull what insects they were. When told that they were buffalo, Kenge laughed and accused Turnbull of lying. Then he strained to see better and inquired what kind of buffalo could be so small. Later, when Turnbull pointed out a fishing boat on the lake, Kenge scoffed at him and insisted it was a piece of floating wood (252).

> **visuality**
> The ways that individuals from different societies learn to interpret what they see and to construct mental pictures using the visual practices that their own cultural system favours.

## Visuality: Learning to Look

Vogel has studied the sculpture of the Baule people of Ivory Coast (see EthnoProfile 3.1) since the early 1970s, and her research has taught her that looking and seeing are culturally learned modes of sensory perception (1997: 108–11). She terms this interpretive process **visuality**. Vogel notes that, for the Baule, objects are powerful and affect the people who see them. Spiritually significant objects, which include much of what Westerners would call *sculpture*, are

---

*EthnoProfile 5.1* | **Mbuti (Bambuti)** ·······································

**Region** Central Africa

**Nation** Ituri Forest (>70,000 km²) in the northeastern Democratic Republic of the Congo

**Language** Mbuti are actually three distinct cultures differentiated by the dialects they speak: Efe Kango, and Asoa

**Population** 30,000–50,000 (c. 2010, estimated)

**Environment** Dense tropical rainforest with a two-month dry season

**Livelihood** Hunting and gathering

**Political organization** Traditionally, communal bands of 7 to 30 families (average 17 families with 15–60 members); today, part of a modern nation-state

**For more information** Turnbull, Colin. 1961. *The Forest People* (New York: Simon & Schuster); 1983. *The Mbuti Pygmies: Change and Adaptation* (New York: CBS College Publishing).

thus potentially dangerous. 'Even an inadvertent glimpse of a forbidden object can make a person sick, can expose them to huge fines or sacrifices, or can even be fatal' (110).

For the Baule, looking is the most important of all perceptual activities: seeing something is potentially more significant and more dangerous than touching, eating, or drinking something. There is an explicit etiquette governing how one ought to look at things, and staring is highly disapproved of. It is disrespectful for younger people to look directly at their elders, for example (110), and the rules for looking actually limit the 'visibility' of sculpture. For example, while Western worshippers might feel free to gaze intently at the adorned altar of a medieval Christian cathedral, the Baule would consider analogous behaviour to be highly improper:

> If someone stopped and looked for a whole minute at the altar erected in plain view in Nguessan's courtyard, they would be called before the chief to explain. The fact that the altar stands in a public place, where a hundred people pass daily, does not mean it can be stared at. In fact the only motives for looking hard at such an object would be malevolent: a desire to kill someone in the courtyard, or to nullify the altar's powers. The stare itself is not the means of achieving either of these ends; it merely accumulates information for later use. (111)

The language Baule speakers use to talk about visuality is also highly revealing. You may recall from Chapter 4 that speakers of a language shape its vocabulary to reflect their cultural preoccupations. The Baule language contains four words for looking and seeing. These terms distinguish among objects that anyone can look at, objects that must never be deliberately looked at, and all degrees in between:

**cognition**
(1) The mental process by which human beings gain knowledge, and (2) the 'nexus of relations between the mind at work and the world in which it works'.

1) The most common verb translated as 'to look' is *nian*, which can also mean 'to watch'. It connotes intentional watching and is used for watching mask dances intended for entertainment and for watching television.

2) The noun *nyin* means 'a stare' or 'a good hard look'. The phrase *nyin kpa*, 'a real stare', is used to describe looking at a useful decorated object with no sacred meaning.

3) The noun *kanngle* means 'evil looks from the corner of the eye'.

4) *Nian klekle* means 'to look clandestinely', to 'cast a rapid glance' (91).

The most awesome objects and events—the men's sacred masks, divination dances, and funerals—are not spoken of with any of these words. 'One never says one has seen or looked at these potent things; one merely says *N'wo se bo*, "I went to the funeral", or *N'su ko awebo*, "I went to the divination dance"' (92).

For the Baule, life is lived knowing that sculptures—powerful objects—are present but cannot be examined, cannot be looked at closely. As a result, when these objects are visible, even though they are incompletely seen, they make an extraordinary impression and become mnemonic devices for the retention of important events. Such experiences become part of an oral history and make powerful contributions to the perception of a particular Baule world view.

# Cognition

The study of illusion demonstrates that there can be a gulf between what we see and what we know, what we perceive and what we conceive. In everyday life, these discrepancies seem to be manageable: there is coherence between perceptions and conceptions. Moreover, because our link with the world is a dialectical one, there is no sharp boundary between what we perceive and what we conceive. Not only can new perceptions lead us to modify our conceptions (i.e., we learn), but new conceptions can also lead us to perceive aspects of the world around us that we didn't pay attention to before. We are active meaning-makers, internally negotiating our experiences. As a result, **cognition** is perhaps best understood as 'a nexus of relations between the mind at work and the world in which it works' (Lave 1988: 1).

Anthropologists began to study cognition in the 1960s, when there was a growing interest in the ways different peoples classified cultural knowledge.

From early studies of *ethnobotany* and *ethnozoology*, anthropologists began doing *ethnoscience*. They used folk taxonomies and generic terms to lump things into categories:

> **Taxonomies** use relations between *kinds of things* which have been recorded into 'configurational attributes'. A *collie* is a kind of *dog*, and 'dogginess' is a configurational attribute—a configuration of large numbers of attributes 'recorded' and 'chunked' into a single gestalt of 'dogginess'. By virtue of being a *kind of dog*, collies 'inherit' all the recorded attributes that make up the chunked quality of 'dogginess'—nose, tail, yelp, and all. (D'Andrade 1995: 93)

Although the classification of different parts of the natural world remains of deep interest, anthropologists have expanded their investigations to incorporate the links between language and culture, focussing on the many ways of 'labelling' the social and cultural worlds of their informants. Recently, cognitive anthropologists have become more interested in the mental processes people use to make sense of their experiences in the world.

## Cognitive Capacities and Intelligence

What makes it possible for us to receive signals from the outside world (or from within our own bodies) and then interpret those signals in a way that makes appropriate action possible? One traditional answer has been that every person either possesses at birth or develops over time certain basic cognitive capacities. At one time, these hypothetical capacities were thought of as substances or properties, and the goal of psychological testing was to measure how much of each cognitive capacity an individual had. Consequently, intelligence has traditionally been 'measured' using an 'instrument' called the *intelligence test*; the 'amount' of intelligence measured is assigned a number called the *intelligence quotient*, or IQ. In the past, some researchers equated differences in performance on intelligence tests with differences in intelligence. Today, such a reductionist approach is subjected to intense scrutiny.

Intelligence texts have proven to be even less useful for studying peoples whose cultural backgrounds differ from those of the researchers. Michael Cole has spent several decades trying to combine psychology and anthropology in his own work (1994: 329). Beginning in the 1960s, he and Sylvia Scribner developed extensive experience in cross-cultural psychological testing. In their fieldwork, they repeatedly encountered situations in which the same psychological test produced results that differed between Western and non-Western subjects. Although the scores of the non-Western subjects were generally lower, Cole and Scribner did not conclude that their non-Western subjects were less intelligent. Indeed, they noted that outside the laboratory setting, in the routine contexts of everyday life, their informants' intelligence and full humanity were obvious.

So why do intelligent informants often perform poorly on psychological tests? In the work of the Russian psychologist Lev Vygotsky, Cole and Scribner (1974) found an approach that pointed toward an answer. Vygotsky distinguished between elementary cognitive processes and the higher systems into which these processes are organized. **Elementary cognitive processes** include the ability to make abstractions, to categorize, to reason inferentially, and so forth. All humans without intellectual cognitive impairment are equipped with these abilities. Different cultures, however, organize these elementary processes into different **functional cognitive systems**. Culture also assigns different functional systems to different tasks in different contexts. There are different ways of defining tasks; once tasks are defined, there are different strategies for carrying them out, and routine strategies for carrying out (or refusing to carry out) tasks cannot be separated from the broader cultural and political contexts in which people live. As a result, administering an adequate psychological test starts to look like a nearly impossible task.

**taxonomies**
Hierarchical systems that sort groups of things (taxonomic units) into subgroups (*taxa*) in a way that the subgroups are mutually exclusive. Thus, all subgroups share the defining characteristic of the group but at least one characteristic that makes them exclusive to their subgroup.

**elementary cognitive processes**
Mental tasks common to all humans without intellectual cognitive impairment.

**functional cognitive systems**
Culturally linked sets of cognitive processes that guide perception, conception, reason, and emotion.

## Cognitive Style

Cultures provide people with a range of **cognitive styles** that are appropriate for different cognitive tasks in different contexts. Psychological anthropologists have attempted to compare cognitive styles cross-culturally. Some have argued that the styles of individuals and of groups can be located on a continuum between a **global style** and an **articulated style**. People who use a global style tend to view the world holistically; they first see a bundle of relationships and only later see the bits and pieces that are related. They are said to be *field dependent* because they consider everything in relation to its context. In contrast, people who use an articulated style tend to break up the world into smaller and smaller pieces, which they can then organize into larger chunks. They also tend to see a sharp boundary between their own bodies and the outside world. People using an articulated style are able to consider whatever they happen to be paying attention to apart from its context and so are said to be *field independent* (Cole and Scribner 1974: 82).

Originally, most people in Western societies were thought to be field independent, whereas most people in most non-Western cultures were thought to be field dependent. However, more detailed research shows that these generalizations are misleading. For instance, the preferred cognitive style of an individual often varies from task to task and from context to context. People who use articulated styles for some tasks also use global styles for other tasks. In fact, they may bring a range of different styles to bear on a single task.

**cognitive style**
Recurring patterns of cognitive activity that characterize an individual's perceptual and intellectual activities.

**global style**
A field-dependent way of viewing the world that first sees it as a bundle of relationships and only later sees the bits and pieces involved in these relationships.

**articulated style**
A field-independent way of viewing the world that breaks it up into smaller and smaller pieces, which can then be organized into larger chunks.

Research by Jean Lave and her colleagues (1988) demonstrated that middle-class North Americans are not field independent in all contexts, even when the task involves mathematics, which would seem to be the most field independent of all cognitive activities. Lave and her associates wanted to test the widespread assumption that cognitive style does not vary across contexts. In particular, they wanted to find out whether ordinary people use the same mathematical skills in the supermarket and the kitchen that they use in the classroom. As part of the research, subjects were given a pencil-and-paper math test to determine how well they could solve certain problems in a school-like context. Researchers also observed how the same subjects used mathematics while making buying decisions at the grocery store. Finally, the subjects were presented with paired grocery items and asked to calculate the best buy.

The results were surprising. First, the subjects averaged only 59 per cent correct on the pencil-and-paper test but achieved averages of 98 per cent on the supermarket experiment and 93 per cent on the best-buy experiment. Second, the researchers found that the high scores on the last two experiments were achieved with very little reliance on mathematics taught in school—shoppers were better able to make wise economic decisions using informal calculation strategies. The three most common informal strategies were *inspection* (recognizing that one item was both lower in price and larger in volume), *best-buy calculations* (comparing two quantities and two prices first and choosing the better value), and a *difference strategy* (deciding whether a marginal difference in quantity was worth the marginal difference in price) (Lave 1988: 107ff.).

Lave notes that some psychologists would conclude from these results that there was something primitive or illogical about the informal strategies—and, by extension, about the people who used them (see, e.g., Lave 1988: 79ff., 107ff.). Yet this conclusion is contradicted by the evidence showing that the shoppers' informal strategies were exceptionally accurate. In addition, shoppers did occasionally use formal mathematics as an alternative to the other informal strategies, but they did so only when the numbers for quantity and price were easy to transform into unit–price ratios. This did not happen very often, however, because units and prices in supermarkets are often given in prime numbers, making rapid mental calculation tedious and complicated. Rather than waste time dividing $5.27 by 13 ounces to obtain the price per ounce, the shoppers preferred to rely on other calculation strategies (Figure 5.8).

These observations point to a major difference between 'school' math and 'grocery store' math. In school, the only purpose of a mathematical exercise is to obtain a single correct answer. 'The puzzles or problems are assumed to be objective and factual. . . . Problem solvers have no choice but to try to solve problems, and if they choose not to, or do not find the correct answer, they "fail"' (Lave 1988: 35). Matters are otherwise in the grocery store. Shoppers do not visit supermarkets to practise formal mathematics; they go to buy food. Consequently, the choices they make are influenced not merely by unit–price ratios but by the family's food preferences, the amount of storage space at home, the amount of time they can spend shopping, and so on. In the supermarket, as Lave puts it, '"problems" are dilemmas to be resolved, rarely problems to be solved' (20). Formal mathematical calculations and knowledge of what costs less per unit may help resolve some dilemmas, but in other cases they may be too troublesome to bother with, or even irrelevant. Shoppers, unlike students in the classroom, are free to abandon calculation, to use means other than formal mathematics to resolve a dilemma (58).

One feature all Lave's subjects shared was the knowledge that pencil-and-paper tests in school-like settings required an articulated, field-independent style. In non-Western societies, attending a Western-style school seems to impart the same knowledge to non-Western people. And most subjects who have been educated in the Western system tend to reserve the Western cognitive style for the classroom, preferring a variety of more global strategies to resolve the dilemmas of everyday life. We have seen how some of these dilemmas can be generated by a lack of fit between the background information we take for granted and sensory signals that are ambiguous (e.g., recall Figure 5.5). In any case, our awareness of the cognitive dilemmas we face should make us more sympathetic to cognitive 'errors' we see being made by people from different cultures who may be employing different cognitive styles.

These observations reinforce the conclusion that competent members of all societies employ a range of cognitive styles. We cannot speak of abstract thinking and concrete thinking as mutually exclusive. Anthropologists have found that many non-Western peoples are not used to thinking about things without relating them to some kind of context. Members of those societies can learn to use a context-free cognitive style if they attend school, but this does not mean that they never use abstract categories

*Figure 5.8* | Shoppers often rely on informal mathematical strategies to calculate the best buy because numbers for quantity and price are not often easy to transform into unit–price ratios.

outside the classroom. As Lave's research demonstrates, the full range of her shoppers' calculating skills were displayed only when she studied mathematics in the supermarket rather than in the classroom and became aware of the range of factors in addition to price that influenced buying decisions.

Levinson's research (1998) concludes with the observation that individuals can acquire cognitive styles through social interaction, essentially adopting the *viewpoint* manifest in the interaction. He notes that such viewpoints can be either dependent (relative/flexible) or independent(absolute/fixed): 'A system of fixed orientations is a social fact . . . that is arbitrary . . . whose existence constrains individuals. It can be learned only through communication. To use it requires constant background computations of a specialized sort that members of other communities may not indulge in at all' (20). Thus, cross-cultural research in cognition is a delicate business. For the researcher, the first trick is to devise a test that will give people who use different cognitive styles an opportunity to show what they know and what they can do. The researcher must also discover whether different groups of subjects share the same understanding of tasks they are being asked to perform. In recent years, a number of researchers have worked to develop methods to assess cognition that are not bound to the traditional psychological testing laboratory or to the classroom.

## Reason and the Reasoning Process

In the early days of Europeans' 'discovery' of other societies—and for many years thereafter—a common topic of debate was the extent to which non-literate non-Western peoples might be said to possess reason. In the context of Western colonialism, this debate was rarely disinterested, for Europeans often justified their position of dominance on the grounds that those dominated were irrational. Faced with this problematic history, how might anthropologists study rational thinking?

Most cognitive psychologists have adopted Jerome Bruner's famous definition of **thinking** as 'going beyond the information given'. This distinction suggests that thinking is different from remembering (which refers to information already given) and also from learning (which involves acquiring information that was not given beforehand). Going beyond the information given thus implies a complex interrelationship between information already at hand and the cognitive processes of the person who is attempting to cope with that information. This definition also reminds us of the nature of cognition as the 'nexus of relations between the mind at work and the world in which it works'. Thinking is open and active, and it has no predetermined outcome.

**thinking**
The active cognitive process of 'going beyond the information given'.

**syllogistic reasoning**
A form of reasoning based on the syllogism, a series of three statements in which the first two statements are the premises and the last is the conclusion, which must follow from the premises.

## Culture and Logic

One set of cognitive tests has to do with verbal reasoning ability. These tests present subjects with three statements in the form of a syllogism—for example, 'All men are mortal, Socrates is a man, therefore Socrates is mortal.' The first two propositions are called the *premises*, and the third statement is the *conclusion*. For a syllogism to be sound, the conclusion must follow from the premises.

**Syllogistic reasoning** is enshrined in Western culture as the quintessence of rational thought. In the past, some researchers suggested that the rational capacities of non-Western peoples could be tested using logical problems

*Map 5.2* | **Kpelle**

in syllogistic form. Presumably their rationality would be confirmed if they could deduce correctly when the conclusion followed logically from the premises and when it did not.

Cole and Scribner (1974) presented logical problems involving syllogistic reasoning to their Kpelle subjects in Liberia (see Map 5.2). Typically, the logical problem was embedded in a folktale-like story. The experimenter read the story to the subjects and then asked them a series of follow-up questions designed to reveal whether the subjects could draw a correct conclusion from the premises given.

Here is one story Cole and Scribner prepared: 'At one time Spider went to a feast. He was told to answer this question before he could eat any of the food. The question is: Spider and Black Deer always eat together. Spider is eating. Is Black Deer eating?' (1974: 162). Given the two premises, the conclusion should be that Black Deer is eating. Now consider a typical Kpelle response to hearing this story:

Subject: Were they in the bush?
Experimenter: Yes.
Subject: Were they eating together?
Experimenter: Spider and Black Deer always eat together. Spider is eating. Is Black Deer eating?
Subject: But I was not there. How can I answer such a question?
Experimenter: Can't you answer it? Even if you were not there, you can answer it. (Repeats the question.)

Subject: Oh, oh, Black Deer is eating.

Experimenter: What is your reason for saying that Black Deer was eating?

Subject: The reason is that Black Deer always walks about all day eating green leaves in the bush. Then he rests for a while and gets up again to eat. (162)

The subject's answer to the question and subsequent justification for that answer seem to have nothing whatsoever to do with the logical problem the subject is being asked to solve.

The experimenters devised this story the same way schoolteachers devise mathematical word problems. That is, the contextual material is nothing more than a kind of window dressing. Schoolchildren quickly learn to disregard the window dressing and seek out the mathematical problem it hides. In the research setting, Cole and Scribner expected the Kpelle subjects to act in a similar way and disregard the contextual material about the feast and seeking out the syllogism embedded within it. However, Kpelle subjects did not understand that they were being read this story in a test situation for which considerations of context or meaningfulness were irrelevant. In the example transcribed above, the subject seemed to have difficulty separating the logical problem both from the introductory material about the feast and from the rest of his experiential knowledge.

Cole and Scribner interpreted their subject's response to this problem as being due not to irrationality but to a 'failure to accept the logical task' (162). In a follow-up study, Cole and Scribner discovered that Kpelle high-school children responded 'correctly' to the logical problems 90 per cent of the time. This finding suggests a strong correlation between Western-style schooling and a willingness to accept context-free analytic tasks in testing situations (164).

But this is not all. David Lancy, one of Cole and Scribner's colleagues, discovered that Western-style syllogisms are very similar to certain forms of Kpelle riddles. Unlike syllogisms, however, those riddles have no single 'logically correct' answer. 'Rather, as the riddle is posed to a group, the right answer is the one among many offered that seems most illuminating, resourceful, and convincing as determined by consensus and circumstance. This emphasis on edification as a criterion for "rightness" is found in Kpelle jurisprudence as well' (Lancy, cited in Fernandez 1980: 47–8). In other words, the 'right' answer cannot be extracted from the form of the riddle by logical operations. Rather, it is the answer that seems most enlightening and informative to the particular audience in the particular setting where the riddle is posed. This approach to identifying the correct answer also reinforces the concept of consensus—inclusion of all in the process—thus making problem solving a group activity.

There is no question that all humans come equipped with the same elementary cognitive processes: the ability to make abstractions, the ability to create conceptual categories, and the ability to reason inferentially. The difficulty is to understand how these elementary cognitive processes are put to work within culturally shared schemas to produce different, functional cognitive systems known as **reasoning styles**.

**reasoning style**
How we understand a cognitive task, how we encode the information presented to us, and what transformations the information undergoes as we think. Reasoning styles differ from culture to culture and from context to context within the same culture.

## Emotion

Psychological anthropologists who try to define emotion in cross-cultural terms run into a familiar problem: they discover that not all languages possess a term that might be translated as *emotion*. To get out of this tangle, they have tried to develop a theory of cognitive functioning that accounts for the experiences that some cultures recognize as emotional.

We return to Western dualism where reason and thought are associated with the mind and emotion with the body. Any attempt to explain emotion must deal with the nature of the bodily arousal we associate with it. But there is more to emotion, as we commonly understand it, than mere bodily arousal. Recall the butcher knife scenario referred to near the beginning of this chapter. What do we feel when we see a butcher knife sitting beside mushrooms on a cutting board in our kitchen? What do we feel when we see that same knife in the hands of an intruder bent on attacking us? The knife alone does not trigger our feeling. The *context* in which

110   *Part II* | The Resources of Culture
**emotion**
The product of a dialectic between bodily arousal and cognitive interpretation. It comprises states, values, and arousals.

we encounter the knife is equally important. The context itself can be ambiguous, and our emotional experience changes as our interpretation of the context changes.

Emotion engages both bodily arousal and cognitive interpretation. Cognitive psychologist George Mandler suggests that bodily arousal can trigger an emotional experience by attracting our attention and prompting us to seek the source of arousal (Mandler 1975: 97). Conversely, a particular interpretation of our experience can trigger bodily arousal. Arousal may heighten or diminish depending on how we interpret what is happening around us.

Mandler describes emotions as *functional systems* in much the same way that Cole and Scribner described cognition in terms of functional systems. Each emotion links elementary processes that involve the body's arousal system to other elementary processes that play a role in the construction of perception, conception, and reasoning. 'Emotions are not something that people "have"; they are constituted of people's states, values, and arousals' (Mandler 1983: 151). Approaching emotion from this perspective accomplishes three things:

1) it integrates mind and body in a holistic fashion;
2) it acknowledges ambiguity as a central feature of emotional experience (recall that ambiguity is also central to linguistic, perceptual, and conceptual experience); and
3) it suggests how different cultural interpretive frameworks might shape not only what we think but also what we feel.

Therefore, we can understand **emotion** as the product of a dialectic between bodily arousal and cognitive interpretation.

Why should we experience emotion at all? The role of emotion in human life may be rooted in our evolutionary history. Bodily arousal alerts us to something new and unexpected in our environment, something that does not easily fit into any conventional schema. Once our attention is caught in this way, the rest of our cognitive processes can focus on the interrupting

phenomenon and decide how we should react to it. From this perspective, a person would be foolish to ignore his or her 'gut feelings' when trying to sort out a confusing experience. Indeed, 'gut feelings' are usually what alert us to confusion in the first place. Our emotions help us engage with the world to develop a full understanding of a situation. Mandler notes, 'Just telling people what a situation is going to be like isn't enough, and it isn't good enough training when you encounter the real situation' (1983: 152). Generations of new spouses, new parents, and anthropological fieldworkers can testify to the overwhelming truth of this statement (Figure 5.9).

In sum, we experience bodily arousal when our familiar world is somehow interrupted. Such arousal may either fade away or develop into an emotional experience depending on the meaning we assign to it. Possible meanings arise out of cultural interpretations of recurring experiential schemas. We should not be surprised

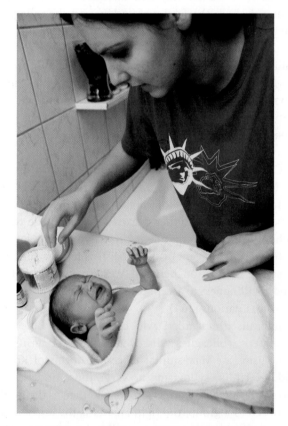

*Figure 5.9* | **New parents must learn through whole-body experience how to care for their newborns.**

to find some overlap in the categories of feeling recognized by different cultures. After all, certain experiential schemas that interrupt the familiar world—birth and death, for example—are human universals. At the same time, the wider cultural context will, in each case, modify the perspective from which such experiences are understood and, thus, the categories of feeling associated with them.

### Emotion in an Eastern African Culture

David Parkin (1984) has studied the cultural construction of emotion among the Giriama of coastal Kenya (see Map 5.3). Their theory of human nature does not recognize a mind–body dualism of the Western sort. They are unwilling to set up sharp, mutually exclusive oppositions of any kind when discussing human nature. Therefore such behaviour as spirit possession, madness, hysteria, witchcraft, persistent violence, drunkenness, and thieving are explained

> as the result of what we might call imbalances in human nature. . . . [They] do not believe that a person can be intrinsically or irredeemably evil: at some stage, usually remarkably quickly, he will be brought back into the fold, even if he subsequently leaves it again. A large number of terms, roughly translatable as greed, lust, envy, jealousy, malice, resentment, anger, are used to refer to these imbalances of character and the accompanying behaviour. (Parkin 1984: 14)

**Map 5.3 | Giriama**

As with Westerners, the Giriama associate different feelings with different parts of the body. In the West, people conventionally connect the brain with reason and the heart with emotion. For the Giriama, however, the heart, liver, kidneys, and eyes are the seat of reason and emotion. They may distinguish thinking from feeling in discussing the actual behaviour of real people, but they nevertheless presume a common origin for both (17). What about particular emotions? Although the categories of feeling recognized by the Giriama overlap in some respects with the experiences labelled by English terms for emotions, Parkin suggests that there are important differences that stem from the nature of recognized Giriama schemas and from the prototypical thoughts and feelings that are appropriate to those schemas. Consider the term *utsungu*:

> *Utsungu* means poison, bitterness, resentment, and anger, on the one hand, but also grief on the other. It is the feeling experienced at a funeral of a loved or respected relative or friend. A man or woman is grieved at the loss but also bitter that it has happened at all, and angry with the witch who caused the death. Since the witch will be made to pay, the sentiment carried with it both the consequences of the loss of a dear one and the intention to avenge his or her death. (118)

In Western societies, people also feel 'grief' at the death of a loved one. But the prototypical Western experience of grief does not contain the additional meaning involving anger at witchcraft and the desire for vengeance. Perhaps one would have to be a Giriama—or have lived in another culture in which witchcraft was understood as the usual cause of death and in which such wrongful death could be avenged—to experience the emotional configuration that Parkin describes.

# Motivation

Perception and cognition are psychological processes that acquaint us with the inner and outer 'worlds' of our experiences and assist us in making sense of those worlds. But human life involves activity, agency: we set goals and pursue the means to achieve them. Even when those goals and means are culturally prescribed, we have to be induced to accept them as valid and to pursue them. Anthropological approaches to **motivation** have always embedded the sources of motivation within a cultural matrix. In the early years of the discipline, when Freudian theory was influential, many psychological anthropologists accepted Freud's idea that all human beings were motivated to seek pleasure in a world that frequently made that goal unattainable. Freud spoke of two basic kinds of 'instincts', the erotic and the aggressive, which were present in all human beings. Unregulated pursuit of satisfaction of these instincts would lead to social chaos. Thus, culture entered the picture as a set of humanly invented arrangements that allowed these otherwise destructive instincts to be curbed or channelled into socially useful activities (Bock 1994: xii).

However, many anthropologists have found speaking of 'instinct' to be unhelpful, particularly when the culturally defined goals of different societies seem so different from one another that tying these goals to the same instinct is implausible. In the 1930s, Ruth Benedict argued that each culture had its own set of motives, its own models of ideal behaviour, which members of a particular society adopted and which motivated them to pursue some kinds of behaviours rather than others. Anthropologists have focussed on how people interact with one another and how they talk about those interactions, in an attempt to uncover the local 'ethnopsychology of motives' (Bock 1994: xii–xiii). As Catherine Lutz's (1988) study demonstrates, achieving this goal, in turn, requires anthropologists to pay close attention to the social and cultural contexts in which individuals learn to interact with other members of their society, learn to understand the local discourse about vice and virtue, and come to terms with local practices and values when attempting to exercise their own agency. That is, anthropologists can uncover the mainsprings of motivation by studying socialization and enculturation.

**motivation**
The inner impulse to set (or accept) and accomplish goals.

**socialization**
The process by which human beings learn to become members of a group, both by interacting appropriately with others and by coping with the behavioural rules established by the group.

**enculturation**
The process by which human beings living with one another must learn to come to terms with the ways of thinking and feeling that are considered appropriate in their respective cultures.

## Socialization and Enculturation

Children use their own bodies and brains to explore their world, but other people actively steer their activity and attention in particular directions. Consequently, their exploration of the world is not merely trial and error: the path is cleared by others who shape their experiences—and their interpretations of their experiences—for them.

Two terms in the social sciences refer to this process of culturally and socially shaped cognitive development: **socialization** and **enculturation**. Becoming human involves both these processes, for children learn how to act, think, feel, and speak at the same time as they participate in the joint activities carried out by social groups to which they belong. These two processes are closely related; thus, cultural anthropologists recognize that the study of one is intimately connected to the study of the other.

Anthropologists seek a theory of cognitive development that is holistic; therefore, many have been attracted to the ideas of George Herbert Mead (1863–1931) and, more recently, to the work of Lev Vygotsky (1896–1934). For Mead and Vygotsky alike, human life is social from the outset. As Vygotsky wrote, 'The social dimension of consciousness is primary in time and in fact. The individual dimension of consciousness is derivative and secondary' (1978: 30). Like Vygotsky, Mead (1934) believed that human nature is completed and enhanced, not curtailed or damaged, by socialization and enculturation. Indeed, the successful humanization of human beings lies in people's mastery of symbols, which begins when children start to learn language. As children come to control the symbolic systems of their cultures, they gain the ability to distinguish objects and relationships in the world and come to see themselves as objects as well as subjects. Mead focussed primarily on face-to-face interaction. However, Vygotsky, in an attempt to be compatible with a Marxian analysis of society, was more interested in the wider social, cultural, and historical context in which face-to-face interaction is embedded. This awareness of context makes Vygotsky's work particularly appealing to anthropologists.

As we suggested earlier in this chapter, Vygotsky's theoretical distinction between elementary cognitive processes and functional cognitive systems is useful in anthropology because it provides a way of describing the similarities and differences observed when we compare how people from different cultures think and feel. These differences have implications for cognitive development as well. The functional systems employed by adult members of society must be acquired during childhood. For Vygotsky, acquisition takes place in a context of face-to-face interactions between, typically, a child and an adult. When children learn about the world in such a context, they are not working on their own to create an entirely new system of understanding; on the contrary, they are learning from another person the symbolic forms (usually language) that others use to represent the world.

This learning process creates in the child a new plane of consciousness resting on the dialogue-based, question-and-answer format of social interaction. From this, Vygotsky inferred that our internal thought processes would also take the format of a dialogue. Mead suggested something similar when he spoke of every person as being able to carry on internal conversations between the *I* (the unsocialized self) and the *me* (the socially conditioned self). Only on this basis can an individual's sense of identity develop as the self comes to distinguish itself from the conversational other.

Vygotsky also developed the related concept of the *zone of proximal development*, which is the distance between a child's 'actual development level as determined by independent problem solving' and the level of 'potential development as determined through problem solving under adult guidance or in collaboration with more capable peers' (Vygotsky 1978: 86). Psychologists everywhere have long been aware that children can often achieve more when they are coached than when they work alone. Western psychologists with individualist biases have viewed this difference in achievement as contamination of the testing situation or as the result of cheating. Vygotsky and his followers, however, see it as an indispensable measure of potential growth that simultaneously demonstrates how growth is rooted in social interaction, especially in educational settings (Moll 1990). The concept of the zone of proximal development enables anthropologists and comparative psychologists to link cognitive development to society, culture, and history because practices of coaching or formal instruction are shaped by social, cultural, and historical factors (Figure 5.10). To the extent that these factors can vary, we can expect cognitive development to vary as well.

## Is Cognitive Development the Same for Everyone?

Most theories, including Mead's, portray cognitive development as a progression through a series of stages. With the exception of Vygotsky's theory, these theories ordinarily assume that the stages are the same for all human beings or at least all human beings in a particular society. A Vygotskian perspective helps us explain not only cross-cultural differences in development but also differences in the cognitive development of different subgroups in a single society.

Consider the following illustrative example. In Cuba, a team of researchers followed a sample of 4,299

*Figure 5.10* | A Japanese woman and child at the Sanja festival in Tokyo, Japan. Practices of coaching or formal instruction are shaped by social, cultural, and historical factors.

children from their birth in 1973 through the late 1980s, periodically collecting information on each child's cognitive, social, economic, physical, and academic development (Gutierrez Muñiz, Hurtado, and Beatón 1997). The researchers identified a series of correlations between levels of education, wage employment, living standards, and health of mothers and levels of development and achievement of the children. Put in Vygotskian terms, the data show that the zone of proximal development is greater for children of mothers with higher levels of education and participation in the paid workforce than it is for children of mothers with lower educational levels who do not work outside the home. These findings contradicted popular beliefs that the children of educated working mothers would suffer as a result of their mothers' activities (Beatón, personal communication).

Carol Gilligan's (1982) comparative study on the moral development of women and men in North American society offers another example. Gilligan argues that middle-class boys and girls begin their moral development in different socio-cultural contexts. Boys are encouraged from an early age to break away from their mothers and families and make it on their own. In this context, they learn that independence is good, that dependency is weakness, and that their first duty is to themselves and what they stand for. In contrast, girls mature in a socio-cultural context in which their bond to their mothers and families is never sharply ruptured. They learn that connection to others is good, that the destruction of relationships is damaging, and that their first responsibility in any difficult situation is to ensure that nobody gets hurt.

Gilligan did not adopt a Vygotskian perspective in this study, although she was influenced by Mead. But the Vygotskian concept of the zone of proximal development provides a useful tool for describing how the differential moral development of boys and girls is accomplished. In Vygotskian terms, the moral development of boys and girls proceeds in different directions because boys and girls are coached differently by more mature members of society. That is, when faced with the same dilemmas but unsure of how to act, boys are encouraged to make one set of choices, girls another. In this way, each gender category builds up a different set of schemas as to what constitutes the 'good'. As a result, North American men and women consistently see one another acting immorally. For example, when men and boys try to be true to themselves and strike out on their own, women and girls may condemn such action as being highly destructive to personal relationships. When women and girls try to encourage intimacy and closeness, men and boys may view such ties as confining and repressive.

Like Vygotsky, Gilligan situates the development of moral reasoning in socio-cultural and historical contexts. She argues that men are able to present their moral perspective as universally correct because men as a group hold power over women as a group in North American society. As women continue to gain social power and status, however, their 'different voice' may acquire ever more legitimacy, and the culturally embedded paths of moral development may themselves eventually be altered.

# Personality/Self/Subjectivity

Socialization and enculturation produce a **self** capable of functioning successfully in society. But what sort of entity is a self? Many Western psychologists have assumed that the mature self was a bounded, independent, self-contained entity with a clear and non-contradictory sense of identity that persisted through time. Anthropologists working in other societies, however, often found that the development of such an independent self was not always the goal of socialization and enculturation. On the contrary, socialization and enculturation were often designed to shape selves that did *not* think of themselves as independent and self-sufficient; the mature individual was one motivated to look out for others and work for the well-being of the family or the lineage rather than in pursuit of his or her own individual self-interest.

Early psychological anthropologists often spoke of individual **personality** rather than the self; this is seen in the name adopted by the early *culture and personality school* of the mid-twentieth century. Bock points out that in such formulations,

**self**
The result of the process of socialization and enculturation for an individual.

**personality**
'The relative integration of an individual's perceptions, motives, cognitions, and behaviour within a socio-cultural matrix.'

personality involves the relative *integration* of an individual's perceptions, motives, cognitions, and behaviour within a socio-cultural matrix (the subjective view of this unity is more often referred to as the *self*). The importance of consistent social feedback to individual functioning has been demonstrated. . . . Personality is thus revealed as part of a dynamic interactive system between a human organism and its physical–social environment. (1994: xiv)

Many psychological anthropologists, including Bock himself, have argued that an individual's personality, understood in this way, is not merely a reflection of a culturally ideal type, but is regularly shaped by 'quasi-universal' factors such as 'the individual's position in the social structure, including his or her social class, gender, occupational role, and even birth order' (xiv).

The notion of an integrated personality, or self, harks back to Enlightenment ideas; as a result, it is hardly surprising that the postmodern critique of Enlightenment ideas questioned the existence of integrated, harmonious personalities or selves. Postmodern thinkers began to see the integrated self as an illusion or an effect of powerful political ideologies that worked to mask the heterogeneity and contradictory features of individual experience. Thus they began to pay attention to the different dimensions of one's personality or self that were activated (or de-activated) in different contexts, and people began to speak of 'decentred' selves as the norm rather than the exception. Contemporary scholars in many fields continue to disagree about the extent to which anyone's self is integrated or coherent, and few anthropologists would defend an unreflective Enlightenment view of the self. Psychological anthropologists have shifted away from any attempt to relate an individual's behaviour to internal experiences of the self. Instead, they examine social discourse about people's behaviour, arguing that 'culture is (largely) created by people in the discourse justifying their behaviour as rational and moral' (Bock 1994: xv). But anthropologists who recognize the uneven and contradictory features of individual self-experience also often draw attention to the attempts individuals make. In the most difficult or bewildering situations in a disorderly world, and even if our understandings are inevitably imperfect and partial, we struggle to find patterns and strive to achieve ordered, coherent understandings of the world and of ourselves.

Many psychological anthropologists and others have come to speak not of individual personality or individual self but of individual **subjectivity**, which has been described as 'the felt interior experience of the person that includes his or her positions in a field of relational power' (Das and Kleinman 2000: 1). To think of individuals as *subjects* has much to recommend it in a postmodern climate. It points to individual agency with each of us as the initiating subject of our actions. However, individual agency is not absolute since our agency is circumscribed by various limitations that result from the deployment of social, economic, and political power in the societies in which we live. These limitations may be greater or lesser, depending on social variables such as class, gender, occupation, or birth order. That is, we are *subject to* the workings of institutionalized power in the various *subject positions* we occupy. Our subject positions are formed in and through our cultural context; consequently, they reflect certain social, economic, and political circumstances, both past and present. The fact that all people in all societies occupy a variety of different subject positions reflects our 'decentred' selves: a particular individual may, in different contexts, be positioned in terms of gender, ethnicity, occupation, class, or some combination of these positions. At the same time, however, all of us can potentially play the insights gained from each subject position against the others and thus gain a measure of reflexive awareness and understanding of our own situations.

**subjectivity**
An individual's awareness of his or her own agency and position as a subject.

**gender roles**
Sets of behaviours that are commonly perceived as masculine or feminine within a specific culture.

## Subject Positions of Sexuality and Gender

In many ways, our subject positions are shaped by our sexual orientation and our adoption of a **gender role** or roles (see, e.g., Peletz 2006). Many people live in cultural realities that separate the worlds of men and women from each other. Some of these separations can be seen in differential rules on the use of public space, conventions of dress, and definitions of maleness and femaleness. As Alice Schlegel comments, gender definitions are concerned with the 'ways members of the two sexes are perceived, evaluated, and expected to behave' (1990: 23).

Before we proceed, we must differentiate among three terms that are fundamental to our discussion: **sex**, **gender**, and **sexuality**. In short, sex is biology, gender is role, and sexuality is orientation or preference and the state of being sexual. Fundamentally, our sex, sexuality, and gender role identities form essential subject positions, sorting each of us into categories—and often hierarchies—defined by our cultures. Kulick (2000: 243) suggests that such sorting is not an inconsequential matter. For example, consider the openness of the identity categories suggested by the acronym LGBTQ (lesbian, gay, bisexual, transgender, queer or questioning), which is now commonly used by sexual and gender-rights activists to draw attention to 'less traditional' gender identities. Indeed, the range of sexual behaviours and identities found within and between cultures makes us question how definitive any categorizations of sex or gender can be.

Biological determiners of sex may not always be obvious, and physical sex differences do not always help us to predict the roles than an individual will play in any particular society. For example, sometimes genetic or hormonal factors produce ambiguous external genitalia, a phenomenon called *hermaphroditism*. Steroid 5-alpha-reductase deficiency (5ARD), a rare hormonal condition, is an example where genetic males are born with ambigious genitalia and at puberty display male morphological changes. Herdt (1994) investigated 5ARD in the Dominican Republic and New Guinea. In both places, the sexually anomalous individuals were assigned to a locally recognized third sex called *guevedoche* ('testicles at twelve') in the Dominican Republic and *kwolu-aatmwol* ('changing into a male thing') among the Sambia of New Guinea. (Jeffrey Eugenides' 2002 Pulitzer Prize–winning *Middlesex* is a fictionalized representation of the author's own struggle with sexual identity as a 5ARD intersexed person.)

The existence of *supernumerary*—that is, more than two sexes and/or gender pluralism/transgenderism (Peletz 2006)—in cultures where the presence of ambiguous genitalia at birth seems to play no obvious role has been documented. In the Byzantine civilization of late antiquity, phenotypic differences were deliberately created in the case of eunuchs, whose testicles were removed or destroyed, often before puberty (Ringrose 1994). With the *hijras* of Gujarat, India, adult males deliberately cut off both penis and testicles in order to dedicate themselves to the mother goddess Bahuchara Mata (Nanda 1994; Figure 5.11). In both cases, members of the wider society understand these third gender roles to be distinct from feminine and masculine gender roles.

Perhaps the most famous example of supernumerary without morphological sex anomalies is that of the so-called berdache. Roscoe points out that the role can be marked by cross-dressing (1994: 332). Individuals in such a role are accepted and respected members of their communities, and their economic and religious

**sex**
The biological distinction between male and female based on *morphological sex* (the appearance of external genitalia and observable secondary sex characteristics), *gonadal sex* (ovaries in females; testes in males), and chromosomal sex (♀ XX chromosomes; ♂ XY chromosomes).

**gender**
The cultural constructions of beliefs and behaviours considered appropriate for each sex.

**sexuality**
An individual's sense of his or her own sexual orientation and preferences.

*Figure 5.11* | In hijra communities, third gender roles—distinct from traditional masculine and feminine gender roles—are considered appropriate for third-sexed individuals. Above, a hijra onlooker watches another hijra apply makeup.

pursuits frequently are culturally more significant than their sexual practices:

> the key features of male and female berdache roles were, in order of importance, *productive specialization* (crafts and domestic work for male berdaches; and warfare, hunting, and leadership roles in the case of female berdaches), *supernatural sanction* (in the form of an authorization and/or bestowal of powers from extra-societal sources), and *gender variation* (in relation to normative cultural expectations for male and female genders) (332)

Early French explorers in the Americas used *berdache* to mean 'male prostitute'. Thus many contemporary anthropologists refuse to use the term, as do those members of contemporary Indigenous societies who want to reclaim this alternative gender role for their cultures. No single term, however, has yet reached universal acceptance, although *two spirit* has been gaining support. Perhaps no single term is adequate; after all, two-spirited males have been described in almost 150 Indigenous North American societies and two-spirited females in perhaps half that number. For a deeper understanding, see the work of Goulet (1996), who discusses personhood and gender, arguing that 'anthropologists have conceptualized gender variance among Native North Americans without paying attention to the ways in which Indigenous practices "construct members of a community 'as' woman or 'as' man (or member of other gender category)"' (683).

In Canada, sex and gender have been topics of public discussion only in relatively recent years. Even today, little of this public discourse focusses on intersexuality (biological manifestation of male and/or female physical characteristics in one individual) or the transgendered (any person whose internal gender identity differs from that suggested by their physiology). Indeed, most Canadians still hold to the traditional view that the existence of only two sexes, each with its own gender role, is both natural and obvious. Yet Laqueur (1990) has shown that the 'two-sex model' only took root after the Renaissance. Prior to that, the bodies of all human beings were evaluated in terms of a 'one-sex model' based on the Platonic notion that there

was one ideal human form, which all actual human beings embodied to greater or lesser degrees. Moreover, as Roscoe points out, 'the presence of multiple genders does not require belief in the existence of three or more physical sexes but, minimally, a view of physical differences as unfixed, or insufficient on their own to establish gender, or simply less important than individual and social factors' (1994: 342). These observations sustain Collier and Yanagisako's key assertion: 'there are no "facts", biological or material, that have social consequences and cultural meanings in and of themselves' (1987: 39).

## Sexual Practices

The range of sexual practice in the world is vast. So too in our culture, as evidenced some years ago in the *Kinsey Reports* (1948 on males and 1953 on females) and more recently in various large-scale studies on sexuality. Indeed, contemporary anthropologists recognize that sexual intercourse is an essential part of social behaviour and that a desire for sex is a strong motivation in most individuals. As such, they have made observations on how sexual practices, as situated within the sexual norms of a culture, influence an individual's identity and social position. Here, we will examine some of those observations.

Some cultures take a relatively open approach to sexuality, and the sexual desires of women and men are equally recognized. For example, consider the Ju/'hoansi, who begin sexual activity at an early age. As a result of this early sexual openness, the social and sexual constraints of marriage represent quite a shock at first, especially for young women. Some Ju/'hoansi are strictly faithful to one another, but a significant minority take lovers. The Ju/'hoansi have no double standard; both men and women are free to take lovers, and women are sometimes eloquent about the time they spend with lovers. However, discretion is necessary when taking a lover because both husbands and wives can become very jealous and start fights. Sexual satisfaction is important to the Ju/'hoansi; female orgasm is known, and women expect both husbands and lovers to satisfy them sexually. Yet not all societies are as accepting of female expressions of sexuality. For the Mundurucu of the Brazilian Amazon, female orgasm is more accidental than expected (Murphy and Murphy 1974). Many societies require a woman's virginity at marriage; in some Arab societies, a couple must produce bloodstained sheets the morning after the consummation of their marriage to demonstrate that the bride was a virgin.

Many cultures place taboos on certain sexual activity, and individuals are expected to respect these taboos. For example, Karl Heider (1979) observed a strict postpartum sex taboo among the Dani, a people of highland New Guinea (see Map 11.8). For five years after the birth of a child, Dani parents do not have sexual intercourse with each other. Such taboos are found in all cultures, but they generally last for only a few weeks or months. (In North America, we say that the mother needs time to heal; other societies have other justifications.) Yet to most Westerners, the Dani's five-year wait would seem to be exceptional. What could explain this difference in opinion? Heider points out that Westerners assume that the sex drive is perhaps the most powerful biological drive of all; the Dani do not share this assumption. The Dani are not celibate, and they certainly have sexual intercourse often enough to reproduce biologically, yet they do not seem very interested in sex (78–81). It seems that the Dani represent an extreme in the cultural construction of sexuality.

Of course, not all sexual practices map onto the Western heterosexual model. Indeed, the fact that people in almost every society have developed complex ideological and ritual structures to encourage heterosexual practices, ostensibly to promote procreation, suggests that human sexual expression would resist such confinement if it were not under strict control. As we mentioned in our previous discussion, anthropological information about supernumerary sexes and genders undermines the 'two-sex model' that is hegemonic in Euro-American cultures. Anthropologists Blackwood and Wieringa have similarly undermined Western heterosexual assumptions in their exploration of how culture shapes female desires. These researchers concluded that focussing on the ways that female bodies are assigned cultural meanings in different historical and ethnographic settings, and on how those meanings affect the way females constitute their relations with other females, reveals a wide range of 'varied and rich cultural identities and same-sex practices between those with female bodies' (1999: ix). Significantly, they note that this sort of research does not assume that having a male body or a female body necessarily determines any individual's traits, feelings, or experiences (x). As a result, it provides a vital comparative context that can illuminate our understanding of sexual practices that Euro-Americans call *homosexuality* and *bisexuality*.

Consider the Nicaraguan concept of *cochónes* within the greater social construct of *machismo* (aggressive masculinity). As anthropologist Roger Lancaster learned while he was doing fieldwork in Nicaragua in the 1980s, working-class Nicaraguans admire *machistas*—'real men' who are active, violent, and dominant. They see the penis as a weapon that can dominate a sexual partner—male or female—who is thereby rendered passive, abused, and subordinate. A 'passive' male who allows a 'manly man' to have sexual intercourse with him is called a *cochón*. Thus the identity and social position of a *cochón* differs greatly from that of a man who is perceived as sexually dominant. While the 'passive' *cochón* is stigmatized, the male who takes the 'active' role in sexual intercourse with other males and with females is seen as 'normal'. These distinctions pervade social interactions, as public challenges for dominance are a constant of male–male interaction in Nicaragua, even when sexual intercourse is not involved. *Cochón* may be used as an epithet not only for a man who yields publicly to another man but also for cats that don't catch mice or indeed anything that somehow fails to perform its

*Map 5.4* | **Dani**

proper function. As Lancaster notes, *cochónes* are made, not born:

> Those who consistently lose out in the competition for male status . . . discover pleasure in the passive sexual role or its social status: these men are made into *cochónes*. And those who master the rules of conventional masculinity . . . are made into *machistas* (1992: 249).

As with the gender roles we recognize in Western cultures, the position of the *cochón* is a social construct. Ideas about sexuality and gender created an unanticipated roadblock for the Sandinista government that passed a series of 'new family laws' in the 1980s designed to discourage irresponsible sex, inappropriate parenting, and familial dislocation while encouraging men to support their families economically. But Lancaster repeatedly got the following: 'First the interrogative: "What do the Sandinistas want from us? That we should all become *cochónes*?" And then the tautological: "A man has to be a man." That is, a man is defined by what he is not—a *cochón*' (1992: 274).

The examples we have discussed in this section reveal that the physical activity we call *sexual intercourse* is not just doing what comes naturally. Like many things in human life, sex does not speak for itself nor does it have only one meaning. Sexual practices can be used to give concrete form to more abstract notions we have about the place of men and women in the world. They may serve as a metaphor for expressing differential power within a society. That is, sexual practices can be used as an excuse to enact, in unmistakable physical terms, the reality of differential power. As anthropologists, we must remember that sexual practices never occur in a vacuum. They are entrenched in other social practices such as food production, political organization, legal protection, and kinship, all of which act to shape who we are, how we see ourselves, and how we are perceived by others.

## Structural Violence and Social Trauma

Earlier in this chapter, we noted that individual subjectivity and identity are heavily influenced by the forces of socialization and enculturation. But social and cultural

expectations are sometimes overturned by experiences that intrude on predictable daily routines, and these experiences, too, will shape individuals' subjectivities. Among the most powerfully intrusive experiences are those occasioned by **structural violence** and **trauma**, both social and individual.

**structural violence**
Violence that results from the way that political and economic forces structure risk for various forms of suffering within a population.

**social trauma**
Individual and group experience of negative physical, mental, and emotional effects resulting from powerfully disturbing occurrences caused by forces and agents external to the person or group,. Social trauma is commonly the result of armed conflict or war, widespread drought and famine, and/or an epidemic.

As you read through the following examples, consider your responses to such violence and trauma, and keep in mind Susan Sontag's observation on the role of compassion in our 'society of spectacle': 'Compassion is an unstable emotion. It needs to be translated into action, or it withers' (2003: 101).

Paul Farmer is an anthropologist and medical doctor who has worked in Haiti since 1983 (see Map 5.5; Figure 5.12). In his position, he has witnessed extreme forms of human suffering that are part and parcel of everyday life for those at the bottom of Haitian society. Much of this suffering is in the form of infectious and parasitic disease, but it can also include other forms of extreme suffering such as hunger, torture, and rape (Farmer 2002 [1996]: 424). In Haiti, the operations of structural violence create circumscribed spaces in

*Map 5.5 | Haiti*

***Figure 5.12* | Dr Paul Farmer treats a patient at Clinique Bon Sauveur in Haiti.**

which the poorest and least powerful members of society are subjected to highly intensified risks of all kinds, increasing the likelihood that sooner or later they will experience one or more varieties of social suffering. The structural aspect of this violence is important to emphasize since the attention of most Western outside observers, even those who want to alleviate suffering, is often trained on individuals and their personal experiences, with the resulting temptation to blame the victims for their own distress.

Farmer relates the story of a Haitian woman, Acéphie Joseph, who died of AIDS in 1991, when she was 25. Acéphie's parents had been prosperous peasant farmers selling produce in village markets until 1956, when the fertile valley in which they lived was flooded after officials built a dam to generate electricity. They lost everything and became 'water refugees' forced to try to grow crops on an infertile plot in the village where they were resettled. Acéphie and her twin brother were born in the village and attended primary school there. Farmer writes that Acéphie's 'beauty and her vulnerability may have sealed her fate as early as 1984' (426). She began to help her mother carry produce to the market along a road that went past the local military barracks, where soldiers liked to flirt with the passing women, and one soldier in particular approached her. 'Such flirtation is seldom unwelcome, at least to all appearances. In rural Haiti, entrenched poverty made the soldiers—the region's only salaried men—ever so much more attractive' (427). Although Acéphie knew that the soldier had a wife and children, she nevertheless did not rebuff him; indeed,

he visited her family, who approved of their liaison. '"I could tell that the old people were uncomfortable, but they didn't say no . . . I never dreamed he would give me a bad illness . . . it was a way out, that's how I saw it"', Acéphie explained. Only a few weeks after the beginning of their sexual relationship, the soldier died, and Acéphie sought training as a cook in order to qualify for work as a servant in the city, for she had no other viable alternative. Eventually she found work as a maid and began a relationship with a young man, who drove a bus, whom she planned to marry. After three years as a maid, Acéphie became pregnant; she went home to her village to give birth, but she had a very difficult delivery. When she finally sought medical help for a series of infections, she was diagnosed with AIDS. Following her death, her father hanged himself.

Acéphie was an individual, and so it is natural to ask how representative her experiences might be. Farmer's work with many poor women with AIDS allowed him to recognize that all of their cases, including Acéphie's, showed 'a deadly monotony'. The women he interviewed 'were straightforward about the non-voluntary aspect of their sexual activity'. They had been driven to it by poverty (431). Farmer concludes, the agony of Acéphie was, in a sense, 'modal' suffering. In Haiti, AIDS is a leading cause of death among young adults (431). And all this suffering and death is the outcome of structural violence; all the key events that contributed to Acéphie's death were the consequences of human agency that, in turn, severely circumscribed her agency no matter what she did. Farmer identifies specifically the relations of power in which Acéphie was embedded, for these contributed to the likelihood that her suffering and death would take the forms it took. For example, 'gender helps explain why Acéphie died of AIDS'(433). Race or ethnicity helps explain why illness is more likely to be suffered by the descendants of enslaved Africans, and social class helps explain why they were more likely to be poor. Acéphie was 'at risk' of such a fate long before she met the soldier who altered her destiny. She was, from the outset, a victim of structural violence. (431)

Anthropologists are also interested in identifying the causes and effects of large-scale, collective violence. After all, incidents of warfare, genocide, ethnic cleansing, mass rape, and other such forms of mass violence were distinctive features of the twentieth century, leading to widespread death, the disruption of social institutions, the destruction of economic and political arrangements, and the displacement of surviving populations into unfamiliar and often hostile new settings. Hayden (2000), who investigates occurrences of mass rape in times of ethnic or nationalist conflicts, argues that mass rape is likely when the state itself is liminal, with both its territory and its governance uncertain. However, when the state is not itself threatened, there is some evidence that rape is avoided, even when murder is accepted. In approaching such topics, some have chosen to speak in terms of social trauma: 'events in life generated by forces and agents external to the person and largely external to his or her control and . . . generated in the setting of armed conflict and war', including such phenomena as 'separation and loss, imprisonment and exile, threats of annihilation, even death and mutilation' (Apfel and Simon 2000: 103). Apfel and Simon distinguish these sorts of experiences from the less devastating 'ordinary traumas' or 'necessary losses' that all people are likely to face, 'such as the birth of a sibling, natural death of a parent or sibling, divorce, illnesses, and accidents, whether man-made or natural' (103).

Anthropologists investigating the causes and consequences of such large-scale trauma regularly work together with other specialists, including psychoanalysts such as Apfel and Simon, because such phenomena are so complex. The causes of large-scale collective violence involve psychic, social, political, economic, and cultural factors, and this sort of violence aims to destroy not just individual psychological functioning but also the physical body and the social order. Individual and cultural factors together bring about the trauma and are equally implicated in the ways in which survivors come to deal with trauma's aftermath (Suárez-Orozco and Robben 2000: 1).

This means, of course, that attempts to reduce explanations of large-scale collective forms of violence to either 'nature' or 'culture' are bound to be inadequate. Like many anthropologists, Suárez-Orozco and Robben seek analysis in the intermediate zone 'somewhere between those two analytical dead ends' (2). For example, attributing large-scale, collective forms of violence to some innate *individual* capacity for violence ignores the many differences between small-scale, face-to-face violent

interchanges and the massing of armies and technology to wreak havoc on an 'enemy' that is often not known personally. To grasp the complexities involved requires 'processual multi-level approaches' that combine 'solid understandings of the inner psychic processes as well as the social and cultural contexts of large-scale violence and trauma' (4).

Western scholarly and medical understanding of large-scale trauma developed over the course of the twentieth century. Phenomena called *shell shock* or *battle fatigue* were first identified in some soldiers during World War I (Figure 5.13). Although initially these soldiers were vilified as cowards who were morally corrupt, some researchers, including anthropologists W.H.R. Rivers and Abram Kardiner, eventually proposed that the suffering these soldiers experienced could not be attributed to individual psychological or moral deficiency but needed to be seen as a consequence of the trauma inflicted by battlefield experience itself. The commitment in World War II to 'total war' made the destruction of civilian populations and support structures as important as, or more important than, the destruction of soldiers on the battlefield. Indeed, the number of civilian casualties rose from 5 per cent in World War I to 50 per cent in World War II (Suárez-Orozco and Robben 2000: 15). After World War II, attention was for the first time directed to the massive trauma to which civilians had been subjected, with particular attention focussed on the experiences of those who had survived Nazi concentration camps. Suárez-Orozco and Robben note that the pioneering work by psychoanalyst Bruno Bettelheim, for example, highlighted the 'complex social dynamics between perpetrators and victims of violence' (17). This dynamic was revealed to be even more complex in later wars—for example, in the Vietnam War, during which the number of civilian casualties was over 80 per cent (15) and after which more than one-third of individual veterans suffered from what was officially designated as 'post-traumatic stress disorder' (PTSD) in 1980 (20).

Suárez-Orozco and Robben note that societies as well as individuals need to heal. In both cases, successful healing requires the re-establishment of 'basic trust': individuals need to find ways to trust other individuals, and all survivors need to be able to find ways to develop trust in

*Figure 5.13* | World War I Canadian soldiers are brought to the field dressing station at Vimy Ridge, April 1917.

the institutions of their society, which are also implicated in the management of (or in failing to manage) collective violence. Some dimensions of healing can be successfully promoted by the efforts of psychiatrists and medical specialists who focus on individuals; for example, interpreting the suffering of veterans in medical terms acknowledges that their suffering was not a consequence of their own personal defects but a consequence of the trauma they had experienced in war. At the same time, a continuing focus on individuals diverts attention away from the socio-cultural dimensions of such trauma. 'Combat trauma shatters the meaningfulness of the self and the world, and makes its sufferers put their bodies and minds on constant alert for any possible attack. They become distrustful of others, their own memories, and visual perceptions' (Suárez-Orozco and Robben 2000: 20). The taken-for-grantedness of everyday social life is destroyed, allowing 'the uncanny'—'the

dread and horror of social violence'—to become a recurring and unassimilable feature of their lives:

> Those who experience such traumas are faced with an unbelievable and unreal reality that is incompatible with anything they knew previously. As a result, they can no longer fully believe what they see with their own eyes; they have difficulty in distinguishing between the unreal reality they have survived and the fears that spring from their own imagination . . . . When one experiences the uncanny . . . what has been hidden becomes visible, what is familiar becomes strange and frightening. (Gampel 2000: 49–50)

We all experience a mild form of 'the uncanny' when we find ourselves in situations of ambiguity—for example, when learning a new language or living in an unfamiliar society. But 'the uncanny' experienced by war refugees, concentration camp survivors, or victims of state repression is more intense. 'The feeling of uncanniness overwhelms us when we are thrust into a fragmented, violent social context, one without any continuity and which transmits extremely paradoxical messages' (55).

Individuals' responses to experiences of social trauma vary. For example, many survivors of Nazi death camps did not explicitly show signs of their severe trauma, but they revealed the lasting effects of their experiences through their general anxiety and over-protectiveness toward their children. Psychoanalysts can be effective in helping individuals who suffer from traumatic experiences in such ways, but many believe it is naïve and overly optimistic to imagine that a total 'cure' is possible (Langer 1997). Other survivors exhibit (and pass on to their children) a remarkable resiliency, 'the capacity to survive violence and loss, and moreover, to have flexibility of response over the course of a life time' including 'a sense of agency and a sense of capacity to choose—among courses of action and among conflicting moral values' (Apfel and Simon 2000: 103).

In still other cases, traumatized persons and groups turn to 'hatred and violence as ways of coping with traumatic wounds' (102). Vamik Volkan has described one way in which this can happen, in terms of what he calls a group's *chosen trauma*. A chosen trauma arises, Volkan argues, from experiences of collective violence and loss that survivors are unable to mourn. This can lead to a collective focus on the group's past experiences of victimization or humiliation, and the entire identity of the group's members may come to centre on the chosen trauma. Moreover, the chosen trauma can be passed on to subsequent generations along with the expectation that it is up to them to right past wrongs, using violence if necessary. 'While the group does not consciously choose to feel victimized, it does choose to psychologize losses and to transform them into powerful cultural narratives which become an integral part of the social identity' (Suárez-Orozco and Robben 2000: 23). Volkan studied Christian Serbs, who elaborated and passed on for hundreds of years their chosen trauma: the loss of their empire to the Ottoman

Turks in the early 1500s. Although this chosen trauma was not always in the forefront of Serbian actions during those centuries, it remained a powerful cultural resource that Slobodan Milosevic and his cronies successfully exploited for their own political purposes in the 1990s, as the former Yugoslavia broke apart (23).

The power of chosen traumas derives in large part from the fact that they remain unmourned, thus cutting off possible forms of social and cultural healing that can rebuild trust in social institutions. Suárez-Orozco and Robben note, for example, that 'institutional acknowledgement—in the form of "truth" commissions and reparations (monetary and symbolic)—and justice—in the form of trials of perpetrators—can begin partially to restore the symbolic order that is another casualty of the work of violence' (2000: 5). These kinds of institutional acknowledgements, most often initiatives taken on the level of the nation-state, may coincide with more local actions designed to reduce the trauma of massive social disruption, through healing rituals and other collective symbolic activities designed to aid recovery and rebuild social trust (22, 24).

The residential school trauma of First Nations peoples in Canada is an example of a large-scale social trauma that went unmourned for many years (see the 'In Their Own Words' box). Today the Canadian federal government is moving to compensation and various forms of reconciliation. Yet has this 'institutional acknowledgement' gone far enough? Perhaps healing can only emerge once all Canadians become engaged—at some level—in the process and once the conditions that have resulted from the original trauma no longer limit the agency of the survivors.

## Individual Psychology and Context

Cross-cultural studies of human psychological functioning all stress the vital importance of *context*—not just the immediate context of the laboratory situations or fieldwork encounters but also the displaced context of culture and history that may be invisible in local settings but present in people's habits of thought and feeling. Sometimes researchers can identify contextual factors with little effort. When administering a psychological test on visual illusions to the Fang in Gabon, for

## *In Their Own Words* | **A Place for Memory**

*Michael G. Kenny from Simon Fraser University discusses residential schools to which First Nations children were sent.*

Boarding schools were seen as a practical necessity if Indian children were to be acculturated to the new European order. Government and church authorities thought it best for children to be taken away from their families and cultural milieu so that they could be 'civilized', meaning that they would be taught to work and to be good Christians. While the Nazi concentration camp guards regarded Jewish inmates as *Urzgeziefer* (vermin), Native children often remember being regarded as dumb, dirty, lousy Indians. Seen in a certain light, the schools were a Dickensian horror: squalid, oppressive, and violent.

The Canadian Federal Government has responsibility for Native affairs. Given the vast size of the country, underfunding, and the absence of constitutional barriers limiting sectarian involvement in public education, the Canadian state in effect farmed Indian education out to the churches and most particularly to the Roman Catholic Church (the United Church of Canada and the Anglican Church were also involved, among others). The schools were often highly regimented, a discipline of much work and, at least at first, little play, insufficient food, and a high mortality rate—particularly from tuberculosis—brought about by the harsh and overcrowded conditions. Children were taken from their families, sometimes with consent, sometimes coercively. While in school, boys were separated from girls, sibling from sibling. The speaking of Indigenous languages was prohibited and little place made for Native culture.

This widely shared school experience has in recent times led to a sense of collective victimization and, inversely, to renewed self-assertion among Canadian Native peoples: 'The residential school issue has united Native people across Canada like no other issue in recent history.' But the way in which the residential school story has come to be told is a sign of our times. Sexual abuse allegations about what went on in the schools have multiplied, accompanied by numerous confessions and convictions, extending even to a Roman Catholic bishop: 'What people make of their places is closely connected to what they make of themselves as members of society.' What Native peoples now make of the residential schools has been accompanied by a sea-change in political consciousness.

It is now possible to speak of a Residential School Syndrome, of Native people as its survivors, and of what Euro-Canadians tried to do to them as 'cultural genocide'. Political and therapeutic discourse have become thoroughly intertwined around the central metaphor of 'healing'. It is said that, as the white world tried to deny Native history, so recovery of the hidden history of the residential schools affirms the persistence and constitutional status of the First Nations as a necessary step toward the restoration of integral personal and cultural identity. One such account actually attempts to drop the 'healing' metaphor since, in the view of its authors, it tends to psychologize what is at root a political issue. What happened in the schools was not the product of an honest mistake on the part of misguided churches and a paternalistic government; instead, it was attempted genocide, as defined by the UN Genocide Convention—an Indian Holocaust. . . .

Source: Kenny, Michael G. 1999. 'A Place for Memory: The Interface between Individual and Collective History', *Comparative Studies in Society and History* 41, 3: 420–37.

example, James Fernandez (1980) discovered that many questioned his explanation of the 'real' reason behind such a bizarre activity as psychological testing. He deduced that years of colonial domination and exploitation at the hands of outsiders made these people suspicious of his research motives.

Contextual factors shape human experiences in subtle ways as well, contributing to nuanced, holistic ethnographic understandings of other ways of making meaning. An excellent description of this kind of holistic experience is given by anthropologist Michael Gilsenan (1982), who worked for a time among urban Muslims in Cairo, Egypt (see Map 5.6). Gilsenan spent many hours with his informants observing their prayers in the local mosque. Along the inside wall of the mosque were verses from the Quran shaped out of bright green neon tubing.

Green is the colour of the prophet Muhammad, so finding that colour used prominently in mosque decoration is not surprising. However, Gilsenan's experiences in Western culture did not include schemas in which neon lights and serious worship went together, and for several months the neon interfered with his attempts to assume a properly reverential attitude. Then one day, Gilsenan reports, 'I turned unthinkingly away from the swaying bodies and the rhythms of the remembrance of God and saw, not neon, but simply greenness. . . . No gaps existed between colour, shape, light, and form. From that unreflecting and unsuspecting moment I ceased to see neon at all' (1982: 266).

Nothing had happened to Gilsenan's eyes or his other senses, which continued to receive the same signals they had always received, but the meaning of the signals had been altered. Gilsenan's experience in the mosque situated neon light within a new schema, and his growing familiarity with that schema made the neon seem more and more natural. Eventually, Gilsenan was noticing only the colour green. He was still able to report, of course, that the green light was produced by green neon tubing; however, that fact seemed irrelevant given the new schema he used to interpret his experience.

Map 5.6 | **Cairo**

These transformations of perception and understanding remain mysterious, but they seem to occur whenever we have an insight of any kind. Insights, like apt metaphors, reshape the world for us, throwing new aspects into sharp focus and casting other aspects into the background. Our ability to achieve insights, like our ability to create apt metaphors, remains a central and highly mysterious aspect of human psychological processes.

# Key Terms

**articulated style**   106

**cognition**   104

**cognitive style**   106

**elementary cognitive processes**   105

**emotion**   110

**enculturation**   112

**functional cognitive systems**   105

**gender**   116

**gender roles**   115

**global style**   106

**motivation**   112

**perception**   99

**personality**   114

**prototypes**   100

**reasoning style**   109

**schemas**   100

**self**   114

**sex**   116

**sexuality**   116

**socialization**   112

**social trauma**   119

**structural violence**   119

**subjectivity**   115

**syllogistic reasoning**   108

**taxonomies**   105

**thinking**   108

**visuality**   103

# Chapter Summary

1. Anthropologists have long been interested in the many ways in which individuals engage in cultural learning. They have tried to find out what all members of our species have in common, what features are limited to specific groups of humans, and how individual unique-ness might be understood. This effort has involved co-operation with other disciplines, such as psychology. Anthropologists have tested universal assumptions about human psychology in different cultural settings and have found them to be problematic.

2. The field of psychological anthropology is complex and difficult to summarize, but it can be grouped into four basic areas of human experience: perception, cogni-tion, emotion, and motivation. Research overwhelmingly sustains the view that human psychological processes are open to a wide variety of influences.

3. Human psychological perception always takes place in a cultural context. Researchers use concepts such as schemas and prototypes to describe some of the ways in which meaning is mapped onto our experience. Clas-sic research on cross-cultural variations in perception showed that variation in responses to psychological tests depended on the meanings subjects brought to the testing situation, especially whether they under-stood the tests the same way Western subjects typically understood them. Alternative understandings are pos-sible because of the ambiguity of many perceptual signals, a phenomenon that is illustrated in the study of visual illusions. In addition, looking and seeing are culturally learned modes of sensory perception, as illus-trated in Vogel's study of Baule visuality.

4. Human beings are active meaning-makers, striving to make sense of our experiences; these processes are a focus of anthropological studies of cognition. Anthro-pologists have been critical of so-called intelligence tests on which non-Western subjects perform poorly because outside the laboratory setting the same individ-uals' intelligence and full humanity are obvious. Today, it is unclear exactly what the results of intelligence tests represent. Consequently, research has shifted its focus to cognitive processes and the way these are organized into culturally shaped functional systems.

5. Some anthropologists argue that people in different cul-tures have different cognitive styles that can be located on a continuum ranging from global style at one end to articulated style at the other. Research suggests that the same individual may use a global style for some tasks and an articulated style for others. In everyday situations, the goal of cognition is not to solve a problem by finding the single correct answer. Instead, people try to resolve dilemmas in a way that allows them to get on with life.

6. Researchers have made several attempts to measure the levels of rational thinking in non-Western populations. The results are problematic. Rational thinking is not the same as logic. Formal Western logic is better understood as a learned reasoning style characteristic of Western culture. Rules of Western logic can be useful, but other logics may be equally valid in other societies—or on other occasions in Western societies—when contextual factors are vital and must be taken into consideration.

7. Our emotions, like our thoughts, are not just something we have; they are culturally constructed of our state of mind, our cultural interpretations, and our levels of bodily arousal. Different cultures recognize different domains of experience and different categories of feel-ing as being appropriate to these domains. For this reason, it is often difficult to translate the language of emotion from one culture to another.

8. Anthropological approaches to motivation have always embedded the sources of motivation within a cultural matrix. Finding the notion of 'instinct' to be unhelpful, anthropologists have had greater success in studying the culturally defined goals that people pursue in differ-ent societies.

9. The mainsprings of motivation are to be uncovered in the study of socialization and enculturation. Humans must learn to pattern and adapt behaviour and ways of thinking and feeling to the standards considered appro-priate in their respective cultures. Vygotsky's concept of the zone of proximal development stresses that cog-nitive development results from a dialogue. Children progress through that process at different rates and in different directions, depending on the amount and kind of coaching they receive from others. This concept makes it possible to explain why people in different cul-tural subgroups are socialized and enculturated in dif-ferent ways.

10. Anthropologists have found that many cultures do not promote the development of the self as a bounded, independent entity with a clear and non-contradictory sense of identity that persists through time. Early psychological anthropologists preferred to speak of individual personality, which always assumed that an individual's psychological processes were integrated within a socio-cultural matrix. Today, some anthropologists prefer to speak not of personality or self but of individual subjectivity, which focusses on internal experiences of individuals as they are shaped by their positions in a field of power relations.

11. Different cultures conceptualize sex and gender roles differently. These roles greatly influence how individuals see themselves, how they define their place with a social group, and how they are perceived by others. Individuals' sexual practices vary greatly—both within a single culture and between different cultures.

12. Patterns of socialization and enculturation are sometimes overturned by experiences that intrude on predictable daily routines. Among the most powerful experiences are those occasioned by structural violence and social trauma, the investigation of which has become a significant topic for some contemporary psychological anthropologists.

# Critical Thinking Questions

1. Developmental Systems Theory (DST) recognizes that a developing organism is subject to many environments, identifiable at different levels of analysis, as it lives out its life cycle. What are some of the reciprocal influences important in the first year of life for the human child? How does DST 'fit' with a Vygotskian perspective?

2. Language, like human psychology, is an open system. How can the linguistic design features of *displacement* and *prevarication* help us to better understand human psychology?

3. A standard IQ test cannot be applied cross-culturally. Why do you suppose this is the case?

4. Why is it sometimes difficult for individuals from different cultures to discuss specific emotions? Which aspects of emotion seem universal to the human experience? Which are defined by the culture in which a person lives?

5. Distinguish between socialization and enculturation. Why are both needed to become 'human'?

6. How would you distinguish among sex, gender, and sexuality? How is gender culturally defined? What role do legislative decisions play in defining the boundaries of what the general population perceives as 'normal' sexual behaviour?

# Suggested Readings

Berlin, Brent, and David G. Casagrande. 2000. 'Cognitive Prototypes in Tzeltal Maya Medicinal Plant Selection', available at http://gravlee.org/ang5091/proposals/casagrande_nsf.pdf. This article, an example of applied anthropology, discusses bridging the gap between traditional medicinal plant knowledge and Western biomedical knowledge, an important example of coming to understand taxonomies.

Bock, Philip K. 1999. *Rethinking Psychological Anthropology: Continuity and Change in the Study of Human Action*, 2nd edn (Prospect Heights, IL: Waveland Press). A thorough introduction to psychological anthropology, tracing developments from the early twentieth century to current directions in the field.

Boellstorff, Tom, and Johan Lindquist. 2004. 'Bodies of Emotion: Rethinking Culture and Emotion through Southeast

Asia', *Ethnos* 69, 4: 437–44, available at www.anthro.uci.edu/faculty_bios/boellstorff/Boellstorff-Emotion.pdf. This article, and the volume it comes from, attempts to develop analyses that treat emotion as cultural—and culturally specific—while recognizing the dogged persistence of the individual/social binarism (dualism).

Cole, Michael, and Sylvia Scribner. 1974. *Culture and Thought: A Psychological Introduction* (New York: Wiley). A clear, readable survey of the literature and case studies on the cultural shaping of cognition.

D'Andrade, Roy G. 1995. *The Development of Cognitive Anthropology* (Cambridge: Cambridge University Press). An interesting and comprehensive review of the early application of theories of cognition. Chapter 5, which is on folk taxonomies, gives insight into shared salient cognitive features; of particular use here are the early studies of ethnobotany and ethnozoology.

**Dods, Roberta Robin. 2004.** 'Knowing Ways/Ways of Knowing: Reconciling Science and Tradition', *World Archaeolgy* 36, 4: 547–57. This paper distinguishes two ways of knowing, traditional and scientific, suggesting their compatibility and utility for the development of a wider perspective in both anthropology and archaeology.

**Kenny, Michael G. 1999.** 'A Place for Memory: The Interface between Individual and Collective History', *Comparative Studies in Society and History* 41, 3: 420–37. This paper discusses the 'tricks' of memory and how they are situated in a wider context than the self.

**Miller, Jonathan. 1983.** *States of Mind* (New York: Pantheon). A series of witty and enjoyable interviews in which English actor, writer, physician, and director Jonathan Miller talks to several of the most interesting scholars on the mind, including George Mandler, Richard Gregory, and Clifford Geertz.

**Schwartz, Theodore, Geoffrey M. White, and Catherine A. Lutz, eds. 1992.** *New Directions in Psychological Anthropology* (Cambridge: Cambridge University Press). A survey of psychological anthropology with articles by experts in the fields of cognition, human development, bio-psychological studies, and psychiatric and psychoanalytic anthropology.

# Related Websites

**Anthropological Theories (Cognitive Anthropology)** http://anthropology.ua.edu/cultures/cultures.php

**British Journal of Psychiatry** http://bjp.rcpsych.org/cgi/content/full/185/5/361

**Culture and Personality School** www.encyclopedia.com/doc/1O88-CultureandPersonalitySchl.html

**Optical Illusions** http://allpsych.com/opticalillusions/index.html

**Prototype Theory** www.nationmaster.com/encyclopedia/Prototype-Theory

# 6 | Social Relationships: Marriage, Family, Kinship, and Friendship

## Chapter Outline

Marriage

Family Structure

Families and Change

Kinship and Systems of Relatedness:
Ways of Organizing Human Interdependence

Beyond Kinship

Theories of Relatedness:
Kin-based and Non-kin-based Societies

## Learning Objectives

By the end of Chapter 6, you will be able to

- understand 'marriage' in a cross-cultural perspective,

- appreciate marriage as a social process,

- consider marriage in the context of economic exchange,

- identify variations in family structure,

- consider how families change over time and in response to new global circumstances,

- recognize patterns of descent in kinship,

- reflect on kinship terminology as a statement of rights and obligations,

- realize the importance of extended kin in certain cultures,

- understand friendship and voluntary group membership as extensions of the need for kinship,

- compare and contrast kin-based and non-kin-based societies, and

- appreciate the nuances of the dimensions of group life.

*A Kayapo Indian woman holds her child in a small village in Brazil. Young children develop close ties to members of their kinship group, first to members of their immediate families and then to more distant relatives and acquaintances.*

**Human beings are highly social creatures. As such, we constantly endeavour to establish and maintain relationships with other people, thus warding off feelings of loneliness**. Our need for companionship is well explored in Kurt Vonnegut Jr's science fiction novel *Slapstick, or Lonesome No More!* (1976). In the novel, Dr Wilbur Daffodil-11 Swain presents a plan to end loneliness with a new system of interrelatedness, one in which every person has a large number of relatives on whom they can depend. Swain proposes that everyone will be given a new middle name composed of a noun and a number (e.g., Daffodil-11). Everyone with the same noun will be cousins and everyone with the same noun and number will be siblings. A side effect is the development of clubs based on shared characteristics. While the setting is a fictional reimagining of America, the author's comments on loneliness resonate beyond the American context, illustrating that **relatedness** is a central concern for most of us. We all want to belong. Indeed, we define ourselves and our world based on the relationships we form and the positions we hold within specific groups.

We start life physically and emotionally tied to our mothers; as we grow, we become individuals. To survive on our own we must bind ourselves to others through alliances of **marriage**, **family**, **kinship**, and **friendship**, as well as larger and more complex forms of community that will inform our social, economic, and political lives. Throughout our lives, we become enmeshed in a changing web of relatives—some based on family lines, others on mutual affection. Each person in the web is aware of her or his rights and obligations to all others with whom she or he is connected. In this chapter, we focus on how humans experience relatedness and how relatedness is selectively interpreted and culturally formed into our deeply layered social practices.

## Marriage

Each culture has its own criteria for defining marriage. Some recognize only heterosexual alliances, while others include same-sex partnerships. Some are strictly monogamous, while others are polygamous. Some treat marriage as a prerequisite for sexual activity (at least for females), while others do not. Some insist on a ceremony or a legal document to formalize a marriage, while others accept long-term cohabitation as a marker of such unions. Indeed, the definition of marriage has evolved in Canada over the past decade, particularly after Bill C-38 opened civil marriage to same-sex couples across the country. Today, more and more Western couples are choosing less rigidly defined forms of marriage, as evidenced by the decreasing proportions of married families along with an increase in the proportion of common-law families (see Figure 6.1 and Table 6.1).

Yet in all cases, marriage creates new *relationships*—not only between the individuals marrying one another but

**relatedness**
The socially recognized ties that connect people in a variety of ways.

**marriage**
An institution that prototypically involves a man and a woman, transforms the status of the participants, carries implications about sexual access, gives offspring a position in society, and establishes connections between the kin of a husband and the kin of a wife.

**family**
At minimum, a woman/man and her/his dependent children.

**kinship**
Social relationships that are prototypically derived from the universal human experiences of mating, birth, and nurturance.

**friendship**
The relatively unofficial bonds that people construct with one another that tend to be personal, affective, and, often, a matter of choice.

*Figure 6.1* | **Proportion of common-law families grows while it declines for married families, Canada.**
Source: Adapted from www12.statcan.ca/english/census01/products/analytic/companion/fam/marriedclu.cfm and www.statcan.gc.ca/daily-quotidien/070912/dq070912a-eng.htm.

*Table 6.1* | **Proportion of Couples that Cohabit**

| Country | Year | As % of All Couples |
| --- | --- | --- |
| Sweden | 2000 | 30.0 |
| Norway | 2000 | 24.5 |
| Finland | 2000 | 18.5 |
| Mexico | 2000 | 18.7 |
| New Zealand | 2001 | 18.3 |
| France | 1999 | 17.5 |
| Canada | 2001 | 16.0 |
|    Quebec | 2001 | 29.8 |
|    Other Provinces | 2001 | 11.7 |
| United States | 2000 | 8.2 |

Source: Adapted from Statistics Canada. 2002. '2001 Census: Marital Status, Common-law Status, Families, Dwellings and Households', *The Daily* (22 Oct.), available at www.statcan.gc.ca/daily-quotidien/021022/dq021022a-eng.htm.

also among their relatives and members of the wider society. Indeed, the community must often acknowledge the legitimacy of the new union by participating in the rites of marriage and by accepting the newly married couple into the community. On the familial level, marriages affect *affinal* relationships (relationships created via marriage, therefore based on *affinity*) as well as *consanguineal* relationships ('blood' relationships based on descent, regardless of whether the child is related by birth adoption, sperm/ovum donation, and/or surrogacy) (see Karp 1986). If the couple has children, these children will go on to form relationships of their own. Thus, many anthropologists choose to think of marriage as a social process.

## Marriage as a Social Process

Thinking of marriage as a social process allows us to describe all forms of marriage, including those that do not fit traditional Western definitions (Lamphere 2005) (Figure 6.2). Marriage sets in place alliances that define essential social roles, and it delineates rights and obligations at the core of social life. It is also an evolving social process. As societal concepts of norms change with changing times, roles change in response. For example, before the passing of Bill 16 in 1964, a woman

*Figure 6.2* | **Muslim brides wait for their turn during a mass wedding ceremony in Hyderabad, India. The state government organized this mass wedding for financially poor Muslims.**

who entered marriage in Quebec lost her status as an independent adult unless she had a previously arranged legal contract, similar to what we would call a 'prenup' today, stating otherwise. Under the province's Civil Code, a married woman who did not have such a contract could not inherit property, open a bank account, or sign her children into hospital for treatment; these 'rights' were reserved for her husband. Today, women in Quebec share these rights with their husbands. Emancipation of married women in Quebec came about in large part because of the work of Marie-Claire Kirkland-Casgrain.

In many cultures, a couple's living arrangement after marriage reflects the role each partner is expected to adopt in familial and social relationships (see Table 6.2). In many societies, the couple is expected to live with a specific set of family members. Thus, a married couple's living arrangement also suggests how that culture understands family bonds.

**bridewealth**
The transfer of certain symbolically important goods from the family of the groom to the family of the bride, representing compensation to the wife's lineage for the loss of her labour and for child-bearing capacities.

Some cultures use creative marriage forms to develop specific social relationships. Evans-Pritchard (1951) described two such forms with the Nuer (Nei Ti Naath) of East Africa. In the first, a woman could marry another woman and become the 'father' of the wife's children. It involves the distinction between *pater* (social father role) and *genitor* (biological father, sperm provider). To establish the marriage, the female husband (the *pater*) gave the bride's lineage cattle as **bridewealth** payments. Then, a male kinsman, friend, or neighbour (the *genitor*) impregnated the wife and contributed labour with tasks considered gender specific to men. The female husband played the social role of a man and could marry several women if wealth permitted. She could demand damage payment if any wife engaged in sexual activity (adultery) without her consent. She was the *pater* of her wives' children, who were of her patrilineage and addressed her as

*Table 6.2* | **Patterns of Residence after Marriage**

| Pattern Name | Residence | Comments | Example |
|---|---|---|---|
| Neolocal (major pattern) | In a place of their own choosing | Found in societies that are more or less individualistic in their social organization. | Most Western nations, including Canada and the United States |
| Patrilocal (major pattern) | With (or near) the husband's father's family | Most common in herding and farming societies. Observed by more societies in the contemporary world than any other residence pattern. | China (village life and traditional communities); Turkey (village life and traditional communities) |
| Matrilocal (major pattern) | With (or near) the family in which the wife was raised | Most common in horticultural groups. The core of the social group consists of a woman, her sisters, and their daughters, together with their husbands. | Iroquois (NE North America); Hopi (SW North America); Tlingit (NW Coast North America) |
| Avunculocal (major pattern) | With (or near) the husband's mother's brother | Found in matrilineal societies in which a boy inherits from his mother's brother. | Chamorros of the Mariana Islands; Taíno of Turks and Caicos Islands |
| Ambilocal (minor pattern) | First with the family of one spouse and later with the family of the other | Eventually they choose which family they want to affiliate with permanently. | SE Porno and E Porno (California); Mbuti of the Ituri Forest, Democratic Republic of the Congo |
| Duolocal (minor pattern) | Each partner lives with his or her own lineage even after marriage | Seen where lineage membership is the most important societal aspect. | Nayar of NE India; Minangkabau of Indonesia |

'father'. She administered her compound and her herds as any male head of household would, she was treated by her wives and children with the same deference shown to a male husband and father, and she fulfilled all her duties to her relatives through her role as a man.

The second, *ghost marriage*, was more common. Since a basic obligation of Nuer kinship was for a man to be remembered through and by his sons, a man who died without male heirs became an unhappy, angry spirit. To appease this ghost, a kinsman—a brother or a brother's son—would marry a woman 'to his name'. Bridewealth cattle were paid in the ghost's name. From the marriage ceremony onward, the kinsman acted as husband and the children were commonly referred to as his—but legally they were the children of the ghost husband. The kinsman was *genitor*, but the ghost husband was *pater* and his name would be remembered in the history of the lineage. Marrying a woman 'to his kinsman's name' before he himself married presented difficulties in subsequently contracting a marriage in his own right. Because he was already married, his relatives would want to allocate cattle for bridewealth to unmarried brothers. Even if he eventually accumulated enough cattle to afford to marry, he would feel that those cattle should provide the bridewealth for the sons he had raised for his dead kinsman. He then died without any sons of his own, thus becoming an angry spirit in his own turn. Someone else (in fact, one of the sons he had raised for the ghost) had to marry a woman to *his* name and so the pattern continued.

This practice is similar to the more widely documented practices of levirate (discussed in Deuteronomy 25: 1–5) where a widow marries her deceased husband's brother (conversely sororate, where a widower marries a sister or specific cousin of his deceased wife). There are advantages to such systems when considerable resources are invested in the formalization of the social bonds signified by the marriage. Sororate also has the advantage of the step-mother being a kinswoman of any existing children from the first marriage. (Think of step-mothers in the context of European fairytales!)

Sometimes marriages must be contracted within a particular social group, a pattern called **endogamy**. In other cases, marriage partners must be found outside a particular group, a pattern called **exogamy**. In all societies, some close kin are off limits as spouses or as sexual partners, specifically members of the nuclear family. This pattern is known as the *incest taboo*. Pressure to marry specific partners can be formally defined, covertly manoeuvred, or nebulously sensed in almost all societies. Collective identities of ethnicity, religion, language, class, and caste may be bounded by law or custom. In some cases, marrying outside the prescribed group can lead to disenfranchisement. This was certainly true for Canadian First Nations women under the Indian Act (1876), which denied them certain rights, including residency rights, if they married non-Native men. (This restriction was in effect until 1985, when an amendment to the Act reversed it and reinstated the rights of 16,000 women and 46,000 first-generation dependants.) The great Mohawk activist Mary Two-axe Earley (Figure 6.3) from Kahnawake, Quebec, observed: 'After all these years, I'll be legally entitled to live on the reserve, to own property, die and

> **endogamy**
> Marriage within a defined social group.
>
> **exogamy**
> Marriage outside a defined social group.

*Figure 6.3* | **Mohawk activist Mary Two-axe Earley was a catalyst for the establishment of Bill C-31, which led to the reinstatement of treaty status for First Nations women married to non-Native men.**

**monogamy**
A marriage pattern in which a person may be married to only one person at a time.

**polygamy**
A marriage pattern in which a person may be married to more than one person at a time.

be buried with my own people' (*The Gazette*, 5 July 1985). Here we can understand when Connolly (2009) asks us to consider familial and individual intimate emotional and experiential responses.

## Monogamy and Polygamy

The number of spouses a person may have varies cross-culturally. **Monogamy** is a marriage form in which a person may have only one spouse at a time. This is the form of marriage currently found in Canada. Before the twentieth century, divorce was rare, and people in European-style societies generally married only once unless they were widowed. Today, some observers suggest that we practise *serial monogamy*; we may be married to several different people but only one at a time.

**Polygamy** is a marriage system that allows a person to have more than one spouse. Within the category of polygamy are two subcategories: polygyny (multiple wives) and polyandry (multiple husbands). Polygynous societies

vary in the number of wives a man may have. Islam permits a man to have as many as four wives but only on the condition that he can support them equally. Some Muslim authorities today argue, however, that equal support must be emotional and affective, not just financial. Convinced that no man can feel the same toward each of his wives, they have concluded that monogamy must be the rule. Other polygynous societies have no limit on the number of women a man may marry. Nevertheless, not every man can be polygynous—there are simply not enough women. Polygyny is also expensive, for a husband must support all his wives as well as their children (Figure 6.4).

Polyandry is much rarer than polygyny. Polyandrous societies tend to separate a woman's sexuality from her reproductive capacity, and some researchers have suggested that polyandry is uncommon because, unlike polygyny or even monogamy, it is not concerned with controlling women's sexuality (see, e.g. Levine and Sangree 1980). Anthropologists generally recognize three forms of polyandry: fraternal, associated, and secondary marriage. Fraternal and associated patterns are *alliance intensifying*, as they enhance the ties within and between families; however, secondary marriage is *alliance proliferative*, as it serves to connect diverse kin groups by

*Figure 6.4* | **The wives and children of a polygynous family.**

building extensive networks of marriage-based ties throughout a region (Levine and Sangree 1980).

Anthropologists generally consider fraternal polyandry—particularly that found in Nepal and Tibet—to be the prototype for other forms of polyandry. In this form, the oldest brother serves as the groom, but all brothers, even those yet unborn, are married in a publicly recognized wedding. The wife and her husbands live together patrilocally. All brothers have equal sexual access to the wife, and all act as fathers (*pater*) to the children without distinguishing the identity of the *genitor*. A notable exception is found with the Nyinba of Nepal (Levine 1980; 1988; see Map 6.1), where each child is recognized as having one particular *genitor*. Sexual jealousy is rare, and the brothers have a strong sense of solidarity with one another. (Levine 1988). If the wife proves sterile, the brothers may marry another woman. Solidarity of brothers is a central kinship ideal and focusses on the landholding household as part of the closed corporate structure. Polyandry mitigates against fragmentation of land holdings while limiting population growth (Mishra et al. 2003). Land and resources are limited, so the concentration of resources increases a household's political position and economic viability.

*Associated polyandry* is open to men who are not brothers (Levine and Sangree 1980). There is evidence it was an acceptable marriage variant with some peoples of the Pacific and North and South America. But it is best-described with the Sinhalese, where polyandry begins monogamously and a second husband is brought into the union later. The first husband is the principal husband in terms of authority, while each man looks after his own economic resources. Both husbands are considered fathers to any children the wife bears. Subsequently, two husbands and their wife may decide to take another woman into the marriage—often the sister of the wife—creating a marriage pattern called *polygynandry*. Depending on relative wealth and the availability of economic opportunity, a Sinhalese household may be monogamous, polyandrous, or polygynandrous.

With *secondary marriage*—as practised, for example, in northern Nigeria and northern Cameroon—a woman marries one or more *secondary* husbands while staying married to her first husband (1980: 400). She lives with only one husband at a time, but retains the right to return to a previous husband and to have legitimate children by him at a later date. There is no divorce; marriage is for life. However, men are as polygynous

Map 6.1 | Nyinba

as women are polyandrous. A man marries a series of women and lives with one or more of them at his homestead, while the women independently pursue their own marital careers. Technically, secondary marriage is a combination of polyandry and polygyny, resulting from the overlap of men seeking several wives and women seeking several husbands. Thus, it can build extensive networks of marriage-based ties throughout a region (Levine and Sangree 1980).

## Flexibility and Negotiation in Marriage

At this point, it may seem as though the rules that govern marriage are often rigid, compelling people to adhere to social norms and, at times, do things they do not want to do. Marriage rules, however, are always subject to some negotiation.

Map 6.2 | Iteso

Sometimes, the contrast between the formal rules of marriage and the actual performance of marriage rituals is very revealing. For example, the Iteso take the marriage ritual very seriously, using it as the basis for the physical and social reproduction of Iteso patrilineages (Map 6.2). Knowing this, Karp (1978) was surprised to witness Iteso women laughing at marriage ceremonies, ceremonies carried out entirely by women who are not consanguineal members of the patrilineage. To understand the seemingly incongruent laughter, Karp analyzed the meaning of the marriage ritual from two perspectives: that of the men and that of the women. He found that the men's perspective constitutes the official (or hegemonic) ideology emphasizing how marriage brings the bride's sexuality and reproductive capacity under the control of her husband's lineage.

In contrast, the women's perspective constitutes an unofficial (or counter-hegemonic) ideology. To perpetuate their lineages, men must control women's bodies. But these bodies belong to outsider women. These same outsiders direct the two ritual events crucial to lineage reproduction—marriage and birth—and men of the lineage are not allowed to attend either ritual. In sum, outsider women control the continued existence of a patrilineage whose male members are supposed to control them! Iteso women see the irony in this: they are at once controlled and controlling. In the marriage ritual itself, they comment on this paradox through their laughter. In doing so, they reveal two things:

- that they know the men are dependent on them; and
- even as the men assert their control over women's bodies, the women's ritual actions escape men's control.

The official ideology of male control is subverted, at least momentarily, by women's laughter.

## Marriage and Economic Exchange

Many societies transfer specific categories of symbolically important goods at marriage. These are called *bridewealth* and *dowry*. Bridewealth, briefly noted earlier with Nuer practices, is most common in patrilineal, patrilocal societies,

**Dowry**
The transfer of wealth from parents to their child (usually a daughter) at the time of the child's marriage.

although it is found in other types of societies as well such as matrilineal societies with avunculocal residence rules. The goods exchanged may include shell ornaments, ivory tusks, brass gongs, bird feathers, cotton cloth, and animals. Bridewealth in animals is prevalent in eastern and southern Africa, where cattle have the most profound symbolic and economic value. In these societies, a man's father, and often his entire patrilineage, gives a specified number of cattle (often in instalments) to the patrilineage of the bride. Anthropologists view bridewealth as a way of compensating the bride's relatives for the loss of her labour and child-bearing capacities. Bridewealth formalizes the new affine link. The bride's relatives, in turn, often use the bridewealth to find a bride for her brother in yet another kinship group. In many societies in eastern and southern Africa, a woman gains power and influence over her brother when her marriage brings the cattle that will allow him to marry and continue their lineage; 'Cattle beget children', according to the southern Bantu! (Kuper 1982: 3). This is why Goody describes bridewealth as 'a societal fund, a circulating pool of resources, the movement of which corresponds to the movement of rights over spouses, usually women' (Goody and Tambiah 1973: 17).

**Dowry** is a transfer of family wealth, usually from parents to their daughter, at the time of marriage. It is found primarily in the agricultural societies of Europe and Asia but has been brought to some parts of Africa with the arrival of Islamic sharia law. In societies where both women and men are seen as potential heirs, dowry is sometimes regarded as the buyout of the inheritance. Dowries are often considered the wife's contribution to the establishment of a new household, to which the husband may bring other forms of wealth. In stratified societies, the size of a woman's dowry often ensures that when she marries she will continue to enjoy her accustomed lifestyle. The goods included in dowries vary in different societies and may or may not include land (Goody and Tambiah 1973).

Leigh Minturn (1993) has examined dowry practices among the Khalapur Rajputs of northern India (see Map 6.3). In Rajput society, all land is held and inherited by men living as a patrilocal *joint family*, a group of brothers with their wives and children. Dowries consist of transportable items (chattels) such as money, jewellery, clothing, and household decorations. Rajput marriages are not only village exogamous but also *hypergamous*: that is, women normally marry into lineages of

**Map 6.3 | Khalapur Rajputs**

higher status than the ones into which they were born, living as low-ranking outsiders in the households and villages of their husbands. How well they marry and how well they are treated by their in-laws depend on the size of their dowries. In the 1950s, when Minturn first visited Khalapur, new Rajput wives were under the strict control of their mothers-in-law, who assigned tasks, limited their contact with their husbands, and controlled their dowries. Every time a wife visited her parents, moreover, she was expected to return with more gifts for her husband's family.

In many cases, such practices cause considerable financial strain on the family providing the dowry. As many Rajputs believe, 'It is best to have two sons and one daughter, because then you will receive two dowries, but give only one' (1993: 130). Yet sons do not always receive dowries. Poor people whose sons cannot attract women with dowries often engage in a practice called *buying a wife*, in which the husband's family gives money to the bride's family to purchase her dowry goods.

In 1961, the government of India passed a law prohibiting dowries, but it has proven impossible to enforce. However, dowry violence and death continue to occur with alarming frequency in India, as too the murder of widows to keep them from withdrawing their husband's portion of the land from traditional joint holdings:

> Dowry violence takes a characteristic form. Following marriage and the requisite giving of dowry, the family of the groom makes additional demands for the payment of more cash or the provision of more goods. These demands are expressed in unremitting harassment of the bride, who is living in the household of her husband's parents, culminating in the murder of the woman by members of her husband's family or by her suicide. The woman is typically burned to death with kerosene, . . . hence the use of the term *bride-burning* in public discourse. . . . Police records do not match hospital records for third-degree burn cases among younger married women; far more violence occurs than the crime reports indicate. (van Willigen and Channa 1991: 369)

Dowries are also tied other social problems. Some women 'commit suicide so as to relieve their families of the burden of providing a dowry' (369). Others participate in the widespread practice of 'selective female abortion' to avoid having to pay dowries in the future (370).

## Family Structure

What is a family? At minimum, most anthropologists would point to the **non-conjugal family**: a woman and her dependent children. While some anthropological definitions require the presence of an adult male (the **conjugal family**), related either by marriage or descent (e.g., husband or brother), recent feminist and primatological scholarship has called this requirement into question. Indeed, in a non-conjugal family, the husband/father may be occasionally present or completely absent. Non-conjugal families are never the only form of family organization in a society. In fact, cross-culturally they are usually rather infrequent. In some large-scale industrial societies, including Canada, non-conjugal families have become increasingly common.

In most societies, the conjugal family is co-resident—spouses live in the same dwelling along with their children—but there are some matrilineal societies in which the husband lives with his

**non-conjugal family**
A woman and her children; the husband/father may occasionally be present or completely absent. (*Or*, less commonly, a man and his children; the wife/mother may be present or completely absent.)

**conjugal family**
A family based on marriage; at minimum, a spousal pair and their children.

matrilineage, the wife and children live with theirs, and the husband visits his wife and children.

## The Nuclear Family

The structure and dynamics of neolocal monogamous families are familiar to North Americans. They are called *nuclear families*. Amazingly, this is the prototype for many North Americans even though in 2000 only about 25 per cent of North Americans lived in such families. For anthropologists, a **nuclear family** is made up of two generations: parents and their unmarried children. Each member of a nuclear family has a series of evolving relationships with every other member, and these relationships frequently involve feelings of: jealousy, competition, controversy, and affection. Sibling rivalry, for example, is a form of competition characteristic of nuclear families that is shaped by the relationships between siblings and between siblings and their parents.

> **nuclear family**
> A family made up of two generations: parents and their unmarried children.

## The Polygynous Family

Polygynous families are significantly different in their dynamics. The wives have relationships with each other as individuals and as a group (Figure 6.5). Co-wives, in turn, individually and collectively, interact with the husband. In addition, an important distinction is made between children with the same mother and children with a different mother. In some polygynous cultures, a close connection with a particular brother or sister is emphasized by saying that he or she is 'same father, same mother'. Children also have different kinds of relationships with their own mothers than they do with their fathers' other wives—and with their fathers as well.

Where there is a significant inheritance, these relationships serve as the channels for jealousy and conflict. The children of the same mother, and especially the children of different mothers, compete with one another for their father's favour. Each mother tries to protect the interests of her own children, sometimes at the expense of her co-wives' children. Among the Mende of Sierra Leone (see Map 6.4), co-wives come to compete with each other. Bledsoe (1993) explains that this competition is often focussed on how many children each wife has and how

*Figure 6.5* | **Co-wives in polygynous households frequently co-operate in daily tasks such as food preparation.**

*Map 6.4* | **Mende**

likely it is that each child will obtain things of value, especially education. In polygynous Mende households husbands try to avoid overt signs of favouritism. However, wives are ranked by order of marriage and then by the status of their natal families. Such rankings lay the groundwork for rivalries.

The education of children can be a contentious issue in polygynous families. A child's education matters intensely to a Mende mother because she depends not only on the income that a child may earn to support her but also on the rights her children have to inherit property and positions of leadership from their father. Education often requires a significant cash outlay, and a man may be able to send only one child to school, or he may be able to send one child to a prestigious private school only if he sends another to a trade apprenticeship. These economic realities can lead to bitter feuds—and even divorce—as co-wives blame the husband for disparities in the accomplishments of their children. To avoid these problems, children are frequently sent to live with relatives who will send them to school.

## Extended, Joint, and Blended Families

Some societies have expanded definitions of the central family unit. Two traditional examples are the **extended family** and the **joint family**. In an extended family, the role each member plays in the family dynamic is tied to his or her position as a parent/grandparent, adult child/parent, or child/grandchild. In a joint family, the dynamic is less constant. Upon the death of the father, the eldest son inherits the position of head of the household. Yet his younger brothers may not accept his authority as readily as they did their father's, and they may decide to establish their own households. Each brother whose household splits off from the joint stem usually hopes to start his own joint family; eventually, his sons will bring their wives into the household, and a new joint family will emerge. Something similar happens among the polyandrous Nyinba discussed earlier. The corporation of brothers may take a second wife. At first, all brothers have equal sexual access to her, but in time they tend to form groups around each wife, eventually choosing to split the household in two.

In recent years in North America, anthropologists have observed the emergence of a new family type: the **blended family**. The internal dynamics of such a family—which can come to include his children, her children, and their children—may resemble the dynamics of polygynous families, with complex relations among the children and between each child and each parent.

## Brother–Sister Relationships

In North America, the relationship of the spousal pair ordinarily takes precedence over the brother–sister relationship, which is attenuated at marriage. Yet in some societies, the most important adult relationships a man or a woman can have are those with his or her opposite-sex siblings.

Fortes (1950) gave us the classic illustration from the Ashanti, where the central legal relationship is the tie between brother and sister (see EthnoProfile 6.1 and Figure 6.6). Legal power is vested in males, and brothers have power over the children of their sisters since all belong to a common matriline. A sister has claims on her brother because she is his closest female relative and represents the only source of the continuity of his lineage. 'Men find it difficult to decide which is more important to them, to have children or for their sisters to have children. But after discussion most men conclude that sad as it may be to die childless, a good citizen's first anxiety is for his lineage to survive' (1950: 274–5). More than this, the Ashanti brother and sister are close confidants on matters ranging from property and financial management to matrimonial difficulties (275). This closeness is reinforced by the Ashanti residence pattern: people live in their matrilineages' neighbourhoods, and, often, husbands and wives do not live together.

Clark (1994) reports that in recent years the status of women within Ashanti matrilineages has eroded, although market women she knew could still turn to their matrilineages for support against the risks of divorce, illness, or bankruptcy. Support is not automatic and must be negotiated as Ashanti girls and women 'unfortunately seem to be increasingly marginalized within their lineages, in leadership, residence, and inheritance' (1994: 335).

**extended family**
A family pattern made up of three generations living together: parents, married children, and grandchildren.

**joint family**
A family pattern made up of brothers and their wives (or sisters and their husbands) along with their children living together.

**blended family**
A family created when previously divorced or widowed people marry, bringing with them children from their previous marriages.

## EthnoProfile 6.1 | Ashanti

**Region** Western Africa
**Nation** Ghana
**Language** The Ashanti, part of the Akan peoples, speak various dialects of Twi, a member of the Niger-Congo language group
**Population** 3.7 million (2011 estimate)
**Environment** Slightly inland, partly mountainous
**Livelihood** Farming, fishing, market trading (women)

**Political organization** Traditionally, a kingdom; today, part of a modern nation-state
**For more information** Fortes, Meyer. 1950. 'Kinship and Marriage among the Ashanti', in *African Systems of Kinship and Marriage*, eds A.R. Radcliffe-Brown and Daryll Forde (Oxford: Oxford University Press).

Brother–sister alliances in patrilineal societies are found even in contemporary urban nation-states. In the slums of Naples, Italy, for example, brothers maintain a moral control even over married sisters (Belmonte 1978: 193). In patrilineal societies, the strength of the relationship depends on how the kinship group is organized. Where sisters do not move too far from home upon marriage, and where they are not incorporated into their husbands' lineages, a group of brothers and sisters may control the lineage and its economic,

> **family of choice**
> A family created over time by new kin ties as friends and lovers demonstrate their genuine commitment to one another.

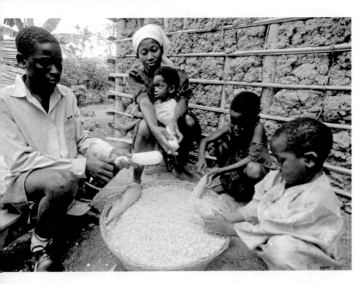

*Figure 6.6* | **The men and women living in the Ashanti's matrilineal society are close confidants, often siding with their opposite-sex siblings over their spouses.**

political, social, and religious aspects. The senior members of the lineage—males and females alike—exercise control over the junior members, although the brothers generally have more control than the sisters.

## Families of Choice

Not everyone defines a family as individuals connected through marriage or genetics. For example, Kath Weston (1991) looked at family forms among gays and lesbians in the San Francisco Bay Area during the 1980s. A lesbian herself, Weston knew that a turning point in the lives of most gays and lesbians was the decision to announce their sexual orientation to their parents and siblings. Sadly, this announcement often resulted in parents turning their child away, thus rejecting the bonds of blood. Living through—or even contemplating—such an experience has been enough to force gays and lesbians to think seriously about the sources of family ties.

By the 1980s, some North American gays and lesbians had reached two conclusions:

- blood ties *cannot* guarantee the 'enduring diffuse solidarity' supposedly at the core of North American kinship (Schneider 1968), and
- new kin ties *can* be created over time as friends and lovers demonstrate their genuine commitment to one another by creating **families of choice**.

'Like their heterosexual counterparts, most gay men and lesbians insisted that family members are people who are "there for you", people you can count on emotionally and materially' (Weston 1991: 113). Some gay kinship ideologies now argue that 'whatever endures is real' as a way of claiming legitimacy for chosen families. Such a definition of family is compatible with understandings of kinship based on nurturance.

# Families and Change

Families change over time. New households branch off from old. The same family can take on different forms and provide different opportunities for the interaction of family members at different points in time. Existing households commonly change through divorce, remarriage, the departure of children, and the break-up of extended families.

Individuals' sense of family belonging changes over time as well. Evans-Pritchard noted that for Nuer women, affinal ties gradually became kinship ties: *ruagh* (in-law relationships) became *mar* (kinship) (1951: 96). The birth of a child gave the wife kinship with her husband's relatives, and it gave the husband kinship with his wife's relatives. In many patrilineal societies, a woman begins to identify with and become more interested in the affairs of her husband's lineage, partly because she comes to be more intimate with the details of the lineage over the years. More significantly, however, what had been her *husband's* lineage becomes her *children's* lineage. The children create a link to the lineage that is independent of her husband.

## Divorce and Remarriage

There are very few societies today in which divorce is not recognized. Depending on the society, nagging, quarrelling, cruelty, stinginess, or adultery may be cited as causes for divorce. In almost all societies, childlessness is grounds for divorce as well.

In some societies, the process is long, drawn-out, and difficult, especially when bridewealth must be returned. A man who divorces a wife in such societies, or whose wife leaves him, expects some of the bridewealth back. But for the wife's family to give the bridewealth back, a whole chain of marriages may have to be broken up. Brothers of the divorced wife may have to divorce to get back enough bridewealth from their in-laws. Sometimes a new husband will repay the bridewealth to the former husband's line, thus letting the bride's relatives off the hook.

In other societies, divorce is easier. For example, the Fulbe of Guider prefer that a man marry his father's brother's daughter (parallel cousin). In many cases, such marriages are contracted simply to oblige the families involved; after a few months, the couple splits up. In general, there is enough dissatisfaction with marriage in Guider to make household transformation through divorce quite common.

Among Muslims in Guider, divorce is controlled by men; women are not legally allowed to initiate divorces. If a husband wants a divorce, he need only follow the simple procedure laid down in the Quran and sanctioned by long practice: he appears before two witnesses and pronounces the formula 'I divorce you' three times. He is then divorced, and his wife must leave his household. She may take an infant with her, but any children at the toddler stage or older stay with the father. If she takes an infant, she must return the child to the father's household by the time the child is six to eight years old. Yet the wives are not entirely powerless. Although a woman cannot ask for a divorce directly, she can facilitate an escape from an unsatisfactory marriage by neglecting her household duties or by going to live in the compound of her father or brother.

For the Ju/'hoansi of the Kalahari Desert, most divorces are initiated by women; the most common reasons for divorce are a woman's displeasure with her husband and her desire to no longer be married (Lee 1992b; Shostak 1981; see EthnoProfile 6.2). After what is often a considerable debate, the couple merely separates. There is no bridewealth to return, no legal contract to be renegotiated. Mutual consent is all that is necessary. The children go with the mother. Ju/'hoansi divorces are generally cordial: ex-spouses may continue to joke with each other and even live next to each other with their new spouses (Lee 1992b).

Traditional north-western Inuit view all kin relationships, including marital ones, as permanent (Burch 1970). A husband and wife who stop having sexual relations and living with each other are considered to be separated and ready for another marriage. If each member of a separated couple remarried, then the two husbands of the wife would become co-husbands; the two wives of the husband, co-wives; and the children of the first and second marriages co-siblings. In such cases, a 'divorce' results in more, not fewer, connections.

## EthnoProfile 6.2 | Ju/'hoansi (!Kung) ········································································

**Region**  Southern Africa
**Nation**  Botswana and Namibia
**Language**  The Ju/'hoansi are speakers of Ju/'hoan of the Ju language family
**Population**  50,000 (1996 estimate)
**Environment**  Desert
**Livelihood**  Hunting and gathering

**Political organization**  Traditionally, egalitarian bands; today, part of modern nation-states
**For more information**  Lee, Richard B. 1992b. *The Dobe Ju/'hoansi*, 2nd edn (New York: Holt, Rinehart, & Winston); Solway, Jacqueline, ed. 2006. *The Politics of Egalitarianism: Theory and Practice* (New York: Berghahn Books).

### International Migration and the Family

Families also change their structure in response to external social pressures. In our globalized world, migration to find work in another country has become increasingly common. Anthropologist Eugenia Georges (1990) examined these effects on people who migrated to the United States from Los Pinos, Dominican Republic (see Map 6.7). Families were divided, with some members moving to New York and some remaining in Los Pinos. Sometimes spouses separated, with the husband migrating and the wife staying home. Consequently, many households in Los Pinos were headed by women. In most cases, the spouse in the United States worked to help his spouse and children migrate, but such migration takes a significant amount of time and money. Children who were close to working age also came to the United States, frequently with their mother, and younger

*Map 6.7* | **Los Pinos**

children were sent for as they approached working age. After several years in the United States, the couple who started the migration cycle would often take their savings and return to the Dominican Republic. Often, their children stayed in the United States and continued to send money home. Even when the husband was geographically separated from his family, he maintained an active role as the breadwinner and the main decision-maker in the household through visits, letters, and occasional telephone calls. Georges found that the divorce rate was slightly lower in migrant families because dense and frequent exchange of information between Los Pinos and New York maintained strong ties of affection that connected husband and wife.

In recent years, the Internet has become increasingly important in the lives of families that are separated by migration, education, work, and so on. Miller and Slater (2000) studied Internet use in Trinidad, finding that email and instant messaging have strengthened considerably both nuclear and extended families, allowing closer relations between distant relatives. They remark on the experiences of a widow they knew who, depressed after her husband's death, was convinced by relatives to learn to use e-mail to contact a beloved grandchild who had gone abroad. This experience was so valuable to her that she began to contact other relatives, and younger members of her family 'swear it has given "new lease of life"' (2000: 61). Overall, the use of the Internet offers anthropologists the opportunity to observe how family separation can be moderated and offers people around the world opportunities for relaxed, expansive, and everyday forms of communication that seem to have important effects on family life.

# Kinship and Systems of Relatedness: Ways of Organizing Human Interdependence

So far, we have discussed systems of relatedness in terms of *marriage* and *family*. But there are other forms of relatedness as well, for example those based on *nurturance* or *invited kinship*. Turning to kinship, we come to the most esoteric of all anthropological studies (Tooker 1992: 357). It is the place to begin understanding socio-cultural transformations and the critical nexus of kinship, gender, and social inequality. Indeed, analyses of the transformations of modernity and post-modernity have their foundation in kinship analysis (Peletz 1995: 366–7).

Anthropologists tend to take a broad approach when they examine relatedness in a particular culture. Some of the key forms of relatedness that anthropologists have studied are those believed to come from shared substance and its transmission (Holy 1996: 171), not only bodily substance (e.g., blood, genetic material, or mother's milk), but also spiritual substance (e.g., soul, rebirth, the spirit world, nurturance, or love). Early anthropologists focussed on relations of biology, believing that Western understandings of 'real' relatives—mothers, fathers, sisters, brothers, sons, daughters, and so on—were universally valid. They saw their job as comparative and formal, and they searched for organizational patterns along genealogical (descent) lines. Their goal was to compare kinship data from different societies in order to discover the universe of genealogical relatives. They tried to specify the formal 'rules' that would be characteristic of, for example, all patrilineal societies. Although this work did bring some important patterns to light, ethnographic evidence indicated that the principles of relatedness that any group of people used to organize themselves were sometimes at odds with genealogical principles. Indeed, in some cases, relatedness based on birth was only one of several ways in which people created strong and enduring ties with one another, some being on nurturance alone (e.g., adoption).

Today, anthropologists continue to focus on relationships that stem from universal human experiences of mating, birth, and nurturance, but they also recognize that definitions of these experiences are not the same in every culture. Many people distinguish between mating and marriage. In addition, all births may not constitute valid links of descent: children whose parents have not been married may not fit the cultural logic of descent, and many societies offer no positions that they can properly fill. Understandings of descent can be even more complicated in cases of surrogacy or children conceived by sperm and/or egg donation. Finally, not all acts of nurturance are recognized as adoption: consider, for example, foster parents in Canada: custody of foster children is officially temporary.

Forms of relatedness are thus selective. One society may emphasize women as the bearers of children and base its kinship system on this fact, while another may trace connections through men, emphasizing the paternal role in conception. A third society may encourage its members to adopt not only children but also adult siblings, blurring the link between biological reproduction and family creation. All three understandings can be justified with reference to the pan-human experiences of relatedness.

Consider our kinship term *aunt*. This term most often refers to a woman occupying a unique position in one of four different ways: father's sister, mother's sister, father's brother's wife, or mother's brother's wife. The women in these positions have something in common: they are sisters or sisters-in-law of your parents. But we may also refer to our mother's best friend as an *aunt*, thereby making her *fictive kin*. By doing so, we recognize the strengths of this system of classification. However, in Chile, children regularly use *tía*, the Spanish term that translates as 'aunt', to refer to female friends of their parents. Indeed, well into early adulthood, Chileans continue to use the term to refer to women who take on the role of 'mother' but with whom they are not as intimate as they are with their own mothers.

Thus anthropologists use *kinship* as an idiom that refers to a selective interpretation of common human experiences—an interpretation resulting in a set of coherent principles people use to assign one another group membership. These principles normally cover several significant issues:

- how to carry out the 'recruiting' of legitimate group members (marriage, birthing, or adoption),
- where group members should live (residence rules),

- how to establish inter-generational links (descent), and
- how to pass on social positions (succession) or material goods (inheritance).

In this way, people are located within social groups in relation to one another both in space and over time.

## Patterns of Descent in Kinship

A central aspect of kinship is descent. Defined by ancestry, existing in time, descent involves the transmission of membership through parent–child links incorporated into groups. In some societies, descent group membership controls how people mobilize for social action. There are two major patterns: **bilateral descent** and **unilineal descent**. Of the two, the unilineal pattern is more common.

**bilateral descent**
The principle that a descent group is formed by people who believe they are related to each other by connections made through their mothers and fathers equally.

**unilineal descent**
The principle that a descent group is formed by people who believe they are related to each other by links made through a father (patrilineal descent) or mother (matrilineal descent) only.

### Bilateral Kindreds

Most Canadians are familiar with the bilateral kindred kinship group, which forms around a particular individual. It includes all the people linked to that individual through kin of both sexes—people conventionally called *relatives* in English (Figure 6.7). These people form a group only because of their connection to the central person or persons, known in the terminology of kinship as *Ego*. Each person within Ego's bilateral kindred has his or her own separate kindred. For example, Ego's father's sister's daughter has kindred that include people related to her through her father and his siblings—people to whom Ego is not related. The major strength of a bilateral kindred is that it can form broad networks; its major weakness is that it does not endure beyond the lifetime of the Ego at its centre.

A classic bilateral kindred is found among the Ju/'hoansi (see Figure 6.8; see also EthnoProfile 6.2). Canadian anthropologist Richard Lee points out that every individual in this society can be linked to every other individual by a kinship term, either through male or female relatives.

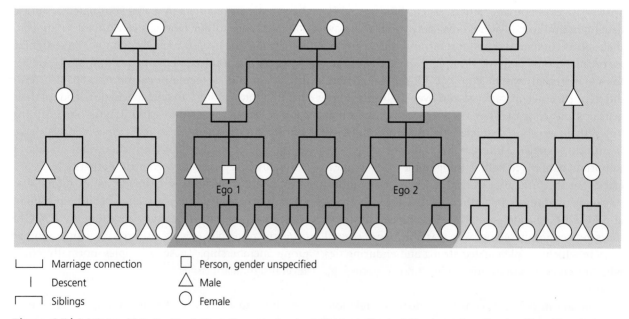

|__| Marriage connection    ☐ Person, gender unspecified
| Descent    △ Male
|‾| Siblings    ○ Female

*Figure 6.7* | **A bilateral kindred includes all recognized relatives on Ego's father's and mother's sides. The dark area in the centre indicates where the kindreds of Ego 1 and Ego 2 overlap.**

*Figure 6.8* | **This Ju/'hoansi grandmother and her grandchild are members of a bilateral kinship group.**

In essence, a Ju/'hoansi camp consists of relatives, friends, and in-laws who have found that they can live and work well together. Under this flexible principle, brothers may be united or divided; fathers and sons may live together or apart. Further, during his or her lifetime a Ju/'hoansi may live at many water holes with many different groups. (1992b: 62)

A wide range of kin-people make this flexibility possible. However, this social flexibility can become problematic in at least four kinds of social circumstances:

- where clear-cut membership in a particular social group must be determined,
- where social action requires the formation of groups that are larger than individual families,
- where conflicting claims to land and labour must be resolved, and
- where people want to perpetuate a particular social order over time.

### Unilineal Descent Groups

Unilineal descent groups, found all over the world, are based on the principle that certain kinds of parent–child relationships are more important than others. In a patrilineal society, women and men belong to a patrilineage formed by father–child links (Figure 6.9); in a matrilineal society, men and women belong to a matrilineage formed by mother–child connections (Figure 6.10). Membership in the group is, on the face of it, unambiguous. Individuals belong to only one lineage. Yet, as

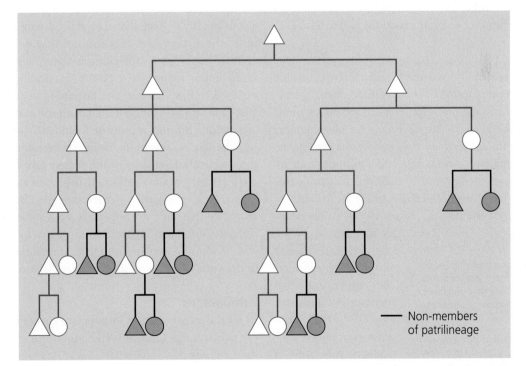

*Figure 6.9* | **Patrilineal descent: all those who trace descent through males to a common male ancestor are indicated in white.**

— Non-members of matrilineage

*Figure 6.10* | **Matrilineal descent: all those who trace descent through females to a common female ancestor are indicated in white.**

Segalen observes, a pattern of unilineal descent is 'no more than a kind of external framework' that can support a wide range of cultural variations (1986: 51–2).

## Lineages

The *-lineal* in patrilineal and matrilineal refers to the nature of the social group formed. They vary in size, ranging from twenty or thirty members to several hundred or more. **Lineages** can endure over time as long as people remember the descent lines. Generally, they survive for five generations (grandparents, parents, Ego, children, and grandchildren). Lineages are *corporate* in their organization—that is, a lineage has a single legal character. As the Ashanti put it, a lineage is 'one person' (Fortes 1953). To outsiders, all members of a lineage are equal *in law* to all others. Lineages are also corporate in that they control property, especially land and water, as a unit.

When members of a group believe that they are related to one another but can no longer actually specify ancient descent links, they arrange themselves in a **clan**. Members of a clan usually believe that they share a common ancestor in the distant past. This ancestor may be a powerful animal/shapeshifter—for example Raven, who is recognized among many Native North American cultures and believed to have lived at the beginning of time. Often, clans transmit beliefs about their common ancestry across generations through stories or legends that offer mythical charters, justifications from the invisible world for the visible arrangements of the society (see Malinowski 1948 [1926]). Many clans apply the incest taboo within their group; among the Nuer, for example, clan members recognize that they cannot marry each other, and they consider sexual relations within the group to be incestuous. In addition, as with lineage, clan membership often brings with it certain political and legal statuses.

### Patrilineages

By far the most common form of lineage organization is the patrilineage. Central is the father–son relationship. Women normally leave when they marry, although they may continue to play an active role in the affairs of their own patrilineages for many years.

**lineages**

A descent group composed of *consanguineal* members, or blood relatives, who believe they can trace their descent from known ancestors.

**clan**

A descent group formed by members who believe they have a common (sometimes mythical) ancestor, even if they cannot specify the genealogical links.

An assumption of hierarchy exists in patrilineal societies: men believe they are superior to women, and many women seem to agree. However, there is a puzzle at the heart of these societies, as we noted earlier in relation to the Iteso. Ironically, the future of the patrilineage depends on people who do not belong to it! A second irony is that women must leave their own lineages to reproduce the next generation of somebody else's lineage. Women in patrilineal societies are often torn between conflicting interests and loyalties (Karp 1986). Should they support their own children or their fathers and brothers?

A classic patrilineal system was found among the Nuer. In the 1930s, Evans-Pritchard noted twenty clans each of which was segmented into separate lineages. The most basic segment constituted the *minimal lineage*, which consisted of three to five generations. Members of one minimal lineage (A) could consider themselves related to another minimal lineage (B) through ancient family connections—for example, if the founder of lineage A. had been the brother of the founder of lineage B. Two minimal lineages related in such a way formed a *minor lineage*, which was composed of all those descended from the common father of the two founders. Minor lineages connected to other minor lineages, by yet another presumed common male ancestor, forming *major lineages*. These major lineages were also believed to share a common male ancestor and thus formed a *maximal lineage*. The members of two maximal lineages believed their founders had been the sons of the clan's founding ancestor; thus, all members of the clan are believed to be patrilineally related.

Disputes among the Nuer emerged and dissipated along lineage lines. If a quarrel erupted between two men whose minimal lineages were in different minor lineages, each would be joined by men who belonged to his minor lineage, even if they were not in his minimal lineage. The dispute would be resolved when the quarrelling minor lineages recognized that they were all part of the same major lineage. Similarly, the minor lineages to one major lineage would ally if a dispute with an opposed major lineage broke out. This process of groups coming together and opposing one another, called **segmentary opposition**, is expressed in kinship terms but represents a very common social process.

Lineages were also important for political purposes for the Nuer. Members of the same lineage were conscious of being in a social group with common ancestors and symbols, corporate rights in territory, and common interests in cattle. When a son in the lineage married, these people helped provide the bridewealth cattle. If the son were killed, they would avenge him and hold his funeral ceremony. Nevertheless, relationships among the members of a patrilineage were not necessarily harmonious:

> segmentary opposition
> A mode of hierarchical social organization in which groups beyond the most basic emerge only in opposition to other groups on the same hierarchical level.

> A Nuer is bound to his paternal kin from whom he derives aid, security, and status, but in return for these benefits he has many obligations and commitments. [However,] duties and rights easily conflict. Moreover, the privileges of [patrilineal] kinship cannot be divorced from authority, discipline, and a strong sense of moral obligation, all of which are irksome to Nuer. They do not deny them, but they kick against them when their personal interests run counter to them. (1951: 162)

In addition, kinship ties can be stressed by societal conflict. In this case, the long period of civil war in Sudan, which led to the separation of South Sudan in 2011, as well as years of drought and famine, caused many deaths and much fragmentation of Nuer kinship (see Hutchinson 1996; 2002).

## Matrilineages

As we have suggested earlier in this chapter, matrilineages are more than just mirror images of patrilineages. While anthropologists find it difficult to generalize on matrilineal societies, and ethnographic evidence suggests a case-by-case approach, we can note a few common features. First, the central relationship is the sister–brother pair; a matrilineage may be thought of as a group of brothers and sisters connected through links made by women. Brothers marry out and often live with the family of their wives, but they maintain essential interest in the affairs of their lineage. Second, a matrilineage is not the same thing as a *matriarchy* (a society in which women rule); brothers often retain controlling interest in the lineage. Thus, inheritances are generally passed to a man from his mother's brother.

A representative example of a matrilineal society comes from the Navajo (Map 6.8). For the Navajo, the basic unit of social organization is the *subsistence residential unit* composed of a head mother, her husband, and some of their children with their spouses and children (Witherspoon 1975: 82). The visible leader of the unit is normally a man, usually the husband of the head mother. He directs livestock and agricultural operations, deals with the outside world, and generally seems to be in charge. In actuality, it is the head mother around whom the unit is organized, as she

> is identified with the land, the herd, and the agricultural fields. All residence rights can be traced back to her, and her opinions and wishes are always given the greatest consideration and usually prevail. In a sense, however, she delegates much of her role and prestige to the leader of the unit. If we think of the unit as a corporation, and the leader as its president, the head mother will be the chairman of the board. . . . When there is a divorce between the leader and the head, it is always the leader who leaves and the head mother who returns, even if the land originally belonged to the mother of the leader. (82–3)

In most matrilineal societies, there are some domains of experience in which men and women are equal, some in which men are in control, and some in which women are in control.

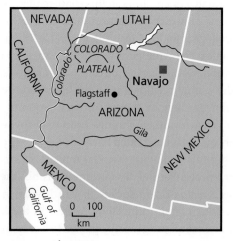

Map 6.8 | **Navajo**

Men living in a matrilineal society may have conflicted feelings surrounding the rules of inheritance. A man may feel great affection for his father, but he will not be his father's heir. He will inherit from his mother's brother, who lives elsewhere. And although a father may wish to have his son inherit from him, he must give to his sister's son (Richards 1954). Malinowski found evidence of such mixed feelings among Trobriand Islanders (see EthnoProfile 7.1). Subsequently, Annette Weiner argued that to understand matrilineal kinship in the Trobriand Islands, one must see the sister–brother pair as an integral unit, with each member making an important contribution to the continuation of the lineage: a boy's mother gives him life, while his mother's brother gives him material inheritance (1980: 286–7).

## Kinship Terminologies

People everywhere use special terms to refer to people they recognize as relatives. Table 6.3 shows the terms in general use in English. Other cultures use different terms—sometimes there are more terms, sometimes fewer. As you might expect, kinship terms do not always retain the same meanings and associations as they are translated across cultures and languages. Greenwood and Stini offer an example: 'Just as the word *father* in English means a great deal more than lineal male ancestor of the first ascending generation, *aita* in Basque has many local connotations irreducible to *father*, as we understand the term' (1977: 333).

Yet despite cross-cultural differences in conceptualizing kinship connections, anthropologists have been able to identify six major prototypical patterns of kinship terminology—Eskimo, Iroquois, Hawaiian, Crow, Omaha, and Sudanese. All provide clues on making sense of a seemingly vast and undifferentiated world of potential kin. External boundaries and internal divisions of the kinship groups outline the structure of rights and obligations and thus roles. Recently, anthropologists have questioned the value of these highly formalized idealized models, mostly because they do not capture the full range of people's actual practices. Nonetheless, they are useful in formal kinship studies insofar as they demonstrate the logic people use to classify and attach importance to their relatives in a society. Table 6.4 lists, in order from most to least common, the main criteria that anthropologists have found people use to classify kinship relationships.

*Table 6.3* | **English Kinship Terms**

|  | **Position and Kinship Chart Abbreviation** |
|---|---|
| Nuclear Family | mother (M) |
|  | father (F) |
|  | son (S) |
|  | daughter (D) |
|  | brother (B) |
|  | sister (Z) |
| Extended Family | uncle (U) |
|  | aunt (A) |
|  | nephew/niece (N) |
|  | cousin (C) |
|  | grandfather (GF) |
|  | grandmother (GM) |
|  | grandson (GS) |
|  | granddaughter (GD) |
|  | great-grandmother (GGM) |
|  | great-grandfather (GGF) |
| Affines (marriage) | wife (W) |
|  | husband (H) |
|  | brother-in-law (WB or HB) |
|  | sister-in-law (WZ or HZ) |
|  | mother-in-law (WM or HM) |
|  | father-in-law (WF or HF) |

Note: The abbreviations given in this chart are generally used in conjunction with symbols that denote gender: Δ (male), ○ (female), or □ (unspecified).

## Kinship and Alliance

Societies based on kinship attempt to resolve the difficulties of intergroup relations by connecting kinship with marriage. Unilineal societies promote or *prescribe* certain kinds of marriage to ensure reproduction of their own memberships and long-term alliances with other groups. Two major types of prescriptive marriage patterns facilitate both these needs: father's sister's daughter (FZD) and mother's brother's daughter (MBD). These patterns are discussed in early alliance theory as 'a rule or practice of marriage between father's sister's child and mother's brother's child (a man's marriage with MBD is "matrilateral cross-cousin marriage"; a man's marriage with FZD is "patrilateral cross-cousin marriage")' (Keesing1975: 148).

In patrilineal systems, the FZD pattern sets up a *direct exchange marriage* where a line that has received a wife from another line in one generation gives a wife back in the next generation. In this system, a man's *father's sister's daughter* is the prototypical spouse, but any woman of the appropriate line can be chosen if both lines agree. In contrast, the MBD system (more common) sets up a pattern of *asymmetrical exchange marriage*. Unlike direct exchange systems, this marriage pattern does not balance out over the generations, as men always find wives in the line their mother came from. This pattern provides a permanent alliance between two lines. While a man's MBD is the prototypical wife in this system, all is not lost if Ego's mother's brother does not have a daughter. In such a case, he could turn to another woman of his generation who is a member of his mother's patrilineage. On the rare occasion that cross-cousin marriage is found in matrilineal systems, men marry out of their lineages, thus creating direct or asymmetrical exchange alliances.

Intergroup relations can also be strengthened by members of the younger generation working to maintain the established alliances they inherit from their kin. Canadian anthropologist Naomi McPherson (2007) notes such inherited alliances in her discussion of trade networks and trade-friendships among the Bariai in Northwest New Britain, Papua New Guinea (see the 'In Their Own Words' box, below). In her analysis, McPherson notes the links between economics, trade networks, friendships (trade partners), and kinship affiliation (particularly that between parents and their first-born child). For example, the ceremonial dress for the first-born becomes a display of trade friendship, as it is constructed out of both locally available raw materials such as red ochre and obsidian and traded 'craft' materials such as the '*poipoi sara* woven armband [which] is only manufactured by the Lolo from a black vine that grows in their particular environment' (2007). In effect, the items used in the ceremonial dress of the first-born advertise the extent of the trade-friendship and the family's access to the network. In the Bariai trade system, first-borns inherit their parents' trade roles; they are exemplars of parental achievement and facilitate the trade partnerships and networks for their younger siblings.

*Table 6.4* | **Criteria of Relatedness**

| Criterion | Distinguishment | Example |
|---|---|---|
| Generation | Place in descent group | *Cousin* conventionally refers to someone who is of the same generation as Ego but who is not considered a sibling. |
| Sex/Gender | Male or female | *Uncle* and *aunt* are distinguished on the basis of both generation and sex. |
| Affinity | Connection through marriage | *Mother* is distinguished from *mother-in-law*. |
| Collaterality | Direct (linking) or indirect (linked) relative | *Mother* and *father* denote direct connections; *aunt* and *uncle* denote relations 'off to one side', linked through the mother or the father. |
| Sex/Gender of Linking Relative | Linking relative is male or female | Not applied in English; some cultures distinguish parallel cousins (Ego's father's brother's children or Ego's mother's sister's children) from cross cousins (Ego's mother's brother's children or Ego's father's sister's children). (See Figure 6.11.) |
| Bifurcation | Relation on mother's or father's side. | Not applied in English; some cultures distinguish the mother's brother from the father's brother. |
| Relative Age | Relatives of the same category who are older or younger than Ego | Not applied in English; Ju/'hoansi separate 'older brother' (*!ko*) from 'younger brother' (*tsin*). |

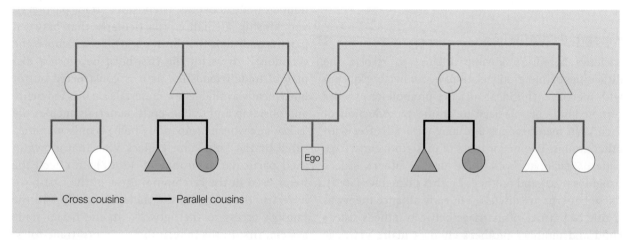

*Figure 6.11* | **Cross-cousins and parallel cousins: Ego's cross-cousins are the children of Ego's father's sister and of Ego's mother's brother. Ego's parallel cousins are the children of Ego's father's brother and of Ego' mother's sister.**

## In Their Own Words | Myth Primogeniture and Long-Distance Trade-Friends in Northwest New Britain, Papua New Guinea

*Trade-friendships form important 'official' bonds, as seen in the trade-friendships of the Bariai of Northwest New Britain, Papua New Guinea. Naomi McPherson examines how trade-friendships, kinship, and economics are intimately intertwined. Note how such integrated analysis offers deep insight into the workings of a society, illustrating our dedication to holism in anthropology.*

Bariai trade-friendships are, in fact, relations between individual women and men (and their spouses) rather than kin groups or communities. Although couched in an idiom of kinship, trade-friendships entail different, albeit parallel, sets of rights, obligations, and motivations from those operating among consanguineal and affinal exchange partners. . . .

Rules for conduct between trade-friends in the Vitiaz Strait include offering one another hospitality and protection, and both parties are under obligation to proffer, to accept, and to reciprocate pre-stations of all sorts. One ought not to lure away the trade-friends of others and, as a trade-friend host, one should act as intermediary for any exchanges between community members and one's trade-friend visitor (Harding 1967: 166–7). Harding characterizes the trade-friend relationship as 'an expression of the social ethic of kinship' (166), an ethic that entails 'generosity and mutual aid' (182). Rather than being the substrate out of which trade-friendships develop, 'kin-like bonds develop partly as a consequence of [these] socially conducive relations' (176). The difference is that a trade-friendship depends on the two parties meeting their obligations; that is, they have a special performance of duty (Harding 1967). Kinship relations, on the other hand, are composed of a variety of acquired obligations and interests, and default in trade specifically does not sever the acquired ties. One can take advantage of kinspeople and get away with it. 'Trading with relatives, therefore, may be burdensome for either side. . . . It is good to have kinsmen in faraway places, but it is better to have good trade-friends' (153). . . .

The analytical conflation of kinship and trade-friendship (prevalent in alliance theories of kinship) has made it difficult to fully appreciate trade-friendships as something other than kinship relations. For example, the idiom of kinship characterizes the Bariai concept of the trade-friend as an affine—indeed, some trade-friends are affinal kin based on contemporary intermarriages—and the trade-friend relationship is also subject to the rights and moral obligations that inform human relations in kinship-based societies. However, the majority of Bariai adults are hard pressed to trace definitive kinship connections with their trade-friends. Rather, a first-born formally inherits his or her mother's and father's trade-friendships within the context of the *mata pau* first-born ceremony. None of the first-born's subsequent siblings is the focus of a *mata pau*, but, as head of the sibling set, the first-born is expected to oversee and facilitate younger siblings' access to inherited trade-friendships. This provides a means for younger siblings to participate in the established trade-friendships while presenting them an opportunity to develop their own trade-friendships through these connections. Not unlike a system of descent reckoning, trade-friendships remain intact over generations while the origin of the relationship, which is of little immediate concern relative to the continuity, substance, and meaning of the relationship itself, is lost in the mists of antiquity. That trade-friendships resemble kinship relations should come as no surprise in societies where human relationships generally are founded on the moral obligations inherent in kinship relations. For the Bariai, trade-friendships can be distinguished from kinship in three important ways. First, the Bariai use the unique, non-kin term *sobo* to encompass the trade-friend relationship. Second, participation in trade-friendships is a household, rather than a descent group or lineage, activity (cf. Harding 1967: 182). Within the framework of day-to-day household activities, it is the spousal partners who, working as a team, produce or procure items of trade and who undertake the transactions involved in trade-friend activities, and it is their first-born who inherits the fruits and friendships of their joint labours. Finally, as noted above, the trade-friendship can be curtailed whereas the kinship relationship cannot. Bariai can and do bring pressure to bear on trade-friends and may even sever a relationship if it is exploitative, an outcome that is next to impossible in the entangled world of affinal and consanguineal relations of kinship. . . .

Exchange relationships with kin and trade-friendships depend upon an ability to manipulate competently the complicated system of debits and credits of the prestige economy and an ability to balance one's own self-interests and the

*Continued*

interests of others according to the principles of morality which structure human relations. The locus of trade (and renown) is the wife/husband team. Transactions between spouses and their kin/affines and between spouses and their trade-friends occur constantly and rather inconspicuously within the context of the household. Similarly, first-born ceremonies are not group efforts but are carried out individually by parents and their *baulo* for their first-born child, when and as they have the wherewithal to do so. These public events effectively deflect individual endeavours onto the person of the first-born who exemplifies parental abilities in forging and maintaining bonds beyond the household. Without a first-born and performance of first-born ceremonies no one can hope to achieve a reputation for renown.

The Bariai distinguish between first-born ceremonies that require 'small work' (K: *ololo kaukau*) and those that require 'big work' (ololo kapei). The difference between the two types is one of relative scale. 'Small work', or minor ceremonies, usually do not require the exchange of pigs, pork, or shell money, and there is no large assembly of witnesses/kin from other villages. Minor ceremonies are contingent upon circumstances and available resources, and none of the key participants (mother and child) is dressed in ceremonial finery. Minor ceremonies celebrate 'firsts' in two senses: they mark the first occasion that others receive a particular food or consumable in the name of the child, and some minor ceremonies confirm phases in the child's physical development (first tooth, first haircut, first fish, first clothing). For these ceremonies, young, inexperienced, first-time parents depend on the resources provided for them by their parents and grandparents who, for example, planned for their descendants by planting stands of sago, coconut, and areca (betel nut) palms for them. Accomplishing certain of the minor ceremonials also serves to release the parents from various taboos on food, mobility, personal hygiene, and appearance that were imposed upon

them when their child was born. Ideally, the minor ceremonies are accomplished by the time the child is four to six years of age. (I have calculated that, in an ideal world, it can take a married couple 15 to 20 years to complete the 17 first-born ceremonies; some parents never do complete them all.)

While the expenditure of energy and wealth required for the performance of minor ceremonials is anything but small, it is only a fraction of that required for major ceremonials. For their proper performance, these ceremonies require vast quantities of one or more of the following: raw/cooked foods (especially taro, sago flour, and coconuts); pigs and/or pork; shell money; and other forms of material wealth such as clay pots, carved bowls, mats, and more. In contrast to the minor ceremonials where the wealth distributed in the child's name was acquired in large part from the child's grandparents and ancestors, the wealth in the major ceremonies is produced and acquired by the child's parents. Parents use their 'strength' to produce more and larger gardens, to acquire and husband numerous pigs, and to access other wealth items by actively developing and engaging in an ever-widening network of social obligations, especially trade networks. Some of the major ceremonies are also concerned with 'firsts', such as the child's first trip to the reef or first wearing of clothes, first excursion to another village. Others focus on a particular item of decorative finery (such as sago fringe, arm bands, red and yellow paint), items that parents and first-born are forbidden to display as personal adornment until the appropriate ceremony is complete. Many of these objects of value are only obtainable through trade; thus, when the first-born is elaborately decorated and paraded through the village to display the item of wealth, the child publicly demonstrates parental ability to forge and maintain relations of trade and exchange.

Source: McPherson, Naomi. 2007. 'Myth Primogeniture and Long-Distance Trade-Friends in Northwest New Britain, Papua New Guinea', *Oceania* 77, 2: 129–57.

## Kinship and Practice

Kinship systems may appear to be fairly rigid sets of rules that use the accident of birth to thrust people into social positions laden with rights and obligations they cannot escape. Yet they are not straitjackets; they offer a flexible series of opportunities for people to choose how to deal with others. They also provide multiple social vectors along which relations of

alliance, association, mutual support, opposition, and hatred may develop. Indeed, the everyday lived experiences of people provide them with the opportunities to *create* cultures of relatedness that are meaningful, that enable them to get on with life, and that allow them to evade the attempts of others who would impose orderly systems of organization, control, or analysis upon them.

## Adoption

The accident of birth thrusts people into prototypical social positions called **ascribed statuses**, laden with rights and obligations. In contrast, **achieved statuses** may be attained as the result of individual or group efforts. Adoption blurs the distinction between ascribed and achieved because it allows people to transform relationships based on nurturance into relations of kinship.

Nurturance is the central theme in Barbara Bodenhorn's (2000) discussion of adoption with the Iñupiat, whalers on the North Slope of northern Alaska. Similar adoption patterns are also found with the Yupik of southwestern Alaska, the Inuit of northern Canada, and the Kalaalit of Greenland. In these polar-region populations, such adoption practices highlight how nurturance overrides 'begetting and bearing'. Most adult Iñupiat have been adopted or have lived in a household in which children have been adopted. The reasons that the Iñupiat gave for adoption included that they 'wanted to', that they had too many boys and wanted a girl (or vice versa), or that all of their 'brothers and sisters [had] adopted'. Often adoption occurred because the child wanted to be adopted. In many cases, the shift was to everyone's satisfaction, but even when it was not, the question of where the child should end up was never based on the argument that he or she belonged with his or her biological parents. After adoption, the degree to which a relationship is maintained between the birth parents and the child is up to the child and ranges from no contact to regular shared activities. Thus, recognition of the biological relationship becomes a matter of choice—there is no social stigma involved if a child ignores his or her biological parents. People do disapprove if the child does not act like a son or daughter to his or her adoptive parents, since they understand that the action of parenting creates parents:

> What is real is acted on and mutually recognized. . . . [B]ecause [relatedness] is disconnected from anything permanent, it must be constantly reconstructed: shared tools, food, labour, political alliance, ceremonial participation, and simply company. . . . It is *this* labour—the work of being related—rather than the labour of giving birth or the 'fact' of shared substance that marks out the kinship sphere from the potentially infinite universe of relatives who may or may not belong (143).

This is kinship based on agency rather than biology.

## Negotiation of Kin Ties among the Ju/'hoansi

Many contemporary kinship studies in anthropology 'tend to devote considerable analytic attention to themes of contradiction, paradox, and ambivalence' (Peletz 1995: 343). These themes appear in Richard Lee's (1992b) analysis of kinship among the Ju/'hoansi, where 'the principles of kinship constitute not an invariant code of laws written in stone, but instead a whole series of codes consistent enough to provide structure but open enough to be flexible' (62). Part of the Ju/'hoansi system of relatedness follows a seemingly straightforward alternating generation bilateral kindred. Kin terms have behavioural correlates, which Lee calls *joking* and *avoidance* (Table 6.5). Joking relationships can be relaxed and affectionate, while avoidance relationships require respect and reserve. Many avoidance relationships may be warm and friendly if the relatives show one another proper respect in public; however, people in an avoidance relationship may not marry one another.

Another, more complex part of the system is structured by the Ju/'hoansi name system, which contains 36 names for men and 32 names for women. A first-born son gets his father's father's name; a first-born daughter gets her father's mother's name. Second-born children

**ascribed statuses**
Social positions people are assigned at birth.

**achieved statuses**
Social positions people may attain later in life, often as the result of their own (or other people's) effort.

Table 6.5 | Generation and Behaviour with the Ju/'hoansi

| Generation | Behaviour |
|---|---|
| Grandparents' | Joking |
| Parents' | Avoidance |
| Ego's | Joking* |
| Children's | Avoidance |
| Grandchildren's | Joking |

*Opposite-gender siblings of Ego's own generation are in the avoidance category.

are supposed to be named after the mother's father or mother. Later children are named after the father's brothers and sisters and the mother's brothers and sisters. All people with the same name will claim to be related. A man older than Ego who shares his or her name is called *!kun!a* ('old name'), which is the same term used for *grandfather*. A man younger than Ego who shares his or her name is called *!kuna* ('young name'), the same term used for *grandson*. By extension, Ego would call anyone with her or his father's name *father* and anyone with her or his mother's name *mother*. Additionally, names restrict potential marriage partners: 'a woman may not marry a man with her father's or brother's name, and a man may not marry a woman with his mother's or sister's name' (Lee 1992b: 74)! Further, an individual may not marry anyone with the name of one of her or his avoidance kin. It does not matter how people are 'really' related to others with the same name or even if they are related at all according to formal kinship terminology; the name relationship takes precedence, making close relatives out of distant ones.

To resolve the apparent 'contradiction, paradox, and ambivalence' of these rules and relationships, the Ju/'hoansi have a third component to their kinship system: *wi*. The principle of *wi* depends on the fact that in any relationship that can be described by more than one kin term, the older party chooses the term to be used. For example, a man may get married only to discover that his wife's aunt's husband has the same name he has. What terms will he and his wife's aunt use for each other? According to the principle of *wi*, the aunt decides because she is older. If she calls him *nephew* (rather than *husband*), he knows to call her *aunt*. The principle of *wi* means that a person's involvement with the kinship system is continually changing over the course of his or her lifetime. For the first half of people's lives, they must accept the kin terms their elders choose. After midlife, however, they begin to impose *wi* on their juniors. For the Ju/'hoansi, kinship connections are open to manipulation and negotiation.

### Compadrazgo in Latin America

An important set of kinship practices in Roman Catholic Latin America is *compadrazgo*, or ritual co-parenthood (Figure 6.12). The baptism of a child requires the

*Figure 6.12* | In Latin America, when a child is baptized, the child's godparents become *compadres*, or ritual co-parents, with the child's birth parents.

presence of a godmother and a godfather as sponsors. In Latin America, godparents are expected to take an active interest in their godchildren and to help them wherever possible. However, the more important relationship is between the godparents and the parents. They become *compadres* ('co-parents'), and they are expected to behave toward each other in new ways. A couple often chooses godparents whose social standing is higher than their own. Participating together in the baptism changes these unequal strangers into ritual kin whose relationship, although still unequal, is now personalized, friendlier, and more open. The co-parents call each other *compadre*, and they help one another: the parents will support the godparents when that support is needed (e.g., politically), and the godparents will do favours for the parents.

Catherine Allen notes that the bonds of *compadrazgo*, in combination with marriage alliances and kinship,

> form constellations of mutual obligation and dependence that shift with time as new *compadrazgo* relationships are formed, young relatives come of age, and old bonds fall into disuse through death or quarrelling. Like kin ties, bonds of *compadrazgo* can become as much a burden as an asset, and like kin ties they can be ignored or honoured in the breach. (1988: 90)

Again we see the flexibility of kinship practices.

### Euro-American Kinship and Reproductive Technologies

In the Euro-American world, kinship is understood as the social construction of natural facts, a logic that both combines and separates the social and natural worlds. Euro-Americans recognize kin related by blood and kin related by marriage; they also believe that procreation—the process that brings kin into existence—is part of nature. Ties of kinship are supposed to stand for what is unalterable in a person's social world in contrast to what is open to change. Yet reproductive technologies such as in vitro fertilization and surrogate motherhood make clear that nothing is unalterable: even the world of natural facts is subject to social intervention.

Contemporary ambiguities surrounding kinship in the United States and Canada have put pressure on the courts to decide what constitutes biological parenthood and how it is related to legal parenthood (see Dolgin 1995). Consider, for example, the case of 'Baby M' in America. It began as a traditional surrogacy arrangement in which the surrogate, Mary Beth Whitehead, was impregnated with the sperm of the husband in the couple who intended to become the legal parents of the child she bore. Whitehead was supposed to terminate all parental rights when the child was born, but she refused to do so. The court faced a dilemma. Existing law backed Whitehead's maternal rights, but the parties had signed a legal contract. Focussing on Whitehead's attempt to break the surrogacy contract, the court terminated her legal rights as biological mother, although they awarded her visitation rights.

More complicated than traditional surrogacy, *gestational surrogacy* deconstructs the role of biological mother into two roles that can be performed by two different women. In another key American case, the Calverts, a childless married couple, provided egg and sperm that were used in a laboratory to create an embryo, which was then implanted in Anna Johnson's uterus. But when Johnson gave birth to the baby, she refused to give it up. As Dolgin points out, this case 'provided a context in which to measure the generality of the assumption that the gestational role both produces and constitutes maternity' (1995: 58). While several previous court cases had emphasized the role of gestation in forming an indissoluble bond between mother and child, in this case the court referred to Anna Johnson 'as a "gestational carrier", a "genetic hereditary stranger" to the child, who acted like a "foster parent"'

(59). The court declared the Calverts and the child a family unit on genetic grounds and ruled that the Calverts were the baby's 'natural' and legal parents.

Dolgin notes that in these cases, the courts awarded legal custody to those parties whose living arrangements most closely approximated the traditional middle-class, North American heteronormative two-parent family. 'Biological facts were called into judicial play only . . . when they justified the preservation of traditional families' (63). Biological facts that might have undermined such families were systematically overlooked. Perhaps the clear-cut biological basis of North American kinship is not so clear-cut after all.

# Beyond Kinship

While kinship may be central to the structure and functioning of some societies, it is not equally important to all groups of people. Consider our own society, for example, where kinship is most often reduced to the realm of personal and family relations. Ultimately, whether living in a kin-based society or a non-kin-based society, all people form significant links with individuals beyond their kin group in order to survive. Thus, to fully understand how human beings relate to one another in any society, we must consider the importance of non-kin relationships in structuring social worlds.

As we will see, the line between 'kin' and 'non-kin' is not always clear; often it is a matter of interpretation. In general, non-kin patterns of social relations do not follow the rules of recruitment or enforce the traditional status distinctions and role obligations that are at the heart of kinship. And yet those involved in non-kin social relations often use a kinship idiom to refer to each other and to define their roles in the relationship. Such relationships can occur on both individual and institutional levels. On the individual level, for example, ritual co-parents refer to themselves as co-parents (*compadres*) and take on the formal role obligations of family members. On the institutional level, members of organizations such as Catholic monastic orders refer to one another as *brother*, *sister*, *father*, and *mother* and model their interactions on those of a family. Such religious orders are parts of international institutions, and the connections established among members reach far beyond the contexts of everyday, face-to-face relatedness.

Schneider (1968) argued that the emotion of North American kinship is the feeling of 'enduring diffuse solidarity'. This definition might just as well apply to friendship or any other form of close companionship. Perhaps enduring diffuse solidarity is something that human beings regularly seek to establish in their relations with other people—kin or not.

## Friendship

A common definition of *friend* is 'one joined to another in intimacy and mutual benevolence independent of sexual or family love' (Brain 1976: 15). Brain points out that the Western belief that friendship and kinship are separate phenomena often breaks down in practice. For example, some husbands and wives in Western societies consider each other 'best friends', and we may be friends with some relatives while treating others as distant acquaintants. Definitions of friendship also differ cross-culturally—recall the example of *compadrazgo*, which many Westerners might interpret as a form of institutionalized friendship rather than kinship.

Bell and Coleman (1999) suggest that typical 'markers' for friendship are the relatively 'unofficial' bonds that people construct with one another—bonds that are personal, affective, and—to a varying extent from society to society—a matter of choice (Figure 6.13). With globalization, the importance of friendship seems to be increasing: 'In many shifting social contexts, ties of kinship tend to be transformed and often weakened [while] new forms of friendship are emerging' (1999: 5). Rezende (1999) observed an example of such a 'new' form of friendship: in Rio de Janeiro, some middle-class women and their maids refer to each other as 'friends' in 'friendships' of affection, care, and consideration. Both sets of women valued these relationships, which establish mutual trust and an 'affinity that brings these people together as parts of the same social world' (1999: 93).

Some cultures also extend their interpretation of the bonds of friendship to apply to entire groups. We can find this perspective in the friendship network that the National Association of Friendship Centres (NAFC) has established. Members of this organization focus their efforts on strengthening the ability of more than 117 Friendship Centres across Canada to respond to the problems of isolation and alienation experienced by First Nations peoples in urban settings. Here we find a contemporary example of the importance of friendship alliances for survival.

## Sodalities

**Sodalities** offer members a more formal organization of non-kin bonds. Such organizations can have various functions,

> among them police, military, medical, initiation, religious, economic, and recreation [Figure 6.14]. Some sodalities conduct their business in secret, others in public. Membership may be ascribed or it may be obtained via inheritance, purchase, attainment, performance, or contract. Men's sodalities are more numerous and highly organized than women's and, generally, are also more secretive and seclusive in their activities. (Hunter and Whitten 1976: 362)

An example of diffuse solidarity in industrial Western societies is the union—an affiliation of workers who seek certain economic and workplace conditions from employers. Sometimes union negotiations highlight

---

**sodalities**
Non-kin forms of social organization; special-purpose groupings that may be organized on the basis of age, sex, economic role, and/or personal interest.

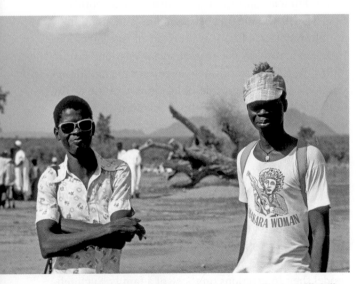

*Figure 6.13* | **Friendships are based on the 'unofficial' bonds that people create with one another, which vary from society to society. These two young men in Cameroon are the best of friends.**

Figure 6.14 | Men of the devil sodality prepare for Carnival parade in Oruro, Bolivia.

issues of human rights, such as pay parity, safe working conditions, protection from harassment in the workplace, or enforcement of child labour laws.

### Age Sets in Eastern Africa

Some groups establish sodalities based on generational distinctions. In eastern Africa, a number of societies assign men from different kinship groups to sodalities composed of **age sets**, which succeed each other in time as their members pass through youth, maturity, and old age. 'Sets are part of the formal social order blessed by tradition, and membership is usually ascribed, and is always obligatory' (Baxter and Almagor 1978: 4). These societies do not establish age-set systems for women, possibly because women are involved in domestic matters from an early age and marry shortly after puberty (11).

In the classic study, Monica Wilson (1951) examined the role of age sets among the Nyakyusa (see Map 6.9).

At the time of Wilson's fieldwork, the Nyakyusa were patrilineal and patrilocal, and their society was divided into many independent chiefdoms. Each Nyakyusa age set began as a group of boys about 10 to 15 years of age. When the members of this junior set were

> **age sets**
> Non-kin forms of social organization composed of young men born within a specified time span, which are part of a sequence of age sets that proceeds through youth, maturity, and old age.

about 33 to 35 years old, an elaborate series of rituals was held to mark their 'coming out'. At that time, the reigning senior generation 'handed the country over to them'. At any point in time, there were three strata in the Nyakyusa age-set system:

1) retired elders,
2) active senior men who carried political and military responsibilities for the entire society, and
3) immature juniors.

Map 6.9 | **Nyakyusa**

Map 6.10 | **Boran**

Age-set systems may play an important cognitive role in the societies where they are found. For example, Baxter (1878) argues that the *gada* age-set system of the Boran of Kenya and Ethiopia (see Map 6.10) provides the idiom the Boran use to describe and debate social and political life. The complex *gada* system recognizes five generation sets that succeed one another over a forty-year period. Every eight years, a new generation set is formed and the oldest set retires. The Boran understand *gada* as a conceptual system that guides their society in social as well as political matters. However, in a classic emic/etic juxtaposition, Baxter rejects the suggestion that the *gada* system ever played an overtly political role in Boran society:

> *Gada* exists primarily . . . in the folk view as well as in mine, to ensure the well-being of the Boran and to regulate the ritual growth and development of individuals and to do so in such a way as to permit all men who survive life's full span to achieve responsible and joyful sanctity. It is this last, joyful aspect of *gada* as an institution which performs rituals that has struck intelligent non-professional observers . . . and not its political ones. (156)

**secret societies**
Non-kin forms of social organization that initiate young men or women into social adulthood and reveal 'secret' knowledge to initiated members.

### Secret Societies in Western Africa

Several neighbouring peoples in western Africa use **secret societies** as a way of drawing members of different kinship groups into crosscutting associations. The most famous secret societies are the Poro and the Sande, which are found among the Mende, Sherbro, Kpelle, and other neighbouring peoples of Sierra Leone, Ivory Coast, Liberia, and Guinea.

Poro is a secret society for men, responsible for initiating young men into social manhood; Sande, a secret society for women, initiates young women into social womanhood. Poro and Sande are responsible for supervising and regulating the sexual, social, and political conduct of all members of the wider society. 'Until he has been initiated in the society, no Mende man is considered mature enough to have sexual intercourse or to marry' (Little 1967: 245). These sodalities are secret in the sense that members of each have certain knowledge that can only be revealed to initiated members. Both sodalities are hierarchically organized. The higher a person's status within the sodality, the greater the secret knowledge revealed. To carry out their regulatory responsibilities, high-status sodality members often impersonate important supernatural figures by donning masks and performing in public. One secret kept from the uninitiated is that these masked figures are not the spirits themselves.

Each community has its own local Poro and Sande congregations, and a person initiated in one community is eligible to participate in the congregations of other communities. Initiates must pay a fee for initiation, and if they wish to receive advanced training and progress to higher levels within the sodality, they must pay additional fees. In any community where Poro and Sande are strong, authority in society is divided between a sodality of mature women and one of mature men. Together, they work to keep society on the correct path. Indeed, the relationship between men and women in societies with Poro and Sande tends to be highly egalitarian.

Anthropologist Beryl Bellman (1984) was initiated into a Poro chapter among the Kpelle of Liberia. He describes the men's initiation as a ritual process that takes place about once each generation. One of the Poro's forest spirits, or 'devils', metaphorically captures and eats the novices—only for them to be reborn metaphorically from the womb of the devil's 'wife' later. Marks incised on the necks, chests, and backs of initiates represent the 'devil's teeth marks'. After this scarification, initiates spend a year living apart from women in a special village constructed for them in the forest. During this period, they carry out various activities under the strict supervision of senior Poro members. Female Sande initiates undergo a similar experience. Bellman notes that, both during and after the process of initiation, members use the idiom of kinship, most importantly MB and ZS terms, to describe certain relationships within their secret society.

MacCormack (1980) studied secret societies among the Sherbro (see Map 6.11). The Sherbro have a third secret society called *Thoma*, which initiates both men and women. Members of one society cannot be initiated into the others, and families with several children usually try to initiate at least one child into each. As with Poro and Sande initiations, Thoma initiations involve elaborate rituals that create kin-like bonds between co-initiates and transform uninitiated, proto-social beings into initiated, fully social adult human beings. Mac-Cormack describes the Thoma as 'a microcosm of the whole': 'Its local congregations or chapters are headed by a man and a woman, co-equal leaders who are 'husband and wife' in a ritual context' (1980: 97). The Sherbro are concerned with the reproduction of their society—not just the production of children but also the continuation of the division of labour between men and women. The Sherbro say that the ritual function of the Thoma sodality is 'to cleanse the land and the village from evil and restore its fertility and well-being' (98).

So what is the secret? Bellman (1984) argued that initiation rituals are primarily concerned with teaching initiates how to be discrete—to know when, how, and even whether to speak about various topics. Discretion is a valued attribute of the social adult.

## Theories of Relatedness: Kin-based and Non-kin-based Societies

For most of our history, kinship or other intimate forms of relatedness organized human interdependence within a fairly restricted local arena. Yet, as we have seen, not all societies are organized around kinship. Indeed, early anthropologists were struck by the ways in which the elaborate kinship systems they found in non-Western societies could regulate social life and organize behavioural patterns. Yet nineteenth-century scholars of classical antiquity recognized that kinship groups had played comparable roles in ancient European societies as well. Somehow, over time, those kin-ordered forms of social life had been displaced by the large-scale, impersonal, bureaucratically ordered forms of social life typical of a modern nation-state.

Sir Henry Maine, an English jurist who studied the roots of Roman law, described the shift as one from *status* to *contract*. Ancient societies organized people's relationships by the particular position, or status, that each person held within the group. Each status carried with it a bundle of rights and obligations, which modern social scientists call a *role*. Statuses and their roles

*Map 6.11 |* **Sherbro**

complemented one another: holders of each status were responsible for particular tasks and could rely on other members of the system to perform different tasks. Ideally these roles fit together like pieces of a puzzle, ensuring that all tasks needed for group survival were carried out.

For Maine, the crucial feature of kinship-based societies was that people were not free to choose their own statuses, nor could they modify the rights and responsibilities associated with those statuses. Status and role were *ascribed*. Status-based societies contrasted with contract-based societies in four major ways:

1) ideally, the parties to contractual relationships enter into them freely;
2) the contracting parties are equally free to specify the rights and obligations between them for the duration of the contract;
3) the range of possible statuses and roles is limitless, bound only by the imagination and interests of the contracting parties; and
4) once the terms of the contract are met, the parties may choose to terminate their relationship with one another.

In another interpretation, Emile Durkheim described the process as a shift from *mechanical solidarity* to *organic solidarity*. In his view, 'primitive' societies (ancient and contemporary) were held together on the basis of mechanical solidarity that assigned the same social tasks to everybody who occupied the same kinship status. Tasks were based on age and sex, with each kinship group containing the full range of roles necessary for survival. Keeping kin groups together as parts of a larger whole was problematic, as nothing bound these groups together except 'mechanical' similarities in language, mode of livelihood, and so on. Mechanical solidarity, therefore,

was brittle. Groups could split and go their own way without seriously affecting their ability to survive.

In contrast, 'modern' societies were held together by organic solidarity, which depended on a highly developed *division of labour* rather than established kinship roles. In the 'modern' system, each non-kin group specialized in a particular task needed for the survival of the larger whole. With organic solidarity the division of labour became more elaborate, some people specializing in food production and others in trade, government, and so on. Full-time specialization meant that each group had to depend on other groups to provide it with things it could not provide for itself, and if any one specialized group were to disappear, the society as a whole would suffer.

Essentially, Maine and Durkheim were asking the same question: What is the social glue that ensures social co-operation? Anthropologists as well as sociologists have suggested many answers to this question over the years. Zygmunt Bauman argues that all human groups of a significant size 'are first and foremost processes of collectivization of friends and enemies . . . individuals sharing a common group or category of enemies [who] treat each other as friends' (1990: 152). Benedict Anderson (1983) suggests that the bonds of nationalism that hold citizens of nation-states together are 'imagined', as they have not existed for all time but are rather social constructions arising from historical circumstances (we will return to this interpretation in Chapter 12). In this chapter, we have discussed a number of cohesive forces, notably Schneider's (1968) interpretation that it is our need for 'enduring diffuse solidarity'—between kin and non-kin—that holds society together. Whatever the binding glue, it is clear that people in all societies have developed patterned social relationships that aim to bind them for the long term, and some of these reach beyond, and even cut across, ties forged in terms of everyday relatedness.

# Key Terms

achieved statuses   153

age sets   157

ascribed statuses   153

bilateral descent   144

blended family   139

bridewealth   132

clan   146

conjugal family   137

dowry   136

endogamy   133

## Chapter Summary

1. Human life is group life; we depend upon one another to survive. We organize this interdependence through relationships of marriage, family, kinship, and friendship.

2. Marriage is a social process that transforms the status of the participants, stipulates the degree of sexual access the married partners may have to each other, positions children, and creates relationships between the kin of the partners.

3. Not all societies agree on a standard definition of marriage; thus, marriage patterns differ across the globe. A number of modern societies, including Canada, recognize same-sex marriages, while others do not. Some cultures promote monogamy, while others promote polygamy—either polygyny (multiple wives) or, less frequently, polyandry (multiple husbands).

4. Bridewealth is a payment of symbolically important goods by the husband's lineage to the wife's lineage, often as compensation for the loss of the wife's productive and reproductive capacities. Dowry is typically a transfer of family wealth from parents to their daughter at the time of her marriage. Dowries are often considered the wife's contribution to the establishment of a new household.

5. Not all cultures share a standard understanding of the central family. Different family structures produce different internal patterns and tensions. Families may change from one type to another over time and with the birth, growth, and marriage of children.

6. Most human societies permit divorce, although it is not always easy. The grounds for divorce differ across cultures, but often include childlessness. In some societies, only men may initiate a divorce; in others, it is the woman who controls divorce.

7. Kinship principles are based on, but irreducible to, the universal experiences of mating, birth, and nurturance. Descent (bilateral or unilateral) links members of different generations with one another. Unlike bilateral kindreds, partrilineages and matrilineages are corporate groups that collectively control important property.

8. Anthropologists traditionally recognize six basic systems of kinship terminology. In recent years, however, anthropologists have become quite skeptical of the value of these idealized models because they are highly formalized and do not capture the full range of people's actual practices. Kinship terminologies pay attention to certain attributes of people that are then used to define different classes of kin.

9. By prescribing certain kinds of marriage, lineages establish long-term alliances with one another. Two major types of prescriptive marriage patterns in unilineal societies are a father's sister's daughter marriage system and a mother's brother's daughter marriage system.

10. Kinship systems are governed by many rules, but they also offer flexibility. Achieved kinship statuses can be converted into ascribed kinship statuses by means of adoption. In some cultures, kin ties are open to negotiation; they can also be formed through relationships other than those of blood or marriage. In many ways, kinship is a cultural construction that cannot be reduced to biology.

11. Every society provides ways of establishing links with non-kin. It is sometimes difficult to draw a neat line between kinship and non-kin relationships because kinship terms may be used between friends and/or kinship roles may be the prototypes for the roles expected of friends. Close relationships—such as those between friends or co-members of a sodality—cultivate a sentiment of enduring diffuse solidarity.

12. Early anthropologists described and explained the differences they saw between kin-based and non-kin-based human societies. They thought of kin-based societies as 'primitive', characterized by personalized, face-to-face relationships, ascribed statuses, and mechanical solidarity. In contrast, they considered non-kin-based societies to be 'modern' and characterized by impersonal relationships, achieved statuses, and organic solidarity. They found that larger societies require more complex, specialized divisions of labour; they also found that specialized divisions of labour make it more likely that institutionalized relationships will develop between non-kin. Thus, it is not surprising that kinship plays a reduced role in most contemporary Western societies.

## Critical Thinking Questions

1. What is the 'prototypical' marriage? Is the prototype the same in all cultures?

2. Distinguish between *pater* and *genitor*. Are they always the same person? Indeed, are gestational and social mothers always the same person? Do adopted children struggle with such categories?

3. How are joint, extended, and blended families different from nuclear families?

4. In what way is kinship an idiom? How is it peculiar to a specific group of people?

5. What are the criteria that people use to indicate relatedness? What criteria might people use to designate kinship or friendship? How do you distinguish between relationships of family, kinship, and friendship in your own life?

6. What are some of the organizational differences between kin-based and non-kin-based societies?

## Suggested Readings

Chute, Janet E. 1999. 'Frank G. Speck's Contributions to the Understanding of Mi'kmaq Land Use, Leadership, and Land Management', *Ethnohistory* 46, 3: 481–540. An interesting article on an early Canadian ethnographer's work with an Algonquian group.

Ginsburg, Faye D., and Rayna Rapp, eds. 1995. *Conceiving the New World Order: The Global Politics of Reproduction* (Berkeley: University of California Press). An important collection of articles by anthropologists who address the ways human reproduction is structured across social and cultural boundaries.

Jamieson, Kathleen. 1986. 'Sex Discrimination and the Indian Act', in *Arduous Journey: Canadian Indians and Decolonization*, ed. J. Rick Ponting (Toronto: McClelland & Stewart), 112–36. A discussion of the discrimination toward First Nations women found in the Indian Act and government policies associated with this Act.

Sacks, Karen. 1979. *Sisters and Wives* (Urbana: University of Illinois Press). *A Marxian analysis of the notion of sexual equality.* This book includes very important data and analysis on sister–brother relations.

Shostak, Marjorie. 1981. Nisa: The Life and Words of a !Kung Woman (New York: Vintage). *A wonderful book that tells the story of a Ju/'hoansi (!Kung) woman's life in her own words.* Shostak provides background for each chapter, and there is much here on marriage and everyday life.

Smith, Mary F. 1981 [1954]. Baba of Karo (New Haven: Yale University Press). *A remarkable document: the autobiography of a Hausa woman born in 1877.* This text provides much information about Hausa patterns of friendship, clientage, adoption, kinship, and marriage.

Stone, Linda, ed. 2001. *New Directions in Anthropological Kinship* (Lanham, MD: Rowman & Littlefield Publishers, Inc.). An excellent collection of recent articles on kinship.

Tooker, Elisabeth. 1992. 'Lewis H. Morgan and His Contemporaries', *American Anthropologist* 94, 2: 357–75. An excellent review article on the early development of kinship studies in anthropology.

## Related Websites

Bill C-38: The Civil Marriage Act www.parl.gc.ca/common/bills_ls.asp?Parl=38&Ses=1&ls=c38

Kinship and Social Organization www.umanitoba.ca/faculties/arts/anthropology/tutor/kinmenu.html

National Association of Friendship Centres (NAFC) www.nafc.ca

Navajo Nation Government www.navajo-nsn.gov

Vanier Institute of the Family www.vifamily.ca

# 7 | Making a Living

## Learning Objectives

By the end of Chapter 7, you will be able to

- recognize how human beings have devised a
  variety of subsistence strategies,

- understand the relationship between
  production, distribution, and consumption,

- detail various forms of economic theory as
  they relate to anthropological concerns,

- identify various forms of exchange,

- compare and contrast internal (needs)
  and external (resources) explanations of
  consumption patterns,

- consider the cultural and symbolic nature
  of consumption in the dialectic between the
  meaningful and the material, and

- appreciate distribution and exchange at local
  and global levels.

*This Kashmiri woman participates in the economic life
of her community by separating green chilies from red
chilies during a drying process. Kashmiri chilies are
highly valued in local and global markets—a kilogram
generally sells for two hundred rupees (about four
Canadian dollars).*

Ethnographer Richard Lee arrived in the Dobe Ju/'hoansi area in the central Kalahari Desert of southern Africa in 1963 (see EthnoProfile 6.2). On his first morning there, his neighbours, including a man named N!eishi, asked him to give them a ride in his Land Rover to get some food. They said there was little left in their area—mostly bitter roots and berries. They wanted to collect mongongo nuts—a staple of their diet and a great favourite—in a nearby grove (Figure 7.1). Lee agreed to take them to their destination. They drove for several hours, progressing at a slow pace as they carefully navigated around aardvark holes and fallen trees, through landscapes 'where no truck had ever been before' (1992b: 39). By the time they stopped, Lee figured they were about 16 kilometres (10 miles) north of Dobe. He was amazed by how fast the Ju/'hoansi, both men and women, were able to gather the nuts. After two hours, they left the grove. He later weighed the food collected in that short time: the women had gathered loads weighing 30 to 50 pounds each; the men, 15 to 25 pounds each. Lee calculated: 'That worked out to about 23,000 calories for food for each woman collector, and 12,000 for each man. Each woman had gathered enough to feed a person for 10 days and each man enough for five days. Not at all a bad haul for two hours' work!'

*Figure 7.1* | **Richard Lee gathers mongongo with the Ju/'hoansi.**

Thus, Lee found strong evidence to counter the Western stereotype of human beings who forage for a living as leading lives that are, in Thomas Hobbes's famous phrase in *Leviathan*, 'nasty, brutish, and short':

> My first full day of fieldwork had already taught me to question one popular view of hunter–gatherer subsistence: that life among these people was precarious, a constant struggle for existence. My later studies were to show that the Ju/'hoansi in fact enjoyed a rather good diet and that they didn't have to work very hard to get it . . . only 20 hours a week in subsistence. But what about the fact that N!eishi had come to me that morning saying that they were hungry and that there was no food nearby? Strictly speaking, N!eishi spoke the truth. October is one of the harder months of the year, at the end of the dry season, and the more desirable foods had been eaten out close to Dobe. What N!eishi did not say was that a little farther away food *was* available, and, if not plentiful, there was enough to see them through until the rains came. When N!eishi came to me with his proposition, he was making an intelligent use of his resources, social and otherwise. Why hike in the hot sun for a small meal when the bearded white man might take you in his truck for 10 large ones? (40–1)

Lee observed that the Ju/'hoansi were well nourished, with balanced diets. What is more, they were choosy about what they ate, unwilling to settle for food they disliked. Such behaviour is entirely familiar to us. Much has changed in the Dobe area since the 1960s, and the Ju/'hoansi no longer forage as they once did. Until relatively recently, however, the cultural, indeed traditional, knowledge of the Ju/'hoansi enabled them to live rather well in what many see as a marginal environment.

In recent years, anthropologists have taken an increasingly holistic view on issues of livelihood, recognizing the interrelationships between the physical, biological, environmental, economic, and cultural aspects of human existence. Indeed, cross-disciplinary research such as that of physicist Peter Finke (2005) calls us to recognize that human culture is not *apart from* the natural world—rather it is *a part of* this world and is contextualized by and interdependent with ecological processes and the energy cycles of nature. It is our cultural responses and our capacity for reflexivity that allow for adaptive responses.

## Culture and Livelihood

Anthropologist Richard Wilk has defined *economic anthropology* as 'the part of the discipline that debates issues of *human nature* that relate directly to the decisions of daily life and making a living' (1996: xv). In ordinary conversation, when we speak of making a living we usually mean doing what is necessary to obtain the material things—food, clothing, shelter—that sustain human life, seldom distinguishing needs from wants. Making a living thus encompasses what is generally considered economic activity. However, anthropologists and other social scientists disagree about what the term *economy* ought to represent.

The rise of the capitalist market led to one view of what economy might mean: buying cheap and selling dear. That is, economy means maximizing utility—obtaining the greatest possible satisfaction for the smallest possible cost. This view is based on the assumption of **scarcity** of both goods and services. Many economists and economic anthropologists came to focus their analyses on how economizing individuals set priorities and allocate resources rationally to maximize economic outcomes. Economic anthropologists also extended their investigations to the societal level to study how societal priorities affect the maximizing decisions of individuals.

Other economic anthropologists regard this way of thinking about economic life as ethnocentric. They present evidence to show that different societies use different principles to organize economic life, and they argue that the job of economic anthropology should be to describe and explain these cultural variations. This view of economy focusses on **institutions**. From an institutional point of view, a society's **economy** consists of the culturally specific processes its members use to provide themselves with material resources. Therefore, economic processes cannot be considered apart from the cultural institutions in which they are embedded (Halperin 1994). Thus, culturally, decisions that seem to be based on 'wants' may actually be based on 'needs'.

## Subsistence Strategies

*Subsistence* often refers to the satisfaction of the most basic material survival needs: food, clothing, and shelter. The different ways that people in different societies go about meeting these needs are called **subsistence strategies**. Subsistence strategies are the intricate ways of actualizing relationships in specific physical environments. Anthropologists have devised a typology of subsistence strategies that has gained wide acceptance (Figure 7.2). The basic division is between **food collectors** and **food producers**. Yet, although this typology suggests a clear delineation between food collectors and food producers, the two systems are not always separated in practice. For example, archaeological evidence shows that some of the first food producers in the world continued food collection for many generations, raising a few crops on the side and occasionally abandoning food production to return to full-time foraging.

The strategies followed by food collectors depend on the availability of resources in the environments in which they live. Small-scale food collectors, such as the Ju/'hoansi throughout the 1960s, live in environments poorly endowed with resources and are likely to change residence often in search of new resources. In contrast, complex food collectors live in environments richly endowed with dependable food sources and may even, like the Native peoples of the northwest coast of North America, build settlements with permanent architecture.

**scarcity**
The assumption that resources (e.g., money) will never be plentiful enough for people to obtain all the goods or services they desire.

**institutions**
Stable and enduring cultural practices that organize social life.

**economy**
From an institutional perspective, the material-means provisioning process in a cultural system.

**subsistence strategies**
The patterns of production, distribution, and consumption that members of a society employ to ensure the satisfaction of their basic material survival needs.

**food collectors**
Those who gather, fish, or hunt for food.

**food producers**
Those who depend on domesticated plants and/or animals for food.

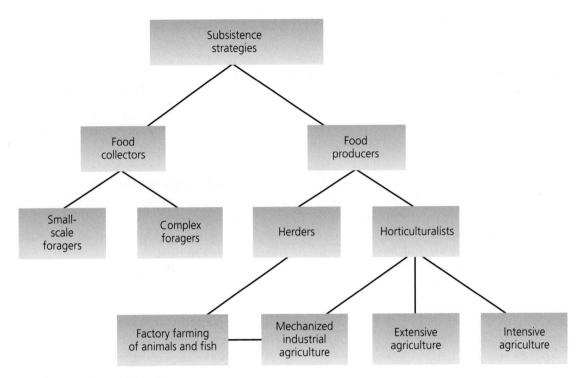

*Figure 7.2* | **Subsistence strategies.**

**extensive agriculture**
A form of cultivation that depends on slash-and-burn techniques, rainwater, human muscle power, and a few simple tools such as digging sticks, hoes, and/or machetes; it exhausts the land, requiring farmers to move plots every few years.

**intensive agriculture**
A form of cultivation that employs plows, draft animals, irrigation, fertilizer, and such, to bring much more land under cultivation at one time.

**mechanized industrial agriculture**
Large-scale farming, often found in conjunction with factory farming of animals, that is highly dependent on industrial methods of technology and production.

Food producers may farm or herd, or both. Pastoralists are often nomadic, moving their herds from place to place in search of fresh pasture. Today, they are often in conflict with settled farmers who own the lands—and often the water—that they traditionally used to sustain their herds. Among those who farm, there are three major distinctions:

1) **extensive agriculture**,
2) **intensive agriculture** (Figure 7.3), and
3) **mechanized industrial agriculture**.

In extensive agriculture, farmers clear plots of uncultivated land, burn the brush, and plant their crops in the

ash-enriched soil that remains. The method of clearing involved is called *slash-and-burn* or *swidden*. Eventually these techniques exhaust the soil, and the plot must lie fallow as a new plot is cleared and the process repeated. (This cycle may range from two years, as in Yucatán, Mexico, to twenty or thirty years, as with the

*Figure 7.3* | **Some farmers use plows and animals for intensive agriculture to reduce the amount of time it takes them to cultivate a large plot of land.**

Iroquoian peoples at the time of European contact.) In intensive agriculture, farmers use more complex tools and technologies (e.g, crop rotation, irrigation, and fertilizers) to work on the same plot for a longer period of time. In mechanized industrial agriculture, farming is organized along industrial lines. Most often, this type of crop production is found alongside the factory farming of animals. Agribusiness 'factories in the field' and animal feedlots transform food production into a large-scale, technology-dependent industry.

## Phases of Economic Activity

Economic activity is usefully subdivided into three distinct phases:

1) **production**,
2) **distribution**, and
3) **consumption**.

Anthropologists differ in the importance they attach to each phase. For example, the distributive process known as *exchange* is central to the functioning of capitalist free enterprise. Some anthropologists have assumed that exchange is equally central to the functioning of all economies and have tried to explain the economic life of non-Western societies in terms of exchange. Anthropologists of a Marxian bent, however, have argued that we cannot properly understand exchange without first studying the nature of production. They point out that production shapes the context in which exchange can occur, determining which parties have how much of what kind of goods to exchange. Other anthropologists have suggested that neither production nor exchange patterns make any sense without first specifying the consumption priorities of the people who are producing and exchanging. Consumption priorities, they argue, are designed to satisfy material needs. But the recognition of needs, and appropriate ways to satisfy them, is shaped by arbitrary cultural patterns. Still others argue that patterns of production, exchange, and consumption are all seriously affected by the kind of *storage* used in a particular society (Figure 7.4).

## Distribution and Exchange

### Neo-classical Economic Theory and the Rise of Capitalism

In the eighteenth century, as capitalist enterprises continued to rise across western Europe at an increasing pace, thinkers such as Adam Smith and his disciples struggled to devise theories to explain the profound changes in European economic and social life. Their work became the foundation for **neo-classical economic theory**, a theory that some economic anthropologists continue to support today.

Capitalism differed in many ways from the preceding feudal economic system, particularly in distribution. Feudal economic relations allotted goods and services to individuals on the basis of their position in society, or their *status*. Because lords had high status and many obligations, they had a right to more goods and services. Peasants, with low status and few rights, were allowed far less. This distribution of goods was time-honoured and not open to modification. The new capitalist economic relations, in contrast, were considered 'free' precisely because they swept away all such traditional restrictions. Distribution under capitalism was negotiated between buyers and sellers in the market.

In Smith's ideal market, everyone has something to sell (if only his or her willingness to work), and everyone is also a potential buyer of the goods (or services) brought to the market. There is economic exchange. Ideally, because there are many buyers, many sellers, and no traditional restrictions governing who should get how much of what, prices can fluctuate depending on levels of supply and demand. Distribution is carried out in line with the preferences of individuals (needs/wants = desired goods). High demand for certain items raises the price for those items, as many buyers bargain to obtain few goods. This high demand, in turn, entices more people to produce

**production**
The transformation of nature's raw materials into a form suitable for human use.

**distribution**
The allocation of goods and services.

**consumption**
Using up material goods necessary for human survival.

**neo-classical economic theory**
A formal attempt to explain the workings of capitalist enterprise, with particular attention to distribution.

*Figure 7.4* | **A seventeenth-century drawing of storage warehouses built at the height of the Inca (Tawantinsuyu) Empire (above). At left, the plan of Huánuco Pampa shows the location of these storage warehouses. Some anthropologists argue that food storage practices buffer a population from ecological fluctuations, making considerable cultural manipulation of the economic relations of consumption possible.**

those goods to take advantage of their higher prices. As competition between suppliers increases, however, prices go down, as each supplier attempts to obtain a greater share of the market. Ideally, prices stabilize as suppliers begin offering 'desired' goods at a cost sufficiently high to allow a profit but sufficiently low for buyers to afford.

Capitalist market exchange of goods and services (labour) for other goods, services, or cash was an important development in Western economic history. It is not surprising, therefore, that eighteenth-century Western economic theory was preoccupied with explaining how the capitalist market worked.

Markets clearly had a new, decisive importance in the functioning of society. Western neo-classical economics is based on the assumption that market forces are the central forces determining levels of both production and consumption in society. Thus, neo-classical economic analysis focusses on markets, scarcity hypotheses, and 'laws' of supply and demand. In such a system everything has a price.

## Modes of Exchange

Some anthropologists have argued, however, that to take self-interested, materialistic decision-making in the

*Figure 7.5* | In his book *The Gift*, Marcel Mauss examines the Kula dance, a ritual exchange ceremony. Here, men perform the Kula dance at a celebration in the Trobriand Islands, Papua New Guinea.

capitalist market as the prototype of human rationality is both reductionist and ethnocentric. Further, such analyses frequently encourage the use of unilineal evolutionary and neo-evolutionary models of organization and interaction in the discussion of cultures defined as 'other'. Thus, Morgan's ethnical stages of savagery, barbarism, and civilization (discussed in Chapter 3) become embedded, overtly or covertly, in the categories used in such discussions.

We must remember that the capitalist market and the neo-classical economic theory are relatively recent cultural inventions specific to societies with certain basic values, institutions, and assumptions about the human condition. In other words, they are specific to peoples with a certain shared world view on the nature of the political economies in which they live. Non-Western, non-capitalist societies also have devised modes of exchange that distribute material goods in ways that are in accordance with their basic values, institutions, and

assumptions about the human condition—their world view.

Characteristic of the Western-centric analysis of non-Western cultures, and suggesting how unilineal evolutionary biases can be embedded in economic theory, is the work of French anthropologist Marcel Mauss (2000 [1950]). Mauss contrasted non-capitalist *gift exchanges* with impersonal *commodity exchanges* typical of the capitalist market (Figure 7.5). Gift exchange is deeply embedded in social relations of kinship, partnerships, and acquaintanceships, always requiring a return 'gift'. Commodity exchange only links the participants by cash—the cost of and payment for an item. However, what Mauss did not fully address is the fact that cultures are not compartmentalized into one of these forms of economic activity but may well engage in various permutations of both. Similarly, the work of Marshall Sahlins (1972) has this ancient–modern directional tone. He drew on the writings of economic historian

Karl Polanyi to propose three **modes of exchange**: reciprocity, redistribution, and market exchange. Polanyi argued that these modes could be identified historically in many cultures; he also recognized that different modes of exchange often coexist within a single society.

## Reciprocity

The most ancient mode of exchange, **reciprocity** is characteristic of egalitarian societies, as the Ju/'hoansi once were. Sahlins identified three kinds of reciprocity:

1) generalized,
2) balanced, and
3) negative.

*Generalized reciprocity* is found when those who exchange do so without expecting an immediate return and without specifying the value of the return. Everyone assumes that the exchanges will eventually balance out. *Balanced reciprocity* is found when those who exchange expect a return of equal value within a specified time limit. For example, Lee noted that the Ju/'hoansi distinguish between barter, which requires an immediate return of an equivalent value, and *hxaro*, which is a kind of generalized reciprocity that encourages social obligations to be extended into the future (1992b: 103). *Negative reciprocity* is an exchange of goods and services in which at least one party attempts to get something for nothing without suffering any penalties. These attempts can range from haggling over prices to outright seizure.

## Redistribution

The second mode of exchange, **redistribution**, requires some form of centralized social organization. Those who occupy the central position receive economic or material contributions from all members of the group. It is then their responsibility to redistribute the goods they receive in a way that provides for every member of the group. The Canada Revenue Agency is probably the institution of redistribution that Canadians come to know best.

The potlatch (Ýaqʷ qʷa), or gift-giving ceremony, of First Nations peoples of Canada's west coast has frequently been used erroneously to illustrate redistribution (Figure 7.6). While there are elements of exchange involved, reducing the event to a venue for redistribution of wealth ignores the complexity of the social interactions the potlatch represents: members of a community coming together to bear witness to specific culturally significant events such as births, marriages, deaths, and remembrances. (Note Daisy Sewid-Smith's discussion in the 'In Their Own Words' box, below.) Further, Tollefson observes that politics plays a very large part in the potlatch:

> certain clan goals could only be fulfilled through potlatching. These include (1) installation of clan leaders, (2) evaluation and verification of clan titles to resources, (3) bestowal of clan titles, (4) resolution of inter-clan disputes, (5) establishing or reaffirming clan alliances, (6) investment and

**modes of exchange**
Patterns according to which distribution takes place: reciprocity, redistribution, and market exchange.

**reciprocity**
A mode of exchange in which individuals exchange goods and/or services 1) under the assumption that the exchanges will eventually balance out, 2) with the expectation of immediate balance, or 3) in the hope that at least one party will get something for nothing.

**redistribution**
A mode of exchange in which a centralized social organization receives contributions from all members of the group and redistributes them in a way that provides for every member.

*Figure 7.6* I **The potlatch of the Kwakiutl was a highly complex social event that held deep cultural importance for all involved in the gathering. The ceremony was banned by the Canadian government from 1884 to 1951 although it continued in the villages even in the face of arrests and punishment through the Canadian courts.**

## In Their Own Words | The Continuing Reshaping of Our Ritual World by Academic Adjuncts

*Daisy Sewid-Smith, a daughter of the late Chief James Sewid, is a member of the Mamaliliq la tribe of Village Island, British Columbia. She was formerly the head of the First Nations Education Department of School District 72 in Campbell River, an advisory council member for the Centre for Studies in Religion and Society at the University of Victoria, and author of Prosecution or Persecution (1979).*

My great-uncle joined with the other nobility to lament the loss of the great economic institutions of the past when he stated to Dr Wolcott, 'It's no use giving a potlatch any more. The old people don't do it; so nobody pays you back, and the young people don't even understand what it's all about.' He was referring to the grossly misunderstood economic system we called *Pǝssa*. This was the investing institution of the Kʷakʷakǝwakaʷ and Liǧʷidaxʷ League of Nations. This institution charged interest, called in debts, gave credit, and kept records of all transactions for future generations. Both my father and my great-uncle held hereditary positions in this complex system. It was to this institution that my great-uncle was referring when he spoke of the young not understanding and the investment not being repaid.

Most of our people today have only seen what was known as Ýaqʷ qʷa, meaning *gift-giving*. That is the reason why the term *potlatch*, a Chinook word meaning *to give*, was assigned to this system by the Chinook speakers of our old trade world. The Ýaqʷ qʷa, or potlatch, was a system that paid witnesses to validate such events as marriages, memorials, and the succession of ancestral names. The Ýaqʷ qʷa, or potlatch system, did not have the same principles, purpose, laws, or membership as the *Pǝssa*.

Unfortunately, my great-uncle understood too well the changing landscape of his ritual world. He and the nobility he came from had struggled so hard to keep the culture alive despite the institutionalized oppression of our beliefs by the state and by religious zealots; the loss of their sacred land and resources by the encroachment and laws of the newcomers; the loss of life due to disease, social breakdown, and the very personal identity struggles of the younger generation; and the diminished use of our precious language that holds the keys to our past, our values, and our religion. Today, our struggle is not just of legal or religious prosecution. Today our struggle is sadly the reshaping of our ritual world by academic interpretations.

The academic world must, in its need to publish accounts of my Nation, begin to subscribe to rules that are consistent with our ritual structure. They must begin to identify the trained specialists who are working within our culture and use the same rules we have of validation and authority to ensure an accurate view of our ritual world. It is not enough to read and cite from previous misinterpretations to make a theory right. When a house is built on a foundation of sand, its structure is weak and unstable. So is it for our ritual world within academic rendering. We have sorrily witnessed the reshaping of the foundations of our old institutions, the validation of those within our Nation unschooled in our complexes, and the loss of our precious rights and privileges so embedded in our history.

The last words belong to one of our chiefs addressing the first academic to come among us, Franz Boas, when he said in 1894, 'It is a strict law that bids us dance. It is a strict law that bids us distribute our property among our friends and neighbours. It is a good law. Let the white man observe his law, we shall observe ours.'

Source: Sewid-Smith, Daisy. 1997. 'The Continuing Reshaping of Our Ritual World by Academic Adjuncts', *Anthropology & Education Quarterly* 28, 4: 594–602.

diversification of clan wealth, (7) social removal of shame, and (8) maintenance of regional stability. (1995: 71)

Thus we see the interconnections among power, politics, cultural priorities, social interaction, and economic exchange; these ties should remind us of the necessity of looking at cultural processes through the anthropological lens of holism. (Note that we will revisit in Chapter 11 the issues of power and politics involved in such network–corporate exchanges.)

## Market Exchange

Invented in capitalist society, **market exchange** is the most recent mode of exchange, according to Polanyi. Polanyi was well aware that trade, money, and market institutions had developed independently of one another, historically. He also knew that they could be found in societies outside the West. The uniqueness of capitalism was how all three institutions were linked to one another in the societies of early modern Europe.

# Production

Some economic anthropologists see production as the driving force behind economic activity. Production creates supplies of goods to which demand must respond, and it determines levels of consumption. Anthropologists who stress the centrality of production borrow their perspective on economic activity, as well as many key concepts, from the works of Karl Marx. They argue that this perspective is far more insightful than the one taken by neo-classical theorists of market exchange.

*Figure 7.7* | **Women weave rope out of coir, a fibre extracted from coconut husks, in Kerala, India. Human beings continuously labour to turn natural substances into useful products.**

**market exchange**
A mode of exchange in which the exchange of goods (trade) is calculated in terms of a multi-purpose medium of exchange and standard of value (money) and carried on by means of a supply–demand–price mechanism (the market).

**labour**
The activity linking human social groups to the material world around them; human labour is therefore always social labour.

**mode of production**
'A specific, historically occurring set of social relations through which labour is deployed to wrest energy from nature by means of tools, skills, organization, and knowledge'.

**means of production**
The tools, skills, organization, and knowledge used to extract energy from nature.

**relations of production**
The social relations linking the people who use a given means of production within a particular mode of production.

## Labour

**Labour** is perhaps the most central Marxian concept these anthropologists have adopted. Through labour, human beings actively struggle together to transform natural substances into forms they can use. This is most clear in the case of food production but includes the production of clothing, shelter, and tools (Figure 7.7). Marx emphasized the importance of human physical labour in the material world, but he also recognized the importance of mental or cognitive labour. Human intelligence allows us to reflect on and organize productive activities. Mentally and physically, human social groups struggle together to ensure their material survival. In struggling, they reproduce patterns of social organization, production, and thought.

## Modes of Production

Marx attempted to classify the ways different human groups carry out production. Each way is called a **mode of production**. Anthropologist Eric Wolf defined a mode of production as 'a specific, historically occurring set of social relations through which labour is deployed to wrest energy from nature by means of tools, skills, organization, and knowledge' (1982: 75). Tools, skills, organization, and knowledge constitute what Marx called the **means of production**. The social relations linking human beings who use a given means of production within a particular mode of production are called the **relations of production**. That is, different productive tasks (clearing the bush, planting, harvesting, and so on) are assigned to different social groups, all of which must work together for production to be successful.

The concept of mode of production is holistic, highlighting recurring patterns of human activity in which certain forms of social organization, production practices, and cultural knowledge co-determine one another. Wolf notes that Marx speaks of at least eight different modes of production in his own writings, although he focussed mainly on the capitalist mode. Wolf finds the concept of mode of production useful. But like most anthropologists inspired by Marx's work, he does not feel bound to accept Marx's conclusions as a matter of course. He suggests that three modes of production have been particularly important in human history:

1) a *kin-ordered mode* in which social labour is deployed on the basis of kinship relations (e.g., husbands/fathers clear the fields, the whole family plants, mothers/wives weed, children keep animals out of the field);
2) a *tributary mode* 'in which the primary producer, whether cultivator or herdsman, is allowed access to the means of production while tribute is exacted from him by political or military means' (79); and
3) the *capitalist mode*.

The capitalist mode has three main features:

1) the means of production are property owned by the capitalists,
2) workers are denied access to such ownership and must sell their labour to the capitalists in order to survive, and
3) this labour for capitalists produces surpluses of wealth that capitalists may retain or plow back into production to increase output and generate further surpluses.

An overlap exists between this classification of modes of production and the traditional anthropological classification of subsistence strategies. The kin-ordered mode of production is found among foragers and those farmers and herders whose political organization does not involve domination by one group. The tributary mode is found among farmers and herders living in a social system that is divided into classes of rulers and subjects. Subjects produce both for themselves and for their rulers, who take a certain proportion of their subjects' product as tribute.

The capitalist mode, the most recent to develop, is found in industrial societies around the world, but particularly those of North America and western Europe.

Thus, in some ways the mode-of-production concept simply recognizes the same variation in the arts of subsistence that Lewis Henry Morgan recognized in the nineteenth century. Yet the concept of mode of production also highlights certain attributes of subsistence strategies that Morgan's approach tended to downplay. For example, modes of production have as much to do with forms of social and political organization as with material productive activities. That is, the kin-ordered mode of production is distinctive as much for its use of the kinship system to allocate labour to production as for the kind of production undertaken, such as farming. In a kin-ordered mode of production, the *relations of kinship* serve as the *relations of production* that enable a particular *mode of production* to be carried out.

## The Role of Conflict in Material Life

Traditionally anthropologists have emphasized the important links between a society's social organization (kinship groups, chiefdom, or state) and the way that society meets its subsistence needs, either to demonstrate the stages of cultural evolution or to display the functional interrelationships between parts of a particular society. In both cases, however, the emphasis of the analysis was on the harmonious fashion in which societies either changed or stayed the same. This focus implied that social stability should not be tampered with. Social change was possible, but it would take place in an orderly fashion, in the fullness of time, according to laws of development beyond the control of individual members of society.

Many anthropologists have not been persuaded that social change is orderly or that social organization is by nature harmonious. They find the Marxian approach useful because it treats conflict as a natural part of the human condition. The concept of mode of production makes a major contribution to economic anthropology precisely because of the very different interpretation it gives to conflict, imbalance, and disharmony in social life.

Marx pointed out, for example, that the capitalist mode of production incorporates the workers and the owners in different and contradictory ways.

These groups, which he called *classes*, have different interests, and what is good for one class may not be good for all classes. The workers' economic desires (higher wages to purchase more goods) are inevitably opposed to the owners' economic desires (lower wages to increase their profits or to reinvest in tools and raw materials).

This does not mean that warfare is constant between the different classes engaged in a particular mode of production; however, it does mean that the potential for conflict is built into the mode of production. The more complex and unequal the involvement of different classes in a mode of production, the more intense the struggle between them is likely to be. Such struggle may not always lead to outright rebellion for sound political reasons, but minor forms of resistance—from sluggish efforts at work to intentional disruption of the status quo—are not uncommon. Marx was one of the first social analysts, and certainly one of the most eloquent, to document the high level of human suffering generated by certain modes of production, particularly the capitalist mode.

Wolf's three modes of production (kin-ordered, tributary, and capitalist) describe not only a society's subsistence strategy but also that society's social organization. As a result, they accent the lines of cleavage along which tension and conflict may develop—or may have developed historically—between different segments of the society: between, say, parents and children or husbands and wives in the kin-ordered mode; between lords and peasants in the tributary mode; and between capitalists and workers in the capitalist mode.

## Applying Production Theory to Social and Cultural Life

Economic anthropologists who focus on production as the prime causal force in material life tend to apply the metaphor of production to other areas of social life as well. They see production as involving far more than short-term satisfaction of material

**ideology**
According to Marx, those products of consciousness—such as morality, religion, and metaphysics—that purport to explain to people who they are and to justify the kinds of lives they lead.

survival needs. If a given *mode* of production is to persist over time, the *means* and *relations* of production must also persist.

For example, farmers produce grain and leave behind harvested fields. They exchange some grain with cattle herders for milk and meat, and they permit the herders' cattle to graze in the harvested fields in exchange for manure they need to fertilize their fields. Consequently, farmers and herders alike end up with a mix of foodstuffs to sustain human life (i.e., to reproduce the producers). In addition, each group has what it needs in the coming season to renew its means of production. Both groups will want to ensure that similar exchanges are carried out by their children; to achieve this goal, they must find a way to ensure that the next generation will consist of farmers and cattle herders producing the same goods and willing to exchange them. Therefore, not only must the means of production perpetuate but so must the relations of production. The result, then, is the reproduction of society from generation to generation.

People also produce and reproduce *interpretations* of the productive process and their roles in that process. Marx used the term **ideology** to refer to the cultural products of conscious reflection. As used in Marxian analysis, *ideology* refers in particular to those beliefs that explain and justify the relations of production to those who engage in them. For Marx, ideology was not independent of the productive process itself. On the contrary, 'men, developing their material production and their material intercourse, alter, along with this their real existence, their thinking and the products of their thinking. Life is not determined by consciousness, but consciousness by life' (Marx 1977 [1932]: 164). As a result, Marxian economic anthropologists investigate the kinds of ideas, beliefs, and values that are produced and reproduced in societies with different modes of production. Members of the class in power usually hold to an ideology that justifies their domination. Those who are dominated may assent publicly to the ideology of the rulers, but in private they are likely to be highly critical and to offer alternative interpretations.

The use of the production metaphor in the analysis of social and cultural life highlights certain processes and relationships that the exchange metaphor tends to downplay or ignore. For example, exchange theorists generally are not interested in *why* the different parties to an exchange have different quantities of resources with which to bargain. Production theorists, in contrast, aim to show that access to resources is determined *before* exchange by the relations of production, which decide who is entitled to how much of what. In particular, they reject the assumption that access to valued resources is open to anyone with gumption and the spirit of enterprise. Different modes of production stack the deck in favour of some classes and against others. This is most clear in the capitalist mode, where owners have disproportionate access to wealth, power, and prestige and where workers' access to these goods is sharply restricted. Thus, the classes who fare poorly do so not because of any inherent inferiority, laziness, or improvidence; they fail to get ahead because the rules of the game (i.e., of the mode of production) were set up in a way that keeps them from winning.

The production metaphor also provides an especially dynamic perspective on cultural persistence and cultural change. Production theory relates peoples' preferences for different goods to the interests and opportunities of the different classes to which they belong. People buy and sell as they do not out of idiosyncratic whimsy but because the choices open to them are shaped by the relations of production. From this perspective, poor people purchase cheap goods not because they have poor taste and cannot recognize quality when they see it but because their deprived position within the mode of production provides them with very limited income, and they must make do with the only goods they can afford.

Finally, production theory focusses on people as much as or more than it focusses on the goods they produce. It views human beings as social agents involved in the construction and reconstruction of human society on all levels in every generation. Traditions persist but only because people labour to reproduce them from one day to the next. Linking production (and reproduction), social relations, and ideologies highlights the contingent nature of social life, even as it suggests how traditions are carried on.

# Consumption

*Consumption* usually refers to using up material goods necessary for human survival. These goods include—at a minimum—food, drink, clothing, and shelter; they can and often do include much more. The study of consumption by economists and others was, until recently, much neglected. To some extent, this is because many observers assumed that there were no interesting questions to ask about consumption. That is, it seemed clear that people either consume goods for obvious reasons, such as survival, or as a result of idiosyncratic personal preferences. Today, consumption is often a central focus in studies of economic practices.

## Explanations for Consumption Patterns

Anthropologists who make cross-cultural comparisons have always noticed striking differences in consumption patterns in different societies. Historically, they have taken three basic approaches to account for these patterns:

1) the internal explanation,
2) the external explanation, and
3) the cultural explanation.

### The Internal Explanation

The internal explanation for human consumption patterns comes from the work of Malinowski. His version of functionalist anthropology explains social practices by relating them to the basic human needs that can be biological or psychological. Whatever their origin, if they go unmet, the society might not survive. Malinowski proposed a list of basic human needs, which includes nourishment, reproduction, bodily comforts, safety, movement, growth, and health. Every culture responds in its own way to these needs with some form of the corresponding institutions: food-collecting techniques, kinship, shelter, protection, activities, training, and hygiene (Malinowski 1944: 91).

Malinowski's approach had the virtue of emphasizing human beings' dependency on the physical world in order to survive. Further, Malinowski was able to show that many customs that appear bizarre to uninitiated Western observers are in fact 'rational' because they help people satisfy their basic human needs. Nonetheless, this approach fell short of explaining why all societies do not share the same consumption patterns.

### The External Explanation

Later anthropologists looked at human consumption patterns from the perspective of *cultural ecology*—that is, in terms of the ways in which humans and their cultural constructs adapt in response to the physical environment in which they exist. From this perspective, human consumption patterns form in response to what is obtainable in the given environment. In order to survive, people must learn to make use of the available resources. This perspective draws on the field of **ecology**, making note of how different **ecozones** and **ecotones** (Figure 7.8) influence the range of **econiches** available to the human population. It also draws on the findings of socio-ecologists, who investigate the features of ecozones to explain why a particular animal population—a troop of baboons, for example—organizes itself the way it does in a particular environment.

The term *cultural ecology* comes to us from Julian Steward (1972), who was influenced by the earlier work of Franz Boas and the teachings of Alfred Kroeber. Steward did fieldwork among the Shoshone in the highly inhospitable Great Basin region of the United States. In conducting his research, he developed an approach that involved

1) outlining the subsistence technologies and methods of environmental exploitation used by local peoples,
2) seeking patterns of behavior/culture (strategies) tied to such exploitations, and
3) investigating how these strategies (and their associated technologies) affect other areas of the culture.

**ecology**
The study of the ways in which living species relate to one another and to their natural environment.

**ecozones**
The particular mixture of plant and animal species occupying any particular region of the earth.

**ecotones**
A transition area between two different ecozones that displays characteristics of both ecozones.

**econiche**
The plants and animals in an ecozone on which a species relies for survival; essentially a place in the natural world where a species is 'at home'.

*Figure 7.8* | **The composition of ecozones is highly variable. In the top diagrams, the brown square has the most potential, as it has resources from all three ecozones (red, blue, yellow); the orange, purple, and green areas are the ecotones. In the bottom diagram, we can see more specifically the many 'tones' of transition between two ecozones—the forest through to the coast line into the depths of the a river, lake, or the ocean.**

His approach has been seminal for researchers in various disciplines.

For example, principles from Steward's approach appear in economic anthropologist Rhoda Halperin's (1994) examination of the relationship between ecological anthropology (itself an extension of the cultural ecology perspective) and economic anthropology. Borrowing concepts from Polanyi, Halperin argued that every economic system can be analyzed in terms of two kinds of movements: *locational movements*, or 'changes of place', and *appropriational movements*, or 'changes of hands'. In her view, ecological relationships that affect the economy are properly understood as changes of place, as when people must move into the grasslands, gather mongongo nuts, and transport them back to camp. Economic relationships, in contrast, are more properly understood as changes of hands, as when mongongo nuts are distributed to all members of the camp, whether or not they helped to gather them. Thus, ecological (locational) movements involve transfers of energy; economic (appropriational) movements, in contrast, involve transfers of rights (1994: 59). Analyzed in this way, people's rights to consume mongongo nuts cannot be derived from the labour they expended to gather them.

Another way of seeing the difference between ecological and economic arrangements is to pay attention to the connection between food storage and food sharing. A socio-ecologist might argue that those who gather mongongo nuts are obliged to share them and consume them immediately because they have no way to store them. Ecological anthropologist Tim Ingold (1983) agrees that the obligation to share makes storage unnecessary, but he also points out that sharing with others today ordinarily obligates them to share with you tomorrow (reciprocity). Put another way, sharing food can be seen not only as a way of avoiding spoilage but also as a way of storing IOUs for the future!

Once societies develop ways to preserve and store food and other material goods, however, new possibilities open up (Figure 7.9). Archaeological evidence indicates that the more food there is to store, the more people invest in storage facilities (such as pits or pottery vessels), and the more quickly they become sedentary. Large-scale food storage techniques involve a series of 'changes of place' that buffer a population from ecological fluctuations for long periods of time. But techniques of food storage alone predict nothing about the 'changes of hands' that food will undergo once it has been stored. Food storage techniques have been associated with all subsistence strategies, including that of complex food collectors. These findings suggest that economic relations of consumption, involving the transfer of rights in stored food, have long been open to considerable cultural elaboration and manipulation (Halperin 1994: 178).

From these examples, we can see that both ecological and economic relationships affect human consumption patterns. However, economic transfers of rights

Figure 7.9 | Traditional facilities for storing food in Sulawesi, Indonesia.

to material resources cannot be separated from wider political forces that impinge on those rights. Thus, according to anthropologist Elliot Fratkin, 'a shift in theoretical understanding from *cultural* ecology to *political* ecology' (1997: 236) is necessary. For example, the current adaptations of eastern African pastoralists and their herds to the semi-arid environment is strongly affected by political pressures coming from the nation-states and the politicization and militarization of the shifting ethno-religious landscape of eastern Africa. As a result, Fratkin says, contemporary anthropological studies of pastoralists explain human–livestock interactions 'less in terms of "carrying capacity" or "desertification" and more in terms of loss of common property rights, increased economic differentiation and social stratification, and incorporation and domination of tribal pastoral groups by larger state systems' (236).

### The Cultural Explanation

From the perspective of cultural anthropology, the explanations for human consumption patterns that we have discussed so far have definite limitations. Consider how each would respond to the following question: Why do people X raise peanuts and sorghum? The internal, Malinowskian explanation would be 'to meet their basic human need for food'. The external, socio-ecological explanation would be 'because peanuts and sorghum the only food crops available in their ecozone that, when cultivated, will meet their subsistence needs'. Both these answers are suggestive, but they remain incomplete. We might ask whether the local food sources that people X choose to exploit are the *only* local food sources available to them. Ethnographic data show that no society exploits every locally available food source to meet its consumption needs. Quite the contrary, consumption needs are selective; in other words, they *are culturally shaped*.

Thus, we can see that major shortcoming of both internal and external explanations for human consumption patterns is that they ignore or deny the possibility of *human agency*. Malinowski, and many cultural ecologists, assumed that patterns of consumption were dictated by an iron environmental necessity that did not allow for alternatives. From such a perspective, individuals in most non-Western societies have little to no control over what they consume; they simply have no choice. Yet to rob people of choice is to dehumanize them.

Sahlins urged anthropologists to pay close attention to consumption because consumption choices reveal what it means to be a human being. Human beings are *human*, he tells us,

> precisely when they experience the world as a concept (symbolically). It is not essentially a question of priority but of the unique quality of human experience as meaningful experience. Nor is it an issue of the reality of the world; it concerns *which worldly dimension becomes pertinent*, and in what way, to a given human group. (1976a: 142; emphasis added)

Thus, by focussing on cultural beliefs and behaviours as the forces behind consumption, and by acknowledging that all people have at least some control over what they consume, we highlight agency as central to the human experience.

## The Cultural Construction of Needs

'Needs' is a vague concept. Hunger can be satisfied by beans and rice or steak and lobster. Thirst can be quenched by water or beer or soda pop. In effect, culture defines needs and provides for their satisfaction according to its own logic. And cultural logic is irreducible to biology, psychology, or ecological pressure.

By adopting this cultural approach to consumption, the distinctions between needs and wants, or between necessities and luxuries, disappear. As Mary Douglas and Baron Isherwood propose,

> Let us put an end to the widespread and misleading distinction between goods that sustain life and health and others that service the mind and heart—spiritual goods. . . . The counter-argument proposed here is that all goods carry meaning, but none by itself. . . . The meaning is in the relations between all the goods, just as music is in the relations marked out by the sounds and not in any one note. (1979: 72–3)

For instance, a good's meaning may have to do with its edibility, but edibility is often culturally determined. Furthermore, the meaning of any individual item of food cannot be explained in isolation. That meaning only becomes clear when the item is compared with other consumption items that are also marked by the culture as edible or inedible.

### The Abominations of Leviticus

Consider the prohibition against eating pork. For Jews and Muslims, pork is inedible, culturally speaking. According to Mary Douglas (1966), this restriction has nothing to do with ecological problems associated with pig raising in southwestern Asia nor with defects in the digestive systems of Jews or Muslims. Douglas analyzed the Jewish dietary prohibitions detailed in the biblical Book of Leviticus. She argued that certain animals were prohibited as food because something about them violated the prototypes for edibility recognized in ancient Hebrew culture (Table 7.1). Prototypically 'clean' land animals were supposed to have four legs and cloven hooves and to chew the cud; pigs were an 'abomination' because they were four-legged, cloven-hoofed beasts that did not chew the cud. 'Clean' beasts of the air were supposed to have feathers and to fly with wings; therefore, hopping insects were 'unclean' because they had six legs, neither walked nor flew, and lacked feathers. 'Clean' water animals were supposed to have fins and scales; shrimp were forbidden because, although they lived in the sea, they lacked fins and scales.

Table 7.1 | Jewish Dietary Prohibitions

| Realm | Class Prototype | Clean Examples | Unclean Examples | Reason Prohibited |
|---|---|---|---|---|
| Earth | Four-legged animals that hop, jump, or walk (i.e., cloven-hoofed, cud-chewing ungulates) | Cattle, camels, sheep, goats | Hare, hyrax | Cud-chewing but not cloven-hoofed |
| | | | Pig | Cloven-hoofed but not cud-chewing |
| | | | Weasel, mouse, crocodile, shrew, chameleon, mole | Two legs, two hands, but go about on all fours |
| Air | Two-legged fowl that fly with wings | Chickens | Grasshoppers | Six legs, cannot walk or fly, and lack feathers |
| Water | Scaly fish that swim with fins | Carp, whitefish | Shrimp, clams | Possess neither fins nor scales but still live in water |

Source: Adapted from Douglas 1966: 41–57.

By itself, Douglas argued, a prohibition against eating pork is meaningless and appears irrational. However, when this prohibition is taken together with other dietary prohibitions in Leviticus, and when these are compared with the foods that were permitted, a pattern emerges. Douglas and Isherwood write, 'Goods assembled together in ownership make physical, visible statements about the hierarchy of values to which their chooser subscribes' (1979: 5). Thus, Jews who consume only 'clean' foods that meet the ritual requirements laid down by their tradition are doing more than procuring the means to satisfy their hunger; they are also making a social declaration of solidarity with their religious community, and the care with which they adhere to the dietary laws is a measure of their commitment. Their need for food is being met, but selectively, and the selection they make carries a social message.

Dietary laws deal with food and drink and so might still be explained in biological or ecological terms. Such explanations are more difficult to construct, however, when we consider the role of banana leaves in the Trobriand Islands.

### Banana Leaves in the Trobriand Islands

Anthropologist Annette Weiner travelled to the Trobriand Islands more than half a century after Malinowski carried out his classic research there (see EthnoProfile 7.1). To her surprise, she discovered a venerable local tradition involving the accumulation

### EthnoProfile 7.1 | Trobriand Islanders

**Region** Oceania
**Nation** Milne Bay, Papua New Guinea
**Language** Trobriand Islanders speak Kilivila of the Kilivila-Louisiades language family
**Population** 40,000 (2009 estimate)
**Environment** Tropical rainforest on main islands of Kiriwina, Kaileuna, Vakuta, and Kitava
**Livelihood** Subsistence horticulturalists (yams as main crop)

**Political organization** Traditionally, chiefs and others of rank in matriclans; today, part of a modern nation-state
**For more information** Malinowski, Bronislaw. 1984 [1922]. *Argonauts of the Western Pacific* (Long Grove, IL: Waveland Press); Weiner, Annette. 1988. *The Trobrianders of Papua New Guinea* (New York: Holt, Rinehart, & Winston).

*Figure 7.10* | In the Trobriand Islands, banana leaves, like the ones this woman is shaping, are recognized as women's wealth, a marker of economic, political, and social status.

and exchange of banana leaves, or women's wealth (Figure 7.10). Malinowski had never described this tradition, even though there is evidence from photographs and writing that it was in force at the time of his fieldwork. There are probably two reasons why Malinowski overlooked these transactions:

1) they are carried out by women, and Malinowski did not view women as important actors in the economy; and

2) Malinowski only labelled activities that satisfied biological survival needs as 'economic', and banana leaves are inedible.

However, explaining transactions involving women's wealth turns out to be crucial for understanding Trobriand kinship obligations.

Banana leaves might be said to have a 'practical' use in that women make skirts out of them. These skirts are highly valued, but the transactions involving women's wealth more often involve the bundles of leaves themselves. Why bother to exchange great amounts of money or other goods to obtain bundles of banana leaves? This would seem to be a classic example of irrational consumption. And yet, as Weiner demonstrates, banana bundles play exactly the role Douglas and Isherwood have

suggested that consumption goods play in society: 'As an economic, political, and social force, women's wealth exists as the representation of the most fundamental relationships in the social system' (Weiner 1980: 289).

Trobrianders are matrilineal, and men traditionally prepare yam gardens for their sisters. After the harvest, yams from these gardens are distributed by a woman's brother to her husband. Weiner's research suggests that what Malinowski took to be the *redistribution* of yams, from a wife's kin to her husband, could be better understood as a *reciprocal exchange* of yams for women's wealth. The parties central to this exchange are a woman, her brother, and her husband. The woman is the person through whom yams are passed from her own kin to her husband and also the person through whom women's wealth is passed from her husband to her own kin.

Transactions involving women's wealth occur when someone in the woman's kinship group dies. Surviving relatives must 'buy back', metaphorically speaking, all the yams or other goods that the deceased person gave to others during his or her lifetime. Each payment marks a social link between the deceased and the recipient, and the size of the payment marks the importance of their relationship. All the payments must be made in women's wealth.

The dead person's status, as well as the status of her or his family, depends on the size and number of the payments made, and the people who must be paid can number into the hundreds. Women make women's wealth themselves and exchange market-bought trade goods to obtain it from other women, but when someone in their matrilineage dies, they collect it from their husbands. Indeed, a woman's value is measured by the amount of women's wealth her husband provides. Furthermore,

> if a man does not work hard enough for his wife in accumulating wealth for her, then her brother will not increase his labour in the yam garden. . . . The production in yams and women's wealth is always being evaluated and calculated in terms of effort and energy expended on both sides of production. The value of a husband is read by a woman's kin as the value of his productive support in securing women's wealth for his wife. (Weiner 1980: 282)

Weiner argues that women's wealth upholds the kinship arrangements of Trobriand society. It balances out exchange relationships between lineages linked by marriage, reinforces the pivotal role of women and matriliny, and publicly proclaims, during every funeral, the social relationships that make up the fabric of Trobriand society. The system has been stable for generations, but Weiner suggests that it could collapse if cash ever became widely substitutable for yams. Under such conditions, men might buy food and other items on the market; they would no longer be dependent on yams from their wives' kin, and they could therefore refuse to supply their wives' kin with women's wealth. This had not yet happened at the time of Weiner's research, but she saw it as a possible future development.

### The Original Affluent Society

As the previous example suggests, Western definitions of wealth are not universal. Lee came to a similar conclusion in his research with the Ju/'hoansi in the 1960s. Many Westerners believe that foraging peoples lead miserable lives, spending all their waking hours searching for enough food to survive (see, e.g., Wilmsen 1989; 1991; Gordon 1992). Yet Lee and other ethnographers have shown that the Ju/'hoansi were able, until relatively recently, to maintain a lifestyle that was very rich according to their own culturally informed definition of **affluence** (see Lee 1992a; 1992b; Solway and Lee 1990).

The Ju/'hoansi provided themselves with a varied and well-balanced diet based on a *selection* from the food sources available in their environment. Although they classified more than 100 species of plants as edible, only 14 were primary or major sources of food (Lee 1992b: 45ff.). Some 70 per cent of this diet consisted of vegetable foods; 30 per cent was meat. Mongongo nuts alone made up more than one-quarter of the diet. Women provided about 55 per cent of the diet and men provided 45 per cent, including the meat. The Ju/'hoansi spent an average of 2.4 working days—or about 20 hours—per person per week in food-collecting activities (Figure 7.11). Ju/'hoansi bands periodically suffered from shortages of their preferred foods and were forced to resort to less desired items; most of the time, however, their diet was balanced and adequate and consisted of foods of preference (56ff.).

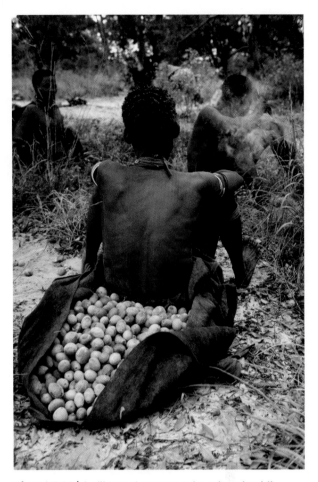

*Figure 7.11* | **Ju/'hoansi women take a break while gathering mongongo nuts.**

Sahlins (1972) coined the expression 'the original affluent society' to refer to the Ju/'hoansi and other foragers like them. Affluence, he argued, is having more than enough of whatever is required to satisfy consumption needs. There are two ways to create affluence:

1) to *produce much* (the path taken by Western capitalist society) and
2) to *desire little* (the option, Sahlins argues, that foragers have taken).

Their wants are few compared to those of most Westerners, but they are abundantly supplied by nature.

> **affluence**
> The condition of having more than enough of whatever is required to satisfy consumption needs.

Moreover, foragers do not suppress their natural greed; rather, their society simply does not institutionalize greed or reward the greedy. As a result, foragers cannot be considered poor, even though their material standard of living is low by Western standards. Poverty is not an absolute condition nor is it a relationship between means and ends; it is a relationship between people and a cultural definition of needs and wants.

## The Cultural Construction of Utility

Just as culture shapes needs, so too does it offer standardized ways of satisfying them. No social exchange can occur unless all parties are able to assess the value of the items to be exchanged. Because of the openness of culture and the ambiguity inherent in many social situations, values and exchange rates may well be bargained over. Such exchanges ultimately rest on cultural principles for assessing value and fairness.

By understanding consumption as the use of goods and services to communicate cultural values, we can arrive at a new understanding of wealth and poverty. We have noted Sahlins's comment that foragers with simple needs and ample means of satisfying those needs are affluent—rich, not poor. Douglas and Isherwood also refuse to use the sheer amount of material possessions as a universal measure of wealth or poverty. They write:

> Many of the countries that anthropologists study are poor on such material criteria—no wall-to-wall carpets, no air conditioning—but they do not regard themselves as poor. The Nuer of the Sudan in the 1930s would not trade with the Arabs because the only things they had to sell were their herds of cattle, and the only things they could possibly want from trade were more cattle. (1979: 17–18)

For the Nuer, to have few or no cattle constituted poverty because cattle mattered as much for their use as markers of social relations as for their use as food. 'To be rich means to be well integrated in a rich community. . . . To be poor is to be isolated' (160).

### Institutionalized Sharing

Capitalist societies have passed laws and created social institutions that reward individuals for accumulating wealth. The economic practices of some non-capitalist societies, in contrast, prevent individual accumulation; the goal is to spread any wealth that exists throughout the community. This pattern is called *institutionalized sharing.*

People accustomed to capitalist practices are often either incredulous or cynical when it is suggested that institutionalized sharing can be the backbone of economic life. They assume that such widespread 'generosity' can only be expected of saintly altruists, not of ordinary human beings. Nevertheless, people in societies with institutionalized sharing are not saints who never experience greed any more than people in capitalist societies are devils who never experience compassion. Both societies, however, make it difficult to get away with practices that undercut established social arrangements.

Institutionalized sharing can be found among the Plains Cree of North America (see Map 7.2), studied by Niels Braroe (1975: 143ff.). In the past, the Cree were bison hunters living in bands. Each band had a leader who provided his followers with the materials necessary for hunting. This leader was the focus of a redistributive mode of exchange, and generosity in redistribution qualified him to be the band leader. At the time of Braroe's fieldwork, the Cree no longer hunted bison, but they still practised the institutionalized sharing of consumption items such as food, clothing, beer, or cigarettes. For example, Braroe tells us that 'it is not considered improper, as it is among whites, to ask for someone's last cigarette; to refuse a request, however, is

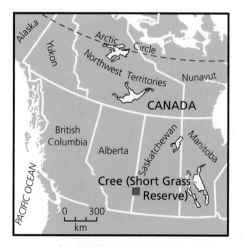

*Map 7.2* | **Cree (Short Grass Reserve)**

frowned upon' (145). Generosity is further reinforced in ceremonies known as *giveaway dances*. The central event in these ceremonies is dancing around the room and giving away material goods, such as clothing, to other guests. Dancers aim to give away more than they receive. It is an insult to shower someone with gifts in the course of such an event.

The Cree ideal is that generosity should be spontaneous and contempt for material goods genuine. Nevertheless, Braroe observed that band members sometimes possessed consumption goods or money that they clearly wanted to keep for themselves. Individuals could enjoy such goods in private, but only if they kept the existence of those goods secret. Men sometimes hid beer to avoid having to share it with others. A woman once asked Braroe's wife to keep a sizable amount of cash for her so others would not know she had it and demand some. The rule seemed to be that 'any visible resource may legitimately be requested by another' (146), and Braroe reported that direct refusals of such requests were rare.

For the Cree, institutionalized sharing is supposed to ensure that consumption goods are not hoarded but spread out and enjoyed by all in the band. This consumption pattern clashes with that of the capitalist, who views accumulation and consumption by individuals in a positive light. Some individual Cree earned money off the reserve and tried to save it in order to get ahead—by capitalist standards. Those people were considered stingy by other Cree and were resented; they could not hope to gain a position of leadership in the band.

## Consumption Studies in the Age of Globalization

The foregoing examples focus attention on distinctive consumption practices in different societies and remind us forcefully not to take the Western market as the measure of all things. These studies also encourage respect for alternative consumption practices that, in different times and places, have worked as well or better than capitalist markets to define needs and provide goods to satisfy those needs. They have also often drawn attention to the way in which the arrival of capitalism, usually in the context of colonialism, has regularly undermined such alternatives, attempting to replace them with new needs and goods defined by the market. This helps explain why, as Daniel Miller summarizes, 'much of the early literature on consumption is replete with moral purpose', emphasizing the ways in which vulnerable groups have resisted commodities or have developed ritual means of 'taming' them, based on an awareness at some level of their capacity to destroy (1995: 144–5). In an era of globalization, however, the consumption of market commodities now occurs everywhere in the world. Moreover, the evidence is mounting that not only are Western commodities sometimes embraced by those whom we might have expected to reject them (e.g., video technology by Indigenous peoples of the Amazon), but this embrace frequently involves making use of these commodities for local purposes to defend or to enrich local culture rather than to replace it (e.g., the increasing popularity of sushi in North America).

Miller, a pioneer in this kind of consumption study, has therefore urged anthropologists to recognize that these new circumstances require that they move beyond a narrow focus on the destructive potential of mass-produced commodities to broader recognition of the role commodities play in a globalizing world. 'Desire for goods is not assumed to be natural nor goods per se as either positive or negative. Poverty is regarded as a relative lack of resources rather than the preservation of authenticity' (143). But this shift does not mean that concern about the negative consequences of capitalist practices disappears. In a global world in which everyone everywhere increasingly relies on commodities provided by a capitalist market, Miller believes that critical attention needs to refocus on 'inequalities of access and the deleterious impact of contemporary economic institutions on much of the world's population' (143).

# A Dialectic between the Meaningful and the Material

As we have seen in this chapter, material goods carry culturally defined meanings, and what is viewed as meaningful (as stipulated by culture) can have material consequences. It is out of this dialectic between the meaningful and the material that the modes of livelihood followed by human beings everywhere emerge.

# Key Terms

affluence   181
consumption   167
distribution   167
ecology   176
econiche   176
economy   165
ecotones   176
ecozones   176
extensive agriculture   166
food collectors   165
food producers   165
ideology   174
institutions   165
intensive agriculture   166

labour   172
market exchange   172
means of production   172
mechanized industrial agriculture   166
mode of production   172
modes of exchange   170
neo-classical economic theory   167
production   167
reciprocity   170
redistribution   170
relations of production   172
scarcity   165
subsistence strategies   165

# Chapter Summary

1.  Our cultures suggest a range of options for making a living as well as furnishing the tools to pursue those options. Human beings have devised a variety of subsistence strategies to satisfy their material survival needs.

2.  Human economic activity is usefully divided into three phases: production, distribution, and consumption. Some anthropologists argue that storage practices affect these phases. In capitalist societies, market exchange is the dominant mode of distribution, yet many non-Western societies have traditionally carried out distribution without money or markets.

3.  Formal neo-classical economic theory developed in an attempt to explain how capitalism works. Building on the emphasis that this theory gives to market exchange, economic anthropologists showed that non-capitalist societies regularly relied on non-market modes of exchange, such as reciprocity and redistribution, which still play restricted roles in societies dominated by the capitalist market.

4.  Marxian economic anthropologists view production as more important than exchange in determining the patterns of economic life in a society. They argue that societies can be classified in terms of their modes of production. Each mode of production contains within it the potential for conflict between classes of people who receive differential benefits and losses from the productive process.

5.  The internal explanation for consumption patterns argues that people produce material goods to satisfy basic human needs. The external explanation argues that consumption patterns depend on the particular external resources available within the ecozone to which a particular society must adapt. Ethnographic evidence demonstrates that both internal and external explanations for consumption patterns are inadequate because they ignore how culture defines our needs and provides for their satisfaction according to its own logic—a logic that is irreducible to biology, psychology, or ecological pressure.

6.  Particular consumption preferences that may seem irrational make sense when considered in the context of other consumption preferences and prohibitions in the same culture. Examples include Jewish dietary prohibitions, the role of banana leaves in the Trobriand Islands, and institutionalized sharing of consumption goods among the Plains Cree.

7.  In our era of globalization, the consumption of Western market commodities is often embraced by those whom we might have expected to reject them. Moreover, this embrace frequently involves making use of market commodities for local purposes to defend or enrich local culture rather than to replace it. In a global world in which everyone everywhere increasingly relies on commodities provided by a capitalist market, we need to pay critical attention to inequalities of access and the negative impact of contemporary economic institutions on most of the world's population.

# Critical Thinking Questions

1.  Anthropologists distinguish between *food collectors* and *food producers*. How does this division hearken back to the ethnical stages proposed by Lewis Henry Morgan in the nineteenth century?

2.  Is reciprocity in all its forms an efficient way of distributing material goods for consumption? Support your answer with examples.

3.  Compare and contrast Wolf's *kin-ordered*, *tributary*, and *capitalist* modes of production. How would you explain the overlap between this classification of modes of production and the traditional anthropological classification of subsistence strategies?

4.  Rhoda Halperin has argued that every economic system can be analyzed in terms of *locational movements*, or 'changes of place', and *appropriational movements*, or 'changes of hands'. How would you distinguish these two forms of 'movements'? How can the relationship between them inform our understanding of human consumption patterns?

# Suggested Readings

Douglas, Mary, and Baron Isherwood. 1996. *The World of Goods: Towards an Anthropology of Consumption*, rev. edn (New York: Routledge). A discussion of consumption, economic theories about consumption, and what anthropologists can contribute to the study of consumption.

Finke, P. 2005. *Die Ökologie des Wissens. Exkursionen in eine gefährdete Landschaft* (The Ecology of Knowledge) (Freiburg and Munich: Alber). Finke asks us to consider ecology as an integrative paradigm for understanding culture as well as science. He sees cultural knowledge and our perceptions of the natural cycles of energy as interdependent while still maintaining the idea that cultural processes, through humans, maintain a self-reflexive dynamic.

Jok, Jok Madut, and Sharon Elaine Hutchinson. 1999. 'Sudan's Prolonged Second Civil War and the Militarization of Nuer and Dinka Ethnic Identities', *African Studies Review* 42, 2: 125–45. A must-read for those who want to understand the political–military–ethno-religious divides that have fuelled the past and present conditions of displacement and deprivation in the Horn of Africa.

Lee, Richard. 2002. *The Dobe Ju/'hoansi*, 3rd edn (Belmont, CA: Wadsworth). This highly readable ethnography contains important discussions about foraging as a way of making a living.

McIntosh, Roderick J. 1996. 'Intellectual History of Archaeology', in *The Oxford Companion to Archaeology*, ed. Brian M. Fagan (Oxford: Oxford University Press), 280–5. A brief but comprehensive look at how we consider the act of 'knowing' in the Western tradition and how we have wrestled with this problem of what we can never come to know.

Miller, Daniel, ed. 1995. *Acknowledging Consumption: A Review of New Studies* (New York: Routledge). Groundbreaking essays that reconfigured the study of consumption anthropology.

Plattner, Stuart, ed. 1989. *Economic Anthropology* (Palo Alto, CA: Stanford University Press). A readable collection of articles by economic anthropologists. Displaying the achievements of formalist-inspired research, it also reconciles with substantivism and recognizes the contribution of Marxian analyses.

Sahlins, Marshall. 1972. *Stone Age Economics* (Chicago: Aldine). A series of classic essays on economic life, written from a substantivist position; the collection includes 'The Original Affluent Society'.

Steward, Julian H. 1972. *Theory of Culture Change: The Methodology of Multilinear Evolution* (Urbana: University of Illinois Press). A collection of twenty papers in which Steward presents culture change as a complex ongoing process, arguing that continuity rather than isolated acts are the driving force of change.

Wilk, Richard. 1996. *Economies and Cultures* (Boulder, CO: Westview). A current, accessible 'theoretical guidebook' to the conflicting views of human nature that underlie disputes in economic anthropology.

# Related Websites

**Cultural Ecology** www.environment.gen.tr/ecology-writings/484-cultural-ecology.html

**Kwakiutl Peoples** www.kwakiutl.bc.ca

**Mongongo Nuts** www.naturalhub.com/natural_food_guide_nuts_uncommon_Ricinodendron_rautanenii.htm

**L.H. Morgan's Ethnical Stages** www.sociologyguide.com/thinkers/lh-morgan.php

**Pictures of Nuer Culture** www.dlib.indiana.edu/collections/nuer/slides

**Gifting and Feasting in the Northwest Coast Potlatch** www.peabody.harvard.edu/potlatch/page2.html

## Chapter Outline

Play
Art
Myth

Ritual
Combining Play, Art, Myth, and Ritual

..................................................................................................................

## Learning Objectives

By the end of Chapter 8, you will be able to

- perceive play as an open system that relates to cognition,
- consider the nature of metacommunication as framing and reflexivity,
- understand the effects of play,
- consider sport as play embedded in the prevailing social order,
- recognize sport as metaphor,
- appreciate art as 'play' producing transformation-representation,

- think about the nature of 'authenticity' in art,
- distinguish the nature of the mythic as providing stories of truth and thus paramount reality,
- regard myths as conceptual tools or charters for social action,
- perceive ritual as a culturally defined schema that brings text and performance together,
- integrate play and ritual as complementary forms of metacommunication, and
- see the connections between play, art, myth, and ritual.

↓ *Masqueraders perform at the annual Carnival in Port of Spain, Trinidad. Cultural festivals bring members of a community together by combining elements of play, art, myth, and ritual in a meaningful way.*

During her fieldwork in Botswana in the late 1970s, Roberta Robin Dods took time off from the work to drive over to a cattle station called Red Shields. On one side of the road a group of children, three boys and eight girls about nine years of age, were gathered. One boy was drawing shapes in the red, dusty earth with a long stick. He had inscribed nine small circles inside a large circle. The boy stood in the middle of the large circle and pointed his stick at each girl saying 'You will be the mommy.' He concluded, 'I will be the daddy.' Each of the girls went to one of the smaller circles, and two of the boys retired to the remaining circle. And so the game of 'playing house' was inscribed in the dust and described by the children playing what all children play—family.

These children were members of a culture where polygyny is practised and where adult sons may live in separate quarters in a family compound. Children at play tell us so much about how play is culturally defined and defining. Childhood is a time when adult roles can be 'tried on' with little or no consequences. Think of the role-playing games you may have engaged in as a child (let's pretend school, house, doctor, etc.); they often involve working through specific aspects of potential adult roles. Play can be fun, but for the observer it is more than fun—it is a window into many aspects of cultural identity. Children's play can reflect the changing realities in which they live—the emerging new realities in a culture. **Play** is one of four elements (along with **art**, **myth**, and **ritual**) in which the interplay of openness and creativity with rules and constraints enables people to produce powerful and moving phenomena.

As we study these sensitive aspects of culture, Riddington cautions that theorizing occurs as a genre of Western academic expression and is not necessarily founded on the constructs of the peoples who provided the data (1998: 345). So we must keep in mind what he describes as 'sharing ethnographic authority':

> The reasons for sharing authority are more than political and aesthetic. An ethnography that places the ethnographer's monologue above the voices of people being represented risks sacrificing effective engagement with its subject. . . . Its claim to objectivity may actually disguise the subjectivity of its singular isolated author. . . . A. Irving Hallowell [Anishinaabe (Ojibwe)], for instance, wrote that 'a higher order of objectivity' may be obtained by 'adopting a perspective which includes an analysis of the outlook of the people themselves as a complementary procedure'. (1998: 344–5)

It is the 'voices' of those living in and through their engagement with play, art, myth, and ritual that resonate with meaning.

## Play

For the anthropologist, play has the characteristic of *openness*—the ability to think, talk, and act about the same things in different ways and about different things in the same way—that we first discussed in relation to language in Chapter 4. Play is a generalized form of behavioural openness.

Many species play, but we believe that humans play the most throughout their lives. Robert Fagen sees animal play as the product of natural selection that gives young animals (including young human beings) needed exercise, preparing them for the rigours of adulthood that might include fighting, hunting, or fleeing when pursued. Importantly, during a brief period of neural development, peak brain developments associated with motor skills and peak periods of play occur at the same time. The development of cognitive and motor skills may be affected by play behaviour. Playful exploration of the environment aids

**play**
A framing (or orienting context) that is (1) consciously adopted by the players; (2) somehow pleasurable; and (3) systemically related to what is non-play by alluding to the non-play world and by transforming the objects, roles, actions, and relations of ends and means characteristic of the non-play world.

**art**
'Play with form producing some aesthetically successful transformation-representation' (Alland 1997: 39).

**myth**
A representative story that embodies a culture's assumptions about the way society, or the world in general, must operate.

**ritual**
A repetitive social practice set off from everyday routine and composed of a sequence of symbolic activities that adhere to a culturally defined ritual schema and are closely connected to a specific set of ideas central to the culture.

learning and allows for the development of behavioural versatility (see Fagen 1981: 350–5). It also seems to have a connection with the repair of developmental damage caused either by injury or by trauma. All of these functions of play may have significant value for the survivability of individuals.

Fagen proposes an additional social function of play: the communication of the message 'all's well' (1992: 48–9). 'It seems likely that a frequent consequence and possible biological function of play is to convey information about short-term and long-term health, general well-being, and biological fitness to parents, littermates, or other social companions' (51).

### Thinking about Play

Joking, which can be verbal or physical (practical jokes, pranks, horseplay), is a good example of how play operates within its cultural context. Anthropologist Andrew Miracle discusses joking behaviour among Aymara people in Bolivia (see EthnoProfile 8.1). He notes that the Aymara do not laugh in the presence of strangers because it is considered disrespectful. They laugh and joke only within a circle of acquaintances and friends; this kind of joking reinforces existing social bonds (1991: 151).

Much of the joking Miracle observed took place on the crowded buses or trucks that transport rural people around the country. Ordinarily, Aymara personal space extends about one arm's length. Where there is any choice, people do not get any closer to one another. They also show respect and honour other people's privacy by not staring. Miracle notes that in everyday situations, 'when stared at, the Aymara may yell at the one staring and become quite rude' (146). On buses or trucks, however, the context changes, and people who are strangers to one another are forced into artificial intimacy. They must sit or stand very close to one another for long periods of time, frequently looking right at one another. Their response, Miracle writes, is often to joke and laugh, behaviour normally reserved for intimates. Put another way, they choose to do 'different things' (passing time with close friends and passing time with strangers in unusually close quarters) in the same way—by joking. This altered definition of context gives joking among strangers a new meaning, playfully changing strangers, if only for a short time, into friends and thus making a socially unpleasant situation more tolerable.

Moving from everyday reality to play reality requires a radical transformation of perspective. To an outside observer, the switch may go undetected. However, when there is potential for the switch to have serious consequences for other people and their activities, play and non-play must be signalled clearly so that one is not mistaken for the other. According to Gregory Bateson (1972), this shift requires a level of communication called **metacommunication**, which provides information about the relationship between those who are communicating. In play there are two kinds of metacommunication: **framing** and **reflexivity**.

---

**metacommunication**
Communicating about the process of communication.

**framing**
A cognitive boundary that marks certain behaviours as 'play' or as 'ordinary life'.

**reflexivity**
Critically thinking about the way one thinks; reflecting on one's own experience.

---

### *EthnoProfile 8.1* | Aymara

**Region** South America
**Nations** Bolivia, Peru, Chile
**Language** The Aymara speak Aymar, which is one of the three official languages of Bolivia and Peru
**Population** 2,500,000 (2011 estimate)
**Environment** The Andes and Altiplano lake basin regions with many living near Lake Titicaca

**Livelihood** Peasant farmers
**Political organization** Pre-conquest state societies conquered first by Incas and later by Spanish; today, part of modern nation-states
**For more information** Miracle, Andrew. 1991. 'Aymara Joking Behaviour', *Play and Culture* 4, 2: 144–52.

Framing is a cognitive boundary that marks certain behaviours as 'play' or as 'ordinary life'. Dogs, for example, have a *play face*, a signal understood by other dogs indicating a willingness to play. If dogs agree to play, they bare their fangs and one animal attacks the other. But the bite is not consummated; it becomes a nip. Both dogs have agreed to enter the *play frame*, an imaginative world in which bites don't mean bites. To put it another way, a basic element of Western logic—that A = A—does not apply in play; the same thing is being treated in different ways. Human beings have many ways of marking the play frame: a smile, a particular tone of voice, a referee's whistle, or the words 'Let's play', 'Let's pretend', or 'You can be the king.' The marker says that 'everything from now until we end this activity is set apart from everyday life'.

Reflexivity is the process of thinking about the social and cultural dimensions of the world in which we find ourselves. Because play tells us that ordinary life can be understood in more than one way, play can be a commentary on the nature of ordinary life (Handelman 1977: 186). It communicates about what *can be* rather than about what *should be* or what *is* (186). This is what we mean when we say that jokes keep us from taking ourselves too seriously. Through jokes, we see that there are alternative, even ridiculous, explanations for our experience.

## Some Effects of Play

Some scholars view children's play as a simple imitation of adult activities. Others see play as rehearsal for the 'real world' (Figure 8.1). According to this view, play can validate the adult role the child is trying on, demonstrating the 'rightness' of being a Mommy or a Daddy or the 'rightness' of preparing meals to eat. It can also give children the opportunity to try on a number of roles and ways of being that may come close to their reality later in life. In North America, various forms of children's 'edutainment'—cultural materials with the dual purpose of entertaining and educating—expose children to circumstances that may be beyond their first-hand experiences. For example, the children's book *The White Swan Express* (2002) gives young children a fictionalized window into international adoption practices and the situations of several non-traditional families as it tells the story of four Chinese baby girls who await adoption by four different families from across North

American—a lesbian couple, a single woman, and two heterosexual married couples.

Several interpretations of play emphasize that it encourages creative interpretations of reality. Some scholars have suggested that play (especially make-believe play) increases children's creativity and originality by allowing them to overcome their limitations of age, experience, and maturity and by permitting a richer reproduction of adult life potential (Schwartzman 1978: 116). Psychologist Brian Sutton-Smith suggests that play activities are important because they allow for innovation (1992; summarized in Schwartzman 1978: 124ff.). Schwartzman has demonstrated how play, through satire and clowning, may allow children to comment on and criticize the world of adults (1978: 232–45). Some adult play forms, such as the pre-Lenten Carnival or Halloween, also act as a commentary on the 'real world'. They sanction insults and derision of authority figures, inversions of social status, clowning, parody, satire, stepping outside of everyday life, and the like (124).

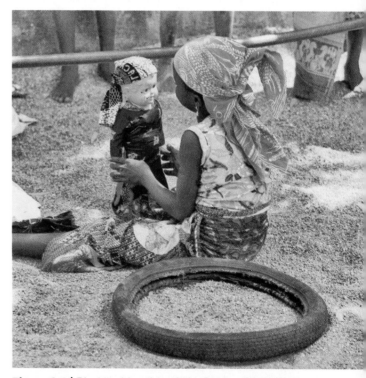

*Figure 8.1* | **Play enables this girl in Guider, Cameroon, to incorporate her European doll into the world she knows.**

Societies contain the threat posed by play by defining it as 'unserious', 'untrue', 'pretend', 'make-believe', or 'unreal' (Handelman 1977: 189). Many political figures recognize that play can undermine the established political order. Repressive political regimes frequently attempt to censor humour critical of their rulers, with the result that such humour becomes an accepted mode of political resistance. Here joking can become satirical comment on the nature of what is and what can be.

### Play and Alternative Views of Reality

We can easily see how humour shows an alternative view of reality, but what about non-joking play? For example, what about adults who climb rocks? 'Is climbing a vertical face of rock at the risk of one's life play, or is it done in earnest?' (Csikszentmihalyi 1981: 16). On the one hand, it fits our definition of play—it is consciously adopted by the player, it is somehow pleasurable, it transforms the relations of ends and means characteristic of the non-play world. On the other hand, it is a serious activity, as a rock climber risks bodily injury and is at all times 'as immersed in reality as anyone can be in this world' (17). These contrasting interpretations suggest that one's perspective on reality can vary. Each person's view of reality 'is relative to the goals that cultures and individuals create' (17). Reality is defined in terms of the goals toward which each player directs his or her attention at any given time. In rock climbing, the goal is to find hand and toeholds in order to get to the top of the rock; it is to put one's body at risk rather than to *avoid* putting one's body at risk. In other words, people do not always submit to the rules of paramount reality (the everyday social order), which is their basic referential perspective.

Play allows us to recognize that *no referential perspective is absolute*. Play exists when there is an awareness of alternatives, 'of two sets of goals and rules, one operating here and now, one that applies outside the given activity' (19), a set of rules that are different from those of our paramount reality. Thus, play creates the awareness of alternatives and demonstrates the openness in human experience and all its ambiguity.

**sport**
An aggressively competitive, often physically exertive activity governed by game-like rules that are ritually patterned and agreed-upon by all participants.

## Sport

**Sport** is

> a physically exertive activity that is aggressively competitive within constraints imposed by definitions and rules. A component of culture, it is ritually patterned, game-like, and of varying amounts of play, work, and leisure. In addition, sport can be viewed as having both athletic and non-athletic variations, *athletic* referring to those activities requiring the greater amount of physical exertion. (Blanchard and Cheska 1985: 60)

It is play embedded in the prevailing social order. Sports reflect the basic values of the cultural setting in which they are performed.

Beyond play, sport can be work for the players and an investment for the owners of professional teams. It also offers a form of personal and social identification for fans, who are invited into a make-believe world in which they may playfully identify with their heroes, rage at the opponents, imagine coaching the team, suffer, and rejoice. It is framed as play, but conflict in games and sports is different from conflict in ordinary life (although game metaphors are often used for serious conflicts such as war). Competitors agree 'to strive for an incompatible goal—only one opponent can win—within the constraints of understood rules' (Lever 1983: 3). As with all forms of play, the relationships of means and ends in sport are altered. Sport is struggle for the sake of struggle.

Because they can reflect a culture's values, some sports change form when they transfer from one cultural setting to another. Cricket in the Trobriand Islands (see EthnoProfile 7.1) offers us an excellent example of this transformation. An English missionary introduced the sport of cricket to the Trobrianders in the early twentieth century. By the 1970s, in the more rural parts of the islands, it had become a different game. Played between two villages, it became a substitute for warfare and a way of establishing political alliances. If the hosts had 40 men ready to play and the visitors had 36, then there were 36 to a side instead of the conventional 11. The game was always won by the home team—but not by too many runs because that would shame the visitors. War magic was employed to aid batsmen and bowlers. Teams had dances and chants for taking the field, leaving it, and celebrating outs. These dances and chants were used to comment on current events and became fertile ground for additional competition beyond that of the sporting event itself. The bat was redesigned for greater accuracy, and the entire activity was associated with the ceremonial exchange of food and other goods. Cricket, the sport of empire, was radically transformed.

From the perspective of some Trobrianders, in fact, their version of cricket was a way of taking the English colonizers' favourite game—a game that was supposed to teach Trobrianders how to become 'civilized'—and using it to express their rejection of the colonial world. As one Trobriand leader says in the film *Trobriand Cricket* (1974), 'we rubbished the white man's game; now it's our game'. Here is the 'openness' of play: sport can transcend its function as an enjoyable way to pass the time and become a venue for social commentary and even collective rebellion against oppression.

### Sport in the Nation-State

The full institutionalization of sport seems to have taken place in the nation-state fairly recently. The most important and universal feature of sport in the nation-state is that it helps complex modern societies cohere (Lever 1995: 3). In her study of soccer in Brazil (see Map 8.2), aptly titled *Soccer Madness*, Janet Lever argues that large-scale organized sport presents a mechanism for building political unity and allegiance to the nation (Figure 8.2). 'Sport's paradoxical ability to reinforce societal cleavages while transcending them makes soccer, Brazil's most popular sport, the perfect means of achieving a more perfect union between multiple groups . . . [by giving] dramatic expression to the strain between groups while affirming the solidarity of the whole' (5, 9).

In Brazil, there is at least one professional soccer team in every city. The larger cities have several teams representing different social groups. In Rio de Janeiro, for example, separate teams tend to be supported by the old rich, the modern middle class, the poor, the blacks, the Portuguese, and a number of neighbourhood communities. The teams come to represent these different groups in a concrete, visible fashion. Through these teams, separate groups maintain their identities. At the same time, the teams bring their opposing fans together through a shared enthusiasm for soccer. City and national championships similarly unify the socio-economically and geographically diverse groups of Brazil.

For many Brazilians—indeed, for many people around the world—the experience of supporting a sports team may be their first and perhaps only experience of a loyalty beyond the local community. Unity is achieved by demonstrating that different teams, and the groups they represent, are in conflict only at one level. At a higher level, the fans of those teams are really united; for example, fans of all Rio teams support the team that

Map 8.2 | **Brazil**

*Figure 8.2* | **Brazilian supporters cheer on their team during the 2007 Women's World Cup tournament.**

goes on to represent Rio in the national championships. This process reaches a climax in international competition as the supporters of the many local teams back the national team. At this highest level of integration, soccer provides a way of affirming one's 'Brazilianness'.

There is one important exception to the mass culture of sport: it regularly separates women from men. Although women have become more visibly involved in the world of sport in recent decades, sport is generally less important to women than it is to men. The gender segregation of sport has significant consequences for the experience of growing up male or female. It also affects relationships later in life between men and women who do not share the same experiences. There is a fundamental ambiguity in the relation of sports and integration: as sports bring people together in one domain, they separate them in another. Sports can maintain and sharpen distinctions that are already significant in many other areas of a culture.

### Sport as Metaphor

Why soccer? Why is it so important in Brazil and other parts of the world? French anthropologist Christian Bromberger (1995), writing about soccer based on field research in Marseille, France, and Naples and Turin, Italy, observes that soccer is fascinating because 'it lays bare the major symbolic horizon of our societies: the course of a match, of a competition, resembles the uncertain fate of people in the contemporary world. Further, the combination of rules that mould the genre give this uncertainty an *acceptable* feel' (197). It all becomes a metaphor for the fragility and the mobility of both individual and collective status. The complexity and sudden changes of a single game or a tournament offer what Bromberger calls 'a shortcut to the joys and dramas that make up a life' (197). A match or a championship season feature not only achievement on the basis of merit but also uncertainties introduced by strategy, luck, law, (in)justice in the form of the referee, trickery, and unfairness. It offers the fan the opportunity to compare players, to reflect, to plan, to strategize, and to be surprised. As one of Bromberger's informants put it, 'At bottom, what most fascinates me is when a player chooses a solution which I had not thought of . . . and it works!' And, as in life, the most innovative strategies don't always work and the best team doesn't always win.

## Art

When anthropologists talk about art in non-Western societies, they begin by focussing on activities or products that resemble art in the West. Whether non-Western peoples refer to such activities or products as 'art', the activities and products themselves are universal. They seem rooted in playful creativity, a birthright of all human beings. And yet, like sport, those activities defined as 'art' differ from free play because they are circumscribed by rules. Artistic rules direct particular attention to, and provide standards for evaluating, the *form* of the activities or objects that artists produce.

### A Definition of Art

Anthropologist Alexander Alland defines art as 'play with form producing some aesthetically successful transformation-representation' (1977: 39). 'Form' refers to the rules of the art game: the culturally appropriate restrictions on the way this kind of play may be organized in time and space, the culturally acceptable style and media. A style is a schema (a distinctive patterning of elements) that is recognized within a culture as appropriate to a given medium. The media in which art is created and executed are culturally recognized and characterized (Anderson 1990: 272–5). A painting is a form: it is two-dimensional; it is done with paint; it is intentionally made; it represents or symbolizes something in the world outside the canvas, paper, or wood on which it is created; it can be displayed. There are different kinds of paintings as well. For example, there is the painting form called *portrait*—a portrait depicts a person in some culturally appropriate way.

By 'aesthetic', Alland means appreciative of, or responsive to, form in art or nature (xii). 'Aesthetically successful' means that the creator of the piece of art (and possibly its audience as well) experiences a positive or negative response. Indifference is the sign of something that is aesthetically unsuccessful. It is probably the case that the aesthetic response is a universal feature in all cultures and, as with play, may be part of the human condition.

Aesthetic response is holistic, involving all our faculties, including emotion, especially as these are shaped by our social and cultural experience. Voloshinov argues that aesthetic response to form in a work of art is based largely on a culturally shaped evaluation of the appropriateness of form to content. He observed that artistic form allows both creator and audience to exert agency: although 'the form in and of itself need not necessarily be pleasurable . . . what it must be is a *convincing evaluation* of the content . . .' (1987 [1926]: 108). Evaluations of appropriateness and of technical perfection involve a broad range of intellectual, emotional, and moral judgments on the part of the viewer.

Aesthetic value judgments guide the artist's choice of form and material; they also guide the observers' evaluations. This implies that art involves more than just the end product of an artist's labour. As Voloshinov notes, art is a creative 'event of living communication' involving the work, the artist, and the artist's audience (107). Artists create their works with an audience in mind, and audiences respond to these works as if the works were addressed to them. Sometimes the response is enthusiastic; sometimes it is highly critical. In either case, the aesthetic event does not leave its participants indifferent. In this sense, it is similar to the experience of intersubjectivity in fieldwork.

Art also involves the *process* through which some product is made. In a practical way, archaeologists can tell us about this process by studying material culture. In the making of things there is an order, essentially a syntax, archaeologists term a *chaîne opératoire*; when followed, this order produces a specific repeatable result, such as a Clovis point (Figure 8.3). Of course, there is a certain amount of variability and creativity involved even within the constraints of artistic convention; creators of art follow a series of steps, but they do so with artistic licence.

## Transformation-Representation

To understand the term **transformation-representation** in Alland's definition of art, we must recall that symbols represent something other than themselves. They are arbitrary in that they have no necessary connection with what they represent. This means that they can be cut away from the object or idea represented and appreciated for their own sake. They may also be used to represent a totally different meaning. When a Javanese leather puppet maker makes a puppet of the mythic hero Bhima, for example, he is representing the traditional form of the hero in his work, but he is also *transforming* a three-dimensional human form into a two-dimensional flat puppet made of buffalo hide in which the colours, style, inclination of the head, and adornment stand for the internal state of the hero at a specific moment (Figure 8.4). At the same time, he is carrying out this work more or less skilfully and is embodying the meanings that Bhima has for the Javanese.

> **transformation-representation**
> The process in which experience is transformed as it is represented symbolically in a different medium.

Because transformation and representation depend on each other, Alland (1977: 35) refers to them as *transformation-representations*; they are *metaphors*. A drawing, for example, is a metaphoric transformation of experience into visible marks on a two-dimensional

*Figure 8.3* | A Clovis point.

*Figure 8.4* | Bhima, the great mythic hero of Javanese wajang, is represented in this leather puppet.

surface. Similarly, a poem metaphorically transforms experience into concentrated and tightened language. This transformation-representation process is one place where the technical skill of the artist is involved.

## But Is It Art?

Alland's definition of art attempts to capture something universal about human beings and their cultures. As Errington observes, all human cultures have '"symbolic forms": artifacts, activities, or even aspects of the landscape that humans view as densely meaningful' (1998: 84).

In the Western prototype of art, there is a distinction between art and non-art. Some paintings, songs, stories, carvings, dances, and the like are considered art; some are not. People who accept this perspective might argue, for example, that the *Mona Lisa* is art but paintings of Elvis Presley on black velvet are not. Why? Part of the answer may have to do with how successfully the artist has captured something that he or she considers to be important about Elvis and the culture to which both the artist and Elvis belong—that is, how aesthetically successful is the transformation-representation? But part of the answer also involves the high degree of specialization in Western societies, which has led to the emergence of an 'art establishment' that includes critics, art historians, art teachers, journalists, schools, and museums—as well as professional artists. These people define what art is and what it is not, as well as the appropriate styles, media, and forms. They distinguish between art and craft. That a painter may in fact have created an image of Elvis that is important and meaningful to the many people who have purchased the paintings—that it speaks to them both in style and medium—does not change the art establishment's opinion that the paintings are not art.

Thus, to them Elvis on velvet is not art because it does not address problems in art theory, because it does not refer to the beautiful and the true, because it does not portray the artist's struggle to produce a new expressive style or, indeed, because the artist seems ignorant or disdainful of the stylistic experimentation that makes up Western art history.

Nevertheless, many people—anthropologists included—have resisted the notion that art is only what a group of Western experts define as art. To highlight the ethnocentrism of Western art experts, they stressed that the division of art and non-art is not universal. In many cultures, there is no category of art distinct from other human activities. On the other hand, convinced that all people were endowed with the same aesthetic capacities, anthropologists felt justified in speaking of art and of artists in non-Western societies. Their goal was to recognize a fully human capacity for art in all societies and to redefine art until it became broad enough to include, on an equal basis, aesthetic products and activities that Western art experts would qualify, at best, as 'primitive', 'ethnic', or 'folk' art.

Some anthropologists focussed on the evaluative standards that artists use for their own work, and other work in the same form, and how these may differ from the standards used by non-artists. Forge, for example, notes that Abelam carvers in New Guinea discuss carvings in a language that is more incisive than that of non-carvers (1967). Other anthropologists pointed out that artists in traditional non-Western societies created objects or engaged in activities that presented and represented the central values of a culture. Thus their work helped maintain the social order, and they did not see themselves as (nor were they understood to be) alienated critics of society as they are in modern Western societies.

Recent work in the anthropology of art, however, has prompted many anthropologists to rethink this position. They have turned their attention to the way certain kinds of material objects made by tribal peoples flow into a global art market where they are transformed into 'primitive' or 'ethnic' art. Some anthropologists, such as Shelly Errington (1998), point out that even in the West many of the objects in fine arts museums today, no matter where they came from, were not intended by their makers to be 'art'. They were intended to be masks for ritual use; paintings for religious contemplation; reliquaries for holding the relics of saints, ancestor figures, furniture, jewellery boxes, architectural details, and so on. They are in fine arts museums today because at some point they were designated as 'art' by someone with the authority to put them in the museum.

For these reasons, Errington distinguishes 'art by intention' from 'art by appropriation'. Art by intention includes objects that were made to be art, such as Impressionist paintings. Art by appropriation, however, consists of all the other objects that 'became art' because at a certain moment certain people, usually those in power situations in colonial settings, decided that they belonged to the category of art. Because museums, art dealers, and art collectors are found everywhere in the world, it is now the case that potentially any material object crafted by human hands can be appropriated by these institutions as 'art'. For an example of such conflicting ideas about the nature of a specific piece of 'art', we can consider the Haisla Nation's Mis'kusa G'psgolox totem pole (Figure 8.5). It was cut down in 1929 by Indian agent Iver Fougner and sold to Sweden's Museum of Ethnography, where it was preserved as a piece of art. For members of the Haisla Nation, however, the pole was a reminder of a significant event in their culture's history. They understood the pole to be situated in a specific time and place, with a 'life' that had a beginning and an end—essentially, it was meant to decay over time and thus move into the realm of the ancestors.

To transform an object into art, Errington argues, it must have *exhibition value*—someone must be willing to display it. Objects that somehow fit into the Western definition of art will be selected for the art market. Looking at the collection of objects that have been defined as 'art' over the years, Errington sees that the vast majority show certain elements to be embedded rather deeply in the Western definition of art: the objects are 'portable (paintings preferred to murals), durable (bronze preferred to basketry), useless for practical purposes in the secular West (ancestral effigies and Byzantine icons preferred to hoes and grain grinders), representational (human and animal figures preferred to, say, heavily decorated ritual bowls)' (1998: 116–17). Errington further notes that the objects people make and 'imbue with meaning' are 'worthy of deep study', but they are not art until someone who carries around a particular definition of art says they are (103).

This process of definition (or, as is often the case, redefinition) is successful when the artifacts in question can be metaphorically transformed and represented as Western art objects. In their original contexts, most meaningful symbolic forms involve more than one sense: an audience hears drumming while looking at masked dancers and feeling the warm breeze carrying the smell of palm oil while hearing the shouts of children frightened by the dancers. But some of the sensory experiences that make richly symbolic performances do not last. As masks, audio recordings, and other objects are moved into the international art market, 'they slough off their . . .

*Figure 8.5* | **Members of the Haisla Nation look at the Mis'kusa G'psgolox totem pole in the Museum of Anthropology at the University of British Columbia after it was returned from Sweden's Museum of Ethnography in 2006.**

performance contexts, . . . retaining only the durable part that can be set aside in a frame or on a pedestal' (84) or can be burned onto a CD and sold in the World Music section of a music store.

Traditionally, the cultural role of art was similar to that of play—it presented its creators and participants with alternative realities, a separation of means from ends, and the possibility of commenting on and transforming the everyday world. In today's global art market, however, the role is often more commercial. Errington observes that the people who make 'primitive art' are no longer 'tribal' but have become

> modern-day peasants or a new type of proletariat. . . . They live in rain forests and deserts and other such formerly out-of-the-way places on the peripheries . . . within national and increasingly global systems of buying and selling, of using natural and human resources, and of marketing images and notions about products. Some lucky few of them make high ethnic art, and sell it for good prices, and obtain a good portion of the proceeds. Others make objects classed as tourist or folk art, usually for much less money, and often through a middleperson. (268)

Others fulfill orders from elsewhere, 'producing either masses of "folk art" or expensive handmade items designed by people in touch with world taste and world markets' (269). Errington points out the bitter irony that international demand for 'exotic' objects is growing at the very moment when the makers of these objects are severely threatened by international economic policies and resource extraction projects that impoverish them and undermine the ways of life that give the objects they make their 'exotic' allure. And, what counts as fashionable decoration this year—'world taste'—may be unfashionable next year, leaving the producers with very little to fall back on.

### 'She's Fake': The Problem of the Authentic

Michelle Bigenho is an anthropologist and violinist whose multi-sited ethnography examines music performance in Bolivia, in part through her experiences performing with *Música de Maestros*. This ensemble has chosen to perform the works of master Bolivian composers and also attempts to recreate accurate performances of contemporary cultural originals that they have studied in the countryside (Bigenho 2002: 4). The ensemble was made up of both classically trained and traditionally trained musicians as well as three foreigners: a Japanese who played the Andean flute, a Cuban who played violin, and Bigenho, from the United States, who also played

**Figure 8.6 |** *Música de Maestros* **in costume performing in a folklore festival in France.**

violin. Along with a dance ensemble, the musicians were invited to represent Bolivia in a folklore festival in France (Figure 8.6). As the bands were lining up, a member of the Belgian delegation walked over to Bigenho and announced in French, 'She's fake.' The Belgian woman then 'pointed to one of the Bolivian dancers dressed in her dancing costume with her long fake braids worked into her short brown hair. As she pointed, she said "She's real"' (88).

In this way, Bigenho raises the question of 'authenticity'. What is real when it comes to music, painting, sculpture, dance, or other 'folk' art forms? How do the images that people in dominant nations have of 'folk' or Indigenous peoples affect the production and circulation of art? And, finally, who gets to decide what is authentic? To address these issues, Bigenho distinguishes three different forms of authenticity:

1) *experiential authenticity*, which exists in the entire, often shared sensory experience connected with a piece of art;
2) *cultural–historical authenticity*, which stems from the way in which a piece of art is represented in relation to the historical or mythical history of the art form; and
3) *unique authenticity*, which is tied to the individual artist's new, innovative, and personal production of a work of art.

Bigenho expands on these forms by relating them to her experience with music. In music performances, *experiential authenticity* is 'connected to a shared experience with others, a fleeting moment of the groove, a listener's great night at a concert' (18). *Cultural–historical authenticity* makes a claim to a connection with the origin of the music. For example, the performances of *Música de Maestros* were authentic in the sense that the musicians sought to perform culturally and historically authentic renditions of Bolivian music. They performed music from the Chaco War (1932–5), as well as music from different regions and ethnic groups in Bolivia, and seemed to be quite successful in performing authentically in the different styles. Bigenho also points out that in terms of Indigenous art, the power of cultural–historical authenticity derives from the Indigenous artist's position in relation to the nation-state. *Unique authenticity* is the creative activity of composing musicians. This form of authenticity raises the issue of who owns cultural products and whether it is possible to talk about collective creation and ownership of the music of a community, a people, or an ethnic group.

Issues surrounding ownership are particularly significant in relation to questions of who owns experiences and representations. Bigenho came face to face with such questions when she compiled a cassette of music from one of the villages in which she worked. She discussed with the villagers how to register the copyright on the cassette. While the villagers recognized that the music they played was composed by individuals, they felt strongly that ownership of the performed music was collective. In doing so, they moved from uniquely authentic individual compositions—intellectual property—to collective ownership of a 'culturally authentic representation'—cultural property (217). When Bigenho went to La Paz to register the copyright, however, she found that it was impossible to register the cassette under collective authorship or ownership. In fact *she*, as the compiler, could register the work, but the people who created the work could not, unless they were willing to be recognized as individuals. What she discovered was that according to Bolivian law, the music on the cassette was legally folklore,

> the set of literary and artistic works created in national territory by unknown authors or by authors who do not identify themselves and are presumed to be nationals of the country, or of its ethnic communities, and that are transmitted from generation to generation, constituting one of the fundamental elements of traditional cultural patrimony of the nation. (221)

As a result, the music was part of the 'National Patrimony' and belonged to the nation-state. But in the context of Bolivian cultural and ethnic politics, Bigenho observes, the villagers gained visibility and connections as a collective Indigenous entity, which they believed would provide them with possible economic advantages. Whether they were correct remains to be seen, but this example of the connections of art and authority is being repeated all over the world.

*Figure 8.7* | **A Baule wood sculpture from the nineteenth century.**

### Sculpture and the Baule Gbagba Dance

The Baule of the Ivory Coast are renowned for their sculpture (see Figure 8.7). Susan Vogel (1997), who has been studying Baule sculpture for over thirty years, identifies four forms of Baule sculpture:

1) art that is watched (performances featuring carved masks),
2) art that is seen without looking (sacred sculpture),
3) art that is glimpsed (private sculptures of personal figures for hunting and sculpture for spirit spouses), and
4) art that is visible to all (the profane; everyday objects that Baule see as beautiful trifles).

As we saw in Chapter 5, Baule visuality is distinctive; people learn to look in a way that is different from that of people in the West—'the more important a Baule sculpture is, the less it is displayed' (Vogel 1997: 108). The Western concept of 'art' does not exist in Baule villages. Rather, 'to approach art from a Baule perspective entails speaking of experiences that are not primarily visual and of art objects that are animate presences, indistinguishable from persons, spirits, and certain prosaic things'. The Baule attribute great powers to their artwork—powers that Westerners would consider incredible. The meaning of most art objects, as well as the emotional responses that these objects evoke, derives from their ability to act. For the Baule, what Western museum-goers call *sculpture* contains enormous powers of life and death, and Baule people do not consider their sculpture apart from these powers (85).

We will consider one use of art objects in performance: the Gbagba dance, described by Vogel. While anthropologists have often studied dance as an independent art form, we are looking here at the intersection of sculpture and dance. The Gbagba dance is an entertainment performance that lasts much of a day and may also be performed for the funeral of an important woman. The style of mask that is used in the performance is called *Mblo*, and in the past, a village may have had as many as a dozen or more such masks—some representations of animals, some portraits of people. Gbagba also includes singing, and two of the songs that are repeated throughout the day refer to death. They are sung both when Gbagba is danced for women's funerals and when it is danced for entertainment.

The Gbagba begins with skits that include unmasked performers, young dancers who are just getting started. The skits are supposed to be funny as they present scenes from everyday life from which a moral is drawn. They often feature masks of domestic animals—generally sheep and goats. These skits are followed by more dance-based skits in which older, more skilled dancers don masks representing the large wild animals that the Baule hunt; these dance skits always end with the successful 'killing' of the portrayed animal.

At the same time that the first masks appear so too does a costumed figure of the trickster Ambomon, who wears a cloth hood rather than a mask and who dances in a rapid and acrobatic way that includes somersaults and tumbling. Ambomon is a completely ambiguous figure, even to the Baule who speculate as to whether or not he is a god. He has no respect for possessions, rank, and decent behaviour. While comical, he also takes things from people, sits on the ground, and gets things dirty. He never does any real damage, and people regard him as an amusing nuisance. He stands in direct contrast to the orderly vision of the world, as expressed by the masks; he is the spirit of disorder. Yet at the same time, Ambomon is the only figure in the dance that *must* appear—he can appear without any of the other masks, but the other masks cannot appear without him. When Gbagba is danced for a funeral, only Ambomon enters the courtyard to pay his respects to the deceased and to greet the mourners. Vogel proposes that the obligatory presence of Ambomon suggests to the Baule that the only certainty in life is the threat of disorder and death (167).

Vogel notes that Ambomon's style of dance is quite different from the ideal Baule dance style, which seems to minimize movement. For example, in a female solo dance, the performer moves forward very slowly in a curved line, with body and neck held upright, hands in front, palms up. Sometimes the dancer carries something in her hand. The dancer's facial features are impassive, her eyes are downcast, and the main movement is in her neck, shoulders, and back, often marking two different rhythmic patterns in the polyrhythmic music. A male dancer may be a bit more vigorous, but

> Baule dancing in general can be characterized as symmetrically balanced and essentially vertical (the dancer's knees may be flexed but the head and torso are held upright). As in so many other Baule creations, the dancer's body is closed in outline. These qualities are also characteristic of Baule sculpture and must be recognized as expressing an aesthetic preference with moral connotations that is deeply embedded in Baule culture and is expressed in myriad ways. (156)

Finally, at the end of the day, one or more portrait masks appear, one by one, These portrait masks are usually of a specific woman, and the subject of the portrait always dances alongside the male who dances the mask. Only the best dancers wear these masks. During these final performances, the finest skills in the community are on display—the best dancers, the most beautiful masks, the best drummers and singers—and the distinguished women who are represented now take their places (Figure 8.8).

The Baule use the term *double* to refer to the portrait mask and its subject. The portrait mask is considered the person's true double; the mask never performs unless the person is there to dance. Vogel tells us that the 'relationships between individuals and their portrait masks are close, complex, and lifelong and become elements of their identities' (166). When the subject of a portrait mask dies or cannot dance any more, a relative becomes the new double or the mask is never danced again.

In sum, Vogel proposes that a Gbagba performance is a joyous occasion that brings everyone in the village, of all ages and persuasions, together in a happy celebration.

> The performance teaches basic lessons about the Baule world—about hierarchies and mysteries. Each skit has a simple moral lesson, evident even to children: that humans, for example, with skill and supernatural aid, can dominate even the largest and most awesome wild animals, while the portrait masks present a model of human accomplishment and beauty. At the same time, the dance provides deeper insights about blurred boundaries—about the interpenetration of bush and village and the complexity of gender. The subject of a portrait, most often a woman, sees herself impersonated by a man dancing 'like a woman' and wearing a mask that is her double or namesake. A frequent theme of Baule art is opposite-sex doubling, meaning that two figures appear not as a pair of complementary beings but as manifestations of a single being having qualities of both sexes. The concept is too troubling to articulate openly in words, but in Gbagba it is available to wordless contemplation. (167–8)

Thus the Gbagba dance event is not merely a form of entertainment; it has deep social and cultural significance for the Baule.

### Dance and Gender in Northern Greece

Jane Cowan has explored how dance may play a role in the social construction of gender in northern Greece. She considers three different kinds of dance events in the town of Sohos (see Map 8.3): the wedding dance, the formal evening dance, and the private dance at home. At each dance event, individuals

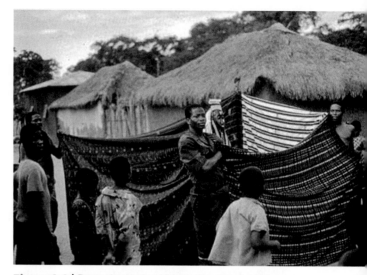

**Figure 8.8** | Portrait mask of Moya Yanso about to enter the Gbagba dance in the Baule village of Kami in 1972. The mask—an important object—is hidden by the cloths until the last moment when the mask, its dancer, and its subject will appear dramatically in the performance.

*Map 8.3* | **Sohos**

present themselves publicly by eating, drinking, and talking, as well as dancing, and other people at the event evaluate them. Men and women, however, do not present themselves in the same way nor are they evaluated in the same way. They perform and experience themselves as gendered subjects—that is, as males or females, as these roles are defined in Sohos. 'In dance events associated with pleasure, sensual intensity, and public sociability, gender inequalities and other social hierarchies are constituted and even celebrated' (Cowan 1990: 4).

Culturally specific images of male and female sexuality in northern Greece are given a particular public form in the dance. From the perspective of the women, dances are places where they can 'escape' and 'forget' their relatively restricted everyday lives. Everyone at the dance—men and women alike—encourages them to do this in order to be good, carefree celebrants. But dance presents problems for women: they are keenly aware that they are being watched, that they not only act but are also acted upon. So women know they must control themselves emotionally and physically. They learn the limits of appropriate bodily expression when they are young and continue to internalize these expressions throughout their lives. A woman's expressions of 'letting go' may be at the boundaries of those limits but rarely overstep them in any fundamental way (228).

Dance provides a place where northern Greek women play with the boundaries of 'good' and 'bad' female sexuality. Should she take the first position in a circle dance or is that too forward? How intense should her *tsifte teli* (belly dance) be? Should she move closer to her partner, lean toward him, and playfully shimmy her shoulders? When a man dances an intense *tsifte teli*, should she break plates at his feet, a conventional statement of deep understanding of, and empathy with, the dancer's inner state? 'In this dance space, ambivalent attitudes toward female sexuality are juxtaposed. Girls and women are not necessarily expected to mute or hide their sexuality. Flirtation, energy, the display of beauty, and even subtle seduction are acknowledged and valued aspects of female performance in these events' (228). But there is always a potential problem: a female who is thought to lack control in these displays can be censured.

> A female celebrant's experience of the dance, then, is rooted in her position in gender relations, but it is not only men who keep her 'in her place'. Women do as well. Only when she believes that everybody is truly 'all together' can the female celebrant

really feel free to let go; for girls, everybody being 'all together' is both the precondition for, and the expression of, collective *kefi* [high spirits]. (229)

### The Mass Media: A Television Serial in Egypt

Contemporary anthropologists recognize the importance of the mass media as a venue for cultural productions. The anthropological study of mass media can go in several different directions, including studies of globalization (Chapter 13), but here we want to highlight the creativity of producers and consumers of media in the interpretation and incorporation of these art forms. This is, perhaps, the most important thing anthropology can add to the study of media: the fine-grained ethnographic assessment of the effects and impact of popular media among the people who watch, listen, read, and interpret, and some of whom also create, those media (cf. Herzfeld 2001: 298).

In many nations in the world, soap operas or television serials are among the most popular mass entertainments, watched by millions. These programs are seen by their creators in some parts of the world not simply as entertainment but also as tools, useful for teaching certain people in their societies what they need to learn to be modern citizens. But what the intended audience gets from the program is not always the message the creators thought they were transmitting.

Anthropologist Lila Abu-Lughod studied an Egyptian television serial called *Hilmiyya Nights* that was broadcast during Ramadan (the Islamic holy month) over five successive years. The serial followed the fortunes and relationships of a group of characters from the traditional Cairo neighbourhood of Hilmiyya, taking them from the late 1940s, when Egypt was under the rule of King Farouk and the British, up to the early 1990s, even incorporating Egyptian reaction to the first Gulf War. The central action revolved around the rivalry, financial wheeling–dealing, and love interests of two wealthy men, and the narrative tied the lives of its characters to Egyptian national political events. Above all, the show promoted the theme of national unity. With few exceptions, all the characters were shown to be basically good and patriotic.

Abu-Lughod studied two separate groups of Egyptians during the 1990s: poor working-class women in Cairo and villagers in Upper Egypt. When she asked poor women in Cairo what they liked about the show, they volunteered not the serious political or social messages but two female characters: the glamorous, aristocratic femme fatale and the arrogant belly dancer turned cabaret-owner. Although these two characters were hardly respectable, they were nevertheless favourites because they defied the moral system that kept good women quiet. Indeed, Abu-Lughod found that both the urban women and the villagers accepted the moral stances presented in the program only when they resonated with their own worlds and ignored those aspects of the serial that were not part of their experiences.

Most interestingly, she argues that television, especially for the villagers, created its own world, one that was a small part of their daily lives. 'What they experienced through television added to, but did not displace, whatever else already existed. They treated the television world not as a fantasy escape but as a sphere unto itself with its familiar time slots and specific attitudes' (Abu-Lughod 1995: 203–4). Moreover, the villagers did not compartmentalize the 'modernity' that television serials present in order to preserve a 'traditional' community untouched by the outside world. On the contrary, these villagers were deeply affected in a wide variety of ways by the outside world, whether through local government policies or through multinational corporations' advertisements. 'Television is, in this village, one part of a complex jumble of life, and the dramatic experiences and visions it offers are surprisingly easily incorporated as discrete—not overwhelming—elements in the jumble' (205).

Television in Egypt, she notes, has had measurable social effects: for example, families prefer to stay home to watch television rather than visit among households in the evenings. Television may also have increased the number of 'experiences' shared across generation and gender as young and old, men and women, now spend time together watching television.

Ultimately, the intended impact of *Hilmiyya Nights* was undermined, but not because nobody was watching television: both urban poor and villagers had their sets on almost constantly. Rather, the positive messages that the creators of *Hilmiyya Nights* and similar serials intended were lost because they were only part of the complex flow of programming in Egypt, which included many other kinds of information: news, entertainment, advertising, and so on. More important, watchers evaluated all these messages in terms of their own life experiences; hence, the messages were often neutralized or contradicted by the watchers' powerful everyday realities. Soap operas are equally contested productions, open for multiple interpretations, not simply places for the transmission of messages from the elite to the masses. This situation is not unique to the Egyptian experience.

## Myth

We have suggested that play lies at the heart of human creativity. However, because the openness of play is random and thus just as likely to undermine the social order as to enhance it, societies tend to circumscribe play with cultural rules, channelling it in directions that appear less destructive. Rules designed to limit artistic expression are one result of this channelling process. Artists who challenge the rules are often viewed negatively by those in power who believe they have the right to restrict artistic expressions that question social, religious, or sexual precepts that ought not to be questioned. All societies depend on the willingness of their members not to question certain assumptions about the way the world works. Because the regularity and predictability of social life might collapse all together if people were free to imagine, and act upon, alternatives to the local version of paramount reality, most societies find ways to persuade their members that the local version of reality is the only reality—period. The most venerable way of doing this is through the use of myth.

Myths are stories whose truths seem self-evident because the narrative does such a good job of integrating personal experiences with a wider set of assumptions about the way society, or the world in general, must operate. Traditionally, these stories involve a teller and an audience; thus, myths are products of high verbal art. Frequently the official myth tellers are the ruling groups in society: the elders, the political leaders, the religious specialists. They may also be considered master storytellers. The content of myths usually concerns past events (usually at the beginning of time) or future events (usually at the end of time). Myths are socially important because they tell people where they have come from, where they are going, and, thus, how they should live right now (Figure 8.9).

In some societies, myths play a relatively informal role in laying out the guidelines of social conduct. This is the case in most complex Western societies such as that of Canada, where many different groups, each with its own mythic tradition, often live side by side. Because the Canadian government supports cultural diversity, or multiculturalism, it regularly prohibits one group from silencing an opposing group. Yet Canada is not without its myths. For many Canadians, the notion of multiculturalism itself is the dominant myth, and our assumption is that it makes us more tolerant. Yet, as is the case with most myths, the ideal it represents is not always reflected in reality.

Myths and related beliefs that are taken to be self-evident truths are sometimes codified in an explicit manner. When this codification is extreme and deviation from the code is treated harshly, we sometimes speak of **orthodoxy**. Societies differ in the degree to which they require members to adhere to orthodox interpretations of key myths. But even societies that place little emphasis on orthodoxy are likely to exert some control over the interpretation of key myths because myths have implications for action. They may justify past action, explain present action, or generate future action. To be persuasive, myths must offer plausible explanations for our experience of human nature, human society, and human history. The power of myths comes from their ability to make life meaningful for those who accept them.

The success of Western science has led many members of Western societies to dismiss non-scientific myths as flawed attempts at science or history. Only recently have some scientists come to recognize the similarities between scientific and non-scientific storytelling about events such as the origin of life on earth. Scientific stories about origin—*origin myths*—must be taken to the *natural* world to be matched against material evidence; the success of this match determines whether they are accepted or rejected. By contrast, non-scientific origin myths get their vitality from how well they match with the *social* world.

## Myth as a Charter for Social Action

Early in the twentieth century, Bronislaw Malinowski introduced a new approach to myth. He believed that to understand myths, we must understand the social context in which they are embedded. Malinowski argued that myths serve as 'charters' or 'justifications' for present-day social arrangements. Myths contain some 'self-evident' truth that explains why society is as it is and why it cannot be changed. If the social arrangements justified by the myth are challenged, the myth can be used as a weapon against the challengers.

Malinowski's (1948 [1926]) famous example is of the origin myths of the Trobriand Islanders (see EthnoProfile 7.1). Members of every significant kinship group know, mark, and retell the history of

**orthodoxy**
'Correct doctrine'; the prohibition of deviation from approved mythic texts.

*Figure 8.9* | **A vase painting illustrating part of the Popul Vuh, the Mayan creation story.**

the place from which their group's ancestress and her brother emerged from the depths of the earth. These origin myths are set in the time before history began. Each ancestress–brother pair brought a distinct set of characteristics that included special objects and knowledge, various skills, crafts, spells, and the like. On reaching the surface, the pair took possession of the land. That is why, today, the people on a given piece of land have rights to it. It is also why they possess a particular set of skills, crafts, and spells. Because the original sacred beings were a woman and her brother, the origin myth can also be used to endorse present-day social arrangements. Membership in a Trobriand clan depends on a person's ability to trace his or her kinship to that clan's original ancestress through matrilineage. A brother and a sister represent the prototypical members of a clan because they have both descended from the ancestress through female links. Should anyone question the wisdom of organizing society in this way, the myth can be cited as proof that this is indeed the correct way to live.

In Trobriand society, clans are ranked relative to one another in terms of prestige. In the Trobriand myth that explains rank, one clan's ancestor, the dog, emerged from the earth before another clan's ancestor, the pig, thus justifying ranking the dog clan above the pig clan in terms of prestige. To believe in this myth, Malinowski asserted, is to accept a transcendent justification for the ranking of clans. He made it clear, however, that if social arrangements change, the myth changes too—in order to justify the new arrangements. At some point, the pig clan became more prominent than the dog clan. This social change resulted in a change in the mythic narrative. The dog was said to have eaten food that was taboo. In doing so, the dog gave up its claim to higher rank. Thus, to understand a myth and its transformations, one must understand the social organization of the society that makes use of it.

## Myth as a Conceptual Tool

Beginning in the mid-1950s, a series of books and articles by French anthropologist Claude Lévi-Strauss (1967 [1962]) transformed the study of myth. Lévi-Strauss argued that myths have meaningful structures that are worth studying in their own right, quite apart from the uses to which the myths may be put. He suggested that myths should be interpreted the same way we interpret musical scores. In a piece of music, the meaning emerges not just from the melody but also from the harmony. In other words, the structure of the piece of music, the way in which each line contributes to the overall sound and is related to other lines, is a form of syntax that carries the meaning.

For Lévi-Strauss, myths are tools for overcoming logical contradictions that cannot otherwise be overcome. They are put together in an attempt to deal with the oppositions of particular concern to a particular society at a particular moment. Using a linguistic metaphor, Lévi-Strauss argued that myths are composed of smaller units—phrases, sentences, words, relationships—that are arranged in ways that give both narrative (or 'melodic') coherence and structural (or 'harmonic') coherence. These arrangements represent and comment upon aspects of social life that are thought to oppose each other. Examples include the opposition of men to women, of the natural world to the cultural world, of life to death, of spirit to body, of high to low, and so on.

The complex syntax of myth works to relate those opposed pairs to one another in an attempt to overcome their contradictions. However, these contradictions can never be overcome; for example, the opposition of life to death is incapable of any earthly resolution. But myth can transform an insoluble problem into a more accessible, concrete form. Mythic narrative can then provide the concrete problem with a solution. For example, a culture hero may bridge the opposition between life and death by travelling from the land of the living to the land of the dead and back. Alternatively, a myth might propose that the beings who transcend death are so horrific that death is clearly preferable to eternal life. Perhaps a myth describes the journey of a bird that travels from the earth, the home of the living, to the sky, the home of the dead. This is similar to Christian thought, where the death and resurrection of Jesus may be understood to resolve the opposition between life and death by transcending death.

From this point of view, myths do not just talk about the world as it is; they also describe the world as it might be. To paraphrase Lévi-Strauss, myths are good to think with; mythic thinking can propose other ways to live

## *In Their Own Words* | The Grizzly Gave Them the Song

*Wendy Wickwire, in discussing the fieldwork of James Teit and Franz Boas, provides some insights into bear ritual in Aboriginal British Columbia. So many aspects of culture highlighted in this chapter can be seen in this article—myth, ritual, art (song), and the transmission of cultural knowledge from person to person.*

Teit's field notes, by way of contrast (to those of Boas), present a much fuller picture of bear culture. Through the medium of songs and stories about direct encounters with bears, this source highlights the nurturing/protective role of the bear. Teit recorded 12 songs associated with bears along with contextual notes drawn from the commentary of seven singers (four men and three women). All seven focus on the close physical and spiritual bond between bears and humans. This source also highlights the prominent role of the female grizzly.

Six of the 12 songs, for example, are lullabies or cradle songs said to have been given to the Nlaka'pamux by female grizzlies. Such songs, according to Teit, were closely associated with women (CMC, cylinder collection VI.M.58). Kax.pítsa's song, catalogued by Teit as VI.M.125 'cradle song', is typical. A member of the Spences Bridge Band, Kax.pítsa told Teit that she had obtained this directly from the bear when she was a young woman.

> She had a vision in which she saw a female grizzly bear with four children under a tree. The children (or cubs) were all males and all of them were in birch bark carriers. The children were crying much and the mother was singing trying to stop them from crying. When the grizzly woman saw Kax.pítsa she called on her to come over and sing to the children. Kax.pítsa told her she did not know how to sing to them properly and the grizzly told her she would teach her. Kax.pítsa took up one after the other and sang to them as the grizzly directed and one after another they quit crying. When all were pacified (or asleep) the grizzly told Kax.pítsa, 'You will now have this song for a cradle song

and by singing it to children when they cry, you will have the power of quickly pacifying them.' Kax.pítsa claims to have this power but only for male children. (VI.M.125)

The song is similar to another in the collection sung by NsEl-kapéskEt, a young Spences Bridge man. Teit catalogued it as a 'lullaby song called the "Black Bear's Lullaby"' (CMC, cylinder collection VI.M.195) and noted that it

> Is said to be old and is said to have originated or been introduced by some person who had heard the black bear singing it. The person saw a black bear come over a hill carrying her baby. The latter was crying and as the mother came along travelling down the hill she sang this song to her baby thus quieting it. Since then the women of the Up.Ntlak (Thompson) have used the song when travelling to quiet their babies when they cried.

Chief TetlEnítsa of Spences Bridge also sang a 'cradle song' with close links to the female bear. He told Teit that he had received the song in a dream in which a 'dark woman and her baby' had appeared to him and led him to her den. Teit believed that this woman 'was likely simply a different manifestation of the black bear woman who became manitou [a guardian spirit] of TetlEnítsa when he was a young man. She appears in different forms in his dreams. . . . [She] often carries baby' (CMC, cylinder collection VI.M.49–50). Although TetlEnítsa claimed this as his own song, he explained that the women of his band liked it and so adopted it as their cradle song. These examples . . . underscore the importance of the *female* bear in the Nlaka'pamux world. Her songs and instructions were a key component of women's culture, especially motherhood.

Source: Wickwire, Wendy. 2001. 'The Grizzly Gave Them the Song: James Teit and Franz Boas Interpret Twin Ritual in Aboriginal British Columbia, 1897–1920', *American Indian Quarterly* 25, 3: 431–52.

our lives. He insists, however, that the alternatives myths propose are ordinarily rejected as impossible. Thus, even though myths allow for play with self-evident truths, this play remains under strict control.

Is Lévi-Strauss correct? There has been a great deal of debate on this issue since the 1955 publication of his article 'The Structural Study of Myth' (note Lévi-Strauss 1967 [1962]). But even those who are most critical of his analyses of particular myths agree that mythic structures are meaningful because they display the ability of human beings to play with possibilities as they attempt to deal with basic contradictions at the heart of human experience.

For Malinowski, Lévi-Strauss, and their followers, those who believe in myths are not conscious of how their myths are structured or of the functions their myths perform for them. More recent anthropological thinking takes a more reflexive approach. This research recognizes that ordinary members of a society *are* often aware of how their myths structure meaning, allowing them to manipulate the way myths are told or interpreted in order to make an effect, to prove a point, or to buttress a particular referential perspective on human nature, society, or history. Therefore myths are, to paraphrase Riddington, the poetics by which people create meaning through language. The stories of a people are metonyms—where parts can stand for wholes (more on this in Chapter 10), and 'each story is connected to every other and to a highly contextualized discourse that assumes familiarity with biography and shared experience' (1998: 346).

# Ritual

Play allows unlimited consideration of alternative referential perspectives on reality. Art permits consideration of alternative perspectives but imposes certain limitations restricting the form and content. Myth aims to narrow radically the possible referential perspectives and often promotes a single, orthodox perspective presumed to be valid for everyone. It thus offers a kind of intellectual indoctrination. But because societies aim to shape action as well as thought to orient all human faculties in the approved direction, art, myth, and ritual are often closely associated with one another.

## A Definition of Ritual

Our definition of ritual has four elements.

1) Ritual is a repetitive social practice composed of a sequence of symbolic activities in the form of dance, song, speech, gestures, the manipulation of certain objects, and so forth.
2) It is set off from the social routines of everyday life.
3) Rituals adhere to a characteristic, culturally defined ritual schema. This means that members of a culture can tell that a certain sequence of activities is a ritual even if they have never seen that particular ritual before.
4) Ritual action is closely connected to a specific set of ideas that are often encoded in myth. These ideas might concern the nature of evil, the relationship of human beings to the spirit world, how people ought to interact with one another, and so forth.

The purpose for which a ritual is performed guides how these ideas are selected and symbolically enacted. What gives a ritual its power is that the people who perform it assert that the authorization for the ritual comes from outside themselves—from their state, society, God, ancestors, or 'tradition'. These people have not made up the ritual themselves; rather, it connects them to a source of power that they do not control but that controls them.

The Western prototype of ritual includes the notion that it is 'religious'. However, in anthropological terms, ritual includes a much broader range of activities. According to the definition given in the preceding paragraph, a scientific experiment, a graduation ceremony, procedures in a court of law, and a child's birthday party are rituals just as much as weddings, bar mitzvahs, Hmong sacrifices to their ancestors, and Catholic Mass.

Consider the example of a young child's birthday party in North America. Several children are formally invited to help celebrate the birthday. Each arrives bringing a wrapped gift, which is handed to the birthday child and then set aside. The children often put on birthday hats. They then play group games of some kind, some of which are now *only* played at birthday parties. The games culminate with the appearance of a birthday cake, illuminated by candles (one for each year of the child's life) and accompanied by the singing of 'Happy Birthday'. The birthday child makes a wish and blows out the candles. Following the cake and ice cream, the birthday child opens the presents. There is much commotion as the guests urge the birthday child to open theirs first. As the birthday child opens each gift, he or she examines it and thanks the guest (often with an adult's prompting). Shortly after the presents are opened, the guests' parents or guardians appear and the guests receive party favours and leave. The ritual order of these events matters. The central events of the party—the giving of gifts; the events associated with the cake, the candles, the singing of 'Happy Birthday', the wish; and the opening of the gifts—must occur in this order. Additionally, if you come from a tradition in which birthday parties are celebrated, it is likely that you cannot remember *learning* how to celebrate a birthday party—it is something you have always known. It's what everyone does. It's just how it is. Its authority comes from 'tradition'.

In the birthday party ritual, children (both hosts and guests) learn to associate receiving gifts with important moments in life. They discover the importance of exchanging material objects in defining significant social relations. They learn to defer gratification (the presents cannot be opened immediately). They live out patterns of sociability and friendship (as anyone who has heard the ultimate preschool threat, 'I'm not inviting you to my birthday party', knows) while recognizing the centrality of the individual (there are few things worse than sharing your birthday party with someone else!). Finally, the children participate in patterns of sharing, of celebrating the self, and of recognizing relationships with friends and kin that are important in other areas of North American life.

## Ritual as Action

A ritual has a particular sequential ordering of acts, utterances, and events: that is, ritual has a *text*. Because ritual is action, however, we must pay attention to the way the ritual text is performed. The *performance* of a ritual cannot be separated from its text; text and performance shape each

**rite of passage**
A ritual that serves to mark the movement and transformation of an individual from one social position to another.

other dialectically. Through ritual performance the ideas of a culture become concrete, take on a form, and, as Bruce Kapferer (1983) puts it, give direction to the gaze of participants. At the same time, ritual performance can serve as a commentary on the text to the extent of transforming it. For example, Jewish synagogue ritual following the reading of the Torah (the Hebrew Bible) includes lifting the Torah scroll, showing it to the congregation, and then closing it and covering it. In some synagogues a man and a woman, often a couple, are called to lift and cover the Torah: the man lifts it and after he seats himself the woman rolls the scroll closed, places the tie around it, and covers it with the mantle that protects it. Robert Lavenda once observed a performance of this ritual in which the woman lifted the Torah and the man wrapped it; officially, the ritual text was carried out, but the performance became a commentary on the text—on the role of women in Judaism, on the Torah as an appropriate subject of attention for women as well as for men, on the roles of men and women overall, and so on. The performance was noteworthy—indeed, many of the regular members of the congregation seemed quite surprised—precisely because it violated people's expectations and in doing so directed people's attention toward the role of men and women in religious ritual at the end of the twentieth century.

Ritual performers are not robots but active individuals whose choices are guided by, but not rigidly dictated by, previous ritual texts (see, e.g., Drewal 1992). After all, human behaviour is fundamentally open. Rituals highlight the fact that human understanding of the world is not just mental and not just physical but a holistic coming together of mind and body, thought and feeling. By performing our ideas, by feeling the implications of our myths, their truths become self-evident.

### Rites of Passage

Let us examine how ritual action can reaffirm certain fundamental truths by looking at one kind of ritual performance: the **rite of passage**. At the beginning of the twentieth century, Belgian anthropologist Arnold Van Gennep noted that certain kinds of rituals around the world had similar structures. These were rituals associated with the movement (or passage) of people from one position in the social structure to another. They included births, initiations, confirmations, weddings, and funerals (Figure 8.10).

Van Gennep (1960) found that all these rituals began with a period of *separation* from the old position and from normal time. During this period, the ritual passenger left behind the symbols and practices of his or her previous position. For example, military recruits leave their families behind and are moved to a new place. They are forced to cut their hair and leave behind the clothing and activities that marked who they were in civilian life.

The second stage in rites of passage involves a period of *transition*, in which the ritual passenger is neither in the old life nor in the new one. This period is marked by rolelessness, ambiguity, and perceived danger. Often, the person involved is subjected to ordeal by those who have already passed through this stage. In the military service, this is the period of basic training, in which recruits (not yet soldiers but no longer civilians) are forced to dress and act alike. They are subjected to a grinding-down process, after which they are rebuilt into something new.

During the final stage—*re-aggregation*—the ritual passenger is reintroduced into society in his or her new position. In the military this involves the graduation from basic training and a visit home, but this time in uniform, on leave, and as a member of the armed forces, a new person. A more familiar rite of passage in North America is high-school graduation, which is understood as a movement from one social position to another.

The work of Victor Turner has greatly increased our understanding of rites of passage. Turner concentrated on the period of transition, which he saw as important both for the rite of passage and for social life in general. Van Gennep referred to this part of a rite of passage as the **liminal period**, from the Latin *limen* ('threshold'). During this period, the individual is on the threshold, betwixt and between, neither here nor there, neither in nor out. Turner notes that the symbolism accompanying the rite of passage often expresses this ambiguous state. Liminality, he tells us, 'is frequently likened to death, to being in the womb, to invisibility, to darkness, to bisexuality, to the wilderness, and to an eclipse of the sun or moon' (1969: 95). We are familiar with this concept

**Figure 8.10 | This funeral procession in Kyoto, Japan, bears resemblance to North American funeral processions. Certain kinds of rituals around the world have similar structures.**

from the tales by the Brothers Grimm. Many of what we call *fairytales* were originally folktales and have rites of passage and liminality as part of the story. Consider the original versions of *Snow White*, *Sleeping Beauty*, and *Rapunzel*. People in the liminal state tend to develop an intense comradeship with each other in which their non-liminal distinctions disappear or become irrelevant. Turner calls this modality of social relationship **communitas**.

Turner contends that all societies need some kind of communitas as much as they need structure. Communitas gives 'recognition to an essential and generic human bond, without which there could be no society' (97). That bond is the common humanity that

**liminal period**
The ambiguous transitional state in a rite of passage in which the person or persons undergoing the ritual are outside their ordinary social positions.

**communitas**
An unstructured or minimally structured community of equal individuals frequently found in rites of passage.

underlies all culture and society. However, periods of communitas (often in ritual context) are brief. Communitas is dangerous, not just because it threatens structure but because it threatens survival itself. Lost in a world of communitas, an individual is cut off from the things that structure ensures—production of food and physical and social reproduction of society. Communitas gives way to structure, which in turn generates a need for the release of communitas. The feeling of oneness associated with communitas is also possible in play and art. Indeed, it may well be that for people in contemporary nation-states the experience of communitas comes through a shared experience of witnessing the climactic winning moments of a sports team, attending a large-scale rock concert, or participating in a mass public event such as Toronto's Caribbean Carnival (Caribana), Carnaval de Québec, or the Calgary Stampede.

## Play and Ritual as Complementary

How does play differ from ritual? Play and ritual (like metaphorical and literal language) are complementary forms of metacommunication (Handelman 1977). Just as the movement from non-play to play is based on the premise of metaphor ('let's make-believe'), the movement to ritual is based on the premise of literalness ('let's believe'). From the perspective of paramount reality, the result of these contrasting premises is the 'inauthenticity' of play and the 'truth' of ritual.

Because of the connection of ritual with self-evident truth, the metacommunication of the ritual frame ('this is ritual') is associated with an additional metacommunication: 'all messages within this frame are true.' It is ritual that asserts *what should be* to play's *what can be*. The ritual frame is more rigid than the play frame. Consequently, ritual is the most stable liminal domain, whereas play is the most flexible. Players can move with relative ease into and out of play, but such is not the case with ritual.

**orthopraxy**
'Correct practice'; the prohibition of deviation from approved forms of ritual behaviour.

Finally, play usually has little effect on the social order of ordinary life. Thus play is allowed a wide range of commentary on the social order. Ritual is different: its role is explicitly to maintain the status quo, including the prescribed ritual transformations. Societies differ in the extent to which ritual behaviour alternates with everyday, non-ritual behaviour. When nearly every act of everyday life is ritualized and other forms of behaviour are strongly proscribed, we sometimes speak of **orthopraxy**. Traditionally, observant Jews and Muslims, for example, lead a highly ritualized daily life, attempting from the moment they awaken until the moment they fall asleep to carry out even the humblest of activities in a manner that is ritually correct. In their view, ritual correctness is the result of God's law, and it is their duty and joy to conform their every action to God's will.

Ritual may seem overwhelming and all-powerful. Yet individuals and groups within a society can sometimes manipulate ritual forms to achieve non-traditional ends. This can range from pushing against tradition as far as it can go without actually destroying the ritual (as when a bride and groom have an alternative wedding outdoors, write their own vows, and still have a member of the clergy officiating), to emphasizing the importance of one ritual and ignoring or downplaying another (as when Protestant Baptists downplayed the communion ritual and emphasized the baptism ritual as a way of articulating their challenge to Roman Catholicism), to exchanging one set of rituals for another (as when lone rural migrants of northern Cameroon converted to Islam shortly after their arrival, abandoning their traditional rituals together with the rural way of life into which they were born).

Margaret Drewal argues that, at least among the Yoruba, play and ritual overlap (see Map 8.4). Yoruba rituals combine spectacle, festival, play, sacrifice, and so on, and integrate diverse media—music, dance, poetry, theatre, sculpture (1992: 198). They are improvisatory events, spontaneous individual moves in which the mundane order is not only inverted and reversed but may also be subverted through power play and gender play. In Yoruba life, gender roles are rigidly structured. Yoruba rituals, however, allow some cross-dressing by both men and women, providing institutionalized opportunities for men and women to cross gender boundaries and to

Map 8.4 | **Yoruba**

Map 8.5 | **Sinhalese**

express the traits that Yoruba consider to be characteristic of the opposite sex, sometimes as parody but sometimes seriously and respectfully (190).

## Combining Play, Art, Myth, and Ritual

As we noted earlier, play, art, myth, and ritual are often experienced together. To reiterate through example, consider Kapferer's study of demon exorcism in Sri Lanka (see Map 8.5). The demon exorcism ceremonies of the Sinhalese Buddhist working class and peasantry last an entire night and are designed to cure disease. The performance combines in 'a marvellous spectacle' ritual, comedy, music, and dance. Its goal is 'to change the experiential condition of [the] patients and to bring patients back into a normal conception of the world' (1983: 177, 236). In other words, the entire performance is transformative. During the course of the ceremony, a demonic reality is created and then destroyed.

At the beginning of the exorcism, the patient and the audience are in different realities. The audience is in the paramount reality of everyday life; the patient is in the alternative reality of his or her illness. In that reality, demons are central and powerful actors. During the Evening Watch, through music, song, and eventually dance, the audience becomes increasingly engaged in

this alternative reality. In this part of the ceremony, the demons are portrayed as figures of horror.

At midnight, the process is complete: the audience has joined the patient's reality. The demons, played by actors, appear. At this point, the Midnight Watch begins. This part of the ceremony is a comic drama that lasts until nearly 3 a.m. The eruption of comedy into what had been an intensely serious ceremony transforms the demons into figures of ridicule. Through the comedy, the demonic reality begins to fragment as the gods appear and reassert their dominance. As this occurs, the sick person begins to see that the demons are really subordinate to the gods, not superior to them.

The last part of the exorcism is the Morning Watch, which continues until 6 a.m. During this period, the patient and audience become re-engaged in the reality of ordinary life. The final comic drama of the performance 'confirms the demonic absurdity and destroys the demonic as powerful and relevant to normal experience in daily life' (220). Having played on the mind, body, and emotions of the patient and the audience, the performance ends.

To understand the performance as a whole, the interactions of all aspects of the performance must be grasped. Kapferer calls this the ceremony's *aesthetics*. He argues that the ceremony succeeds because it is composed of many different parts that fit together in

Page 210, Part II | The Resources of Culture

a way that is satisfying to the Sinhalese. Only in the aesthetic realm are ideas, symbolic objects, and actions brought into the relationship from which their meaning comes.

Play, art, myth, and ritual are different facets of the holistic human capacity to view the world from a variety of perspectives. The human capacity to play is channelled in different directions in different cultures, but it is always present. When the products of this containment process come together in key cultural productions, such as the Sinhalese curing ceremony, they display both the opportunities and dangers that result from open human creativity.

# Key Terms

art   187
communitas   207
framing   188
liminal period   207
metacommunication   188
myths   187
orthodoxy   202

orthopraxy   208
play   187
reflexivity   188
rite of passage   206
ritual   187
sport   190
transformation-representation   193

# Chapter Summary

1.  Play is a generalized form of behavioural openness. Play can be thought of as a way of *organizing* activities, not merely a set of activities. We put a frame that consists of the message 'this is play' around certain activities, thereby transforming them into play. Play also permits reflexive consideration of alternative realities by setting up a separate reality and suggesting that the perspective of ordinary life is only one way to make sense of experience.

2.  The functions of play include exercise, practise for the real world, increased creativity, and commentary on the real world.

3.  The fate of national sports teams can come to represent the nation itself, and the devotion of sports fans becomes a way of affirming patriotism. When sports are translated from one culture to another, they are frequently transformed to fit the patterns appropriate to the new culture.

4.  Art is a kind of play that is subject to certain culturally appropriate restrictions on form and content. It aims to evoke a holistic, aesthetic response from the artist and the observer. It succeeds when the form is culturally appropriate for the content and is technically perfect in its realization. Aesthetic evaluations are culturally shaped value judgments. We recognize art in other cultures because of its family resemblance to what we call *art* in our own culture. Although people with other cultural understandings may not have produced art by intention, we can often successfully appreciate what they have created as art by appropriation. These issues are addressed in ethnographic studies that call into question received ideas about what counts as 'authentic' art.

5.  Myths are stories whose truths seem self-evident because they do such a good job of integrating personal experiences with a wider set of assumptions about the way the world works. As stories, myths are the products of high verbal art. A full understanding of myth requires ethnographic background information.

6.  Ritual is a repetitive social practice composed of sequences of symbolic activities such as speech, singing, dancing, gestures, and the manipulation of certain

objects. In studying ritual, we pay attention not just to the symbols but also to how the ritual is performed. Cultural ideas are made concrete through ritual action.

7.  Rites of passage are rituals in which members of a culture move from one position in the social structure to another. These rites are marked by periods of separation, transition, and re-aggregation. During the period of transition, individuals occupy a liminal position. Those in this position frequently develop an intense comradeship and a feeling of oneness, or communitas.

8.  Ritual and play are complementary. Play is based on the premise 'let's make-believe', while ritual is based on the premise 'let's believe'. As a result, the ritual frame is far more rigid than the play frame. Although ritual may seem overwhelming and all-powerful, individuals and groups can sometimes manipulate ritual forms to achieve non-traditional ends.

## Critical Thinking Questions

1.  What adult roles do you remember learning through childhood play? Did the games you played reflect dominant cultural stereotypes within the culture (for example, that a 'standard' family has both a mommy and a daddy)? In what ways did the games creatively diverge from the reality of adult life?

2.  In what ways do Janet Lever's observations on soccer's 'paradoxical ability to reinforce societal cleavages while transcending them' echo the function of hockey in Canadian culture?

3.  How are art and play alike in presenting alternative realities?

4.  Consider the three different forms of authenticity from Michelle Bigenho. What would you consider authentic in your cultural context?

5.  How do you think that the multiculturalism myth impact the ways Canadians act and interpret their place in the world? What other myths do you see at work in your society?

6.  How would you describe your experience of becoming a university or college student as a rite of passage? Did you venture through periods of separation, transition, and re-aggregation? What were your experiences with liminality and communitas?

## Suggested Readings

Alland, Alexander. 1977. *The Artistic Animal* (New York: Doubleday Anchor). An introductory look at the biocultural bases for art. This work is very well written, clear, and fascinating.

Archetti, Eduardo P. n.d. 'Anthropology of Sport', available at www.forskningsradet.no/servlet/Satellite?blobcol=urldata&blo bheader=application%2Fpdf&blobheadername1=Content-Disp osition%3A&blobheadervalue1=+attachment%3B+filename% 3DEduardoArchetti01.pdf&blobkey=id&blobtable=MungoBlob s&blobwhere=1274460305123&ssbinary=true. A consideration of sport as a field of analysis for understanding rituals, complex processes of identity construction, rites of passage, and bodily performances.

Blanchard, Kendall. 1995. *The Anthropology of Sport*, rev. edn (Westport, CT: Bergin & Garvey). An excellent introduction to the field.

Errington, Shelly. 1998. *The Death of Authentic Primitive Art and Other Tales of Progress* (Berkeley: University of California Press). A sharp and witty book about the production, distribution, interpretation, and sale of 'primitive art'.

Halliday-Scher, Kathy, Kathryn A. Urberg, and Melissa Kaplan-Estrin. 1995. 'Learning to Pretend: Preschoolers' Use of Meta-communication in Socio-dramatic Play', *International Journal of Behavioural Development* 18, 3: 451–61. This article explores how children's ability to structure socio-dramatic play may depend on their ability to communicate pretense transformations effectively.

Hallowell, A. Irving. 1960. 'Ojibwa Ontology, Behavior, and World View', *in Culture and History: Essays of Paul Radin, ed. Stanley Diamond* (New York: Columbia University Press), 19–52. This work focusses on Anishinaabe (Ojibwe) organization of various knowledge domains—what we describe as schemas and proto-types in the context of this text.

King, Thomas. 1993. *Green Grass, Running Water* (Toronto: HarperCollins). This exploration of contemporary Native American culture and North American literature and literary theory juxtaposes the real and the magical, showing how the magical gives essential meaning to the real. It is an engaging example of both metacommunication and transformation-representation.

**Riddington, Robin. 1998. 'Coyote's Canon: Sharing Stories with Thomas King',** *American Indian Quarterly* 22, 3: 343–62. The counterpoint of Coyote is King as he presents a Native American perspective on the American literary and cultural canon.

**Steiner, Christopher. 1994.** *African Art in Transit* **(Cambridge: Cambridge University Press).** This work traces the social life of objects made in rural West African villages from their creation to their resting places in galleries, museums, tourist shops, or private Western art collections, highlighting the role of African merchants who make this transit possible.

**Turner, Victor. 1969.** *The Ritual Process* **(Chicago: Aldine).** An important work in the anthropological study of ritual, this text is an eloquent analysis of rites of passage.

**Vogel, Susan. 1997. Baule:** *African Art/Western Eyes* **(New Haven: Yale University Press).** A book of extraordinary photographs and beautifully clear text, this work explores both Baule and Western views of Baule expressive culture.

**Wickwire, Wendy. 2001. 'The Grizzly Gave Then the Song: James Teit and Franz Boas Interpret Twin Ritual in Aboriginal British Columbia, 1897–1920',** *American Indian Quarterly* 25, 3: 431–52. Compares and contrasts the ethnographic information collected and interpreted by two researchers in British Columbia. The focus of this comparison is the songs of the Bear.

## Related Websites

*The Antiquity of Man* www.antiquityofman.com/Solomon_myth_ritual.html

*Canadian Art* www.canadianart.ca

*Illinois State Museum* www.museum.state.il.us/muslink/nat_amer/post/htmls/il_am.html

*Turtle Island Native Network* www.turtleisland.org/culture/culture-haisla.htm

# 9 | States of Being in Wellness and Illness

*Roberta Robin Dods*

## Chapter Outline

Beyond the Science–Tradition Divide

Integrated Approaches and Holism in Medical Anthropology

Cultural Interpretations and Labels of Illness and Disease

Environments and Well-Being

Health Care Delivery Systems

Epidemiology

Being Applied

## Learning Objectives

By the end of Chapter 9, you will be able to

- understand that medical anthropology draws on many disciplines to study well-being, health, illness, and disease,

- identify the roles of traditional knowledge and Western scientific knowledge in the management of wellness and illness,

- consider that interpretations of illness and disease, health care systems, clinical realities, and care providers vary considerably within and between cultures,

- recognize the patchy delivery of medical intervention based on class, gender, age, and geographical location,

- appreciate that human wellness and illness are affected by three interacting environments: the biotic (biological), the abiotic (physical), and the cultural, and

- detail the role of anthropological epidemiologists in learning about the cross-cultural distribution of diseases.

*These Puri Puri men in Papua New Guinea follow the path laid out by a bamboo stick after asking for guidance to find a guilty party. Like many traditional healers, these men also offer traditional cures for illnesses and diseases by mediating forces in the physical as well as the spiritual world.* →

In *Childhood in the Middle Ages* (1990), Shulamith Shahar writes about the lives (and deaths) of children in Europe from the twelfth through the fifteenth century. She also notes the case of one sixteenth-century English woman who had given birth to 17 children, none of whom survived to adulthood. This woman was a member of the upper class and had access to the best her society could offer in terms of education, housing, food, and health care, yet her resources were not enough to save her children from diseases and medical conditions that we would find easily treatable today. Indeed, considering the low life expectancy (35 years) and the high rates of maternal death related to childbirth she faced, we could marvel that this woman survived birthing so many children in the first place.

Now you may say this woman's situation is simply a product of the time in which she lived. In some sense, you would be right. After all, in Western nations, life expectancies have increased dramatically since the Middle Ages, and maternal mortality ratios are low. Yet we must also remember that we view the situation from a privileged position. In Canada, we have access to public and private institutions that offer cutting-edge medical technologies (vaccines, medications, procedures, machines, etc.). Most of us live in communities that provide adequate sanitation programs to regulate the quality of drinking water and the disposal of sewage and garbage. Not only is our life expectancy at birth over 80 years, our quality of life is quite high well into old age. We desire relatively small families, and various birth control and fertility technologies allow us to choose when and under what conditions we will have children. Most of us take immunization for granted, and we seldom think of diseases such as diphtheria, polio, or measles—all of which contributed to high infant and childhood mortality rates in past centuries (Figure 9.1). And smallpox is unimaginable for most of us, since it was eradicated worldwide by 1979. Overall, our landscape of health and well-being has improved in ways never imagined by previous generations.

*Figure 9.1* | This 1898 *memento mori* photograph of an infant from Hull, Quebec, suggests the preoccupation with high infant mortality rates—more than 20 per 100 live births in some regions—at the turn of the twentieth century. Infectious diseases were a common cause of death.

Yet conditions are much different for people in less affluent regions of the world. In many areas, for example, a high proportion of children and adults still die of diseases transmitted through unclean water. As Tables 9.1 and 9.2 show, maternal mortality ratios and under-five death rates—both measures of a population's overall health—vary greatly across the globe. All too often, when it comes to issues of health and wellness, the divide between rich and poor is starkly evident. This division was apparent when cholera broke out in Haiti in 2010; the poorest segments of the population had the least access to uncontaminated water and life-saving resources. We see this division within wealthy nations as well, as the disenfranchised of all societies face greater health challenges, exacerbated by poor nutrition, than do their more affluent neighbours. Thus, while we may look at the world of the English woman who lost 17 children so long ago as frozen in history, there are millions of people today who would recognize that world and who would understand what it is like to face the threat of deadly contagious diseases on a daily basis.

Ultimately, an individual's expectations of wellness depend on the cultural context in which she or he lives. Think about how important context is in your day-to-day

*Table 9.1* | Countries with Highest and Lowest Maternal Mortality Ratios (MMRs), 2008

| 20 Countries with Highest Ratios | MMR (per 100,000 live births) | 20 Countries with Lowest Ratios | MMR (per 100,000 live births) |
|---|---|---|---|
| Afghanistan | 1,400 | Greece | 2 |
| Chad | 1,200 | Ireland | 3 |
| Somalia | 1,200 | Austria | 5 |
| Guinea Bissau | 1,000 | Belgium | 5 |
| Liberia | 990 | Denmark | 5 |
| Burundi | 970 | Iceland | 5 |
| Sierra Leone | 970 | Italy | 5 |
| Central African Republic | 850 | Sweden | 5 |
| Nigeria | 840 | Japan | 6 |
| Mali | 830 | Poland | 6 |
| Niger | 820 | Slovakia | 6 |
| United Republic of Tanzania | 790 | Spain | 6 |
| Zimbabwe | 790 | Germany | 7 |
| Sudan | 750 | Israel | 7 |
| Guinea | 680 | Norway | 7 |
| Democratic Republic of the Congo | 670 | Portugal | 7 |
| Angola | 610 | Australia | 8 |
| Cameroon | 600 | Czech Republic | 8 |
| Congo | 580 | Finland | 8 |
| Lao People's Democratic Republic | 580 | France | 8[a] |

[a] The estimated ratios for Malta, Qatar, and Serbia were also 8.

Note: Canada's estimated ratio was 12.

Source: Adapted from the World Health Organization's 'Global Health Observatory Data Repository', MDG 5: Maternal Health, Maternal Mortality Ratio, available at http://apps.who.int/ghodata/.

experiences with health matters. For example, consider the different ways in which you would describe your sense of un-wellness to your doctor, your grandmother, your instructor, or your boss, particularly if you want a day off. What words would you choose to make each understand your symptoms and the validity of your perception of un-wellness? How would your sex, gender, age, or class influence your selection of terms? Undoubtedly your statements will be informed by the paradigms of your culture and subculture; they will also be suited to the relationship you have with the person to whom you are talking. You are situated in a world of cultural concerns, a world with historic context that you participate in from a uniquely situated position.

*Table 9.2* | Countries with Highest and Lowest Under-Five Mortality Rates, 2009

| 20 Countries with Highest Rates | Under-Five Mortality Rate (per 1,000 live births) | 20 Countries with Lowest Rates | Under-Five Mortality Rate (per 1,000 live births) |
|---|---|---|---|
| Chad | 209 | Luxembourg | 2 |
| Afghanistan | 199 | San Marino | 2 |
| Democratic Republic of the Congo | 199 | Cyprus | 3 |
| Guinea-Bissau | 193 | Finland | 3 |
| Sierra Leone | 192 | Iceland | 3 |
| Mali | 191 | Japan | 3 |
| Somalia | 180 | Singapore | 3 |
| Central African Republic | 171 | Slovenia | 3 |
| Burkina Faso | 166 | Sweden | 3 |
| Burundi | 166 | Andora | 4 |
| Angola | 161 | Czech Republic | 4 |
| Niger | 160 | Denmark | 4 |
| Cameroon | 154 | France | 4 |
| Equatorial Guinea | 145 | Germany | 4 |
| Guinea | 142 | Greece | 4 |
| Mozambique | 142 | Ireland | 4 |
| Zambia | 141 | Italy | 4 |
| Nigeria | 138 | Norway | 4 |
| Congo | 128 | Portugal | 4 |
| Uganda | 128 | Spain | 4[a] |

[a] The estimated rate for Switzerland was also 4.

Note: Canada's estimated rate was 6.

Source: Adapted from the World Health Organization's 'Global Health Observatory Data Repository', MDG 4: Child Mortality, Under-Five Mortality Rate, available at http://apps.who.int/ghodata/.

# Beyond the Science–Tradition Divide

In this complex world, there is always a dynamic tension between **traditional knowledge** and Western scientific modes of inquiry. This tension plays out in all of our lives, and it is increasingly intensified by concepts of 'modernization'. Thus, it is naturally a central concern in **medical anthropology**. Note that the term *medical* does not refer specifically to the field of 'medicine' as it is strictly defined in the West. Rather, *medical* here points to a wider array of concerns that relate more broadly to human ideas of **well-being, health, illness,** and **disease**.

In the 1970s and 1980s, many medical anthropologists saw a binary opposition between medical systems based on traditional knowledge and those based on 'modern' Western science. Some anthropologists even saw the characterization of these two primary categories as the 'broad aims of the research' (Colson and Selby 1974: 246). In one category, there is the Western biomedical approach in which a team of medical professionals, working within an institutionalized system, combat a disease-produced illness with little reference to the social and/or cultural conditions of the 'client'. Allan Young (1976) called this an *internalizing* system, as it focusses on the physiological pathology of the individual. In the other category, there are traditional ethnomedical approaches in which a wise, often spiritually powerful specialist fights an illness based on the knowledge and beliefs of his or her specific cultural group, generally with an awareness of the context of social relationships (Fabrega 1971: 167). Young called such systems *externalizing*, as they often humanize or anthropomorphize the agents of illness as purposive. Today, this rudimentary typology continues to have some use within the discipline, but primarily as a backdrop against which we can begin to understand anthropology's current approach to studies of wellness and illness.

Contemporary medical anthropologists try to move beyond such 'either/or' approaches for a number of reasons. First, they understand that the two systems are not mutually exclusive; indeed, many cultures in the modern world incorporate both traditional and Western concepts into their medical systems. Second, they see that they can arrive at a more holistic appreciation of all knowledges by examining the traditional in terms of the scientific and the scientific in terms of the traditional. Third, they perceive that biomedical knowledge is actually a form of traditional knowledge—after all, such knowledge is rooted in Western history, it developed as Western society developed, and it is passed along within Western cultures. Fourth, they note that the lines between 'folk' medicine and 'scientific' medicine are not always clear. For example, Dr Irwin Ziment, of the UCLA Collaborative Centers for Integrative Medicine, observes that

> chicken soup contains drug-like agents similar to those in modern cold medicines. For example, an amino acid released from chicken during cooking chemically resembles the drug acetylcysteine, prescribed for bronchitis and other respiratory problems. (quoted in Day 2010)

Finally, they understand that 'modern' is a relative concept. Each culture defines its own 'modernity' based on its own interpretations and techniques rooted deep in time and emergent ideas in the 'now'. Thus it is ethnocentric to see the Western version of modernity, along with its biomedical approaches, as more modern than the modernities of cultures that support ethnomedical approaches. Whether we call it 'science' or 'tradition', knowledge is constantly advancing, as cultures are always in flux. Traditional peoples are open to new concepts, and they have often incorporated elements from Western science into their treatment regimes. At the same time, there are ideological reasons for limiting such borrowings: 'linguistic and cultural diversity gives rise to different degrees of acceptance. . . [and] in some cases, reaffirmation of traditional medicine is enacted as a defence of ethnic identity' (Menegoni 1996: 382).

Ultimately, although Western biomedical approaches can be very effective when it comes to saving lives, they have their limitations. As Sobo puts it, they are 'asocial and highly technologized, bureaucratized, and industrialized' (2004: 5). Consequently, they stand in opposition to the anthropologist's goal of understanding individuals and their lives as situated in specific *contexts*. Medical anthropologists recognize this opposition and actively seek to remain open to non-Western, culturally defined ways of knowing and being. They understand the need to contextualize all situations. Thus they value qualitative along with quantitative data and consider various aspects of cultural

---

**traditional knowledge**
Knowledge that is culturally held and passed on from generation to generation.

**medical anthropology**
An area of anthropological inquiry that focusses on issues of well-being, health, illness, and disease as they are situated in their wider cultural contexts.

**well-being**
A state (or role) of general physical and mental comfort and good health; a lack of illness.

**health**
A cross-cultural term to describe a person's general social, psychological, and physical condition. Generally, good health is what allows an individual to function within his or her society.

**illness**
A culturally identified state (or role) of general physical and/or mental discomfort; a personal experience of suffering that prompts the afflicted to seek intervention and that underlies all culturally defined interventions to alleviate suffering.

**disease**
A biomedical condition characterized by a harmful biological irregularity in an organism.

systems engaging from the local through to the global. Perhaps most importantly, they understand that the relationship between traditional and biomedical approaches is often very complex; in practice, the two have a lot to offer one another, but they successfully work together only when cultural contexts are taken into account.

This final observation is perhaps most significant when contrasted with the Western-centric approaches of many foreign aid workers, particularly those operating in the mid-to-late twentieth century, who believed they could effectively introduce Western medical technologies around the globe without considering potential social, economic, and cultural impacts on local populations. Not surprisingly, their efforts failed in many cases, resulting in ineffective, patchy distributions of medical supplies and treatments. To avoid similar cultural bias when investigating health issues, we must keep in mind three questions at the heart of medical anthropology: How do cultures define what constitutes wellness? How do people characterize different illnesses? What degree of intervention is considered appropriate?

# Integrated Approaches and Holism in Medical Anthropology

Medical anthropology is highly interdisciplinary. With roots in overlapping social, cultural, and medical studies of the late nineteenth and early twentieth centuries, the field has evolved into a productive melding of the biological sciences, the social sciences, and the humanities. Today, medical anthropologists draw on such diverse disciplines as biology, ecology, biochemistry, sociology, psychology, political science, economics, linguistics, ethics, and religious studies. While not all of these disciplines are centrally concerned with health issues, they all have components that can inform our understanding of wellness and illness. For example, a researcher interested in linguistics might record a list of plant names that could instruct us on not only local concepts of the environment and human ecology but also the medicinal uses of plants and their place in religious practices (see Dobkin De Rios 1976). Additionally, a medical researcher who studies the transmission of a disease from person to person might offer us valuable information on

the inner workings of families or larger kinship, social, or economic groups. In other cases, medical anthropologists might make useful observations on how an individual's age, sex, gender, class, geographic location, and economic status affect his or her access to treatment.

Because the approach medical anthropologists take is so broad, we often find it in venues that are not overtly anthropological. A good example comes from journalist Ingrid Peritz's recent exposé on lack of equal access to abortion clinics in Canada. As Peritz (2010) notes, 'While decades of court battles and debates have led Canadians to view abortion access as a given, the on-the-ground reality looks like a country carved into have and have-not communities'. Peritz takes a holistic approach to the topic, considering factors such as the social stigma attached to abortion, insufficient government funding, unsupportive public policy, and low numbers and geographically patchy distributions of abortion clinics. Peritz's findings reflect those of Fried (2000) for the United States, where abortion access for very young women, low-income women, and women of colour is relatively lacking. In both countries, although national public policy has been defined by court cases that ruled on access, federal and local authorities that control medical resources do not always facilitate access in practice.

Such integrated approaches are equally informative when we consider health issues on a global scale. As Dressler notes, biological disease is 'socially distributed between and within societies, especially societies being transformed by their increased dependency within international capitalist market systems' (2001: 456). Consider that, in many cases, the rate at which a disease spreads within a region is tied to transnational decisions based on political, economic, and ideological considerations. Whiteford points out that decisions made in one powerful nation can have an intense impact on health and well-being around the globe:

> Without doubt, global health policies reflect national priorities; the role of the UN and other international agencies, such as the World Health Organization (WHO), is shaped by funders' priorities. Likewise the role of the US government in influencing global reproductive health programs is also clear. The most overtly negative impacts of US policies originated in the early 1980s . . . [and]

Reagan's 'Mexico City' policy [that] cut funding from NGOs that used any funds, from any source, to do anything related to abortion. New policy impact studies now show that the global gag rule effectively increased the disastrous effects of HIV/AIDS and contributed to the deterioration of women's health globally. (2009: 106–7)

Thus we see that an integrative anthropological perspective can contribute much-needed cultural context to the discussion of international health concerns.

## Openness to Traditional Knowledge

Medical anthropologists' openness to a variety of integrated perspectives makes their approach particularly suited to examining both traditional knowledge and Western scientific (medical) knowledge (Dods 2004). For example, in the non-Western context, early medical anthropologists observed medico-religious practitioners, such as **shamans** and **witchdoctors**, in traditional healing roles (Figure 9.2). In previous contexts, researchers had considered shamanistic and witchdoctoring practices as responses to general physical complaints (Mair 1969), as expressions of social values (Wilson 1951), or more often, forms of religious rituals. Yet some saw such systems as analogous to science, and medical anthropologists came to see such practices as legitimate forms of healing. Their research has advanced our understanding of the importance of folk practitioners as Indigenous healers.

By accepting traditional knowledge as a source of wisdom, we open ourselves up to new discovery. Such was the case for ethnobotanist Paul Alan Cox when he was working in Samoa with a team of researchers from the United States' National Cancer Institute. In his discussions with local healers, Cox learned of prostratin, an antiviral chemical compound found in the bark of the mamala tree. The compound's antiviral properties had long been known to traditional Samoan healers who use the bark of the mamala tree to treat hepatitis. Western researchers have since found that prostratin shows potential to be effective in the treatment of HIV. In a letter published in the journal *Science* in 2008, Cox and his colleagues recognize their debt to the Samoan healers:

Because knowledge of prostratin's antiviral activity originated from ethnobotanical studies with Samoan

*Figure 9.2* | **A medicine man in Oku, Cameroon, walks down the road carrying the supplies he needs to treat various ailments.**

healers, the AIDS Research Alliance (ARA) and the Government of Samoa agreed that 20 per cent of ARA's profit from prostratin will be returned to the Samoan people (4). Similarly, Samoa and the University of California, Berkeley, agreed to share equally in commercialization of the prostratin gene sequences (5). In the spirit of these previous agreements, we encourage future developers of prostratin analogs for antiviral therapy to negotiate fair and equitable benefits with the Samoan people. (Cox et al. 2008)

Here we are reminded that respecting traditional knowledge also means behaving ethically toward those who share that knowledge.

As we remain open to the views of other cultures, we must always be aware that our own perceptions are rooted in the conventions of Western medicine. As Foster (1976) points out,

anthropologists filter the data of all exotic systems through the lens of belief and

**shaman**
An individual who is an expert on cultural definitions and treatments of medical as well as spiritual issues.

**witchdoctor**
An individual who deals with psychological aspects of illness, often administering treatments that Westerners might describe as 'placebos'; the position is found mainly in Africa with groups that practise ancestor worship.

practice of the people they know best. Whether it be causality, diagnosis, the nature and role of the curer, or the perceptions of illness within the wider supernatural and the social universe, general statements seem strongly influenced by the writers' personal experiences. (733)

In effect, Foster's words remind us of the importance of remaining reflexive when we consider medical approaches within the cultures we are studying.

# Cultural Interpretations and Labels of Illness and Disease

As we have suggested, interpretations of illness and even disease differ across cultures. To begin, Foster (1976) notes that we can identify two principal interpretations of **etiology** (Table 9.3) when we compare traditional medical systems cross-culturally:

1) the personalistic, in which people believe that illness is caused by supernatural forces (e.g., magical powers, an evil spirit, or a deity), and

2) the naturalistic, in which people believe that the causes of illness are rooted in the physical world (e.g., dampness, cold, or an imbalance in bodily substances).

**etiology**
The study of the causes of a disease and/or an illness.

In the personalistic interpretation, all misfortune is explained by

referring to illness, religion, and magic as indivisible, and a cure must be brought about by an individual with access to the supernatural. The sick are victims, and death is frequently defined as 'unnatural'. In the naturalistic interpretation, disease comes from *natural forces* or *conditions in nature*, and a cure can thus be found in nature. Foster observes that the naturalistic form was found in many prominent cultures of the past—for example, in ancient Chinese civilizations. (Note the similarities between this distinction and Allan Young's distinction between *internalizing systems* and *externalizing systems*, discussed above.)

Similar systems of interpretation exist in contemporary societies as well. In the West, medical conditions are interpreted through the paradigms of Western medicine (Table 9.4). The Western interpretations tend to focus on *biological causes* of medical conditions, with a single classification covering a wide array of symptoms. Increasingly, first as a consequence of colonization and subsequently as a result of globalization, these interpretations are being accepted as definitions of illness and disease in other cultures as well. Yet traditional definitions still hold sway in many areas of the world (e.g., in Sri Lanka; see Table 9.5), particularly in places where first-response and long-term care remain with traditional healers. In more traditional systems of classification, the focus tends to be on the *effect* a disease has on the person who is suffering.

Of course, cultural interpretations of disease and illness change over time. In the West, we can find evidence of such change in the evolution of the words we use to describe certain medical conditions. For example, in English what was once called *apoplexy* (with connotations

---

*Table 9.3* | **Foster's Two Principal Interpretations of the Causes of Illness**

| | **Personalistic** | **Naturalistic** |
|---|---|---|
| Causation | Active (supernatural) agent | Equilibrium loss |
| Illness | Special case of misfortune that can be named from a 'typology' of misfortunes | Unrelated to misfortune, although it is unfortunate that something has happened |
| Religion, Magic | Ultimately tied to illness | Largely unrelated to illness |
| Causality | Multiple levels | Single level |
| Prevention | Positive action | Avoidance |
| Responsibility | Beyond patient control | Resides with patient |

Source: Based on Foster 1976: 781.

Table 9.4 | Western Medicine's Systems of Disease Classification

| Term | Description |
| --- | --- |
| Allergy | Abnormality of immune mechanisms that normally act to protect the body against foreign proteins; also includes autoimmune diseases |
| Developmental or Congenital Disease | Malfunction of an organ or system resulting from an abnormal environment within the uterus during fetal development |
| Functional Defect | Disease for which there is no obvious anatomical explanation; includes psychosomatic diseases (emotional or social stress interacting with somatic functioning) |
| Genetic Disease | Malfunction of an organ or system resulting from a mutation or inheritance of a deleterious gene or an alteration in the number or arrangement of chromosomes |
| Infection | Disease produced by viruses, prions, bacteria, or other invasive biological entities; arbitrarily distinguished from infestation with parasitic insects |
| Metabolic Disease | Disease due to faulty biochemical processes, including nutritional, endocrine, and poisoning |
| Neoplasm | 'New growth', including benign tumours and malignancies (cancers) |
| Psychiatric Disease | Mental illness, including psychosis (a severe mental and emotional disorder, probably caused by a biochemical imbalance), neurosis (a moderate emotional disorder involving obsessive-compulsive behaviours, probably caused by learned behaviours in combination with biochemical factors), and addiction (a dependence on substances or behaviours that alter moods) |
| Thrombosis | Blood clot that forms in a blood vessel and blocks the flow of blood to an organ |
| Trauma | Injury produced by mechanical stress (e.g., fracture), a physical agent (e.g., frostbite), or a chemical agent (e.g., burn from a strong acid) |

Source: Adapted from McElroy and Townsend 1996: 46.

of being overwhelmed by a powerful state) is today called *stroke* (suggesting a physical assault from a tangible source). As historian Barbara Duden (1991) suggests, understandings of disease and illness are tied to the social reality at a particular period in time.

In many societies that suffered under European colonialism, Indigenous peoples developed new categories to describe disease as new pathogens invaded their world. For example, the Anishinaabe (Ojibwe) of Canada continue to divide diseases into two types:

• 'white man's sickness' and
• 'Anishinaabe sickness'.

In the first category, they place the diseases of the colonial and neo-colonial reality. This category first included smallpox, measles, chickenpox, and tuberculosis (TB); now it also includes high blood pressure, diabetes, cancer, and AIDS. The Anishinaabe believe that these diseases are best treated by Western medical personnel and techniques. In the second category are illnesses the Anishinaabe consider to be situated in 'discrete and identifiable, or potentially knowable, actions of human beings, alive or dead' or in 'breaches of certain rules that govern social relationships'. For these conditions, sufferers can find help only through 'guidance of other-than-human persons' (Garro 2004: 910–11).

The boundaries between different cultural interpretations of disease and illness can become blurred in practical situations. For example, Jeffrey Ehrenreich (1996) describes the sickness and eventual treatment of an Awá woman named Rosa in Ecuador. Both Rosa and her husband, Ishmael, believed she was dying from

*Table 9.5* | **An Example of a Traditional Ethnomedical System of Disease Classification (from Sri Lanka)**

| Demon (*Sanniya*) | Literal Translation | Associated Conditions |
|---|---|---|
| Amukku | Vomiting bouts | Vomiting and stomach diseases |
| Abutha | Non-spirit related | Non–spirit-related insanity |
| Butha | Spirit related | Spirit-related insanity |
| Bihiri | Deaf | Deafness |
| Deva | Divine | Epidemic diseases |
| Gedi | Lumps | Boils and skin diseases |
| Gini Jala | Great fire or flame | Malaria and high fevers |
| Golu | Dumb | Dumbness |
| Gulma | Worms (especially hookworm) | Parasitic worms and stomach diseases |
| Jala | Water or diarrhea | Cholera and chills |
| Kana | Blind | Blindness |
| Kora | Lame | Lameness and paralysis |
| Maru | Death | Delirium and death |
| Naga | Snake (especially cobra) | Bad dreams about snakes |
| Pissu | Insanity | Temporary insanity |
| Pith | Bilious | Bilious diseases |
| Slesma | Phlegm | Phlegm and epilepsy |
| Vatha | Wind humour or rheumatic | Flatulence and rheumatism |

Source: Bailey and de Silva 2006: 1,327.

a disease caused by **witchcraft**, as a consequence of the malice of a *brujo* (witch). Ishmael had insulted a specific man in their community, and he now believed that this man was a witch who had brought revenge illness on Rosa for Ishmael's social mistake. Initially, Rosa underwent traditional treatment in the form of shamanic curing ceremonies. When traditional approaches failed, Ishmael carried Rosa on his back for five days to reach the post at which Ehrenreich and his fellow anthropologist Judith Kempf were working. From a Western perspective, Rosa's symptoms suggested a parasitic worm infestation and resulting starvation.

**witchcraft**
The performance of innate, non-human powers—which may be for evil or good—by human beings, whether or not the act is intentional or self-aware. Note that perceptions of and definitions of witchcraft differ across cultures.

**folk illness**
A culture-bound illness; a set of symptoms that are grouped together under a single label only within a particular culture.

Western medical approaches were unsuccessful at first, potentially because Rosa vomited up both the food and the medication she consumed. But this changed when the anthropologists adopted shamanistic methodology in addition to the Western treatment regimes. A combination of incantations (in this case Hebrew prayers), chicken soup, and anti-parasitic medication resulted in Rosa becoming well again (1996: 137–9). Thus, while each culturally defined interpretation of Rosa's condition led to a different treatment, it was a combination of the two—made possible by the anthropologists' openness to traditional knowledge—that cured Rosa.

Historically, conflicting cultural interpretations of an illness and its appropriate treatment have not always been reconciled so harmoniously. Consider the historical debate surrounding the condition (or **folk illness**) Western medicine today refers to as Wendigo-psychosis (Figure 9.3). In Algonquian culture, the Wendigo is a

*Figure 9.3* | **Swift Runner, a Cree man from Alberta, killed and ate his family during a cold winter in 1878. He claimed that he was suffering from the influence of the Wendigo at the time of the murders. He later confessed, was remorseful, and was executed at Fort Saskatchewan.**

malevolent cannibalistic spirit that can influence human action. The Algonquians also believe that, under certain conditions, a human can transform into the Wendigo. When such a transformation occurs, the group recognizes that the afflicted individual is in need of treatment. The purpose of treatment is not only to alleviate the suffering of the individual but also, and more importantly, to protect the group as a whole. Traditionally, a shaman must treat the condition by defeating the Wendigo, and the only way to defeat the Wendigo is to kill the afflicted individual (in our culture, we might think of this treatment as a form of euthanasia). In the late nineteenth and early twentieth centuries, non-Native authorities began hearing stories of the Wendigo condition and its treatment. According to the interpretation of those authorities, the afflicted

were suffering from a form of psychosis; according to this interpretation, the proper treatment could be found in a mental institution, and the traditional treatment was a form of murder. Thus in 1907 Jack Fiddler, an Anishinini (Severn) chief and powerful shaman known for defeating the Wendigo, was prosecuted for murder in a Canadian court. He was found guilty but later pardoned when the cultural constructs were considered.

As these examples suggest, anthropologists can look to a culture's interpretation of illness to find deeper insight into how members of that culture collectively interpret their world and their place in that world. As Migliore (2001) notes in his examination of illness narratives surrounding a condition called 'nerves' among Sicilian-Canadians, 'Such narratives are an important means by which people, often in collaboration with one another, give meaning to various life experiences' (100). Migliore further notes that, when looking for meaning in cultural interpretations of illness, we need to

- address ambiguity, vagueness, and variability as central concerns in the anthropological quest for understanding;
- focus on how people use 'folk' concepts (and discourse in general) in their everyday thoughts and actions;
- recognize that our definitions and explanations do not capture the essence of a particular 'folk' concept but, rather, give us an insight into some of the more common or popular uses of that concept within a given group; and
- examine the decision-making processes that lead people to use or generate certain meanings rather than others. (2001: 119)

An important part of this process of investigation is looking at the labels—along with the meaning attached to those labels—that people use to describe their experiences.

## Medical Labels as Signifiers

Western medicine prides itself in its efficiency in grouping together a wide array of symptoms under a single medical label. Medical labels are mutually agreed upon signifiers; they denote clusters of symptoms that are understood to be related within a medical taxonomy. As such, they facilitate medical research. Without labels, epidemiologists, for example, would not be able to track patterns of occurrence, prevalence of outbreaks, attack rates, modes of transmission, and virulence for diseases such as the newly identified prion infections of kuru and bovine spongiform encephalopathy (mad-cow disease). In all cultures, medical labels help people identify and interpret illness. Naming is the first step to understanding and thus 'illuminating relationships among illness, social forms, and social thought' (Lindenbaum 2001: 363).

Nonetheless, medical labels can be constricting on the personal level. From the perspective of the person who is unwell, the labels often reflect a position of dependence or marginalization. An afflicted individual might be defined as *the sick family member*, *the supplicant*, *the patient*, or even *the client*. Each label suggests a perceived role. More specific medical labels often carry a stigma associated with suffering, contagion, or death. As such, they can lead to stereotyping, separation, status loss, and discrimination of persons and populations who are thus labelled (Link and Phelan 2001). Consider the longstanding cross-cultural response to the term *leprosy* (Figure 9.4). For thousands of years the name of this disease has triggered feelings of fear, not only because of the nature of the disease itself but also because of the historical 'treatment', which consisted of segregating individuals afflicted with the disease into 'leper colonies' for the benefit of the wider population. Thus, to be labelled as 'a leper' was to be cast as a marginalized figure, someone to be feared as an outsider. Even after the discovery of effective treatments of leprosy in the early twentieth century, the disease still

carries a social stigma. Today, leprosy is often referred to by its alternative name—Hansen's disease, named so after the doctor who first identified the bacterium responsible for the disease—to evoke fewer negative associations.

In a recent study at McMaster University in Hamilton, Ontario, researchers have shown that the label used to name a disease influences the perceived seriousness of a specific set of symptoms. They investigated synonymous terms such as *erectile dysfunction disorder* and *impotence* and found that participants who were presented with a 'newer' medicalized term perceived the condition to be more severe. They conclude: 'A simple switch in terminology can result in a real bias in perception' (Young et al. 2008). Such findings also suggest that simple, non-medicalized terms might be best for disseminating medical information to the general public.

The act of labelling can itself have significant social outcomes for individuals and communities. Sarah E. Castle (1994) illustrates this in her discussion of two folk illnesses that result in the death of children in a rural Malian village. Local peoples refer to these illnesses as *foondu* ('the bird') and *heendu* ('the wind'), and they understand both to be caused by supernatural forces and 'untreatable, particularly with modern medicine'. As Castle observes,

> Foondu and heendu are rarely seen in living children but are frequently discussed in relation to child death. In a survey of mothers of children who had died before the age of five years . . . about half the deaths were attributed to these two illnesses. These folk illnesses act as explanatory mechanisms in this high mortality area. (314)

Labelling an illness as either *foondu or heendu* exonerates the child's caretakers from any fault (e.g., lack of care or effort to bring about a cure), as the label could not have been applied while the child was still alive. Here we see the psychotherapeutic value of the folk illness—it can offer a deflection of failure (e.g., failure to keep the child alive) from the self to other sources. Additionally, when the child is ill, family members are not resigned to the death of the child as inevitable; they have hope for a positive outcome. Such hope would be destroyed if the disease were labelled before death. Finally, because the post-mortem diagnoses are conferred by senior women in a patrilineage, they also

*Figure 9.4* **| Leprosy has always carried a stigma, even after effective treatments were developed.**

## In Their Own Words | Indigenous Medicine and Identity in Nicaragua

*Hugo De Burgos, assistant professor at the University of British Columbia Okanagan, discusses survival of ethnic identity and the use of traditional medical terminologies to reinforce concepts of identity and mediate place in a wider community.*

Rescuing our Indigenous medicine is to recover our Indigenous identity and culture. Using our traditional medicine is expressing our Indigenous identity.

—Antonio Guzmán, Nicaraguan Indigenous leader

Medical systems are more than social schemes for healing. They are also systems of ecological adaptation; explanatory models for physical and social suffering; and mechanisms for social control. The practical and symbolic functions of a medical system are not restricted to medical concerns. Their multiple implications pervade non-medical spheres of social life, shaping in this way their initially medical purpose. Medical beliefs and practices constitute cultural configurations that inform, shape, and mediate human experience in ways that go beyond purely medical functions.

The people of Veracruz del Zapotal, or Veracruceños, are a Spanish-speaking Indigenous community of Nahua descent from Nicaragua. Currently figuring approximately 3,800, they inhabit the Veracruz del Zapotal valley and the mountain region between the rivers of El Camarón, Guachipilin, and Rio Grande in the department of Rivas, in southern Nicaragua. In their struggle to remain culturally distinct, Veracruceños have been able to direct their medical behaviour, articulate their medical ideas, and organize their medical resources for political purposes. Since the early 1990s, they have used their Indigenous medicine as a strategy to claim and assert their precariously kept ethnic identity. In the past, these people made use of medical knowledge according to tradition, but not in a political manner. With the introduction of the 'revival of Indigenous medicine', a new disposition toward their Indigenous medicine emerged.

Claiming ethnic identity through the use of medicine is informed by an elaborate discourse on how traditional medicine *is* Indigenous identity and on how Indigenous identity is conversely embedded in traditional medicine. Through the use Indigenous medicine as both *materia medica* and a symbolic system, Veracruceños promote community practices that enhance an Indigenous world view. Indigenous medicine is for Veracruceños, as W.H.R. Rivers noted so long ago, a symbolic system, and all symbolic systems are valuable sites for meaning-making, at the level of the individual as well as the community. Indigenous medicine is seen by Veracruceños as a cultural trait, a part of the repertoire of practices and knowledge that makes Veracruceños culturally distinct. This sharply contrasts with the construction of scientific biomedicine, which is, categorically, non-specific to any particular people or culture.

Source: De Burgos, Hugo. 2009. 'Indigenous Medicine and Identity in Nicaragua', guest editorial.

reinforce hierarchical power relationships among women while encouraging 'social support from affines for the woman whose child has died' (1994: 314).

## Environments and Well-Being

Researchers in many disciplines are becoming increasingly aware of the impact of physical, social, and cultural environments on human well-being. Using the integrative approach that is characteristic of their discipline, medical anthropologists examine not only the influence of environments on human health but also the many human factors—political, economic, social, and cultural—that shape those environments. Consider the landscapes that arise with the disposal of unwanted electronic goods. Such 'dead' gear does not simply disappear. Rather, it is transported to less affluent nations where it sits in vast wastelands—digital dumps of frightening contamination. These dumps are mined by the poor for recyclable resources. Case in point: the Agbogbloshie dump in Accra, Ghana (Figure 9.5). Here the discarded technology of the West is burned for the retrieval of materials such as copper, brass, aluminum, and zinc; in the process, the surrounding soil and water are contaminated with lead, cadmium, antimony, PCBs, beryllium, mercury, and chlorinated dioxins. Many of the scavengers of this lethal detritus are boys who

*Figure 9.5* | Agbogbloshie dump in Accra, the capital city of Ghana, is a vast wasteland of unwanted electronic equipment.

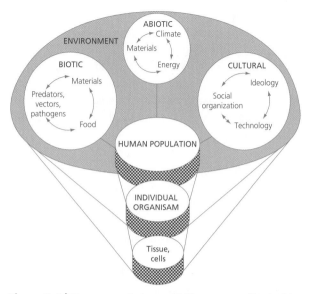

*Figure 9.6* | **Human wellness and illness are affected by three interacting environments: the biotic (biological), the abiotic (physical), and the cultural.**
Source: McElroy and Townsend 1996: 25.

labour to send money home to their impoverished families in northern Ghana. Thus are created the contentious borderlands of wellness and illness.

## Integrated Worlds of the Biotic, the Abiotic, and the Cultural

The environments in which we live are made up of biotic (biological), abiotic (physical), and cultural components (Figure 9.6). Within these environments, all components are interlinked in complex, often invisible ways—if you tinker with one part, you risk disrupting the entire system.

Ecologically, we are tied to our surroundings. From a *medical-ecological* perspective, then, good health often results from living in an environment that is capable of supporting human life in all of its social, psychological, and physical needs. Conversely, bad health—disease and illness—is often the consequence of a disruption in the life-sustaining balance of our environment.

**realized niche**
The portion of the fundamental niche (the complete range of physical and biological conditions under which a species can survive) that a group of people is forced to utilize and to which it becomes highly adapted.

Environmental factors can have consequences for human health on micro and macro levels, with components in the most immediate surroundings having the greatest impact on a population. In terms of physical location, a population's immediate environment is its **realized niche**.

In many cases, realized niches face pressure from large-scale political, economic, and social processes. Certainly these processes featured in the poisoning of

the Wabigoon River and the surrounding area in north-western Ontario. Over the course of the 1960s and early 1970s, Reed International's pulp and paper plant in Dryden, Ontario, released a dangerous amount of mercury into the Wabigoon River. The mercury was a by-product of chemical processing in the plant, and the river seemed to be the most convenient and economical place to dispose of the excess waste. In doing so, the plant's operators were not in violation of any legal restrictions. Before long, the links between the contaminated natural environment and human health were apparent. The Grassy Narrows First Nation peoples (see EthnoProfile 9.1)—who relied on the Wabigoon River for their water, food (fish), and livelihood (fisheries)—began showing signs of extensive mercury poisoning, including Minamata disease; (Figure 9.7). The community went from wellness to severe illness in less than a decade. Yet both the Canadian government and the operators of the plant ignored the evidence for a considerable period of time. When the government did step in, in addition to restricting chemical dumping it also closed the community's commercial fisheries to prevent the distribution of contaminated fish to the wider population. With the closing of the fishery, the community's problems were compounded as it went from 95 per cent employment to 95 per cent unemployment. The ramifications of this poisoning continue

## EthnoProfile 9.1 | Grassy Narrows First Nation (Asubpeeschoseewagong Netum Anishinabek)

**Region** North America

**Nation** Canada; the Anishinaabe Nation

**Language** traditionally Anishinaabe (Ojibwe); today, also English

**Population** 1,402 (910 living on the reserve) (2010)

**Environment** Boreal forest, threatened by deforestation

**Livelihood** Pre-contact, hunting, gathering, and trapping; today, various jobs, inside and outside the community

**Political organization** Elected tribal council operating within a modern nation state

**For more information** 'Free Grassy Narrows: Support Grassy Narrows First Nation', http://freegrassy.org/2011/08/01/grassy-trappers-win-major-legal-victory/; 'Grassy Narrows: Overview', www.amnesty.ca/themes/indigenous_grassy_narrows.php; 'Grassy Narrows First Nation: Protecting Traditional Lands', www.turtleisland.org/news/news-grassy.htm.

today, some fifty years after the mercury began to move up the food chain.

For peoples whose diets contain a considerable amount of 'country foods'—traditional foods such as wild game and fish taken from the natural environment—**bioaccumulation** is a growing concern.

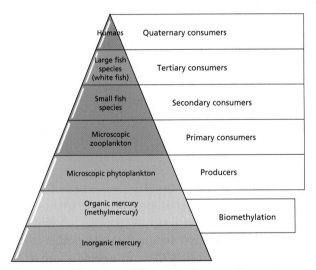

*Figure 9.7* | **Etiology of Minamata disease. Through the process of biomethylation, organic bodies such as fungi and bacteria convert mercury (an inorganic heavy metal) into methylmercury (an organic substance), which is very destructive to the human neurological system. The methylmercury moves up the food chain, from algae to fish to humans, in increasing concentrations.**

Source: Adapted from Vecsey 1987.

When uncontaminated, a traditional, protein-rich 'country food' diet is considerably healthier than a high-carbohydrate European-style diet. Yet today, such traditional diets are not only high in protein and other nutrients but also high in toxic substances. Considering the pervasiveness of environmental toxins, and considering that most contaminated food looks no different from uncontaminated food, it has become nearly impossible for Indigenous peoples to maintain traditional diets without suffering severe consequences to their health. Here medical anthropologists recognize that emerging health problems can be identified and responded to only through the reconciliation of traditional knowledge and Western scientific knowledge, although this reconciliation has not been straightforward or in any way simple.

In nearly every case of severe contamination, the toxins come from sources beyond the affected community. Nowhere is this more distinctly the case than in the Arctic. As Aboriginal Affairs and Northern Development Canada (AANDC) notes,

> **bioaccumulation**
> The accumulation of toxic substances in progressively higher concentrations from the bottom to the top of a food chain.

Many sites in the North have been contaminated due to private sector mining, oil and gas, and government military activities that occurred before their environmental impact was fully understood. In addition, studies in the early 1990s found that a number of pollutants originating from sources outside the Arctic or in some cases outside Canada were reaching unexpectedly high levels in the Arctic ecosystem. (AANDC 2011)

The AANDC has created two programs to assist the peoples of Canada's Arctic: the Northern Contaminated Sites Program (NCSP), which 'focusses on the cleanup and remediation of a number of contaminated sites in the North', and the Northern Contaminants Program (NCP), which 'addresses human exposure to contaminants in wildlife species that are important to the traditional diets of Northern Aboriginal peoples' (2011). Of course, the success of these programs depends on the merger of tradition and science in open cross-cultural discourse.

Large-scale programs such as the NCSP and the NCP are often created in response to the findings of studies conducted by academic researchers. One such anthropological study is Poirier and Brooke's 2000 examination of perceptions of ecological contaminants among the Salluit, one of 16 Inuit communities of Nunavik. In many ways, the traditional Inuit view of the environment is congruent with the anthropological interpretation of the environment as composed of integrated biotic, abiotic, and cultural elements:

> In Inuit ontology, the environment is seen as complex systems of interacting agencies (and variables) and they appreciate well that interface with one part of the system has implications for the other part. . . . As hunters they view and experience their relationship with the environment and the animal world in a particularly intimate, communicative, and reciprocal manner. Human beings, animals, and the environment are all perceived as sharing partners; their modes of becoming are intrinsically linked. . . . [E]very animal [is] a sentient being or other-than-human person . . . not simply as a representative of another wildlife species that needs to be monitored or managed. (2000: 81, 86)

**defensive research**
Research that is designed and conducted by individuals outside the affected community without consulting members of the community about their interests or concerns.

**positive research**
Research that is designed with fair consideration of the interests and concerns of members of the affected community and conducted with consideration of cultural contexts within the community.

With increasing media access in the North, the Inuit have developed an understanding of pollutants. Yet, trusting their traditional knowledge and their world view, many remain convinced of their own ability to perceive and avoid dangerously sick animals and therefore guard their own health. They have not developed a confidence in the southern biologists and their warnings of contaminants in the meat (86). Thus Poirier and Brooke highlight the need for cross-cultural discourse and note the late Daniel Weetaluktuk's distinction between '**defensive research**', which is based on the interests and methodologies of southerners, and '**positive research**', which gives the Inuit the chance to have input in the research process. As Poirier and Brooke conclude, taking a 'positive' approach 'does not mean deterioration of the research quality . . . [but it] would give northern perceptions of southern people a much wider scope and fuller understanding, at least for those who have enough of a broad mind to grasp it' (2000: 89).

## Nutritional Health

A healthy diet must be based on food that is not only free from harmful contaminants but also full of nutrients. The human body requires a regular, balanced supply of carbohydrates, protein, fats, minerals, and vitamins in order to function properly and maintain a strong immune system. Thus, nutritional health is the basis of good health.

Worldwide, the availability of sufficient amounts of nutritious food has been a growing concern for more than a century. While conducting fieldwork in Botswana in the late 1970s, Roberta Robin Dods noted that most local children had enough calories in their diet but not enough nutrition—in particular, they were not getting enough vitamins, minerals, protein, and certain essential amino acids. Their diet was restricted to what was available, and the staple food was mielie-meal, a coarse flour ground from maize. Those who could afford to do so would add small pieces of vegetables and sometimes meat to the main mielie-meal dish. Without these additions, the diet is almost entirely carbohydrate-based. Carbohydrates provide energy by converting to blood sugar, but they do not build bones and tissue. Dods noted that a simple way to enhance this diet would be to add legumes such as beans, which are a good source of protein and essential amino acids (see, e.g., Sellen 2003). Today, medical and nutritional anthropologists continue

*Figure 9.8* | **A health care worker in Rwinkwavu, Rwanda, teaches children and adults about nutrition.**

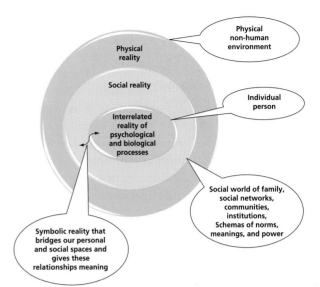

*Figure 9.9* | **'Clinical reality' is constructed based on aspects of physical and social realities—cultural norms, schemas, beliefs, and behaviours, as well as various communication interactions surrounding disease and illness. Central are the practitioner–patient relationships, the therapeutic regimes, and the way outcomes are defined and evaluated.**
Source: Adapted from Kleinman 1980: 28.

to investigate conditions that lead to inadequate nutrition; in many cases, their work is useful to doctors and health care practitioners who work to inform local populations about the importance of nutrition (Figure 9.8).

Anthropologists who study nutritional health tend to have very broad research interests, and their findings often contribute to national and international policies on health and nutrition, food safety and inspection, and world hunger (Mintz and Du Bois 2002: 111). In one notable study, anthropologist Penny Van Esterik (2002) investigated food-safety regulations and the contamination of foods for infants—both breast milk and commercially available baby formulas. Other researchers have addressed issues related to child growth and development in association with nutrition, activity, and health (Dufour 1997). The expanding interest in the role of nutrition in a population's health has led to the development of a new subdiscipline in medical anthropology: nutritional anthropology.

# Health Care Delivery Systems

Health care systems take a variety of forms, based in the specifics of social and physical realities (Figure 9.9). 'Clinical realities'—those realities that are tied to a health care system—vary considerably, based on factors such as

- cultural constructs (e.g., how open a woman is allowed to be in presenting her condition to a male doctor);
- geopolitical circumstances of place (e.g., hinterland or centre place; rural or urban);

- the patient's absolute and perceived situation in time (e.g., biological age in conjunction with attitudes on lifecycle stages and transitions);
- concepts of reality (e.g., whether a disease or a symptom is perceived to be real or imagined);
- social and physical resources available to the afflicted individual or group (e.g., formal or informal restrictions on who is given access to medical treatment);
- depth of interaction with other individuals or groups (e.g., relationships with kin, family, friends, and acquaintances);
- symptom-reporting paradigms (e.g., those based on class, gender, and/or age);
- curative norms (often defined by class, gender, and/or age—e.g., Western treatments of heart disease are different for men than they are for women); and
- level of institutional complexity (e.g., in complex bureaucratic medical practices, patients may face alienation or problems of access).

**placebo effect**
An effect produced in response to an individual's belief that a treatment will have a desired effect, despite evidence that the treatment has no medicinal properties.

Out of these and many other social threads, the fabric of care is woven. For some it is a warm blanket; for others it is gossamer thin indeed.

While health care systems take many different forms across the globe, Kleinman (1980) notes that we can identify five core clinical functions of a health care system from a cross-cultural perspective:

1) the cultural construction of illness or disease as a psychosocial occurrence;
2) the evaluation of treatment approaches based on *general* criteria, independent of the individual incidents of illness;
3) the management of *specific* illness incidents through communicative operations (labelling and explaining);
4) the performance of healing activities (supportive care, healing rituals, psychotherapy, medication, and surgery; also end-of-life palliative care, where healing is not physical but can sustain the human sense of self or 'spirit' and offer closure); and
5) the management of outcomes from cure, recurrence, chronic illness, impairment, to treatment failure and death. (71–2)

Kleinman does not use *clinical* as a Western term but rather as a category intrinsic to all societies, since the 'problem with most ethnomedical studies is not that they impose an alien clinical category on indigenous materials, but rather that they fail to apprehend a profound cross-cultural similarity in clinical interest and praxis' (1980: 83). He notes that his list is a 'summation' and that there can be great variation in the emphasis placed on each of the five functions from culture to culture and from group to group, since 'the cultural construction of illness experience . . . is frequently a personally and socially adaptive response' (72).

## Variety in Curing Practices

When we are faced with a mild disease, illness, or injury, we often take care of the treatment for ourselves. For example, for a cold we might take over-the-counter medication; for a cut, we might use commercial bandages and antiseptics. We might also resort to home remedies or folk cures recommended by a member of our family or our community. On your grandmother's assurance that 'it has always been done that way', you may swallow some vile cough syrup she has concocted or some soothing chicken soup she has prepared with care. Frequently, we find that these home remedies are effective—if only through the **placebo effect**—and we do not need to venture far beyond our home for a cure. Families are often our frontline, our fortitude, our foundation in health care regardless the cultures in which we live.

When we feel that treatment requires more than home remedies, we will seek outside help from someone with advanced knowledge of our condition. If we are part of a culture that relies on traditional knowledge, we might appeal to a medicine woman or man or a shaman (male or female) for assistance. To a Western observer, traditional curative measures may seem no more effective than a home remedy; yet traditional cures can be highly effective for reasons not often considered in Western medicine. Marilyn Walker (2003), for example, notes that shamanistic music used in Siberia induces altered states of consciousness, allowing the shaman to access the patient's unconscious as well as various forces (spirits) in the transcendental world(s). Other cultures use similar ceremonial activities to mediate inner and outer worlds and thus rebalance the patient in these worlds.

In other cases, even trained medical practitioners may not be able to help. For example, if you are bitten by a black mamba (*Dendroaspis polylepis*) in a remote area, you may not be able to find medical assistance before it is too late. The venom of the Black Mamba is full of neurotoxins that quickly shut down voluntary and autonomic nerve functions such as those that control breathing. If left without treatment, an adult who is bitten will generally die within an hour; even with treatment, small children never survive a black mamba bite. What can anyone do for the patient if there is no hope of finding antivenin and medevac to a hospital in time? They can comfort the victim as he or she dies and hope that coma or death will come before the worst of the symptoms can manifest. This is a horrific and, in some sense, extreme example, but similarly hopeless situations may arise after a traffic accident or when a patient is in the final stages of an incurable disease.

## In Their Own Words | Clown Doctors

*Linda Miller Van Blerkom gives us an interesting overview of the shamanistic origins of clowning, situating it in a healing paradigm.*

A review of the literature shows that comparing clowns and shaman is not new. Clowning and other popular entertainment (magic tricks, sword swallowing, juggling, acrobatics, etc.) originated with shamanistic performances (Kirby 1974). Some trace the derivation of all performing arts to shamanism (Flaherty 1988; LaBarre 1979). Turner (1985: 235–6) includes clowns and fools with shamans, tricksters, healers, and other characters in a list of luminal figures found in rites of passage dealing with social crisis and affliction. Both clowns and shamans mediate between order and chaos, sacred and profane, real and supernatural, culture and anticulture, or nature (Charles 1945: 32–3; Willeford 1969: 100–50). This mediation of culture and nature is central to the healing arts and sciences (Moerman 1979: 59). In the language of semiotics, clown performances are metacultural texts, acts of communication about culture, that invent cultural rules, thereby provoking emotional responses (Bouissac 1985: 151–75). Whether the antics of clowns produce mirth or agitation in the observer, such folly has long been associated with psychological healing (Willeford 1969: 29).

Clown figures with healing functions occur in other societies, particularly in Native American cultures. Institutionalized clowning is best developed among the Pueblos. Charles ranks Pueblo clowns with the Commedia dell'Arte as among the 'four major groups of clown societies . . . known to exist or to have existed' (1945: 30). Not all Pueblo clown societies function as healers, but some do. For example, the Zuni Ne'wekwe is a highly regarded medicine society, some of whose members are clowns who improvise farces and burlesques during curing ceremonies (Bunzell 1932: 498). The Laguna Koshare and Santa Clara Kossa are sometimes called on for curing, although most Koshares do not heal (Parsons and Beals 1934: 495). Other clown societies for which curing is a primary function occur among the Yaqui and Mayo Indians of Sonora (Parsons and Beals 1934: 506). Iroquois False Faces use clown-like theatrics to exorcise disease (Towson 1976: 13).

Plains Indian clowning takes the form of 'contrary' behaviour, such as talking or performing actions backward and in other ways violating natural and social conventions (Steward 1931: 198). Modern Plains Indians consider circus clowns similar to contraries (Towson 1976: 13). Some of these contraries function as healers, but only if they are of the comic type or 'buffoon'; 'serious' contraries, such as the Oglala Heyoka, never cure (Ray 1945: 91). Healing buffoons include the Plains Ojibway Windigokan and the Plains Cree Wetigokan, who use contrary behaviour and ragged costumes, as well as dancing, singing, whistling, and shaking rattles in their curing (Ray 1945: 84–7; Steward 1931: 203). The Canadian Dakota (Wahpeton) consider clowns to be the most powerful shamans (Ray 1945: 86).

Source: Miller Van Blerkom, Linda. 1995. 'Clown Doctors: Shaman Healers of Western Medicine', *Medical Anthropology Quarterly*, New Series, 9, 4: 462–75.

Sometimes—all too often in some places—the treatment a patient seeks may depend on his or her financial resources rather than the severity of the condition. Medical treatment can be very expensive, and the harsh reality is that class and geopolitical disparities affect an individual's access to and quality of treatment. As McGill University researchers Nguyen and Peschard (2003) note,

high levels of socioeconomic inequality correlate with worsened health outcomes across an entire society. . . . [A]ffliction must be understood as an embodiment of social hierarchy, a form of violence that for modern bodies [individual and group] is increasingly sublimated into differential disease rates and can be measured in terms of morbidity and mortality between social groups. (447).

The reality of such disparities is clear when we examine the various statistics on HIV/AIDS generated by national and pan-national organizations. Consider that in excess of 95 per cent of all new infections of HIV/AIDS occur in countries commonly classified as 'developing' and that at least 50 per cent of these infections are in women. Consider also that the number of childhood cases being reported is increasing, not only among children born to infected mothers but also among children forced to work in the sex trade. Indeed, we can wonder what 'development' can mean to communities where so many people are dead or dying of this disease. Socioeconomic disparity is also a significant factor in HIV transmission in more affluent Western nation-states. In Canada, rates of transmission are highest in Aboriginal communities, where many live in what could be considered 'developing' conditions. Health Canada (2010) estimates that between 6 and 12 per cent of new HIV/AIDS infections occur in Aboriginal people, while Aboriginal people make up only 3.3 per cent of the Canadian population.

## Patient–Practitioner Interactions

All systems of treatment have a two-step process: 1) diagnosis and 2) treatment. Both are based on effective communication between patients and their health care providers. To effectively interact with one another, all parties must be conversant in the languages of their culture's health and treatment institutions. For the patient, there is a need to develop an intersubjective space where meanings can be negotiated, much as anthropologists do in fieldwork. Not infrequently, negotiations are incomplete, and there remains an unresolved disconnect between what are, essentially, two or more cultures—the one of the patient and at least one of the medical practitioners.

Naming is very important in this process, as it communicates the symptoms, frames the diagnosis, and dictates the range of available treatments. Yet naming can be problematic in some instances, such as when a population considers a disease to be newly introduced from the outside world. Consider how cancer is understood among Indigenous peoples in Australia:

> Many Indigenous languages do not have a word for cancer, making it difficult to conceptualize. This emphasizes the belief that it is a 'white man's disease' that only came about after colonization. Whether this is true or whether it was never labelled as cancer until colonization is unknown; however, many signs point to the fact that the change in Indigenous lifestyle from traditional

to Westernized has increased the risk of cancer. (Shahid et al. 2010)

All systems begin by naming. We structure and make sense of our world using schema and prototypes. The naming process is universal, but the contents are culture specific. Named is the 'condition' and named is the 'cure'.

While all health care systems recognize the importance of patient–practitioner communication, there are considerable differences between traditional systems and Western institutionalized systems in terms of how they perceive the patient's place in the system. In traditional systems, practitioners form personal relationships with their patients, investing considerable time in getting to know the patient and imparting a sense of concern. Traditional practitioners also situate the treatments in an environment that is deeply familiar to the patient—in effect their home turf. In Western medical systems, where time is money and the volume of patients affects the bottom line in a doctor's medico-business practice, the patient is viewed as a client. Doctors keep their distance from their patient/clients, and they administer treatment only in official medical environments. Of course, Western systems have their benefits: the act of 'industrialization' affords a wide range of interventions supported by medical institutions, technologies, and highly trained personnel. Nevertheless, institutionalized treatment is removed from the familiar and can be very discomforting and alienating for the patient/client. Feelings of alienation can be particularly intense when the patient/client is crossing cultural and/or class boundaries and moving from traditional systems to industrialized medical systems.

Patient–practitioner relationships also differ between urban and rural locations. In the urban setting, unlike in the rural, the curer may not be a member of the community in which she or he works. Press (1978) has found that most urban curers do not become spokespersons for these communities and that they seldom know the majority of their patients on a personal level. Thus it rests with the patient to provide the symptoms and suggest the causality, while it is up to the practitioner to provide a diagnosis based on his or her understanding of the symptoms. The rural curer, in contrast, 'often directs the patient's search for a diagnosis in directions required by community knowledge of the patient's socioritual condition' (1978: 78). And Press notes that folk practices associated with rural environments are actually flexible and capable of changing to meet the needs of the urban clients. The curers also can 'shift to accommodate *modern* health elements where these reflect the patient needs' (81). Of particular value is the potential of urbanized folk practices to provide an 'ideational and behavioural outlet for new migrants or poorly acculturated individuals who find the city traumatic, inhospitable, and unhealthy' (80).

By recording patients' narratives on illness and treatment, medical anthropologists offer us important insight into the culture clash the patient experiences when entering a systems of care. Of central concern are the ways in which patients are treated—as humans or as numbers—and practitioners' willingness to incorporate elements of the patient's culture into the system of treatment. In such narratives, with embedded critique of treatment, patients are empowered to maintain or regain human identity and a sense of control over their lives.

## SEARCH as an Integrative Model

Maintaining or regaining human identity and a sense of control is the objective of SEARCH (Society for Education, Action, and Research in Community Health), an NGO established in 1986 by Dr Abhay Bang and his wife, Dr Rani Bang, in the Gadchiroli district of Maharashtra, India. Two of the NGO's stated goals are promoting the reproductive health of women and improving the health of mothers, infants, and children. In rural India, infant and maternal mortality rates are very high. According to one statistic, one woman dies every five minutes giving birth to a child in rural India. Yet most of these deaths are preventable. SEARCH has addressed this problem by establishing public health programs in 39 villages in Maharashtra, each of which combine grassroots fieldwork with sophisticated medical monitoring, research, and advocacy. The result is a community-based health system that combines the best features of folk medicine with appropriate modern medical interventions. At the village level, the system is administered by a literate woman, herself a mother, who is trained to identify problems early and provide basic care. Physicians visit the villages every two weeks to supervise the care in place but do not give additional treatments. In the years since its inception, SEARCH has been an overwhelming success. Between 1988 and 2003, the infant mortality rate dropped from 121 to 30 deaths per 1,000 live births, and policy makers from Bangladesh, Nepal, and many African countries are currently investigating how the SEARCH approach can be implemented in their communities (Shetty 2011).

An understanding of the principles of SEARCH can help us interpret the efficacy of different approaches to health care seen elsewhere. For example, consider Sargent and Bascope's (1996) study on birthing practices in Mexico, USA (Texas), and Jamaica. In their study, the researchers focussed on 'ways of knowing' about birthing and technology in high- and low-technology settings. They also considered the relationship between authoritative (biomedical) knowledge and social status. The collaborative birthing system of the Mayan women in Mexico incorporated midwives and other adult women who used their knowledge in a low-tech response. In general, patients felt at ease with their place in the system. By contrast, the women in Texas felt alienated from their public hospital system, although they appreciated the technology that provided needed caesarean deliveries. In Jamaica, the lack of communication between the English-speaking staff and the Spanish-speaking patients distanced patients from caregivers in a system dominated by authoritative knowledge but lacking adequate access to and use of biomedical technology. In each situation, the SEARCH model can help us reassess the relationship between authoritative (biomedical) knowledge and patient comfort and security. By extension, we can apply such reassessment techniques beyond birthing practices to all medicalized situations.

## Political Intervention: Population Control and Management

The structure and focus of health care delivery systems frequently reflect local or national political interests, particularly when health care systems receive government funding. Most often, political and medical arenas intersect over issues surrounding population control and management. When the government's interests are aligned with those of its citizens, the health care system can function smoothly and contribute to social cohesion. But a clash between national and personal health interests can result in an array of social problems.

One example of a government's attempt to regulate health-related issues for political reasons is China's controversial one-child policy. Implemented in 1979, the policy aims at bringing control of individuals' reproduction and family size under the central government in order to lower the rate of population growth. At the local level, the program is administered by community functionaries, and health care systems must operate in line with governmental regulations. While most citizens abide by the national policy, some families attempt to circumvent the law by hiding pregnancies and births from government administrators. The 2000 national census found that 8,052,484 people were unregistered (Zhou 2005). Without official registration, these people are left without legal rights to health care or education. Additional social issues have emerged, including the preference for male children, increased female infanticide, and abandoned infant girls (Brookes 2001) as well as forced abortions for women pregnant with their second child and forced sterilizations in some rural areas. The imbalance in the sex ratio has steadily increased over the past three decades, with current estimates ranging from 117 to 131 males for every 100 females. Further, it is estimated that by 2020 China will have a 'bachelor army' (Ross 2010) consisting of 30,000,000 to 40,000,000 single men (Figure 9.10). With the policy still in place, we are left to wonder what additional social problems will emerge in the future. For example, what will become of the millions of men who have no prospects for marrying a woman? Or, what will happen if, as some have predicted, women are designated as a scarce resource?

A number of countries, including China, are facing a very different problem: how to manage the health issues of an aging population. This problem has come to the fore in recent years for a number of reasons. One major factor is the worldwide increase in life expectancy: the UN has estimated an increase in the mean global life expectancy from 58 years in 1975 to 67 years in 2010, and it projects a rise to 75 years by 2050 (UN 2007). Additionally, the shift from rural (with traditional family structures) to urban (with smaller family units) living situations means that aging individuals have fewer family members to rely on for support. In the West, the demographic shift brought about by the aging of the 'baby boomers' is beginning as well.

**managed care**
A system of care, tied to the market-based delivery of medicine, particularly in the US, in which a patient's choice of treatment and of practitioner is directed by an intermediary organization that claims to provide the most cost effective services available while generating profits for its members.

*Figure 9.10* I **China's one-child policy has caused a crisis in the country. Soon, men could outnumber women by as much as 1.3 to 1.**

Elderly people face increasing rates of physical as well as cognitive conditions—for example, Alzheimer's disease and certain forms of dementia. Part of the struggle is to find financial resources to support this growing sector of patients, particularly in nation-states where universal and near universal medical interventions have been the norm. Yet the challenge is not only financial; social systems must also arrange for care that will allow the elderly to maintain their identities when they enter systems of care. Latimer notes that clinical staff do categorize older people according to how they perform in response to staff's moves. 'If individuals participate in the authoring of the categories to which they are assigned, then selfhood is preserved' (1999: 205). If they suffer from forms of dementia, then the bedside interaction area does not develop 'as a site through which the medical domain as a quality space is produced and reproduced . . . [where] patients, and practitioners themselves are classified . . . [into categories that] incarnate wider sociocultural relations' (205).

Paul Farmer has investigated the intersections between politics and health care in his work with the NGO Partners in Health, in his role as UN special envoy to Haiti, in his advocacy in the Americas and Africa, and in a number of his extensive writings (see Farmer 2005; 2006; Farmer et al. 2009). As a physician and a medical anthropologist, Farmer explores the depth and breadth of health care issues through specific and general analysis. Additionally, with Rylko-Bauer (2002), he has discussed **managed care** and the form of inequities that are generated when market forces focus on the management of inequality rather than the provision of the tools for delivery of care. Farmer and his colleagues direct our attention to the urban–rural divide and to the global have–have not chasm. They do not just report on conditions but seek reasons for what they see. Arguably, the most important issue is found in the succinct epilogue of *Global Health in Times of Violence*:

> If ethics are the embodiment of beliefs that individuals, groups, and cultures use to guide their behaviours and actions then we must question the violence of these ethics. We must question and challenge the contemporary moral economies that . . . tolerate the failure to provide needed and available medical assistance, and that exacerbate social and economic inequalities. . . . Connecting global violence to health requires that our analysis shift from a structural and geopolitical scale to a place that is intimate and experiential. . . . Finding the intimacy on the global requires new ways to assess, analyze, and present information . . . [that connects] the global to the personal. (Farmer et al. 2009: 224–5)

Farmer and his colleagues argue against complacency; they challenge us to act on what they have found. They also remind us of the individuals who are affected by all the sociopolitical conditions that lead to patchy health care delivery, from the structure of political economies to the rural–urban divide to social class placement. For anthropologists, the actualities of individual lives remain as the foundation of study from which we can come to connect the personal to the global.

## Epidemiology

Because disease spreads along social networks, and because social structures can facilitate this spread, collaboration between anthropologists and medical epidemiologists can be productive. Today, a number of anthropologists are looking at the cross-cultural distribution of diseases and the variables determining these distributions (race, class, religion, time, etc.). These anthropologists understand that knowledge about cultural responses can offer insight into cultural biases and how these biases play out in surveillance systems and treatment regimes for epidemics. Trostle and Sommerfeld (1996) have suggested the term *cultural epidemiology* for this type of interdisciplinary research.

To prevent or at least slow the spread of a disease, medical personnel must identify the major paths of transmission; they must also try to anticipate how, where, and when people are most likely to become infected; and they must try to inform the general population of the risks involved in certain activities. All of these goals can be accomplished most effectively if the medical personnel understand the habits and cultural situation of the affected people. For example, consider the response to the 2003 SARS (Severe Acute Respiratory Syndrome) epidemic. On a global scale, the WHO targeted travellers by advising against travel to sites where there were known infections, primarily Hong Kong, China, Taiwan, Singapore, and Toronto (see WHO 2003). Within affected countries, local regulatory bodies targeted populations most at risk. In Hong Kong, where the rate of infection was greatest, this involved shutting down schools and placing more than a thousand people under quarantine across the country (Cheng 2004: 71). In Canada, where transmission was traced to contact with recent travellers and mainly restricted to the city of Toronto, the response included selective quarantining of individuals, increased screening for symptoms at airports, and the cancellation of many non-essential conferences and conventions in Toronto (Figure 9.11). In most countries,

**epidemiology**
The study of the occurrence, spread, management, and prevention of infectious diseases

*Figure 9.11* | **A Toronto resident dons a medical mask to protect herself from the SARS virus.**

popular radio, print, and television media spread information about the disease and how to avoid infection. While the disease ultimately killed fewer people than did influenzas in the same period, the rapid emergence of the disease and the relative youth of its victims suggested a serious threat and a potentially devastating global pandemic.

While the widespread threat from SARS turned out to be fairly short-lived, other epidemics have proven to be more persistent. The most recent epidemic-level infections to have arisen on a global scale are Ebola and HIV/AIDS, both currently the subject of much research. Malaria remains of particular concern, as it leads to nearly 300 million clinical cases and about one million deaths every year (2008 estimates; see WHO 2010). A first step toward fighting the disease is understanding its ecology—how it affects and is affected by its environment. Such understanding led researchers to identify that malaria is spread by mosquitoes that live in tropical and subtropical regions; subsequently, knowledge of global warming has allowed researchers to predict how the disease will spread into areas that did not support malaria-carrying mosquitoes in the past. Also important is knowledge of the social and cultural practices of the people who have to live in regions affected by the disease. Together, medical and cultural knowledge have led to successful control of mosquitoes through water clean-ups and the use of prophylactics such as insecticides and sleeping nets (Figure 9.12). The ultimate goal is to develop a vaccine.

Past successes provide hope for future break-throughs—after all, we have managed to eradicate smallpox, the disease that was largely responsible for the depopulation of the Americas shortly after European contact. At the same time, the celebration of this success is tempered by the fear that smallpox could be used as a biological weapon. Although the disease was eradicated in the general population, samples are still held in at least two controlled medical research facilities (see Chapter 14 for more on this), and few people born after 1980 have been vaccinated against the disease.

## Being Applied

In some sense, this area of study we now call medical anthropology is more 'applied' than many of the other areas of anthropological research. This is appropriate, as health issues affect us all on a personal level and are also tied to biological, environmental, economic, and political influences beyond our control. Taking an integrated approach to health issues allows us to avoid becoming too closely aligned with any one set of interests—for example, the interests of powerful biomedicine industries. Our approach must also be global in nature, as studying the micro-cultural involves placing it in macro-cultural contexts. After all, the local has become the global; it is situated in a wider political and economic milieu.

Being applied requires us to be present in the real world and aware of all of the factors that shape that world. When we approach a medical issue, we must place scientific knowledge in its sociohistorical context, and we must balance unbiased social science methodologies with critical applications of Western scientific

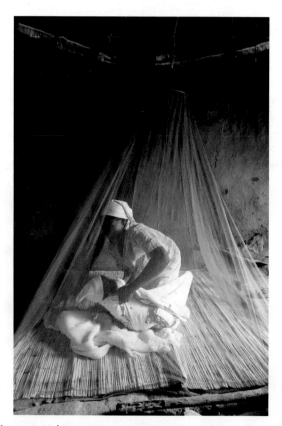

*Figure 9.12* | **A woman puts her baby to bed under an insecticide-protected mosquito net in Gutu, Zimbabwe. Mosquito nets are one of the ways to prevent the spread of diseases such as malaria.**

principles while honouring traditional knowledge. This approach can help clarify health issues that are situated in a socio-political colonial heritage. Consider the way we as a society offer support for Aboriginal peoples living within Canada's political boundaries. We have done little to counter the inequality that results from the urban–rural divide. We have only begun to reconcile traditional Aboriginal knowledge of medicine with Western biomedical practices. We have continued to invade and pollute the Canadian 'wilderness', contaminating the environments in which many Aboriginal peoples live. Additionally, we have failed to provide adequate assistance to Aboriginal individuals who are forced into moving to substandard urban areas. And these conditions are not unique to Canada—they are repeated to varying degrees in postcolonial contexts around the world.

Through their health-related research, medical anthropologists can and do contribute to policy and programming at both local and international levels. Their aim is not just to understand but to work to change cultural patterns related to health care that can be seen as inappropriate, oppressive, and/or exploitive (Singer 1995: 81). For example, medical anthropologists have contributed to the global awareness of culturally situated forms of violence against women such as female genital mutilation, sex-selective abortion and infanticide, and dowry abuse and murder (see CAPMAS 2009). Here one of the core ethical issues in applied anthropology arises: How do we reconcile our commitment to the principle of cultural relativism with our moral obligation to preserve the well-being of the peoples with whom we work?

The anthropological tradition of cultural relativism (whatever its limitations) and the discipline's enduring concern with insider understanding . . . [results in] . . . an appreciation of and commitment to the principle of self-determination. Support of self-determination is further supported by the anthropological obligation to counter Western, colonial ethnocentrism and to create opportunities for the voices of so-called people without history (i.e., oppressed third world populations) to be heard on the contemporary world stage. (Singer 1995: 98–9)

Certainly self-determination and consent are taken as core rights in the UN's Universal Declaration of Human Rights (UN 2011; see also Mackie 2003).

Can we help bring about change when asked? Of course! We can effect transformations by focussing on conscious-raising and empowering objectives directed toward 'unmasking the structural roots of suffering and ill health' (Singer 1995: 99). By taking a critical approach in which we appreciate the intersubjective space of social relationships and social action, we can also foster collaborative, respectful relationships with the peoples who are the centre of our studies. Respectful interaction rests in recognizing that we all live in our own modernity and define our contemporaneousness with the bricolage of our personal and cultural historic pasts and realities of the present. Ultimately, we find that a mixture of tradition and innovation may lead us to new ways to solve the age-old problems of disease and illness.

## Key Terms

bioaccumulation  227
defensive research  228
disease  217
epidemiology  235
etiology  220
folk illness  222
health  217
illness  217
managed care  234

medical anthropology  217
placebo effect  230
positive research  228
realized niche  226
shaman  219
traditional knowledge  217
well-being  217
witchcraft  222
witchdoctor  219

# Chapter Summary

1. Individual expectations of wellness differ cross culturally. In Western nations, expectations are high; most people have access to health-promoting resources such as clean water, nutritious food, medicines, and medical treatment. Yet not everyone is in an equal position, and the disenfranchised often lack access to sufficient resources. In many poorer countries today, health conditions resemble those of past centuries, and many people continue to suffer from diseases we rarely encounter in the West.

2. Medical anthropologists recognize the tension between traditional knowledge and 'modern' Western science, but they also recognize that the two approaches intersect in many ways. In the past, the systems were depicted as in binary opposition, as in the conception of *internalizing* systems (e.g., Western biomedical systems) versus *externalizing* systems (e.g., traditional ethnomedical approaches). Today, medical anthropologists try to move beyond such 'either/or' interpretations.

3. Medical anthropology is highly interdisciplinary, drawing on and influencing such diverse fields as biology, ecology, biochemistry, sociology, psychology, political science, economics, linguistics, ethics, and religious studies. Thus medical anthropologists value integrated approaches and holism in their work, and they are always open to a variety of perspectives.

4. Some of our greatest learning and ethical challenges have come from studying traditional knowledge in systems of wellness that transcend the constructed dichotomy between 'folk' medicines and Western biomedicine. Examples from medical anthropologists work in the field remind us that the sharing of traditional knowledge is a gift—from local experts to visiting anthropologists—and needs to be recognized in all ways.

5. Interpretations of illness and disease differ across cultures. Some interpretations are personalistic, while others are naturalistic, and yet others are a blend of the two. Over time, these interpretations change to reflect new knowledge, changing perceptions, and cultural events. As interpretations change, labels and their meanings change as well.

6. Medical anthropologists are aware that physical (biotic and abiotic), social, and cultural environments can have a dramatic impact on human well-being. Within every environment, all components are linked in complex, often indivisible ways. Thus, researchers examine the influence of environments—especially *realized niches*—on human health as well as the many human factors that shape those environments. Two areas of particular interest are environmental contamination and access to a balanced diet.

7. Health care systems take many different forms around the world. Yet medical anthropologists recognize three conditions in medical treatment that occur cross culturally, regardless of the approach to affecting a cure: medical procedures sometimes help the patient recover, while other times they do not; a patient sometimes gets well regardless the interventions taken by caregivers since the disease/illness/injury was, in effect, self-correcting or self/healing; and the placebo effect sometimes works to bring about a cure, simply because the patient believes that it will be effective.

8. Within and between cultures, curing practices range from home remedies or folk cures to intensive treatment by a traditional or medical healer. In some cases, no treatment is possible; in other cases, factors such as geographical location or financial resources may limit an individual's access to treatment.

9. Doctor–patient relationships differ cross culturally. In traditional health care systems, practitioners try to form personal relationships with their patients and make the patient feel at home with the treatment. In Western medical systems, doctors often see patients as clients and offer treatment only in formal institutions.

10. Political interventions—such as those meant to control population growth or to managing changing population demographics—can also affect individuals' access to health care. Social problems can arise when citizens feel that official policies are preventing them from achieving their health-related goals.

11. Medical anthropologists can offer valuable insight into how diseases spread along social networks and how cultures respond to threats from disease. Such insights are valuable in the field of epidemiology. As an 'applied' discipline, medical anthropology has much potential for making valuable contributions to the resolution of real-world problems.

# Critical Thinking Questions

1. How does context affect your understanding of wellness, both in general and in terms of your own health?

2. How is the medical system in Canada an externalizing system? What evidence can you find of internalizing approaches to wellness in Canada? How can these two approaches complement one another?

3. What are your perceptions of the link between environmental contamination and health? Is this an important issue in your life?

4. How do socioeconomic and geopolitical disparities affect treatment options? Why are Western nations often slow to act in response to the health crises such as that of HIV/AIDS in less affluent regions of the world? What can be done about such disparities within relatively affluent Western nations?

5. Bruce Lincoln has observed that the human body in sickness transcends its individual psychological and physical vulnerability, becoming the 'site where social pressures and tensions are experienced most acutely' and various community 'contradictions and lacerations that divide a community' are played out (2001: 791). How have social pressures and tensions factored into your own experiences with disease and illness? How might Lincoln's observations relate to an epidemic within a community?

# Suggested Readings

Berkes, F., P. George, R. Preston, and J. Turner. 1992. 'The Cree View of Land and Resources: Indigenous Ecological Knowledge', report prepared for taso (Technology Assessment in Subarctic Ontario), Second Series, no. 8 (Hamilton: McMaster University). An interesting paper that discusses the traditional values of the James Bay Cree with respect to their land base and the resources they use (animals, fish, and birds).

Dods, Roberta Robin. 2004. 'Knowing Ways/Ways of Knowing: Reconciling Science and Tradition', *World Archaeology* 36, 4: 547–57. This paper discusses the structure of Traditional Ecological Knowledge (TEK) and Western Scientific Knowledge (WSK), concluding that both forms of knowledge offer access to important information and that the greatest insight can come when they are combined.

Farmer, Paul. 2005. *Pathologies of Power: Health, Human Rights, and the New War on the Poor* (Berkeley: University of California Press). A highly respected text in which Paul Farmer investigates the many intersections between politics and health care. Also worthwhile are Farmer's 2006 work *AIDS and Accusation: Haiti and the Geography of Blame* and his 2009 work, co-authored by Barbara Rylko-Bauer and Linda Whiteford, *Global Health in Times of Violence*.

Mackie, Gerry. 2003. 'Female Genital Cutting: A Harmless Practice?', *Medical Anthropology Quarterly, New Series*, 17, 2: 135–58.

This article discusses issues of self-determination and consent in the context of cultural relativism.

Mintz, Sidney W., and Christine M. Du Bois. 2002. 'The Anthropology of Food and Eating', *Annual Review of Anthropology* 31: 99–119. This article links diverse areas of research including food security and social change. The authors note that much remains to be done in examining nutritional practices in many areas of the world.

Rylko-Bauer, Barbara, and Paul Farmer. 2002. 'Managed Care or Managed Inequality? A Call for Critiques of Market-Based Medication', *Medical Anthropology Quarterly* 16, 4: 476–502. This paper challenges us to consider the actual cost of care managed by corporations who base decisions on profit-motive directives.

Stephenson, Peter H. 2001. 'Expanding Notions of Culture and Ethics in Health and Medicine to Include Marginalized Groups: A Critical Perspective', *Anthropologica* 43, 1: 3–17. A nuanced and historically contextualized paper that examines the ethical challenges involved in practising medicine—both Western and traditional—in a globalizing world.

Van Esterik, Penny. 2002. 'Contemporary Trends in Infant Feeding Research', *Annual Review of Anthropology* 31: 257–78. An informative investigation into health and nutrition concerns related to infant care and feeding.

# Related Websites

Aboriginal Affairs and Northern Development Canada www.ainc-inac.gc.ca

Abortion, Province by Province www.theglobeandmail.com/news/abortion-province-by-province/article1609885

Health Canada: Smallpox www.phac-aspc.gc.ca/ep-mu/smallpox-eng.php

Partners in Health www.pih.org/who/vision.html

UNFPA'S State of World Population www.unfpa.org/swp

UN'S World Population Prospects www.un.org/esa/population/publications/wpp2006/English.pdf

Society for Medical Anthropology www.medanthro.net

Violence against Women in Egypt http://unstats.un.org/unsd/demographic/meetings/vaw/docs/Paper2.pdf

WHO'S HIV/AIDS Data and Statistics www.who.int/hiv/data/en

# 10 | World View

## Chapter Outline

## Learning Objectives

By the end of Chapter 10, you will be able to

- consider the role of metaphor, metonymy, and symbol in constructing world views,

- recognize key metaphors for constructing world views,

- appreciate the nature of religion and religious expression in world views,

- identify the difficulties in maintaining and changing a world view,

- understand world views as instruments of power, and

- compare and contrast the roles of religion and secularism.

← *Facing water shortages due to an uncertain monsoon, these Hindu Brahmins perform a Parjanya Yagna ritual to appease the gods at a temple in Ahmedabad, India. Many world views accept the existence of supernatural forces that can influence conditions in the physical world.*

**What guides us as we attempt to give life meaning? How do we devise cultural forms through which we can make sense of our being and belonging? How do we frame our physical and metaphysical contexts?** In this chapter we attempt to answer these very complex questions by exploring different **world views**.

## The Role of Metaphor, Metonymy, and Symbol

### Metaphor

One way to grasp a particular world view and the cultural patterns that it contains is to 'follow the metaphor'. In Canada, for example, we might examine the cultural metaphor of our country as a cultural mosaic to understand how Canadians interpret their place in the world. We might also contrast this metaphor with the American metaphor of the US as a melting pot to uncover how our cultural perceptions differ from those of our neighbours to the south. Following metaphors successfully, however, requires understanding how metaphors work.

**Metaphor** asserts the existence of a meaningful link between two expressions from different semantic domains. For example, metaphorical statements such as 'Arnold is a turkey' create an ambiguity that can only be resolved in context. If we know

**metaphor**
A form of thought and language that asserts a meaningful link between two expressions from different semantic domains.

**metaphorical subject**
The first part of a metaphor, which indicates the domain of experience that needs to be clarified.

**metaphorical predicate**
The second part of a metaphor, which suggests the familiar domain of experience that may clarify the metaphorical subject.

**metaphorical entailments**
All the attributes of a metaphorical predicate that relate it to the culturally defined domain of experience to which it belongs.

Arnold is characteristically inept, ignorant, and annoying, and that turkeys are prototypically stupid and clumsy, our metaphor becomes intelligible and apt. But why resort to metaphor to represent our opinion of Arnold? Why not simply say 'Arnold is inept, ignorant, and annoying'? When we choose to use metaphoric language instead of literal language, it is usually because literal language is not equal to the task of expressing the depth of meaning we intend. Our experience of Arnold may be complex and difficult to pin down in literal language. That is, there is something about the image of a turkey that encompasses more of what we think about Arnold than can ever be represented by a list of adjectives. We therefore select a figurative image whose features are familiar and use it as a tool to help us express what kind of person Arnold is. The metaphor does not demonstrate unequivocally that Arnold *is* a turkey. Rather, using a particular metaphor simply asserts that a particular link exists and invites those who know both Arnold and turkeys to decide (and perhaps to debate) the extent to which the metaphor is apt. Similarly, the metaphor 'The Lord is my shepherd' links a subject we have trouble describing ('The Lord') to an image ('my shepherd') that is familiar and well understood in Christian societies. This metaphorical statement is an invitation to ponder what it means to be a shepherd, what it means to be *my* shepherd, and then to apply this knowledge to one's understanding of the Lord.

World views aim to encompass the widest possible understanding of how the world works. In constructing world views, people tend to examine what they already know for clues that might help them make sense of what puzzles them. Metaphor is a powerful tool for constructing world views because it clarifies areas of human experience that are vague or poorly understood. The first part of a metaphor, the **metaphorical subject**, represents the domain of experience that needs to be clarified ('The Lord'). The second part of a metaphor, the **metaphorical predicate**, suggests the domain of experience that is familiar (shepherding) and may help us understand what the metaphorical subject is all about (Figure 10.1). To understand the metaphor, we have to list every conceivable attribute of shepherds and then decide which ones describe the Lord. These attributes are called **metaphorical entailments** (Lakoff

## In Their Own Words | House Re-thatching in an Andean Annual Cycle

*Canadian social anthropologist Peter Gose illustrates that Andean roofing can be very complex and, at the same time, provide meaningful insights into many areas of life.*

By Andean standards, house re-thatching is only a moderately ritualized labour process. Its imagery varies considerably from locality to locality, and . . . [it] is best understood through its position in the annual cycle of agrarian labour and ritual. . . . [T]he relatively modest ritual imagery of house re-thatching means little if anything in itself and cannot stand on its own as symbolism. Rather, it is motivated and given most of its significance by the practices that surround and support it in the annual cycle. House re-thatching in the Andes takes place as the dry season is giving way to the growing season. This seasonal shift involves a corresponding change in social relations from an emphasis on private appropriation by individual households during the harvest to an extensive and institutionalized inter-household co-operation that will prevail throughout the growing season. . . . [T]hese seasonally opposed moralities overlap in the house re-thatching and each lay claim to its content. . . . [C]ontradiction animates the imagery of this act and makes it signify in a way that we would miss if we considered it in abstraction from its grounding in the annual cycle. . . . [I]t is only when the imagery of the performance is subsumed by the annual cycle that it acquires the directedness necessary to 'reflect and refract' another part of reality, that is, to become properly symbolic. . . . The . . . images do not function as self-contained 'semantic values' that just happen to crop up around the house re-thatching but as metaphorical vehicles that intervene in and organize the very nature of the act. Put differently, this imagery does not exist

for itself, in isolation from the instrumentality of the house re-thatching as a labour process, but in order to give that labour process a cultural form. And in turn, the seasonal position of the house re-thatching gives this imagery direction and entry into a real context within which it can truly signify. An example of this sort of interaction can be found in the transportation of hay down the mountain on the first day, which at first appears entirely unremarkable but, on further consideration, is seen to be embroiled in the entire 'domestication' complex, including the origins of agriculture in descent. If this theme of 'domestication' were not so thoroughly developed by other aspects of the rite, there would be no justification for this interpretation of the downward movement of hay. But once such a theme is established, it becomes equally hard to deny that the apparently technical act of transporting hay contributes to it. In sum, this rite teaches not only a negative lesson, that it is impossible to separate meaning from practice, but also a positive one, that the two taken together as praxis form a whole that is greater than its parts. Yet the praxis of commoners within the annual cycle is characterized not by a vapid holism but rather by a contradictory interpenetration of opposed moralities of private appropriation and collective production. This contradiction is most evident in the seasonal position of the rite, but it also works through its spatial and sequential organization and can even be identified in each of its individual symbols. Because the source of these contradictions lies beyond the act itself, house re-thatching must be understood as a moment in a larger seasonal process, not as a self-contained 'text'.

Source: Gose, Peter. 1991. 'House Re-thatching in an Andean Annual Cycle: Practice, Meaning, and Contradiction', *American Ethnologist* 18, 1: 38, 57.

**metonymy**
The culturally defined relationship of the parts of a semantic domain to the domain as a whole and of the whole to its parts.

and Johnson 1980). They suggest what follows from, or is entailed by, calling the Lord a *shepherd*. If we were to assert that 'The Lord is my friend', an entirely different set of metaphorical entailments would follow.

## Metonymy

**Metonymy** is the relationship that links the parts of a semantic domain to one another. In the metaphor 'The Lord is my shepherd', the links between the metaphorical predicate *shepherd* and its metaphorical entailments are links of metonymy. The word *shepherd* can stand for any and all attributes connected to the semantic domain defined by shepherding. At the same time, any of these

**Figure 10.1 | An analysis of the metaphor 'The Lord is my shepherd', illustrating the links of metaphor and metonymy.**

attributes (such as protecting sheep from wild animals) may entail the word *shepherd*. Because semantic domains are culturally defined, the meaningful elements that are linked by metonymy within any semantic domain are also culturally defined. Shepherding occurs in many societies, and yet the range of meanings associated with it may vary: compare a society in which shepherds are women, sheep graze freely, and mutton is primarily for family consumption with a different society in which shepherds are men, sheep graze in enclosed fields, and most animals are sold on the market for cash. Of course, members of the first society may think that theirs is the only sensible way to herd sheep and vice versa. Put another way, in any society, semantic domains defined by links of metonymy are viewed as 'natural' or 'true' associations.

The links of metonymy we discover within a particular semantic domain may help us make sense of experiences that seem chaotic and meaningless.

Consider what happens in the case of what some people call *religious conversion*. An individual who is troubled and confused may see his personal situation suddenly come into focus when he starts thinking of himself as a lost sheep. Further, he may reason that a lost sheep must have been lost by someone—the shepherd to whom it belonged. This reflection, in turn, may lead him to ask who his shepherd might be. If he learns that some people believe that the Lord is their shepherd, he may be attracted to them and want to learn more. Thus, his exploration of the links of metonymy within a particular semantic domain in the context of his own life may lead him to conclude that the metaphor 'The Lord is my shepherd' resonates with the power of divine revelation. Such reflections play an important role in religious conversion, but they are equally important in science, for example, when a new theory is adopted because it makes sense of otherwise puzzling data (see Kuhn 1970; Poewe 1989).

## Symbol

As people increase their understanding of themselves and the wider world by creating apt metaphors, they devise *symbols* to remind themselves of their significant insights and the connections between those insights. As noted at the beginning of this book, a symbol is something that stands for something else—be it a word, an image, or an action. Symbols signal the presence and importance of given domains of experience. They are special cases of metonymy. Some symbols—what Sherry Ortner (1973) calls *summarizing symbols*—represent a whole semantic domain and invite us to consider the various elements within it. Others—what Ortner calls *elaborating symbols*—represent only one element of a domain and invite us to place that element in its wider semantic context.

## Key Metaphors

World views are attempts to answer the following question: What must the world be like for my experiences to be what they are? Over the ages, thoughtful people in all cultural traditions have drawn on different metaphors to suggest various answers to this question. Those suggestions that have become entrenched in any particular tradition are based on especially apt metaphors—**key metaphors** that make sense of experience in a variety of circumstances. Over time, as circumstances change and the established metaphors become less apt, new key metaphors replace the old, forming the basis for new world views.

> **key metaphors**
> Metaphors that serve as the foundation of a world view.
>
> **societal metaphor**
> A world-view metaphor whose model for the world is the social order.

Anthropologist Robin Horton suggests that people who construct a world view are 'concerned above all to show order, regularity, and predictability where primary theory [i.e., commonsense experience] has failed to show them'. As they search for key metaphors, therefore, they look at those areas of everyday experience that are most associated with order, regularity, and predictability (1982: 237). Cross-culturally, key metaphors typically relate to three such realms of experience: the societal, the organic, and the technological.

### Societal Metaphors

In societies where human social relations provide great order, regularity, and predictability, the central model for the world is the social order. People within these societies tend to use **societal metaphors** as they try to explain various aspects of their reality. For example, geneticist Richard Lewontin (1984) and his colleagues point out that biologists studying cells have used a societal metaphor almost from the very beginning. These biologists liken cells to a factory assembling the biochemical products needed to support the body's economy. This metaphor recurs in the twentieth-century work of Francis Crick, one of the discoverers of the structure of DNA (deoxyribonucleic acid). Lewontin and colleagues suggest: 'Read any introductory textbook to the new molecular biology and you will find these metaphors as a central part of the cellular description. Even the drawings of the protein synthesis sequence are often deliberately laid out in "assembly-line" style' (1984: 59) (Figure 10.2).

Similarly, contemporary sociobiologists have borrowed certain concepts from modern economic thought and used them to describe the behaviour of genes or of living organisms. Sociobiologists describe the nurturing behaviour of parents toward their offspring as 'parental investment'. They talk about the cost–benefit analyses that people make before deciding whether or not to sacrifice themselves for others and even describe genes as 'selfish'. To some sociobiologists, the natural world is just the capitalist market on a larger scale. Indeed, anthropologist Marshall Sahlins (1976a) and others have argued that, from its inception in the late eighteenth century, modern biology has taken its key metaphors from the social

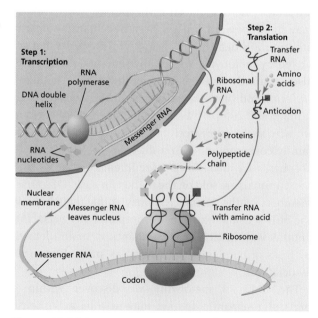

*Figure 10.2* | **An example of a protein synthesis diagram laid out in 'assembly-line' style.**

world familiar to eighteenth-century biologists—the world of early capitalism.

## Organic Metaphors

An **organic metaphor** applies the image of a living body to something. A common organic metaphor is based on an interpretation of the body of a living organism as divisible into different systems (digestive, reproductive, respiratory, and so on), each carrying out a specialized task. When all these systems are functioning in harmony with one another, the organism is said to be healthy. If we compare society to a living organism, for example, we look for the subsystems into which society can be divided, identify the tasks each is supposed to perform, and describe a healthy society as one in which all the subsystems are functioning harmoniously. Indeed, this sort of organic metaphor is responsible for the social-scientific metaphor of society as an organism, with various interlinked components that rely on one another for survival. Alternatively, we can use an organic metaphor to analyze the life course of a society or civilization in terms of its birth, youth, maturity, old age, and death.

*Personification* (attributing human characteristics to non-human entities) is another organic metaphor. The belief that the vending machine in your office has a malevolent and greedy personality or that you can persuade your car to start on a cold morning by speaking gentle and encouraging words to it both involve personification.

## Technological Metaphors

A **technological metaphor** uses objects made by human beings as metaphorical predicates. Technological metaphors that use machines as metaphorical predicates have been prominent in the world view(s) of Western society since the rise of science. For example, in the seventeenth century, René Descartes popularized the notion that the human body was a machine, albeit one inhabited by an immortal soul. Subsequently, Julien La Mettrie carried this metaphor to its radical conclusion in *L'homme-machine* ('man-machine'), where he argued that the concept of the human soul was superfluous because machines do not have souls. As Western science and technology have grown in importance, machine metaphors have also become more widespread.

In the twentieth century, a major revolution in cognitive psychology was brought about by a shift in key technological metaphors. Psychologists rejected the steam engine metaphor of nineteenth-century industrial technology in favour of the **computer metaphor** of twentieth-century cybernetic technology. Computer jargon has become popular among scientists investigating the functions of the brain, the nervous system, and even the whole human body. Today, it seems impossible to avoid such language given the many suggestive insights into human mental functioning that the computer metaphor makes possible.

Using a computer as a model for the mind can produce varying interpretations. Everything depends on the kind of computer you choose as the metaphorical predicate and the aspects of computer operations you emphasize. For example, biological determinists might prefer to think of the mind as a 'dedicated' computer whose functions are fully specified and wired into the hardware, allowing little flexibility. But if we think of the mind as a sophisticated general-purpose computer, we cannot predict the specific tasks it performs simply by knowing the design of its hardware. Rather, by loading different software programs, we direct the computer's hardware to perform particular tasks. Thus, the 'functional processes [of the brain] cannot be guessed at from its design. . . . Although we may have biological origins, these may not be much more relevant than, say, soil for flowers. . . . Soil chemistry tells us remarkably little about orchids' (Gregory 1981: 566).

Were we to extend this kind of computer metaphor to explain the development of culture, we could argue that the co-evolution of brain and culture is the process by which a program hungry for system memory makes demands on hardware design. Random alterations that result in new central processing unit (CPU) chips and hardware design (mutations) allow more applications to be developed. At a certain point, however, the capacity of the CPU chip to access memory is reached. An external 'swap file' to handle the users' ever-increasing memory demands must be created in some sort of external storage system—flash memory or hard disks. The human

**organic metaphor**
A world-view metaphor that applies the image of the body to social structures and institutions.

**technological metaphor**
A world-view metaphor that employs objects made by human beings as metaphorical predicates.

**computer metaphor**
A technological metaphor that employs computers as metaphorical predicates.

cultural equivalent of this swap file would be oral tradition and forms of symbolic inscription such as writing.

# Religion

For many readers of this text, the most familiar form of world view is probably **religion**. The anthropological concept of religion, like many analytic terms, began as a description of a certain domain of Western culture. As a result, it has been very difficult for anthropologists to settle on a definition of religion that is applicable in all human societies.

> **religion**
> 'Ideas and practices that postulate reality beyond that which is immediately available to the senses.'

Scholars have often argued that religion differs from other kinds of world views because it assumes the existence of a supernatural domain: an invisible world populated by one or more beings who are more powerful than human beings and are able to influence events in the 'natural' human world. The problem is that the distinction between 'natural' and 'supernatural' was originally made by non-religious Western observers, where 'real' was equated to the 'natural' world that was separate from their defined 'imaginary' or 'supernatural' world. However, 'humans do not have a world that is fixed for their kind; instead, there is a vital experience of space. . . . The vital functions of a body subject are carried out within a vital space, which is not given as such but is shaped by that being's actions' (Von Maltzahn 1994: 67). These actions are based on belief systems, and the sentient world may be interpreted through a set of mythological constructs that give meaning to the 'animate beings in motion against the backdrop of a terrain that . . . [is] itself continually in process' (Riddington 1982: 473). Thus many anthropologists who study different religious traditions believe that it is less distorting to begin with their informants' statements about what exists and what does not. In this way, they are in a better position to understand the range of forces, visible and invisible, that religious believers perceive as active in their world.

Anthropological inquiry into religious world views needs to begin with broad objectives that can move to increasing specificity as the details of a particular religious tradition are revealed by its adherents. With this approach in mind, Bowen defines religion as 'ideas and practices that postulate reality beyond that which is immediately available to the senses' (2002: 5). These ideas and practices are not individual; they are *social*: they are shared among a group of people and shape how members of the group interact with one another and with the universe in a variety of ways (Figure 10.3). In a society, religion may take the shape of beliefs in spirits and gods, in impersonal forces that affect the world, in the correct practice of ritual, or in the awareness that the ancestors continue to be active in the world of the living. This definition of religion emphasizes that religions involve actions as well as beliefs. Indeed, anthropologist A.F.C. Wallace proposed a set of 'minimal categories of religious behaviour' that describe many of the practices usually associated with religions (1966). Several of the most salient are as follows:

1) *Prayer.* Where there are personified cosmic forces, there is a customary way of addressing them, usually by speaking or chanting out loud. Often people pray in public, at a sacred location and with special apparatuses: incense, smoke, objects (such as rosary beads or a prayer wheel), and so on.

2) *Physiological exercise.* Many religious systems have methods for physically manipulating psychological states to induce an ecstatic spiritual state. Wallace suggests four major kinds of manipulation: drugs; sensory deprivation; mortification of the flesh by pain, sleeplessness, and fatigue; and deprivation of

*Figure 10.3* **| Religious beliefs and practices are social. Here, Muslim men pray together at Shah Mosque (Imam Mosque) in Isfahan, Iran.**

food, water, or air. In many societies, the experience of ecstasy, euphoria, dissociation, or hallucination seems to be a goal of religious effort (Figure 10.4).

3) *Exhortation.* In all religious systems, certain people are believed to have closer relationships with the invisible powers than others, and they are expected to use those relationships in the spiritual interests of others. They give orders, heal, threaten, comfort, and interpret.

4) *Mana.* Mana refers to an impersonal superhuman power that is sometimes believed to be transferable; for example, by laying their hands on a sick person, the power of a healer enters the person's body to remove or destroy an illness. In Guider, Cameroon, some people believe that the ink used to copy passages from the Quran has power. Washing the ink off the board on which the words are written, and drinking the ink, transfers the power of the words into the body of the drinker. The principle here is that sacred things are to be touched so that power may be transferred.

5) *Taboo.* Objects or people that may not be touched are taboo. Some people believe that the cosmic power in such objects or people may 'drain away' if touched or may injure the toucher. Many religious systems have taboo objects. Traditionally, Catholics were not to touch the host (the consecrated bread) during communion; Jews may not touch the handwritten text of the biblical scrolls. In ancient Polynesia, commoners could not touch the chief's body; even an accidental touch resulted in the death of the commoner. Food may also be taboo; many societies have elaborate rules concerning the foods that may or may not be eaten at different times or by different kinds of people.

6) *Feasts.* Eating and drinking in a religious context is very common. The Holy Communion of Catholics and Protestants is a meal set apart by its religious context. The Passover Seder for Jews is another religious feast. For the Huichol of Mexico, the consumption of peyote is set apart by its religious context. Even everyday meals may be seen to have a religious quality if they begin or end with prayer.

7) *Sacrifice.* Giving something of value to the invisible forces or their agents is a feature of many religious systems. This may be an offering of money, goods, or services. It may also be the immolation of animals or, very rarely, human beings. Sacrifices

*Figure 10.4* | **A Hindu devotee makes the painful pilgrimage to Batu Caves, near Kuala Lumpur.**

may be made in thanks to the cosmic forces in hopes of influencing them to act in a certain way or simply to gain general religious merit (Figure 10.5).

## Religion and Communication

Those who are committed to religious world views are convinced of the existence of beings or forces that are ordinarily invisible but actively involved in their lives. Indeed, some of the most highly valued religious practices, such as religious ecstasy or trance, produce outer symptoms that may be perceived by others, but their most powerful effects can be experienced only by the individual who undergoes them personally. If you had such a personal experience and wanted to tell others about it, how would you proceed?

*Figure 10.5* | **This Balinese woman offers a sacrifice of food and flowers in prayer.**

You might well begin by searching for metaphors based on experiences already well known to your audience. One Hindu Tamil worshipper in Kuala Lumpur who successfully went into trance during the festival of Thaipusam described his experience as 'floating in the air, followed by the wind' (*Floating in the Air* 1973; Figure 10.6). And the Hebrew poet who wrote Psalm 23 tried to express his experience of the power and love of his God by comparing God to his shepherd and himself to a sheep. Many contemporary theologians argue that the language human beings use to talk about omnipresent

*Figure 10.6* | **A devotee prays at the Hindu festival of Thaipusam in Kuala Lumpur.**

and omniscient supernatural beings is full of metaphors (see, e.g., Gillman 1992). Even those who claim to have had personal experience of this reality, such as the People of the Book (Jews, Christians, and Muslims who call to Elohim, God, or Allah, respectively), will probably still find themselves forced to resort to poetic, metaphorical language if they want to explain that experience to other people—and perhaps even to themselves.

When societal metaphors are used, members of the tradition are likely to conceive of the force(s) at work in the universe as personified beings with many of the attributes of human agents at work in their own society. As societies differ from one another, so too does the way their members characterize the universe. Thus members of societies organized in strong groups based on kinship usually conceive of a universe peopled with the spirits of powerful ancestral figures who take an interest in the lives of their living descendants. However, members of societies run by vast and complex bureaucracies (e.g., the Roman Empire) are apt to picture the universe as being run by an army of hierarchically ordered gods and spirits, all of which may be supervised by a chief god. It is not likely that 'The Lord is my shepherd' would be accepted as an apt description of cosmic reality by people living in a society that lacks class distinctions and has no experience of shepherding.

Organic metaphors may also figure in the construction of religious understanding. Anthropologist James Fernandez (1977) reports that organic metaphors are common in the Bwiti religion of the Fang (see Map 10.1). The human heart, for example, is an apt metaphor for Bwiti devotees because '(1) it is the heart which is the most alive of the bloody organs, (2) it is traditionally conceived by the Fang to be the organ of thought, and (3) in its bloodiness it is associated with the female principle. . . . Many meanings are at work in this metaphor, for that bloody organ, the heart, has a congeries of useful associations' (1977: 112).

Societies that rely on technological metaphors tend to construct a world view in which the universe is a highly complex machine put together by a skilled builder or builders. When we say that we are only cogs in a machine, or talk about social status and roles as interchangeable parts, we are using machine metaphors. In a mechanical world view, all processes are complex, orderly, predictable, and knowable; thus it is possible for humans to effectively intervene in the world and alter the course of a process without the aid of a spiritual being or force. Therefore,

Map 10.1 | **Fang**

while this world view is popular in Western societies today, many people question whether it can be called *religious*.

## Religious Organization

In the societal metaphor, the forces in the universe are personalized, and people seeking to influence those forces must handle them as they would handle powerful human beings. Thus communication is the central feature. When we address each other we expect a response. The same is true when we address personalized cosmic forces, and this can become a tremendously complex undertaking. It is not surprising, therefore, that some societies have developed complex social practices to ensure that it is done properly. In these societies, religion is institutionalized, and social positions are created for specialists who supervise or embody correct religious practice.

Anthropologists have identified two broad categories of religious specialists: shamans and priests. A shaman is a religious practitioner and healer who is believed to have the power to contact invisible powers directly on behalf of individuals or groups. Shamans are often thought to be able to travel to the cosmic realm to communicate with the beings or forces that dwell there. They can plead with those beings or forces to act in favour of their people and may return with messages for them. In many societies, the training that a shaman receives is long and demanding and may involve the use of powerful psychotropic substances, producing altered states of consciousness to access cosmic beings. This position can embody dangerous ambiguities: someone who can contact such beings for positive benefits may also be able to contact them to produce negative outcomes like disease or death. Barbara Tedlock (2005) observes that shamanism was possibly the domain of women in its earliest forms. Certainly it is the world's oldest form of religion and medicine, and it remains a force for healing today.

Priests, in contrast, are skilled in the practice of religious rituals, which are carried out for the benefit of the group (Figure 10.7). Priests do not necessarily have direct contact with cosmic forces. Often their major role is to mediate such contact by ensuring that the required ritual activity has been performed according to the established tradition. Priests are found in hierarchical societies. Status differences separating rulers and subjects in such societies are reflected in the unequal relationship between priest and laity.

Figure 10.7 | **Priests are experts in carrying out religious rituals. This Shinto priest wears his traditional costume as he carries out his ritualized role in a ceremony in Meiji Shrine, Tokyo.**

# World Views in Operation: Two Case Studies

Anthropologists often say that people of different cultures live in different worlds. This itself is a metaphorical statement. It asserts that our understanding of reality depends on the particular point of view embodied in our culture. Of course, every culture contains subcultures that may draw pictures of reality that conflict with each other. The experience of juggling multiple points of view in our own society helps us to cope with unfamiliar perspectives in different societies.

We have been discussing how world views are constructed, but most of us encounter them fully formed, both in our own society and in other societies. We face a rich tapestry of symbols and rituals and everyday practices linked to one another in what often appears to be a seamless web. Where do we begin to sort things out?

*Figure 10.8* | **A Huichol shaman's violin and arrows, together with a basket of freshly gathered peyote.**

## Mind, Body, and Emotion in Huichol Religious Practice

Barbara Myerhoff (1974) discusses the world view of the Huichol in relation to their sacred peyote hunt (Figure 10.8). The Huichol are maize farmers who live in the Sierra Madre Occidental of northern Mexico (see Map 10.2). Annually, they travel to a desert about 600 kilometres from their homes to hunt peyote. Because peyote is sacred to the Huichol, this journey is also sacred, representing a pilgrimage to Wirikuta, the original Huichol homeland where the First People, both deities and ancestors, once lived. The journey is hard and dangerous, both physically and spiritually. The pilgrims seek to restore and experience the original state of unity that existed at the beginning of the world.

This state of unity is symbolized by deer, maize, and peyote. The deer symbolizes the masculine, hunting past and thus connects the Huichol with their ancestors. In Huichol thought, the deer gave them peyote and appears every year in the hunt in Wirikuta. Blood from a sacrificed deer makes the maize grow and makes it nourishing. The deer is more powerful than human beings but not as remote as the gods. It symbolizes independence, adventure, and freedom.

Although the Huichol have only recently begun to grow maize, it is central to their present-day life. A life based on maize is tedious and precarious: the Huichol have to stay home to watch the crops, and even if they are careful, the maize may not grow. Maize symbolizes the labour of the present: food, domesticity, sharing between

*Map 10.2* | **Huichol**

the sexes, routine, and persistent diligence. It also provides the Huichol with the language of beauty. 'Maize', the Huichol say, 'is our life.'

Peyote, when gathered in the land of its origins, is sacred. It is used to induce private visions, which are not shared with others. It is also used ritually, in which case so little is eaten that no visions are produced. It seems that the purpose of ritual consumption is to reach communion with the deities. The Huichol think of peyote as plant and animal at once; at the climactic moments of the peyote hunt, it is hunted like the deer. 'Peyote is neither mundane, like maize, nor exotic and exciting, like deer. It is that solitary, ahistorical, asocial, asexual, non-rational domain without which [human beings] are not complete, without which life is a lesser affair' (Myerhoff 1974: 227). In Huichol religious thought, deer, maize, and peyote fit together: maize cannot grow without deer blood, the deer cannot be sacrificed until after the peyote hunt, the ceremony that brings the rain cannot be held without peyote, and the peyote cannot be hunted until the maize has been cleaned and sanctified.

### The Peyote Hunt

In 1966, Barbara Myerhoff and Peter Furst accompanied Huichol pilgrims on the peyote hunt. Each pilgrim was given the name of a Huichol god for the duration of the pilgrimage. The pilgrims, under the guidance of a shaman, all followed strict rules about sexual continence and other behaviours, separating themselves from their everyday routine. Once the pilgrims entered Wirikuta, many ways of speaking and acting were reversed. 'Stand up' meant 'sit down'; 'go away' meant 'come here'. The van in which they travelled became a 'burro' that would stop 'if he ran out of tequila'. The shaman who led the pilgrimage told Myerhoff that 'on the peyote hunt, we change the names of things because when we cross over there, into Wirikuta, things are so sacred that all is reversed' (1974: 148).

In the sacred land, the pilgrims became hunters, searching for peyote. Once the first peyote cactus was found, it was trapped by two arrows. The pilgrims then encircled it and presented their offerings. The shaman cut it out of the ground, sliced sections, and put one section in each pilgrim's mouth. The little group was sharply etched against the desert in the late afternoon sun—motionless,

soundless, the once-bright colours of their costumes now muted under layers of dust—chewing, chewing the bitter plant. So Sahagún described the ancient Indians who wept in the desert over the plant they esteemed so greatly. The success of the undertaking was unquestionable and the faces changed from quiet wonder to rapture to exaltation, all without words, all at the same moment. . . . Their camaraderie, the completeness of their communion with one another was self-evident. The companions were radiant. Their love for life and for one another was palpable. Though they did not speak and barely moved, no one seeing them there could call the experience anything less than collective ecstasy. (155–7)

Following this moment of communitas, the pilgrims collected as much peyote as they would need for their community and hastened to depart. The reversals and other requirements remained in effect until they reached home.

The unification of deer, maize, and peyote gives the peyote hunt its power. As Myerhoff puts it, 'In the climactic moments of the rituals in Wirikuta, these symbols provide the Huichols with a formulation of the large questions dealt with by religion, the questions of ultimate meaning and purpose'. She suggests that the way the Huichol's religious system answers these questions is distinctive. Some religions explain present-day moral incoherence by asserting that an original paradise was lost following an ancient sin. Other systems assert that there is an afterlife in which all the suffering of the world will be set right. The Huichol refuse to let go of their past:

Their most precious religious heritage—their beginnings—is idealized and recovered. Even if only for a little while, by means of the peyote hunt, Paradise may be regained. Through the deer–maize–peyote complex, the deer and a life dedicated to hunting the deer is still a fact of present-day life rather than a fading, shabby memory, chewed over by old men at the end of the day. (1974: 262)

The deer–maize–peyote complex and the peyote hunt represent the union of mind, body, and emotion. Through a holistic ritual experience that is profoundly meaningful, deeply moving, and thoroughly physical, the Huichol re-experience the correctness of their way of life.

## Witchcraft, Oracles, and Magic among the Azande

Anthropologist E.E. Evans-Pritchard, in his classic work *Witchcraft, Oracles, and Magic among the Azande* (1976 [1937]), describes how the Azande use witchcraft beliefs to explain unfortunate things that happen to them and how they employ oracles and magic to exert a measure of control over the actions of other people (see EthnoProfile 10.1). Evans-Pritchard was impressed by the intelligence, sophistication, and skepticism of his Azande informants. For this reason, he was all the more struck by their ability to hold a set of beliefs that many Europeans would regard as superstitious.

### Azande Witchcraft Beliefs

The Azande believe that *mangu* (translated by Evans-Pritchard as 'witchcraft') is a substance in the body of witches, generally located under the sternum. Being part of the body, the witchcraft substance grows as the body grows; therefore, the older the witch, the more potent his or her witchcraft. The Azande believe that children inherit witchcraft from their parents. Men and women may both be witches. Men practise witchcraft against other men, women against other women. Witchcraft works when its 'soul' removes the soul of a certain organ

**magic**
A set of beliefs and practices designed to control the visible or invisible world for specific purposes.

in the victim's body, usually at night, causing a slow, wasting disease. Suffering such a disease is therefore an indication that an individual has been bewitched.

Witchcraft is a basic concept for the Azande, one that shapes their experience of adversity (Figure 10.9). All deaths are due to witchcraft and must be avenged by **magic**. Other misfortunes are also commonly attributed to witchcraft unless the victim has broken a taboo, has failed to observe a moral rule, or is believed to be responsible for his own problems. An incompetent potter whose pots break while firing may claim that witchcraft caused them to break, but everyone will laugh because they know there that potter lacks skill. Witchcraft is believed to be so common that the Azande are neither surprised nor awestruck when they encounter it. Their usual response is anger.

To the Azande, witchcraft is a completely natural explanation for events. Consider the circumstances that might lead to someone being crushed by a collapsing granary. Azande territory is hot, and people seeking shade often sit under traditional-style granaries, which are raised on logs. Termites are common in Azande territory, and sometimes they destroy the supporting logs, causing a granary to collapse. Occasionally, when a granary collapses, people sitting under it are killed. Why does this happen? The Azande are well aware that the termites chew up the wood until the supports give way but to them that explanation is not enough. Why, after all, should that particular granary have collapsed at that particular moment? To skeptical observers, the only connection is coincidence in time and space. Western science does not provide any explanation for why these two chains of causation intersect. But the Azande

### EthnoProfile 10.1 | Azande

**Region** Central Africa

**Nations** Northeast Democratic Republic of the Congo, South Sudan, southeast Central African Republic

**Language** The Azande speak Zande (Pazande), an Adamawa-Ubangi language of the Niger-Congo group

**Population** 1,000,000–4,000,000 (early 2000s estimate)

**Environment** Sparsely wooded savanna

**Livelihood** Agriculture with maize, rice, and groundnuts (peanuts); cassava and sweet potatoes as main crops; hunting, fishing, and chicken raising

**Political organization** Traditionally, highly organized, tribal kingdoms; today, part of modern nation-states

**For more information** Evans-Pritchard, E.E. 1976 [1937]. Witchcraft, Oracles, and Magic among the Azande, abr. edn (Oxford: Oxford University Press).

do: witchcraft causes the termites to finish chewing up the wood at just that moment and that witchcraft must be avenged.

### Dealing with Witches

How to expose the witch? For this task, the Azande employ specific trials as **oracles**. Pre-eminent among these is the poison oracle. The poison is a strychnine-like substance imported by the Azande. The oracle 'speaks' through the effect the poison has on chickens. When witchcraft is suspected, a relative of the afflicted person will take some chickens into the bush along with a specialist in administering the poison oracle. This person will feed poison to one chicken, name a suspect, and ask the oracle to kill the chicken if this person is the witch. If the chicken dies, a second chicken will be fed poison, and the oracle will be asked to spare the chicken if the suspect just named is indeed the witch. Thus, the Azande double-check the oracle carefully; a witchcraft accusation is not made lightly.

People do not consult the oracle with a long list of names. They need only consider those who might wish them or their families ill: people who have quarrelled with them, who are unpleasant, anti-social, and whose behaviour is somehow out of line. Indeed, witches are always neighbours because neighbours are the only people who know you well enough to wish you and your family ill.

Once the oracle has identified the witch, the Azande removes the wing of the chicken and has it taken by messenger to the compound of the accused person. The messenger presents the accused witch with the chicken wing and says that he has been sent concerning the illness of so-and-so's relative. 'Almost invariably the witch replies courteously that he is unconscious of injuring anyone, that if it is true that he has injured the man in question he is very sorry, and that if it is he alone who is troubling him then he will surely recover because from the bottom of his heart he wishes him health and happiness' (Evans-Pritchard 1976 [1937]: 42). The accused then calls for a gourd of water, takes some in his mouth, and sprays it out over the wing. He says aloud, so the messenger can hear and repeat what he says, that if he is a witch he is not aware of it and that he is not intentionally causing the sick man to be ill. He addresses the witchcraft in him, asking it to become cool, and concludes by saying that he makes this appeal from his heart, not just from his lips (42).

*Figure 10.9* | **An Azande witchdoctor.**

People accused of witchcraft are usually astounded; no Azande thinks of himself or herself as a witch. However, the Azande strongly believe in witchcraft and in the oracles, and if the oracle says someone is a witch, then that person must be one. The accused witch is grateful to the family of the sick person for letting this be known. Otherwise, if the accused had been allowed to murder the victim, all the while unaware of it, the witch would surely be killed by vengeance magic. The witchcraft accusation carries a further message: the behaviour of the accused is sufficiently outside the bounds of acceptable Azande behaviour to have marked him or her as a potential witch. The accused witch, then, is being told to change his or her behaviour.

**oracles**
Invisible forces to which people address questions and whose responses they believe to be truthful.

### Patterns of Witchcraft Accusation

Compared with the stereotypes of Euro-American witchcraft—old hags dressed in black, riding on broomsticks, casting spells, causing milk to sour or people to sicken— Azande witchcraft seems quite tame. People whose impression of witchcraft comes from Western European images may believe that witchcraft and witch-hunting tear at the very fabric of society. Yet anthropological accounts such as Evans-Pritchard's suggest that practices such as witchcraft accusation can sometimes keep societies together.

Anthropologist Mary Douglas looked at the range of witchcraft accusations worldwide and discovered that they fall into two basic types (1970: xxvi–xxvii): in some cases, the witch is an evil outsider; in others, the witch is an internal enemy, either the member of a rival faction or a dangerous deviant. These different patterns of accusation perform different functions in a society. If the witch is an outsider, witchcraft accusations can strengthen in-group ties. If the witch is an internal enemy, accusations of witchcraft can weaken in-group ties; factions may have to regroup, communities may split, and the entire social hierarchy may be reordered. If the witch is a dangerous deviant, the accusation of witchcraft can be seen as an attempt to control the deviant in defence of the wider values of the community. Douglas concludes that how people understand witchcraft is based on the social relations of their society.

# Maintaining and Changing a World View

What makes a world view stable? Why is a world view rejected? These questions are related to general questions about persistence and change in human social life. Anthropologists recognize that culture change is a complex phenomenon, and they admit that they do not have all the answers.

Changes in world view must, first of all, be related to the practical everyday experiences of people in a particular society. Stable, repetitive experiences reinforce the acceptability of any traditional world view that has successfully accounted for such experiences in the past. When experiences become unpredictable, however, thinking people in any society may become painfully aware that past experiences can no longer be trusted as guides for the future, and traditional world views may be undermined (see Horton 1982: 252).

**syncretism**
The synthesis of old religious practices (or an old way of life) with new religious practices (or a new way of life) introduced from outside, often by force.

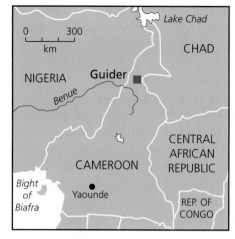

Map 10.4 | **Guider**

## Coping with Change

Drastic changes in experience lead people to create new interpretations that will help them cope with the changes. Sometimes the change is an outcome of local or regional struggles. The Protestant Reformation, for example, adapted the Christian tradition to changing social circumstances in northern Europe during the Renaissance by breaking ties to the Pope, turning Church lands over to secular authorities, allowing clergy to marry, and so forth. Protestants continued to identify themselves as Christians even though many of their religious practices had changed.

In Guider (see Map 10.4), lone rural migrants frequently abandoned old religious practices and took on urban customs and a new identity through conversion to Islam. However, the conflict between new and old need not necessarily lead to conversion. Sometimes the result is a creative synthesis of old religious practices and new ones, a process called **syncretism**. Under the pressure of Christian missionizing, Indigenous people of Central America identified some of their own pre-Christian, personalized superhuman beings with particular Catholic saints. Similarly, Africans brought to Brazil identified Catholic saints with African gods to produce the syncretistic religion Candomblé.

Anthropologists have debated the nature of syncretistic practices, noting that while some may be viewed as a way of resisting new ideas imposed from above, others may be introduced from above by powerful outsiders deliberately making room for local beliefs within their

## In Their Own Words | The Iroquois and the World's Rim

*George Hammel speculates on colour, culture, and contact among the Iroquois.*

Contact between the peoples of the New World and of the Old World had ideational consequences for both. The event of Contact, and more importantly the process of Contact, initiated the reciprocal redefinition of the mythical realities which for centuries, if not millennia, had structured New World and Old World thoughts and behaviours about the other world. Neither the event nor the process of Contact are over. For the Iroquois, dwelling beneath the Great Tree at the centre of Earth-Island, indirect knowledge of Contact at the eastern World's Rim and the indirect receipt of exotic trade goods emanating there, appear to have reified and reinvigorated the traditional ritual meanings and functions of light, bright (reflective), and white things. Not least among these were white marine shell and red, upper Great Lakes native copper, into whose meanings and functions were incorporated and assimilated analogous European trade goods of glazed ceramic, glass, and metal. This seemingly innocuous exchange of European baubles, bangles, and beads along the mid-Atlantic Coast of northeastern North America during the sixteenth century catalyzed profound changes in the ideational, socio-political, and economic subsystems of coastal and interior Native populations.

The lure of exotic and of, literally and figuratively, precious substances brought the mythical reality of the *Old* World into tangential relations with the *New* World. What were among these substances, so precious in the Old World, that lured men in small boats to the ends of the world, as known? Gold, silver, diamonds, and pearls, which had long been and still are traditional Western European material metaphors of value, not only of *economic* value but of *ideational* value as well (cf. Gombrich 1963: 12–29). Before bank books, stocks and bonds, and paper currencies, that is, paper symbols of wealth, these substances comprised tangible and conspicuous metaphors of cultural value, encoded and manifested linguistically and synesthetically within figures of speech, in clothing and adornment, and in works of art and architecture. Invested within these substances and the artifacts made from them was a millennia-old fusion of aesthetic and ideational interest and value.

Like most biological organisms, humans are phototropic:

they grow toward the light. As sentient biological organisms, humans tend toward the light, whether it be the Sun or *the Son*. As sentient biological organisms, humans understand that light is life and that light is the prerequisite to animacy and sentience. This is a fundamental and, I dare say, universal cultural axiom that has generated parallel dependent corollaries manifested cross-culturally in human thought and behaviour, linguistic and physical. Light (sources), bright (reflective), and white things are tangible metaphors for abstractions of greatest cultural value: for life itself, and for positive states of physical, social, and spiritual well-being. We should remind ourselves that the great value that Western culture places upon the Golden Rule, or upon a gem or pearl of wisdom, lies not with their economic worth but with their reflective virtues.

For millennia, in the Old World, such substances and artifacts fashioned from them have represented wealth as weal- or well-being. The Iroquois and other Northeastern Woodland Indian peoples would agree with this characterization of wealth as well-being. Among them, however, wealth as well-being is more generally appreciated as medicine: the insurance and assurance of physical, social, and spiritual well-being, individually or collectively invoked in ritual. Within ritual contexts, these concepts of well-being have traditionally constellated about white shell, and more recently about another, bright, light-reflective, white substance: a 'white metal', silver.

In the interior mid-Atlantic region at Contact, the 'diamonds of the country' were the relatively scarce and small cylindrical or barrel-shaped beads of white marine shell, which were to become recorded in contemporary documents as *sewant* (Dutch), *porcelaine* (French), and *wampumpeague*, shortened to *wampum* (English). It was Jacques Cartier in 1535, who speaking of the St Lawrence Iroquoians, established the convention of making the comparison between the Northeastern Woodland Indians' interest and desire for these seemingly inconsequential, small white (marine) shell beads and that of Western Europeans for gold, silver, diamonds, and pearls.

Among the Northern Iroquoians and the Northeastern Woodland Indians, generally, colour is a semantically organizing principle of ritual states-of-being and of ritual material culture. Three colours predominate: white, black, and red. These colours organize ritual states-of-being into three contrastive and complementary sets: social states-of-being, asocial states-of-being, and anti-social states-of-being, respectively. Ritual is the means to maintain a desired state-of-being or to transform one state-of-being into an at least temporarily more desirable state-of-being. Within ritual contexts, material culture functions to synesthetically manifest through its attribute of colour the present state-of-being of its participants and to synesthetically manifest through colour the desired state-of-being to be ritually effected. This may be the status quo or one of the other two contrastive states-of-being.

The colours white, black, and red potentially organize ritual states-of-being and ritual material culture into either triadic or dyadic contrastive–complementary sets. White social states-of-being, black asocial states-of-being, and red anti-social states-of-being form the one contrastive–complementary, triadic set; white *and* red social states-of-being in contrast to black asocial states-of-being form one dyadic opposition; and white social states-of-being in contrast to black and red anti-social states-of-being form the other. Within these ritual states-of-being, the colours white, black, and red also individually manifest varying valencies (+, 0, or −) of potency, evaluation, and activity (cf. Adams 1973; Osgood, May, and Miron 1975) depending upon the state-of-being being ritually foregrounded and the state-of-being with which it is being contrasted. For example white(ness), the colour of (day)light and thus of life itself, is the most potent colour and the most highly evaluated colour if that potency is consecrated to socially constructive purposes. However, white *and* red are both *potent* colours since they are generally identified with the sentient aspect and the animate aspect (i.e., blood) of life, respectively.

White and red are also positively evaluated colours to the extent that their (life) potency is ritually consecrated to socially constructive functions. However, since red is the most *active* or animate of the three colours, it is also bivalent: if its animacy is consecrated to socially destructive functions, it manifests anti-social states-of-being in contrast to white social states-of-(physical, social, and spiritual)being; if its animacy is consecrated to socially constructive functions, it manifests social states-of-(physical well-)being. When conjoined, white and red manifest the sentient and animate aspects of social states-of-being, respectively, and are most frequently contrasted to black states-of-being, characterized by the absence of sentience and animacy, as in states of mourning. Concepts of greatest

(life) potency, and consequently of greatest positive cultural evaluation—which are semantically identified with whiteness—are the common ideational denominators underlying the ritual functions of white shell throughout the Northeastern Woodlands. Within social states-of-being, white shell, whether freshwater or marine in origin, and regardless of its natural or manufactured form, functions as a metaphor for light and thus for life itself, particularly in its sentient aspect. White shell is a material metaphor for the biological continuity of life in general and for the biological and social continuity of human life in particular (Hamell 1986). This function and meaning of white shell underwrote the intense interest in white marine shell 'ornaments', particularly, in those small cylindrical beads called *sewant*, *porcelaine*, and *wampum*, which became after Contact the medium and the message of social exchanges between Native and Native, and Native and newcomer. Red(-painted) and/or purple ('black') wampum beads, bead strings, and bead belts were the media of socially contrastive messages.

Light, bright, and white were and still are good to think with among the Iroquois and other Northeastern Woodland Indians. This ritual function and meaning of light, bright, and white material culture, shellwork in particular, may with confidence be projected far back into prehistory, as can the contrastive–complementary functions and meanings of black and red material culture. This proposed semantics of colour, ritual, and material culture most probably accounts for the differential and deferential disposal in mortuary contexts during the Terminal Archaic and during the Early and Middle Woodland periods of white (marine) shell, white freshwater pearls, white (= transparent) rock crystal, white chalcedony, white (muscovite) mica, white free-state metals (silver, galena); red cedar, red ocher (hematite), red chalcedony, red jasper, red pipestone (catilinite), red native copper; and black charcoal, black obsidian, black chalcedony (and chert), black (biotite) mica, and black meteoric iron. I suggest that in the reporting of archaeologically recovered ritual material culture, a presentation organized by colour may be as meaningful, and perhaps more so, than its reportage by the traditional analytical categories of raw material and function.

Source: Hamell, George R. 1992. 'The Iroquois and the World's Rim: Speculations on Colour, Culture, and Contact', *American Indian Quarterly* 16, 4: 451, 455–8. Reproduced with permission from the University of Nebraska Press.

own supralocal world view. The Romans, for example, made room for local deities within their imperial pantheon, and post–Vatican II Catholicism explicitly urges non-European Catholics to worship using local cultural forms (Stewart and Shaw 1994).

When groups defend or refashion their own way of life in the face of outside encroachments, anthropologists sometimes describe their activities as **revitalization**—a deliberate, organized attempt by some members of a society to create a more satisfying culture (Wallace 1972: 75). Revitalization arises in times of crisis, most often among groups who are facing oppression and radical transformation, usually at the hands of outsiders (such as colonizing powers). Revitalization movements engage in a 'politics of religious synthesis' that produces a range of outcomes (Stewart and Shaw 1994). Sometimes syncretism is embraced; other times it is rejected in favour of nativism, a return to the old ways. Some nativistic movements expect a messiah or prophet who will bring back a lost golden age of peace, prosperity, and harmony, a process often called *revivalism*, *millenarianism*, or *messianism*.

A classic New World example of a millenarian movement was the Ghost Dance movement among Indigenous peoples on the Great Plains of the United States in the 1890s. When the buffalo were exterminated, Indigenous Plains dwellers lost their independence and were herded onto reservations by numerically superior and better-armed Euro-Americans. Out of this final crisis emerged Wovoka, a prophet who taught that the existing world would soon be destroyed and that a new crust would form on the earth. All settlers and Indigenous people who followed the settlers' ways would become buried. Those Indigenous people who abandoned the settlers' ways, led pure lives, and danced the Ghost Dance would be saved. As the new crust formed, the buffalo would return, as would all the ancestors of the believers. Together, all would lead lives of virtue and joy.

Because the world was going to change by itself, violence against the oppressors was not a necessary part of the Ghost Dance. Nevertheless, the movement frightened settlers and the US Army, who suspected an armed uprising. Those fears and suspicions led to the massacre at Wounded Knee, in which the cavalry troopers killed all the members of a Lakota (Sioux) band, principally women and children, whom they encountered off the reservation.

A revitalization movement that has enjoyed greater longevity is the syncretistic Bwiti religion of the Fang

Figure 10.10 | Fang women perform the Belebele dance during a Bwiti eremony.

in Central Africa (Figure 10.10; Map 10.1). Since the late nineteenth century, the Fang have faced three important challenges to their world view. First, the reality of 'the far away' represented by French colonialism came to challenge the reality of 'the near' and familiar. Second, the protective traditional powers of 'the below' were challenged by Christian missionaries' messages of divinity in 'the above'. Third, the pluralism of colonial life challenged the community's sense if cohesion by establishing a double standard in which the colonized were treated differently from the colonizers (Fernandez 1982: 571). Bwiti allows its members to cope with the

**revitalization**
A conscious, deliberate, and organized attempt by some members of a society to create a more satisfying culture in a time of crisis.

Map 10.5 | Kwaio

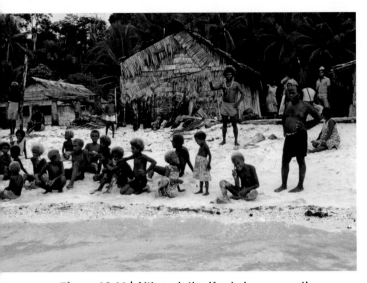

Figure 10.11 | Although the Kwaio have recently adopted some outsider practices, such as wearing manufactured clothing, they continue to adhere to many of their traditional ways.

first challenge by using the drug *eboga* to go out to the far and convert it into the near. In the second case, the Christian god of 'the above' and the traditional gods of 'the below' are both incorporated into the Bwiti pantheon. For the third, Bwiti ritual promotes among members the communal feeling of 'one-heartedness'.

Bwiti has created a world view that allows many Fang to cope with the strains of exploitation. Within Bwiti, some old metaphors (the forest, the body social, the kinship system) have been reanimated, some new ones (red and white uniforms, a path of birth and death, the world as a globe or a ball) have been created, and all have been fitted together in a satisfying way. This world has, however, closed itself off from the wider society of Gabon. Bwiti represents a kind of escape from the pressures of the outside world (566).

Nativistic movements, however, may represent resistance to, rather than escape from, the outside world, actively removing or avoiding any cultural practices associated with outsiders. One such 'anti-syncretistic' group is the Kwaio, living on the island of Malaita in the Solomon Islands (Figure 10.11; see also Map 10.5). Almost all their neighbours have converted to Christianity, and the nation of which they are a part is militantly Christian. Members of other groups wear Western-style clothing, work on plantations or in tourist hotels, attend schools, and live in cities. The Kwaio have refused all this: 'Young men carry bows and arrows; girls and women, nude except for customary ornaments, dig taro in forest gardens; valuables made of strung shell beads are exchanged at mortuary feasts; and priests sacrifice pigs to the ancestral spirits on whom prosperity and life itself depend' (Keesing 1982: 1).

## In Their Own Words | Custom and Confrontation

*In the following passage, the late Roger Keesing recorded the words of one of his Kwaio informants, Dangeabe'u, who defends Kwaio custom.*

The government has brought the ways of business, the ways of money. The people at the coast believe that's what's important and tell us we should join in. Now the government is controlling the whole world. The side of the Bible is withering away. When that's finished, the government will rule, unchallenged. It will hold all the land. All the money will go to the government to feed its power. Once everything—our lands, too—are in their hands, that will be it.

I've seen the people from other islands who have all become Christians. They knew nothing about their land. The white people have gotten their hands on their lands. The whites led

them to forget all the knowledge of their land, separated them from it. And when the people knew nothing about their land, the whites bought it from them and made their enterprises. . . .

That's close upon us too. If we all follow the side of the Bible, the government will become powerful here, too, and will take control of our land. We won't be attached to our land, as we are now, holding our connections to our past. If the government had control of our land, then if we wanted to do anything on it, we'd have to pay them. If we wanted to start a business—a store, say—we'd have to pay the government. We reject all that. We want to keep hold of our land, in the ways passed down to us.

Source: Keesing, Roger. 1992. *Custom and Confrontation: The Kwaio Struggle for Cultural Autonomy* (Chicago: University of Chicago Press), 184.

Keesing (1992) admits that he does not know exactly why the Kwaio responded to colonial influence in this way. He suspects that pre-colonial social and political differences between the Kwaio and their coastal neighbours influenced later developments. The colonial encounter was certainly relevant. In 1927, some Kwaio attacked a British patrol, killing the district officer and 13 Solomon Islands troops. The subsequent massacre of many Kwaio by a police force of other Malaitans, and their marginalization and persecution by the colonial government, contributed to Kwaio resistance.

The Kwaio maintain their old ways deliberately, in the face of alternatives; their traditional way of life is therefore lived in a modern context. 'In the course of anti-colonial struggle, *kastomu* (custom) and commitment to ancestral ways have become symbols of identity and autonomy' (Keesing 1982: 240). In the eyes of the Kwaio, the many Solomon Islanders who became Christianized and acculturated lost their cultural ties and thereby their ties to the land and to their past, becoming outsiders in their own homeland. Thus, maintaining tradition is a form of political protest. From this perspective, many contemporary anti-syncretistic movements in the world, from various religious fundamentalisms to movements for national identity and cultural autonomy, can be understood as having aims very similar to those of the Kwaio, sparked by many of the same forces.

## World Views as Instruments of Power

We have discussed the process that people use to build their world views and have noted how world views vary enormously from culture to culture. But within any particular cultural tradition, there are probably always different world views.

How does a particular picture of reality become the 'official' world view for a given culture? And once that position is achieved, how is it maintained? To be in the running for the official picture of reality, a world view must be able, however minimally, to make sense of some people's personal and social experiences. Sometimes, however, it may seem to some members of society that barely credible views of reality have triumphed over alternatives that seem far more plausible. Thus, something more than persuasive ability alone must be involved, and that something is power. As Lakoff and Johnson put it, 'People in

power get to impose their metaphors' (1980: 157). Powerless people may be unable to dislodge the official world view of their society. They can, however, refuse to accept the imposition of someone else's world view and develop an unofficial world view based on metaphors that reflect their own condition of powerlessness (Scott 1990). Such unofficial world views may even suggest appropriate action for transforming that condition.

How can metaphors, or the symbols that represent them, be used as instruments of power and control? First, a symbol can be used to refer to a self-evident truth when people in power seek to eliminate or impose certain forms of conduct. Thus, a deceased parent, whose memory must be respected, may be invoked to block some actions or to stimulate others. Holy books such as the Quran may also be used in this way. For example, a legal record from Guider indicates that a son once brought suit against his father for refusing to repay him a certain amount of money. The father claimed that he had paid. Both father and son got into an increasingly heated argument in which neither would give ground. Finally, the judge in the case asked the father to take a copy of the Quran in his hand and swear that he was telling the truth. This he did. The son, however, refused to swear on the Quran and finally admitted that he had been lying. In this case, the status of the Quran as the unquestioned word of God, which implied the power of God to punish liars, controlled the son's behaviour.

Second, a symbol may be under the direct control of a person wishing to affect the behaviour of others. Consider the role of official interpreters of religious or political ideology, such as priests or kings. Their pronouncements define the bounds of permissible behaviour. As Keesing points out:

> Senior men, in Melanesia as elsewhere in the tribal world, have depended heavily on control of *sacred knowledge* to maintain their control of earthly politics. By keeping in their hands relations with ancestors and other spirits, by commanding magical knowledge, senior men could maintain a control mediated by the supernatural. Such religious ideologies served too, by defining rules in terms of ancient spirits and by defining the nature of men and women in supernatural terms, to reinforce and maintain the roles of the sexes— and again to hide their nature. (1982: 219)

Keesing's observations remind us that knowledge, like power, is not evenly distributed throughout a society. Just as some people speak or write or carve better than others, so too do some people possess knowledge and control symbols to which others are denied access. Furthermore, this distribution of knowledge is not random: different kinds of people know different things. In some societies, what men know about their religious system is different from what women know, and what older men know may be different from what younger men know. Such discrepancies can have important consequences. Keesing suggested that men's control over women and older men's control over younger men are based on differential access to knowledge (14). It is not just that these different kinds of people know different things; rather, the different things they know (and don't know) enable them (or force them) to remain in the positions they hold in the society.

## Religion and Secularism

The European Enlightenment gave birth to a new world view that has come to be called **secularism**, and the spread of this world view has had repercussions across the globe. The development of secular ideas and practices profoundly transformed the religious and political institutions that had dominated European society in the Middle Ages. Earlier generations of anthropologists took secularism for granted as the expected outcome of cultural evolution. More recently, however, anthropologists have been led to reconsider the nature of both the Enlightenment and secularism, prompted most sharply by resistance to the secular institutions of Western nation-states. Strong resistance has come from some immigrant groups living within those states as well as some groups in non-Western nation-states who insist that citizenship and religious identity belong together.

Perhaps the most difficult struggles to adapt to life in secular Western nation-states have been those of some Muslim groups. The distinction between what the liberal democratic state expects and what some Muslims want has recently been explored by anthropologist Talal Asad. His efforts to develop an 'anthropology of secularism' highlight the ways in which notions

**secularism**
The separation of religion and state, including a notion of secular citizenship that owes much to the notion of individual agency developed in Protestant theology.

of the secular were shaped in the course of European history, particularly by the Protestant Reformation of Christianity, the subsequent wars of religion in the sixteenth and early seventeenth centuries, and the Enlightenment and the French Revolution of the eighteenth century. Secularism is usually defined as the separation of religion and state, and is commonly understood as the Enlightenment solution to the bloody and irresolvable wars of religion that followed the Reformation. But Asad's account shows that European secularism presupposed a specific post-Reformation concept of 'religion' and a very specific post-Enlightenment concept of 'the state', as well as a notion of secular citizenship that owes much to the notion of individual agency developed in Protestant theology. 'The secular', he argues, 'is a concept that brings together certain behaviours, knowledges, and sensibilities in modern life' (2003: 25).

The particularities of modern secularism may be clarified if we return to the distinction made in Chapter 8 between orthodoxy and orthopraxy. Religious disputes in the Reformation and the wars of religion concerned questions of doctrinal *orthodoxy*—that is, correct religious beliefs. In European secularism, thus, *religion* is defined primarily in terms of the beliefs to which its adherents are committed. Similarly, the secular *state* is always understood to be the modern nation-state within a capitalist economy. It is from these understandings of *religion* and *state* that the Enlightenment concept of *citizenship* develops. Secular citizenship, Asad explains, is supposed to 'transcend the different identities built on class, gender, and religion, replacing conflicting perspectives by unifying experience. In a sense, this transcendent mediation *is* secularism' (2003: 5). Secular citizens are first and foremost individuals unencumbered by ties to other social groups who possess *within themselves* the motivation to formulate goals, who have the resources to initiate action to pursue those goals, and who are responsible for the consequences of their actions. This concept of agency, absolutely crucial to the successful functioning of democratic government and the capitalist market, was itself the product of Protestant theology. In the religious context, independent, self-motivating individuals were responsible before God; in their role as citizens of a liberal secular state, they are individually responsible before the law.

Thus, secularism as a political doctrine clearly emerged as a response to specific religious, political, and economic developments in early modern Europe. Secularism depends, for example, on the notion that a 'worldly' domain of social life exists that is distinct from a realm in which religion holds sway. In Christian Europe, this domain was recognized when proponents of what would become 'science', such as Francis Bacon and Robert Boyle, successfully argued that the 'supernatural', spiritual realm of God was separate and distinct from the 'natural', material world of lifeless, inert matter (Keller 1997). This distinction between supernatural and natural worlds 'signals the construction of a secular space that begins to emerge in early modernity' (Asad 2003: 27). That secular space would be the ground to which the modern nation-state would lay claim.

Religion and state remained entangled after the wars of religion, however, since 'religious freedom' was left in the hands of the states themselves. That is, citizens were to profess the faith of their princes, and if their princes changed allegiance, the allegiance of citizens was to follow. But in every state, this arrangement created religious minorities of 'dissenters' whose rights as citizens were regularly curtailed. Protest against these inequalities fuelled the secular democratic political theory of the Enlightenment, embodied in the 'Declaration of the Rights of Man and the Citizen' and secured by the French Revolution. Now religious affiliation was a matter of individual conscience and could not be imposed by the state. But at the time, as Asad notes, 'the decisive movements that helped to break the allegiance of church and state seem to have been religious . . . aimed at securing the freedom of Christ's church from the constraints of earthly power' (174). One consequence of this change 'was the eventual emergence of "minority rights". But this consequence contained a paradox. Religious minorities in a secular state were at once equal to other citizens [and] . . . unequal to the majority, requiring special protection' (174).

Secularism is 'not a simple matter of absence of "religion" in the public life of the modern nation-state. For even in modern secular countries the place of religion varies' (Asad 2003: 5–6). But Asad's analysis suggests that adaptation to life in a liberal secular state is likely to be difficult and painful for those whose religious commitments are rooted primarily in forms of religious *orthopraxy*—correct practice. Many traditions, he notes,

> attribute to the living human body the potential to be shaped (the power to shape itself) for good or ill. . . . The living body's materiality is regarded as an essential means for cultivating what such

traditions define as virtuous conduct and for discouraging what they consider as vice. The role of fear and hope, of felicity and pain, is central to such practices. . . . [The] more one exercises a virtue the easier it becomes; . . . the more one gives into vice, the harder it is to act virtuously. (89–90)

Islamic religious traditions are rooted in such orthopraxy, and cultivation of correct practice depends upon one's embeddedness within a community of like-minded practitioners. When successful, such orthopraxy is understood to produce 'the virtue of faithfulness, [which is] an unquestioning habit of obedience'. Faithfulness is 'a disposition that has to be cultivated like any other and that links one to others who are faithful, through mutual trust and responsibility' (90). Religious orthopraxy of this kind can only be sustained by faithful practitioners whose entire way of life is informed by, and acts to reinforce, these unquestioning habits of obedience. If this is the case, then such forms of orthopraxy would appear to be incompatible with secularism.

> For many Muslim minorities (though by no means all) being Muslim is more than simply belonging to an individual faith whose private integrity needs to be publicly respected by the force of law and being able to participate in the public domain as equal citizens. It is more than the cultural identity recognized by the liberal democratic state. It is being able to live as autonomous individuals in a collective life that extends beyond national borders. (180)

World views represent comprehensive ideas about the structure of the world and the place of one's own group, or one's own self, within that world. The ethnographic record offers a broad array of different world views, each testifying to the imaginative, meaning-making cultural capacity of humans. These models of the world, moreover, do not exist apart from everyday social practices; on the contrary, they are heavily implicated in our interactions with others. And when those interactions lead to crisis, humans respond by seeking ways to make the crisis appear meaningful and therefore manageable. We are meaning-making, meaning-using, meaning-dependent organisms, and nowhere is this clearer than when a meaningful way of life is under assault.

# Key Terms

computer metaphor   244

key metaphors   245

magic   252

metaphor   242

metaphorical entailments   242

metaphorical predicate   242

metaphorical subject   242

metonymy   242

oracles   253

organic metaphor   245

religion   246

revitalization   257

secularism   260

societal metaphor   244

syncretism   254

technological metaphor   245

world view   241

# Chapter Summary

1. People attempting to account for their experiences make use of shared cultural assumptions about how the world works. The encompassing pictures of reality that result are called *world views*. Metaphors are valuable tools for constructing world views by directing attention to certain aspects of experience and downplaying or ignoring others.

2. The distinction between metonymy and metaphor may be said to correspond to the distinction between semantic linkages viewed as literal or true and semantic linkages viewed as hypothetical or false. If the relationships asserted in metaphors fit the rest of our experience, they may be converted into accepted relationships of metonymy.

3. As people create apt metaphors that are transformed into metonymic structures of their world view, they mark the resulting semantic domains by symbols. Symbols that sum up an entire semantic domain are called *summarizing symbols*. *Elaborating symbols*, in contrast, are analytic and allow people to sort out complex and undifferentiated feelings and ideas.

4. Differences in world views derive from differences in experience that people try to explain by means of metaphor. People use at least three kinds of key metaphors as foundations for particular world views: societal metaphors, organic metaphors, and technological metaphors.

5. Anthropological studies of religion tend to focus on the social institutions and meaningful processes with which it is associated. Followers of religions address personalized forces symbolically and expect them to respond. Maintaining contact with cosmic forces is very complex,

and societies have complex social practices designed to ensure that this is done properly. Two important kinds of religious specialists are shamans and priests.

6. Many anthropologists have attempted to display the rich, coherent tapestries of symbols, rituals, and everyday practices that make up particular world views, noting the high degree to which world views vary from one another. They have also studied the ways in which drastic changes in peoples' experiences lead them to create new meanings to explain the changes and to cope with them. This can be accomplished through the elaboration of the old system to fit changing times, conversion to a new world view, syncretism, revitalization, or resistance.

7. A single society may have members who subscribe to different world views. Knowledge, like power, is not evenly distributed throughout a society. More powerful individuals and groups often impose their preferred key metaphors on the rest of society. Those without power can resist this imposition by creating their own contrasting metaphors and constructing alternative world views.

8. Whereas earlier generations of anthropologists took secularism for granted as the expected outcome of cultural evolution, some contemporary anthropologists have begun to re-assess the relationship between religion and secularism as a product of the European Enlightenment. Today, an important issue remains the extent to which life in a liberal secular state is likely to be difficult and painful for those whose religious practices do not recognize any domain of life in which religious considerations do not hold sway.

# Critical Thinking Questions

1. How do *summarizing symbols* and *elaborating symbols* differ? Can you find examples from a Canadian context?

2. Key metaphors that have served as the foundation of world views in different societies include societal, organic, and technological metaphors. What is an example of each type of key metaphor? What types of metaphorical subjects and predicates are involved?

3. Consider the Canadian metaphor of the cultural mosaic. If we 'follow the metaphor', what will we find as the Canadian world view? How might this world view compare to the dominant world view in other countries?

4. Drastic changes in experience lead people to create new interpretations that will help them cope with the changes. How can metaphors, or the symbols that represent them, be used as instruments of power and control in such times?

5. How do the pronouncements of official interpreters of religious or political ideologies define the bounds of permissible behaviour?

6. Keesing observes that some people possess knowledge and control symbols to which others are denied access and different kinds of people know different things. How can such non-random distribution of knowledge affect key metaphors in a society?

# Suggested Readings

Bowen, John. 2002. *Religions in Practice: An Approach to the Anthropology of Religion*, 2nd edn (Needham Heights, MA: Allyn & Bacon). A twenty-first century introduction to the anthropology of religion focussing on religious practice and interpretation, with a very wide range of case studies.

Evans-Pritchard, E.E. 1976 [1937]. *Witchcraft, Oracles, and Magic among the Azande*, abr. edn (Oxford: Oxford University Press). An immensely influential and very readable anthropological classic.

Fernandez, James. 1982. *Bwiti: An Ethnography of the Religious Imagination in Africa* (Princeton: Princeton University Press). A tremendously rewarding and demanding study of a religious movement and its associated rituals in context.

Frazer, James George. 2006 [1922]. *The Golden Bough* (NuVision Publications, llc), available online in various formats. An example of the 'armchair' anthropology of the nineteenth century, this book, nonetheless, developed the theoretical background used for the anthropological analysis of religion.

Keesing, Roger. 1983. *'Elota's Story* (New York: Holt, Rinehart, & Winston). The autobiography of a Kwaio Big Man with interpretative material by Keesing. First-rate, very readable, and involving. We come to know 'Elota by the end of the book.

———. 1992. *Custom and Confrontation: The Kwaio Struggle for Cultural Autonomy* (New York: Columbia University Press).

Based on thirty years of research, Keesing's final book provides a clear, readable, and committed discussion of Kwaio resistance.

Klass, Morton. 1995. *Ordered Universes: Approaches to the Anthropology of Religion* (Boulder, CO: Westview Press). A brief introduction to the issues involved in the anthropological study of religion, with an emphasis on an operational definition of religion.

Lambek, Michael. 2008. *A Reader in the Anthropology of Religion*, 2nd edn (Malden, MA: Blackwell). An excellent collection of classic and contemporary readings in the anthropology of religion.

Malinowski, Bronislaw. 1948 [1926]. *Magic, Science, and Religion, and other Essays* (New York: Doubleday Anchor), excerpt available at www.adolphus.nl/xcrpts/xcmalinow.html. The essays in this book cover many aspects of Malinowski's fieldwork in the Trobriand Islands and subsequently in Africa. His lifelong interest in the ideational life of the people he worked with is evident in this book.

Myerhoff, Barbara. 1974. *Peyote Hunt* (Ithaca, NY: Cornell University Press). A remarkable account of the world view and sacred journey of the Huichol Indians of Mexico. This work is accessible, very well written, and theoretically sophisticated.

Robidoux, Michael A. 2002. 'Imagining a Canadian Identity through Sport: A Historical Interpretation of Lacrosse and Hockey', *The Journal of American Folklore* 15, 456: 209–25. Do we have a key metaphor as a country based on the game of hockey? Here, we can examine this in a historical perspective.

# Related Websites

CBC Digital Archives http://archives.cbc.ca/politics/rights_freedoms/clips/3302

Human Rights Watch www.hrw.org/en/news/2004/02/26/france-headscarf-ban-violates-religious-freedom

National Gallery of Canada on Norval Morrisseau www.gallery.ca/en/about/379.php

Semiotics for Beginners www.aber.ac.uk/media/Documents/S4B/sem07.html

Shamans www.angelfire.com/electronic/awakening101/not_shamans.html

Winnipeg Art Gallery on Inuit Art http://wag.ca/art/inuit

Wounded Knee Museum www.woundedkneemuseum.org/main_menu.html

**Human beings have used their cultural creativity, together with political and economic resources, to create imagined communities that now encompass the entire world.** These communities have complex hierarchical forms of social organization. In the following chapters, we look at some of the most significant ways in which social inequality has been institutionalized, and we turn to the rise of global forms of inequality, particularly as they are associated with European colonial empires and their aftermath. Finally, we examine the work of those anthropologists who have tried to do more than record and analyze contemporary social change and who have taken on the task of applying anthropological information to the solution of contemporary human social problems.

# 11 | Organization and Power

## Chapter Outline

## Learning Objectives

By the end of Chapter 11, you will be able to

- consider that social organization refers to the patterning of human interdependence,
- question why the complexities of human social relations can never be reduced to a single cause,
- understand power as a transformative capacity—at times an independent entity—that is exercised by both coercive and persuasive means,

- distinguish coercive domination from hegemony,
- appreciate the power of the imagination for investing the world with meaning,
- recognize how people bargain for reality,
- see how history can be a prototype for action, and
- think about the power of negotiating the meaning of history and tradition.

*Villagers of the Turkana tribe in northern Kenya hold a crisis meeting under a tree to discuss the drought and lack of food. Traditional peoples living in modern nation-states often struggle to hold on to their traditional social orders and power structures as they face increasing political marginalization.*

In 1992, following twelve years of civil war and two years of intensive negotiation, representatives of the government of El Salvador and of the Salvadorian guerrilla movement known as the Farabundo Martí National Liberation Front (FMLN) signed a peace accord. The civil war had cost over 75,000 lives and had turned a million Salvadorians into refugees. It was one of the bloodiest insurrections in twentieth-century Latin America. How could so many years of fierce fighting end at the negotiator's table?

The roots of the conflict go back to the nineteenth century, when a tiny elite of Salvadorian landowners managed to monopolize 60 per cent of the land in order to raise coffee for export. The result was one of the most highly polarized class structures in all of Latin America. Ninety-eight per cent of the citizens were forced to survive on plots too small to support them, to live as tenant farmers or labourers on land they did not own, or to become landless migrants. When the coffee market crashed during the depression of the 1930s, the majority on the bottom rebelled against their exploitation, and the Salvadorian army crushed them in a brutal massacre known as *la matanza* ('the massacre').

During the Cold War between the United States and the Soviet Union that began in the late 1940s, even comparatively mild efforts to reform the system were repressed. After 1958, the US government interpreted challenges to the Salvadorian government as signs that El Salvador might be vulnerable to a Cuban-style communist revolution and viewed Salvadorian repression of reformers and rebels as a fight against the spread of communism, an explanation the Salvadorian government willingly endorsed. By the late 1970s, convinced that peaceful social change would never occur, political moderates in El Salvador swelled the ranks of five guerrilla groups that united to form the FMLN. The government response in the 1980s was as brutal as it had been in the 1930s and included a new *matanza* in the peasant village of El Mozote in which over two hundred men, women, and children were massacred for their supposed collaboration with the guerrillas (Danner 1994).

By 1990, Salvadorian society was still polarized, but the prospect of endless war caused Salvadorians on both sides to rethink their positions. Members of the National Republican Alliance party (ARENA) had won national elections in 1989 and seemed less hostile to democracy, and their elite supporters had become convinced that continued fighting would only hurt their business interests. The United States was also tiring of the war and could no longer ignore highly publicized human rights violations committed by the Salvadorian government. Furthermore, the notion that supporting the Salvadorian government was stemming the spread of communism lost its force following the collapse of communism in eastern Europe. At the same time, Salvadorian guerrillas concluded that military victory offered no permanent guarantees when the Sandinistas in neighbouring Nicaragua, who had won their revolution a decade earlier, were voted out of office. Led by guerrilla leaders including Rubén Zamora, who had long favoured a negotiated settlement, the FMLN eventually agreed to meet their enemies at the peace table.

What drives people to take up arms against powerful, well-armed government forces? What convinces battle-hardened fighters, who believe that their cause is just, to lay down their arms and negotiate when they have no certainty of success? Historian Peter Winn observes that the 1992 UN-brokered accord in El Salvador 'was a political compromise that allowed both sides to claim victory while leaving the future in doubt' (1992: 535). Not all Salvadorians supported the negotiated settlement, and sporadic violence directed against some guerrillas-turned-politicians after 1992 threatened the fragile peace it brought about. In May of 1994, however, the first national elections held since the signing of the peace accord were peaceful. The ARENA presidential candidate, Armando Calderon Sol, won two-thirds of the vote against the left coalition whose candidate, Rubén Zamora, won one-third of the vote. By late 1996, the FMLN was reflecting on the experiences of its first legislative session and planning on making alliances with other parties for future elections.

To be sure, the absence of violence at one moment of political crisis does not mean that violence will not be used later. The UN accord did not end economic and political inequality in El Salvador. And the damage caused by various natural disasters over the past two decades, most notably Hurricane Mitch in 1998 and a series of

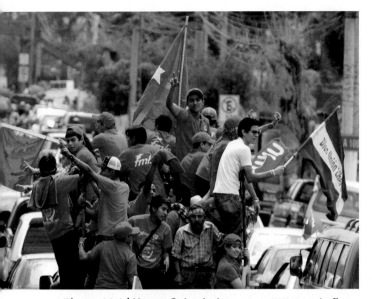

*Figure 11.1* | **Young Salvadorians wave FMLN party flags in a non-violent show of support as they ride through downtown San Salvador in 2009.**

powerful earthquakes in 2001, have only added to these continuing woes. But the political settlement of 1992 has held (Figure 11.1), and the mere fact that violence is not automatic suggests that even the most thoroughgoing systems of political oppression have points of vulnerability and that the exercise of power, even in a highly stratified society, is more complicated than it may appear.

There are always choices to be made about how a society is to be organized or how that organization may be changed. Who has the power to make and enforce these choices? Where does that power come from? What forms can power take? To answer these questions, this chapter focusses on social organization and the power that human beings have to produce, reproduce, or change that organization.

**social organization**
The patterning of human interdependence in a given society through the actions and decisions of its members.

# Varieties of Social Organization

We have already described, in Chapter 3, the variety of forms of human society and some attempts by anthropologists to analyze that variation. Lewis Henry Morgan

urged anthropologists to pay close attention to what he called the *arts of subsistence*. But he ran into difficulties when he observed significant differences in ways of life that were *not* connected with significant differences in ways of making a living. In terms of Morgan's scheme of 'ethnical stages', for example, both barbarians and civilized peoples relied on farming and herding, and in many cases their technologies were quite similar. What did distinguish them were differences in who did what, how it was done, and for whom. That is, they differed from one another in terms of **social organization**.

# The Search for the Laws of Social Organization

Even before the birth of the social sciences, Western thinkers searched for the inflexible laws of society that would explain differences in social organization in a non-arbitrary way. Biological determinists look for biological processes operating deeply within human beings forcing them to act in some ways and forbidding them to act in other ways. Other thinkers explain similarities and differences in social organization as adaptations to particular ecological conditions. In the nineteenth century, unilineal evolutionists such as Lewis Henry Morgan and Karl Marx believed that the laws of society are rooted in the dynamics of history and work themselves out over time for each human group. Although Marxist analysis still has its adherents, the use of the unilineal evolutionary approach is now seen as somewhat counterproductive to understanding the diversity of historical realities manifest in all cultures.

## The Arbitrariness of Social Organization

Perhaps the most important and controversial contribution of anthropology to the debate about laws of social organization is the argument that social relations in any society are ultimately arbitrary. This does not mean that societies are free to do or be whatever they like; rather, there is no way to reduce the complexities of human societies to a single underlying cause.

For example, the demonstrated adaptive flexibility of the human brain and body would be impossible if our behaviour were under rigid genetic control. Environmental determinism is implausible because, historically speaking, no society has ever been left on its own long enough

Map 11.1 | Somalis (Northern)

for so-called environmental pressures to exert their forces without outside human interference. European colonial conquest vividly demonstrated how the most delicately balanced societal adaptation to a given environment can be totally disrupted, if not destroyed, when outsiders arrive with plans of their own and the power to enforce them. Yet even if societies could be isolated from one another and left to work out their own destinies in their own environments, it is unlikely that identical societies would develop in identical environments or in identical step-by-step sequences as Morgan argued. I.M. Lewis points out, for example, that the northern Somalis and the Boran Galla live next to each other in semi-arid scrubland (see Map 11.1) and even herd the same kinds of animals (1967: 166ff.). Despite these similarities, the Somalis and the Boran are quite different in social structure: the Boran engage in much less fighting and feuding than the Somalis; Boran families split up to take care of the animals, whereas Somali families do not; and lineage organization is less significant among the Boran.

## The Power to Act

Human beings actively work to reshape the environments in which they live to suit themselves. Because the resources available in any environment can be used to sustain more than one way of life, however, human beings must choose which aspects of the material world to depend on. Human choice is equally important in the domain of social organization.

Some archaeologists suggest, for example, that population growth is a constant aspect of the human condition that determines forms of social organization. Marshall Sahlins (1976b: 13) reminds us, however, that population pressure determines nothing more than the number of people that can be supported when the environment is used in a particular way. Members of a society can respond to that pressure in various ways: they can try to get along on less, intensify food production by inventing new technologies, reduce their numbers by inventing new social practices (infanticide or forms of birth control), or migrate. Indeed, the manner in which a group might choose to implement any of these options is equally undetermined by population pressure. Which members of the group will have to do with less? Which members will control technological innovation? Who will be expected to migrate? And will the ultimate decision be imposed by force or voluntarily adopted? Population pressure alone cannot determine the answer to any of these questions.

The ability to choose implies the ability to transform a given situation. Thus, the ability to choose implies **power**, which we can understand broadly as 'transformative capacity' (Giddens 1979: 88). When the choice affects an entire social group, we speak of *social power*. In any social situation, we all have some degree of social power, although some people have more influence than do others. When one group is officially recognized as having more social power than any other group has, we speak of *political power*. VeneKlasen and Miller (2002) note three levels of political power: the visible, the hidden, and the invisible. On the visible level are the 'definable aspects of political power—the formal rules, structures, authorities, institutions, and procedures of decision-making' (47). Individuals who are not part of the dominant governing group can observe the operations of visible power, and they can assert their social power in support of or in resistance to visible political decisions. Hidden power is exerted when a group with a great deal of social power discreetly influences the decisions that are made on the visible level, often with negative consequences for groups and individuals with less social power (47–8). Invisible power is 'the most insidious of the three': it is embedded in cultural norms and makes certain issues, interests, and

**power**
Transformative capacity; the ability to transform a given situation.

problems invisible by shaping 'people's beliefs, sense of self, and acceptance of their own superiority or inferiority' (48). This form of power is what keeps certain minorities from protesting when they are treated as less than equal to others.

When thinking about how political power impacts social organization, we can also consider Eric Wolf's concept of *structural power* (introduced in Chapter 3). Structural power organizes social settings themselves and controls the allocation of social labour. Uncovering the patterns of structural power requires paying attention to the large-scale and increasingly global division of labour among regions and social groups, the unequal relations between these regions and groups, and the way these relations are maintained or modified over time. The way in which clothing for sale in wealthy nations is manufactured in countries with cheap labour forces—for example, factory workers in Indonesia, El Salvador, Romania, or China make clothing for markets in Canada, Europe, the United States, and Japan—is an example of structural power. People are hired to work long hours for low wages in unpleasant conditions to make clothing that they cannot afford to buy, even if it were available for sale in the communities where they live.

> **political anthropology**
> The study of social power in human society.

The study of social and political power in human society is the domain of **political anthropology**. In a recent overview, Joan Vincent has argued that political anthropology continues to be vital because it involves a complex interplay between ethnographic fieldwork, political theory, and critical reflection on political theory (2002: 1). Vincent divides the history of political anthropology into three phases. The first phase, from 1851 to 1939, she considers the 'formative' era in which basic orientations and some of the earliest anthropological commentaries on political matters were produced. The second phase, from 1942 to about 1971, is the 'classic' era in the field; it developed under conditions of the post–World War II British Empire through the period of decolonization in the 1950s and 1960s. This phase is most closely associated with the flourishing of British social anthropology rooted in structural-functionalist theory, and it produced well-known works by such eminent figures as E.E. Evans-Pritchard, Max Gluckman, Fredrik Barth, and Edmund Leach. Topics of investigation during this period were also the 'classic' topics of

political anthropology: classifying pre-industrial political systems and attempting to reconstruct their evolution, displaying the characteristic features of different kinds of pre-industrial political systems and demonstrating how these functioned to produce political order, and studying local processes of political strategizing by individuals in non-Western societies (see, e.g., Lewellen 1983).

Decolonization drew attention to emerging national-level politics in new states and the effects of 'modernization' on the 'traditional' political structures that had formerly been the focus of anthropological investigation. But the turbulent politics of the 1960s and early 1970s called into question not only received social forms but also received forms of anthropological scholarship. Beginning in the 1960s, political anthropologists developed new ways of thinking about political issues and new theoretical orientations to guide them, inaugurating in the 1970s and 1980s a third phase in which political anthropology posed broader questions about power and inequality (Vincent 2002: 3). Under conditions of globalization, anthropologists interested in studying power have joined forces with scholars in other disciplines who share their concerns and have adopted ideas from influential political thinkers such as Antonio Gramsci and Michel Foucault to help them explain how power shapes the lives of those they describe in their ethnographies.

The cross-cultural study of social power reveals a paradox of the human condition. On one hand, open cultural creativity allows humans to imagine worlds of pure possibility; on the other hand, we all live in material circumstances that make many of those possibilities profoundly unrealistic. We can imagine many different ways to organize ourselves into groups, but, as Marx claims, the past weighs like a nightmare on the brain of the living—and the opportunity to remake social organization is ordinarily quite limited. Therefore, we will look closely at the ways in which the material circumstances of everyday life generate fields of power that channel and inhibit agency and cultural creativity—and how human beings can sometimes creatively exercise power and agency in order to evade or subvert those restrictions.

## The Role of the State

In the beginning, political anthropologists were strongly influenced by other Western thinkers who had investigated the same topics. Many of these earlier thinkers had assumed that the state was the prototype of 'civilized' social power. The absence of a state, therefore, had to represent anarchy and disorder—what English philosopher Thomas Hobbes (1588–1679) called the 'war of all against all'. Although the state often perpetrated injustice or exploitation as a side effect of its monopoly of force, this could be viewed as a necessary price for social order.

Early anthropologists such as Lewis Henry Morgan, however, showed that kinship institutions organized social life in societies without states. A later generation of political anthropologists showed how different kinship institutions distribute power among their members and how non-kin institutions, such as secret societies, sometimes carry out important political roles. They were able to show repeatedly that societies without states can reach and carry out decisions affecting the entire social group by means of orderly traditional processes. More recently, Feinman et al. (2000) have proposed a network–corporate/hierarchical–egalitarian matrix (see Figure 11.2) that applies to power organization and application in all societies regardless of their complexity. This approach

expands on traditional evolutionary models through the recognition that an unequal distribution and ostentatious display of wealth does not always correlate tightly with the concentration of power or proscribed inheritance rules. It also recognizes a wide range of power-wielding strategies, which in themselves have marked organizational and integrative implications. (2000: 453)

(Note Gary Feinman et al.'s discussion of political hierarchies and organization within societies in the 'In Their Own Words' box, below.)

## Coercion: With and without Traditional State Institutions

The traditional Western prototype of power in human social relations is based on physical coercion. A typical 'natural' manifestation might be a fist fight. This prototype is an exceedingly pessimistic, even cynical, view of human nature. It suggests that co-operative social living is not natural for humans, as innate instincts drive us

## In Their Own Words | Political Hierarchies and Organizational Strategies in the Puebloan Southwest

*Gary Feinman and his colleagues have been working on alternative ways to explain organization within societies. And although this example comes from researchers investigating ancient Puebloan societies, it is informed by ethnography of several contemporary peoples of the southwest US. Thus in attempting to find explanations for the past, they have given us insight for today.*

'The network strategy of political action is associated with heavily personalized or centralized forms of leadership. Wealth is concentrated in the hands of a few, who use their network of personal connections to enhance and expand their individualized power and authority. The network strategy broadly corresponds to descriptions of accumulators (Hayden 1990), aggrandizers (Clarke and Blake 1994), strivers (Maschner 1995), and entrepreneurial elites (Hayden 1995), which are well entrenched in Western leader-centric ideas about power and individualism. In

contrast, the corporate strategy bears certain similarities to Johnson's sequential hierarchies and Saitta's communal mode and adheres closely to descriptions of Renfrew's (1974) group-oriented chiefdoms and Lehman's (1969) concept of systemic power. In corporate organizations, economic resources are more dispersed, leadership is less personalized, and ostentatious displays and individual aggrandizement are less apt to be found. Instead, communal ritual, public construction, large co-operative labour tasks, shared power, social segments that are woven together through broad integrative ritual and ideological means, and suppressed economic differentiation are emphasized. . . . Corporate–network strategies of political action represent a continuous comparative dimension. We stress that these strategies are not an explicit substitute for the familiar dimensions of hierarchical complexity. Instead, corporate–network strategies are an orthogonal comparative dimension to that of hierarchies [see Figure 11.2]. In other

**Table 11.1 | Tendencies of Corporate–Network Modes**

| Network | Corporate |
|---------|-----------|
| Concentrated wealth | More even wealth distribution |
| Individual power | Shared power arrangements |
| Ostentatious consumption | More balanced accumulation |
| Prestige goods | Control of knowledge, cognitive codes |
| Patron/client factions | Corporate labour systems |
| Attached specialization | Emphasis on food production |
| Wealth finance | Staple finance |
| Princely burials | Monumental ritual spaces |
| Lineal kinship systems | Segmental organization |
| Power inherited through personal glorification | Power embedded in group association/affiliation |
| Ostentatious elite adornment | Symbols of office |
| Personal glorification | Broad concerns with fertility, rain |

words, corporate–network tendencies may be found in political organizations with little hierarchical development or in those characterized by complex bureaucracies with multiple levels of decision-making. . . . As a consequence, we propose that there are at least two important comparative dimensions (corporate–network and hierarchical complexity) relevant to explaining long-term change and variation.

**Figure 11.2 | Two comparative dimensions for the examination of social organization.**

Source: Feinman, Gary M., et al. 2000. 'Political Hierarchies and Organization Strategies in the Pueboan Southwest', *American Antiquity* 65, 3: 453–4. Reproduced by permission of the Society for American Archaeology.

toward **free agency**. By extension, political activity is competition between individual free agents over political control. When free agents make decisions, no larger groups, no historical obligations, and no collective beliefs can or ought to stand in their way. In this view, cultural evolution took a giant leap forward when our ancestors first realized that sticks and stones could be used as weapons, not only against non-human predators but especially against human enemies, and human history is a chronicle of the production of better and better weapons. Thus the civilizations we are so proud of have been born and sustained in violence.

> **free agency**
> The freedom of self-contained individuals to pursue their own interests above everything else and to challenge one another for dominance.

Even in stateless societies of the past, coercion played a role in maintaining control. While there was no central political power, other institutions functioned to punish those who deviated from cultural norms. Members of such societies did not fear the king or the police but rather the ancestors, witchcraft, or the lineage elders. Power was still physical coercion, with co-operation resulting largely from the fear of punishment.

In the global systems of today, the violence of power-seeking states—states bent on acquiring control over new territories and resources—impinges on the lives of those who traditionally lived in what were essentially stateless societies. (Note John Wagner's discussion in the 'In Their Own Words' box, below.) Additionally, when political and institutional coercion come into play in an atmosphere of ethnic, racial, religious, and economic power struggles, the Darfurs of the world emerge (Figure 11.3). Nothing can focus our understanding of these power struggles more than the personal accounts of those who have lived through such violence (see, e.g., Bashir 2008).

## Domination and Hegemony

Our reasons for accepting social power structures are often ambiguous. Do we submit to institutionalized power because we have been coerced and fear punishment? Or do we submit because we believe that the power structures in our society are legitimate given our understandings about the way the world works? What leads people to accept coercion by others as legitimate (Figure 11.6)?

Karl Marx argued that rulers consolidate their power by successfully persuading their subjects to accept a ruling-class ideology that portrays their domination as legitimate: that is, dominated groups suffer from *false consciousness*. However, the concept of false consciousness is problematic since it views people as passive and incapable of withstanding ideological indoctrination.

*Figure 11.3* | **The people of regions such as Darfur suffer when power struggles erupt in violence. People displaced by armed conflicts are often forced to live in refugee camps, where they have few resources and little power to improve their situation.**

More promising was the approach taken by Antonio Gramsci (1971). Writing in the 1930s, Gramsci pointed out that coercive rule—what he called **domination**—is expensive and unstable. Rulers do better if they

---

*In Their Own Words* | **Water as Commodity in the Okanagan Valley of British Columbia**

*John Wagner of the University of British Columbia Okanagan works in Papua New Guinea and the Okanagan in Canada. His research interest could be broadly described as environmental but, more specifically, he focusses on water and the consequences of its commodification.*

Conflict is a normal and inevitable part of life in all societies but wars involving the loss of thousands or even millions of human lives are not. Why do human beings go to war? Many recent and ongoing civil wars such as those in Rwanda, Sudan, or the former Yugoslavia are described in the media as either *ethnic* or *religious* in nature. In fact, the causes of war are always more complex than these simplistic explanations indicate and *competition over resources* is almost always a significant, if not a determining, factor. An increasing number of resource conflicts today are also global in scale, an outcome of the increasingly integrated nature of

the world economy. Many analysts including Michael T. Klare (2001), author of *Resource Wars: The New Landscape of Global Conflict*, have proposed that water may well replace oil as the chief source of armed conflict in the twenty-first century.

The economic, military, and technological control of water has, in fact, been essential to the emergence of state-level human societies since they first occurred several thousands of years ago in Mesopotamia, Egypt, China, India, and the Americas. These *hydraulic societies*, as they are often called, typically acquired their economic strength through construction of large irrigation systems that facilitated greater agricultural productivity, food surpluses, and thus the capacity to maintain professional armies and bureaucracies.

As human demands on freshwater resources grow, and clean water in particular becomes an increasingly scarce resource, armed conflicts and other less immediately destructive forms of conflict are likely to become more frequent. Intensive commoditization of water under these conditions can worsen the divide between rich and poor, leaving the poor of many countries without sufficient access to clean water for even their most basic needs. Over the past few decades bottled water has become a billion dollar/year industry, water utility services are being privatized in both affluent and less developed nations, and bulk water transfers are occurring on a massive scale.

The Okanagan Valley of British Columbia illustrates another way in which water is being commoditized within today's global marketplace. Home originally to the *Syilx*, an Indigenous hunting/gathering society, this arid and mountainous region was settled by Europeans in the late nineteenth and early twentieth centuries. Irrigation systems were constructed by land development companies to carry water from upland reservoirs to subdivided lots on the valley bottom. Once irrigated, those lands were ideally suited to the intensive cultivation of tree fruits. A family-farm orchard industry thus emerged and became a dominant feature of Okanagan culture and landscape [Figure 11.4]. That economy is being displaced today, however, by an economy based on the region's growing popularity as a resort destination and retirement centre. Water as

a commodity lies at the heart of this new form of development but in a very different sense than previously. Despite low levels of rainfall in the region, a series of large lakes stretch along the valley bottom, remnants of a glacier that covered the area 10,000 years ago. The lakes are valued for recreational purposes: for boating, scuba diving, and swimming; and waterfront and lakeview properties fetch a high premium in today's booming real estate market [Figure 11.5]. The orchard oases that surround the lakes at lower elevations enhance the aesthetic and economic value of lakeview properties, but, ironically, the orchard industry is in decline precisely because of this new form of commoditization. As a commodity, water has much higher value in the recreational tourism and housing industries than it does in the agricultural industry. As a consequence, land prices have escalated beyond the level at which they are affordable for agricultural purposes. In the Okanagan Valley, as elsewhere in Canada, conflict over water is not likely to result in armed conflict, but it is likely to result in long-term social and economic change and a sharper divide between water haves and have-nots.

Source: Wagner, John. 2009. 'Water as Commodity in the Okanagan Valley of British Columbia', guest editorial.

**Figure 11.4 | Historic apple box image from the Okanagan Valley.**

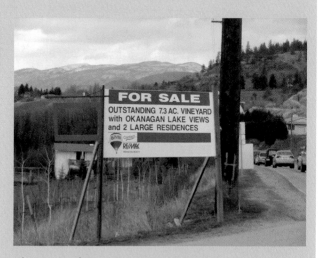

**Figure 11.5 | The conversion of family-farm agricultural land in the Okanagan Valley to waterfront and lakeview properties for affluent hobby-farmers fetches a high premium.**

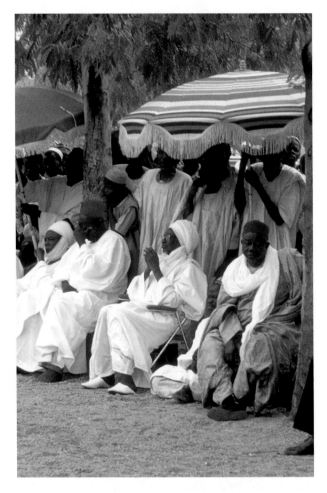

*Figure 11.6* | **Prior to colonial conquest by outsiders, Muslim emirs from northern Cameroon had coercive power.**

can persuade the dominated to accept their rule as legitimate, both by providing some genuine material benefits to their subjects and by using schools and other cultural institutions to disseminate an ideology justifying their rule. If they achieve all this—while also ensuring that none of these concessions seriously undermine their privileged position—they have established what Gramsci called **hegemony**. Hegemony is never absolute but always vulnerable to challenges: struggles may develop between rulers trying to justify their domination and subordinate groups who exercise agency by challenging 'official' ideologies and practices that devalue or exclude them. Hegemony may be threatened if subordinate groups maintain or develop alternative,

or *counter-hegemonic*, cultural practices. Successful hegemony involves linking the understandings of dominant and subordinate groups into what appears to be mutual accommodation.

**domination**
Coercive rule.

**hegemony**
A system of leadership in which rulers persuade subordinates to accept the ideology of the dominant group by offering mutual accommodations that nevertheless preserve the rulers' privileged position.

The concept of hegemony is attractive because it draws attention to the central role of cultural beliefs and symbols in struggles to consolidate social organization and political control. Gramsci's contrast between domination (rule by coercive force) and hegemony (rule by persuasion) was central to his own analysis of the exercise of power (Crehan 2002: 153), and it has been helpful to anthropologists who study the exercise of power in societies with and without traditional state institutions. In analyses of non-state settings, anthropologists are able to avoid some of the tortuous and implausible accounts of power that depend on fear of punishment or false consciousness. In place of these determinants, researchers examine the verbal skills and personal charisma of leaders with limited coercive force at their disposal who can nonetheless persuade others to follow them by skilfully aligning shared meanings, values, and goals with a particular interpretation of events or proposed courses of action.

Consider, for example, how witchcraft is perceived in Azande culture. The Azande believe that people use witchcraft only against those they envy. This seems highly plausible to people who experience daily friction with their neighbours. However, this belief makes it impossible to accuse Azande chiefs of using witchcraft against commoners—because, as the Azande themselves ask, 'Why would chiefs envy their subjects?' In this way, hegemonic ideology deflects challenges that might be made against those in power.

Hegemonic ideology may justify social action in some individuals that would be condemned in others. Consider the example of the Beng of Ivory Coast (see Map 11.2) and the connection between witchcraft and kingship. There are two Beng regions, each ruled by a king and a queen who come from a specific matrilineal clan. The king is said to be the owner of the Earth, which

Map 11.2 | **Beng**

is the primary focus for worship. Violations of taboos concerning the Earth are believed to endanger the entire region and therefore must be dealt with by the king of the region who is said to have the power to foresee those natural calamities that are punishment for sins committed. In general, 'the king is responsible not only for the legal but also the moral and spiritual well-being of the people living in this region' (Gottlieb 1989: 249).

The legitimate power of the king is in direct contrast to the power of witches, who are considered to be utterly immoral. Using illegitimate power, working in secret, they kill and 'consume' their close matrilineal kin. Nevertheless, when a man becomes king, he has one year to bewitch three close relatives in his matriline. If he fails to do so, he will die. Rather than destroying his power, this exercise of illegitimate power legitimates his rule. By killing three close matrilineal relatives, the king shows his commitment to the greater public 'good'. He is demonstrating his control over, and independence from, the narrow interests of his own kinship group. Operating on a plane beyond that of common morality, the king, who has sacrificed part of himself, will rule the kingdom fairly. From the point of view of the Beng, including members of his own matrilineal clan, the king's actions are not only legitimate but also make it possible for him to rule.

As well, Gramsci was interested in how hegemony is (or is not) successfully established in state societies. In a post-colonial and globalizing world, where all people are presumed to be citizens of one nation-state

or another, understanding the effects of decisions and actions of state authorities becomes crucial for making sense of many events on a local level. Anthropologists have often focussed on the processes by which ruling groups in former colonies attempt to build national identities. For example, the British colony of Ceylon became independent in 1948, later changing its name to Sri Lanka. The majority of residents of Ceylon belonged to two populations: the Tamils, concentrated in the northern part of the island, and the Sinhalese, who lived elsewhere and in much greater numbers (see EthnoProfile 11.1). After independence, however, new Sinhalese rulers worked to forge a national identity rooted in their version of local history, which excluded the Tamils. In 1956, Sinhala was made the only official language; in the 1960s and 1970s, the Tamils' access to education was restricted and they were barred from the civil service and the army (Daniel 1997: 316). The Tamils became a persecuted minority. In 1979, when some Tamils began to agitate for a separate state of their own, the Sri Lankan government responded with severe and violent repression, sending many of the Tamils into exile and stimulating the rise of the nationalist Liberation Tigers of Tamil Eelam (LTTE), which grew 'into one of the most dreaded militant organizations in the world' (323) (see Figure 11.7). The period of the Sri Lankan Civil War (1983–2009) was marked by escalating violence, with both sides committing 'gross human rights abuses, including war crimes'; today, instances of 'torture and enforced disappearances' continue to be reported, but still no one is held responsible (Amnesty International 2011).

Over the years, the Sri Lankan government used violent means of coercion to force Tamil residents out of the Sri Lankan. But it has also used violence against Sinhalese citizens who objected to state policies. Between 1987 and 1990, Indian troops were brought into Sri Lanka to supervise a peace agreement between Tamils and Sinhalese. These troops found themselves fighting the LTTE in the north and facing violent resistance in Sinhalese areas:

the rest of the country was convulsed by a wave of terror as young members of a group called the JVP (Janata Vimukti Peramuna, or People's Liberation Front) attacked the government not only for

## EthnoProfile 11.1 | Tamils ·····

**Region** South Asia

**Nation** Northeast Sri Lanka, also southeast India

**Language** The Tamils speak Tamil, one of the many Dravidian languages

**Population** 3.8 million in Sri Lanka (several hundred thousand have fled the country), nearly 70 million in India (2011 estimates)

**Environment** Low plains; tropical monsoon climate

**Livelihood** Planation agriculture; clothing manufacture

**Political organization** Part of a modern nation-state

**For more information** Trawick, Margaret. 2002. 'Reasons for Violence: A Preliminary Ethnographic Account of the LTTE', in *Conflict and Community in Contemporary Sri Lanka*, eds Siri Gamage and I.B. Watson (Thousand Oaks, CA: Sage); Indrapala, K. 2007. The Evolution of Ethnic Identity: *The Tamils of Sri Lanka* (Colombo: Vijitha Yapa).

betraying the nation by allowing the Indian presence but also for its own unjust political and economic policies. . . . The government responded with a wave of terror, directed at young males in particular, which reached its climax with the capture and murder of the JVP leadership in late 1989. As far as we can tell, the government won the day by concentrated terror— killing so many young people, whether JVP activists or not, that the opposition ran out of resources and leadership. (Spencer 2000: 124–5)

After 1990, violence directed by the state against Sinhalese lessened, and in 1994, a new government promised to settle the ethnic conflict by peaceful means. But even before then, Sri Lankan government efforts at nation-building had not rested entirely on violence. Leaders also tried to exercise persuasive power to convince Sinhalese citizens that the state had their welfare in mind and was prepared to take steps to improve their lives. For example, anthropologist Michael Woost (1993) has described how the government of Sri Lanka has used a wide range of cultural media (television, radio, newspapers, the school system, public rituals, and even a lottery) to link the national identity to development. National development strategies are presented as attempts to restore Sinhalese village society to its former glory under the pre-colonial rule of Sinhalese kings. The ideal village, in this view, is engaged in rice-paddy cultivation carried out according to harmonious principles of Sinhala Buddhist doctrine. The villagers Woost

**Figure 11.7 | Sri Lankan Tamil civilians enter a government-controlled area in 2009 after fleeing territory controlled by Liberation Tamil Tigers of Eelam (LTTE) rebels in northeast Sri Lanka.**

knew could hardly escape this nationalist development discourse, but they did not resist it as an unwelcome imposition from the outside. On the contrary, they had incorporated development goals into their own values and had accepted that state-sponsored development would improve their lives.

This acceptance might suggest that the state's attempt to establish hegemony had succeeded, but collaboration with the state was undermined as three different village factions selectively manipulated development discourse in their struggle to gain access to government resources. For example, nationalistic rhetoric connected development with 'improvement of the land'. One village faction claimed it had 'improved the land' first by building houses or planting tree crops. A second faction claimed it had 'improved the land' first by introducing paddy cultivation in the village. A third faction claimed it had 'improved the land' first since its members had intermarried with early settlers who had planted a large mango tree, a sign of permanent residence. Each faction made what the other factions interpreted as unjust claims, and each blamed the lack of village unity on the un-Buddhist greed of its opponents. These disagreements eventually led the state to withdraw its offer of resources, ultimately preventing the implementation of a village development scheme that all factions wanted!

Woost argues that the outcome of this political wrangling demonstrates the contradictory and fragile nature of the hegemonic process: paradoxically, the villagers' active appropriation of nationalist ideology undermined efforts to establish the very social order it was supposed to create. Gramsci himself was well aware that establishing successful hegemony in a nation-state was a difficult process whose outcome was not assured; indeed, it was the very inability of Italians to achieve this goal that stimulated many of his reflections on domination and hegemony. Gramsci's own description of a *colonial* state, emphasized by Indian historian Ranajit Guha as dominance *without* hegemony (Crehan 2002: 125), comes to mind when we consider the Sri Lankan state's repeated resort to violent coercion (e.g., the accusation that it withheld international aid to the Tamil region after the 2004 tsunami).

### Biopower and Governmentality

Is there a set of skills that would bring into existence—and sustain—a peaceful, prosperous nation-state in places like Sri Lanka? This question was addressed by French philosopher Michel Foucault, who looked at the way European thinkers from the end of the Middle Ages onward had posed (and attempted to answer) similar questions. Together with colleagues, he identified the emergence of a new

**governmentality**
The art of governing appropriate to promoting the welfare of populations within a state.

form of power in the nineteenth century. He called this form of power *biopower* or *biopolitics*, and it was preoccupied with bodies—both the bodies of citizens but also the social body itself (Hacking 1991: 183). As Gordon summarizes, biopower refers to 'forms of power exercised over persons specifically insofar as they are thought of as living beings; a politics concerned with subjects as members of a *population* in which issues of individual sexual and reproductive conduct interconnect with issues of national policy and power' (1991: 4–5).

According to Foucault, a state based on biopolitics is very different from states in the Middle Ages based on the rule of law or administrative states of the fifteenth and sixteenth centuries based on regulation and discipline. A major concern in those states, especially, was making sure that the ruler maintained control of the state. Machiavelli's famous treatise *The Prince* is the best known of a series of handbooks explaining what an absolute ruler needed to do to maintain power. But by the seventeenth century, this approach to state rule was proving increasingly inadequate. Machiavelli's critics began to speak instead about *governing* a state, likening such government to the practices that preserved and perpetuated other social institutions, 'a household, souls, children, a province, a convent, a religious order, a family' (Foucault 1991: 90). The example of household management, at that time called *economy*, was a preferred model of government and debate concerned how to incorporate 'the correct manner of managing individuals, goods, and wealth within the family . . . into the management of the state' (92). Thus the concept of *political economy* was born. But running the state in terms of political economy—managing citizens and their relations with goods and resources, with the territory, and with customs, and coping with misfortunes such as famines, epidemics, and death—could not be undertaken effectively until rulers possessed adequate knowledge about such things. In the eighteenth century, such knowledge was produced by state bureaucracies that began to count and measure people and things subject to state control, giving birth to the discipline of *statistics*. Statistics suggested that populations had unique attributes, and rulers concluded that management of the population through the use of statistics was the proper task of government.

The art of governing appropriate to biopolitics—what Foucault calls **governmentality**—relies on tactics of measuring and intervening to prevent calamities or to blunt their effects by using statistics to identify a series of possible and probable events, calculate their cost, and prescribe a form of intervention that would render such events tolerable, such that they would not undermine the security of the state. For example, such interventions include forms of insurance that protect economic activities in the event of a catastrophe that would otherwise curtail or destroy them (Gordon 1991: 18–20).

To an extent, governmentality is a form of power at work in the contemporary world, and institutions that rely on it count and measure their members in a variety of ways (Figure 11.8). Although, as Ian Hacking insists, not all bureaucratic applications of such statistical knowledge are evil (1991: 183), the fact remains that providing the government (or any bureaucratic institution) with detailed vital statistics can be very threatening, especially in cases where people are concerned that the state does not have their best interests at heart. After

all, states want to tax citizens, vaccinate and educate their children, restrict their activities to those that benefit the state, control their movements beyond (and sometimes within) state borders, and otherwise manage what citizens do. In a globalizing world full of nation-states, anthropologists are increasingly likely to encounter both the pressures of governmentality and attempts to evade or manipulate governmentality in their fieldwork.

### The Ambiguity of Power

The contrasts between domination and hegemony and Foucault's explorations of the machinery of governmentality demonstrate that the exercise of power cannot be equated with physical violence alone. Moreover, the occasional violent outburst of one member of a foraging society against another is not the same thing as the organized violence of one army against another in a conflict between modern nation-states. No one can deny that human beings can be violent with one another. But is this the whole story?

'It is useful to accept the proposition that while men have in some sense always been equal (i.e., in that each always has some independent power), they have in another sense never been equal (in that some always have more power than others)' (Adams 1979: 409). Some political anthropologists who think of power as coercion have traditionally emphasized the universality of human inequality. Some have concentrated on power in societies without states, whereas others have taken a more Gramscian approach and reconsidered the nature of independent power available to individuals living in societies with states. The first focus involves looking at power as an independent entity. The second looks at the power of the human imagination to define the nature of social interactions and to persuade other actors to accept these definitions of the situation.

## Power as an Independent Entity

In some of the traditionally stateless societies of Native peoples in North and South America, power is understood to be an entity existing in the universe independent of human beings. As such, it cannot be produced and accumulated through the interactions of human beings. Strictly speaking, power does not belong to human beings at all. At

*Figure 11.8* | **Censuses are one way in which a state collects information in order to govern effectively.**

**resistance**
The power to refuse being forced against one's will to conform to someone else's wishes.

**consensus**
An agreement to which all parties collectively give their assent.

**persuasion**
Power based on verbal argument.

most, people can hope to *gain access* to power, usually through ritual means. From this point of view, 'control over resources is evidence of power rather than the source of power' (Colson 1977: 382).

Societies that see power as an independent force usually embed this understanding within a larger world view in which the universe consists of a balance of different forces. Individuals may seek to manipulate those natural forces to their own ends, but only if they can do so without upsetting the universal balance. As a consequence, coercive means of tapping power sources are ruled out in such societies. Violence threatens to undo the universal balance. Thus, in many Native North and South American societies, gentler measures were required. One approached power through prayer and supplication. The vision quest (as among the Lakota) is a good example of such an approach: through fasting and self-induced suffering, individuals hoped to move the source of power to pity so that the source might then freely bestow on them the power they sought in the form of a vision or a song or a set of ritual formulas. Power freely bestowed would not disrupt the balance of the universe.

In such a world view, violence and access to power are mutually contradictory. Cultures that conceive of cosmic power in this way also tend to view individual human beings as independent entities who cannot be coerced but must be supplicated. Individuals in such societies are not free agents in the Western sense—free of social ties and responsibilities—but they are free in the sense that they can refuse to be forced against their will to conform to someone else's wishes. They exercise the power of **resistance**. The power of individuals to resist emphasizes the importance of **consensus** as the appropriate means to decide issues affecting the group. In seeking consensus, proponents of a particular course of action must use **persuasion** rather than coercion to get other members of the group to support their cause. They resort to verbal argument, not physical intimidation. As a result, the most respected members of stateless societies, those sometimes given the title 'chief' by outsiders,

are persuasive speakers, great orators. Indeed, as Pierre Clastres (1977) points out, such respected individuals are often referred to by other members of their society as 'those who speak for us'. The shamans (or *mara'akate*) of the Huichol Indians of northern Mexico serve this function. By virtue of their verbal ability, they see themselves (and are seen by their fellows) as especially well suited to negotiate for all the Huichol with outsiders, especially representatives of the Mexican state.

Clastres suggests that stateless forms of social organization are strongly resistant to the emergence of hierarchy (1977: 35). Indeed, he argues that members of stateless societies struggle to prevent such authority from emerging. They sense that the rise of state power spells the end of individual autonomy and disrupts beyond repair the harmonious balance between human beings and the forces of the wider world. Richard Lee agrees, arguing that band societies, and some farmers and herders, have found ways to limit

> the accumulation of wealth and power. Such societies operate within the confines of a metaphorical ceiling and floor: a ceiling above which one may not accumulate wealth and a floor below which one may not sink. These limits . . . are maintained by powerful social mechanisms known as levelling devices. . . . Such societies therefore have social and political resources of their own and are not just sitting ducks waiting to adopt the first hierarchical model that comes along. (1992a: 39–40)

Here you may recall our discussion of levelling devices, such as institutionalized sharing, in Chapter 7.

# The Power of the Imagination

Gramsci's discussion of the interplay between coercion and persuasion and Foucault's discussions of governmentality and biopolitics offer more nuanced understandings of the different levels on which social power can operate. Many anthropologists feel that a discussion of social power is incomplete if it does not also pay attention to the way individuals make sense of and use the constraints and opportunities for action open to them, however limited they may be.

All people have the power to interpret their experiences, regardless of the complexity of a social system and whether or not the power of coercion is monopolized by a central authority. People retain this power even under totalitarian dictatorship. It is notoriously difficult to erase the sense of self from human consciousness, even in the face of degradation and imminent death, as can be seen in the art and writings of inmates of the concentration camps of Nazi Germany. Alverson argues that 'a belief in one's power to invest the world with meaning (the "will to believe") and a belief in the adequacy of one's knowledge for understanding and acting on personal experience are essential features of all human self-identity' (1978: 7). This is the power to resist outside influences, to reject alternative choices that others want to impose. This does not mean that individuals work out the meanings of their experiences in isolation. All human activities, including the growth and development of self-identity, take place in a social, cultural, and historical context. Still each individual retains the power to interpret that context from his or her unique vantage point, in terms of his or her unique experiences. Cynics might argue that the power of the imagination must, in the real world, be restricted to private opinions; the mind can resist, but the body must conform. From this perspective, for example, the actions of a miner who labours underground daily for a meagre wage are clear-cut and unmistakable: he works for money to buy food for his family. However, ethnographic data suggest that this may not be the whole story.

The modern prototype of the downtrodden and exploited human being is the industrial labourer, the sufferer of the dislocations of the Industrial Revolution. Social scientists in the early twentieth century attempted to describe these changes. Emile Durkheim coined the term **anomie** to refer to the pervasive feelings of rootlessness and normlessness that people were experiencing. Karl Marx used the term **alienation** to describe the deep separation workers seemed to experience between their innermost sense of identity and the labour they were forced to do in order to earn enough money to live.

Do industrial workers in what used to be called the Third World similarly suffer from anomie and alienation? The issue has been hotly debated. Some argue that their condition could well be far worse than that of Western workers because the context of non-Western industrialization is much more backward. This has been called the *scars of bondage* thesis. This thesis predicts that the more complete the political domination and exploitation of a people, the more deeply they will be scarred, brutalized, and dehumanized by the experience. For people suffering the twin exploitations of colonialism and industrialism, the outcome could only be the most bitter, unrelieved tragedy.

June Nash (1979), working among Bolivian tin miners (see Map 11.4), has made interesting observations about the power of the human imagination to transform experiences by investing them with meaning. The labour force in Bolivian mines has been drawn from local Indigenous populations who have been effectively separated from their involvement in traditional Indigenous communities. Nonetheless, the tin miners of Bolivia have been able to combine elements of the dominant industrial culture with elements drawn from Indigenous traditions. Bolivian miners have created new, cohesive cultural patterns; far from being dissonant and alienating, the miners' culture provides an intact sense of self and belonging and an ability to celebrate life because it is viewed as meaningful (Figure 11.9).

**anomie**
A pervasive sense of rootlessness and normlessness in a society.

**alienation**
The deep separation that individuals experience between their innermost sense of identity and the labour they are forced to perform in order to survive.

Map 11.4 | Bolivian Tin Miners

*Figure 11.9* | **The offerings of cigarettes and coca leaves placed in front of a statue of 'El Diablo', a guardian of a government-run Bolivian tin mine complex, is an example of how the Bolivian miners have created new, cohesive cultural patterns. The roots of this custom date from much earlier Inca times.**

How can we explain, in the lives of Bolivian miners, the combination of what appears to be both genuine suffering and genuine celebration? Exploitation certainly leaves its mark on its victims: poor health, high infant mortality, intra-familial abuse, shattered hopes. Yet many Bolivian miners have not been irrevocably brutalized by these experiences. Their powers to invest their experiences with meaning remain intact, despite crushing conditions of exploitation. Nash notes, 'My experience living in mining communities taught me more than anything else, how a people totally involved in the most exploitative, dehumanizing form of industrialization managed to resist alienation' (1979: 319–20). She argues that the events people experience are less important than how they interpret those events. Nash concludes that the ethnocentrism of Western observers has kept them from recognizing the creative, revolutionary potential embodied in hybrid cultures like that of the Bolivian tin miners.

## Bargaining for Reality

The power that people have to invest their experiences with meanings of their own choosing suggests that a ruler's power of coercion is limited, which was Gramsci's key insight. Thought alone may be unable to alter the material circumstances of coercion, yet it has the power to transform the meaning of those material circumstances.

Any hegemonic establishment runs the risk that the dominated may create new, plausible accounts of their experiences of domination. Political scientist James Scott (1990) refers to these unofficial accounts as 'hidden transcripts'. Occasionally, those who are dominated may be able to organize themselves socially in order to transform their hidden transcripts into a counter-hegemonic discourse aimed at discrediting the political establishment. Those who are dominated may be able to persuade some or all of those around them that their counter-hegemonic interpretation of social experience is better or truer than the hegemonic discourse of the current rulers. Such challenges to incumbent political power are frequently too strong to be ignored and too widespread to be simply obliterated by force. When coercion no longer works, what remains is a struggle between alternative accounts of experience.

Anthropologist Lawrence Rosen worked in the Moroccan city of Sefrou (see Map 11.5). As he listened to the local people discussing and defining their relationships with each other, he realized that none of the traditional concepts they used could be said to have a fixed meaning. Any definition offered by one person would be verbally challenged by another. Rosen concluded that political and social life in Sefrou could not be understood unless one accepted that, for the locals, negotiation was the norm. Rosen (1984) calls this socio-political negotiation *bargaining for reality*.

The reality bargained for is not an impersonal, unchangeable set of truths about the world. Moroccans

*Map 11.5* | **Sefrou**

aim to persuade one another to accept alternative ways of understanding a particular situation. Persuasive accounts must be *coherent*: they must explain events and processes central to the experiences of those to whom they are addressed, they must be expressed in language that other members of society can understand, and they must hang together in a way that is not blatantly contradictory.

The power relationship between men and women in Sefrou illustrates this process. Men view women as less intelligent, less self-controlled, and less altruistic, and they expect women to obey them. Although women often assent to the male account of this relationship, they do not accept it in all circumstances. Women have developed an alternative account that explains elements in their lives that the male account either overlooks or interprets differently.

Women in Sefrou depend on men—first their fathers, later their husbands, and perhaps eventually their sons—for material support. But marriages are fragile, and women often have to rely on males of their patriline when their husbands divorce them (a wife cannot legally divorce her husband). Consequently, security for women depends on strengthening their positions within their families. In particular, women attempt to influence marriage negotiations because marriage automatically rearranges social relationships within the family. Women are eager to protect themselves and their daughters from oppressive demands by a husband and his kin. They view their actions as sensible and compassionate, not as misplaced interference. Nor do they accept the view that men are intellectually and morally superior to women. Indeed, they often view men as self-centred and childish.

In effect, Moroccan men and women live side by side in different worlds. They share experiences but interpret those experiences differently. Because neither gender has much direct contact with the other during everyday life, these different interpretations of experience do not constantly come into conflict. But marriage negotiations inevitably bring these different perspectives into contention. The outcome is reality bargaining, as several different actors attempt to make their definitions of the situation prevail.

Rosen describes one marriage negotiation that he encountered in Sefrou (1984: 40–7). A girl refused to marry the suitor her family chose, and her continued resistance had disrupted the harmony of her father's household. Rosen visited the household in the company of a respected male informant who was an old friend of the family. During their visit, the family friend and the girl's mother discussed the betrothal and the girl's refusal to consent to it. Both parties interpreted the girl's refusal differently. The family friend described the girl's behaviour as a typical case of female selfishness and immorality. What other reason could there be for her refusal to obey her father, as dutiful daughters should? He spoke harshly of her and repeatedly asserted that when her father returned they would force her to come to her senses and make the marriage. Her mother never openly contradicted these assertions. All the while, however, she quietly and insistently continued to make counter-assertions of her own. She reported her daughter's reason for rejecting the match: her intended husband came from a distant city. If she married him she would have to leave her family behind and go live among strangers. It was not that she objected to an arranged marriage; rather, she did not want to marry this particular man because to do so would take her so far away from home. From a woman's perspective, the daughter's anxieties were entirely rational given the powerlessness and isolation that she would endure as a result of the marriage.

As it turned out, after a year and a half of successful resistance, the young girl was eventually persuaded to marry the suitor. She changed her mind when she became convinced that consenting to the marriage was an economically sound move, not a submission to patriarchal authority. So women may agree with the male position in general terms and yet successfully dispute its relevance in a particular situation. Men may get women to comply with their wishes, and yet the women's reasons for doing so may have nothing to do with the reasons men offer to justify their demands.

James Scott carried out two years of ethnographic research among peasant rice farmers in a Malaysian village he called Sedaka (a pseudonym) (see Map 11.6). Poor Malaysian peasants are at the bottom of a social hierarchy, dominated locally by rich farmers and nationally by a powerful state apparatus. These peasants are not kept in line by some form of state-sponsored terrorism; rather, the context of their lives is shaped by what Scott calls *routine repression*: 'occasional arrests, warnings, diligent police work, legal restrictions, and an Internal Security Act that allows for indefinite preventive

Map 11.6 | **Sedaka**

detention and proscribes much political activity' (1985: 274).

Scott wanted to find out how this highly restrictive environment affected political relations between members of dominant and subordinate classes in the village. He quickly realized that the poor peasants of Sedaka were not about to rise up against their oppressors. But this was not because they accepted their poverty and low status as natural and proper. One reason was that organized overt defence of their interests would have

Figure 11.10 | **Until recently, rice harvesting in rural Malaysia was manual labour that regularly allowed poor peasants to earn cash and receive grain from their employers as a traditional form of charitable gift.**

been difficult given the conflicting loyalties generated by local economic, political, and kinship ties. Another reason was that the peasants knew that overt political action in the context of routine repression would be foolhardy. And they had to feed their families. Their solution was to engage in what Scott calls *everyday forms of peasant resistance*: this included 'foot dragging, dissimulation, desertion, false compliance, pilfering, feigned ignorance, slander, arson, sabotage, and so forth' (xvi). These actions may have done little to alter the peasants' situation in the short run; however, Scott argues, in the long run they may have been more effective than overt rebellion in undercutting state repression.

What we find in everyday forms of peasant resistance are indirect attempts to challenge local hegemony. Scott says: 'The struggle between rich and poor in Sedaka is not merely a struggle over work, property rights, grain, and cash. It is also a struggle over the appropriation of symbols, a struggle over how the past and present shall be understood and labelled, a struggle to identify causes and assess blame' (xvii). When peasants criticize rich landowners or rich landowners find fault with peasants, the parties involved are not just venting emotion. According to Scott, each side is simultaneously constructing a world view. Rich and poor alike are offering 'a critique of things as they are as well as a vision of things as they should be. . . . [They are writing] a kind of social text on the subject of human decency' (23).

Scott describes the dynamics of this struggle during the introduction of mechanized rice harvesting in Sedaka. Traditionally, rice harvesting was manual labour (Figure 11.10). In the late 1970s, however, the introduction of combine harvesters eliminated the rich farmers' need for hired labour, a loss that dealt poor families a severe economic blow. When the rich and poor talked about the harvesters, each side offered a different account of their effect on economic life in the village.

While both sides agreed that using the machines hurt the poor and helped the rich, consensus evaporated when each side was asked whether the benefits of the machines outweighed their costs. The poor offered practical reasons against the use of combine harvesters: they claimed that the heavy machines were inefficient and that their operation destroyed rice paddies. They also offered moral reasons: they accused the rich of being 'stingy', of ignoring the traditional obligation of rich people to help the poor by providing them with work and charity. The rich denied both the practical and the moral objections of the poor. They insisted that using harvesters increased their yield. They accused the poor people of bad faith. They claimed that the poor suffered because they were bad farmers or lazy, and they attributed their own success to hard work and prudent farm management.

Rich rice farmers would never have been able to begin using combine harvesters without the outside assistance of both the national government and the business groups who rented the machines to them at harvest time. Poor peasants were aware of this, yet they directed their critique at the local farmers and not at the government or outside business organizations. After all, the rich farmers 'are a part of the community and therefore *ought* not to be indifferent to the consequences of their acts for their neighbours' (161). The stinginess of the rich did not just bring economic loss. It also attacked the social identity of the poor, who vigorously resisted being turned into non-persons. The poor insisted on being accorded the 'minimal cultural decencies in this small community' (xviii). The only weapon they controlled in this struggle was their ability, by word and deed, to undercut the prestige and reputation of the rich.

This strategy worked in Sedaka because rich local farmers were not ready to abandon the traditional morality that had regulated relations between rich and poor. They had not yet become so Westernized that they no longer cared what other villagers thought of them. A shrewd campaign of character assassination may have caused at least some of the rich to hesitate before ignoring their traditional obligations. The improvement might have been minor, strictly in economic terms, but it would have been major in terms of the ability of the poor to defend their claims to citizenship in the local community. In addition, the wider political arena could always change in the future. Scott was convinced that many of the poor peasants he knew might well engage in open, active rebellion if routine repression disappeared.

When disputes are settled in this manner, experience is transformed. As Scott observes:

The key symbols animating class relations in Sedaka—generosity, stinginess, arrogance, humility, help, assistance, wealth, and poverty— do not constitute a set of given rules or principles

that actors simply follow. They are instead the normative raw material that is created, maintained, changed, and above all manipulated by daily human activity. (309)

In a similar way, Rosen refers to central Moroccan values such as intelligence, self-control, and generosity as **essentially negotiable concepts**: 'There is an element of uncertainty inherent in these terms such that their application to any situation by one person can be contested by another' (1984: 43). Bargaining for reality involves just this sort of manoeuvre: 'What is negotiable, then, is less one's view of reality as such than its scope, its impact, and its differential importance' (47). World views articulated in language by different social subgroups aim 'not just to convince but to control; better stated, they aim to control by convincing' (Scott 1985: 23).

> **essentially negotiable concepts** Culturally recognized concepts that evoke a wide range of meanings and whose relevance in any particular context must be negotiated.

The issues arising from the post-colonial environment also extend into basic definitions and negotiations of rights of citizenship and who controls these definitions and negotiations. This is of concern to anthropologists as well as scholars working in other disciplines, such as political science. (Note Joyce Green's discussion in the 'In Their Own Words' box, below.) The rights of those designated by a society as *the least amongst us* are essentially the only rights existing under law for all. What can be granted by authorities to the 'least' can become the reality for the 'most' in any regime of subjugation. This point moves beyond contested world views to contested human rights.

## History as a Prototype of and for Political Action

When individual actors within a particular cultural and situational context attempt to impose their definition of the situation on those with whom they interact, they draw on elements of a shared tradition of values and beliefs. This shared tradition, however, does not consist of values and beliefs divorced from experience and history. To some degree, people in all cultures continue to reshape—to bargain over—not merely which part of an agreed-on tradition is relevant in a particular situation

## *In Their Own Words* | Canaries in the Mines of Citizenship

*Joyce Green, a political scientist from the University of Regina, discusses the issues of citizenship and membership for First Nations women in Canada.*

So what is an excluded Indian woman to do? The standard responses to citizen dissatisfaction with an aspect of the political regime include legal challenge, political activism, partisan activity, and building new social consensus. Indian women concerned about citizenship and membership issues have tried all of these but have not yet found the political leverage to have their concerns ranked high by predominantly white or Aboriginal male politicians, mainstream political parties, and colonial courts.

Law, democratic mainstream politics, and Indigenous politics seem unable or unwilling to contend with the issues raised by this problematic minority. Denied band membership, meaningful exercise of Aboriginal and treaty rights, and, perhaps most importantly, denied the right to practise identity by living and raising children in their own communities, the affected women and their children are exiled to the dominant society where, thanks to racism, they are seen forever as 'Indian'.

Nor will the state apply its emerging view of rights in a way that works to the advantage of these women. Rather, the federal government retreats behind its self-serving rhetoric of respect for 'self' government, washing its hands of any responsibility to guarantee these women's rights. Meanwhile, Indian Act band governments claim to be governments of First Nations, practising a constitutionally recognized Aboriginal and treaty right which includes control of membership or citizenship.

The Sawridge pleadings suggest some of these invoke colonial sexist practices as constitutionally protected 'tradition'. In sum, neither the state nor band governments defended these women with rights discourse, though both use it when it suits them. Neither has affirmed their value as human resources to society. Neither guarantees equality of citizenship by taking the steps needed to permit these women to live in a way that honours their identity and values their participation.

Democracy fails these women. Premised on majority rule, and on the theoretical cultural-neutral and gender-neutral citizen and politician, it is unable to ensure their representation in a political system implicitly premised on their sex and ethnic inferiority. Privileging mythical notions of undifferentiated equality, the ideology grounding Canadian democracy is inherently hostile to affirming rights-bearing specificity, especially where Aboriginal rights may result in constitutional and public policy measures that benefit Aboriginal people in ways not available to non-Aboriginal Canadians; that is, where differing kinds of citizenship result. This hostility has been evident in non-Aboriginal opposition to treaty fishing rights and to land and governance rights sustained by the Supreme Court of Canada.

To date, Canadian law has failed these women, even with rights discourse foregrounded. The Lavell case of 1974, eight years prior to the entrenchment of the Canadian Charter of Rights and Freedoms, is infamous for dignifying sex discrimination as non-discrimination in law. The Sawridge case 21 years later sought to define Indian women's sexual equality rights out of existence. Lawmakers fail to see that any law affirming these women's rights must affirm them in their specificity as Indigenous women, part of colonized societies, to whom the state is historically an oppressor and only potentially an ally. While the Charter protections from discrimination on the basis of gender have motivated the federal government to eliminate the most egregious forms of legislative discrimination against Indian women, the measures are inadequate and stem from incomplete analyses that ignore the centrality to these women of their Aboriginal identities and rights, and their right to be fully acknowledged as part of their communities.

Yet citizenship may have the capacity to transcend the contradictions and pitfalls of decolonization in conditions defined by liberal and neo-liberal ideology and by the realpolitik of contemporary Canada. Even though Aboriginal rights constitute a different kind of right belonging only to members of Aboriginal nations, in addition to other citizenship rights enjoyed by all citizens of Canada, in the final analysis, people are not so incommensurable as to not share fundamental and inalienable human rights. All governments are impositions of authority upon those they govern, no matter how democratic or culturally authentic their processes. Authority must be held accountable for protecting the conditions fundamental to our humanity. In addition to human rights, which may be expressed and practised in different culturally specific fashions, Aboriginal rights must also be protected for all Aboriginal women and men.

Source: Green, Joyce. 2001. 'Canaries in the Mines of Citizenship: Indian Women in Canada', *Canadian Journal of Political Science* 34, 4: 736–8.

but also which version of the tradition ought to be agreed on. The combinations they come up with are sometimes surprising.

Consider the development of rural justice groups called *rondas campesinas* ('peasants who make the rounds') in the northern Peruvian highlands (see Map 11.7). Rondas consist of armed groups of peasants who walk the paths around their hamlets at night keeping an eye out for animal rustlers (Figure 11.11). The rondas began in one small hamlet in the northern Peruvian department of Cajamarca in 1976. During the 1980s, they spread hundreds of miles within Cajamarca and surrounding departments. At the same time, their functions were radically expanded: they became an alternative justice system with open peasant assemblies to resolve problems ranging from wife-beating to land disputes. By the early 1990s, rondas operated in 3,400 hamlets in the northern Peruvian Andes.

Orin Starn (1992) notes that at least five forces spurred campesinas to establish their alternative justice system.

*Figure 11.11* | **Rondas campesinas have become an alternative justice system in highland Peru. Here, a group of ronderos pose with a stolen donkey recovered from rustlers in 1986.**

1) The theft of animals shot up dramatically with the onset of the Peruvian economic crisis of the mid-1970s. The rise in theft was extremely serious for the poor farmers of the northern Andes, most of whom had small flocks and earned less than two thousand dollars per year.

2) Peasants got no relief from the official justice system. As the economy worsened, many government authorities tried to enlarge their shrinking salaries through bribery, kickbacks, and extortion, and poorer peasants were increasingly unable to pay.

3) The government had only a weak presence in the mountains, providing an opportunity for peasants to develop a new form of community organization.

4) Country people in northern Peru value toughness and bravery in the face of violence and were able to channel their aggressiveness into the service of order and discipline in the rondas.

5) Local organizers had outside supporters. In the province where the rondas began, these were activists from the Maoist Red Homeland party. In a neighbouring province, peasant catechists trained in liberation theology became early ronda leaders and were defended by priests and nuns as well as the local bishop.

During the 1980s, rondas were transformed from vigilante groups to dispute-resolution groups. Compared to the expensive, time-consuming, humiliating, and ineffective official justice system, the rondas were inexpensive, efficient, effective, and local. By the late 1980s, rustling was virtually eliminated and rondas in some communities were adjudicating over one hundred cases a month. The rondas also involve the elaboration of political identity and culture. Songs and poems celebrate the rondas and festivals commemorate their anniversaries.

*Map 11.7* | **Northern Peruvian Highlands**

To create the rondas, peasants drew on national and local cultural patterns. Peasants had served on patrols to stop thieves on haciendas (expansive estates) before the haciendas were broken up in the late 1960s. Men in the hamlets who had served in the Peruvian military incorporated military strategies and forms into the rondas. The peasants also employed local patterns, keeping the ronda patrols under the collective authority of the community. Likewise, when the rondas took on adjudication roles, they adopted some forms from the state bureaucracy, using a table like a judge's bench, rubber stamps, a recording secretary with notarized minutes, and so on. But the openness of the ronda system is very different from the state bureaucracy, for the final decision rests on the ronda president's evaluation of the response of the people attending. Assemblies of rondas are often held outside, where the event occurred, such as a farmyard. All attending have detailed knowledge of some kind that may be brought into play, and everyone jumps in to attempt to settle the dispute.

But the rondas, for all their effective innovation, are sometimes still enmeshed in old practices.

- They are connected with political parties in Peru, and squabbles involving the parties have weakened the ronda movement.
- They see themselves as the genuine upholders of the law and the Peruvian constitution. Thus, even though they have challenged the government's monopoly on the administration of justice, they are not working to overthrow the state.
- In some rondas, the leaders stay on for many years, hoard power, and begin to show favouritism. (More often, communities encourage constant rotation of leaders to avoid this problem.)
- The rondas perpetuate patriarchy. Although the rondas have given women a place to censure wife-beating, and a number of offenders have received a stern warning or whipping, only men patrol; female participation in assemblies is limited and mostly passive, and women are never ronda officers.
- The rondas sometimes use violent measures to bring about justice. While their ultimate aim is to create peace and order in a violent environment, the ronderos employ some of the techniques of the Peruvian police—for example, whipping with

barbed wire and hanging accused rustlers by their arms—to achieve their goal.

Starn concludes that, on the whole, the rondas have given Peruvian peasants the vision of an alternative modernity and have renewed among them a powerful sense of independent identity.

# Negotiating the Meaning of History

The meanings of the central symbols of any cultural tradition are essentially negotiable. That is, each symbol evokes a wide range of meanings among those who accept it. But what that symbol means in any particular situation, as well as the appropriateness of applying that symbol to the situation, is never obvious. Such matters are cultural dilemmas that people struggle to resolve. Consider the Moroccan and Peruvian examples and the power to invest experience with one's own meanings. This is a very real power. And yet many anthropologists are divided about the effectiveness of resistance as a solution to the problems of those at the very bottom of society. While there is much ethnographic evidence documenting the ability of some individuals and groups to assert themselves and their view of the world in the face of tremendous oppression, there is also much evidence that other individuals and groups have been destroyed by such oppression. Political anthropologist John Gledhill observes that it would be 'dangerous to be over-optimistic. "Counter-hegemonic" movements exist but much of the world's population is not participating in them' (1994: 198). He is particularly skeptical about the power of everyday forms of peasant resistance: the ability of such practices to undermine the local elite, he warns, may 'merely provide the scenario for the replacement of one elite by another, more effective, dominant group' (92). At the beginning of the twenty-first century, with no utopian solutions in sight, the most that anthropologists may be able to do is agree with historian A.R. Tawney, who wrote about the agrarian disturbances in sixteenth-century England: 'Such movements are a proof of blood and sinew and of a high and gallant spirit. . . . Happy the nation whose people has not forgotten how to rebel' (quoted in Wallerstein 1974: 357).

# Key Terms

alienation   281

anomie   281

consensus   280

domination   275

essentially negotiable concepts   285

free agency   272

governmentality   278

hegemony   275

persuasion   280

political anthropology   270

power   269

resistance   280

social organization   268

# Chapter Summary

1. Social organization refers to the patterning of human interdependence in a given society through the actions and decisions of its members. Unlike biological determinists, environmental determinists, and unilineal evolutionists, anthropologists understand that the complexities of human social organizations can never be reduced to a single cause. The power that human beings have to reproduce or to change their social organization is an important focus of anthropological study.

2. The ability to act implies power. The study of social power in human society is the domain of political anthropology. In most societies, at most times, power can never be reduced to physical force, although this is the Western prototype of power. Power in society operates according to principles that are cultural creations. As such, those principles are basically arbitrary, are affected by history, and may differ from one society to another.

3. Western thinkers traditionally assumed that without a state, social life would be chaotic, if not impossible. They believed that people were free agents who would not co-operate unless forced to do so. Anthropologists have demonstrated that power is exercised both by coercive and by persuasive means. People may submit to institutionalized power because they fear punishment, but they may also submit because they believe it is the right thing to do.

4. Anthropologists interested in how power is exercised in states have been influenced by the works of Antonio Gramsci and Michel Foucault. Gramsci argued that coercion alone is rarely sufficient for social control. He distinguished coercive domination from hegemony.

Successful hegemonic practice deflects challenges to the coercive power of the ruling group, but hegemony is always the outcome of struggle, and success is never guaranteed. Foucault's concept of governmentality addresses practices developed in Western nation-states in the nineteenth century that aimed to create and sustain peaceful and prosperous social life by exercising power over persons who could be counted, whose physical attributes could be measured statistically, and whose sexual and reproductive behaviours could be shaped by the exercise of state power.

5. Anthropological research in societies without states has shown how social obligations can restrict individuals from pursuing their own self-interest to the detriment of the group. In those societies, power is usually seen to be an independent entity to which one may gain access by supplication, not coercion. Likewise, individuals cannot be coerced but must be persuaded to co-operate. They are not free agents in the modern Western sense, but they are empowered to resist conforming to another's wishes.

6. All human beings possess the 'power to invest the world with meaning'. Many anthropologists feel that a discussion of social power is incomplete if it does not also pay attention to the ways individuals make sense of and use the constraints and opportunities for action open to them, however limited they may be. Rulers always face the risk that those they dominate may create new, persuasive accounts of their experience of being dominated, organize themselves to defend and disseminate their account, acquire a following, and unseat their rulers.

7. When people bargain for reality, they draw on elements of a shared culture and shared history in order to persuade others of the validity of their position. But they must often bargain over not merely which part of an agreed-on tradition is relevant but also which version of the tradition ought to be agreed on. Much political debate concerns which lessons from the past are relevant to the present. When disputes are settled in this manner, experience is transformed.

## Critical Thinking Questions

1. Why would the anthropological contention that social relations in any society are ultimately arbitrary be a controversial idea?

2. What are the similarities and differences between domination and hegemony?

3. What was the initial bureaucratic role of statistics, and why were (are) they considered important?

4. If power is part of the natural order of things yet independent of direct human control, what are the consequences that follow? Consider personal access to power, social constructs and relationships related to power, and the individual's ability to change the balance in a power relationship.

5. How would you describe the 'scars of bondage' thesis in the context of the exploitations of colonialism in Canada?

## Suggested Readings

Alverson, Hoyt. 1978. *Mind in the Heart of Darkness* (New Haven: Yale University Press). Difficult in places, but important and gripping: A study of how Tswana miners in South Africa maintain a sense of who they are under the most hellish circumstances.

Arens, W., and Ivan Karp, eds. 1989. *Creativity of Power: Cosmology and Action in African Societies* (Washington, DC: Smithsonian Institution Press). Contains 13 essays exploring the relationship among power, action, and human agency in African social systems and cosmologies.

Bashir, Halima. 2008. *Tears of the Desert: A Memoir of Survival in Darfur* (New York: One World). One woman's description of her survival of torture and gang-rape, inflicted for speaking out about an attack on primary school children. Dr Bashir continues in the work of defending others.

Fogelson, Raymond, and Richard N. Adams, eds. 1977. *The Anthropology of Power* (New York: Academic Press). A collection of 28 ethnographic essays on power all over the world.

Vincent, Joan, ed. 2002. *The Anthropology of Politics: A Reader in Ethnography, Theory, and Critique* (Malden, MA: Blackwell Publishers). A challenging but worthwhile collection of key texts in political anthropology ranging from the eighteenth-century Enlightenment to twenty-first-century critique.

## Related Websites

**The Andean World** www.mundoandino.com/Peru/Ronda-Campesina

**Council on Hemispheric Affairs (COHA)** www.coha.org/2008/10/a-new-face-to-salvadoran-politics/

**Pueblo Indian History and Resources** www.puebloindian.com/

**Sawridge Band v. Canada** www.lawsite.ca/WLSC/AMMSA_w.htm

# 12 | Inequality in the Contemporary World

## Chapter Outline

Class
Caste
Race

Ethnicity
Nation and Nationalism

## Learning Objectives

By the end of Chapter 12, you will be able to

- identify aspects of social stratification resulting in class structures,
- distinguish the stratification created by caste-based societies,

- consider and challenge the concept of race,
- appreciate the forms ethnicity may take, and
- understand aspects of nation-building and nationalism.

⬇ *Members of a Somali family sit in their makeshift hut on the edge of the Hagadera refugee camp in Kenya after fleeing their war-torn homeland. Many refugees face inequality and marginalization in their new settlements, as they often lack close social ties and may be treated as outsiders or even threats.*

While anthropologists have documented some distinctive forms of social organization that are relatively egalitarian, in today's globalizing world we most often find stratified societies. In **stratified societies**, higher-ranking groups have a disproportionate access to wealth, power, and prestige. At times, stratification is minimal—for example, in societies that anthropologists call *chiefdoms*, the chief may be the only person with a permanently superior status, while social and economic relations among non-chief members may remain relatively egalitarian. More elaborate social stratification is found in societies classified as *states*, which are not only much larger than chiefdoms but also employ a variety of mechanisms to bind different subgroups together into a hierarchy that regulates each group's access to wealth, power, and prestige.

All people in the world today, including the stateless and refugees, must deal with the authority of one or another nation-state, and all nation-states are socially stratified. But inequality within nation-states may be constructed out of multiple categories arranged in different, and sometimes contradictory, hierarchies of stratification. We can refer you to the earlier discussions of gender and then consider the problems of sexism, the forms of discrimination that result from sexual orientation, and the biases involved in ageism; however, we shall confine our discussion in this chapter to five categories of inequality:

1) **class**,
2) **caste**,
3) **race**,
4) **ethnicity**, and
5) **nationality**.

It is important to understand that *every one* of these categories is a cultural invention designed to create boundaries around one imagined community or another. *None* of these categories maps onto permanent biological subdivisions within the human species, although members of societies that employ these categories often will invoke 'nature' to shore up their legitimacy.

Some of these patterns (i.e., class, caste) reach back thousands of years. Others (i.e., race, ethnicity, and nationality) appear to be far more recent in origin and are closely associated with changes that began in Europe some five hundred years ago and continued with the spread of capitalism and colonialism. New forms of stratification were introduced to formerly independent, egalitarian societies while forms of stratification that predated European contact were reshaped. Anthropologists and other social scientists have argued with one another about how these categories should be defined and whether or not they can be usefully applied cross-culturally, and we will look at some of their arguments.

## Class

In general, classes are hierarchically arranged social groups defined on economic grounds. That is, higher-ranked social classes have disproportionate access to sources of wealth in the society, whereas members of lower-ranked classes have much more limited access to wealth (Figure 12.1).

The concept of class has a double heritage in modern anthropology, one stemming from Europe, the other from North America. European social scientists lived in states with a long history of social class divisions reaching

---

**stratified societies**
Societies in which there is a permanent hierarchy that accords some members privileged access to wealth, power, and prestige.

**class**
A ranked group within a hierarchically stratified society whose membership is defined primarily in terms of wealth, occupation, and/or access to power.

**caste**
A ranked group whose membership is based on inherited social roles. Caste systems are closed (individuals cannot move from one caste to another), and they combine elements of tribal affiliation, endogamy, class, occupation, mores, and ritual.

**race**
A broad human population category that allegedly corresponds to distinct, heritable sets of biological attributes and often conflates geographic ancestry and physical type.

**ethnicity**
A social classification based on a common cultural heritage and selected cultural features such as language, religion, or dress. Ethnicity emerges from historical processes that incorporate distinct social groups into a single political structure under conditions of inequality.

**nationality**
A sense of identification with and loyalty to a nation-state; membership, defined by citizenship, in a geopolitical sovereign state.

*Figure 12.1* | **Social classes often live within easy sight of one another. Here, luxury apartments and squatter settlements rub shoulders in Caracas, Venezuela.**

back to the Middle Ages and beyond. In their experience, entrenched social classes are relatively closed groups. The Industrial Revolution and the French Revolution promised to end the oppressive privileges of the ruling class and to equalize everyone's access to wealth. However, class divisions did not wither away in Europe during the nineteenth century; they just changed their contours. Followers of Marx judged that, at best, an old ruling class had been displaced by a new one: feudal aristocrats by bourgeois capitalists. The lowest level in European societies—rural peasants—were partially displaced as well with the appearance of the urban working class. But the barriers separating those at the top of the class hierarchy from those at the bottom seemed just as rigid as ever.

Significantly, Marx defines classes in terms of their members' different relations to the means of production. This means that as long as a particular set of unequal productive relations flourishes in a society, the

classes defined by these unequal roles in the division of labour will also persist. The French Revolution had triggered the displacement of aristocrats and peasants who had played the key roles in European feudalism only to replace them with new key classes—industrial entrepreneurs and the industrial working class linked together within the capitalist mode of production. In time, Marx predicted, these industrial workers would become the new 'leading class', rising up to oust capitalists when the socialist revolution came.

As Marx was well aware, all those who are linked to the means of production in the same way (e.g., as workers) do not often recognize what they have in common and may therefore fail to develop the kind of solidarity—the 'class consciousness'—that could, in Marx's view, lead to revolution. Indeed, the possibility of peasant- or working-class solidarity in many of the stratified societies studied by anthropologists is actively undercut by institutions of **clientage**. According to anthropologist M.G. Smith, clientage 'designates a variety of relationships, which all have inequality of status of the associated persons as a common characteristic' (1981 [1954]: 31). Clientage is a relationship between individuals—**patrons** and **clients**—rather than groups. Stratified societies united by links of clientage can be very stable. Low-status clients believe their security depends on finding a high-status individual who can protect them. For example, clientage is characteristic of *compadrazgo* relationships (discussed in Chapter 6), especially when the ritual parents are of higher social status than the biological parents. In fact, the Latin American societies in which *compadrazgo* flourishes are class societies, and parents who are peasants or workers often seek landowners or factory owners as *compadres*.

Marx's view of class is clearly different from the view of class hegemony in North America. For generations, North Americans have assumed that individuals may pursue wealth, power, and prestige unhampered by the unyielding class barriers characteristic of 'Old World' societies. This assumption is the basis for what is commonly referred to as the 'American Dream', but this

**clientage**
The institution linking individuals from upper and lower levels in a stratified society.

**patron**
The party of superior status in a clientage.

**client**
The party of inferior status in a clientage.

'dream' of equal opportunity for upward class mobility has more than a little currency here in Canada as well. As a result, many social scientists trained in North America have tended to define social classes primarily in terms of income level and to argue that such social classes are open, porous, and permeable rather than rigid and exclusionary. Yet the promise of equal opportunity for upward class mobility has not been fully realized.

In the early twentieth century, social scientists began to investigate race as a class mobility–limiting factor in North America. In the United States, black and white social scientists concluded that an unyielding 'colour bar' prevented upward class mobility. First argued for citizens with African ancestry, the analysis could also be extended to Indigenous peoples. One participant in these studies, an anthropologist named W. Lloyd Warner, argued in 1936 that the colour bar looked more like the rigid barrier reported to exist between castes in India than the supposedly permeable boundary separating social classes. With castes, membership is ascribed at birth and each ranked caste is closed such that individuals are not allowed to move from one caste into another. With social classes, membership is also ascribed at birth, but classes are not closed and individual social mobility is possible (Harrison 1995; 1998; Sharma 1999: 15; Warner 1936). Warner's distinction between caste and class became standard for decades in North American cultural anthropology.

Is this a plausible contrast? The aspect of caste that impressed Warner was the reported rigidity of the barrier between castes, which seemed much like the barrier separating blacks and whites in the United States. But in 1948, a black Trinidadian-American sociologist named Oliver Cromwell Cox rejected an equation between caste and race. Cox pointed out that many authorities on caste in India claimed that Hindu castes were harmoniously integrated within a *caste system* shaped by Hindu religious beliefs about purity and pollution. Most importantly, it appeared that members of low-ranked 'impure' castes did not challenge the caste system even though it oppressed them. If this were true, Cox concluded, caste relations were *unlike* race relations in the United

States, and by extension Canada, because whites had imposed the colour bar by force, and only by force had they been able to repress black resistance to the injustice of the system. Ursula Sharma (1999) points out, however, that both Warner and Cox were relying on an understanding of Hindu castes that, today, is considered highly misleading.

# Caste

The word *caste* comes from the Portuguese word *casta*, meaning 'chaste'. Portuguese explorers applied it to the stratification systems they encountered in South Asia in the fifteenth century. They understood that these societies were divided into a hierarchy of ranked subgroups, each of which was 'chaste' in the sense that sexual and marital links across group boundaries were forbidden (endogamy was practised). Most Western scholars have taken the stratification system of India as the prototype of caste stratification, and some insist that caste cannot properly be said to exist outside India. Others, however, do find value in applying the term to forms of social stratification, developed elsewhere, that bear a certain resemblance to the Indian pattern.

## Caste in India

The term *caste*, as most Western observers use it, collapses two different South Asian concepts:

1) **varna**, which refers to the widespread notion that Indian society is ideally divided into four functional subdivisions analogous to the estates of medieval and early modern Europe—priests, warriors, farmers, and merchants (Guneratne 2002; Sharma 1999); and
2) **jāti**, which refers to localized, named, endogamous groups.

Although jāti names are frequently the names of occupations (e.g., farmer, saltmaker), there is no conventional way to group the many local jātis within one of the four varnas, which is why jāti members can disagree with others about where their own jāti ought to belong. In any case, varna divisions are more theoretical in nature, whereas jāti divisions are more significant in most of the local village settings where anthropologists have traditionally conducted fieldwork.

**varna**
A caste that refers to the widespread notion that Indian society is divided into four functional subdivisions: priests, warriors, farmers, and merchants.

**jāti**
A caste that refers to localized, named, endogamous groups.

Map 12.1 | **Gopalpur**

Villagers in the southern Indian town of Gopalpur (see Map 12.1) defined a jāti for anthropologist Alan Beals. They said it was 'a category of men thought to be related, to occupy a particular position within a hierarchy of jātis, to marry among themselves, and to follow particular practices and occupations' (Beals 1962: 25). Beals's informants compared the relationship between jātis of different rank to the relationship between brothers. Ideally, they said, members of low-ranking jātis respect and obey members of high-ranking jātis, just as younger brothers respect and obey older brothers.

Villagers in Gopalpur were aware of at least fifty different jātis, although not all were represented in the village. Because jātis have different occupational specialties that they alone can perform, villagers were sometimes dependent on the services of outsiders. For example, there was no member of the Washerman jāti in Gopalpur. As a result, a member of that jāti from another village had to be employed when people in Gopalpur wanted their clothes cleaned ritually or required clean cloth for ceremonies.

Jātis are distinguished in terms of the foods they eat as well as their traditional occupations. These features have a ritual significance that affects interactions between members of different jātis. In Hindu belief, certain foods and occupations are classed as pure and others as polluting. In theory, all jātis are ranked on a scale from purest to most polluted (Figure 12.2). Ranked highest of all are the vegetarian Brahmins, who are pure enough to approach the gods. Carpenters and Blacksmiths, who also eat a vegetarian diet, are also assigned a high rank. Below the

vegetarians are those who eat 'clean', or 'pure', meat. In Gopalpur, this group of jātis included Saltmakers, Farmers, and Shepherds, who eat sheep, goats, chicken, and fish but not pork or beef. The lowest-ranking jātis are 'unclean' meat-eaters, who include Stoneworkers and Basketweavers (who eat pork) and Leatherworkers (who eat pork and beef). Occupations that involve slaughtering animals or touching polluted things are themselves polluting. Jātis that traditionally carry out such activities as butchering and washing dirty clothing are ranked below jātis whose traditional work does not involve polluting activities.

Hindu dietary rules deal not only with the kinds of food that may be eaten by different jātis but also with the circumstances in which members of one jāti may accept food prepared by members of another. Members of a lower-ranking jāti may accept any food prepared by members of a higher-ranking jāti. Members of a higher-ranking jāti may only accept certain foods prepared by a lower-ranking jāti. In addition, members of different jātis should not eat together. In practice, these rules are not as confining as they appear. In Gopalpur, '"food"

Figure 12.2 | **Gautam Ganu Jadhao, a city worker, removes a cart full of sewage waste from a Mumbai neighbourhood in July 2005. People like him, whose occupations are characterized as polluting, are ranked at the bottom of Hindu caste society.**

referred to particular kinds of food, principally rice. "Eating together" means eating from the same dish or sitting on the same line. . . . Members of quite different jātis may eat together if they eat out of separate bowls and if they are facing each other or turned slightly away from each other' (Beals 1962: 41). Members of jātis that are close in rank and neither at the top nor at the bottom of the scale often share food and eat together on a daily basis. Strict observance of the rules is saved for ceremonial occasions.

The way in which non-Hindus were incorporated into the jāti system in Gopalpur illuminates the logic of the system. For example, Muslims have long ruled the region surrounding Gopalpur; thus, political power has been a salient attribute of Muslim identity. In addition, Muslims do not eat pork or the meat of animals that have not been ritually slaughtered. These attributes, taken together, led the villagers in Gopalpur to rank Muslims above the Stoneworkers and Basketweavers, who eat pork. All three groups were considered to be eaters of unclean meat because Muslims do eat beef.

There is no direct correlation between the status of a jāti on the scale of purity and pollution and the class status of members of that jāti. Beals noted, for example, that the high status of Brahmins meant that 'there are a relatively large number of ways in which a poor Brahmin may become wealthy' (1962: 37). Similarly, members of low-status jātis may find their attempts to amass wealth curtailed by the opposition of their status superiors. In Gopalpur, a group of Farmers and Shepherds attacked a group of Stoneworkers who had purchased good rice land in the village. Those Stoneworkers were eventually forced to buy inferior land elsewhere in the village. In general, however, regardless of jāti, a person who wishes to advance economically 'must be prepared to defend his gains against jealous neighbours. Anyone who buys land is limiting his neighbour's opportunities to buy land. Most people safeguard themselves by tying themselves through indebtedness to a powerful landlord who will give them support when difficulties are encountered' (39).

Although the interdependence of jātis is explained in theory by their occupational specialties, the social reality is a bit different. For example, Saltmakers in Gopalpur are farmers and actually produce little salt, which can be bought in shops by those who need it. It is primarily in the context of ritual that jāti interdependence is given full play. Recall that Gopalpur villagers required the services of a Washerman when they needed *ritually* clean garments or cloth; otherwise, most villagers washed their own clothing.

To arrange a marriage, to set up the doorway of a new house, to stage a drama, or to hold an entertainment, the householder must call on a wide range of jātis. The entertainment of even a modest number of guests requires the presence of the Singer. The Potter must provide new pots in which to cook the food; the Boin from the Farmer jāti must carry the pot; the Shepherd must sacrifice the goat; the Crier, a Saltmaker, must invite the guests. To survive, one requires the co-operation of only a few jātis; to enjoy life and do things in the proper manner requires the co-operation of many (41).

Beals's study of Gopalpur documented three dimensions of caste relations in India that have become increasingly significant over time. First, Beals noted that jāti membership in Gopalpur mattered most on ritual occasions. In the years since Beals completed his study, cultural practices associated with caste in Indian villages have become even more attenuated or have disappeared as increasingly large numbers of Indians have moved to large cities where they are surrounded by strangers whose caste membership they do not know (Sharma 1999: 37). They still use the idiom of purity and pollution to debate the status of particular castes, but otherwise their understanding of caste usually has nothing to do with ritual status.

Second, Beals described members of middle-ranking jātis in Gopalpur who treated one another as equals outside of ritual contexts. Mitra points out that 'By the 1960s, electoral mobilization had led to a new phenomenon called *horizontal mobilization* whereby people situated at comparable levels within the local caste hierarchy came together in caste associations', many of which formed new political parties to support their own interests (1994: 61). Moreover, increased involvement of Indians in capitalist market practices has led to 'a proliferation of modern associations that use traditional ties of jāti and varna to promote collective economic well-being' (65). For example, a housing trust set up for Brahmins in the Indian state of Karnataka recruits Brahmins from throughout the Karnataka region in an effort to overcome 'jāti-based division into quarrelling sects of Brahmins' (66). The interests that draw jātis into coalitions of this kind 'often turn out to be class interests. . . . This does not mean that caste and class are the same, since commentators note caste as blurring class divisions as often as they express them. Rather it tells us that class and caste are not "inimical" or antithetical' (Sharma 1999: 68).

Third, Beals showed that middle-ranking jātis in Gopalpur in the 1960s were willing to use violence to block the upward economic mobility of members of a low-ranking jāti. Similar behaviour was reported in the work of other anthropologists like Gerald Berreman, who did fieldwork in the peasant village of Sirkanda in the lower Himalayas of North India in the late 1950s. Berreman observes that low-caste people in Sirkanda 'do not share, or are not heavily committed to, the "common official values" which high-caste people affect before outsiders. . . . Low-caste people resent their inferior position and the disadvantages which inhere in it', while 'high castes rely heavily on threats of economic and physical sanctions to keep their subordinates in line' such that when low-caste people publicly endorse 'common official values' they do so only out of fear of these sanctions (1962: 15–16).

In recent years, a number of low-caste groups in urban India have undertaken collective efforts to lift themselves off the bottom of society, either by imitating the ritual practices of higher castes (a process called *Sanskritization*) or by converting to a non-Hindu religion (such as Buddhism or Christianity) in which caste plays no role. Typically, however, these moves have had no effect in changing the negative stereotypes of so-called untouchables held by the so-called clean castes. However, the constitution of India prohibits the practice of untouchability, and the national government has acted to improve the lot of the low castes by regularly passing legislation designed to improve their economic and educational opportunities. In some cases, these measures seem to have succeeded, but violent reprisals have been common. In rural areas, many disputes continue to be over land, as in Gopalpur. However, even worse violence has been seen in urban India, as in 1990 when unrest was triggered by the publication of a report recommending increases in the numbers of government jobs and university enrolment quotas for members of low castes. At the end of the twentieth century, relations between low-caste and

high-caste Hindus were described as 'conflictual rather than competitive in some localities', with 'caste violence . . . recognized as a serious problem in contemporary India' (Sharma 1999: 67).

## Caste in Other Societies

Anthropologists have applied the concept of caste to systems of social stratifications outside of India as well. For example, Jacques Maquet (1970) used it to describe the closed, endogamous ranked strata Tutsi, Hutu, and Twa in the central African kingdom of Rwanda prior to 1959. Pierre van den Berghe (1970) documents the history of caste-like relationships dating from the beginnings of white settlement in southern Africa that culminated in the twentieth-century 'colour caste' system, distinguishing Whites, Asians, Coloureds, and Bantu that was enforced in apartheid South Africa. De Vos and Wagatsuma (1966) used the term *caste* to describe the *burakumin* of Japan, low-ranking endogamous groups, traditionally associated with polluting occupations, who have been subject to dehumanizing stereotypes and residential segregation from other Japanese. Sharma suggests that the concept of caste might be fruitfully used to characterize the relations between the Roma (or 'gypsy')

**Figure 12.3 |** Social and economic segregation of the Roma people continue to this day. The problem is particularly problematic in western Europe, where longstanding prejudices against the Roma influence political decisions in many countries.

people of Europe and their non-Roma neighbours, who for centuries have subjected the Roma to stigmatization, social segregation, and economic exclusion (1999: 85–6; Figure 12.3).

A key element recognized by all anthropologists who use the concept of caste is the endogamy that is enforced, at least in theory, on the members of each ranked group. As van den Berghe put it, membership in such groups is 'determined by birth and for life' (1970: 351). Sharma notes the significance of this link between descent and caste, observing that 'in societies where descent is regarded as a crucial and persistent principle (however reckoned, and whatever ideological value it is given), almost any social cleavage can become stabilized in a caste-like form' (1999: 85). She suggests the term *castification* to describe a political process by

which ethnic or other groups become part of a rank order of some kind, probably orchestrated from the top, but which need not result in the construction of a caste system (92–3).

But the principle of descent has also played a central role in the identification and persistence of race, ethnicity, and nationality. As noted above, these three categories are all closely bound with historical developments over the past five hundred years that built the modern world. Indeed, these categories are particularly significant in nation-states, and many contemporary nation-states are of very recent, post-colonial origin. Clearly, to make sense of contemporary post-colonial forms of social stratification, we will also need some understanding of the categories of race, ethnicity, and nationality.

## In Their Own Words | The Slave Narrative in Life History and Myth

*Susan J. Rasmussen draws on her experiences with the Tuareg people of Niger as she speaks to us on the slave 'story' and identity.*

Anthropologists and narrators may become mutually implicated with one another in a variety of ways. As a researcher among the Tuareg, I stood in a relationship of friendship, but also of marginality, to the community. In effect, I became a sign facilitating the storytellers in making their points. The act of constructing a life narrative can expand historical and ethnographic consciousness by compelling the author to move from accounts of discrete experiences to an account of why and how his or her life took the shape it did, at a given time, and why this was revealed from a particular viewpoint. The Personal Narratives Group (1989: 4–5) observes that the dynamics of gender emerge more clearly in personal narratives of women than in those of men. Likewise, it would seem to follow that the dynamics of social differentiation, inequality and domination, negotiation and resistance, would also emerge more clearly in slave narratives than in non-slave narratives. Or do they? Former slave and noble both used the experience of marginality and interdependence as a device by which to express their sense of how they have been treated in the post-colonial era. The tales of Tama the noble woman, as a discourse on servitude, in effect

complement the narrative of the former slave man although they are not mirror images of each other. Gender and age were shown to be significant in both of them, in historical memory as well as social practice. Women and former slaves were also revealed as united in certain contexts, rather than always competing or opposed.

Discourse about past servitude offers an expressive vocabulary that provides not only reflection about social stratification and gender but also meaning for suffering from any basis of declared social difference. Additionally, these slave narratives—both in life history and myth—empower, each in their own manner. They enable an inversion of deprivation and effect a recasting of roles and relationships in a way that does not merely recreate social difference or redirect oppression but that reconciles the interests of all the parties to the narratives. There emerges from them an expanded consciousness, on the part of local residents of diverse origins and outside anthropologists in the audiences. The personal slave narrative/life history and the mythology about slavery constitute a counterpoint through which Atakor and other Tuareg remember, but also recast, their social and political history.

Source: Rasmussen, Susan J. 1999. 'The Slave Narrative in Life History and Myth, and Problems of Ethnographic Representation of the Tuareg Cultural Predicament', *Ethnohistory* 46, 1 (winter): 67–108.

# Race

The concept of race developed in the context of European exploration and conquest beginning in the fifteenth century. Europeans conquered Indigenous peoples in the Americas and established colonial political economies that soon depended on the labour of Africans imported as slaves. By the end of the nineteenth century, light-skinned Europeans had established colonial rule over large territories inhabited by darker-skinned peoples, marking the beginnings of a global racial order (see Harrison 1995; Köhler 1978; Smedley 1993; 1998; Sanjek 1994; Trouillot 1994). Both as a way of explaining the existence of the human diversity they had encountered, and as a way of justifying the domination of Indigenous peoples and the enslavement of Africans, European intellectuals argued that the human species was subdivided into 'natural kinds' of human beings called *races* that could be sharply distinguished from one another on the basis of outward physical (or *phenotypic*) appearance. All individuals assigned to the same race were assumed to share many other common features, of which phenotype was only the outward index.

Belief in the existence of biologically distinct races (sometimes called **racialism**) was then joined to an ancient Western notion called the 'Great Chain of Being', which proposed that all 'natural kinds' could be ranked in a hierarchy. In the latter half of the nineteenth century, European thinkers, including many anthropologists, devised schemes for ranking the 'races of mankind' from lowest to highest. Not surprisingly, the 'white' northern Europeans at the apex of imperial power were placed at the top of this global hierarchy. Darker-skinned peoples, like the Indigenous inhabitants of the Americas or of Asia, were ranked somewhere in the middle. But Africans, whom Europeans had bought and sold as slaves, and whose homelands in Africa were later conquered and incorporated into European empires, ranked lowest of all. In this way, the identification of races was transformed into **racism** (Figure 12.4).

It is important to emphasize once again that all the so-called races of human beings are *imagined communities*. The racial boundaries that nineteenth-century European observers thought they had discovered *do not correspond to major biological discontinuities* within the human species. Although our species as a whole does exhibit

**Figure 12.4 | Racism has been common in countries that were colonized by Europeans. In South Africa, for example, apartheid policies forced the majority population of non-whites into positions of subordination under the ruling white minority.**

variation in phenotypic attributes such as skin colour, hair texture, and stature, these variations *do not* naturally clump into separate populations with stable boundaries that can be sharply distinguished from one another. Put another

> **racialism**
> Belief in the existence of biologically distinct races.
>
> **racism**
> The systematic oppression of one or more socially defined 'races' by another socially defined 'race' that is justified in terms of the supposedly inherent biological superiority of the rulers and the supposed inherent biological inferiority of those they rule.

way, *the traditional concept of race in Western society is biologically and genetically meaningless.*

But even though the concept of race is biologically meaningless, racial thinking persists in the twenty-first century. Anthropologists have long argued that race is a culturally constructed social category whose members are identified on the basis of certain selected phenotypic features (such as skin colour) that all of them are said to share. The end result is a highly distorted but more or less seemingly coherent set of criteria that members of a society can use to assign people they see to one culturally defined racial category or another. Once this happens, members of society can treat racial categories *as if* they reflect biological reality, using them to build institutions that include or exclude particular culturally defined races. In this way, race can become 'real' in its consequences, even if it has no reality in biology.

The social category of race is a relatively recent invention. Audrey Smedley reminds us that in the worlds of European classical antiquity, and through the Middle Ages, 'no structuring of equality . . . was associated with people *because of their skin colour*' (1998: 693; emphasis in original), and Faye Harrison points out that 'phenotype prejudice was not institutionalized before the sixteenth century' (1995: 51). By the nineteenth century, European thinkers were attempting to classify all humans in the world into a few, mutually exclusive racial categories. Significantly, from that time until this, as Harrison emphasizes, 'blackness has come to symbolize the social bottom' (1998: 612; see also Smedley 1998: 694–5).

White domination of Euro-American and Euro-Canadian racial hierarchies has been a constant. However, some anthropologists who study the cultural construction of whiteness point out that, even in North America, 'whiteness' is not monolithic and that the cultural attributes supposedly shared by 'white people' have varied in different times and places. Some members of white ruling groups in the southern United States, for example, have traditionally distanced themselves from lower-class whites, whom they call *white trash*; and the meaning of whiteness in South Africa has been complicated by differences of class and culture separating British South Africans from Afrikaners (Hartigan 1997). Moreover, the sharp 'caste-like' racial divide between blacks and whites in North America is currently complicated by new immigrants identified with so-called brown/Latin American/ Hispanic (or Indian/Pakistani) and yellow/Asian racial categories. Harrison and others recognize that racial categorization and repression take different forms in different places. As we shall see, anthropologists working in Latin America describe racial practices that do not match those characteristic of the United States and Canada.

## Race in Colonial Oaxaca

Anthropologist John Chance studied the development of ideas about race and class in the city of Oaxaca, Mexico (see EthnoProfile 12.1). Oaxaca (known as *Antequera* during the period of Spanish colonial domination) is a highland city founded in an area that was densely populated, prior to the Spanish conquest, by Indigenous people who participated in Mexican high civilization. Chance (1978) examined how social stratification changed from the period of Spanish conquest, in 1521, to the early years of the Mexican war of independence, in 1812. He used an anthropological perspective to interpret census records, wills, and other archival materials preserved in Mexico and Spain. As a result, he was able to show that changes occurred both in the categories used to describe social groups and in the meanings attached to those categories, with associated changes in the dynamics of social stratification itself.

When the Spanish arrived in Mexico in 1521, they found a number of Indigenous societies organized into states. The Aztecs, for example, were divided into an upper ruling stratum of nobles and a lower, commoner stratum. The Spanish conquerors also came from a society stratified into a system of *estates*, which were legally recognized social categories entitled to a voice in

## *EthnoProfile* 12.1 | **Colonial Oaxaca** (1521–1812)

**Region** North America
**Nation** Mexico
**Language** Mixtec, an Oto-Manguean language of Mexico
**Population** 18,000 (1792)
**Environment** High mountain river basin; temperate

**Livelihood** Administrative centre; clothing and textile industries
**Political organization** Colony of Spain
**For more information** Chance, John. 1978. *Race and Class in Colonial Oaxaca* (Stanford: Stanford University Press).

government. European estates prototypically included the nobility, the clergy, and the common people. By 1529, African slaves had been brought to New Spain. The colonizers in colonial Oaxaca reworked the European notion of estates to accommodate these new cleavages by assigning people membership into one or another estate on the basis of their outward phenotypes, the key criterion used to define *race*.

In theory, the clergy and nobility were reserved for the 'white' Spanish; all 'non-white' Indigenous groups were merged together to form the common people, and 'black' African slaves formed a final layer at the bottom of the colonial hierarchy. There were exceptions to this system, however. Indigenous nobles were given special status in post-conquest society and were used by the colonial administration to control the common people. Moreover, the conquistadors, who brought no Spanish women with them, soon established sexual relationships with local Indigenous women. In the early years, if these unions involved marriage, the offspring were usually considered Spanish, but if they were casual or clandestine, the offspring were more likely to be considered Indigenous. Over the years, sexual relations between Europeans, Indigenous peoples, and Africans created a population of mixed descent. According to the system of estates, people of mixed ancestry were not supposed to exist. By the mid-sixteenth century, however, their numbers and their economic importance made them impossible to ignore. As a result, the rulers of New Spain developed the *sistema de castas* to classify all people of mixed racial heritage (Figure 12.5). The first castas recognized were *mestizos* (people of mixed Spanish and Indigenous descent) and *mulatos* (people who showed evidence of African ancestry).

As soon as there were enough mestizos and mulattos to attract attention, the colonial government tried to limit their social mobility by legal means. Yet their status was ambiguous. Mestizos were ranked above mulattos because they had no African ancestry, but they were ranked below the Spanish because of their 'illegitimacy'. In cases where Indigenous and Spanish people were legally married, their children were called *españoles* (creoles). They were distinguished from *españoles europeos* (Spaniards born in Spain). In later years, the term *creole* (*criollo*) was also used to refer to people of presumably 'pure' European ancestry who were born in America.

Figure 12.5 | By the late eighteenth century, the number of castas recognized in Mexico had proliferated. This contemporary painting displays 16 different outcomes of various cross-casta matings. Note that the child of a castizo (who has three Spanish grandparents) and an española (who has four Spanish grandparents) would be an español. The painting attempts to represent not only the phenotypes of different castas but also the relative social statuses their members might occupy, as suggested by the clothing they wear (note especially the presence or absence of shoes).

Some mestizos managed to obtain elite privileges, such as the right to carry arms. Most mulattos were classed with Africans and could be enslaved. Yet free mulattos could also apply for the right to carry arms, which shows that even their status was ambiguous.

During the seventeenth century, the castas were acknowledged as legitimate strata in the system of colonial stratification. A number of new castas were recognized: *castizo* (a person of mixed Spanish and mestizo descent), *mulato libre* ('free mulatto'), *mulato esclavo* ('mulatto slave'), *negro libre* ('free black'), and *negro esclavo* ('black slave'). Perhaps most striking is the castizo category. This seems to have been designed by the colonial elite to stem the tide of ever 'whiter' mestizos who might be mistaken for genuine Spaniards. Chance points out that racial mixing was primarily an urban phenomenon and that the castas perceived themselves, and were perceived by the elite, as belonging to Hispanic rather than Indigenous society (1978: 126). It is perhaps not surprising that lighter-skinned castas became increasingly indistinguishable from middle-class and lower-class creoles. In fact, census records in Oaxaca list creoles as the largest segment of the city's population throughout the entire colonial period.

### Other Stratification Systems

As if the *sistema de castas* were not enough, colonial society in Oaxaca recognized three additional systems of classification that cut across the castas. One distinguished groups required to pay tribute to the Spanish crown (Indigenous groups, Africans, and mulattos) from everyone else. The second distinguished *gente de razon* ('rational people', who practised the Hispanic culture of the city) from *indios* (the rural, culturally distinct Indigenous population). And a third distinguished *gente decente* ('respectable people') from *la plebe* (the 'common people'). Chance suggests that the last distinction, which made most sense in the urban setting, represented an embryonic division into socio-economic classes (1978: 127).

### Mobility in the Casta System

Throughout the colonial period, the boundaries of the stratification system in Oaxaca were most rigid for those of 'unmixed' Indigenous, African, and European descent. Those of mixed background had the most ambiguous status and therefore the greatest opportunity to improve it. For example, when a couple married, the priest decided the casta membership of the bride and groom. The strategy for upward mobility called for choosing a marriage partner who was light-skinned enough for the priest to decide that both spouses belonged in a high-ranking casta. Over time, such manoeuvring swelled the ranks of the creoles.

The growth of the casta population coincided with the transformation of the colonial economy from one based on tribute and mining to one based on commercial capitalism. The prosperity this transformation brought to Oaxaca was greatest in the eighteenth century, when the city became the centre of an important textile and dye-manufacturing industry. Many castas were able to accumulate wealth, which together with light skin and adoption of the urban culture made it possible for them to achieve the status of creole.

Chance argued that during the late colonial period, racial status had become an achieved, rather than an ascribed, status. By that time, the increasing rate of legitimacy in all castas meant that descent lost its importance as a criterion of group membership. Creole status could be claimed by anyone who was able to show that his or her ancestors had not paid tribute. At the same time, in a dialectical fashion, people's image of what high-status people looked like had changed. As people with Indigenous and African ancestry moved up the social scale, their phenotypes widened the range of phenotypes considered prototypical for creoles.

Chance concludes that the *sistema de castas* is best understood as 'a cognitive and legal system of ranked socio-racial statuses' (1978: viii). Anthropologists have used the term **social race** to describe the system of ranking to which it eventually gave birth. The stratification system in Oaxaca was a hybrid, beginning with closed, caste-like racial categories whose 'purity' could not be maintained and ending up with open, class-like categories with racial labels.

## Colourism in Nicaragua

Some observers might expect that once race becomes an achieved status, racism has disappeared. But the situation is not so simple. Let us compare the case of Oaxaca, Mexico, with that of Managua, Nicaragua. Roger Lancaster argues that, in Nicaragua, racism exists but that it is 'not as absolute and encompassing a racism as that

**social race**
An achieved status with a racial label in a system of stratification that is composed of open, class-like categories to which racial labels are assigned.

which one encounters in the United States' even though it remains, in his opinion, 'a significant social problem' (1992: 215). One dimension of Nicaraguan racism contrasts the Spanish-speaking mestizo majority of the highlands with the Indigenous Miskitos and African Caribbeans along the Atlantic coast. Highland mestizos whom Lancaster knew tended to regard these coastal groups as backward, inferior, and dangerous—notions overlain with political suspicions deriving from the fact that some Miskito factions had fought with the contras against the Sandinistas.

But Lancaster came to see racism toward the coastal peoples as an extension of the pattern of race relations internal to highland mestizo culture that he calls **colourism**. In colourism, no fixed race boundaries exist. Instead, individuals negotiate their colour identity anew in every social situation they enter, with the result that the colour they might claim or be accorded changes from situation to situation.

Lancaster's informants used three different systems of colour classification. The first, or *phenotypic*, system has three categories—*blanco* (white), *moreno* (brown), and *negro* (black)—that people use to describe the various skin tones that can be seen among Nicaraguan mestizos:

> Nicaraguan national culture is mestizo; people's physical characteristics are primarily Indigenous; and in the terms of this phenotypic system, most people are *moreno*. In this system, *negro* can denote either persons of African ancestry or sometimes persons of purely Indigenous appearance, whether they are culturally classified as Indio or mestizo. (1992: 217)

Lancaster calls the second system the *polite* system, in which all the colours in the phenotypic system are 'inflated'. That is, Europeans are called *chele* (a Mayan word meaning 'blue', referring to the stereotype that people of European ancestry have blue eyes), *morenos* are called *blanco*, and *negroes* are called *moreno*. Polite terms are used in the presence of the person about whom one is speaking, and Lancaster was told that it was 'a grave and violent offence to refer to a black-skinned person as *negro*' (217). In rural areas, for similar reasons, Indians are called *mestizos* rather than *Indios*.

Lancaster calls the third system of colour terms the *pejorative and/or affectionate* system. This system has only two terms, *chele* (fairer skin, lighter hair) and *negro* (darker skin, darker hair). When the less powerful person in an interaction feels he is being imposed upon by the more powerful person, the former might express his displeasure by addressing the latter as *chele* or *negro*, both of which would be heard as insulting. Paradoxically, members of families call one another *negro* or *negrito mio* as affectionate and intimate terms of address, perhaps precisely because these terms are 'informal' and violate the rules of polite discourse (218).

**colourism**
A system of social identities negotiated situationally along a continuum of skin colours between white and black.

Lancaster discovered that 'Whiteness is a desired quality, and polite discourse inflates its descriptions of people' (219). People compete in different settings to claim whiteness. In some settings, individuals may be addressed as *blanco* if everyone else has darker skin; in other settings, they may be addressed as *moreno* if someone else has lighter skin than theirs.

Because it allows people some freedom of manoeuvre in claiming higher-status colour for themselves, Nicaraguan colourism may seem less repressive than the rigid black–white racial dichotomy traditional in North America. Lancaster points out, however, that all three systems of colourist usage presuppose white superiority and black inferiority. 'Africanos, Indios, and lower-class mestizos have been lumped together under a single term—*negro*—that signifies defeat' (223). Of course, the achieved social races of Oaxaca also oscillated along a continuum with whites on the top and blacks on the bottom. Lancaster is not optimistic about the possibilities of successfully overturning this system in Nicaragua any time soon. Similarly, Harrison argues that racial solidarity and rebellion are hard to achieve or sustain in societies where social race is present, and she is not optimistic that similar systems would have the same effect in other countries. For example, considering race relations in the United States, she fears that a 'more multi-shaded discourse' would be more likely to contribute to 'an enduring stigmatization of blackness' than to 'democratization and the dismantling of race' (1998: 618–19).

*In Their Own Words* | **The Emergence of a New Political Paradigm**

*John Matthiasson first went to Baffin Island, in the Canadian Arctic, to do fieldwork among the Inuit in 1963. He returned a decade later to carry out additional fieldwork and has kept up with events in the Canadian Arctic since then. Here, he writes about a people's name.*

The names by which we refer to ourselves or others can also be used to manipulate our identity and to align with or isolate ourselves from others, as well as to rationalize our treatment of others. When I lived with the Aullativikmiut in the 1960s they referred to themselves as Eskimos, as did all of the Tununermiut. By the 1970s many of them had ceased to use the term, which was now considered pejorative. (Its etymological origins have always been murky, although many sources claim that it means 'eaters of raw meat'.) It was, of course, replaced in both singular and plural by Inuk and Inuit, for 'a person' and 'the people'. The change in terminology of self-reference had, I am convinced, enormous political significance.

Not everyone accepted the change readily, and in some instances it was never adopted. One elderly man who had lived virtually all of his life in the camps told me in 1973, 'I was born an Eskimo and I will die an Eskimo.' However, his was to become a minority position. Others—even of his generation—soon saw the political significance of rejecting the term, and certainly that man's children and grandchildren did. This change, which was so important in the construction of new individual and group identities, was the work of the Inuit Tapirisat of Canada (ITC), or Inuit Brotherhood, a new organization that sought to create a pan-Inuit consciousness. The ITC was external to the Tununermiut, but when it offered them a new political agenda, they responded and, in the process, took further steps toward a renewed sense of self-determination.

Source: Matthiasson, John S. 1992. 'The Emergence of a New Political Paradigm', in *Living on the Land: Northern Baffin Inuit Respond to Change* (Peterborough, ON: Broadview Press), 161–2.

# Ethnicity

For anthropologists, **ethnic groups** are social groups whose members distinguish themselves (and/or are distinguished by others) in terms of *ethnicity*—that is, in terms of distinctive cultural features such as language, religion, or dress. Ethnicity, like race, is a culturally constructed concept. Many anthropologists today would agree with John Comaroff and Jean Comaroff that ethnicity is created by historical processes that incorporate distinct social groups into a single political structure under conditions of inequality (1992: 55–7; see also Williams 1989; Alonso 1994). Comaroff and Comaroff point out that ethnic consciousness existed in pre-colonial and pre-capitalist societies; however, they and most contemporary anthropologists have been more interested in forms of ethnic consciousness that were generated under capitalist colonial domination.

**ethnic groups**
Social groups that are distinguished from one another on the basis of ethnicity.

Ethnicity develops as members of different groups try to make sense of the material constraints they experience within the single political structure that confines them. This is sometimes described as a struggle between *self-ascription* (i.e., insiders' efforts to define their own identity) and *other-ascription* (i.e., outsiders' efforts to define the identities of other groups). In Comaroff and Comaroff's view, furthermore, the ruling group turns both itself and the subordinated groups into *classes* because all subordinated social groupings lose independent control 'over the means of production and/or reproduction' (1992: 56).

One outcome of this struggle is the appearance of new ethnic groups and identities that are not continuous with any single earlier cultural group (Comaroff and Comaroff 1992: 56). In northern Cameroon, for example, successive German, French, and British colonial officials relied on local Muslim chiefs to identify significant local social divisions for them, and they adopted the Muslim practice of lumping together all the myriad non-Muslim peoples of the hills and plains and calling them *Haabe* or *Kirdi*—that is, 'Pagans'. To the extent, therefore, that Guidar, Daba, Fali, Ndjegn, or Guiziga were treated the same by colonial authorities and came to share a common situation and set of interests, they developed a new, more inclusive level of ethnic identity. This new, post-colonial identity, like many others, cannot be linked to any single pre-colonial cultural reality but has been constructed out of cultural materials borrowed from a variety of non-Muslim Indigenous groups who were incorporated as 'Pagans' within the colonial political order.

Comaroff and Comaroff argue that a particular structure of nesting, opposed identities was quite common throughout European colonies in Africa. The lowest and least inclusive consisted of local groups, often called *tribes*, who struggled to dominate one another within separate colonial states. The middle levels consisted of a variety of entities that crossed local boundaries, sometimes called *supertribes* or *nations*. For example, the British administered the settler colony of Southern Rhodesia (later to become Zimbabwe) according to the policy of 'indirect rule', which used Indigenous 'tribal' authorities to maintain order on the local level. The effect of indirect rule was thus both to reinforce 'tribal' identities where they existed and to create them where they had been absent in pre-colonial times. Two such tribal identities, those of the Shona and the Ndebele, became pre-eminent, and each gave rise to its own '(supratribal) nationalist movement'.

Both movements joined together in a 'patriotic front' to win a war of independence fought against white settlers. This confrontation took place at the highest level of the ethnic hierarchy, which Comaroff and Comaroff call *race*. At this level, 'Europeans' and 'Africans' opposed one another, and each group developed its own encompassing ethnic identity. For example, Africans regularly dealing with Europeans began to conceive of such a thing as 'African culture' (as opposed to European culture) and 'pan-African solidarity' (to counter the hegemony of the European colonizers). Conversely, in the British settler colonies of southern and eastern Africa, European immigrants defined themselves in opposition to Africans by developing their own 'settler–colonial order' based on a caricature of aristocratic Victorian English society (1992: 58).

Because ethnic groups are incorporated into the colony on unequal terms (and, if we follow Comaroff and Comaroff, in different class positions), it is not surprising to discover that many individuals in colonies attempted to achieve upward mobility by manipulating ethnicity. Anthropological studies of such attempts at ethnic mobility constitute, as Comaroff and Comaroff put it, 'the very stuff of the ethnography of urban Africa' (1992: 63).

Emily Schultz investigated ethnic mobility in Guider, Cameroon, in 1976 (Figure 12.6). Guider began as a small settlement of non-Muslim Guidar. In 1830 it was brought into the Muslim Fulbe empire of Yola and remained a Fulbe stronghold under subsequent colonial rule. The Fulbe remained numerically dominant in town until after World War II; by 1958, individuals from over a dozen non-Fulbe groups had migrated to town, primarily from the neighbouring countryside. By 1976, 83 per cent of household heads in town were recent migrants, and 74 per cent did not claim Fulbe origins.

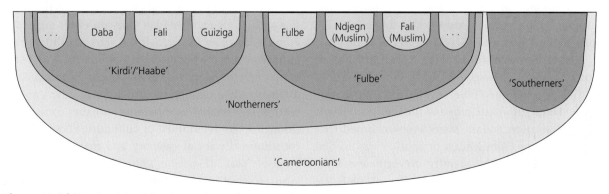

*Figure 12.6* | **Nesting identities in northern Cameroon in 1976.**

In Comaroff and Comaroff's terms, all these groups, including the Fulbe, had lost political and economic independence with the coming of colonial rule and, under conditions of inequality, were incorporated as ethnic groups into first the German and later the French colony of Cameroon. The colonizers uniformly admired the political, cultural, and religious accomplishments of the Muslim Fulbe. In their own version of indirect rule, they allowed Fulbe chiefs to administer territories they had controlled prior to colonization and, in some cases, handed over additional territories, whose residents had successfully resisted Fulbe domination in pre-colonial times.

In 1976, the local ethnic hierarchy in Guider placed Fulbe at the top and recent non-Muslim, non-Fulfulde-speaking migrants from rural areas at the bottom. But in the middle were numerous individuals and families of Fulfulde-speaking Muslims who could claim, and in some cases be accorded, recognition as Fulbe by others in the town. For example, two young men Schultz hired as field assistants first described themselves as '100 per cent Fulbe'. As she got to know them better, however, she learned that the family of one was Ndjegn, and the family of the other was Fali. Neither young man saw anything contradictory about being both Fulbe and Ndjegn, or Fulbe and Fali. And in fact, each ethnic identity was emphasized in different situations. Ndjegn and Fali ethnicity mattered to them in the domain of family and kinship; these ethnic identities nested within the broader Fulbe ethnicity that mattered in urban public settings, especially high-status ones associated with education and cash salaries.

Indeed, by 1976, Fulbe identity had become an achieved status; it was the ethnicity claimed by the upwardly mobile in Guider. People born outside the dominant Fulbe ethnic group could achieve Fulbe status in their lifetimes (Schultz 1984). To do this, they had to be successful in three tasks: they had to adopt the Fulbe language (Fulfulde), the Fulbe religion (Islam), and the Fulbe 'way of life', which was identified with urban customs and the traditional high culture of western Sudan. Many Fulbe claimed that descent from one Fulbe lineage or another was needed in order to claim Fulbe identity. Nevertheless, they seemed willing to accept 'Fulbeized Pagans' as Fulbe (e.g., by giving their daughters to them as brides)

because those people were committed defenders of the urban Fulbe way of life. Those who were 'Fulbeizing', however, came from societies in which descent had never been an important criterion of group membership. For those people, ethnic identity depended on territorial affiliation of the group to which they were currently committed. In becoming Fulbe, they had simply chosen to commit themselves to Fulfulde, Islam, and life in 'Fulbe territory'—the town.

This example illustrates some of the key attributes often associated with ethnicity: it is fluid, malleable, and something that can be voluntarily embraced or successfully ignored in different situations. Ambitious individuals and groups in an ethnically stratified society can manipulate ethnicity as a resource in order to pursue their interests. When nesting identities are present, people may regularly alternate between different identities in different contexts. Ethnic Fulbeization in northern Cameroon might be described as the formation of a 'supertribe'. Like the formation of caste alliances in India, it involves the expansion of group boundaries, allowing for the creation of stronger solidarity linkages among more people of different backgrounds. When such expanded alliances actually achieve increased success in political, economic, and social struggles, they may affect the very structures that gave rise to them (as the Shona–Ndebele alliance did in Zimbabwe) (Comaroff and Comaroff 1992: 61).

For dominant groups, however, defence of ethnic identity can be a way of defending privilege. They may be threatened rather than flattered by subordinate groups who master elite cultural practices. Members of the dominant ethnic group may stress their cultural superiority and question the eligibility (and even the humanity) of subordinate groups who challenge them. It is at this point that anthropologists like Faye Harrison would argue that ethnicity becomes *racialized*. In her view, race differs from ethnicity precisely because it is used to 'mark and stigmatize certain peoples as essentially and irreconcilably different, while treating the privileges of others as normative. This quality of difference, whether constructed through a bio-determinist or culturalist idiom, is what constitutes the social category and material phenomenon of "race"' (Harrison 1998: 613). Racialization in Western societies would thus bear a family resemblance to castification in South Asian societies.

Harrison argues that by the middle of the nineteenth century white northern Europeans, connecting their growing colonial power with their whiteness, began to racialize ethnic, religious, or class stereotypes associated with other Europeans (e.g., Irish, Jews, Italians, Poles, Slavs), viewing them as less human or, at any rate, differently human from themselves and attributing this difference to biologically inherited factors (1995: 52). Conversely, some racialized ethnic groups, such as the Irish, were able to reverse this process once they moved to the United States, shedding their stigma and *ethnicizing* into just another American ethnic group. Some social scientists might argue, or at any rate hope, that all racialized groups should be able to ethnicize sooner or later. But such a perspective risks ignoring the plight of racialized groups whose status never seems to change. Historians argue, for example, that the Irish were able to ethnicize precisely because they accepted the racialization of black Americans (Allen 1994–97). Indeed, operating under material conditions that presuppose white privilege, non-white races in the United States 'historically have defined layers of the social bottom vis-à-vis several successive waves of immigrants' (Harrison 1995: 49; see also Smedley 1998: 690).

For these reasons, Harrison argues that attempts to interpret race relations in the United States as ethnic relations 'euphemized if not denied race' by failing to address the social, political, and economic factors responsible for keeping groups like African Americans excluded and stigmatized at the bottom of society (1995: 48). Harrison agrees that African Americans do engage in 'ethnicizing practices emphasizing cultural heritage', but in her view such practices have never been able to overcome the 'caste-like assumptions of the most systematically oppressive racial orders' like that of the United States (1998: 613; 1995: 54; see also Sharma 1999: 91).

As we have seen, anthropologists have argued about which technical terms ought to be used to describe which forms of identity under which circumstances. We would agree with Sharma that social scientists should use a particular term only if it highlights a dimension of social relationships that would otherwise go unnoticed (1999: 93). Thus, ethnicity probably needs to be supplemented by the notion of race in order to distinguish the dehumanizing confinement of certain social groups to the bottom layers of society, and caste's emphasis on endogamy and hierarchical ranking highlights features of social organization that elude the usual scope of race, class, or ethnicity.

**objectification**
The intentional construction of a collective public identity; it is the process that produces what we commonly think of as ethnicity.

**reification**
A form of negative racial or ethnic absolutism that encourages the violent elimination of targeted groups and is central to the practice of racism.

Anthropologist Pnina Werbner (1997) further builds on these distinctions when she argues that in order to make progress in analyzing ethnic violence as a social force, practices of 'everyday' ethnic identification need to be distinguished from racism.

Based on her research on multicultural social relations in Britain, Werbner distinguishes two different social processes: **objectification** and **reification**. Objectification simply refers to the intentional construction of a collective public identity; it is the process that produces 'everyday' or 'normal' ethnicity. Ethnic identities are distinguished by the fact that they are 'evoked situationally . . . highlighted pragmatically, and objectified relationally and contingently' and by the fact that they focus on two key issues: 'a demand for ethnic rights, including religious rights, and a demand for protection against racism' (1997: 241). Social relations between objectified ethnic groups are based on a 'rightful performance' of multiple, shifting, highly valued forms of collective identification based on religion, dress, food, language, and politics. Interaction between groups that differentiate themselves along such lines ordinarily do not lead to violent confrontations (229). Reification, in contrast, is a form of negative racial or ethnic absolutism that encourages the violent elimination of targeted groups and is central to the practice of racism. Reification 'distorts and silences'; it is 'essentialist in the pernicious sense' (229). Violence differentiates racism from everyday ethnicity, and if ethnic confrontation becomes violent, then it turns into a form of racism (234–5). For Werbner, making this distinction is crucial in multi-ethnic situations because when people fail to distinguish non-violent forms of everyday ethnicity from racism, they are, in effect, criminalizing valid ethnic sentiments and letting racists off the hook (233).

# Nation and Nationalism

As we saw earlier, state societies are not new social forms. **Nation-states**, however, are a far more recent invention. Prior to the French Revolution, European states were ruled by kings and emperors whose access to the throne was officially believed to have been ordained by God. After the French Revolution in 1789, which thoroughly discredited the divine right of kings, rulers needed to find a new basis on which to found legitimate state authority. The solution that was eventually adopted rooted political authority in **nations**: groups of people believed to share the same history, culture, language, and even the same physical substance. Nations were associated with territories, as were states, and a nation-state came to be viewed as an ideal political unit in which national identity and political territory coincided.

The building of the first nation-states is closely associated with the rise and spread of capitalism and its related cultural institutions during the nineteenth century. Following the demise of European colonial empires and the end of the Cold War, the final decades of the twentieth century witnessed a scramble in which former colonies or newly independent states struggled to turn themselves into nation-states capable of competing successfully in what anthropologist Liisa Malkki has called a 'transnational culture of nationalism' (Malkki 1992).

On the one hand, the ideology of the nation-state implies that every nation is entitled to its own state. (Here we could consider the aspirations of the Kurds to establish their own nation-state in West Asia.) On the other hand, it also suggests that a state containing heterogeneous populations *might be made into a nation* if all peoples within its borders could somehow be made to adopt a common nationality: a sense of identification with and loyalty to the nation-state. The attempt made by government officials and state institutions to instill this sense of nationality into the citizens of a state has been called **nation-building**, or **nationalism**.

As we learned in our discussion of ethnicity, states are the very political structures that generate ethnic identities among the various cultural groupings unequally incorporated within them. Thus, anthropologists studying state formation often find themselves studying ethnicity as well as nationalism (Alonso 1994). However, groups with different forms of identity that continue to persist within the boundaries of the nation-state are often viewed as obstacles to nationalism. If such groups successfully resist assimilation into the nationality that the state is supposed to represent, their very existence calls into question the legitimacy of the state. Indeed, if their numbers are sufficient, they might well claim that they are a separate nation, entitled to a state of their own!

To head off this possibility, nationalist ideologies typically include some cultural features of subordinate cultural groups. Thus, although nationalist traditions are invented, they are not created out of thin air. The prototype of national identity is usually based on attributes of the dominant group, into which specially chosen elements of the cultural practices of other, subordinated groups are integrated. That is, those who control the nation-state will try to define nationality in ways that 'identify and ensure loyalty among citizens . . . the goal is to create criteria of inclusion and exclusion to control and delimit the group' (Williams 1989: 407). The hope seems to be that if at least some aspects of their ways of life are acknowledged as essential to national identity, subordinated groups will identify with and be loyal to the nation. Following Gramsci, Williams calls this process a **transformist hegemony** in which nationalist ideologues are attempting to 'create purity out of impurity' (1989: 429, 435).

National leaders will measure the trustworthiness and loyalty of citizens by how closely they copy (or refuse to copy) the cultural practices that define national identity (Williams 1989: 407). Unfortunately, the practices of subordinated groups that do not get incorporated into nationalist ideology are regularly marginalized and devalued, and continued adherence to such practices may be viewed as subversive. Some groups, moreover, may be totally ignored. Alonso points out, for example, that Mexican nationalism is 'mestizo nationalism' rooted in the official doctrine that the Mexican people

---

**nation-state**
An ideal political unit in which national identity and political territory coincide.

**nations**
Groups of people believed to share the same history, culture, language, and even the same physical substance.

**nation-building, or nationalism**
The attempt made by government officials to instill a sense of nationality into the citizens of a state.

**transformist hegemony**
A nationalist program to define nationality in a way that preserves the cultural domination of the ruling group while including enough cultural features from subordinated groups to ensure their loyalty.

are a hybrid of European whites and the Indigenous people they conquered. As we saw in colonial Oaxaca, African slaves were also a part of early colonial Mexican society. Nationalist ideology, however, erases their presence entirely (1994: 396).

## Australian Nationalism

Australia began its existence as a settler colony of Great Britain. Over the past two hundred years, the prototype of Australian national identity was based on the racial and cultural features of the settler population. The phenotypically distinct Indigenous people, called *Aborigines* by the settlers, were completely excluded from citizenship. Settlers' claims to land and other resources rested on the doctrine of *terra nullius*: the idea that before the arrival of the Europeans, the land had been owned by nobody. In European capitalist terms, 'ownership' meant permanent settlement and 'improvement' of the land by clearing it and planting crops or grazing animals. Since the Aboriginal peoples living on the continent of Australia were foraging peoples who did not depend on domesticated plants or animals, European settlers felt justified in displacing them and 'improving' the land as they saw fit. Aborigines were viewed as a 'dying race', and white settler domination was taken as a foregone conclusion.

But times change and, currently, Australians are seriously rethinking the nature of Australian national identity. Indeed, according to Robert Tonkinson (1998), two kinds of nation-building are going on at the same time. First, an intense national debate has developed in recent years that favours creating a new Australian Republic whose constitution would affirm the existence and rights of the country's Indigenous peoples. For that to happen, however, 'the nation as a whole must re-imagine itself via a myth-making process, in which the search for distinctively Australian national symbols may well include elements drawn from Indigenous cultures' (Tonkinson 1998: 287–8).

And this will not be easy because such a myth-making process (or transformist hegemony) immediately runs up against a second, alternative myth-making process generated by Australia's Indigenous minorities who have, for decades, struggled to construct a sense of 'pan-Aboriginal' identity. Since the 1970s, a central theme in this struggle has been the demand for land rights, which was given an enormous boost by the decision handed down by the High Court of Australia in 1992 in the case of *Eddie Mabo*

*and Others* v. *The State of Queensland*. The so-called *Mabo* decision rejected the doctrine of *terra nullius*, proclaiming that the Native title of Australia's Indigenous people was part of Australian common law.

The symbolic significance of the *Mabo* decision has been enormous. For those Australians who want to remake Australian nationalism, *Mabo* clears ground for constructing a multicultural national identity. The Australian federal government has therefore made reconciliation with Indigenous minorities a major policy goal, well aware that 'unless Australia achieves a formal and lasting reconciliation with its Indigenous people, its self-image as a fair and just land will continue to be mocked by the history of its oppression of them' (Tonkinson 1998: 291). Many white Australians and the national government are seeking ways of incorporating Aboriginality into Australian national identity. A measure of success is indicated by increasing interest on the national level in the artistic, literary, and athletic accomplishments of Aboriginal people. As a popular reconciliation slogan puts it, 'White Australia Has a Black History' (Figure 12.7).

While all this might augur favourably for a reconstructed Australian national identity that includes Aboriginal people, many problems remain. Some come from white Australians who reject a multicultural national identity or who see their economic interests threatened

*Figure 12.7* | Australian Aboriginal people marching in protest over the Australian Bicentennial celebrations, which, they argued, did not pay appropriate attention to them.

**naturalizing discourses**
The deliberate representation of particular identities (e.g., caste, class, race, ethnicity, and nationality) as if they were a result of biology or nature rather than history or culture, making them appear eternal and unchanging.

by the *Mabo* decision. But even Aboriginal people, whom it is supposed to help, criticize the *Mabo* decision because of its limitations and unresolved complexities. For example, the only lands eligible for Indigenous claims turn out to be those that have demonstrable historical connection to contemporary Aboriginal groups who continue to practise 'traditional' Aboriginal customs. This not only exempts most of Australia from Indigenous land claims, but it also means that most of Australia's quarter of a million Aboriginal people will be barred from making land claims because they live in Australia's large towns and cities and have, for generations, been separated from the lands of their ancestors.

Since the *Mabo* decision, however, expressions of Aboriginality seem to be moving toward 'a more culture-centred—and to non-Aboriginal Australians more easily accommodated—emphasis on Aboriginal commonalities, continuity, and survival' (Tonkinson 1998: 289). The *Mabo* decision has ratified the legitimacy and revival not only of Aboriginal land rights but also of Aboriginal customs. This has stimulated the explosion of Aboriginal cultural expression that white Australians have come to appreciate, as well as numerous programs that have brought urban Aboriginals into remote areas to work, to learn about rural Aboriginal traditions, and to contribute to the growth of biculturalism among rural Aboriginal people. Even in a multicultural Australia, however, many Aboriginal people would insist that they must not be lumped together with other 'ethnic minorities', given their special status as descendants of the original inhabitants and victims of centuries of exploitation. Tonkinson concludes that, at the end of the twentieth century, 'despite the limitations of *Mabo* . . . its symbolic force is such that it may provide the basis for reconciliation between Indigenous and other Australians' (300).

## Naturalizing Discourses

We have emphasized that all the social categories under discussion—class, caste, race, ethnicity, and nationality—are culturally created and cannot be justified with reference to biology or nature. At the same time, many members of the societies anthropologists study argue just

the opposite, employing what some anthropologists call **naturalizing discourses**.

Naturalizing discourses rely on the imaginary reduction, or *conflation*, of identities to achieve persuasive power (Williams 1989). For example, every one of the forms of identity we have discussed in this chapter has been described or justified by someone, at some time, in terms of *shared bodily substance*. Thus, living within the same borders is conflated with having the same ancestors and inheriting the same culture, which is conflated with sharing the same blood or the same genes. Culture is reduced to blood, and 'the magic of forgetfulness and selectivity, both deliberate and inadvertent, allows the once recognizably arbitrary classifications of one generation to become the given inherent properties of reality several generations later' (Williams 1989: 431).

Nation-states frequently use trees as national symbols, rooting the nation in the soil of its territory (Figure 12.8). Sometimes they use kinship imagery, referring to the nation-state as a 'motherland' or 'fatherland'; sometimes the territory of a nation-state itself can be a unifying image, especially when portrayed on a map (Alonso 1994). The case of Australia shows, however, that doctrines like *terra nullius* enable newcomers to deny the 'natural' links to the land of Indigenous inhabitants while specifying how newcomers may proceed to establish their own 'natural' links to the land through 'improvement'.

## The Paradox of Essentialized Identities

The struggle of Aboriginal people to defend themselves and claim their rights after centuries of exploitation and neglect was extraordinarily important in making the *Mabo* decision possible. In response to dominant groups that attempted to conflate their humanity with a narrow, unflattering stereotype, they chose to accept the racial designation but to view it as a positive *essence*, an 'inner something or distinctive "spirituality" possessed by everyone who is Aboriginal' (Tonkinson 1998: 294–5). Similar kinds of essentialist rhetoric have helped many stigmatized groups build a positive self-image and unite politically.

Many anthropologists and other observers would argue that the essentialist rhetoric of Aboriginal activists does not, in fact, reflect what those activists believe about Aboriginality at all. They would describe what the activists are promoting as *strategic essentialism*: that is, essentialist

*Figure 12.8* | The tree-like symbol at the centre of the Mexican coat of arms (the cactus on which an eagle perches holding a snake in its beak) is a pre-Conquest Aztec symbol. In the national seal, the image is encircled by the Spanish words *Estados Unidos Mexicanos* (United Mexican States). These combined elements stand for the officially mixed ('mestizo') Mexican people the state is supposed to represent—the offspring of Spanish conquerors and the Indigenous people they conquered.

rhetoric is being used as a conscious political strategy. Most activists are perfectly aware that essentialized racial or ethnic identities have no scientific validity. Nevertheless, they press their claims, hoping that by stressing their difference they may be able to extract concessions that the national government cannot refuse without violating its own laws and sense of justice. The concessions may be substantial, as in the case of the *Mabo* decision. At the same time, strategic essentialism is troubling to many observers and participants in these struggles, for those who promote it as a political strategy risk 'reproducing the same logic that once oppressed them' (Hale 1997: 547) and, rather than bringing about a more just society, may simply 'serve to perpetuate an ethnically ordered world' (Comaroff and Comaroff 1992: 62).

## Nation-building in a Post-colonial World: The Example of Fiji

While the citizens of nation-states need to construct a shared public identity, they also need to establish concrete legal mechanisms for taking group action to influence the state. That is, as John Kelly and Martha Kaplan (2001) argue, nation-states are more than imagined communities; they are also *represented* communities. For this reason, nation-building involves more than constructing an image of national unity; it also requires institutions of political representation that channel the efforts of citizens into effective state support. But what happens when citizens of a nation-state do not exactly agree about what nation they are building or what kinds of legal and political structures are necessary to bring it about? One answer to this question can be seen in the South Pacific island nation of Fiji, which became independent from Britain in 1970 and has experienced four political coups in the last twenty years, the most recent being the coup d'état of December 2006.

At independence, the image of the Fijian nation was that of a 'three-legged stool'; each 'leg' was a separate category of voters: 'general electors' (a minority of the population including Europeans), 'Fijians' (ethnic Fijians, descended from the original inhabitants of the island), and 'Indians' (or Indo-Fijians, descendants of indentured labourers brought to Fiji by the British from Mumbai [Bombay] and Kolkata [Calcutta] in the nineteenth century). Kelly and Kaplan show that these three categories have deep roots in the colonial period, where they were said to correspond to separate 'races'. In the British Empire, race was an accepted way to categorize subordinated peoples, even though in many cases—as in the case of the Indo-Fijians—the people so labelled had shared no common identity prior to their arrival in Fiji.

These racial distinctions were concretized in colonial law, and the legal status of ethnic Fijians was different from the legal status of Indo-Fijians. The status of ethnic Fijians was determined by the Deed of Cession, a document signed by some Fijian chiefs with the British in 1874, which linked ethnic Fijians to the colonial government through their hierarchy of chiefs. The status of Indo-Fijians, in contrast, was determined by the contracts of indenture (*girmit*) that each individual labourer had signed in order to come to Fiji. Thus, ethnic Fijians were accorded a hierarchical, collective legal identity, whereas Indo-Fijians had the status of legal individuals, with no legally recognized ties to any collectivity.

Inspired by the freedom movement in India in the early twentieth century, Indo-Fijians began to resist racial oppression and struggle for equal rights in Fiji, but their efforts were repeatedly quashed by the British. When it became possible for them to vote after 1929, for example, Indo-Fijians lobbied for equal citizenship and the abolition of separate racial voting rolls, and they lost: the voting rolls were divided by race in order to limit representation for Indo-Fijians in government. At the time of World War II, Indo-Fijians agreed to serve in the armed forces, but only if they were treated as equals with white soldiers, and their efforts were resisted: they spent the war serving in a labour battalion for very low wages, while ethnic Fijians joined a Fijian Defence Force. It was primarily Indo-Fijians who pushed for independence in the late 1960s, and once again they engaged in difficult negotiations for equal citizenship and a common voting roll but finally consented to separate race-based voting rolls in 1969 in order to obtain independence.

> Thus, when Fiji's independence became real in 1970, the constitution insisted that races still existed in Fiji and had to vote separately. Since then parties have generally and increasingly followed racial lines, and the army has remained an enclave of Indigenous Fijians. When political parties backed mostly by Indo-Fijian voters won Fiji's 1987 election, this army took over the country after only a month. The constitution that was then installed in 1990 returned to even more naked discrimination against Indo-Fijians in regard to voting rights. (Kelly and Kaplan 2001: 77)

The constitution was revised yet again, in a manner that favoured ethnic Fijian chiefly interests and seemed guaranteed to prevent parties backed by Indo-Fijian voters from winning control of the government in the 1999 election. To everyone's surprise, parties backing ethnic Fijians lost again. A second coup came on 19 May 2000. Finally, after new elections in 2001, ethnic Fijians won control of the government. The military coup d'état of 2006 was a direct result of the continuing consequences of the coup of 2000. It focussed primarily on the Reconciliation, Tolerance, and Unity Bill that proposed amnesty legislation for those involved in the 2000 coup. The coup of 2006 resulted in the military effectively taking control of the country (Figure 12.9). In October 2008, the Fijian High Court ruled that the resulting government was the legal government.

What lessons does this history suggest about nation-building in post-colonial states? The issues are many and

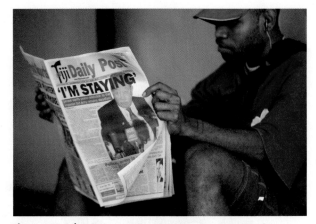

**Figure 12.9 | A Fijian citizen reads a newspaper in November 2006 as tensions rise between Prime Minister Laisenia Qarase and the Fijian military. The military took control of the government on 6 December 2006.**

complex. But one key factor emphasized by Kelly and Kaplan is that the image of a united Fijian nation projected at independence was severely undermined by legal mechanisms of political representation carried over from the colonial period, particularly the race-based voting rolls. What became apparent in the years after independence was the fact that Indo-Fijians and ethnic Fijians had imagined very different national communities. Indo-Fijians had supported the image of a Fijian nation in which all citizens, Indo-Fijian or ethnic Fijian or 'general elector', would have equal status, voting on a single roll, working together to build a constitutional democracy. However, 'few among the ethnic Fijians have yet come to see themselves as partners with immigrants' (2001: 41). Ever since independence, and particularly after each coup, ethnic Fijians worked to construct an image of the Fijian nation based solely on chiefly traditions in which Indo-Fijians had no meaningful place. Thus, Kelly and Kaplan conclude, in Fiji (and in many other parts of the world) '"the nation" is a contested idea, not an experienced reality' (142).

## Nationalism and Its Dangers

The most horrifying consequence of nation-building movements in the twentieth century has been the discovery of just how far the ruling groups of some nation-states are willing to go in order to enforce their version of national identity.

After World War II, the world was shocked to learn about Nazi programs to 'liquidate' Jews, Roma, and other groups that failed to conform to Nazi ideals of Aryan purity (Linke 1997). Many people hoped that the Nazi Holocaust was exceptional, but subsequent developments suggest that it may have been the most dramatic example of an exterminationist temptation that accompanies all drives to nationalism. Sociologist Zygmunt Bauman argued in his book *Modernity and the Holocaust* (1989) that modern nation-states with rationalized bureaucracies and industrial technology were the first societies in history to make efficient mass extermination of deviants technically possible. In a transnational culture of nationalism, not to belong to a nation-state made up of loyal, ambitious, like-minded citizens is a severe, possibly fatal, handicap. Using violence against all citizens who undermine claims of national homogeneity and common purpose may thus be a peculiarly modern way for insecure rulers of embattled nation-states to try to bring about solidarity and stability. In the late twentieth century, warring nationalities in the former Yugoslavia deployed selective assassinations and forced migration to rid their fledgling nation-states of unwanted others, a policy known as *ethnic cleansing* (Figure 12.10). Thus, rather than relics of a barbarian past, ethnic cleansing, *ethnocide* (the destruction of a culture), and *genocide* (the extermination of an entire people) may constitute a series of related practices that are all signs of things to come. All are measures of the high stakes for which rulers of these nation-states see themselves competing.

Inevitably, such policies create populations of immigrants and refugees whose social status is anomalous and ambiguous in a world of nation-states and whose presence as new pockets of heterogeneity in a different nation-state sets the stage for new rounds of social struggle that may lead to violence. As we will see in the next chapter, the economic, political, and cultural processes that made this possible have undergone important shifts in the last few decades.

*Figure 12.10* | Relatives of 8,000 Muslim men and boys slaughtered in the 1995 Srebrenica massacre walk between rows of coffins next to freshly dug graves, looking for those belonging to their relatives, in a field in the town on 31 March 2003.

## *In Their Own Words* | Past Wars, Present Dangers, Future Anthropologies

*With the 'War on Terrorism', what of Native and minority populations and their aspirations for political justice? David Price questions the position of the Canadian government on the issue of who is defined as a terrorist.*

It is imperative that anthropologists critically evaluate and speak out about the dangers the War on Terrorism will present to Native and minority populations around the world if the governments managing them and their lands are given a new international legitimacy to repress them as 'terrorists'. The United Nations' support for new anti-terrorist policies is helping to establish new forms of co-operation among member nations, yet these arrangements proceed with explicit agreement that terrorism shall remain strategically undefined. International human rights groups and even the German Foreign Ministry have raised concerns that these policies will usher in renewed state terrorism against minority populations. But for the most part these objections have been suppressed in the interest of the Western world's new unity of purpose.

There are signs that the US Secretary of State, Powell-the-coalition-builder, is purchasing the co-operation and approval of the world leaders by adopting policies whereby the United States will not protest or intervene when these states suppress or attack their own ethnic minority populations. As the United States signals President Putin that it can learn to see Russia's bloody war in Chechnya as part of the global War on Terrorism, this signal is welcomed by other world leaders hoping for a free hand to deal with domestic Indigenous troubles.

Anthropologists know that most of the world's nation-states are in internal conflict with one or more domestic groups contesting power relations; and these conflicts are frequently marked by violence and counter-violence. The idiom of power dictates that the violence of the state is legitimized as peace-keeping, while that of the dispossessed becomes terrorism. It is this hypocrisy that prevents the formation of a coherent behavioural definition of terrorism—and without such a definition the War on Terrorism must be viewed with informed skepticism.

Anthropologists also know that colonial powers and nation-states have long designated a wide range of cultural practices as terrorist threats. Historically, activities categorized as 'terrorism' have not been limited to acts of violence. The historical range of non-violent practices defined as terrorism includes certain forms of speech, teaching Native languages, and a wide range of religious or cultural ceremonies. North American examples of this include outlawed cultural and religious practices associated with resistance or non-assimilation such as the Ghost Dance, potlatch, peyote rituals, and lodge ceremonies. As terrorism remains undefined we are left to wonder if world leaders will be freely allowed to oppress their own minority populations for engaging in similar non-violent acts of rebellion.

There is a present danger of the wholesale categorization of people who resist domination as 'terrorists'—thereby sidestepping all issues that an in-depth cultural and historical analysis would raise. Whether it is the Basques in Spain, the Irish Catholics in Northern Ireland, the Tamils in Sri Lanka, Zapatistas in Mexico, Chechens in Russia, post-colonial wars of Africa smouldering along ethnic lines, or struggles of other excluded groups, there are contentious battles for power that will rapidly become even more lopsided if the currently ill-defined anti-terrorism campaign continues. . . .

Source: Price, David. 2002. 'Past Wars, Present Dangers, Future Anthropologies', *Anthropology Today* 18, 1 (Feb.): 3–5.

# Key Terms

caste  292
class  292
client  293
clientage  293
colourism  303
ethnic groups  304
ethnicity  292
jāti  294
nationality  292
nation-building, or nationalism  308
nations  308
nation-state  308

naturalizing discourses  310
objectification  307
patron  293
race  292
racialism  299
racism  299
reification  307
social race  302
stratified societies  292
transformist hegemony  308
varna  294

# Chapter Summary

1. All people in the world today, even refugees, must deal with the authority of one nation-state or another, each of which contains multiple, and sometimes contradictory, hierarchies of stratification. Every one of these hierarchies is a cultural invention designed to create boundaries around different kinds of imagined communities. Some patterns of stratification may reach back thousands of years, but others are closely associated with the rise of European capitalism and colonialism.

2. The concept of class in anthropology has a double heritage: Europeans tended to view class boundaries as closed and rigid, whereas North Americans tended to view them as open and permeable. Class solidarity may be undercut by clientage relations that bind individuals to one another across class boundaries.

3. The stratification system of India has been taken as the prototype of caste stratification, although anthropologists have applied the concept to social hierarchies encountered elsewhere in the world. Local caste divisions in Indian villages adhere to rules of purity and pollution defined in terms of the occupations their members perform and the foods they eat; these divisions also govern whom an individual may marry. Members of jātis of similar rank do not observe such distinctions with

one another, especially in urban settings. Caste associations in large cities of India use jāti ties to promote their members' economic well-being. At times, higher-ranking jātis have used violence to block the advance of lower-ranking jātis. Contemporary anthropologists reject views of caste in India that portray it as internally harmonious and uncontested by those at the bottom of the caste hierarchy, pointing to the rise in caste violence in recent years.

4. The contemporary concept of race developed in the context of European exploration and conquest beginning in the fifteenth century, as light-skinned Europeans came to rule over darker-skinned peoples in different parts of the world. The so-called races whose boundaries were forged during the nineteenth century are imagined communities; human biological variation does not naturally clump into separate populations with stable boundaries. Despite variations in opinions and practices regarding race over the centuries, a global hierarchy persists in which whiteness symbolizes high status and blackness symbolizes the social bottom.

5. Although ethnic consciousness existed in pre-colonial and pre-capitalist societies, contemporary anthropologists have been most interested in forms of ethnicity that

were generated under capitalist colonial domination, when different groups were subordinated within a single political structure under conditions of inequality. This process can produce ethnic groups not continuous with any single earlier group and is often characterized by nesting, opposed identities that individuals often manipulate in order to achieve upward mobility. When dominant ethnic groups feel threatened, they may attempt to stigmatize subordinate groups by 'racializing' them.

6.  Nation-states were invented in nineteenth-century Europe, but they have spread throughout the world along with capitalism, colonialism, and political decolonization. Nationalist thinking aims to create a political unit in which national identity and political territory coincide, and this has led to various practices designed to force subordinate social groups to adopt a national identity defined primarily in terms of the culture of the dominant group. When subordinate groups resist, they may become the victims of genocide or ethnic cleansing. Alternatively, the dominant group may try to recast its

understanding of national identity in a way that acknowledges and incorporates cultural elements belonging to subordinate groups. If the creation of such an imagined hybrid identity is not accompanied by legal and political changes that support it, however, the end result may be political turmoil, as shown in the recent history of Fiji.

7.  Because membership in social categories such as class, caste, race, ethnicity, and nationality can determine enormous differences in peoples' life chances, much is at stake in defending these categories and all may be described as if they were rooted in biology or nature rather than history or culture. Conceptualizing these forms of identity as essences is one way of stereotyping and excluding, but it has also been used by many stigmatized groups to build a positive self-image and as a strategic concept in struggles with dominant groups. Although strategic essentialism may be successful in such struggles, it also risks repeating the same logic that justifies oppression.

## Critical Thinking Questions

1.  How has the 'American Dream' been realized in the Canadian context? Does our interpretation of class hegemony differ from that of our neighbours to the south?

2.  Which aspects of social stratification would you consider to be associated with capitalism?

3.  Discuss open and closed stratification systems. Beyond their permeable or non-permeable boundaries, what would you consider to be their main differences?

4.  How and why do dominant ethnic groups stigmatize subordinate groups by 'racializing' them?

5.  Nationalist thinking aims to create a political unit in which national identity and political territory coincide. How would you consider this statement as it applies to Quebec?

6.  What are naturalizing discourses? Give some examples and include explanatory comments.

## Suggested Readings

Anderson, Benedict. 1991. *Imagined Communities*, rev. edn (London: Verso). The classic discussion of the cultural processes that create community ties between people—such as citizens of a nation-state—who have never seen one another, producing the personal and cultural feeling of belonging to a nation.

Domhoff, G. William. 2009. *Who Rules America? Challenges to Corporate and Class Dominance*, 6th edn. New York: McGraw-Hill. First published in 1967, this book has become a classic in sociology; it is also important for the anthropologist interested in theory on elites, as it discusses how power and politics operate in the United States.

Dusenbery, Verne A. 1997. 'The Poetics and Politics of Recognition: Diasporan Sikhs in Pluralist Polities', *American Ethnologist* 24, 4: 738–62. A discussion of political identity in Sikh overseas communities, cogent to the analysis of the Air India bombing.

McAlpine, Lynn, Alice Eriks-Brophy, and Martha Crago. 1996. 'Teaching Beliefs in Mohawk Classrooms: Issues of Language and Culture', *Anthropology & Education Quarterly* 27, 3: 390–413. The importance of teaching language is examined in the context of culture retention for a First Nations community.

Magat, Ilan N. 1999. 'Israeli and Japanese Immigrants to Canada: Home, Belonging, and the Territorialization of Identity', *Ethos* 27, 2: 119–44. This article investigates identity formation, management, and change, and the interrelationship of the personal, the cultural, and the national for immigrants to Canada from Israel and Japan, both nations with a strong sense of uniqueness central to their national discourse.

Malkki, Liisa. 1995. *Purity and Exile: Memory and National Cosmology among Hutu Refugees in Tanzania* (Chicago: University of Chicago Press). This ethnography chronicles the bloody consequences of nationalist politics in Africa and explores the connections between the conditions of refugee resettlement and the development of refugee identities.

Nash, Manning. 1989. *The Cauldron of Ethnicity in the Modern World* (Chicago: University of Chicago Press). Nash looks at ethnicity in the post-colonial world and sees more of a seething cauldron than a melting pot. He examines the relations between Ladinos and Maya in Guatemala, Chinese and Malays in Malaysia, and Jews and non-Jews in the United States.

Razack, Sherene. 2000. 'From the "Clean Snows of Petawawa": The Violence of Canadian Peacekeepers in Somalia', *Cultural Anthropology* 15, 1: 127–63. Discusses the violence of Canadian peacekeepers in the context of gender roles and racist responses.

Schryer, Frans J. 2001. 'Multiple Hierarchies and the Duplex Nature of Groups', *The Journal of the Royal Anthropological Institute* 7, 4: 705–21.

Examines the links between multiple hierarchies and broad-based groups to create a theoretical framework for integrating group phenomena, social identities, and political mobilization.

Sharma, Ursula. 1999. *Caste* (Philadelphia: Open University Press). A brief, up-to-date survey of recent anthropological scholarship dealing with caste in South Asia.

Smedley, Audrey, and Brian Smedley. 2011. *Race in North America: Origin and Evolution of a World View*, 4th edn (Boulder, CO: Westview Press). This book offers a comprehensive historical overview of the development of the concept of race in North America, beginning in the late eighteenth century. Smedley shows how the concept of race is a cultural construct that over time has been used in different ways, for different purposes.

## Related Websites

**French Canadian Nationalism** www.thecanadianencyclopedia.com/index.cfm?PgNm=TCE&Params=A1ARTA0003061

**The History of Racism in Canada** www.hopesite.ca/remember/history/racism_canada_1.html

**The Immigration and Refugee Board of Canada** www.irb-cisr.gc.ca

**The Inuit Tapirisat of Canada** www.itk.ca

**The Politics of Racism** www.japanesecanadianhistory.ca

**Who Rules America** Power Structure Research and the Hope for Democracy: http://sociology.ucsc.edu/whorulesamerica/methods/power_structure_research.html

# 13 | A Global World

## Chapter Outline

Views of the Political Economy
Cultural Processes in a Global World
Globalization and the Nation-State

Human Rights and Globalization
Cultural Imperialism, Cultural Hybridization,
 and Cosmopolitanism

## Learning Objectives

By the end of Chapter 13, you will be able to

- understand the history of the development of
  political economies,
- appreciate cultural process as the global world
  emerged,

- consider globalization and the pressures on the
  nation-state,
- recognize the challenges of human rights in a
  'globalized world', and
- compare and contrast cultural imperialism, cultural
  hybridization, and cosmopolitanism.

↓ *These Yao women send text messages to their friends as they take a break from their work near the Longsheng
rice terraces in southern China. Around the world, modern technologies are reshaping traditional ways of life.*

Orlando, Claudio, and Leonardo Villas Bôas were middle-class Brazilians who took part in an expedition that explored central Brazil in the early 1940s. Their experiences led them to dedicate their lives to protecting Brazil's Indigenous peoples from the ravages of contact with Western society. They were instrumental in persuading the government to create Xingu National Park, in 1952, a large area in the state of Mato Grosso where Indigenous groups could live undisturbed by outsiders. For much of the twentieth century, they continued to work to contact threatened Indigenous groups and to persuade them to move to Xingu.

One such group was the Kréen-Akaróre, now known as the Panará, whose existence was menaced by a highway being built through their traditional territory. In February 1973, after years of avoiding outsiders, the Panará finally made contact with Claudio Villas Bôas, who had been following them in hopes of finding them before the highway builders did. Shortly after this, Orlando Villas Bôas gave a press conference in which he forcefully urged that a reserve be created for the Panará by the Brazilian government. The reserve was not located in traditional Panará territory, however, and it was bounded by the Santarém-Cuiabá Highway. Within months, the 300 remaining Panará who settled there had abandoned their gardens; sick and in despair, they were begging for food from truck drivers. Finally, in October 1974, the Villas Bôas brothers were able to fly the 135 surviving Panará to Xingu National Park (Davis 1977: 69–73). Within a year, there were only 79 left.

Disease, devastation, and misery have been all too common for Indigenous peoples who have encountered Western expansion. Many observers, including anthropologists, have long feared that Indigenous Amazonian peoples were destined for extinction. After all, of a population of 5 million in 1500, only 280,000 remain today, and some groups have already died out (Gomes 1996). Recent history, however, suggests a reversal of fortune. During the last thirty to forty years, the 220 surviving Indigenous groups have seen their populations grow. Although some members still strive to keep free of outside entanglements, others have been educated and

live in cities; one has even been elected to the Brazilian National Congress (Gomes 1996). Even the Panará population has rebounded to over 160 people, and they recently received title to a 1.2 million-acre tract of the land they had originally inhabited, as well as a legal settlement for damages resulting from unsupervised contact with outside society. This was the first time that the Brazilian state has had to pay an Indigenous people for pain and suffering (Schwartzman 1998; Rainforest Foundation 2003).

This remarkable and heartening turn of events is illustrated by more recent events involving the Kayapó (see EthnoProfile 13.1). In March 1989, the *Anthropology Newsletter* published a report from anthropologist Terence Turner describing how Indigenous Amazonians had organized themselves to resist outside encroachment on their traditional lands. They were the people most directly affected by continued destruction of the Amazonian rainforest, but no one could have imagined that they might be leaders in defence of the environment, working successfully with national and international allies. Yet they brought some 28 Indigenous nations together in a huge inter-tribal village built in the path of a proposed hydroelectric dam complex at Altamira, on the Xingu River. The Kayapó leader Payakan combined traditional Indigenous political skills with a knowledge of Portuguese and a keen understanding of the international media. He and other Kayapó chiefs, such as Raoni, toured Europe and appeared publicly with well-known celebrities, including Sting, who supported their cause (see Figure 13.1). The Brazilian government, moreover, has still not built its dam. As Turner observes, 'The boldness and global vision of this project are breathtaking; nothing like such a concerted action by even a few, let alone 28 unrelated Indian societies, has ever taken place in the Amazon. The Indians are trying to tell us something important; we should listen' (1989: 21–2).

By 1992, the Kayapó had established legal and physical control of 28.4 million acres of their traditional land, but some Kayapó had been illegally selling very valuable mahogany trees, in part to buy boats and radios to protect their borders. In that year, one Kayapó village began working with Conservation International to create a sustainable and income-generating research station to replace cutting trees. By 2002, all 15 Kayapó

*EthnoProfile 13.1* | **Kayapó** ·······················································

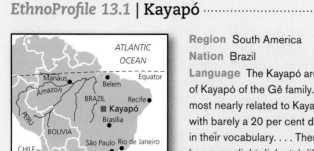

**Region** South America

**Nation** Brazil

**Language** The Kayapó are speakers of Kayapó of the Gê family. 'The language most nearly related to Kayapó is Apinayé, with barely a 20 per cent difference in their vocabulary. . . . There are, however, slight dialectal differences between the various groups' (Advameg Inc. 2008)

**Population** 7,096 (2003)

**Environment** Rainforest and savannah; wet and dry seasons

**Livelihood** Extensive agriculture and hunting and gathering

**Political organization** Headmen with no formal power; age grades

**For more information** Rabben, Linda. 1999. *Unnatural Selection: The Yanomami, the Kayapó and the Onslaught of Civilization* (London: Pluto Press); 'Language Family Trees: Macro-Ge, Ge-Kaingang, Ge, Northwest, Kayapó', www.ethnologue.com/14/show_family. asp?subid=2136; 'Encyclopedia—Kayapo', www.nationmaster.com/encyclopedia/Kayapo.

villages had signed agreements with Conservation International for conservation-based development projects, and Conservation International was also helping to develop a system for effective border surveillance (Conservation International 2003).

Peoples like the Panará and the Kayapó have struggled with the effects of European contact for over five hundred years, but rather than disappear forever, they have now moved out of the forest and into the thick of

*Figure 13.1* | **The Rainforest Foundation was founded in 1989 by filmmaker Jean-Pierre Dutilleux, musician Sting, and actress Trudie Styler to help the Kayapó resist outside encroachment on their lands.**

Brazilian national life. Indeed, they and other Indigenous people elsewhere in the world have been able to create global alliances by making use of contemporary Internet technology (Ribeiro 1998). Anthropological research on Amazonian peoples has also changed. Today, Gomes observes, 'one's living objects of research are easy to find, not more than a few hours away by plane, at the most a few days away by boat. They are on the outskirts of cities, in hospitals and medical centres, and even in the corridors of the National Congress. . . . They will also be available in the future' (1996: 19).

In this chapter, we take up the story of how the Western world and the societies where anthropologists work are interrelated, how those interrelationships have changed over the last sixty years, and with what consequences. We look at ourselves as much as we look at the peoples on which anthropological research traditionally focusses. Through this reflexive exercise, we try to establish a context for contemplating the common fate of humankind.

## Views of the Political Economy

It has become evident as we have moved through the chapters of this book that anthropologists have made use of a variety of theoretical perspectives over the years to explain the relationship between the West and the rest of the world. Looking back over the last sixty or so years, we can distinguish two important phases of anthropological theorizing.

The first phase corresponded to the period of the Cold War—from the end of World War II to the break-up of the Soviet Union in 1989—which was also the period in which European colonial empires were dismantled. The struggle between the First World (the Western capitalist 'free world') and the Second World (the Soviet 'communist world', which sometimes included communist China as well) focussed on the Third World (or 'non-aligned world'), which included the new nation-states being formed out of former European colonies. The larger political struggle between First and Second worlds affected anthropologists working in what had become the Third World, and the major debates were between proponents of modernization theory and proponents of dependency theory and its various offshoots.

The second phase began in 1989, with the end of the Cold War and the dismantling of economic and political barriers that had separated the First, Second, and Third worlds from each other, events that unleashed new patterns of movement and exchange that have come to be called *globalization*. Issues connected to globalization now dominate anthropological discussions related to matters of political economy. However, the three-world analysis structure still has some currency. Although the Second World is no longer strictly represented by the USSR's successor states, there are still nation-states such as China and North Korea that fit more or less in the 'communist' mold. And perhaps here we could now place those states and societies in conflict with First World 'development' and 'democratization' aspirations—for example, radical Islamic societies whose ideologies oppose those of the West. This system of categorization would fit with the original First/Second World construct because that construct was based on an ideological framework as well. Then again we can question if the First World is not also represented by a new ideology, an ideology of elites— the ideology of globalization. This ideological conflict is not merely characterized as economic but as the conflict between tribalism and globalization. Political theorist Benjamin R. Barber (1995) sees both of these ideologies as dangerous to the survival of democracy.

More importantly, there has been an expansion of the analytical framework to include a Fourth World— the world of Indigenous peoples living in neo-colonial/ ex-colonial areas of the world, such as the First Nations and Inuit peoples of Canada. Renée Sylvain, a Canadian researcher working like Lee in southern Africa, puts emphasis on issues of Indigenous identities (2003) and culture and globalization (2002). The range of analytical expansion in this Fourth World domain of concern challenges all of us, as it addresses core issues of human survival. Thus the analysis of alignments is evolving to a more inclusive perspective.

Nonetheless, in order to understand the anthropological discussion of globalization, we must review past perspectives on global relationships.

## Modernization versus Dependency: The Colonial Legacy

In the early days of decolonization through to the period of the Cold War, many Western leaders and scholars interpreted the meaning of colonialism and its consequences through **modernization theory**. As colonial empires were reframed as newly independent states, Western thinkers postulated that these states would become prosperous, self-sustaining countries so long as they imitated the policies and practices believed to have been responsible for the successes of 'modern' Western nation-states. In this model, colonization was viewed as a positive process because it had taught backward peoples the (capitalist) skills and Western-style institutions they needed to move forward.

Former colonies were viewed as 'young' nation-states in need of paternal guidance from 'mature' modern states such as the US, which emerged from World War II as the richest and most powerful capitalist country in the world. Paternalistic supervision seemed particularly necessary after the successful communist revolution in Cuba in 1959, and modernization theory became the foundation of US foreign-aid policy in the 1960s. It was presented as a road map that promised to guide newly decolonized nations to self-sustaining prosperity, but only if they avoided revolution. There were no shortcuts to the future.

Many observers, particularly those living in former colonies, rejected such a view, as they

**modernization theory**
A theory that argues that the social change occurring in non-Western societies under colonial rule was a necessary and inevitable prelude to higher levels of social development that had been reached by the more 'modern' nations.

**dependency theory**
A theory that argues that the success of 'independent' capitalist nations has required the failure of 'dependent' colonies or nations whose economies have been distorted to serve the needs of dominant capitalist outsiders.

**world-system theory**
A theory that argues that, from the late fifteenth and early sixteenth centuries, European capitalism began to incorporate other regions and peoples into a world system whose parts were linked economically but not politically.

saw that the prosperity of Western nations had *depended on* the exploitation of cheap raw materials, cheap labour, and the captive markets that colonies provided. **Dependency theory** was developed in the 1960s by Latin American economists and social scientists who wanted to explain why, after more than a century of independence from colonial domination, their countries were still poor and weak. They challenged the assumption that nations are naturally autonomous and independently responsible for their own success or failure at modernizing. If colonies and other peoples' resources are necessary for a nation to become modern, then countries without colonies can never hope to become modern. In short, the West would never have prospered if colonial powers had not expropriated the wealth of other people to fuel their own development. The success of a few has required the failure of many. Indeed, the prophetic view was that the capitalist nations of the world would remain prosperous only as long as others were dependent on them for economic direction. Of course, the 2008 meltdown of the market economy of Western nation-states and its continuing and deepening consequences may indicate that we are currently witnessing the fulfillment of this prophesy.

While modernization theory rested on the metaphor of individual growth, many dependency accounts were based on the *metaphor of sexual violation*. Colonialism was seen as a violent rape of the colonies. Dependency theory drew attention to the way that dependent colonies or nations endure the reshaping of their economic structures to meet demands generated outside their borders. For example, land that could be used to raise food crops for local consumption is used to grow export goods such as flowers, bananas, or coffee; local needs are pushed into the background. Thus the international capitalist economic order was directly responsible for distorting the economies of these nations. (This

is a theme in documentaries such as *Man Made Famine* [1987] and *Amor, Mujeres y Flores* [*Love, Women, and Flowers*; 1988] and in novels such as *One Hundred Years of Solitude* [1967], by Gabriel García Márquez, where the foreign-owned banana company plays a role in the police massacre of plantation workers.) Such an analysis suggested that 'underdevelopment' would persist until dependent countries took control of their own destinies and restructured their economies and societies to meet local needs. Thus the 1960s, 1970s, and 1980s were notable for the attempts of anti-capitalist revolutionary movements in various Third World countries, as in the Cuban example.

Wallerstein's functionalist **world-system theory**, based on the metaphor of society as a living organism, compared the shared patterns of domination and dependency found in Third World countries. In *The Modern World System* (1974), Wallerstein set forth a global framework for understanding problems of development and underdevelopment, rejecting modernization theory. He argued that exploitative relations between First World and Third World countries took shape and were fine-tuned during the colonial era, embedding these developments within a broader and deeper historical narrative. Beginning in the late fifteenth and early sixteenth centuries, emerging European capitalism began incorporating other regions and peoples into a world economy based on the capitalist mode of production. We might think of the rise of the Hudson's Bay Company as a Canadian example of this process. Wallerstein deliberately chose to speak of a world economy rather than a world empire or other political entity because a world economy

> precisely encompasses within its bounds empires, city-states, and the emerging 'nation-states'. It is a 'world' system, not because it encompasses the whole world but because it is larger than any juridically defined political unit. And it is a 'world *economy*' because the basic linkage between the parts of the system is economic. (1974: 15)

At the time, the European world economy was not the only world economy in existence. Perhaps its most important competitor centred on China. Nevertheless, the European world economy was able to surpass these other world economies because of capitalism. 'The secret of capitalism was in the establishment of the division of labour within the framework of a world economy that was *not* an empire' (1974: 127). Banking, finance, and highly skilled industrial production became central, and nations with these specialties became the **core** of the European world economy. The core exploited the **periphery** to support highly skilled 'free' labour and a high standard of living in the West. The periphery, in contrast, practised various forms of coerced labour to produce goods to support core industries, and the standard of living for coerced workers was generally low. In this model, there was also a **semi-periphery** consisting of states like Mexico and Brazil that played peripheral roles in the past but that seemed to have accumulated sufficient industrial capacity and other resources to possibly achieve core status in the future.

The main critique of this model is that it only offers two possibilities for change:

1) units within the system may change roles (a semi-peripheral state may move to the core, or vice versa), or

2) the system as a whole may be transformed into something else as the result of a system-wide socialist revolution.

In its abstraction, the model misses the actual vibrancy of local activity.

## Globalization: Post–Cold War Debates

No part of the world after the Cold War was unaffected, to some extent, by capitalist economic practices. For some, this period of uncertainty seemed to present an opportunity to challenge the previously unquestioned truths about development and underdevelopment. Such challenges were seen in what were called *new social movements*. From vigilante movements (such as the *rondas campesinas* of Peru) to squatter movements in cities to movements defending the rights of women and homosexuals to movements defending the rainforests, people were attempting to construct cultural institutions that met their needs in ways that often bypassed national governments or development agencies (Figure 13.2). Anthropologist Arturo Escobar (1992) argued that such social movements in Latin America were struggles over meanings as well as material conditions.

Further, Escobar and anthropologists like James Ferguson attacked the notion of 'development' supported and promoted by Western governments and international aid agencies. They argued that the source of the problems in 'underdeveloped' countries was misidentified. 'By uncompromisingly reducing poverty to a technical problem, and by promising technical solutions to the sufferings of powerless and oppressed people, the hegemonic problematic of "development" is the principal means through which the question of poverty is de-politicized in the world today' as well as being 'a machine for reinforcing and expanding the exercise of bureaucratic state power, which incidentally takes "poverty" as its point of entry' (Ferguson 2002: 407).

Yet while the critique of Western efforts at modernization via development continued, the world toward which

**core**
In world-system theory, the nations specializing in banking, finance, and highly skilled industrial production.

**periphery**
In world-system theory, those exploited former colonies that supply the core with cheap food and raw materials.

**semi-periphery**
In world-system theory, states that have played peripheral roles in the past but that now have sufficient industrial capacity and other resources to possibly achieve core status in the future.

*Figure 13.2* | Following the Cold War, a number of 'new social movements' developed around the world, including Wangari Maathai's Green Belt Movement, a tree-planting project in Kenya, run mostly by women.

such arguments were aimed was already disappearing. The apparent triumph of capitalism reanimated the defenders of modernization theory, now repackaged as *neo-liberalism*, while the Marxian analysis was called into question. Now, states would be encouraged by international institutions like the World Bank and the International Monetary Fund to accept that prosperity depended on their finding a niche in the growing global capitalist market. Market discipline would force state bureaucrats, first, to support economic enterprises that would earn them income in the market and, second, to eliminate the role of state institutions and subsidies that had provided a safety net for the poor. Western leaders enthusiastically embraced the beckoning opportunity to bring the entire world within the compass of the capitalist economy. Less enthusiastic observers began to suspect that forces unleashed were remaking the global political economy in unprecedented ways, with outcomes that no one could predict or control.

## Cultural Processes in a Global World

The theories discussed above presuppose a world of relatively clear-cut geographic and cultural boundaries. However, the cybernetics revolution led to advances in manufacturing, transportation, and communications technology that removed the seemingly insuperable barriers to communication and contact that characterized much of the period of capitalist development. We live with a phenomenon called 'space–time compression' (Harvey 1990), where changes are easier, cheaper, and faster than ever before. It is now possible to stretch social relationships of all kinds over huge distances that previously would have been unbridgeable (Giddens 1990). No part of the globe escaped the effects of these changes—changes called **globalization**. The local is reshaped by powerful global forces on an ever-intensifying scale. Globalization is 'the intensification of global interconnectedness'; it involves 'a world full of movement and mixture, contacts and linkages, and persistent cultural interaction and exchange' (Inda and Rosaldo 2002: 2).

Globalization does not affect all individuals

**globalization**
Reshaping of local conditions by powerful global forces on an ever-intensifying scale.

and cultures in equal ways. After all, 'there are large expanses of the planet only tangentially tied to the webs of interconnection that encompass the globe' (Inda and Rosaldo 2002: 4). Thus different groups and actors interpret and experience global processes in different—often very personal and unique—ways. Anthropologists Faye Ginsburg and Rayna Rapp (1995), for example, describe the global process of *stratified reproduction*, in which some categories of people (Westerners, the wealthy) are empowered to nurture and reproduce, while others (non-Westerners, the poor) are not. Consider, for example, how members of the elite in some nations 'import' childcare workers; these workers then send their earnings home to support their own children, who are raised by parent surrogates. Globalization has created new opportunities for some groups, like the Kayapó and other Indigenous peoples, to build worldwide organizations to defend their interests (Kearney 1995: 560). At the same time, global forces can also reinforce old constraints. Evaluating the record of new social movements in Latin America, for example, Gledhill writes that 'to date the challenge that popular forces have been able to mount to the remorseless progress of the neo-liberal, neo-modernization agenda, has remained limited' (1994: 198).

It would be difficult to find any research project by contemporary cultural anthropologists that does not in some way acknowledge the ways in which global forces affect the local societies in which they work. For them it is a truism that *the global articulates with the local*. Therefore 'globalizing processes exist in the context of, and must come to terms with, the realities of particular societies' (Inda and Rosaldo 2002: 4). So 'while everyone might continue to live local lives, their phenomenal worlds have to some extent become global' (9).

Globalization is seen in the growth of transnational corporations that relocate their manufacturing operations from core to periphery or that appropriate local cultural forms and turn them into images and commodities to be marketed throughout the world. It is seen in tourism, which has grown into the world's largest industry, and in migration from periphery to core on such a massive scale that observers now speak of the 'de-territorialization' of peoples and cultures that, in the past, were presumed to be firmly attached to specific geographical locations (Figure 13.3). Not only that: de-territorialized people always 're-territorialize' in a new location. Such

*Figure 13.3* | **Tourism has grown into the world's largest industry, and tourists have begun to encroach on people and cultures all over the world. This Bonda woman presents her handmade necklaces for sale to Western tourists in a market in Orissa, India.**

re-territorialization regularly sparks social conflicts and generates new forms of cultural identity, as nation-states try to retain control over citizens living beyond their borders and as relocated populations struggle both for recognition in their new homes and for influence in their places of origin. Globalization has drawn the attention of many anthropologists to regions such as the borderland between northern Mexico and the southwestern US, where struggles with contradictory social practices and ambiguous identities have long been the rule rather than the exception. Such contexts exhibit a 'diffusion of culture traits gone wild, far beyond that imagined by the Boasians' (Kearney 1995: 557). Since borderland conditions are now becoming worldwide, they undermine views of culture that depend upon settled peoples with distinct cultural attributes.

Where does Wallerstein's portrayal of the global processes as part of a world *system* fit now? Anthropologist Arjun Appadurai points out that ever-intensifying global flows of people, technology, wealth, images, and ideologies are highly contradictory, generating global processes that are fundamentally disorganized and unpredictable (1990). Meanwhile Jonathan Friedman argues that the disorder may be real but it is also a predictable consequence of the breakdown of Western global hegemony (1994). In his view, these developments exemplify a pattern of commercial expansion and contraction that began at least five thousand years ago with the rise of the first commercial civilizations—world systems in Wallerstein's sense—each of which was characterized by its own form of 'modernity'. Thus, the capitalist world system of the West 'tends, as in previous mercantile civilizations, to become decentralized and more competitive. Weakened and crisis-ridden, the centre is likely to decline and lose its hegemonic power to new rising centres of imperialist accumulation' (1994: 2–3). As a result, 'modernity in this sense is just another tradition, labile and fragile, that has emerged, however partially, and disappeared numerous times on the stage of human history'—for example, in ancient Greece, Rome, China, India, and the Arab Middle Ages (229–30). Awareness of this oscillating pattern reveals that 'the variety of social structures documented in the anthropological literature can be understood as transformations of one or two basic types of organization in changing conditions of marginality in larger systems' based on whether they occur as a new commercial civilization begins to spread or as that civilization begins to decline (40).

Recognition of this pattern makes Friedman even more pessimistic than Wallerstein about possibilities for the future. He sees current changes in the capitalist world system as simply the latest example of 'a more cyclically sinister history of civilizational systems' that have risen and fallen repeatedly throughout history (99; cf. Abu-Lughod 1991). Friedman remains unmoved by those who suggest that anything new or hopeful might emerge from the current state of the world: 'The capacity to even conceive of consciously changing the world for the better lies, perhaps, in changing the system as a whole, a system whose more general properties have eluded the storms of innumerable revolutions and

## In Their Own Words | Cofan: Story of the Forest People and the Outsiders

*Randy Borman is president of the Centro Cofan Zabalo. He was born to missionary parents and grew up in Cofan culture in the Ecuadorian Amazon. Borman briefly attended school in North America and then returned to Ecuador to become a leader in the Cofan fight for economic and cultural survival. He has written in* Cultural Survival Quarterly *about the development of ecotourism in the Cofan area of Ecuador. The results of tourism elsewhere in the world are not always as positive as they have been for the Cofan people, in part because tourism is often imposed from the outside.*

I had the fortune to grow up as a forest person, enjoying the clean rivers and unlimited forests, learning the arts and skills of living comfortably in a wonderland of the marvellous, beautiful, and deadly. I experienced first-hand both the good and the bad of a world, which will never again be possible, at least in the foreseeable future. And I also experienced the crushing physical, psychological, and spiritual impact of the invasion of the outside that erased our world.

In 1955, the Cofan people were the sole inhabitants of more than 1,000,000 hectares of pristine forest in northeastern Ecuador. By 1965, oil exploration and exploitation had begun. And by 1975, the forest was fast disappearing before a massive mestizo colonization, which was brought in by roads created to access vast quantities of oil. The rivers were fouled with chemicals and raw crude; the animals disappeared; boom towns sprung up all over; and the Cofan struggled to survive on less than 15,000 hectares of badly degraded forest. The old life was gone forever, and my companions and I faced the numbing prospect of discarding our culture and way of life, and becoming peasant farmers like so many others, trying to eke out a living from crops and animals which were never meant to grow in this environment. We had been powerless to maintain our forests in the face of outsider pressures to make every given piece of land profitable. If we were to save anything from the wreckage we needed alternatives, and quickly. . . .

[As the only member of his community with an outsider education, Borman worked with the community in trying to develop strategies for community survival, including those associated with marketing forest products. These strategies did not work.]

As we were wrestling with these possible alternatives, we were also acting as boatmen for the slowly increasing economy on the river. Several of us had managed to buy outboard motors with carefully saved returns from corn fields, animal skins, and short stints as trail makers with the oil companies. We had a long tradition of carving dugouts, and soon our canoes were travelling up and down the rivers with loads of lumber, corn, and coffee; occasional trips carrying cattle provided excitement and variety. This was not an alternative for the entire community, and it was only viable until roads were built, but it worked as a stop-gap measure for some of us. And unexpectedly, it led us directly into the alternative, which we have adopted as our own in the years since.

Travellers were coming to our region. The roads made it easier than at any previous time, and people from First World countries—the US, Canada, England, Germany, Israel, Italy—began to come, searching for the vanishing rainforest. Most of them were primarily interested in seeing wildlife. This fit with our view of the situation precisely. We had our motorboats. There was still a lot of good forest out there, but it was hard to access with regular paddling and poling expeditions. So when these travellers arrived and wanted to go to 'wild jungle', we were delighted to take them. They paid the transportation cost, and we took our shotguns and spears along to go hunting. Our attitude was that if the traveller wanted to go along with us, and didn't mind that we were hunting, why, we were happy to have them along to help carry the game home! From such a pragmatic beginning, we slowly developed our concept of tourism.

There were changes. We soon learned that the traveller had a lot more fun if we modified our normal hunting pattern a bit, and we even got paid extra for it. We found out that the average tourist didn't mind if we shot birds that looked like chickens, even if they were rare. But if we shot a toucan they were outraged, despite the fact that toucans are very common. Tourists preferred a board to a stick as a seat in the canoe, and a pad made them even happier. Tourists' food needed to be somewhat recognizable, such as rice, rather than the lumpy, thick manioc beer we normally eat and drink. But the community as a whole decided early that our role would be that of guides and service providers for tourists interested in the forest. We would not dress up and do dances, or stage fake festivals, or in any way try to sell our traditions and dress. We would not accept becoming the objects of tourism—rather, we would provide the skills and knowledge for the tourist to understand our environment. We would sell our education at a price that was in line with the importance to the outsiders who wanted to buy it, such as lawyers, biologists, doctors, teachers, and other professionals the world over do.

Being guides for the tourism experience, not the objects of it, has provided both a very real economic alternative and a very solid incentive for the younger generation to learn the vast body of traditional knowledge, which lies at the heart of our culture. A deep conservation ethic—the roots of which lie at the hearts of most cultures who maintain a viable relation with their environments—has helped the Cofan community to create a number of projects which combine outsider science with our traditional knowledge. Interestingly enough, this has also turned out to be an economic success, as many of our projects began to receive funding in recognition of their innovation and replicability in other communities throughout Amazonia.

At present, the Cofan community most involved in both tourism and conservation is my community, Zabalo. Located in what is now part of the Cuyabeno Wildlife Reserve near the northern border of Ecuador with Peru, this community owns and manages over 100,000 hectares of forest in coordination with the Ecuadorean national parks system. With four community-operated cabins, an interpretation centre, and a series of trails and camps both in deep forest and on the black water streams of the area, Zabalo plays host in varying scale to over 3,000 visitors annually. Most of these visitors come via an Ecuadorean tourism agency, Metropolitan Touring, which operates a floating hotel in the region (appropriately the Flotel), and spend only a few hours at the interpretation centre and market. However, perhaps 200 visitors per year spend up to 10 days enjoying the village's programs—trekking, canoeing, birding, wildlife watching; learning to know the forest intimately in the company of Cofan guides, cooks, and administrators. Both the cabins and the interpretation centre generate income for the community. Working as crew and as guides for the groups provides individual income. And the sale of crafts both directly to tourists and to retailers elsewhere in the country is a steady and important source of cash for the families of the community. . . .

Tourism is not for everyone. Some of our experiences have been negative. One of our biggest and most constant headaches is effective commercialization. To operate a community-based tourism business while maintaining our cultural heritage is not possible using the outsider formula of a tour operator. The implied hierarchy of manager, finance department, buyers, transport specialists, etc., all working eight hours a day, five days a week, with an office and a fax machine is clearly not applicable. Instead, we rely on teams, which rotate in their work, leaving time for farms, family duties, crafts, fishing, hunting, and the garden. But the lack of a full-time office makes it difficult to commercialize effectively, and we walk the precarious line between too much tourism (no time left over to live a normal life, and possible loss of our cultural way of life) and too little (not enough jobs, not enough income, lack of attraction for a forest-based life and education for our young people). If we commercialize effectively, we run the risk of the operation snowballing, with more and more tourists arriving, and eventually we are all wealthy in outsider goods and income but without our culture's wealth of time and interpersonal relationships that we all value so much now. If we don't commercialize effectively, we will wake up tomorrow back at the beginning, with the need to destroy our forest for short-term survival.

But in the overall scheme of things, our experiment with tourism has been overwhelmingly positive. Contact with people who wish to know what we can teach, who value our forests and are willing to pay to help us maintain them has been very important. Our increased awareness of the conservation imperatives facing us has led to many changes in our way of life, all aimed at preserving core values for future generations.

Source: Borman, Randy. 1999. 'Cofan: Story of the Forest People and the Outsiders', *Cultural Survival Quarterly* 23, 2: 48–50.

cataclysm' (1994: 41). Not all anthropologists accept Friedman's arguments, as his conclusions cannot account for the 'local structures' and 'autonomous cultural schemes' that appear at any point in the cycle. It is this historically specific local detail—what Inda and Rosaldo (2002: 27) call 'the conjunctural and situated character of globalization'—that anthropologists aim to document and analyze.

# Globalization and the Nation-State

## Are Global Flows Undermining Nation-States?

In the recent past, one of the fundamental suppositions about global social organization was that it consisted of an international order of independent nation-states. This is an assumption rooted in the nineteenth-century nationalist struggles in Europe, although it came fully into its own after World War II as former colonies achieved independence. The United Nations presupposed a world of nation-states. Modernization theorists and dependency theorists alike assumed that the world was a mosaic of nations that were entitled to self-determination and a state of their own. The flows of people, technology, wealth, images, and ideologies unleashed by globalization, however, have undermined the ability of nation-states to police their boundaries effectively and has seemed to suggest that the conventional ideas about nation-states require revision. Further, many nation-states are actually composed of disparate ethnic groups with diverging self-interests. National governments are virtually powerless to control what their citizens read or watch in the media: satellite services and telecommunications and the Internet elude the censor. Nation-states allow migrants or students or tourists to cross their borders because they need their labour or tuition or vacation dollars, but in doing so states must contend with the political values or religious commitments or families that these outsiders bring with them (Figure 13.4). Is the weakening of boundaries between states a good thing?

Massive global displacements of people have characterized Western modernity, starting with the slave trade and the movement of indentured labour to the

*Figure 13.4* | A foreign-born student sits among her Japanese classmates. Japan is an example of a nation-state where foreigners struggle to understand cultural values, customs, and beliefs that often differ from their own.

colonies. In the nineteenth century, as developing capitalist markets pushed and pulled waves of European and Asian emigrants out of their homelands and installed them in different parts of the globe, colonial authorities revived the institution of indentured labour to rearrange populations within their dominions. For example, consider that over 100,000 'home children'—orphans and other children from Great Britain—were shipped to Canada between 1869 and 1930. When volumes of immigration were lower and moved at a slower pace, and jobs were plentiful, comfortable assimilation into the society of re-territorialization was often possible. But globalization has changed all that. Today, desperate economic and political situations in migrants' home territories, plus ease of transportation, have increased the volume and speed of migration, while market crises in the countries where migrants have settled have sharply reduced the economic opportunities available to them. Thus migrants often find themselves caught between the hope for better opportunities and the threat of failure. Additionally, their visibility in enclaves of settlement, often in the poorer areas of cities, and the hostility, sometimes with violence, directed against them by locals promotes the sense that hopes of assimilation are unrealistic. In such an atmosphere it is difficult to break off ties to the homeland.

## Migration, Transborder Identities, and Long-distance Nationalism

The term *diaspora* is commonly used to refer to migrant populations with a shared identity who live in a variety of different locales around the world, but Nina Glick Schiller and Georges Fouron point out that not all such populations see themselves in the same way. They describe different types of *transborder identities* that can characterize different groups of migrants. They prefer to use the term *diaspora* to identify a form of transborder identity that does not focus on nation-building. Should members of a diaspora begin to organize in support of nationalist struggles in their homeland, or to agitate for a state of their own, they become **long-distance nationalists** (2002: 360–1).

*Long-distance nationalism* is a term coined by political scientist Benedict Anderson to describe the efforts of émigrés to offer moral, economic, and political support to the nationalist struggles of their countries of origin. In his original discussion, Anderson emphasized the dangerous irresponsibility of the 'citizenshipless participation' of long-distance nationalists: 'while technically a citizen of the state in which he comfortably lives, but to which he may feel little attachment, he finds it tempting to play identity politics by participating (via propaganda, money, weapons, any way but voting) in the conflicts of his imagined *Heimat* [homeland]' (2002 [1992]: 269–70). Schiller and Fouron argue, however, that the conditions of globalization have led to new forms of long-distance nationalism that do not correspond to Anderson's original description. They point to the emergence of the **transborder state**: a form of state 'claiming that its emigrants and their descendants remain an integral and intimate part of their ancestral homeland, even if they are legal citizens of another state' (2002: 357).

In today's global world, political leaders of many states sending emigrants not only accept the likelihood that those emigrants will permanently settle elsewhere but also insist that such permanently settled émigrés will retain full membership in the nation-state from which they came. This form of long-distance nationalism creates what Schiller and Fouron call a **transborder citizenry**: 'Citizens residing within the territorial homeland and new emigrants and their descendants are part of the nation, whatever legal citizenship the émigrés may have' (2002: 358).

Transborder states and transborder citizenries are more than symbolic identities: they have become concretized in law. Canadians can hold dual citizenship; and several Latin American countries, including Mexico, Colombia, the Dominican Republic, Ecuador, and Brazil, permit emigrants who have become naturalized citizens in countries such as the US to retain dual nationality and even voting rights in their country of origin. Some countries go so far as to set up special government ministries to address the needs of citizens living abroad. This situation is very different from Anderson's notion of 'citizenshipless participation'. Schiller and Fouron stress that transborder states and citizenries 'cannot be seen as top-down fostering of elite beliefs' but that they spring instead 'from the life experiences of migrants of different classes' and are 'rooted in the day-to-day efforts of people in the homeland to live lives of dignity and self-respect that compel them to include those who have migrated' (2002: 359).

But some transborder citizenries face difficulties.

- First, their efforts at nation-building are sometimes blocked by political forces in the homeland who do not welcome their contributions. This has been the case for Haitians living abroad while Haiti was ruled by the Duvalier dictatorship and for Cubans living abroad whose efforts are blocked by Castro's revolutionary government.
- Second, the states in which immigrants have settled may not welcome the continued involvement of transborder citizens in the affairs of another state. Such involvement has often been seen as even more threatening since terrorists destroyed the World Trade Center and attacked the Pentagon in the US on 11 September 2001.

Yet in an era of globalization, attempts to control migration threaten to block the global flows of people that

**diaspora**
Migrant populations with a shared identity who live in a variety of different locales around the world; a form of transborder identity that does not focus on nation-building.

**long-distance nationalists**
Members of a diaspora who begin to organize in support of nationalist struggles in their homeland or to agitate for a state of their own.

**transborder state**
A form of state in which it is claimed that those people who left the country and their descendants remain part of their ancestral state, even if they are citizens of another state.

**transborder citizenry**
A group made up of citizens of a country who continue to live in the homeland plus the people who have emigrated from the country and their descendants, regardless of their current citizenship.

**legal citizenship**
The rights and obligations of citizenship accorded by the laws of a state.

**substantive citizenship**
The actions people take, regardless of their legal citizenship status, to assert their membership in a state and to bring about political changes that will improve their lives.

**transnational nation-states**
Nation-states in which the relationships between citizens and their states extend to wherever citizens reside.

**flexible citizenship**
The strategies and effects employed by managers, technocrats, and professionals who regularly move across state boundaries and who seek both to circumvent and benefit from different nation-state regimes.

keep the global economy going. Moreover, the vulnerability of transborder citizens in these circumstances often increases the appeal of long-distance nationalism (Schiller and Fouron 2002: 359–60).

The globalizing forces that produce long-distance nationalism and transborder states and citizens have undermined previous understandings of what a world made up of nation-states should look like. In addition, unacknowledged contradictions and weaknesses of actual nation-states are revealed. For example, the existence and strength of transborder states and citizenries show that some nation-states—especially those sending migrants—are actually what Schiller and Fouron call *apparent states*: they have all the outward attributes of nation-states (government bureaucracies, armies, a seat in the UN), but in fact they are unable to meet the needs of their people (2002: 363). The strength of long-distance nationalism and transborder citizenries also exposes inconsistencies and paradoxes in the meaning of citizenship in the nation-states where migrants settle.

Schiller and Fouron contrast **legal citizenship** with what they call **substantive citizenship** and point out that, for transborder citizens, the two do not often coincide. Legal citizenship is accorded by state laws and can be difficult for migrants to obtain. But even those transborder citizens who obtain legal citizenship often experience a gap between what the legal citizenship promises and the way they are treated by the state. For example, people of colour and women who are US citizens are not treated by the state the same way white male citizens are treated. In contrast, substantive citizenship is defined by the actions people take, regardless of their legal citizenship status, to assert their membership in a state and to bring about political changes that

will improve their lives. Some transborder citizenries call for the establishment of fully fledged **transnational nation-states**. That is, 'they challenge the notion that relationships between citizens and their state are confined within that territory' and work for the recognition of a new political form that contradicts the understandings of political theory, but which reflects the realities of their experiences of national identity (Schiller and Fouron 2002: 359).

The contrast between formal and substantive citizenship suggests that conventional notions of citizenship that previously seemed straightforward begin to break down in the context of globalization. Anthropologist Aihwa Ong suggests these contradictions and ambiguities speak to **flexible citizenship**: 'the strategies and effects of mobile managers, technocrats, and professionals seeking both to circumvent *and* benefit from different nation-state regimes by selecting different sites for investment, work, and family relocation' (2002 [1999]: 174).

Ong's research concerns diaspora communities of elite Chinese families who have played key roles in the economic successes of the Pacific Rim in recent years. Although their success is often attributed by outsiders to 'Chinese culture', Ong's research calls this simplistic explanation into question. She documents the ways in which Chinese families have responded creatively to opportunities and challenges they have encountered since the end of the nineteenth century, when Chinese merchants first became involved in overseas commercial capitalism in the economic centres of European colonial empires in East and Southeast Asia. Their success has come because they were able to cultivate values and practices that allow them to evade or exploit the governmentality of three different kinds of institutions: Chinese kinship and family, the nation-state, and the marketplace.

The break from mainland Chinese ideas of kinship and Confucian filial piety came when Chinese first moved into the capitalist commercial circuits of European empires. Money could be made in these settings, but success required Chinese merchant families to cut themselves off from ties to mainland China and to reinforce bonds among family members and business partners in terms of *guanxi* ('relationships of social connections built primarily upon shared identities such as native place, kinship, or attending the same school' [Smart 1999: 120]). Shaped primarily by the pressures of intense economic competition and tight state restrictions on permissible economic and political activity, diaspora Chinese merchant and industrial families developed a set of values and practices that centred on the well-being of the family.

> An individual's sense of moral worth is based on endurance and diligence in income-making activities, compliance with parental wishes, and the making of sacrifices and deferral of gratification, especially on the part of women and children. . . . Children, especially sons, are expected to collect symbolic capital in the form of educational certificates and well-paying jobs that help raise the family class position and prestige. (Ong 2002 [1999]: 178)

Having managed to evade the discipline of mainland Chinese kinship and family practices, the family discipline of overseas Chinese enabled them to become wealthy and provided the resources to subvert the governmentality of the nation-state. The orientation of these wealthy families toward national identity and citizenship, Ong explains, is 'market-driven'. In Hong Kong, for example, in the years leading up to its return to mainland China in 1997, many wealthy Chinese thought of citizenship 'not as the right to demand full democratic representation but as the right to promote familial interests apart from the well-being of society' (178). None of the overseas Chinese she knew expressed any commitment to nationalism, either local or long-distance.

Rather, relying on family discipline and loyalty, and buttressed by considerable wealth and strong interpersonal ties, they actively worked to evade the governmentality of nation-states. For example, Chinese from Hong Kong who wanted to migrate to Britain in the 1960s were able to evade racial barriers that blocked other 'coloured' immigrants because of their experience with capitalism and their reputation for peaceful acquiescence to British rule. When the British decided to award citizenship to some Hong Kong residents in the 1990s, they used a point system that favoured applicants with education, fluency in English, and training in professions of value to the economy, such as accountancy and law. These

attributes fit the criteria for citizenship valued under the government of Margaret Thatcher, while other applicants for citizenship who lacked such attributes were excluded. Citizenship, or at least a passport, could be purchased by those who had the money: 'well-off families accumulated passports not only from Canada, Australia, Singapore, and the US but also from revenue-poor Fiji, the Philippines, Panama, and Tonga, which required in return for a passport a down payment of US $200,000 and an equal amount in instalments' (Ong 2002: 183) (Figure 13.5).

Wealthy overseas Chinese families had thus managed to evade or subvert both the governmentality of Chinese kinship and family and the governmentality of nation-states. But they remained vulnerable to the discipline of the market. To be sure, market discipline under globalization was very different from the market discipline

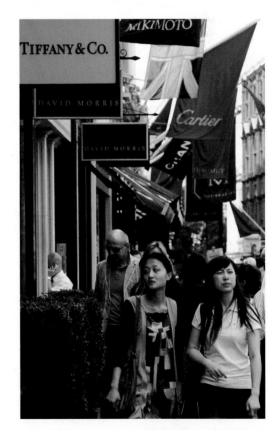

*Figure* 13.5 | Chinese shoppers flock to the luxury stores in London's West End. Historically, wealthy Chinese families have been able to use their money, along with their business experience, to succeed in Western society.

typical in the 1950s and 1960s, before the development of the transportation, communication, and manufacturing technologies that enabled people to move money and factories with ease around a world no longer divided by the Cold War. Making money in the context of globalization required the flexibility to take advantage of economic opportunities wherever and whenever they appeared; accordingly, overseas Chinese took steps to position family members in different settings. Ong describes one family in which the eldest son remained in Hong Kong to run part of the family hotel chain located in the Pacific region while his brother lived in San Francisco and managed the hotels located in North America and Europe. Children can be separated from their parents when they are, for example, installed in one country to be educated while their parents manage businesses in other countries on different continents. Yet these flexible business arrangements are not without costs. 'Familial regimes of dispersal and localization . . . discipline family members to make do with very little emotional support; disrupted parental responsibility, strained marital relations, and abandoned children are such common circumstances that they have special terms.' At the same time, individual family members truly do seem to live comfortably as citizens of the world. A Chinese banker in San Francisco told Ong: 'I can live anywhere in the world, but it must be near an airport' (2002: 190).

The values and practices to which overseas Chinese adhere, and which seem responsible for their tremendous achievements in a globalized capitalist economy, suggest to Ong that, for these elite Chinese, the concept of nationalism has lost its meaning. Instead, she says, they seem to subscribe to a **post-national ethos** in which they submit to the governmentality of the capitalist market while trying to evade the governmentality of nation-states,

ultimately because their only true loyalty is to the family business (2002: 190). Ong notes, however, that flexible citizenship informed by a post-national ethos is not an option for non-elite migrants: 'whereas for bankers, boundaries are always flexible, for migrant workers, boat people, persecuted intellectuals and artists, and other kinds of less well-heeled refugees, this . . . is a harder act to follow' (190).

She also points out that, on the way to their success, contemporary Chinese merchants 'have also revived pre-modern forms of child, gender, and class oppression, as well as strengthened authoritarianist regimes in Asia' (190). Yet neither the positives nor the negatives should, she insists, be attributed to any 'Chinese' essence; instead, she thinks these strategies are better understood as 'the expressions of a habitus that is finely tuned to the turbulence of late capitalism' (191).

# Human Rights and Globalization

## Human Rights Discourse as the Global Language of Social Justice

The original UN Declaration on Human Rights in 1948 and numerous subsequent declarations, accompanied by the intensification of processes of globalization, have created conditions for growing discussions of **human rights**. The challenge has been the emerging, different understandings about what it means to be human, or what kinds of rights people may be entitled to under radically changed conditions of everyday life. Questions of human rights become most salient in settings defined by **multiculturalism**, a situation found everywhere in today's globalized world but of particular interest to Canadians. Multicultural settings combine different cultural understandings of what it means to be human and what rights humans are entitled to.

Human rights discourses now extend into areas of gender politics. For example, in 1992, the Committee on the Elimination of Discrimination against Women (CEDAW) declared that violence against women was a form of gender discrimination that violated the human rights of women. This declaration was adopted by the UN General Assembly in 1993 and became part of the rights

---

**post-national ethos**
An attitude toward the world in which people submit to the governmentality of the capitalist market while trying to evade the governmentality of nation-states.

**human rights**
A set of rights that should be accorded to all human beings everywhere in the world.

**multiculturalism**
Living permanently in settings surrounded by people with cultural backgrounds different from your own and struggling to define the degree to which the cultural beliefs and practices of different groups should or should not be accorded respect and recognition by the wider society.

platform at the Fourth World Conference on Women in Beijing, China, in 1995. Anthropologist Sally Merry observes that this declaration 'dramatically demonstrates the creation of new rights—rights which depend on the state's failure to protect women rather than its active violation of rights' and that 'the emergence of violence against women as a distinct human rights violation depends on redefining the family so that it is no longer shielded from legal scrutiny' (2001: 36–7). Although CEDAW has proved particularly contentious, other human rights documents have been signed without controversy by many national governments.

Signing on to a human rights declaration ostensibly binds governments to take official action to implement changes in local practices that might be seen to violate the rights asserted in the declarations. Human rights discourses are common currency in all societies, at all levels. As Jane Cowan, Marie-Bénédicte Dembour, and Richard Wilson write, it is 'no use imagining a "primitive" tribe which has not yet heard of human rights . . . what it means to be "Indigenous" is itself transformed through interaction with human rights discourses and institutions' (2001: 5).

Because of the wide adoption of human rights discourses throughout the world, some people have come to speak of an emerging 'culture of human rights' that has now become 'the pre-eminent global language of social justice' (Merry 2001: 38). These developments mean that anthropologists need to take note of the important influence this human rights discourse is having in the various settings where they do their research. What counts as 'human rights' has changed over time, due not only to the action of international bodies like the UN but also to the efforts of an increasing number of non-governmental organizations (NGOS) that have become involved in various countries of the world, many of them deeply committed to projects designed to improve people's lives and protect their rights. As Merry says, these developments 'have created a new legal order' that has given birth to new possibilities throughout the world for the elaboration and discussion of what human rights are all about (2001: 35). In addition, because the 'culture of human rights' is increasingly regarded, in one way or another, as the 'culture of globalization', it would seem to be a topic well-suited to anthropological analysis.

As we shall see, human rights discourse is not as straightforward as it seems. On the face of things, defending human rights for all people would seem unproblematic. Few people who are aware of the devastation wrought by colonial exploitation, for example, would want to suggest that the victims of that exploitation did not have rights that needed to be protected at all costs. And yet, when we look closely at particular disputes about human rights, the concept no longer seems so simple. Jane Cowan and her colleagues (2001) have noted that there are two major arguments that have developed for talking about the way human rights and culture are related:

1) that *human rights are opposed to culture* and that the two cannot be reconciled, and
2) that a key universal human right is precisely one's *right to culture*.

We will consider each in turn.

## Rights versus Culture

Arguments that pit human rights against culture depend on the assumption that 'cultures' are homogeneous, bounded, and unchanging sets of ideas and practices and that each society has only one culture, which its members are obligated to follow. As we saw in Chapter 1, this view of culture has been severely criticized by cultural anthropologists. But it is a view of culture that is very much alive in many human rights disputes. For if people have no choice but to follow the rules of the culture into which they were born, international interference with customs said to violate human rights would seem itself to constitute a human rights violation: disrupting a supposedly harmonious way of life and preventing those who are committed to such a way of life from observing their own culturally specific understandings about rights. Thus, cultures should be allowed to enjoy absolute, inviolable protection from interference by outsiders. This has been the position adopted, for example, by some national governments that have refused to sign the CEDAW declaration that violence against women violates women's human rights. As of 2011, 187 of 193 UN member countries are party to CEDAW, although some countries, such as the US, have yet to ratify, thus not moving as a nation to full implementation. The US remains the only industrialized nation to be in this position of non-ratification.

Sometimes the reasons for defending culture against rights discourses are explicitly linked to the nineteenth-century struggle between defenders and opponents of the European Enlightenment. Thus, representatives of non-Western nation-states may feel free to dismiss rights talk as an unwelcome colonial imposition of ideas that, far from being universal, reflect ethnocentric European preoccupations. But such dismissal of human rights discourse needs to be closely examined. In the case of the right of women to protection from violence, for example, Merry points out that although some forms of violence against women may be culturally sanctioned in some societies, there are many forms that violence against women can take even in those societies, and not all of these are accorded the same amount of cultural support. Even practices like wife-beating or female genital cutting (Figure 13.6), which in the past could be justified in some circumstances as appropriate cultural actions, are now being questioned and even outlawed in the societies where they were practised. This suggests 'culture values' cannot be held responsible for everything that people do in any society and that members of

**Figure 13.6 | Among many East African people, including the Maasai, female genital cutting is an important part of the transformation of girls into women.**

the same society can disagree about these matters and sometimes change their minds.

As talk about human rights has become incorporated into local cultural discussions in recent decades, anthropologists are not surprised to discover that the notion undergoes transformation as people try to make sense of what it means in their own local contexts (Cowan et al. 2001: 8). Being forced to choose between rights *or* culture, however, seems increasingly unviable in a globalizing, multicultural world. In their own anthropological work on these matters, Cowan and her colleagues are convinced that the rights-versus-culture debate exaggerates cultural differences. Like many cultural anthropologists today, they find that 'it is more illuminating to think of culture as a field of creative interchange and contestation' (2001: 4).

Finally, it is worth asking if 'culture' is sometimes used as a scapegoat to mask the unwillingness of a government to extend certain rights to its citizens for reasons that have nothing to do with culture. Cowan, Dembour, and Wilson observe that states like Indonesia and Singapore, which position themselves as stout defenders of 'Asian values', have welcomed Western industrial capitalism. To reject human rights discourse because it contradicts 'Asian values' would, at the very least, suggest 'an inconsistent attitude toward Westernization', which, in turn, feeds suspicions that the defence of 'Asian values' may be a political tactic designed 'to bolster state sovereignty and resist international denunciations of internal repression and political dissent' (Cowan et al. 2001: 6–7).

## Rights to Culture

A second popular argument about the relationship between rights and culture begins from very different premises. Far from viewing universal 'human rights' as alien and opposed to 'cultures', this argument states that all peoples have a universal human right to maintain their own distinct cultures. This right has been made explicit in a number of international rights documents, and it draws strength from the ideas, popularized by earlier generations of anthropologists, that cultural diversity is intrinsically valuable and that people should be free to observe their own cultural practices without outside interference. The right-to-culture argument is an interesting twist on the rights-versus-culture argument since it seems to involve conceding that such things as universal human rights do exist after all. Still, the list of rights deemed to be universal is itself amended to include the right to one's culture, which calls into question the common understanding that people frequently have to be *freed* from the constraints of local cultures in order to enjoy their full human rights. The right-to-culture position therefore shows exactly the kind of transformation that the ideas of rights and culture undergo when caught in the mangle of global–local struggles provoked by globalization.

One of the key issues in the struggle to protect the right to culture—as well as any human rights deemed worthy of protection—concerns the kinds of legal mechanisms needed to ensure such protection. The great promise of international documents like the UN Declaration on Human Rights seems to be that people are now free to bring allegations of human rights abuses to an international forum to seek redress. But in fact, this is not the case.

- First, as human rights activists have discovered, human rights are legally interpreted as *individual* rights, not group rights.
- Second, the way in which people are to seek protection of their individual human rights is to demand that the *governments of the nation-states in which they are citizens* recognize and enforce the individual rights defended in international documents. International institutions like the UN have been unwilling to challenge the sovereignty of individual nation-states.

This second factor—which makes the defence of all human rights, including a right to culture, depend on the policies of particular national governments—has been viewed by activists and others as a serious contradiction in human rights discourse that undermines its effectiveness (see the letter from the Assembly of First Nations to the Canadian government in the 'In Their Own Words' box, below).

Anthropological disciplinary commitments have allowed anthropologists to approach debates about rights and culture in ways that contribute something new to the discussion. These anthropological contributions are primarily of two sorts:

1) anthropologists have addressed the ways in which human rights discourse can be seen as culture, and
2) they have mounted a critique of some of the ways that the concept of culture has been mobilized in the discussion of human rights.

## Rights as Culture

The ways that anthropologists have developed to study cultural patterns in other contexts seem well suited as tools for investigation of the extent to which a 'culture of human rights' can be said to have emerged in recent years. As in the cultures traditionally studied by anthropologists, the culture of human rights is based on certain ideas about human beings and their needs and their ability to exercise agency, as well as the kinds of social connections between human beings that are considered legitimate and illegitimate. The entire question of 'legitimacy' in human rights discourse points to the central role played by *law*, both as a way of articulating specific human rights and as a tool for defending those rights. Cowan, Dembour, and Wilson (2001) have drawn on earlier anthropological work in which systems of law were analyzed as cultural systems.

One important source has been the 'law and culture' framework developed by anthropologists Clifford Geertz, Laura Nader, and Lawrence Rosen and non-anthropologists like Boaventura de Sousa Santos. In this framework, 'law is conceived as a world view or structuring discourse . . . "facts" . . . are socially constructed through rules of evidence, legal conventions, and the rhetoric of legal actors' (Cowan et al. 2001: 11). Analysts who talk about a 'culture of human rights' as the new culture of a globalizing world point out that the key features of the human rights world view clearly indicate its origins in Western secular discourse: it focusses on the rights of individuals; it proposes to relieve human suffering through technical rather than ethical solutions, and it emphasizes rights over duties or needs (11). To the extent that this is the case, human rights culture is well designed to function as what anthropologist James Ferguson has called an 'anti-politics' machine (2002: 407).

As we saw in our discussion of post–cold war debates, Ferguson had a negative view of technical solutions to political problems. They not only failed to solve the problems of poverty, they also reinforced the power

## *In Their Own Words* | **Open Letter to All Political Parties**

*Living with the contradictions between international policy and governmental implementation, the Assembly of First Nations, with their significant allies, wrote an 'Open Letter to All Political Parties' on the one-year anniversary of the UN's adoption of its Declaration on the Rights of Indigenous Peoples.*

'Tomorrow, 13 September 2008, we celebrate the one-year anniversary of the United Nations Declaration on the Rights of Indigenous Peoples. The Declaration was adopted by the UN General Assembly on 13 September 2007 after more than two decades of negotiation and debate.

Despite having previously played a positive role in building international support for this human rights instrument, Canada was one of only four states to oppose the Declaration.

There are over 370 million Indigenous people worldwide. Indigenous peoples urgently require international affirmation and protection of their human rights. Their rights are routinely ignored and trampled by national governments, even when these rights are entrenched in domestic laws.

The Declaration affirms minimum human rights standards necessary for the 'survival, dignity, and well-being of the Indigenous peoples of the world'. These include the right of self-determination, protections from discrimination and genocide, and recognition of rights to lands, territories, and resources that are essential to the identity, health, and livelihood of Indigenous peoples.

The Declaration also explicitly requires that all provisions are to be balanced with the rights of others and interpreted in accordance with principles of justice, democracy, non-discrimination, good governance, and respect for the human rights of all.

On 8 April 2008 the Canadian House of Commons passed a resolution to endorse the UN Declaration and calling ON Parliament and the Government of Canada to 'fully implement the standards contained therein'. Unfortunately, the minority Conservative government has persisted with its unfounded claims that the Declaration cannot be applied in Canada and should not be used as a standard of human rights protection in countries that voted against it.

Human rights declarations become universally applicable upon their adoption by the UN General Assembly, regardless of how individual states vote. To claim that countries should be exempt from principles and standards they vote against flies in the face of six decades of Canadian human rights advocacy at the United Nations and sets a dangerous example for other countries of the world.

Indigenous peoples and human rights organizations urge Canada to join the global community in implementing this long overdue and much needed universal human rights instrument. To continue in any other manner undermines Canada's commitment to human rights at both the domestic and international levels.

In June a private members bill was introduced in the House of Commons calling for concrete measures to advance the Declaration in Canada. This includes requiring the Minister of Indian Affairs and Northern Development to report regularly to Parliament on implementation. Regretfully, Parliament will not have the opportunity to vote on this bill before the 14 October election. We recommend that this worthy initiative be re-introduced and embraced by all political parties in the new Parliament.

In February 2009, Canada's human rights record will be examined as part of the un Human Rights Council's Universal Periodic Review process. As a sign of its commitment to respecting the human rights of all, Canada should endorse the Declaration.

Our organizations take the occasion of the anniversary of the adoption to call on all political parties to affirm their support for the UN Declaration on the Rights of Indigenous Peoples. In accordance with the 8 April 2008 Motion, all parties should commit themselves to take action to ensure effective implementation of the Declaration when the new Parliament begins its work.

Source: Union of BC Indian Chiefs. 2008. 'First Nations Pressure Canada to Endorse the UN Declaration on the Rights of Indigenous Peoples' (12 Sept.), available at www.ubcic.bc.ca/News_Releases/UBCICNews09120801.htm.

of the state to interfere in and control the lives of its poor citizens. In the early twenty-first century, however, where state structures are under stress and the dynamics of transnational and multicultural living sometimes provoke violent and bloody political confrontations, a human rights discourse—or discourses—capable of 'depoliticizing' such confrontations might have an important role to play. Indeed, some anthropologists see the development of such discourses as a vital necessity and a key challenge in a globalized world, as we discuss below.

In the meantime, to the extent that human rights discourse is conceived to be a 'culture', most anthropologists would probably agree that this culture concept would be more illuminating if it reflected current anthropological understandings of culture (Cowan et al. 2001: 13). An understanding of culture as open, heterogeneous, and supple can become an effective analytic tool to help us understand how human rights processes work.

## Culture as a Way of Thinking about Rights

To use the culture concept as a tool for analyzing human rights processes means looking for 'patterns and relationships of meaning and practice between different domains of social life' that are characteristic of the culture of human rights (Cowan et al. 2001: 13). Since human rights are articulated in legal documents and litigated in courts, one of the most important patterns that becomes visible in the culture of human rights is the way these rights are shaped to accommodate the law. Groups and individuals who assert that their human rights have been violated regularly take their cases to courts of law. But this means that in order to get the courts to take them seriously, they need to understand how the law operates. A key feature of this understanding involves a realistic awareness of the kinds of claims that the law pays attention to and the kinds of claims that will be dismissed.

Looking at human rights law as culture reveals that only certain kinds of claims are admissible. As we saw above, the culture of human rights as currently constituted is best suited to redress the grievances of individuals, not groups, and to provide technical, not ethical, remedies; it also emphasizes rights over duties or needs. Plaintiffs are therefore likely to have a difficult time if they want to claim that their group rights have been violated, that

they want the violator exposed and punished, or that the state itself has failed to fulfill its responsibilities toward them. Part of the human rights process therefore involves learning how to craft cases that will fit the laws, and this can be tricky if the categories and identities recognized in human rights law do not correspond to categories and identities that are meaningful to the plaintiffs.

Many social groups among whom anthropologists work have engaged in political struggles with national governments in which they argue for protection of their rights to practise their culture freely. This portrayal of a group's culture in these kinds of political struggles regularly includes claims about protecting the culture's distinct and unchanging values and practices from state policies. As we saw in Chapter 12, these kinds of arguments for a right to culture are often cases of 'strategic essentialism' in which the unity and unchanging homogeneity of a particular 'culture' is deliberately constructed in order to build group solidarity and to engage the state in a focussed and disciplined way. But the 'essentialism' that often comes to dominate discussions of group rights is not due entirely to the strategies of activists. Once they choose to make their case in a court of law, they become subject to the 'essentializing proclivities of the law' (Cowan et al. 2001: 11).

Because human rights law only recognizes certain kinds of rights violations, groups with grievances must tailor those grievances to fit the violations that human rights law recognizes. According to Merry (2001), for example, groups like the Hawaiian Sovereignty Movement have successfully achieved some of their political goals by making claims based on the requirements of their 'traditional culture' (Figure 13.7). Their approach is effective because they live in a society that is 'willing to recognize claims on the basis of cultural authenticity and tradition but not reparations based on acts of conquest and violation' (2001: 42–3). Outside the courtroom, many members of Indigenous groups think of their culture the way contemporary anthropologists think about culture: there are some common patterns but culture is basically unbounded, heterogeneous, and open to change. But human rights law is ordinarily written in such a way that claims for cultural rights will only be considered if the culture in question is presented as bounded, homogenous, and unchanging. As a result, Indigenous peoples are often forced to portray themselves and their

*Figure 13.7* | **Members of Hawaiian sovereignty groups protest in the streets of Honolulu.**

cultures in ways that are very different from their own everyday understandings of who they are. While doing so may enable them to win legal judgments in their favour, it can also reshape their ideas about what their culture is. Groups that enter into the human rights process, thus, are entering into ethically ambiguous territory that is 'both enabling and constraining' (Cowan et al. 2001: 11).

### Human Rights in Thailand: Child Prostitution

Reaching successful accommodations between human rights discourse and local cultural practices is not always easy. A particularly difficult set of issues must be confronted when attempting to enforce the rights of children. Anthropologist Heather Montgomery (2001) did field research in a slum settlement in Baan Nua, Thailand, that was located near a prosperous seaside resort catering to foreign tourists (see Map 13.2). Those who lived in this settlement had broken all ties to other kin and other places from

---

*In Their Own Words* | **AFN Praises Sharon McIvor on 6 October, First Nations Women's Day**

*In 2008, AFN National Chief Phil Fontaine and AFN Women's Council Chair Kathleen McHugh called on women across Canada to celebrate First Nations Women's Day by making donations to support 'one of the longest standing and important human rights cases in Canadian history'.*

'McIvor's case, which will be heard by the BC Court of Appeal on 14 October 2008, could restore the right to Indian Status to more than 30,000 First Nations women and children. Thousands of First Nations women and their children do not have the legal right to vote in band elections or to own or inherit property on reserves because of a clause in the Indian Act that continues to discriminate against First Nations women by removing their ability to pass Indian Status on to their children. The clause has existed in varying forms in the Indian Act since 1869.

Sharon McIvor, a descendant of the Lower Nicola Valley Band, first launched her case in 1989, hoping to win Indian Status for her own children. Shortly before her case reached the courts in 2006, the federal government agreed to restore status to McIvor's children.

'Sharon could have dropped the case at that point, once her own children were granted their rights. Instead she

pushed forward on behalf of all First Nations women and children', says AFN Women's Council Chair, Kathleen McHugh. 'She is a true champion and heroine.'

McIvor has had trouble funding the case since October 2006, when the federal government cancelled the Court Challenges program. The government's decision came just after McIvor won her preliminary case in the BC Supreme Court, and just before the government decided to appeal her victory. The AFN Women's Council has led several fundraising events among chiefs to support McIvor's case.

'This is not only a First Nations issue, and it is not only a woman's issue. It's an issue of fairness and human rights that I believe all Canadians care about. Our preference always is to negotiate rather than litigate to achieve resolution. However, by choosing litigation the federal government denies our peoples the full expression of our fundamental human rights', said afn National Chief Phil Fontaine.

Source: Assembly of First Nations. 200 8. 'AFN Praises Sharon McIvor on 6 October, First Nations Women's Day', article released online at www.afn.ca.

Map 13.2 | Thailand

which they had migrated, which meant, Montgomery tells us, that the bonds linking parents and children in the settlement had become especially strong. Of overriding importance among these families was the duty of children to work to help support their families. Children did their best to fulfill this duty as soon as they were able, trying many different jobs, including begging. But none of these options earned very much. And so, sooner or later, children began working as prostitutes for wealthy foreign tourists who visited the resort. At the time of her research, 65 children in the community were working as prostitutes.

Children could earn five times as much money working as prostitutes as they could get from begging; plus they were able to visit fancy hotels and were well fed. Many of the clients, moreover, developed long-term relationships with the families of the child prostitutes, often lending them large sums of money—in one case, enough to rebuild the family home. It was friends and neighbours of the children, not their mothers, who recruited them into prostitution. When faced with the reality of the nature of their children's employment, mothers were able to claim that they had not found out until it was too late, and they interpreted the children's acts as evidence of their strong sense of filial duty in fulfilling obligations to help support the family. 'Both adult and child were aware of the child's duties, but there was a degree of unease about how far a child had to go to fulfill them' (Montgomery 2001: 90). The children claimed not to hate the men whom they worked for, especially those who kept

in touch even when not in Thailand and who continued to send money to the children. Because of the financial generosity and long-term involvement of these men with their children, mothers said they felt the men were trustworthy. The actual sexual acts for which the children are paid take place outside the settlement and are never publicly discussed, and the obvious physical consequences for the children are, to a point, studiously ignored.

Commercial sex and even child prostitution are not new in Thailand, and the situation in Baan Nua is not unique. On the basis of estimates from UNICEF, between 60,000 and 200,000 Thai children are prostitutes, and HIV/AIDS is a serious and continuing issue. In recent years, many Thais working in the media and for NGOS have denounced child sex tourism and have tried to force the national government to put a stop to it. Human rights discourse—particularly discourse about the rights of the child—have played a prominent role in this campaign (Figure 13.8). Montgomery points out that, since 1924, international bodies have issued nine separate documents dealing with human rights and the rights of the child.

Children's rights, like human rights in general, are based on Western ideas about what constitutes an acceptable human childhood and when childhood begins and ends. For example, the 1989 Convention on the Rights of the Child defines a child as anyone under 18 years of age, and Anti-slavery International has claimed that child-marriage is a form of slavery and therefore violates human rights. But as Montgomery observes, 'it does not take an anthropologist to recognize that a child marrying at 15 in full accordance with traditional norms and local custom in India is very different from a child marrying at 15 in the UK' (2001: 82). In common with other forms of human rights discourse, declarations on the rights of the child normally emphasize the importance of rights over duties, although this is not universal. But this is the issue that needs to be emphasized, Montgomery argues, in order to talk meaningfully about the rights of the children working as prostitutes in the Baan Nua slum.

The model of ideal Western childhood contained in the UN Convention on the Rights of the Child includes the idea that, as Montgomery puts it, 'every child has a right to a childhood that is free from the responsibilities of work, money, and sex' (83). The problem with this standard is that it fits so poorly with understandings of childhood in which, for example, children are expected

*Figure 13.8* | **Doctors without Borders runs a rehabilitation centre for child prostitutes in Thailand.**

(or needed) to work for money to support the family, and it seems unable to imagine situations in which the entire support of a family depends on a child's earnings from prostitution. Yet that is an accurate description for many families and children in Baan Nua.

Local Thai activists have been particularly interested in enforcing Article 34 of the Convention, which aims to protect children 'from all forms of sexual exploitation and sexual abuse' (Montgomery 2001: 86). But the Convention also recognizes many other children's rights, including the notion that the child's best interests must always be kept uppermost and that they have a right to live with their families. The problem is that 'the assurance of one right often occurs at the expense of others. How these rights are prioritized is not culturally neutral' (85). 'Too often . . . Article 34 is quoted in isolation, decontextualizing sexual abuse and presenting it as the paramount difficulty that poor children face without linking it to global issues of poverty, cultural background, and discrimination' (86–7). The child's best interests are certainly compromised through prostitution, but they are also compromised when children are removed from their families and communities or when they have nothing to eat. This is particularly poignant in the case of the children of Baan Nua, many of whom claimed that they were not exploited, and all of whom were strongly motivated to engage in

prostitution based on the cultural belief that children are obliged to support their parents. Montgomery concludes:

> By ensuring that their families could stay together and have a sustainable income, it would be possible to eradicate child prostitution without enforcing punitive measures against their parents. . . . Thailand's positions in globalized political and economic relations are as important as cultural specificities in perpetuating that sexual exploitation. . . . Article 34 would be redundant if the other rights enshrined in the convention . . . could be reliably enforced. (97–8)

The lesson of these and other examples suggest two important conclusions:

1) it is possible to find ways of accommodating the universal discourse of human rights to the particularities of local conditions, and
2) no single model of the relationship between rights and culture will fit all cases.

Moreover, as the culture of human rights becomes better established, it increasingly becomes enmeshed in political and legal institutions that go beyond the local level. As activists become more experienced operating in globalized circumstances, they are likely to become more sophisticated about making use of these different settings as they plan their human rights strategies (Cowan et al. 2001: 21). Struggles over human rights are hardly likely to go away; indeed, along with struggles over global citizenship, they can be seen as the prime struggles of our time (Mignolo 2002). Anthropologists are well positioned to help make sense of these complex developments as they unfold.

# Cultural Imperialism, Cultural Hybridization, and Cosmopolitanism

## Cultural Imperialism or Cultural Hybridization?

The *impact* of the global spread of people, technology, wealth, images, and ideologies in local social settings has clearly been profound, as illustrated by the preceding examples. But how should anthropologists characterize the processes by which these changes have come about? One explanation, formulated during the Cold War debates about modernization and dependency, was in the concept of **cultural imperialism**. Cultural imperialism is based on two notions.

1) The idea that some cultures dominate other cultures. In recent history, it is the culture(s) of 'the West' that are seen to have come to dominate all other cultures of the world, due to the spread of colonialism and capitalism.
2) The idea that cultural domination by one culture leads inevitably to the destruction of subordinated cultures and their replacement by the culture of those in power.

Thus, Western cultural imperialism is seen as responsible for destroying, for example, local music, technology, dress, and food traditions and replacing them with rock and roll, radios, flashlights, cellphones, T-shirts, blue jeans, McDonald's hamburgers, and Coca-Cola. The inevitable outcome of Western cultural imperialism is seen to be 'the cultural homogenization of the world', with the unwelcome consequence of 'dooming the world to uniformity' (Inda and Rosaldo 2002: 13, 14).

The discourse of cultural imperialism developed primarily outside anthropology, but anthropologists could not ignore it because it purported to describe what was happening to the people they studied. Anthropologists, too, were aware that Western music, fashion, food, and technology had spread among those they worked with. But cultural imperialism did not seem to be a satisfactory explanation for this spread for at least three reasons (Inda and Rosaldo 2002: 22–4).

1) Cultural imperialism denies *agency* to non-Western peoples who make use of Western cultural forms. It assumes that they are passive and without the resources to resist anything of Western origin that is marketed to them.
2) Cultural imperialism assumes that non-Western cultural forms never move 'from the rest to the West'. Yet non-Western music, food, and material culture have large and eager followings in western Europe and North America.
3) Cultural imperialism ignores the fact that cultural forms and practices sometimes move from one part of the non-Western world to other parts of the non-Western world, bypassing the West entirely. Movies made in India have been popular for decades in northern Nigeria (Larkin 2002), Mexican soap operas have large followings in the Philippines, and karaoke is popular all over the world.

Thus anthropologists began to search for alternative ways of understanding global cultural flows.

From the days of Boas and his students, anthropologists had not only recognized the significance of cultural borrowing but had emphasized that borrowing cultural forms or practices from elsewhere always involves *borrowing-with-modification*; that is, people never adopt blindly but always adapt what they borrow for local purposes. Put another way, people rarely accept ideas or practices or objects from elsewhere without *domesticating* or *indigenizing* them—finding a way of reconciling them with local practices in order to serve local purposes.

> **cultural imperialism**
> The idea that some cultures dominate other cultures and that cultural domination by one culture leads inevitably to the destruction of subordinated cultures and their replacement by the culture of those in power.

In the 1980s, for example, weavers in Otavalo, Ecuador, who were making a lot of money selling textiles to tourists, organized small production firms and purchased television sets to entertain their employees while they worked at their looms. In addition, some men had so much business that they encouraged their wives to take up weaving, even though women were not traditionally weavers. In order to spend more time weaving, women started to use indoor cookstoves, which relieved them from the time-consuming labour of traditional meal preparation over an open fire (Colloredo-Mansfeld 1999). From the perspective of anthropologist Rudi Colloredo-Mansfeld, these adoptions of items of Western technology could not be understood as the consequences of Western cultural imperialism because they clearly had nothing to do with trying to imitate a Western lifestyle. It made more sense to interpret these changes as Otavalan *domestication* or *indigenization* of televisions and cookstoves, since these items from elsewhere were adopted precisely in order to promote Indigenous Otavalan weaving. Thus borrowing-with-modification involves *customizing* that which is borrowed to meet the purposes of the borrowers, which may be quite remote from the purposes of those among whom the form or practice originated (Inda and Rosaldo 2002: 16). This form of cultural change is very different from having something from elsewhere forced upon you against your will (Figure 13.9).

At the same time, it also is necessary to recognize that the consequences of borrowing-with-modification can never be fully controlled. Thus, Otavalan weavers may start watching television because local reruns of old American television series relieve the tedium of weaving, but once television-watching becomes a habitual practice, it also exposes them to advertising and news broadcasts, which may stimulate other local changes that nobody can predict. The domestication or indigenization of cultural forms from elsewhere makes it possible *both* to do old things in new ways *and* to do new things as well. Cultural borrowing is double-edged; borrowed cultural practices are both amenable to domestication and yet able to escape it. No wonder that cultural borrowing is often viewed with ambivalence. The challenges are particularly acute in globalizing conditions—colonial or postcolonial—where borrowed ideas, objects, or practices remain entangled in relationships with donors

**hybridity**
Cultural mixing.

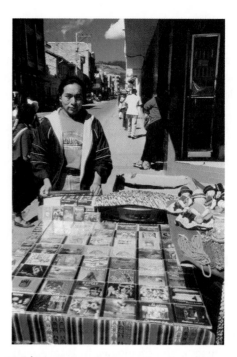

*Figure 13.9* | Musical performance has become an important part of the Otavalo economy, as musicians from Otavalo travel throughout the world performing and selling woven goods. They have domesticated CD production as well and have been quite successful in selling CDs of their music to tourists in Otavalo and to listeners abroad.

even as they are made to serve new goals by recipients (Thomas 1991). It is not surprising, therefore, that people in multicultural settings who must deal with tempting cultural alternatives emanating from more powerful groups regularly struggle to control processes of cultural borrowing and to contain domesticated cultural practices within certain contexts or in the hands of certain people.

Many social scientists have borrowed a metaphor from biology to describe this complex process of globalized cultural exchange and speak of *cultural hybridization* or **hybridity**. For example, sociologist Jan Nederveen Pieterse writes that 'Dependency theory may be read as a theory of structural hybridization in which dependent capitalism is a mélange category. . . . The contested notion of semi-periphery may also be viewed as a hybrid formation' (1995: 50–1). Anthropologist Ulf Hannerz, in contrast, objects to the 'biologistic' overtones of hybridity metaphors and prefers to borrow the concept of *creolization* from linguistics (see Chapter 4): 'Creolist concepts suggest that cultural mixture is not necessarily deviant, second-rate, unworthy of attention, matter out of place. . . . What is at the core of the concept of creole culture, I think, is a combination of diversity, interconnectedness, and innovation in the context of global centre-periphery relations' (1996: 66–7). Both cultural hybridization and creolization were meant to highlight forms of cultural borrowing that produced something new that could not be collapsed or subsumed, either within the culture of the donor or within the culture of the recipient. In addition, both terms stressed the positive side of cultural mixing: rather than indicating a regrettable loss of original purity, hybridity and creolization draw attention to positive processes of cultural creativity.

The move from talk of dependency and cultural imperialism to talk about globalization and cultural hybridization is widely seen as a move from *modernist* discourse to *postmodernist* discourse. Modernist discourse embodies Enlightenment assumptions about rationality, science, progress, capitalism, and democracy. Postmodernist discourse calls all these Enlightenment assumptions into question. The 'writing against culture' movement in anthropology was a postmodernist critique of modernist social science assumptions that portrayed 'authentic' non-Western societies and cultures as bounded, orderly, and unchanging. Postmodernists argued that all social and cultural borders were porous, and thus open to people, ideas, and practices from elsewhere. This postmodern position is not confined to academic contexts, but has had important implications regarding everyday cultural choices. For example, if hybridity is a normal part of all human social experience, then the idea that 'authentic' traditions never change can legitimately be challenged. For members of a social group who wish to revise or discard cultural practices that they find outmoded or oppressive, hybridity talk is liberating. Choosing to revise or discard, borrow or invent, *on terms of one's own choosing* also means that one possesses agency, the capacity to exercise at least some control over one's life. And exercising agency calls into question charges that one is succumbing to cultural imperialism or losing one's cultural 'authenticity'.

However, as anthropologist Nicholas Thomas puts it, 'hybridity is almost a good idea, but not quite' (1996: 9). Close examination of talk about cultural hybridization or creolization reveals at least three problems. First, it is not clear that either concept actually frees anthropologists from the modernist commitment to the existence of

bounded, homogeneous, unchanging 'cultures'. That is, the idea of cultural hybridity is based on the notion of cultural mixing. But what is it that is mixed? Two or more non-hybridized, original, 'pure' cultures! But such 'pure', homogeneous, bounded, unchanging cultures are not supposed to exist. Thus we are caught in a paradox. For this reason Jonathan Friedman, among others, is highly critical of discussions of cultural hybridity; in his view, cultures have *always* been hybrid and it is the existence of *boundaries*, not cultural borrowing, that anthropologists need to explain. Besides, hybrid cultural mixtures often get transformed into new, unitary cultural identities. This process can be seen, Friedman argues, in the way in which the 'mixed race' category in the US has been transformed into a 'new, unitary group of mixtures for those who feel "disenfranchised" by the current single-race categories' (1997: 83). Friedman also points out that hybrid identities are not liberating when they are thrust upon people rather than being adopted freely. He draws attention to cases in Latin America where the 'mestizo' identity has been used 'as a middle-/upper-class tool' against Indigenous groups by '"creolizing" them from above': that is, criticizing their claims to a common Indian identity in order to undermine their sense of solidarity as members of a single group. 'We are all part-Indian, say members of the elite who have much to lose in the face of minority claims' (81–2).

These examples highlight a second difficulty with hybridity talk: those who celebrate cultural hybridization often ignore the fact that its effects are experienced differently by those with power and those without power. As Friedman says, 'the question of class becomes crucial' (1997: 81). The complexity of this issue is seen in many popular discussions of 'multiculturalism' that celebrate cultural hybridization and that, in the context of globalizing capitalism, turn hybridity into a marketable commodity. The commodification of hybridity is problematic because it smooths over differences in the experience of cultural hybridization, offering multiculturalism as an array of tempting consumables for outsiders. 'Multiculturalism is aimed at nourishing and perpetuating the kind of differences which do not [threaten]', writes Nira Yuval-Davis (1997: 197). International folk festivals, festivals of nations, and the like—events that emphasize costume, cuisine, music, and dance—spring to mind (Figure 13.10). But the troubling fact is that cultural hybridity is experienced as

*Figure 13.10* | **Youth performers dance and cheer at the Kitchener–Waterloo Oktoberfest celebrations.**

both non-threatening and very threatening, depending on the terms on which it is available. Because of power differences among groups challenged by cultural hybridization, any globalized 'multicultural' setting reveals active processes of cultural hybridization *together with* the defence of discrete cultural identities that seem to *resist* hybridization (Werbner 1997: 3). Cultural hybridization is unobjectionable when actors perceive it to be under their own control, but cultural hybridization is resisted when it is 'perceived by actors themselves to be potentially threatening to their sense of moral integrity' (Werbner 1997: 12). The threat is greatest for those with the least power who feel unable to control forms of cultural hybridization that threaten to undermine the fragile survival structures on which they depend in an unwelcoming multicultural setting.

And this point leads to a third problem with the concept of cultural hybridization. Fashionable hybridity talk hides the differences between elite and non-elite experiences of multiculturalism. Anthropologist John Hutnyk, for example, deplores the way 'world music' is marketed to middle-class consumers, noting that such sales strategies divert attention 'from the urgency of anti-racist politics' (1997: 122). When cultural hybridization becomes fashionable, it easily turns the experiences of hybridized elites into a hegemonic standard, suggesting that class

exploitation and racial oppression are easily overcome or no longer exist. But to dismiss or ignore continuing non-elite struggles with cultural hybridization can spark dangerous confrontations that can quickly spiral out of control.

Anthropologist Peter van der Veer argues that such a dynamic ignited the furor in Britain that followed the publication of Salman Rushdie's novel *The Satanic Verses* (1988). Rushdie is an elite, highly educated South Asian migrant to Britain who experienced cultural hybridity as a form of emancipation from oppressive religious and cultural restrictions. His novel contained passages describing Islam and the Prophet Muhammad that, from his elite point of view, embodied 'transgression' that was liberating. But migrants from South Asia in Britain are not all members of the elite. Most South Asian Muslim immigrants in Britain are workers, and they saw *The Satanic Verses* not as a work of artistic liberation but as a deliberate attempt to mock their beliefs and practices. 'These immigrants, who are already socially and culturally marginalized, are thus double marginalized in the name of an attack on "purity" and Islamic "fundamentalism"' (van der Veer 1997: 101–2). Even more important, however, may be the way popular interpretations of their objections in the press and among Western intellectuals ignored these immigrants' own, very different but very real, *non-elite* experiences of cultural hybridization. Van der Veer stresses that British Muslims who objected to the novel were

> not necessarily fundamentalists at all; their religious ideas are just as hybrid and syncretic as those of the author. They, too, are migrants, but the sources of their identity are authenticated not by profane literary texts but by what are to them sacred religious traditions. It is ironic, therefore, to find that migrants who are at the vanguard of political resistance to the assimilationist tendencies of the nation-state, who have their own cultural project for living hybrid cultural lives in a non-Islamic nation—expressed, for example, in demand for state-funded Muslims schools or the extension of the blasphemy laws—are condemned, while the postmodernist hybrid novelist is celebrated by liberals and the state, extolled for his struggle against that very oppositional resistance, against the supposed 'backwardness' of the 'fundamentalist' British Muslim community. (1997: 102)

Put simply, elites experience cultural hybridization in ways that are often very different from the ways non-elites experience cultural hybridization. We all ignore this fact at our peril.

## From Cultural Hybridity to Cosmopolitanism

The era of globalization in which we live is an era of uncertainty and insecurity. Possibilities for emancipatory new ways of living are undercut by sharpening economic and political differences and the looming threat of violence. Is it possible, in the midst of all this confusion and conflict, to devise ways of coping with our circumstances that would provide guidance in the confusion or moderation to the conflict? No one expects such efforts to be easy. But anthropologists and other concerned scholars are currently struggling to come up with concepts and practices that might be helpful.

Our era is not the first to have faced such challenges. Walter Mignolo (2002) argues that multiculturalism was born in the sixteenth century when Iberian conquest in the New World first raised troubling issues among Western thinkers about the kinds of relationships that were possible and desirable between the conquerors and the Indigenous peoples whom they had conquered. During the ensuing centuries, the challenges posed by a multicultural world did not disappear. In the context of eighteenth-century Enlightenment promises of human emancipation based on the *Declaration of the Rights of Man and of the Citizen*, philosopher Immanuel Kant concluded that the achievements of the Enlightenment offered individuals new opportunities for developing ways of being at home in the world wherever they were.

To identify this orientation, Kant revived a concept that was first coined by the Stoic philosophers of ancient Rome: **cosmopolitanism** (Mignolo 2002). Kant's cosmopolitanism was firmly embedded within the values and practices of Enlightenment civilization, which meant, in the terms of our preceding discussion, that it was embedded in Western elite forms of cultural hybridization. That is, Kantian cosmopolitanism 'by and large meant being versed in Western ways, and the vision of "one world" culture was only a sometimes unconscious, sometimes unconscionable, euphemism for "First World" culture' (Abbas 2002: 210). To the extent that discussions of cosmopolitanism continue to focus on Western elites only, they would seem to offer little to anthropologists and others who are

interested in finding a place for non-elite and non-Western experiences of cultural hybridization. Perhaps it is for this reason that Friedman has written that those who celebrate their own cultural hybridity are simply 'all those who can afford a cosmopolitan identity' (1997: 81).

But is it possible to rework our understandings of cultural hybridity to stretch the notion of cosmopolitanism beyond its traditional association with privileged Western elites? Many anthropologists have become comfortable talking about 'alternative' or 'minority modernities' that depart from the western European norm. In a similar fashion, any new anthropological understanding of cosmopolitanism would have to be plural, not singular, and it would have to include non-elite experiences of cultural hybridization—'minoritarian' or 'discrepant' cosmopolitanisms—that reflect the experiences of those who have been the victims of modernity (Abu-Lughod 1991: 134; Breckenridge et al. 2002: 6, 8). The goal would be to develop new concepts and new skills enabling one to handle difficult cultural situations with grace 'by juggling with multiple perspectives' (Abbas 2002: 223), new ways of thinking 'beyond the local' or 'ways of living at home abroad or abroad at home—ways of inhabiting multiple places at once, of being different beings simultaneously, of seeing the larger picture stereoscopically with the smaller' (Breckenridge et al. 2002: 1, 10–11).

Does anthropological talk about a world of 'cosmopolitanisms' offer any advantage over earlier anthropological talk about a world of 'cultures'? It might, if anthropologists can find a way to think about cultural hybridization (and resistance to hybridization) that moves beyond the current stalemate. Pnina Werbner (1997) suggests that this might be possible if we can think about cultural hybridization as a *process* rather than as a series of momentary, shocking 'transgressive' challenges that periodically disrupt the ongoing, tense standoff among defenders of different cultural positions. Rather than assuming that all hybridity (or all resistance to hybridity) is the same—either all 'good' or all 'bad'—Werbner's approach would make it possible to distinguish *different processes* of cultural hybridization and cultural resistance. To illustrate, Werbner insists on distinguishing between cultural processes that lead to ethnicity and cultural processes that lead to racism (see Chapter 12). A processual theory of cultural

**cosmopolitanism**
Being at ease in more than one cultural setting.

hybridization 'must differentiate . . . between a politics that proceeds from the legitimacy of difference [ethnicity] and a politics that rests on coercive unity [racism]', and it 'must explain how and why cultural hybrids are still able to disturb and "shock" . . . in a postmodern world that celebrates difference' (Werbner 1997: 21). Previous anthropological work can suggest how such a processual analysis might proceed. For example, Victor Turner's analysis of rites of passage (see Chapter 8) demonstrated that 'liminality is itself structured processually . . . categories are exaggerated and caricatured *in order to be worked upon and reconfigured.* . . . By analogy we need to think . . . of the way discourses interact to create bridges or precipitate polarizing processes' (Werbner 1997: 21; emphasis added).

Werbner's approach to cultural hybridization as a process has much in common with what Walter Mignolo calls *border thinking*. That is, in a globalized world, concepts like 'democracy' and 'justice' can no longer be defined within a single Western logic—or, for that matter, from the perspective of the political left or the political right. Border thinking involves detaching these concepts from their hegemonic 'Western' meanings and practices, and using them as 'connectors'—tools for imagining and negotiating new, cosmopolitan forms of democracy or justice informed by the ethical and political judgments of non-elites (Mignolo 2002: 179, 181).

Finally, in re-imagining what cosmopolitanism might mean, it is important not only to go beyond Kantian limitations but also to go beyond standard anthropological orientations to other ways of life. An understanding of cosmopolitanism that is limited to being open to other cultures or to being inclusive—the traditional orientation of cultural relativism—is insufficient to cope with the challenges presented by a globalizing world. For one thing, 'Otherness has lost its innocence as a result of the colonial experience' (Abbas 2002: 226). For another, 'silenced and marginalized voices are bringing themselves into the conversation of cosmopolitan projects rather than waiting to be included' (Mignolo 2002: 174).

The hope is that border thinking can produce a *critical cosmopolitanism* capable of negotiating new understandings of human rights and global citizenship in ways that can dismantle barriers of gender and race that are the historical legacies of colonialism (Mignolo 2002: 161, 180). In many cases, this may require seriously revising Western modernist ideas and practices, if that is the only honourable way of overcoming power differentials and threats to moral

integrity experienced by non-elites. But because cosmopolitanism involves border thinking, this means that ideals and practices with Enlightenment credentials may also turn out to be valuable counterweights to extremism and violence.

This potential value of Enlightenment ideals is realized in the stance taken by those citizens of Mumbai (Bombay), India, who resist attempts by radical Hindus to banish Muslims from the city and to turn India into a Hindu state. Relationships between Hindus and Muslims in India took a severe turn for the worse after Hindu vandals destroyed a mosque in the city of Ayodhya in 1992. Appadurai, who has followed these developments closely, notes that the brutal Hindutva movement pushing to turn India into a Hindu state 'violates the ideals of secularism and inter-religious harmony enshrined in the constitution' (2002: 73–4). Appadurai writes of Indians from many walks of life, rich and poor, Muslim and Hindu, who have shown 'extraordinary displays of courage and critical imagination in Mumbai', who have 'held up powerful images of a cosmopolitan, secular, multicultural Bombay'. Their 'radical moderation' in resisting violent religious polarization is, he argues, neither naïve nor nostalgic: 'These utopian visions and critical practices are resolutely modernist in their visions of equity, justice, and cultural cosmopolitanism' (79). Secularism, as we saw in Chapter 10, is a notion with impeccable Enlightenment credentials, and this notion arrived in India with British colonialism. And yet it is this 'situated secularism'—indigenized, customized, domesticated, *Indian* secularism that is opposed to *Indian* inter-religious violence—that Appadurai and many other Indian citizens see as a key element of a form of local Indian cosmopolitanism that has been effective in preventing religious strife in the past and may be able to do so again.

Many of the cases in this chapter demonstrate the human ability to cope creatively with changed life circumstances. They remind us that human beings are not passive in the face of the new, that they actively and resiliently respond to life's challenges. Nevertheless, the example of the Panará reminds us that successful outcomes are never ensured. Modes of livelihood that may benefit some human groups can overwhelm and destroy others. Western capitalism and modern technology have exploded into a vortex of global forces that resist control. A critical cosmopolitanism involving concerted practical action to lessen violence and exploitation may be all that can prevent these forces from destroying us all.

# Key Terms

core  323
cosmopolitanism  345
cultural imperialism  341
dependency theory  322
diaspora  329
flexible citizenship  330
globalization  324
human rights  332
hybridity  342
legal citizenship  330
long-distance nationalists  329

modernization theory  321
multiculturalism  332
periphery  323
post-national ethos  332
semi-periphery  323
substantive citizenship  330
transborder citizenry  329
transborder state  329
transnational nation-states  330
world-system theory  322

# Chapter Summary

1. Anthropologists have made use of a variety of theoretical perspectives to explain the relationship between the West and the rest of the world. During the Cold War, anthropologists debated the relative merits of modernization theory and dependency theory. Later, they were influenced by world system theory, which divided the territories controlled by capitalism into core, periphery, and semi-periphery and argued that the relationships between these regions had been established during the years when capitalism was first introduced outside Europe. The end of the Cold War and the fall of communism led to a crisis in Marxian thought, and many of the tenets of modernization theory were revived in neo-liberal economic theory, which promised to bring prosperity to any nation-state that could find its niche in the globalizing capitalist market.

2. Globalization is understood and evaluated differently by different observers, but most anthropologists agree that the effects of globalization are uneven. In a globalizing world, people, technology, wealth, images, and ideologies are de-territorialized. Some groups in some parts of the world benefit from global flows, contacts, and exchanges, whereas others are bypassed entirely.

3. Anthropologists and others disagree about whether these global processes are systemic or not or whether they are only the latest in a series of expansions and contractions that can be traced back to the rise of the first commercial civilizations several thousand years ago. But none of these overall schemas can, by itself, account for the historically specific local details of the effects of global forces in local settings, which is what most anthropologists aim to document and analyze.

4. The flows unleashed by globalization have undermined the ability of nation-states to police their boundaries effectively, suggesting that conventional ideas about nation-states require revision. Contemporary migrants across national borders have developed a variety of transborder identities. Some become involved in long-distance nationalism that leads to the emergence of transborder states claiming emigrants as transborder citizens of their ancestral homelands, even if they are legal citizens of another state. Some transborder citizenries call for the establishment of fully fledged transnational nation-states.

5. The contrasts between formal and substantive citizenship suggest that conventional notions of citizenship are breaking down in the context of globalization. Diaspora communities of elite Chinese families have developed a strategy of flexible citizenship that allows them to both circumvent and benefit from different nation-state regimes by investing, working, and settling their families in different sites. For these elite Chinese, the concept of nationalism has lost its meaning, and they seem to subscribe instead to a post-national ethos in which their only true loyalty is to the family business.

6. Discussions of human rights have intensified as global flows juxtapose and, at least implicitly, challenge different understandings of what it means to be human or what kinds of rights people may be entitled to under radically changed conditions of everyday life. But different participants in this discourse have different ideas

about the relationship that human rights and culture have with one another. As talk about human rights becomes incorporated into local cultural discussions, the notion is transformed to make sense in local contexts. Sometimes, 'culture' may be used as a scapegoat for a government unwilling to extend certain rights to its citizens.

7. Some arguments about human rights include the right to one's culture. But most international human rights documents only protect individual human rights, not group rights. And even those who seek to protect their individual rights are supposed to appeal to the governments of their own nation-states to enforce rights defended in international documents. Many activists, and others, view this factor as a serious contradiction in human rights discourse that undermines its effectiveness.

8. Some anthropologists argue that a 'culture of human rights' has emerged in recent years that is based on certain ideas about human beings, their needs, and their abilities that originated in the West. Some consider this culture of human rights to be the culture of a globalizing world that emphasizes individual rights over duties or needs and that proposes only technical rather than ethical solutions to human suffering. Anthropologists disagree about the value of such a culture of human rights in contemporary circumstances.

9. Groups and individuals who assert that their human rights have been violated regularly take their cases to courts of law. But because human rights law only recognizes certain kinds of rights violations, groups with grievances must tailor those grievances to fit the violations that human rights law recognizes. Groups that enter into the human rights process are entering into ethically ambiguous territory that is both enabling and constraining.

10. Debates about children's rights in Thailand show both that it is possible to accommodate the universal discourse of human rights to local conditions and that no single model of the relationship between rights and culture will fit all cases. Struggles over human rights, along with struggles over global citizenship, can be seen as the prime struggles of our time.

11. The discourse of cultural imperialism tried to explain the spread of Western cultural forms outside the West. But anthropologists reject cultural imperialism as an explanation because it denies agency to non-Western peoples, because it assumes that cultural forms never move 'from the rest to the West', and because it ignores flows of cultural forms that bypass the West entirely. Thus anthropologists prefer to speak about borrowing-with-modification, domestication, indigenization, or customization of practices or objects imported from elsewhere. Many anthropologists describe these processes as examples of cultural hybridization or hybridity.

12. Talk of cultural hybridization has been criticized because the very attempt to talk about cultural mixtures assumes that 'pure' cultures existed prior to mixing. Others object to discussions of cultural hybridization that fail to recognize that its effects are experienced differently by those with power and those without power. Cultural hybridization is unobjectionable when actors perceive it to be under their own control but is resisted when they see it threatening their moral integrity.

13. Some anthropologists are working to devise ways of coping with the uncertainties and insecurities of globalization. Some would like to revive the notion of cosmopolitanism originally associated with Western elite forms of cultural hybridization and rework it in order to be able to speak about alternative or discrepant cosmopolitanisms that reflect the experiences of those who have been the victims of modernity. The ideal end result would be a critical cosmopolitanism capable of negotiating new understandings of human rights and global citizenship in ways that can dismantle barriers of gender and race that are the historical legacies of colonialism.

# Critical Thinking Questions

1. What would you consider to be the main factor(s) in the emergence of globalization?

2. What do you consider to be some of the key factors in the local variations on the acceptance of globalization?

3. How would you compare and contrast formal and substantive citizenship?

4. Are national boundaries being challenged by the ubiquitous and non-censorable nature of the Internet? How and to what possible ends?

5. What are some of the ways elites and non-elites experience cultural hybridization in different ways? Why do you suppose there are differences?

# Suggested Readings

Barber, Benjamin R. 1995. *Jihad versus McWorld: How Globalism and Tribalism Are Reshaping the World* (New York: Times Books). This book examines the basis for the misunderstanding between the Muslim world and the capitalist Western world.

Dyck, Noel, and James B. Waldram. 1993. *Anthropology, Public Policy, and Native Peoples in Canada* (Montreal and Kingston: McGill-Queen's University Press). A comprehensive review of governmental policy issues and the present conditions experienced by First Nations peoples.

Hobart, Mark, ed. 1993. *An Anthropological Critique of Development* (London: Routledge). Anthropologists from Britain, Holland, and Germany challenge the notion that Western approaches to development have been successful. They use ethnographic case studies to demonstrate how Western experts who disregard Indigenous knowledge contribute to the growth of ignorance.

Inda, Jonathan Xavier, and Renato Rosaldo, eds. 2007. *The Anthropology of Globalization: A Reader*, 2nd edn (Malden, MA: Blackwell). A recent, comprehensive collection of articles by anthropologists who address the process of globalization from varied points of view and different ethnographic situations.

Márquez, Gabriel García. 1998. *One Hundred Years of Solitude* (New York: HarperCollins). Noble Prize–winning author Márquez chronicles the history of a family and their fictional town of Macondo. The story emphasizes the fact that in the life of humans, time has a nebulous quality—it lapses, repeats, speeds up, and can even stop altogether.

Murray, David A.B. 2000. 'Between a Rock and a Hard Place: The Power and Powerlessness of Transnational Narratives among Gay Martinican Men', *American Anthropologist* 102, 2: 261–70. Murray argues that Quebec is signified as utopic in specific gay narratives in terms that are antithetical and therefore profoundly connected to impressions of social life in France and Martinique.

No'eau Warner, Sam L. 1999. '"Kuleana": The Right, Responsibility, and Authority of Indigenous Peoples to Speak and Make Decisions for Themselves in Language and Cultural Revitalization', *Anthropology & Education Quarterly* 30, 1: 68–93. This paper addresses the issue of Hawaiian language revitalization becoming highly politicized by non-Indigenous Hawaiian language educators. This is characterized as colonization of the field in an attempt to control specific resources.

Rigney, Lester-Irabinna. 1999. 'Internationalization of an Indigenous Anti-colonial Cultural Critique of Research Methodologies: A Guide to Indigenist Research Methodology and Its Principles', *Wicazo Sa Review* 14, 2: 109–21. The author states: 'Indigenous peoples' interests, knowledge, and experiences must be at the centre of research methodologies and construction of knowledge about Indigenous peoples.'

Sylvain, Renée. 2002. '"Land, Water, and Truth": San Identity and Global Indigenism', *American Anthropologist* 104, 4: 1074–85. This article discussed how some international ideas of indigenism are counter to essential concepts of culture and ethnic identity for the San in their struggle for recognition of identity and land claims.

Wallerstein, Immanuel. 1974. *The Modern World System* (New York: Academic Press). A difficult but tremendously influential work that started the world-system approach to understanding and explaining patterns of social change in recent world history.

Wolf, Eric. 1999 [1969]. *Peasant Wars of the Twentieth Century* (Norman: University of Oklahoma Press). An important, readable study of the commonalities of last century's major wars of revolution.

# Related Websites

AIDS Portal www.aidsportal.org

Arjun Appadurai www.appadurai.com/homebio.htm

Conservation International www.conservation.org

Division for the Advancement of Women (DAW) www.un.org/womenwatch/daw/daw/index.html

Doctors without Borders www.doctorswithoutborders.org

Home Children www.collectionscanada.gc.ca/databases/home-children/index-e.html

International Bureau for Children's Rights www.ibcr.org

International Women's Rights Project (IWRP), CEDAW www.iwrp.org/projects/cedaw

Native Planet: Indigenous Communities in Brazil www.nativeplanet.org/indigenous/ethnicdiversity/latinamerica/brazil/indigenous_data_brazil_kayapo.shtml

SIL International www.sil.org

UNAIDS www.unaids.org

UNICEF Thailand www.unicef.org/infobycountry/Thailand.html

Women Activities & Social Services Association www.counterpart-afg.org/wassa.html

# 14 | Applying Anthropology in Everyday Life

## Chapter Outline

Anthropology beyond the University

Anthropology and the Challenges of
   Global Citizenship

Awareness and Uncertainty

Freedom and Constraint

........................................................

## Learning Objectives

By the end of Chapter 14, you will
be able to

- understand the value of applied
  anthropology,

- appreciate anthropology as
  a portal to effective global
  citizenship,

- consider the world of uncertainty
  and the awareness needed to
  confront it (reflexivity), and

- challenge views on freedom and
  constraint.

← *Tourists and locals explore the popular
shopping district of Petit Champlain in
Quebec City. When viewed through
the anthropological perspective, even
seemingly commonplace situations
here in Canada can be a source of
new insight into the many ways in
which beliefs and behaviours are
shaped by culture.*

# How do the narratives of men and women of diverse cultures inform us in today's world? How do these stories find a place in the practice of anthropology?

The answers are found in a relatively recent development in cultural anthropology—applied anthropology. In this chapter, we examine some of the ramifications of seeing anthropology as an 'action' social science in the examination of modern issues in a 'global' world made up of a multitude of local traditions. We also look at what anthropology can teach us about ourselves (Figure 14.1). And as a student of anthropology, whether or not you intend to continue in the field after you graduate, you can rely on your studies to help you find personal answers to questions about your place as a global citizen.

## Anthropology beyond the University

Why study anthropology? The response usually comes in three parts. The first part is practical.

Figure 14.1 | Studying anthropology can help us understand our own culture. Here, anthropology graduate students help Professor Bill Rathje examine the dirt at a landfill in San Francisco in an effort to understand local human behaviour through waste habits.

Today, many anthropologists work in the area called *applied anthropology*. As we saw in Chapter 9, medical anthropologists often engage in practical research with significant applied results. Some are involved in issues of aging and gerontology, designing programs for the elderly and doing research on aging in different cultures. Others work in public or community health, medical education, nursing, or hospital planning. Additionally, medical anthropologists draw attention to practical issues of medical ethics. As Margaret Lock (2001) notes in her discussion of medicalization and resistance,

> Recognition of moral economies permits us to pose questions about scientific knowledge, its production and application, and its methods of relegating other methodologies, including ethnography, to the sidelines. Ethnography makes it possible to examine the way in which scientific knowledge is selectively deployed in different global contexts by drawing on morals and value systems that are historically, politically, and culturally informed. . . . Here medical anthropologists join forces with historians and sociologists of science to tackle some of the most pressing questions of our day involving moral conundrums requiring debate. . . . I find culture (used reflexively and in conjunction with a political/economy framework) a necessary concept for most research projects, especially when culture is explicitly made to do work by the particular people or institutions that one is studying. (488)

Of particular interest here are the health and well-being of women and children in a world where access to prenatal care, adequate nutrition, clean water, and immunization programs is patchy, while diseases like malaria and HIV are rampant (Figure 14.2). Indeed, many applied anthropologists work on aids-related projects. Consider Holly Wardlow's work on HIV infections in rural Papua New Guinea. Demonstrating how a researcher's site-specific observations often point to broader cultural concerns, she notes that 'married women are at risk for HIV primarily because of their husbands' extramarital sexual liaisons, and wives have little control over this risk, which is not lessened by their own fidelity. . . . [T]he dynamics of marital HIV transmission [are embedded in] economic,

*Figure 14.2* **| Medical anthropologist Andrea Wiley (left) in the Himalayas of Ladakh (India) where she studied maternal and child health.**

social, and cultural factors that propel and structure men's extramarital sexuality' (2007: 1006).

Applied anthropology takes a number of non-biomedical forms as well. Some anthropologists have gone into public policy and planning as interpreters,

*Figure 14.3* **| Millet, a cereal grown in warm countries and regions with poor soils, is one of the crops studied in the INTSORMIL research project.**

mediators, civil servants, or urban planners. A few are psychotherapists, employing the insights of anthropologist Gregory Bateson and others on family systems and family therapy, while others are cross-cultural social workers. Yet others have begun to work with Indigenous peoples' organizations or with human rights organizations such as Survival International and Cultural Survival. Still others are actively involved in international development, working with various agencies on projects such as devising appropriate technologies, resolving fuel shortages, locating potable water, establishing agricultural and micro-credit (as with the work of Nobel Peace Prize–winner Muhammad Yunus and his Grameen Bank), developing new lands, conducting feasibility studies for dams and other enterprises, implementing bilingual education programs, and improving and managing livestock (for more examples, see Partridge 1984; van Willigen 1991). Below, we examine in greater detail three cases that illustrate the value of applied anthropology.

## Sorghum and Millet in Honduras and Sudan

Applied anthropologists carry out much work in international development, often in agricultural programs. The US Agency for International Development (USAID) is the principal instrument of US foreign development assistance. One new direction taken by USAID in the mid-1970s was to create multidisciplinary research programs to improve food crops in 'developing' countries. An early research program—the International Sorghum/Millet Research Project (INTSORMIL)—dealt with sorghum and millet, important grains in some of the poorest countries in the world (Figure 14.3). In this program, selected American universities investigated one of six areas: plant breeding, agronomy, plant pathology, plant physiology, food chemistry, and socio-economic studies.

Anthropologists from the University of Kentucky, selected for the socio-economic study, used ethnographic field research techniques to gain first-hand knowledge of the socio-economic constraints on the production, distribution, and consumption of sorghum and millet among limited-resource agricultural producers in western Sudan and in Honduras. They intended to make their findings available to INTSORMIL as well as to scientists and government officials in the host countries. They believed sharing such knowledge could lead to more effective research and development.

## In Their Own Words | What Can You Learn from an Anthropology Major?

*The Career Development Center at SUNY Plattsburgh developed a document that highlights what students typically learn from a major in anthropology.*

### 1. Social agility

In an unfamiliar social or career-related setting, you learn to quickly size up the rules of the game. You can become accepted more quickly than you could without this anthropological skill.

### 2. Observation

You must often learn about a culture from within it, so you learn how to interview and observe as a participant.

### 3. Analysis and planning

You learn how to find patterns in the behaviour of a cultural group. This awareness of patterns allows you to generalize about the group's behaviour and predict what they might do in a given situation.

### 4. Social sensitivity

Although other people's ways of doing things may be different from your own, you learn the importance of events and conditions that have contributed to this difference. You also recognize that other cultures view your ways as strange. You learn the value of behaving toward others with appropriate preparation, care, and understanding.

### 5. Accuracy in interpreting behaviour

You become familiar with the range of behaviour in different cultures. You learn how to look at cultural causes of behaviour before assigning causes yourself.

### 6. Ability to appropriately challenge conclusions

You learn that analyses of human behaviour are open to challenge. You learn how to use new knowledge to test past conclusions.

### 7. Insightful interpretation of information

You learn how to use data collected by others, reorganizing or interpreting the data to reach original conclusions.

### 8. Simplification of information

Because anthropology is conducted among publics as well as about them, you learn how to simplify technical information for communication to non-technical people.

### 9. Contextualization

Although attention to details is a trait of anthropology, you learn that any given detail might not be as important as its context and can even be misleading when the context is ignored.

### 10. Problem solving

Because you often function within a cultural group or act on culturally sensitive issues, you learn to approach problems with care. Before acting, you identify the problem, set your goals, decide on the actions you will take, and calculate possible effects on other people.

### 11. Persuasive writing

Anthropologists strive to represent the behaviour of one group to another group and continually need to engage in interpretation. You learn the value of bringing someone else to share—or at least understand—your view through written argument.

### 12. Assumption of a social perspective

You learn how to perceive the acts of individuals and local groups as both shaping and being shaped by larger socio-cultural systems. The perception enables you to 'act locally and think globally'.

Source: Omohundro, John. 2000. 'What Can You Learn from an Anthropology Major?', in *Careers in Anthropology* (New York: McGraw-Hill).

The principal investigators from the University of Kentucky were Edward Reeves, Billie DeWalt, and Kathleen DeWalt. They took a holistic and comparative approach, called Farming Systems Research (FSR). This approach attempts to determine the techniques used by farmers with limited resources to cope with the social, economic, and ecological conditions under which they live. FSR is holistic because it examines how the different crops and livestock are integrated and managed as a system. It also relates farm productivity to household consumption and off-farm sources of family income (Reeves, DeWalt, and DeWalt 1987: 74). Thus the FSR approach is very different from the traditional methods of agricultural research, which grow and test one crop at a time in an experiment station. The scientists at INTSORMIL are generally acknowledged among the best sorghum and millet researchers in the world, but their expertise comes from traditional agricultural research methods. They have spent little time working on the problems of limited-resource farmers.

The anthropologists saw their job as facilitating 'a constant dialogue between the farmer, who can tell what works best given the circumstances, and agricultural scientists, who produce potentially useful new solutions to old problems' (Reeves, DeWalt, and DeWalt 1987: 74–5). However, this was easier said than done in the sorghum/millet project. The perspectives of farmers and scientists were very different from one another. The anthropologists found themselves having to learn the languages and the conceptual systems of both the farmers and the scientists for the two groups to be able to communicate. The FSR anthropologists had four research goals:

1) to discover what was holding back the increased production of sorghum and millet so that they could identify areas that needed attention from the agricultural researchers;

2) to discover which aspects of new technology the farmers thought might benefit them the most;

3) to suggest how new crop 'varieties and/or technologies might most easily and beneficially be introduced into communities and regions'; and

4) '[t]o suggest the long-term implications that changing production, distribution, and consumption patterns might have on these communities' (1987: 74).

The anthropologists began their research in June 1981 in western Sudan and in southern Honduras. They were in the field for 14 months of participant-observation and in-depth interviewing, as well as survey interviewing of limited-resource farmers, merchants, and middlemen. They discovered that the most significant constraints the farmers faced were uncertain rainfall, low soil fertility, and inadequate labour and financial resources (Reeves, DeWalt, and DeWalt 1987: 80). Equally important were the social and cultural systems within which the farmers were embedded. Farmers based their farming decisions on their understanding of who they were and what farming meant in their own cultures.

As a result of the FSR group's research, it became increasingly clear that 'real progress in addressing the needs of small farmers in the Third World called for promising innovations to be tested at village sites and on farmers' fields under conditions that closely approximated those

which the farmers experience' (Reeves, DeWalt, and DeWalt 1987: 77). Convincing the scientists and bureaucrats of this necessity required the anthropologists to become advocates for the limited-resource farmers. Billie DeWalt and Edward Reeves ended up negotiating INTSORMIL's contracts with the Honduran and Sudanese governments and succeeded in representing the farmers. They had to learn enough about the bureaucracies and the agricultural scientists so they could put the farmers' interests in terms the others could understand.

As a result of the applied anthropologists' work, INTSORMIL scientists learned to understand how small farmers in two countries made agricultural decisions. They also learned that not all limited-resource farmers are alike. The poorest third of the Sudanese farmers, for example, have to decide during the cropping season whether to weed their own gardens or someone else's for a wage. If they choose the former, they realize a long-term gain but they and their families go hungry. The latter choice enables them to buy food in the short run but lowers their own harvests later. The decisions farmers make, and the needs they have, are context-sensitive.

Together with INTSORMIL, the Honduran and Sudanese governments have increased funding for projects aimed at limited-resource farmers. Staff have been assigned to work with INTSORMIL, new programs have begun, and the research results of the anthropologists are guiding the breeding of sorghum.

Reeves, DeWalt, and DeWalt warn that it is too early to demonstrate gains in sorghum or millet production and use in either country.

> Nevertheless, INTSORMIL scientists are clearly coming to accept the farming systems research goals and the value of anthropological fieldwork. The FSR group has argued that on-site research is both desirable and necessary for the problems of farmers to be correctly identified and that eventually on-farm testing of new plant varieties and technologies will be essential to ensure that farmers are going to accept them. (1987: 79)

The INTSORMIL staff was so impressed by the anthropologists' work that it has begun funding long-term research directed at relieving the constraints that limited-resource farmers face. Rather than trying to develop and then introduce hybrids, INTSORMIL research is now aimed at modifying existing varieties of sorghum. The goal is better-yielding local varieties that can be grown together with other crops.

In summary, Reeves, DeWalt, and DeWalt point out that without the anthropological research, fewer development funds would have been allocated to research in Sudan and Honduras. More important, the nature of the development aid would have been less holistic.

## Doing Business in Japan

Anthropologist Richard Reeves-Ellington (1993) designed and implemented a cross-cultural training program for a North American company doing business in Japan (see Map 14.1). He found that many of the traditional methods of anthropology—cultural understanding, ethnographic data, and participant-observation—helped managers conduct business in Japan. Reeves-Ellington began the training program by having employees first gather general cultural information artifacts ('How are things classified? What are the artifacts of an agreed classification system?'), social knowledge ('What are proper principles for behaviour? What are the values that drive the categories and artifacts?'), and cultural logic. Social knowledge or values are based on an underlying, taken-for-granted cultural logic. Coming to understand Japanese cultural logic is of great importance to foreigners wishing to live and work in Japan.

The managers at the company decided to learn how to carry out introductions, meetings, leave-taking, dinner, and drinking in Japan. Each practice was analyzed according to the framework of artifacts, social knowledge, and cultural logic and was taught by a combination of methods that included the general observations that the managers collected while visiting Japanese museums, theatres, shrines, baseball games, and business meetings. The managers analyzed these observations and discussed stories that show how badly things can go when cultural knowledge is not sufficient. For example, one thing Reeves-Ellington's students needed to learn about introductions involved the presentation of the business card (*meishi*). The proper presentation and use of the *meishi* is the central element in the practice of making introductions at business meetings (Figure 14.4). Reeves-Ellington explained that, to a Japanese business person, the *meishi* is an extension of the self. Damage to the card is damage to the individual. Therefore, mistreatment of a *meishi* will ruin a relationship. Reeves-Ellington

Map 14.1 | **Japan**

*Figure 14.4* | **A Japanese man presents his *meishi* to a colleague. The *meishi* exchange is a central part of Japanese business culture.**

notes that his students did not fully appreciate the consequences of these beliefs until he told them a story:

A major US company was having problems with one of its distributors, and the parties seemed unable to resolve their differences. The president of the US company decided to visit Japan, meet with his counterpart in the wholesaler organization, and attempt to resolve their differences. The two had not met previously and, upon meeting, each followed proper *meishi* ritual. The American, however, did not put the Japanese counterpart's *meishi* on the table; instead he held on to it. As the conversation became heated, the American rolled up the *meishi* in his hand. Horror was recorded on the face of the Japanese businessman. The American then tore the *meishi* into bits. This was more than the Japanese could stand; he excused himself from the meeting. Shortly afterward the two companies stopped doing business with each other. (1993: 209)

Table 14.1 shows the information regarding introductions and the use of the *meishi* that Reeves-Ellington's students derived from their work based on their analytic framework of artifacts, social knowledge, and cultural logic.

On three critical measures—effective working relationships with Japanese executives, shortened project times, and improved financial returns—the anthropologically based training program that Reeves-Ellington designed was a success. Both employees and their Japanese counterparts felt more comfortable working with each other. Prior to the program, joint projects required an average of 15 months to complete; projects run by executives applying the methodologies of the program cut completion time to an average of 8 months. Financial returns based on contracts negotiated by personnel who had not participated in the program averaged gross income of 6 per cent of sales, whereas those negotiated by personnel applying the anthropological techniques averaged gross income equal to 18 per cent of sales.

*Table 14.1* | Introductions at Business Meetings

| Artifacts | Social Knowledge | Cultural Logic |
|---|---|---|
| Technology<br>• Business cards.<br>• *Meishi*. | • Once given, a card is kept—not discarded.<br>• *Meishi* are not exchanged a second time unless there is a position change. | Human relations<br>• *Meishi* provide understanding of appropriate relations between parties.<br>• *Meishi* take uncertainty out of relationships. |
| Visual behaviour<br>• Presentation of *meishi* by presenting card, facing recipient.<br>• Senior people present *meishi* first.<br>• Guest presents first, giving name, company affiliation, and bowing.<br>• Host presents *meishi* in same sequence.<br>• Upon sitting at conference table, all *meishi* are placed in front of recipient to assure name use. | • Before the next meeting between parties, the *meishi* are reviewed for familiarization with the people attending the meeting.<br>• The *meishi* provide status for the owner. | Environment<br>• *Meishi* help establish insider/outsider environment.<br>• *Meishi* help establish possible obligations to environment.<br><br>Human activity<br>• *Meishi* help to establish human activities. |

Source: Reeves-Ellington, Richard H. 1993: 203–16.

## Urban Social Planning and Restructuring in Canada

Alexander Ervin is an anthropologist in Saskatoon, Saskatchewan, who has had considerable experience in collaborative, community-based research in social service and health agencies (see EthnoProfile 14.1). In his view, anthropologists seem to be particularly well-suited for this kind of applied work since they 'have been trained conceptually and methodologically to seek linkages among behaviours, institutions, and values, and to attempt to construct integrated overviews of whatever is the phenomenon under investigation' (1996: 324). As government policy-makers move to cut costs by downsizing, few policy disciplines are able to provide information about how the different social service providers and their services fit together, and few are able to listen effectively to grassroots perceptions of issues, needs, and solutions. Anthropologists, however, are trained to do precisely these things.

To illustrate, Ervin discusses his work with the Saskatoon Social Planning Council. The council was established in 1992 with a push from activists from the approximately two hundred human service delivery organizations in Saskatoon. In Canada, social planning councils focus attention on local social issues. They are involved with an extremely wide range of policies and issues and carry out policy research, including needs assessment, program evaluations, and problem-focussed investigations. Ervin's main task has been to design a plan for an annual investigation of a specific policy domain or issue to be carried out by the council. The goal of the research would be to provide the data that the human service organizations could use to solve effectively some of the problems the research identified. The pilot investigation has been a multi-dimensional study of the well-being of children in the city in relation to poverty, hunger, recreation, education, family, Native and immigrant issues, substance abuse, and general health concerns. Several organizations have collaborated in the project, including the regional health board, the Catholic and public school boards, and the social services district office. A working group of representatives of each organization has been formed to analyze the data, much of which was collected by three anthropology students at the University of Saskatchewan. When the report of the research has been written, the council will call together those organizations and people that are involved with children's issues in Saskatoon to consider the results and discuss possible solutions.

Ervin believes that anthropologists can make important contributions in urban policy contexts, especially in needs assessment, 'the process of identifying and seeking solutions to problems of particular populations, irrespective of whether programs have already been designed to address them' (330). Anthropologists seem particularly well placed for these projects, given their commitment to participatory research and holism. Indeed, from his point of view, the major need in the kinds of urban policy research that he has been engaged in is for flexible generalists—anthropologists who can move from one policy domain to another and construct integrated overviews of the phenomenon under investigation.

*EthnoProfile 14.1* | **Saskatoon**

**Region** North America
**Nation** Canada
**Language** English is the official language, but Cree is also spoken as there is a large population of First Nations peoples, mostly from Plains Cree communities, in Saskatoon
**Population** 224,300 (2010)
**Environment** Northern plains

**Livelihood** Industrial, commercial, agricultural, educational centre
**Political organization** City in contemporary nation-state
**For more information** 'City of Saskatoon', www.saskatoon.ca/; 'Saskatoon Treaty Indians Supported by Chiefs', www.sicc.sk.ca/saskindian/a88feb04.htm.

## Anthropology and Policy

In all this work—and there is much more—the anthropological perspective illustrated throughout this text has been employed. Applied anthropologists do their work using holism, comparison, relativism, and a concern for particular cases.

Nevertheless, anthropologists are hesitant to make detailed policy recommendations that other professional disciplines make. This may be because anthropologists are particularly aware of the problems in applied work, the problems in trying to make people, or systems, change. Anthropologists are trained to analyze social and cultural systems, but when they are asked how to change them, they begin to ask questions. These questions are based on an awareness of the enormous complexity of human life when it is viewed from ground level. Anthropologists have developed a keen awareness that not everyone makes the same basic assumptions about the world that planners and officials make. They know that sometimes technical experts providing help in other cultures know less than the people they are advising or give advice that is culturally inappropriate. Anthropologists realize that no change benefits everyone equally and that some gain as others lose. They also understand that even if they get involved in planning a program, implementation depends on external factors over which they have no control: cash flow problems to government agencies, fear over a legislator's response, political issues, elections, budget reductions, lack of interest, and so on.

Anthropologists believe they have much to contribute in helping build a better world, yet they are also highly sensitive to the kinds of issues that arise when dealing with the complex human systems we have discussed throughout this text. Applied anthropologists are well aware of the ambiguities of the human experience.

# Anthropology and the Challenges of Global Citizenship

One of the challenges faced by people everywhere in the world at the beginning of the twenty-first century is that of defining citizenship in a complex, diverse, and difficult world. Can anthropologists provide ways for people to understand the issues involved?

## Anthropology and Democracy

As we saw in the previous chapter, the end of the Cold War appears to have marked a turning point in the world system. The capitalist market has spread into all parts of the globe, and many observers have assumed that other Western institutions are bound to follow. The fall of dictatorial political regimes in a number of Latin American and central European countries, for example, was viewed as an opportunity to introduce Western political practices, including political parties and formal elections. Many members of the Western political and economic elite eagerly proclaimed the arrival of democracy as soon as the first elections were held and have often been very suspicious of political movements—such as some of the new social movements we described in the previous chapter—that challenge formal electoral institutions in the name of democracy.

But anthropologists and other social scientists working in these same countries are often able to present a different perspective on the 'transition' to democracy. Fieldwork brings them into close, regular contact with citizens who have their own ideas about what kinds of social institutions do or do not operate in a democratic fashion. Taking these observations seriously has drawn anthropologists into a growing debate about what democracy has been and can be. In particular, their work has helped to show that formal Western electoral politics may produce less democratic outcomes than other, traditional institutions.

For example, anthropologist Serge Tcherkézoff (1998) has followed debates about the shape democracy ought to take in the independent nation of Samoa (see Ethno-Profile 4.1). Traditionally, Samoa has been a land of villages, each of which was governed by a council of *matai*, or 'sacred chiefs'. This system had survived Christian missionaries, German colonization, and the effects of 42 years while the area was a protectorate of New Zealand. A referendum sponsored by the un in 1962 led to independence, and the people then voted to set up a parliamentary system of national government (Figure 14.5). However, their constitution specified that only *matai* could vote and run for office. In 1990, the law was changed to allow all citizens to vote, but *matai* were still the only ones allowed to run for office.

Does this hybrid of a Western parliamentary system and the Samoan *faamatai*, or 'chief-system', represent an undemocratic attempt by chiefly 'aristocrats' to maintain power within formally democratic political institutions? In Tcherkézoff's opinion, the question is deeply misleading because it rests on a fundamental misunderstanding of how the Samoan chief-system functions. He points out that if outsiders insist on thinking of *matai* as aristocrats, then there are no families in Samoa who are not aristocratic. This is because each *matai* is actually the head of an extended family. Each extended family is held together by kinship connections, joint ownership of land, and joint participation in rituals directed to their founding ancestor. *Matai*, in fact, means 'the one who bears the family name', and members of each extended family choose the person who will be ritually invested with this title. It is the job of each *matai* to serve his family and his *matai* name by leading worship directed to the ancestor and engaging in other activities designed to elevate the reputation of his extended family. If a *matai* fails to live up to these expectations, his extended family can strip him of his title and give it to someone else. Every family has a *matai*, which is why Tcherkézoff says that there are no families that are not chiefly families; and *matais* serve at the will of the kin who choose them, which is why, he tells us, 'when Samoans heard about "democracy", they said that they "already have it"' (1998: 423).

So why are Samoans arguing about the connection between the *matai* system and democracy? As Tcherkézoff explains, this debate involves a variety of different ideas about what democracy means and which kinds of institutional arrangements are most likely to ensure it. Those who want universal suffrage favour a view of democracy in which the emphasis is on individual freedom: anyone can run for office and anyone can vote. They point out, for example, that traditionally nobody becomes a *matai* until he has served his family for many years and his predecessor has died, which limits the field of possible parliamentary candidates to one (relatively) old man per extended family. How can it be democratic to restrict the opportunities of younger people to run for office? These sorts of arguments fit well with traditional Western arguments that speak of democracy in connection with individual freedom from arbitrary restrictions.

But those Samoans who want the *matai* system to continue stress that it is more democratic than universal suffrage because it creates representatives who can never forget that they are responsible to those who elected

Figure 14.5 | The parliament building in Samoa. Today, Samoans are taking part in a debate that involves a variety of ideas about what democracy means and what kinds of institutional arrangements are most likely to ensure it.

them—the other members of their extended family. In thinking about democracy in this way, these Samoans are refusing to reduce democratic citizenship to the right to vote. Rather, they take the view that democracy involves not just being treated as an equal by others but also the obligation of those who make political decisions for others to remain accountable and accessible to those whom they represent (O'Donnell and Schmitter 1986; Rubin 1997). Thus, the *matai* system can be viewed as more democratic than universal suffrage because it ensures that every extended family will be represented in some form in the electoral process and that any *matais* elected to parliament will not be able to ignore the wishes of those who put them in office.

Politics in Samoa also has a regional dimension. Tcherkézoff points out that Samoa was primarily a nation of villages in the past, but the capital city has been growing in size in recent years. Many of those who live in the growing urban area depend more on wage labour and less on agriculture and fishing, the activities central to village life where *matais* traditionally exercised their authority. Thus, those who want to preserve the *matai* system also defend it as a way of maintaining equality between those who live in the city and those who still live in rural areas. They fear that if parliamentary elections were to operate in terms of universal suffrage, Samoa would be fractured into two societies: an urban sector with a Western political system, and no way to hold their parliamentary representatives accountable, and a rural sector in which *matais* still exist but only as powerless guardians of local folklore. Should this happen, 'then some Samoans say that "democracy" will not be achieved and will even go backwards' (Tcherkézoff 1998: 427).

As Tcherkézoff makes clear, the debate about democracy in Samoa is complex and nuanced: Samoans have a sophisticated understanding of the advantages and drawbacks of different democratic political forms, some of which are indigenous to Samoa and some of which came from elsewhere.

> The problem is that Samoa has the chance to build its future on ideas and experiences that come both from the *faamatai* tradition and from the Western tradition of democracy and to maybe create a new synthesis where the advent of democracy will not just be the replacement of hierarchy (in the *faamatai*) by inequality (in the Western-style politics). There lies the real question of the future of the country. (430)

## Anthropology and Multicultural Politics in the New Europe

One of the more interesting things about the early twenty-first century is that Europe, the continent that gave birth to the Enlightenment and colonial empires and to anthropology itself, has now become a key setting for the anthropological study of social and cultural changes. During the last half of the twentieth century, the countries of Europe were the target of large waves of migration from all over the world. As a result, Europeans are struggling with the concept of multiculturalism in ways we in Canada can recognize. Indeed, we are the people with the Canadian Multiculturalism Act, passed in Parliament in 1988, which recognizes 'the diversity of Canadians as regards race, national or ethnic origin, colour, and religion as a fundamental characteristic of Canadian society . . . while working to achieve the equality of all Canadians in the economic, social, cultural, and political life of Canada' (Preamble). How is Europe dealing with the influx of people they consider non-European?

Let us look at an example from Italy. In 1999, anthropologist Michael Herzfeld moved into Rione Monti, a working-class Roman neighbourhood close to the Coliseum (see Map 14.3), to do fieldwork exploring social change in the way people use the concept of the past (2003). Long-time residents of Monti share a common local culture, which includes use of the *romanesco* dialect rather than standard Italian and a strong sense of local identity that distinguishes them from 'foreigners', including diplomats and non-Roman Italians. Their identity survived Mussolini's demolition of part of the neighbourhood in the early twentieth century. They successfully dealt with a local criminal underworld by mastering a refined urbane code of politeness. The underworld had faded away by the 1970s, but beginning in the 1980s, residents began to face two new challenges to their community.

1) Historic Roman neighbourhoods became fashionable, and well-to-do Italians began to move into Rione Monti, pushing many workers into cheaper housing elsewhere.
2) In the 1990s, another group of newcomers arrived: immigrants from eastern Europe.

Italy is one of the more recent destinations of immigration into Europe, reversing the country's historical experience as a source, rather than a target, of immigration. After Germany, France, and Britain passed

*Map 14.3* | **Rione Monti**

laws curtailing immigration in the 1970s, Italy became an increasingly popular destination for immigrants from Africa, Asia, Latin America, and, after the Cold War, other European nations, particularly those of eastern Europe. Until recently, laws regulating immigration were few, and the country appeared welcoming. But this is changing (Figure 14.6). 'Italy has not historically been a racist country, but intolerant attitudes toward immigrants have increased. To a large extent, this seems to be the result of a long-standing underestimation of the magnitude of the changes and thus poor policy implementation for a lengthy period, in spite of the best intentions officially proclaimed' (Melotti 1997: 91).

Umberto Melotti contrasts the distinctive ways in which immigration is understood by the governments of France, Britain, and Germany. According to him, the French project is *ethnocentric assimilationism*: since the early nineteenth century, when French society experienced a falling birth rate, immigration was encouraged and immigrants were promised all the rights and privileges of native-born citizens as long as they adopted French culture completely, dropping other ethnic or cultural attachments and assimilating the French language, culture, and character (1997: 75). The British project, in contrast, is *uneven pluralism*: that is, the pragmatic British expect immigrants to be loyal and law-abiding citizens, but they do not expect immigrants to 'become British', and they tolerate private cultivation of cultural differences as long as these do not threaten the British way of life (79–80). Finally, Melotti describes the German project as *the institutionalization of precariousness*, by which he means that despite the fact that Germany has within its borders more immigrants than any other European country, and began receiving immigrants at the end of the nineteenth century, its government continues to insist that Germany is not a country of immigrants. Immigrants were always considered 'guest workers', children born to guest workers are considered citizens of the country from which the worker came, and it still remains very difficult for guest workers or their German-born children to obtain German citizenship. (This contrasts with France, for example, where children of immigrants born on French soil automatically become French citizens.)

Figure 14.6 | In recent years, intolerance toward immigrants has increased in Italy. As part of a 2002 protest in Rome against increased restrictions on immigration, this young immigrant from Africa displayed a silencing sticker that reads 'never more racism'.

Some European countries face issues of multiculturalism that are rooted in longstanding tensions between two or more ethnic groups that are equally established within the same country. This is the case in Belgium, for example, where there has been historic conflict between the Dutch-speaking Flemings in the north and the French-speaking Walloons in the south. The country has found a partial solution to cultural tension by allowing both groups to enjoy considerable autonomy, and the state's role is to protect the rights of each community in the public sphere. This system, known as *pillorization*, bears some similarity to the way separate religious communities were organized under the Ottoman Empire (Modood 1997: 22–3).

Coming to terms with increasing numbers of Muslims living in countries where Christianity has historically been dominant is a central theme in multicultural debates within Europe. Although all European states consider themselves secular in orientation, the relation between religion and state is far from uniform. France is unusual because of its strict legal separation between religion and state. In Britain, the combination of a secular outlook with state funding of the established Anglican Church has allowed citizens to support forms of religious inclusion that first involved state funding of Catholic schools for Irish immigrants and now involve state funding of Muslim schools for Muslim immigrants (Lewis 1997; Modood 1997). In Germany, where a secular outlook also combines with state-subsidized religious institutions, the state has devised curricula for elementary schools designed to teach all students about different religious traditions, including Islam, in ways that emphasize the possibility of harmonizing one's religious faith with one's obligations as a citizen. Although this approach may be seen as presumptuous or paternalistic, its supporters counter that its advantages outweigh its costs. Perhaps as a result of their own history, many contemporary Germans have less faith than the British that a civic culture of religious tolerance will automatically lead to harmony without state intervention and less faith than the French in the existence of a separate secular sphere of society from which religion can be safely excluded (Schiffauer 1997).

These are, of course, thumbnail sketches of more complex attitudes and practices. But they illustrate the fact that there is no single 'European' approach to the challenges posed by immigration and multiculturalism. In a way, each European state, with its own history and institutions, is experimenting with different ways of coping, and their failures and successes will influence the kinds of multicultural relations and institutions that develop in the future. This experimentation is particularly significant in light of the fact that European nation-states have joined together in the European Union (EU), a superstate with 27 members as of 2011. Reconciling the diverse, culturally informed interests and needs of member states poses enormous challenges for the EU as a whole.

Many scholars and activists hope that solutions can be found that will involve extensions of social justice throughout the EU (see, e.g., Ben-Tovim 1997; Brewin 1997). But there is still a lot of work to be done, and there are no guarantees about the outcome. Modood points out, for example, that European multiculturalism requires supporting conceptions of citizenship that allow the 'right to assimilate' as well as the 'right to have one's "difference" . . . recognized and supported

in the public and the private spheres'; multiculturalism must recognize that 'participation in the public or national culture is necessary for the effective exercise of citizenship' while at the same time defending the 'right to widen and adapt the national culture' (1997: 20). The potential and actual contradictions among some of these goals are apparent, but insofar as they are seen as necessary, the challenge becomes finding ways to move forward. And here, with no blueprint to follow, all parties find themselves involved in creating new cultural practices. Based on her experience in France, Dembour is convinced that 'we need to accept the discomfort of moving in-between, as a pendulum' (2001: 71–2). Modood agrees: 'There is indeed a tension here, and perhaps it can only be resolved in practice through finding and cultivating points of common ground between dominant and subordinate cultures, as well as new syntheses and hybridities. The important thing is that the burdens of change . . . are not all dependent on one party to this encounter' (1997: 20).

Anthropologists are inevitably drawn into these discussions, not only because they carry out research in the communities struggling for resolution but also because many of them are citizens of the societies whose future depends on the solutions that are implemented. As a result, theoretical debates in the field are intertwined with political debates in society, and scholars can disagree with one another just as political activists do. For example, Norwegian anthropologist Thomas Eriksen reports on the outcome of a formal debate organized by the Department of Anthropology at the University of Oslo in 1997, in which the thesis to be contested was the assertion that cultural freedom protects not only a group but also the rights of every individual within a group (2001: 144). 'Speaking from very different ethnographic horizons, the antagonists not only reached opposite conclusions but also failed to engage in a proper dialogue: they tended to depict each other . . . as hopeless Romantics and cynical modernists, respectively' (2001: 144). In the end, Eriksen observes, the debate raised the same kinds of issues and provoked the same kinds of responses and stand-offs that can be found in the wider society. After the debate, the audience was invited to vote for the side they thought had made the best case. The results were 78 in favour of the motion, 75 against. This almost perfect standoff, Eriksen points out, is very different from what the outcome would likely have been 10 or 15 years earlier, when there would have been 'almost certainly a massive "yes" vote. . . . [P]erhaps the tide will turn again' (145).

Thus, the struggles and dilemmas facing residents of Rione Monti are widespread across the new Europe. But the specifics of the situation in Rione Monti, and the cultural resources available to longstanding residents, have their own particularity. Thus, the traditionally left-wing Monti residents have resisted attempts by neo-fascist politicians to get them to turn against immigrant families in the neighbourhood. Still, they are unhappy with many of the ways in which immigration has impacted their lives. For example, they do not like the location of the Ukrainian church in a building that overlooks the neighbourhood's central square because churchgoers gather there twice a week, invading 'their' space (Herzfeld 2003: 4) (Figure 14.7). Herzfeld reports that the residents of Monti, like other Romans, claim not to be racist (which accords with Melotti's views of Italians in general) and that they seem less hostile to immigrants of colour than to Ukrainians. Ukrainians are more numerous in Monti and more threatening because they look like local people and compete with local people for work and space in the neighbourhood (5). At the same time, the Monti code of politeness 'underlies the facility with which democratically inclined residents today construct a popular street democracy, a system of neighbourhood associations' (2). Currently, immigrants are not able to deploy this code, a fact that signals their outsider status and can lead to misunderstandings and bad feelings. If they could learn to use the code, however, fresh opportunities for political co-operation might be forged. This arrangement could be decisive, for the code of politeness is the foundation of local democratic processes and 'may also eventually be the only generally available means of denying access to manipulative party politics and land speculation alike' (6).

*Figure 14.7* | In the neighbourhood of Rione Monti in central Rome, long-time residents and new immigrants are negotiating new forms of relationships.

## Anthropology and Human Rights

Recently, anthropologists have been involved in expanding the understanding of human rights and have participated in organizations for the defence of human rights. In particular, they have contributed to the recognition by human rights legal advocates that the collective rights of groups (such as Indigenous peoples) deserve as much attention as the rights of individuals. Ellen Messer observes that anthropologists have examined, and continue to examine,

the contexts of human rights abuses to understand how the political economic conditions that create cultural customs such as infanticide, underfeeding of women and children, and other abuses of women might be improved and make the customs of less evident utility. They also continue to work with interpreters of local traditions, so that through persuasion and contextualization, and by drawing on the authority of multiple traditions, people might be empowered to improve human rights in their own lives. (1993: 241)

Perhaps one of the foremost anthropologically oriented organizations involved with human rights is Cultural Survival, founded in 1972 by anthropologists Pia Maybury-Lewis and David Maybury-Lewis and dedicated to helping Indigenous people and ethnic minorities deal as equals in their encounters with industrial society. Anthropologist Carolyn Nordstrom (1993) writes about the efforts of the Ministry of Education in Mozambique and the Mozambican Woman's Organization to begin programs to assist children and women traumatized, raped, displaced, and impoverished by the 16-year war in that country. She discusses how Indigenous healers have come to develop specialties in war trauma, 'to take the violence out of people', and are being brought into the national health care system.

Biological anthropologists, most notably Clyde Snow, have also contributed in an important way to the defence of human rights in the world. Snow is a consulting forensic anthropologist who is often called on by police departments, medical examiners, and other law enforcement officials to try to identify human remains and to determine the cause of death. Snow has been involved in a number of international human rights cases. Beginning in 1984, he worked with the American Association for the Advancement of Science to help the Argentinian National Commission on Disappeared Persons to determine the fate of some of the more than 10,000 people who had vanished during the 'dirty war' waged by the Argentine military government against supposed subversives. Snow began his work in Argentina by training a team of medical and anthropology students in the techniques of forensic investigation, both skeletal and archaeological, and then helped them exhume and examine scores of the remains of the *desaparecidos* ('those who have disappeared'). By 1988, only 25 victims had been positively identified, but those identifications helped convict seven members of the former ruling junta and other high-ranking military and police officers (Huyghe 1988).

The Argentine team Snow trained has gone on to investigate sites of massacres in Guatemala, Bolivia, Panama, Iraq, and the site of the massacre at El Mozote, El Salvador. Snow himself was in Chiapas in February 1994 to investigate the deaths of peasants following the Mexican army's battle with Emiliano

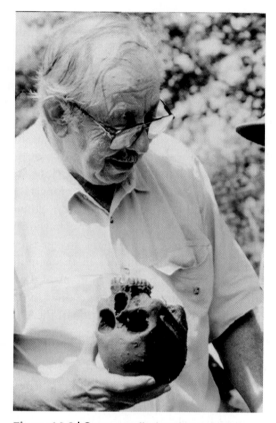

*Figure 14.8* | **Some applied anthropologists, like Clyde Snow (shown here), use their knowledge and skills in skeletal identification.**

Zapata's Liberation Army in early January of that year (Figure 14.8). Snow states, 'There are human rights violations going on all around the world. But to me murder is murder, regardless of the motive. I hope that we are sending a message to governments who murder in the name of politics that they can be held to account' (Huyghe 1988).

Paul Oldham and Miriam Frank (2008) consider the adoption of the UN's 2007 Declaration on the Rights of Indigenous Peoples. Declarations are important, but only so far as they become the road map for action. They challenge us to consider the role that anthropology might play in promoting human rights. In Canada, for example, we might ask what anthropologists can do to help ease the suffering of Aboriginal peoples who continue to struggle with the aftereffects of the residential school system.

*In Their Own Words* | **Into the Warp and Woof of Multicultural Worlds**

*Changes in the contemporary world are producing what anthropologist George Marcus calls 'transcultural "traditional" peoples', whose members live in many different places and whose sense of cultural identity involves a mix of many cultural elements.*

The power of global cultural homogenization in the late twentieth century challenges the conventions and rationales by which anthropology has so far produced its knowledge of other cultures. The reorganization of the world economy through technological advances in communication, production processes, and marketing has thoroughly de-territorialized culture. For example, the Tongan Islanders of Polynesia that I studied in the early 1970s now constitute a diaspora of communities in locales around the Pacific Rim. As many, if not more, Tongans now live permanently in Australia, New Zealand, and the United States as in the islands themselves. One might fairly ponder where both the cultural and geographical centre of the Tongan people resides. Their identity is produced in many locales and through the mix of many cultural elements. And their conditions are similar to those of numerous other peoples that anthropologists have traditionally studied. It is no longer just the most powerful, large-scale, and most modern societies, such as the United States and Japan, that exist in international, transcultural science.

Among such transcultural 'traditional' peoples, levels of cultural self-consciousness and alternatives increase. The authenticity of performances, rituals, or apparently deep-seated norms like those of kinship cannot be merely assumed, either by locals or by visitors such as anthropologists. To some extent, media documentaries have absorbed anthropology's function of presenting vividly the lifeways of other cultures to Euro-American publics that themselves can no longer be considered as homogeneous or mainstream. And, finally, the subjects of anthropological study independently and articulately translate their own perspectives with sensitivity to the effects of different media.

Peoples who in particular have become classic anthropological subjects, such as the Samoans, Trobriand Islanders, Hopi of the Southwest USA, and Todas of India, know their status well, and have, with some ambivalence, assimilated anthropological knowledge about them as part of their sense of themselves. A recent example was the visit of a Toda woman to Houston. A trained nurse among her people, as well as a cultural broker, she was on tour in the United States giving talks about the Todas, of the sort that anthropologists might have given in past decades. By chance, she was visiting the home of a colleague just as a British documentary about the Todas appeared on the television—a documentary in which the visitor was featured prominently as the filmmaker's prime source of information. The visitor's comments as she watched the program along with my colleague did not much concern the details of Toda culture but rather dealt with the ironies of the multiple representations of her people—by herself, by anthropologists, and by the British Broadcasting Corporation.

The lesson of this story is compelling. The penetrations of a world economy, communications, and the effects of multiple, fragmented identities on cultural authenticity, once thought restricted to advanced modernity, have increased markedly among most local and regional cultures worldwide. They have thus engendered an ethnography in reverse among many peoples who not only can assimilate the professional idioms of anthropology but can relativize them among other alternatives and ways of knowledge. This does not mean that the traditional task of anthropology to represent distinctive and systematic cultural forms of life has been fundamentally subverted by its own subjects. Rather, anthropology's traditional task is now much more complicated, requiring new sensibilities in undertaking fieldwork and different strategies for writing about it.

Source: Marcus, George. 1990. 'Into the Warp and Woof of Multicultural Worlds', guest editorial in *Cultural Anthropology: A Perspective on the Human Condition*, 2nd edn, eds Emily Schultz and Robert Lavenda (St Paul: West), 254–5.

# Awareness and Uncertainty

Why study anthropology? The second part of our answer is personal.

Studying cultural anthropology brings students into contact with different ways of life. It makes them aware of just how arbitrary their own understanding of the world is as they learn how other people have developed satisfying but different ways of living. In addition, if they are from Western countries that were responsible for colonialism and its consequences, it makes them painfully aware of just how much their own tradition has to answer for in the modern world.

Knowing and experiencing cultural variety gives rise, perhaps inevitably, to doubt. We come to doubt the ultimate validity of the central truths of our own cultural tradition, which have been ratified and sanctified by the generations who preceded us. We doubt because a familiarity with alternative ways of living makes the ultimate meaning of any action, of any object, a highly ambiguous matter. Ambiguity is part and parcel of the human condition. Human beings have coped with ambiguity from time immemorial by means of culture, which places objects and actions in contexts and thereby makes their meanings plain. This doubt can lead to anxiety, but it can also be liberating.

This liberation leads to a recognition of themes of central concern for informed global citizens—freedom, health, divisions of wealth, environment, personhood, governance, transnationalism, and the like. An excellent example is how these themes combine in the context of the debate about who should control the remaining samples of the 'eradicated' disease smallpox (see the 'In Their Own Words' box on this topic). Western scientists

## In Their Own Words | Homes for the Smallpox Virus

*This editorial article considers the efficacy of keeping samples of the most deadly virus known to humans decades after its eradication from human populations. Such ethical discussions will arise in other world health situations.*

20 January 2011

At a May meeting of the World Health Assembly—a gathering of delegates from all WHO member states—the United States and Russia will once again face a clamour, led by African countries, to eliminate the last known live samples of the smallpox virus—thirty years after the WHO declared it eradicated. Unfortunately, humanity cannot dispense with this destroyer of life so easily.

The scourge is believed to have killed more people over the millennia than any other, its victims running into the hundreds of millions. Legions more were blinded and permanently disfigured. The last natural outbreaks occurred in Africa as late as the 1970s, within living memory, and it is understandable that African countries are pushing most vehemently to bring about its extinction.

The fact of smallpox's survival three decades after its eradication through a global program of vaccination, even in maximum-containment, 'biosafety level 4' laboratories at the US Centers for Disease Control and at a research institution in Russia, constitutes a real and constant danger. But the elimination of the live virus would not remove that threat. On the contrary, it might serve in a perverse way to exacerbate it.

Live viruses might well persist in unknown laboratories, or even, it has been theorized, lie in wait in permafrost cemeteries. It is also possible that the virus could be artificially reconstructed and used in a bioterrorism attack. For that reason, the US ordered the emergency production of 168 million doses of smallpox vaccine after 11 September 2001 and continues to add to its stocks.

This is not bioterror hysteria. It is a sensible precaution. Such a threat is much greater than any risk posed by the collections maintained at two WHO-authorized high-security laboratories. These samples, frozen in liquid nitrogen, are the source of anxiety for those who want to declare total victory in the war against smallpox. But such chest-thumping would harm research into the human immune system and undermine the capacity of science to identify and research antiviral agents and next-generation vaccines. Surely this is a case of its being better to know thy enemy.

Source: 'Homes for the Smallpox Virus'. 2011. Editorial in *The Globe and Mail* (19 Jan.), available at www.theglobeandmail.com/news/opinions/editorials/homes-for-the-smallpox-virus/article1876412/. © The Globe and Mail Inc. All Rights Reserved.

and politicians argue that the samples are necessary for research purposes. Yet other people—especially people living in Africa, where the disease was most devastating during the twentieth century—argue that all samples should be destroyed to prevent them from leaking out into the public. Between these two positions, other individuals and groups have developed their own unique perspectives based on their own unique situations. As students of anthropology, you can understand the many sides of the debate, and you can respect the validity of the many perspectives involved.

## Freedom and Constraint

So why study anthropology? The third part of our response is humanistic—it relates to our interest in our fellow human beings and our desire learn about and from the diversity of humanity.

All human beings live in culturally shaped worlds, enmeshed in webs of interpretation and meaning. It has been the particular task of anthropologists to go out into the world to bear witness to and record the vast creative diversity in world-making that has been the history of our species. In our lifetimes, we will witness the end of many of those ways of life. This loss is tragic, for as these worlds disappear so too does something special about humanity: variety, creativity, and awareness of alternatives.

Our survival as a species, and our viability as individuals, depends on the possibility of choice, of perceiving and being able to act on alternatives in the various situations we encounter during our lives. If, as a colleague has suggested, human life is a minefield, then the more paths we can see and imagine through that minefield, the more likely we are to make it through—or at least to have an interesting time trying. As alternatives are destroyed, wantonly smashed, or thoughtlessly crushed, *our* own human possibilities are reduced. A small group of men and women have, for the last century, laboured in corners of the world, both remote and nearby, to write the record of human accomplishment and bring it back and teach it to others.

Surely our greatest human accomplishment is the creation of the sometimes austerely beautiful worlds in which we all live. Anthropologists have rarely given in to the romantic notion that these other worlds are all good, all life-enhancing, all fine or beautiful. They are not. Ambiguity and ambivalence are, as we have seen, hallmarks of the human experience. There are no guarantees that human cultures will be compassionate rather than cruel or that people will agree they are one or the other. There are not even any guarantees that our species will survive. But all anthropologists have believed that these are *human* worlds that have given those who have lived in them the ability to make sense out of their experiences and to derive meaning for their lives, that we are a species at once bound by our culture and free to change it.

This is a perilous and fearsome freedom, a difficult freedom to grasp and to wield. Nevertheless, the freedom is there, and in this dialectic of freedom and constraint lies our future. It is up to us to create it.

## Chapter Summary

1. Anthropological research can be challenging to conduct in today's world, but it is also very rewarding. Applied anthropology can contribute to contemporary solutions of various social issues. Applied anthropologists do their work using holism, comparison, relativism, and a concern for particular cases.

2. At the beginning of the twenty-first century, people everywhere face the challenge of defining citizenship in a complex, diverse, and difficult world. At this point in your studies, you can consider how you can apply what you have learned about anthropology to your own position, and you can anticipate your potential efficacy as a global citizen. Anthropology is not just an esoteric exercise. Even if you do not go on to work as an anthropologist, you can refer to your knowledge of anthropology as a guide for a way of living in the world in a state of reflexivity—a state of constant engagement and growth.

3. Recently, anthropologists involved in expanding the understanding of human rights have participated in organizations for the defence of human rights. In particular, they have contributed to the recognition by human

rights legal advocates that the collective rights of groups (such as Indigenous peoples) deserve as much attention as the rights of individuals. Additionally, forensic anthropologists have worked to uncover evidence of genocides and ethnic cleansings in various parts of the world.

4.  Cultural anthropology brings us into contact with different ways of life and challenges our awareness of just how arbitrary our own understanding of the world is as we learn how other people have developed satisfying but different ways of living.

5.  In addition, anthropology helps us understand our place in and responsibility for the historical and present-day worlds of colonialism and post-colonialism. The consequences of colonialism resonate, and we can become aware of just how much the Western tradition has to answer for in the modern world.

6.  Our survival as a species, and our viability as individuals, depends on the possibility of choice, of perceiving and being able to act on alternatives in the various situations we encounter during our lives.

# Critical Thinking Questions

1.  How would you describe the potential of applied anthropology to address various issues of concern in today's world? Give at least three specific examples.

2.  Review the list of the 12 main skills you can learn from a major in anthropology (p. 353). Which have been the greatest challenges for you?

3.  How can coming to understand the social knowledge or values based on an underlying, taken-for-granted cultural logic of another culture be of importance to you?

4.  Why do you suppose anthropologists are particularly aware of the problems in applied work—the problems in trying to make people, or systems, change? What is it about anthropology that engenders such sensitivity?

5.  How would you describe the ambiguity and ambivalence of the human experience in the sometimes austerely beautiful worlds in which we all live?

# Suggested Readings

Lock, Margaret. 2001. 'The Tempering of Medical Anthropology: Troubling Natural Categories', *Medical Anthropology Quarterly* 15: 478–92. A continuation of Lock's work on the relationship of emerging bioscientific knowledge and associated technologies with the social, political, and moral order, and with the subjectivity of categories (typologies).

Oldham, Paul, and Miriam Anne Frank. 2008. '"We the People . . .": The United Nations Declaration on the Rights of Indigenous Peoples', *Anthropology Today* 24, 2: 5–9. A report on the adoption of the UN document of the rights of Indigenous people worldwide. Note that not all states have signed on!

Rodman, William L. 1991. 'When Questions Are Answers: The Message of Anthropology, According to the People of Ambae', *American Anthropologist* 93, 2: 421–34. The story of a young man who established an important social movement in Ambae based on his allegorical interpretation of Rodman's questions in the New Hebrides archipelago.

Salzman, Philip Carl. 1986. 'Is Traditional Fieldwork Outmoded?', *Current Anthropology* 27, 5: 528–30. Challenges the view that research is conducted by a lone observer and calls anthropologists to adopt a team approach—this would include the 'informant' as the specialist as well.

Wardlow, Holly. 2007. 'Men's Extramarital Sexuality in Rural Papua New Guinea', *American Journal of Public Health* 97, 6: 1006–14. Considers the role of extramarital activity in the spread of HIV/AIDS.

Warry, Wayne, S. Smith, and N. Johnson, eds. 1997. *Nurtured by Knowledge: Learning to Do Participatory Action Research* (New York/Ottawa: The Apex Press and the International Development Research Centre [IDRC Books]). Discussion of PAR (Participatory Action Research), a methodology that enables people to take control of their lives through the integration of formal and informal knowledge and by using this integrated knowledge in a transformative way to challenge their assumed realities. Now that suggests reflexivity!

# Related Websites

**Canadian Multiculturalism** www.cic.gc.ca/english/multiculturalism/citizenship.asp

**CBC's Making the Mosaic** http://archives.cbc.ca/society/celebrations/topics/3517

**CIDA's International Youth Internship Programs** www.acdi-cida.gc.ca/IYIP; www.acdi-cida.gc.ca/acdi-cida/ACDI-CIDA.nsf/eng/FRA-621103243-K3H

**Cultural Survival** www.culturalsurvival.org

**Truth and Reconciliation Commission of Canada** www.trc.ca

INTSORMIL **http://**intsormil.org

**Grameen Bank: Muhammad Yunus** www.grameen-info.org

**Society for Applied Anthropology** www.sfaa.net

**Survival International** www.survival-international.org

USAID www.usaid.gov

# REFERENCES

AAA (American Anthropological Association). 2009. *Code of Ethics of the American Anthropological Association*, available at www.aaanet.org/issues/policy-advocacy/upload/AAA-Ethics-Code-2009.pdf.

AANDC (Aboriginal Affairs and Northern Development Canada). 2011. *Contaminants in the North*, available at www.ainc-inac.gc.ca/nth/ct/index-eng.asp.

Abbas, Ackbar. 2002. 'Cosmopolitan Description: Shanghai and Hong Kong', in *Cosmopolitanism*, eds Carol A. Breckenridge et al. (Durham, NC: Duke University Press), 209–28.

Abley, Mark. 2005. *Spoken Here: Travels among Threatened Languages* (New York: Mariner Books).

Abu-Lughod, Lila. 1991. 'Writing against Culture', in *Recapturing Anthropology*, ed. Richard Fox (Santa Fe, NM: SAR), 137–62.

——. 1995. 'The Objects of Soap Opera: Egyptian Television and the Cultural Politics of Modernity', in *Worlds Apart: Modernity through the Prism of the Local*, ed. Daniel Miller (London: Routledge), 109–210.

Adams, Richard Newbold. 1979. *Energy and Structure: A Theory of Social Power* (Austin: University of Texas Press).

Advameg Inc. 2008. 'Xikrin: Orientation', from World Culture Encyclopedia, available at www.everyculture.com/South-America/Xikrin-Orientation.html.

Agar, Michael. 1996. *The Professional Stranger: An Informal Introduction to Ethnography*, 2nd edn (San Diego: Academic Press).

Alland, Alexander. 1977. *The Artistic Animal* (New York: Doubleday Anchor).

Allen, Catherine J. 1988. *The Hold Life Has: Coca and Cultural Identity in an Andean Community* (Washington, DC: Smithsonian Institution Press).

Allen, Theodore. 1994–7. *The Invention of the White Race*, 2 vols (London: Verso).

Allen, Timothy F.H., and T.W. Hoekstra. 1991. 'Role of Heterogeneity in Scaling of Ecological Systems under Analysis', *Ecological Heterogeneity (Ecological Studies)*, vol. 86, eds J. Kolasa and S. Pickett (New York: Springer Verlag), 47–68.

Alonso, Ana María. 1994. 'The Politics of Space, Time, and Substance: State Formation, Nationalism, and Ethnicity', *Annual Review of Anthropology* 23: 379–405.

Alverson, Hoyt. 1978. *Mind in the Heart of Darkness* (New Haven: Yale University Press).

Amnesty International. 2011. 'Sri Lanka Human Rights', available at www.amnestyusa.org/our-work/countries/asia-and-the-pacific/sri-lanka.

Anderson, Benedict. 1983. *Imagined Communities.* (London: Verson).

——. 2002 [1992]. 'The New World Disorder', in *The Anthropology of Politics*, ed. Joan Vincent (Malden, MA: Blackwell), 261–70.

Anderson, Richard L. 1990. *Calliope's Sisters: A Comparative Study of Philosophies of Art* (Englewood Cliffs, NJ: Prentice-Hall).

Apfel, Roberta J., and Bennett Simon. 2000. 'Mitigating Discontents with Children in War: An Ongoing Psychoanalytic Inquiry', in *Cultures under Siege: Collective Violence and Trauma*, eds Antonius C.G.M. Robben and Marcelo M. Suárez-Orozco (Cambridge: Cambridge University Press), 102–30.

Appadurai, Arjun. 1990. 'Disjuncture and Difference in the Global Cultural Economy', in *Global Culture*, ed. Mike Featherstone (London: Sage), 295–310.

——. 2002. 'Grassroots Globalization and the Research Imagination', in *The Anthropology of Politics*, ed. Joan Vincent (Malden, MA: Blackwell), 271–84.

Asad, Talal, ed. 1973. *Anthropology and the Colonial Encounter* (London: Ithaca Press).

——. 2002. 'From the History of Colonial Anthropology to the Anthropology of Western Hegemony', in *The Anthropology of Politics*, ed. Joan Vincent (Malden, MA: Blackwell), 133–42.

——. 2003. *Formations of the Secular: Christianity, Islam, Modernity* (Palo Alto, CA: Stanford University Press).

Atwood, M. 1972. *Survival: A Thematic Guide to Canadian Literature* (Toronto: House of Anansi Press Ltd).

Bailey, A.G. 1969 [1937]. *The Conflict of European and Eastern Algonquian Cultures, 1504–1700*, 2nd edn (Toronto: University of Toronto Press).

Bailey, Mark S., and H. Janaka de Silva. 2006. 'Sri Lankan *Sanni* Masks: An Ancient Classification of Disease', BMJ, 333(7582), 1327–1328. BMJ by British Medical Association. Reproduced with permission of BMJ Publishing Group in the format Journal via Copyright Clearance Center.

Bailyn, Bernard. 1986. *The Peopling of British North America: An Introduction* (New York: Knopf).

Bakhtin, Mikhail. 1981. *The Dialogical Imagination* (Austin: University of Texas Press).

Ball, M.S., and G.W.H. Smith. 1992. 'Analyzing Visual Data', *Qualitative Research Methods* series, vol. 24 (Newbury Park: Sage Publications).

Barad, Karen. 1999. 'Agential Realism: Feminist Interventions in Understanding Scientific Practices', in *The Science Studies Reader*, ed. Mario Biagioli (New York: Routlege), 1–11.

Barber, Benjamin R. 1995. *Jihad versus McWorld: How Globalism and Tribalism Are Reshaping the World*. Published originally in *The Atlantic Monthly*, March 1992, as an introduction to *Jihad vs. McWorld* (Ballantine paperback, 1996), a volume that discusses and extends the themes of the original article. (New York: Times Books).

Barrett, Stanley R., Sean Stokholm, and Jeanette Burke. 2001. 'The Idea of Power and the Power of Ideas: A Review Essay', *American Anthropologist*, New Series, 103, 2: 468–80.

Basham, Richard. 1978. *Urban Anthropology* (Palo Alto, CA: Mayfield).

Bashir, Halima. 2008. *Tears of the Desert: A Memoir of Survival in Darfur* (New York: One World).

Bateson, Gregory. 1972. 'A Theory of Play and Fantasy', in *Steps to an Ecology of Mind*, ed. Gregory Bateson (New York: Ballentine Books), 177–93.

Bauman, Zygmunt. 1989. *Modernity and the Holocaust* (Ithaca, NY: Cornell University Press).

——. 1990. 'Modernity and Ambivalence', in *Global Culture*, ed. Mike Featherstone (London: Sage), 143–69.

Baxter, P.T.W. 1978. 'Boran Age Sets and Generation Sets: *Gada*, a Puzzle or a Maze?', in *Age, Generation, and Time*, eds P.T.W. Baxter and Uri Almagor (New York: St Martin's Press), 151–82.

——, and Uri Almagor, eds. 1978. *Age, Generation, and Time* (New York: St Martin's Press).

Beals, Alan. 1962. *Gopalpur, A South Indian Village* (New York: Holt, Rinehart, & Winston).

Bell, Sandra, and Simon Coleman, eds. 1999. 'The Anthropology of Friendship: Enduring Themes and Future Possibilities', in *The Anthropology of Friendship* (Oxford: Berg), 1–19.

Bellman, Beryl. 1984. *The Language of Secrecy* (New Brunswick, NJ: Rutgers University Press).

Belmonte, Thomas. 1978. *The Broken Fountain* (New York: Columbia University Press).

Benhabib, Seyla. 2002. *The Claims of Culture: Equality and Diversity in the Global Era* (Princeton, NJ: Princeton University Press).

Benedict, Ruth. 1934. *Patterns of Culture* (New York: Houghton Mifflin).

Ben-Tovim, Gideon. 1997. 'Why "Positive Action" Is "Politically Correct"', in *The Politics of Multiculturalism in the New Europe: Racism, Identity, and Community*, eds Tariq Modood and Pnina Werbner (Cambridge: Cambridge University Press), 209–22.

Berkes, F., P. George, R. Preston, and J. Turner. 1992. 'The Cree View of Land and Resources: Indigenous Ecological Knowledge', report prepared for TASO (Technology Assessment in Subarctic Ontario), Second Series, No. 8 (Hamilton: McMaster University).

Bernhardt, B., J. Ball, and J. Deby. 2007. 'Cross-cultural Interaction and Children's Speech Acquisition', in *The International Guide to Speech Acquisition*, ed. S. McLeod (Clifton Park, NY: Delmar), available at www.ecdip.org/dialects/index.htm.

Berreman, Gerald D. 1962. *Behind Many Masks: Ethnography and Impression Management in a Himalayan Village* (Lexington, KY: Society for Applied Anthropology).

Betts, Wendy. 2008. Review in *Notes from the Windowsill*, available at www.armory.com/~web/gaybooks.html.

Bickerton, Derek. 1981. *Roots of Language* (Ann Arbor, MI: Karoma).

Bigenho, Michelle. 2002. *Sounding Indigenous: Authenticity in Bolivian Music Performance* (New York: Palgrave).

Bishop, C.A. 1970. 'The Emergence of Hunting Territories among the Northern Ojibwa', *Ethnology* XI, 1: 1–15.

——. 1973. 'Ojibwa Cannibalism', paper presented at the IX International Congress of Anthropological and Ethnological Sciences (Chicago).

——. 1981. 'Northeastern Indian Concepts of Conservation and the Fur Trade: A Critique of Calvin Martin's Thesis', in *Indians, Animals, and the Fur Trade*, ed. S. Krech III (Athens: University of Georgia Press), 39–58.

Blackwood, Evelyn, and Saskia E. Wieringa, eds. 1999. 'Preface', in *Female Desires:Same-Sex Relations and Transgender Practices across Cultures* (New York: Columbia University Press), ix–xiii.

Blanchard, Kendall, and Alyce Cheska. 1985. *The Anthropology of Sport* (South Hadley, MA: Bergin & Garvey).

Bledsoe, Caroline. 1993. 'The Politics of Polygyny in Mende Education and Child Fosterage Transactions', in *Sex and Gender Hierarchies*, ed. Barbara Diane Miller (Cambridge: Cambridge University Press), 170–92.

Boaz, Noel T., and Linda Wolfe, eds. 1995. *Biological Anthropology: The State of the Science* (Bend, OR: International Institute for Human Evolutionary Research).

Bock, Philip K., ed. 1994. *Psychological Anthropology* (Westport, CT: Praeger).

Bodenhorn, Barbara. 2000. '"He Used to Be My Relative": Exploring the Bases of Relatedness among Iñupiat of Northern Alaska', in *Cultures of Relatedness: New Approaches to the Study of Kinship*, ed. Janet Carsten (Cambridge: Cambridge University Press), 128–48.

Boesch-Achermann, H., and C. Boesch. 1994. 'Hominization in the Rain Forest: The Chimpanzee's Piece of the Puzzle', *Evolutionary Anthropology* 3, 1: 9–16.

Bohannan, Paul, and Fred Plog, eds. 1967. *Beyond the Frontier* (Garden City, NY: Natural History Press).

—— and ——. 1968. *Marriage, Family, and Residence* (New York: Natural History Press).

Borman, Randy. 1999. 'Cofan: Story of the Forest People and the Outsiders', *Cultural Survival Quarterly* 23, 2: 48–50. Cultural Survival Quarterly by Cultural Survival Inc. Copyright 1999. Reproduced with permission of Cultural Survival Inc.

Bowen, John. 2002. *Religions in Practice: An Approach to the Anthropology of Religion*, 2nd edn (Needham Heights, MA: Allyn & Bacon).

Bradburd, Daniel. 1998. *Being There: The Necessity of Fieldwork* (Washington, DC: Smithsonian Institution Press).

Brain, Robert. 1976. *Friends and Lovers* (New York: Basic Books).

Braroe, Niels. 1975. *Indian and White* (Stanford: Stanford University Press).

Breckenridge, Carol A., et al. 2002. 'Cosmopolitanisms', in *Cosmopolitanism* (Durham, NC: Duke University Press), 1–14.

Brenneis, Donald, and Ronald K.S. Macauley, eds. 1996. *The Matrix of Language* (Boulder, CO: Westview Press).

Brewin, Christopher. 1997. 'Society as a Kind of Community: Communitarian Voting with Equal Rights for Individuals in the European Union', in *The Politics of Multiculturalism in the New Europe: Racism, Identity, and Community*, eds Tariq Modood and Pnina Werbner (Cambridge: Cambridge University Press), 223–39.

Briggs, Jean. 1980. 'Kapluna Daughter: Adopted by the Eskimo', in *Conformity and Conflict: Readings in Cultural Anthropology*, 4th edn, eds J. Spradley and D. McCurdy (Glenview, IL: Scott Foresman), 44–62.

Bromberger, Christian. 1995. *Le match de football: Etnologie d'une passion partisane à Marseille, Naples et Turin* (Paris: Éditions de la maison des sciences de l'homme).

Brookes, Adam. 2001. 'China's Unwanted Girls', *BBC News* (23 Aug.), available at http://news.bbc.co.uk/2/hi/asia-pacific/1506469.stm.

Broom, Leonard, et al. 1954. 'Acculturation: An Exploratory Formulation', *American Anthropologist* 56: 973–1000.

Burch Jr, Ernest S. 1970. 'Marriage and Divorce among the North Alaskan Eskimos', in *Divorce and After*, ed. Paul Bohannan (Garden City, NY: Doubleday), 152–81.

Canadian Multiculturalism Act. 1988. Revised Statutes of Canada, 1985, c. 24 (4th Supp.), available at http://laws.justice.gc.ca/en/C-18.7/.

CAPMAS (Central Agency for Public Mobilization and Statistics Egypt). 2009. 'Violence against Women in Egypt', report prepared for the United Nations Statistical Division, available at http://unstats.un.org/unsd/demographic/meetings/vaw/docs/Paper2.pdf.

Carsten, Janet, ed. 2000. 'Introduction: Cultures of Relatedness', in *Cultures of Relatedness: New Approaches to the Study of Kinship* (Cambridge: Cambridge University Press), 1–36.

Carter, S. 1997. *Capturing Women: The Manipulation of Cultural Imagery in Canada's Prairie West* (Montreal and Kingston: McGill-Queen's University Press).

Castle, Sarah E. 1994. 'The (Re)negotiation of Illness Diagnoses and Responsibility for Child Death in Rural Mali', *Medical Anthropology Quarterly* 8, 3: 314–35.

Chance, John K. 1978. *Race and Class in Colonial Oaxaca* (Stanford: Stanford University Press).

Cheng, Cecilia. 2004. 'To Be Paranoid Is the Standard? Panic Responses to SARS Outbreak in the Hong Kong Special Administrative Region', *Asian Perspective* 28, 1: 67–98.

Cheyfitz, E. 1991. *The Poetics of Imperialism: Translation and Colonization from the Tempest to Tarzan* (New York: Oxford University Press).

Chomsky, Noam. 1957. *Syntactic Structures* (The Hague: Mouton).

——. 1965. *Aspects of the Theory of Syntax* (Cambridge, MA: MIT Press).

Chrisjohn, R., S. Young, and M. Maraun. 1997. *The Circle Game: Shadows and Substance in the Indian Residential School Experience in Canada* (Penticton: Theytus Books Limited).

Christopher, F. Scott, and Susan Sprecher. 2000. 'Sexuality in Marriage, Dating, and Other Relationships: A Decade Review', *Journal of Marriage and Family* 62, 4: 999–1017.

CIHR, NSERC, SSHRC (Canadian Institutes of Health Research, Natural Sciences and Engineering Research Council of Canada, Social Sciences and Humanities Research Council of Canada). 1998 (with 2000, 2002, and 2005 amendments). *Tri-Council Policy Statement: Ethical Conduct for Research Involving Humans.*

——. 2010. *Tri-Council Policy Statement: Ethical Conduct for Research Involving Humans*, available at www.pre.ethics.gc.ca/pdf/eng/tcps2/TCPS_2_FINAL_Web.pdf.

Clark, Gracia. 1994. *Onions Are My Husband* (Chicago: University of Chicago Press).

Clastres, Pierre. 1977. *Society against the State*, trans. Robert Hurley (New York: Urizen Books).

Cohen, I.B., ed. 1994. 'An Analysis of Interactions between the Natural and Social Sciences', *Boston Studies in the Philosophy of Science* 150 (Dordrecht: Kluwer), 1–99.

Cole, Michael. 1994. *Cultural Psychology: A Once and Future Discipline* (Cambridge, MA: Harvard University Press).

——, and Sylvia Scribner. 1974. *Culture and Thought: A Psychological Introduction* (New York: Wiley).

Collier, Jane, and Sylvia Yanagisako, eds. 1987. 'Toward a Unified Analysis of Gender and Kinship', in *Gender and Kinship: Essays Toward a Unified Analysis* (Stanford: Stanford University Press), 14–50.

Colloredo-Mansfeld, Rudi. 1999. *The Native Leisure Class: Consumption and Cultural Creativity in the Andes* (Chicago: University of Chicago Press).

Colson, Anthony C., and Karen E. Selby. 1974. 'Medical Anthropology', *Annual Review of Anthropology* 3: 245–63.

Colson, Elizabeth. 1977. 'Power at Large: Meditation on "The Symposium on Power"', in *The Anthropology of Power: Ethnographic Studies from Asia, Oceania, and the New World*, eds R. Fogelson and R.N. Adams (New York: Academic Press), 375–86.

Comaroff, John, and Jean Comaroff. 1992. *Ethnography and the Historical Imagination* (Boulder, CO: Westview Press).

Connolly, J. 2009. 'Forbidden intimacies: Christian–Muslim Intermarriage in East Kalimantan, Indonesia', *American Ethnologist* 36, 3: 492–506.

Conservation International. 2003. 'Kayapó Indigenous Territories: Preserving Ancestral Lands', *Conservation International Online*, available at www.conservation.org/xp/frontlines/2003/fall/features/parkprofiles/parkprofile5.xml.

Côté, J.E. 2000. 'The Mead–Freeman Controversy in Review', *Journal of Youth and Adolescence* 29, 5: 525–38.

Cowan, Jane. 1990. *Dance and the Body Politic in Northern Greece* (Princeton: Princeton University Press).

——, Marie-Bénédicte Dembour, and Richard A. Wilson, eds. 2001. 'Introduction', in *Culture and Rights: Anthropological Perspectives* (Cambridge: Cambridge University Press), 1–26.

Cox, Oliver Cromwell. 1948. *Caste, Class, and Race: A Study in Social Dynamics*. Garden City, NY: Doubleday.

Cox, Paul Alan, Holly E. Johnson, Gaugau Tavana. 2008. 'Giving Samoan Healers Credit for Prostratin', *Science*, New Series, 320, 5883: 1589.

Crehan, Kate. 2002. *Gramsci and Cultural Anthropology* (Berkeley: University of California Press).

Crick, Malcolm. 1976. *Explorations in Language and Meaning: Towards a Semantic Anthropology* (New York: Wiley).

Csikszentmihalyi, Mihalyi. 1981. 'Some Paradoxes in the Definition of Play', in *Play and Context*, ed. Alyce Cheska (West Point: Leisure Press), 14–25.

D'Andrade, Roy G. 1992. 'Cognitive Anthropology', in *New Directions in Psychological Anthropology*, eds Theodore Schwartz, Geoffrey M. White, and Catherine A. Lutz (Cambridge: Cambridge University Press), 47–58.

——. 1995. *The Development of Cognitive Anthropology* (Cambridge: Cambridge University Press).

Daniel, E. Valentine. 1997. 'Suffering Nation and Alienation', in *Social Suffering*, eds Arthur Kleinman, Veena Das, and Margaret Lock (Berkeley: University of California Press), 309–58.

Danner, Mark. 1994. *The Massacre at El Mozote* (New York: Vintage).

Darnell, Regna. 2001. *Invisible Genealogies: A History of Americanist Anthropology* (Lincoln: University of Nebraska Press), 16–17.

Das, Veena, and Arthur Kleinman. 2000. 'Introduction', in *Violence and Subjectivity*, eds Veena Das et al. (Berkeley: University of California Press), 1–18.

Davies, B., and R. Harré. 1990. 'Positioning: The Discursive Production of Selves', *Journal for the Theory of Social Behaviour* 20, 1: 44–63.

Davis, Shelton. 1977. *Victims of the Miracle* (Cambridge: Cambridge University Press).

Day, Chet. 2010. 'Chicken Soup: Nature's Best Cold and Flu Remedy', available at http://chetday.com/coldfluremedy.htm.

Deacon, Terrence W. 1997. *The Symbolic Species: The Co-evolution of Language and the Brain* (New York: Norton).

de Gobineau, A. 1967 [1915]. *The Inequality of Human Races*, trans. A. Collins, with Introduction by O. Levy (New York: Howard Fertig).

Dembour, Marie-Bénédicte. 2001. 'Following the Movement of a Pendulum between Universalism and Relativism', in *Culture and Rights: Anthropological Perspectives*, eds Jane Cowan, Marie-Bénédicte Dembour, and Richard A. Wilson (Cambridge: Cambridge University Press), 26–79.

de Saussure, F. 1993. *Saussure's Third Course of Lectures in General Linguistics (1910–1911): From the Notebooks of Emile Constantin*, Language and Communication Series 12, trans. R. Harris and ed. E. Komatsu (Oxford: Pergamon).

Dettwyler, Katherine A., and Claudia Fishman. 1992. 'Infant Feeding Practices and Growth', *Annual Review of Anthropology* 21: 171–204.

De Vos, George, and Hiroshi Wagatsuma. 1966. *Japan's Invisible Race* (Berkeley: University of California Press).

Dingwall, Robert. 1980. 'Anthropology in Britain', *Medical Anthropology Newsletter* 11, 2: 9–12.

Dobkin De Rios, Marlene. 1976. *The Wilderness of Mind: Sacred Plants in Cross-Cultural Perspective* (Beverley Hills, CA: Sage Publications).

Dods, Roberta Robin. 2003. 'Wondering the Wetland: Archaeology through the Lens of Myth and Metaphor in Northern Boreal Canada', *Journal of Wetland Archaeology* 3: 17–36 (Oxbow Books).

———. 2004. 'Knowing Ways/Ways of Knowing: Reconciling Science and Tradition', *World Archaeology* 36, 4: 547–57.

———. 2007. 'Pyrotechnology and Landscapes of Plenty in the Northern Boreal', in *The Archaeology of Fire: Understanding Fire as Material Culture*, eds D. Gheorghiu and G. Nash (Budapest: Archaeolingua).

Dolgin, Janet. 1995. 'Family Law and the Facts of Family', in *Naturalizing Power*, eds Sylvia Yanagisako and Carol Delaney (New York: Routledge), 47–67.

Douglas, Mary. 1966. *Purity and Danger* (London: Routledge & Kegan Paul).

———. 1970. 'Introduction', in *Witchcraft Confessions and Accusations*, ed. Mary Douglas (London: Tavistock), vi–xxxviii.

———, and Baron Isherwood. 1979. *The World of Goods: Towards an Anthropology of Consumption* (New York: Norton).

Dozier, E.P. 1960. 'The Pueblos of the Southwestern United States', *Journal of the Royal Anthropological Institute* 90: 146–60.

———. 1970. *The Pueblo Indians of North America* (New York: Holt, Rinehart, & Winston).

Dressler, William W. 2001. 'Medical Anthropology: Toward a Third Moment in Social Science?', *Medical Anthropology Quarterly* 15: 455–65.

Drewal, Margaret. 1992. *Yoruba Ritual* (Bloomington: Indiana University Press).

Driver, Harold E. 1961. *Indians of North America* (Chicago: University of Chicago Press).

Duden, B. 1991. *The Woman beneath the Skin: A Doctor's Patients in Eighteenth-Century Germany* (Cambridge, MA: Harvard University Press).

Dufour, Darna L. 1997. 'Nutrition, Activity, and Health in Children', *Annual Review of Anthropolgy* 26: 541–65.

Duranti, Alessandro. 1994. *From Grammar to Politics: Linguistic Anthropology in a Western Samoan Village* (Berkeley: University of California Press).

Eggan, F. 1950. *Social Organization of the Western Pueblos* (Chicago: University of Chicago Press).

Ehrenreich, Jeffrey David. 1996. 'Worms, Witchcraft, and Wild Incantations: The Case of the Chicken Soup Cure', *Anthropological Quarterly* 69, 3: 137–41.

Elliot, Alison. 1981. *Child Language* (Cambridge: Cambridge University Press).

Ember, Carol R., and Melvin Ember, eds. 2004. *Encyclopedia of Medical Anthropology: Health and Illness in the World's Cultures*, vols 1 and 2 (New York: Springer Science + Business Media, Inc.).

Eriksen, Thomas Hylland. 2001. 'Between Universalism and Relativism: A Critique of the UNESCO Concept of Culture', in *Culture and Rights: Anthropological Perspectives*, eds Jane Cowan, Marie-Bénédicte Dembour, and Richard A. Wilson (Cambridge: Cambridge University Press), 127–48.

Errington, Shelly. 1998. *The Death of Authentic Primitive Art and Other Tales of Progress* (Berkeley: University of California Press).

Ervin, Alexander M. 1996. 'Collaborative and Participatory Research in Urban Social Planning and Restructuring: Anthropological Experiences from a Medium-sized Canadian City', *Human Organization* 55, 3: 324–33.

Escobar, Arturo. 1992. 'Culture, Economics, and Politics in Latin American Social Movements Theory and Research', in *The Making of Social Movements in Latin America*, eds Arturo Escobar and Sonia Alvarez (Boulder, CO: Westview Press), 62–85.

Etienne, Mona. 1980. 'Women and Men, Cloth and Colonization: The Transformation of Production–Distribution Relations among the Baule (Ivory Coast)', in *Women and Colonization: Anthropological Perspectives*, eds Mona Etienne and Eleanor Leacock (New York: Praeger), 270–93.

Evans, Mike. 2004. 'Ethics, Anonymity, and Authorship in Community Centred Research, or Anonymity and the Island Cache', *Pimatisiwin: A Journal of Aboriginal and Indigenous Community Health* 2, 1: 60–75.

Evans-Pritchard, E.E. 1951. *Kinship and Marriage among the Nuer* (Oxford: Oxford University Press).

———. 1963. *Social Anthropology and Other Essays* (New York: Free Press).

——— 1976 [1937]. *Witchcraft, Oracles, and Magic among the Azande*, abr. edn (Oxford: Oxford University Press).

Fabrega, Horacio. 1971. 'Medical Anthropology', in *Biennial Review of Anthropology*, ed. J. Siegel (Stanford, CA: Stanford University Press), 167–229.

Fagen, Robert. 1981. *Animal Play Behavior* (New York: Oxford University Press).

———. 1992. 'Play, Fun, and Communication of Well-being', *Play and Culture* 5, 1: 40–58.

Farkas, Carol. 1979. *Survey of Northern Canadian Indian Dietary Patterns and Food Intake* (Waterloo: University of Waterloo).

Farmer, Paul. 2002 [1996]. 'On Suffering and Structural Violence: A View from Below', in *The Anthropology of Politics*, ed. Joan Vincent (Malden, MA: Blackwell), 424–37.

———. 2005. *Pathologies of Power: Health, Human Rights, and the New War on the Poor* (Berkeley: University of California Press).

———. 2006. *AIDS and Accusation: Haiti and the Geography of Blame*, 2nd edn (Berkeley: University of California Press).

Feinman, Gary M., Kent G. Lightfoot, and Steadman Upham. 2000. 'Political Hierarchies and Organizational Strategies in the Puebloan Southwest', *American Antiquity* 65, 3: 449–70.

Ferguson, James. 2002. 'The Anti-politics Machine', in *The Anthropology of Politics*, ed. Joan Vincent (Malden, MA: Blackwell), 399–408.

Fernandez, James W. 1977. 'The Performance of Ritual Metaphors', in *The Social Use of Metaphors*, eds J.D. Sapir and J.C. Crocker (Philadelphia: University of Pennsylvania Press).

———. 1980. 'Edification by Puzzlement', in *Explorations in African Systems of Thought*, eds Ivan Karp and Charles Bird (Bloomington: Indiana University Press), 44–69.

———. 1982. *Bwiti: An Ethnography of the Religious Imagination in Africa* (Princeton: Princeton University Press).

Fiddler, Thomas, and James R. Stevens. 1985. *Killing the Shamen* (Manotick, ON: Penumbra Press).

Finke, P. 2005. *Die Ökologie des Wissens. Exkursionen in eine gefährdete Landschaft* (*The Ecology of Knowledge*) (Freiburg and Munich: Alber).

Firth, Raymond. 1984 [1936]. *We, the Tikopia* (Stanford: Stanford University Press).

Fischer, Michael M.J. 1999. 'Emergent Forms of Life: Anthropologies of Late or Postmodernities', *Annual Review of Anthropology* 28: 455–78.

*Floating in the Air, Followed by the Wind*. 1973. Film distributed by Indiana University Instructional Support Services. Produced by Michigan State University.

Foley, Douglas. 1989. *Learning Capitalist Culture: Deep in the Heart of Tejas* (Philadelphia: University of Pennsylvania Press).

Forge, Anthony. 1967. 'The Abelam Artist', in *Social Organization: Essays Presented to Raymond Firth*, ed. Maurice Freedman (London: Cass), 65–84.

Fortes, Meyer. 1950. 'Kinship and Marriage among the Ashanti', in *African Systems of Kinship and Marriage*, eds A.R. Radcliffe-Brown and Daryll Forde (Oxford: Oxford University Press).

———. 1953. 'The Structure of Unilineal Descent Groups', *American Anthropologist* 55: 25–39.

———, and E.E. Evans-Pritchard. 1940. *African Political Systems* (Oxford: Oxford University Press for the International African Institute).

Foster, George M. 1976. 'Disease Etiologies in Non-Western Systems', *American Anthropologist* 78, 4: 773–82.

Foucault, Michel. 1991. 'Governmentality', in *The Foucault Effect: Studies in Governmentality*, eds Graham Burchell, Colin Gordon, and Peter Miller (Chicago: University of Chicago Press), 87–104.

Fouts, Roger. 1997. *Next of Kin: What Chimpanzees Have Taught Me about Who We Are* (New York: William Morrow & Company).

———. 1999. *The Fateful Hoaxing of Margaret Mead: A Historical Analysis of Her Samoan Research* (Boulder, CO: Westview Press).

Fratkin, Elliot. 1997. 'Pastoralism: Governance and Development Issues', *Annual Review of Anthropology* 26: 235–61.

Freeman, Derick. 1983. *Margaret Mead and Samoa: The Making and Unmaking of an Anthropological Myth* (Cambridge: Harvard University Press).

———. 1998. *The Fateful Hoaxing of Margaret Mead: A Historical Analysis of Her Samoan Research* (Boulder, CO: Westview Press).

Fried, Marlene Gerber. 2000. 'Abortion in the United States: Barriers to Access', *Health and Human Rights* 4, 2: 174–94.

Friedman, J. 1994. *Cultural Identity and Global Process* (London: Sage).

———. 1997. 'Global Crises, the Struggle for Cultural Identity, and Intellectual Porkbarrelling: Cosmopolitans versus Locals, Ethnics ,and Nationals in an Era of Dehegemonisation', in *Debating Cultural Hybridity: Multicultural Identities and the Politics of Anti-racism*, eds Pnina Werbner and Tariq Modood (London: Zed Books), 70–89.

Frye, N. 1971. *The Bush Garden: Essays on the Canadian Imagination* (Toronto: House of Anansi Press Ltd).

Gampel, Yoland. 2000. 'Reflections on the Prevalence of the Uncanny in Social Violence', in *Cultures under Siege: Collective Violence and Trauma*, eds Antonius C.G.M. Robben and Marcelo M. Suárez-Orozco (Cambridge: Cambridge University Press), 48–69.

Garro, Linda C. 2004. 'Overview of Culture: Ojibwa', in *Encyclopaedia of Medical Anthropology: Health and Illness in the World's Cultures*, vol. 2, eds Carol R. Ember and Melvin Ember (New York: Springer Science + Business Media, Inc.), 903–15.

Geertz, Clifford. 1973. *The Interpretation of Cultures* (New York: Basic Books).

Geertz, Hildred, and Clifford Geertz. 1975. *Kinship in Bali* (Chicago: University of Chicago Press).

Georges, Eugenia. 1990. *The Making of a Transnational Community: Migration, Development, and Cultural Change in the Dominican Republic* (New York: Columbia University Press).

Giddens, Anthony. 1979. *Central Problems in Social Theory* (Berkeley: University of California Press).

——. 1990. *The Consequences of Modernity* (Stanford: Stanford University Press).

Gilligan, Carol. 1982. *In a Different Voice* (Cambridge, MA: Harvard University Press).

Gillman, Neil. 1992. *Sacred Fragments: Recovering Theology for the Modern Jew* (New York: Jewish Publication Society).

Gilsenan, Michael. 1982. *Recognizing Islam: Religion and Society in the Modern Arab World* (New York: Pantheon).

Ginsburg, Faye D. 1998. *Contested Lives: The Abortion Debate in an American Community*, rev. edn (Berkeley: University of California Press).

——, and Rayna Rapp, eds. 1995. *Conceiving the New World Order: The Global Politics of Reproduction* (Berkeley: University of California Press).

Gledhill, John. 1994. *Power and Its Disguises* (London: Pluto Press).

Gomes, Mercio. 1996. 'Indians and Brazil: Holocaust and Survival of a Native Population', unpublished translation of *Os indios e o Brasil*, 2nd edn (Petropolis: Editora Vozes).

Goody, Jack, and S. Tambiah. 1973. *Bridewealth and Dowry* (Cambridge: Cambridge University Press).

Gordon, Colin. 1991. 'Governmental Rationality: An Introduction', in *The Foucault Effect: Studies in Governmentality*, eds Graham Burchell, Colin Gordon, and Peter Miller (Chicago: University of Chicago Press), 1–52.

Gordon, Robert. 1992. *The Bushman Myth* (Boulder, CO: Westview Press).

Gose, Peter. 1991. 'House Re-thatching in an Andean Annual Cycle: Practice, Meaning, and Contradiction', *American Ethnologist* 18, 1: 38, 57. Reproduced by permission of the American Anthropological Association. Not for sale or further reproduction.

Gottlieb, Alma. 1989. 'Witches, Kings, and the Sacrifice of Identity, or the Power of Paradox and the Paradox of Power among the Beng of Ivory Coast', in *Creativity of Power: Cosmology and Action in African Societies*, eds W. Arens and Ivan Karp (Washington, DC: Smithsonian Institution Press), 245–72.

Goulet, Jean-Guy A. 1996. The "Berdache"/"Two-Spirit": A Comparison of Anthropological and Native Constructions of Gendered Identities among the Northern Athapaskans', *Journal of the Royal Anthropological Institute* 2, 4: 683–701 (published by Royal Anthropological Institute of Great Britain and Ireland).

Gramsci, Antonio. 1971. *Selections from the Prison Notebooks*, trans. Q. Hoare and G.N. Smith (New York: International Publishers).

Green, Joyce. 2001. 'Canaries in the Mines of Citizenship: Indian Women in Canada', *Canadian Journal of Political Science* 34, 4: 736–8. *Canadian Journal of Political Science* by Canadian Political Science Association. Reproduced with permission of Cambridge University Press in the format Journal via Copyright Clearance Center.

Greenwood, David, and William Stini. 1977. *Nature, Culture, and Human History* (New York: Harper & Row).

Gregory, Richard. 1981. *Mind in Science: A History of Explanations in Psychology and Physics* (Cambridge: Cambridge University Press).

——. 1983. 'Visual Perception and Illusions: Dialogue with Richard Gregory', in *States of Mind*, ed. Jonathan Miller (New York: Pantheon), 42–64.

Guneratne, Arjun. 2002. 'Caste and State', in *South Asian Folklore: An Encyclopedia*, eds Peter Claus and Margaret Mills (New York: Garland).

Gupta, Akhil, and James Ferguson. 1997. 'Discipline and Practice: "The Field" as Site, Method, and Location in Anthropology', in *Anthropological Locations: Boundaries and Grounds of a Field Science*, eds Akhil Gupta and James Ferguson (Berkeley: University of California Press), 1–46.

Gutierrez Muñiz, Jose A., Josefina Lopez Hurtado, and Guillermo Arias Beatón. 1997. 'La educacion ambiental en el proceso docente educativo en las montañas de Cuba', available at www.monografias.com/trabajos11/eduamb/eduamb.shtml?monosearch.

Hacking, Ian. 1991. 'How Should We Do the History of Statistics?', in *The Foucault Effect: Studies in Governmentality*, eds Graham Burchell, Colin Gordon, and Peter Miller (Chicago: University of Chicago Press), 181–96.

Hale, Charles. 1997. 'Cultural Politics of Identity in Latin America', *Annual Review of Anthropology* 26: 567–90.

Hallowell, A. Irving. 1932. 'Kinship Terms and Cross-cousin Marriage of the Montagnais-Naskapi and the Cree', *American Anthropologist* 34, 2: 171–99.

——. 1960. 'Ojibwa Ontology, Behavior, and World View', in *Culture and History: Essays of Paul Radin*, ed. Stanley Diamond (New York: Columbia University Press), 19–52.

Halperin, Rhoda. 1994. *Cultural Economics: Past and Present* (Austin: University of Texas Press).

Handelman, Don. 1977. 'Play and Ritual: Complementary Frames of Metacommunication', in *It's a Funny Thing, Humour*, eds A.J. Chapman and H. Foot (London: Pergamon), 185–92.

Hanks, William. 1996. *Language and Communicative Practices* (Boulder, CO: Westview Press).

Hann, Christopher. 2002. 'All Kulturvölker Now? Social Anthropological Reflections on the German–American Tradition', in *Anthropology beyond Culture*, eds Richard Fox and Barbara J. King (Oxford: Berg), 259–76.

Hannerz, Ulf. 1996. *Transnational Connections: Culture, People, Places* (New York: Routledge).

Haraway, Donna. 1991. *Simians, Cyborgs, and Women: The Reinvention of Nature* (New York: Routledge).

Harding, Sandra. 1991. *Whose Science? Whose Knowledge?: Thinking from Women's Lives* (Ithaca, NY: Cornell University Press).

Harding, T.G. 1967. *Voyagers of the Vitiaz Strait: A Study of a New Guinea Trade System*. University of Washington Press: Seattle and London.

Harris, M. 2001 [1968]. *The Rise of Anthropological Theory: A History of Theories of Culture* (London: AltaMira Press).

Harrison, Faye. 1995. 'The Persistent Power of "Race" in the Cultural and Political Economy of Racism', *Annual Review of Anthropology* 24: 47–74.

——. 1998. 'Introduction: Expanding the Discourse on "Race"', *American Anthropologist* 100, 3: 609–31.

Hartigan Jr, John. 1997. 'Establishing the Fact of Whiteness', *American Anthropologist* 99, 3: 495–504.

Harvey, David. 1990. *The Condition of Postmodernity* (Malden, MA: Blackwell).

Hastrup, Kirsten, and Peter Elsas. 1990. 'Anthropological Advocacy: A Contradiction in Terms?', *Current Anthropology* 31, 3: 301–11.

Hayden, Robert M. 2000. 'Rape and Rape Avoidance in Ethno-National Conflicts: Sexual Violence in Liminalized States', *American Anthropologist*, New Series, 102, 1: 27–41.

Health Canada. 2010. *First Nations, Inuit, and Aboriginal Health*, available at www.hc-sc.gc.ca/fniah-spnia/diseases-maladies/aids-sida/index-eng.php.

Hedican, Edward J. 2000. *Applied Anthropology in Canada: Understanding Aboriginal Issues* (Toronto: University of Toronto Press).

Heider, Karl. 1979. *Grand Valley Dani* (New York: Holt, Rinehart, & Winston).

Herdt, Gilbert, ed. 1994. 'Mistaken Sex: Culture, Biology, and the Third Sex in New Guinea', in *Third Sex, Third Gender* (New York: Zone Books), 419–45.

Herring, D.A. 1994. '"There Were Young People and Old People and Babies Dying Every Week": The 1918–1919 Influenza Pandemic at Norway House', *Ethnohistory* 41, 1: 73–105.

Herskovits, Melville. 1973. *Cultural Relativism*, ed. Frances Herskovits (New York: Vintage).

Herzfeld, Michael. 2001. *Anthropology: Theoretical Practice in Culture and Society* (Malden, MA: Blackwell Publishers).

——. 2003. 'Competing Diversities: Ethnography in the Heart of Rome', *Plurimundi* 3, 5: 147–54.

Hess, David J. 1997. *Science Studies: An Advanced Introduction* (New York: New York University Press).

Hill, Jane, and Judith Irvine. 1992. *Responsibility and Evidence in Oral Discourse* (Cambridge: Cambridge University Press).

Hockett, C.F. 1966. 'The Problems of Universals in Language', in *Universals of Language*, ed. J.H. Greenberg (Cambridge, MA: MIT Press), 1–29.

Holm, John. 1988. *Pidgins and Creoles: Theory and Structure*, vol. 1 (Cambridge: Cambridge University Press).

Holy, Ladislav. 1996. *Anthropological Perspectives on Kinship* (London: Pluto Press).

Horton, Robin. 1982. 'Tradition and Modernity Revisited', in *Rationality and Relativism*, eds M. Hollis and Steven Lukes (Cambridge, MA: MIT Press), 201–60.

Howell, Nancy. 1988. 'Health and Safety in the Fieldwork of North American Anthropologists', *Current Anthropology* 29, 5: 780–7.

Høygaard, A. 1941. *Studies on the Nutrition and Physiopathology of Eskimos*. [Skrifter utgitt av Det Norske Videnskaps-Akademi i Oslo. I. Mat.-Naturv. Klasse 1940, No. 9.] (Oslo: I Kommisjon Hos Jacob Dybwad).

Hudson, R.A. 1980. *Sociolinguistics* (Cambridge: Cambridge University Press).

Hunter, David, and Phillip Whitten, eds. 1976. *Encyclopedia of Anthropology* (New York: Harper & Row).

Hutchinson, Sharon. 1996. *Nuer Dilemmas* (Berkeley: University of California Press).

——. 2002. 'Nuer Ethnicity Militarized', in *The Anthropology of Politics*, ed. Joan Vincent (Malden, MA: Blackwell), 39–52.

Hutnyk, John. 1997. 'Adorno at Womad: South Asian Crossovers and the Limits of Hybridity-talk', in *Debating Cultural Hybridity: Multicultural Identities and the Politics of Anti-racism*, eds Pnina Werbner and Tariq Modood (London: Zed Books), 106–36.

Huyghe, Patrick. 1988. 'Profile of an Anthropologist: No Bone Unturned', *Discover* (Dec.), 51–6.

Hymes, Dell. 1972. 'On Communicative Competence', in *Sociolinguistics: Selected Readings*, eds J.B. Pride and J. Holmes (Baltimore: Penguin), 269–93.

Ignace, Ron, George Speck, and Renee Taylor. 1993. 'Some Native Perspectives on Anthropology and Public Policy', in *Anthropology, Public Policy and Native Peoples in Canada*, eds Noel Dyck and James B. Walram (Montreal and Kingston: McGill-Queen's University Press), 166–91.

Inda, Jonathan Xavier, and Renato Rosaldo, eds. 2002. 'Introduction: A World in Motion', in *The Anthropology of Globalization* (Malden, MA: Blackwell).

Ingold, Tim. 1983. 'The Significance of Storage in Hunting Societies', *Man* 18: 553–71.

———. 2000. *The Perception of the Environment: Essays on Livelihood, Dwelling, and Skill* (London: Routledge).

Jarvenpa, Robert. 2004. 'Silot'ine: An Insurance Perspective on Northern Dene Kinship Networks in Recent History', *Journal of Anthropological Research* 60, 2: 153–78.

Jourdan, Christine. 1991. 'Pidgins and Creoles: The Blurring of Categories', *Annual Review of Anthropology* 20: 187–209.

Kahn, Susan Martha. 2000. *Reproducing Jews: A Cultural Account of Assisted Conception in Israel* (Durham, NC: Duke University Press).

Kapferer, Bruce. 1983. *A Celebration of Demons* (Bloomington: Indiana University Press).

Karp, Ivan. 1978. *Fields of Change among the Iteso of Kenya* (London: Routledge & Kegan Paul).

———. 1986. 'Laughter at Marriage: Subversion in Performance', in *The Transformation of African Marriage*, ed. David Parkin (London: International African Institute).

———, and Martha B. Kendall. 1982. 'Reflexivity in Field Work', in *Explanation in Social Science*, ed. P. Secord (Los Angeles: Sage).

Kearney, M. 1995. 'The Local and the Global: The Anthropology of Globalization and Transnationalism', *Annual Review of Anthropology* 24: 547–65.

Keesing, Roger. 1975. *Kin Groups and Social Structure*. New York: Holt, Rinehart, & Winston.

———. 1982. *Kwaio Religion* (New York: Columbia University Press).

———. 1983. *'Elota's Story* (New York: Holt, Rinehart, & Winston).

———. 1992. *Custom and Confrontation: The Kwaio Struggle for Cultural Autonomy* (Chicago: University of Chicago Press).

Keller, Evelyn Fox. 1997. 'Secrets of God, Nature, and Life', in *The Gender/Sexuality Reader*, eds Roger Lancaster and Micaela di Leonardo (New York: Routledge), 209–18.

Kelly, John D., and Martha Kaplan. 2001. *Represented Communities: Fiji and World Decolonization* (Chicago: University of Chicago Press).

Kenny, Michael G. 1999. 'A Place for Memory: The Interface between Individual and Collective History', *Comparative Studies in Society and History* 41, 3: 420–37. © 1999 Society for Comparative Studies in Society and History.

Kesterton, Michael. 2007. 'Stone Age Campaign', in 'Social Studies' column, *The Globe and Mail*, sec. L6 (18 July).

Kirby, Peter. 1985. 'Marrying Out and Loss of Status: The Charter and the New Indian Act Legislation', *Journal of Law and Social Policy* 1: 77–95.

Kleinman, Arthur. 1980. *Patients and Healers in the Context of Culture* (Berkeley: University of California Press).

Knorr Cetina, Karin. 2000. *Epistemic Cultures* (Cambridge, MA: Harvard University Press).

Köhler, G. 1978. *Global Apartheid* (New York: Institute for World Order).

Kopytoff, Igor, and Suzanne Miers, eds. 1977. 'Introduction: African "Slavery" as an Institution of Marginality', in *Slavery in Africa* (Madison: University of Wisconsin Press), 3–84.

Kroeber, Alfred L. 1939. 'Cultural and Natural Areas of Native North America', *University of California Publications in American Archaeology and Ethnology* 38: xii.

Kuhn, Thomas. 1962. *The Structure of Scientific Revolutions* (Chicago: University of Chicago Press).

———. 1970. *The Structure of Scientific Revolutions*, 2nd edn (Chicago: University of Chicago Press).

———. 1979. 'Metaphor in Science', in *Metaphor and Thought*, ed. Andrew Ortony (Cambridge: Cambridge University Press), 409–19.

Kulick, Don. 2000. 'Gay and Lesbian Language', *Annual Review of Anthropology* 29: 243–85.

Kumar, Nita. 1992. *Friends, Brothers, and Informants: Fieldwork Memoirs of Banaras* (Berkeley: University of California Press).

Kunitz, S.J. 1983. *Disease, Change, and the Role of Medicine in the Navajo Experience* (Berkeley: University of California Press).

Kuper, Adam. 1982. *Wives for Cattle: Bridewealth and Marriage in Southern Africa* (London: Routledge & Kegan Paul).

———. 1999. *Culture: The Anthropologists' Account* (Cambridge, MA: Harvard University Press).

Labov, William. 1972. *Language in the Inner City: Studies in the Black English Vernacular* (Philadelphia: University of Pennsylvania Press).

Lakoff, George, and Mark Johnson. 1980. *Metaphors We Live By* (Berkeley: University of California Press).

Lamphere, Louise. 2005. 'Replacing Heteronormative Views of Kinship and Marriage', *American Ethnologist* 32, 1: 34–6.

Lancaster, Roger. 1992. *Life Is Hard: Machismo, Danger, and the Intimacy of Power in Nicaragua* (Berkeley: University of California Press).

Langer, Lawrence L. 1997. 'The Alarmed Vision: Social Suffering and Holocaust Atrocity', in *Social Suffering*, eds Arthur Kleinman, Veena Das, and Margaret Lock (Berkeley: University of California Press), 47–65.

Laqueur, Thomas. 1990. *Making Sex* (Cambridge, MA: Harvard University Press).

Larkin, Brian. 2002. 'Indian Films and Nigerian Lovers: Media and the Creation of Parallel Modernities', in *The Anthropology of Globalization*, eds Jonathan Xavier Inda and Renato Rosaldo (Malden, MA: Blackwell), 350–78.

Latimer, Joanna. 1999. 'The Dark at the Bottom of the Stairs: Performance and Participation of Hospitalized Older People', in *Medical Anthropology Quarterly* 13, 2: 186–213.

Lave, Jean. 1988. *Cognition in Practice* (Cambridge: Cambridge University Press).

Lee, Richard B. 1992a. 'Art, Science, or Politics? The Crisis in Hunter–Gatherer Studies', *American Anthropologist* 94: 31–54.

———. 1992b. *The Dobe Ju/'hoansi*, 2nd edn (New York: Holt, Rinehart, & Winston). © 1994 Wadsworth, a part of Cengage Learning, Inc. Reproduced by permission. www.cengage.com/permissions

———. 2002. *The Dobe Ju/'hoansi*, 3rd edn (Belmont, CA: Wadsworth).

Lever, Janet. 1983. *Soccer Madness* (Chicago: University of Chicago Press).

———. 1995. *Soccer Madness*, rev. edn (Prospect Heights, IL: Waverland Press).

Levine, Nancy. 1980. 'Nyinba Polyandry and the Allocation of Paternity', *Journal of Comparative Family Studies* 11, 3: 283–8.

———. 1988. *The Dynamics of Polyandry: Kinship, Domesticity, and Population on the Tibetan Border* (Chicago: University of Chicago Press).

———, and Walter Sangree. 1980. 'Women with Many Husbands', *Journal of Comparative Family Studies* 11, 3: 283.

Levinson, S.C. 1998. 'Studying Spatial Conceptualization across Cultures', *Ethos:*

*Journal of the Society for Psychological Anthropology* 26, 1: 7–24.

Levi-Strauss, Claude. 1967 [1962]. *L'antropologie structurale* (Paris: Plon), trans. under the title *Structural Anthropology*, eds Claire Jacobson and Brooke Grundfest Schoepf (New York: Doubleday Anchor).

Lewellen, Ted. 1983. *Political Anthropology: An Introduction*. Reproduced with permission of ABC-CLIO INC. (South Hadley, MA: Bergin & Garvey).

Lewis, I.M. 1967. *A Pastoral Democracy: A Study of Pastoralism and Politics among the Northern Somali of the Horn of Africa* (London: Oxford University Press).

Lewis, Philip. 1997. 'Arenas of Ethnic Negotiations: Co-operation and Conflict in Bradford', in *The Politics of Multiculturalism in the New Europe: Racism, Identity, and Community*, eds Tariq Modood and Pnina Werbner (London: Zed Books), 126–46.

Lewontin, Richard, Steven Rose, and Leon J. Kamin. 1984. *Not in Our Genes* (New York: Pantheon).

Liebersohn, Harry. 1994. 'Discovering Indigenous Nobility: Tocqueville, Chamisso, and Romantic Travel Writing', *American Historical Review* 99, 3: 746–66.

Lincoln, Bruce. 2001. 'Revisiting "Magical Fright"', *American Ethnologist* 28, 4: 778–802.

Lindenbaum, Shirley. 2001. 'Kuru, Prions, and Human Affairs: Thinking about Epidemics', *Annual Review of Anthropology* 30: 363–85.

Link, Bruce G., and Jo C. Phelan. 2001. 'Conceptualizing Stigma', *Annual Review of Sociology* 27: 363–85.

Linke, Uli. 1997. 'Gendered Difference, Violent Imagination: Blood, Race, Nation', *American Anthropologist* 99, 3: 559–73.

Little, Kenneth. 1967. *The Mende of Sierra Leone* (London: Routledge & Kegan Paul).

Lock, Margaret. 2001. 'The Tempering of Medical Anthropology: Troubling Natural Categories', *Medical Anthropology Quarterly* 15: 478–92.

Lukács, Georg. 1971. *History and Class Consciousness: Studies in Marxist Dialectics* (Cambridge, MA: MIT Press).

Lutz, Catherine. 1988. *Unnatural Emotions: Everyday Sentiments on a Micronesian Atoll and Their Challenge to Western Theory*. Chicago: University of Chicago Press.

Lyotard, J.-F. 1987. 'The Postmodern Condition', in *After Philosophy: End or Transformation?*, eds K. Baynes, J. Bohman, and T McCarthy (Cambridge, MA: MIT Press).

McCay, Bonnie J. 1978. 'Systems Ecology, People Ecology, and the Anthropology of Fishing Communities', *Human Ecology* 6, 4: 397–422.

MacCormack, Carol P. 1980. 'Proto-social to Adult: A Sherbro Transformation', in *Nature, Culture, and Gender*, eds Carol MacCormack and Marilyn Strathern (Cambridge: Cambridge University Press), 95–118.

McElroy, Ann, and Patricia K. Townsend. 1996. *Medical Anthropology in Ecological Perspective*, 3rd edn (Boulder, CO: Westview Press). Reprinted by permission of Westview Press, a member of the Perseus Books Group.

McGregor, G. 1985. *The Wacousta Syndrome* (Toronto: University of Toronto Press).

Mackie, Gerry. 2003. 'Female Genital Cutting: A Harmless Practice?', *Medical Anthropology Quarterly*, New Series, 17, 2: 135–58.

McPherson, Naomi. 2007. 'Myth Primogeniture and Long-Distance Trade-Friends in Northwest New Britain, Papua New Guinea', *Oceania* 77, 2: 129–57.

Mafeje, A. 1976. 'The Problem of Anthropology in Historical Perspective: An Inquiry into the Growth of the Social Sciences', *Canadian Journal of African Studies* 10, 2: 307–33.

Mair, Lucy Philip. 1969. *Witchcraft* (New York: McGraw-Hill).

Malinowski, Bronislaw. 1944. *A Scientific Theory of Culture and Other Essays* (New York: Oxford University Press).

———. 1948 [1926]. *Magic, Science, and Religion, and Other Essays* (New York: Doubleday Anchor).

Malkki, Liisa. 1992. 'National Geographic: The Rooting of Peoples and the Territorialization of National Identity among Scholars and Refugees', *Cultural Anthropology* 7, 1: 24–44.

Mandler, George. 1975. *Mind and Emotion* (New York: Wiley).

———. 1983. 'The Nature of Emotion: Dialogue with George Mandler', in *States of Mind*, ed. Jonathan Miller (New York: Pantheon), 136–52.

Mann, Charles C. 2005. *1491: New Revelations of the Americas before Columbus* (New York: Random House).

Maquet, Jacques. 1970. 'Rwanda Castes', in *Social Stratification in Africa*, eds Arthur Tuden and Leonard Plotnicov (New York: Free Press).

Marcus, George. 1995. 'Ethnography in/of the World System: The Emergence of Multi-sited Ethnography', *Annual Review of Anthropology* 24: 95–117.

Marks, Jonathan. 1995. *Human Biodiversity* (New York: Aldine).

Marx, Karl. 1963. *The 18th Brumaire of Louis Bonaparte* (New York: International Publishers).

———. 1977 [1932]. 'The German Ideology', selections reprinted in *Karl Marx: Selected Writings*, ed. David McLellan (Oxford: Oxford University Press).

Mason, O.T. 1896. 'Influence of Environment upon Human Industries or Arts', in *Annual Review of the Smithsonian Institution of 1895* (Washington: Smithsonian Institution), 639–65.

———. 1902 [1985]. *A Study of Industry among Primitive Peoples* (London: Walter Scott Publishing Co.).

Matthiasson, John S. 1992. 'The Emergence of a New Political Paradigm', *Living on the Land: Change Among the Inuit of Northern Baffin Island* (Peterborough, ON: Broadview Press). Reprinted with permission of the publisher.

Mauss, Marcel. 2000 [1950]. *The Gift: The Form and Reason for Exchange in Archaic Societies* (New York: W.W. Norton).

Mead, George Herbert. 1934. *Mind, Self, and Society* (Chicago: University of Chicago Press).

Meisch, Lynn. 2002. *Andean Entrepreneurs: Otavalo Merchants and Musicians in the Global Arena* (Austin: University of Texas Press).

Melotti, Umberto. 1997. 'International Migration in Europe: Social Projects and Political Cultures', in *The Politics of Multiculturalism in the New Europe: Racism, Identity and Community*, eds Tariq Modood and Pnina Werbner (London: Zed Books), 73–92.

Menegoni, Lorenza. 1996. 'Conceptions of Tuberculosis and Therapeutic Choices in Highland Chiapas, Mexico', *Medical Anthropology Quarterly* 10: 381–401.

Merry, Sally Engle. 1992. 'Anthropology, Law, and Transnational Processes', *Annual Review of Anthropology* 21: 357–79.

———. 2001. 'Changing Rights, Changing Culture', in *Culture and Rights: Anthropological Perspectives*, eds Jane Cowan, Marie-Bénédicte Dembour, and Richard A. Wilson (Cambridge: Cambridge University Press), 31–55.

Messer, Ellen. 1993. 'Anthropology and Human Rights', *Annual Review of Anthropology* 22: 221–49.

Michelson, Truman. 1916. 'Terms of Relationship and Social Organization', *Proceedings of the National Academy of Sciences of the United States of America* 2, 5: 297–300.

Migliore, Sam. 2001. 'From Illness Narratives to Social Commentary: A Pirandellian Approach to "Nerves"', *Medical Anthropology Quarterly* 15, 1: 100–25.

Mignolo, Walter D. 2002. 'The Many Faces of Cosmopolis: Border Thinking and Critical Cosmopolitanism', in *Cosmopolitanism*, eds Carol A. Breckenridge et al. (Durham, NC: Duke University Press), 157–87.

Miller, Daniel, ed. 1995. *Acknowledging Consumption: A Review of New Studies* (New York: Routledge).

———, and Don Slater. 2000. *The Internet: An Ethnographic Approach* (Oxford: Berg).

Mills, Anthony J. 2010. 'Dakhleh Oasis Project', *Monash University Arts*, available at http://arts.monash.edu.au/archaeology/excavations/dakhleh/index.php.

Miner, Horace. 1956. 'Body Ritual among the Nacirema', *American Anthropologist* 58, 3: 503–7, available at www.msu.edu/~jdowell/miner.html.

Minturn, Leigh. 1993. *Sita's Daughters* (New York: Oxford University Press).

Mintz, Sidney W., and Christine M. Du Bois. 2002. 'The Anthropology of Food and Eating', *Annual Review of Anthropology* 31: 99–119.

Miracle, Andrew. 1991. 'Aymara Joking Behaviour', *Play and Culture* 4, 2: 144–52.

Mishra, Charudutt, Herbert H.T. Prins, and Sipke E. Van Wieren. 2003. 'Diversity, Risk Mediation, and Change in a Trans-Himalayan Agropastoral System', *Human Ecology* 31, 4: 595–609.

Mitra, Subrata. 1994. 'Caste, Democracy, and the Politics of Community Formation in India', in *Contextualizing Caste: Post-Dumontian Approaches*, eds Mary Searle-Chatterjee and Ursula Sharma (Oxford: Blackwell Publishers/The Sociological Review), 49–71.

Modood, Tariq. 1997. 'Introduction: The Politics of Multiculturalism in the New Europe', in *The Politics of Multiculturalism in the New Europe: Racism, Identity, and Community*, eds Tariq Modood and Pnina Werbner (Cambridge: Cambridge University Press), 1–25.

Moll, Luis, ed. 1990. *Vygotsky and Education* (Cambridge: Cambridge University Press).

Montgomery, Heather. 2001. 'Imposing Rights? A Case Study of Child Prostitution in Thailand', in *Culture and Rights: Anthropological Perspectives*, eds Jane Cowan, Marie-Bénédicte Dembour, and Richard A. Wilson (Cambridge: Cambridge University Press), 80–101.

Morgan, L.H. 1871. *Systems of Consanguinity and Affinity of the Human Family* (Washington: Smithsonian Institute).

———. 1877. *Ancient Society: Researches in the Lines of Human Progress from Savagery through Barbarism to Civilization* (New York: Holt).

Morgan, Marcyliena. 1995. 'Theories and Politics in African American English', *Annual Review of Anthropology* 23: 325–45.

Morris, A. 1877. *The Treaties of Canada with the Indians of Manitoba and the North-West Territories, including the Negotiations on Which They Were Based, and Other Information Relating Thereto* (Toronto: Belford, Clarke, & Co.).

Murphy, Robert, and Yolanda Murphy. 1974. *Women of the Forest* (New York: Columbia University Press).

Myerhoff, Barbara. 1974. *Peyote Hunt* (Ithaca, NY: Cornell University Press).

Naiman, R.J., J.M. Melillo, and J.E. Hobbie. 1986. 'Ecosystem Alteration of Boreal Forest Streams by Beaver (*Castor Canadensis*)', *Ecology* 67, 5: 1254–69.

Nanda, Serena. 1994. 'Hijras: An Alternative Sex and Gender Role', in *Third Sex, Third Gender*, ed. Gilbert Herdt (New York: Zone Books), 373–417.

Nash, June. 1979. *We Eat the Mines, and the Mines Eat Us* (New York: Columbia University Press).

Nguyen, Vinh-Kim, and Karine Peschard. 2003. 'Anthropology, Inequality, and Disease: A Review', *Annual Review of Anthropology* 32: 447–74.

Nordstrom, Carolyn. 1993. 'Treating the Wounds of War', *Cultural Survival Quarterly* 17: 28–30.

Odling-Smee, F.J. 1994. 'Niche Construction, Evolution, and Culture', in *Companion Encyclopedia of Anthropology: Humanity, Culture, and Social Life*, ed. Tim Ingold (London: Routledge).

O'Donnell, Guillermo, and Philippe Schmitter. 1986. *Tentative Conclusions about Uncertain Democracies* (Baltimore: Johns Hopkins University Press).

Oldham, Paul, and Miriam Anne Frank. 2008. '"We the People. . .": The United Nations Declaration on the Rights of Indigenous Peoples', *Anthropology Today* 24, 2: 5–9.

Oliver, Kelly. 2008. 'Response to Reviews of "The Colonization of Psychic Space: Toward a Psychoanalytic Social Theory"', *Symposia on Gender, Race, and Philosophy* 4, 1, available at http://web.mit.edu/sgrp/2008/no1/Oliver0108.pdf.

Omohundro, J. 2000. 'What Can You Learn from an Anthropology Major?', *Careers in Anthropology*. Used with permission of The McGraw-Hill Companies.

Ong, Aihwa. 2002 [1999]. 'The Pacific Shuttle: Family, Citizenship, and Capital Circuits', in *The Anthropology of Globalization*, eds Jonathan Xavier Inda and Renato Rosaldo (Malden, MA: Blackwell), 172–97.

Ortner, Sherry. 1973. 'On Key Symbols', *American Anthropologist* 75, 5: 1338–46.

———, ed. 1999. *The Fate of 'Culture': Geertz and Beyond* (Berkeley, CA: University of California Press).

Overholt, T.W., and J.B. Callicott. 1982. *Clothed-in-Fur and Other Tales: An Introduction to an Ojibwa World View* (Washington: University Press of America).

Oyama, Susan. 1985. *The Ontogeny of Information* (Cambridge: Cambridge University Press).

Palley, Howard A. 2006. 'Canadian Abortion Policy: National Policy and the Impact of Federalism and Political Implementation on Access to Services', *Journal of Federalism* 36, 4: 565–86.

Parkin, David. 1984. 'Mind, Body, and Emotion among the Giriama', paper presented at Humanity as Creator lecture series (St Cloud State University).

Parsons, E.C. 1939. *Pueblo Hzdian Religion*, 2 vols (Chicago: University of Chicago Press).

Partridge, William L., ed. 1984. 'Training Manual in Development Anthropology', special publication of the American Anthropological Association and the Society for Applied Anthropology 17 (Washington, DC: American Anthropological Association).

PBS. 2001. 'Sex: Unknown', *NOVA* (30 Oct.), available at www.pbs.org/wgbh/nova/transcripts/2813gender.html.

Peletz, Michael. 1995. 'Kinship Studies in Late Twentieth-century Anthropology', *Annual Review of Anthropology* 24: 343–72.

———. 2006. 'Transgenderism and Gender Pluralism in Southeast Asia since Early Modern Times', *Current Anthropology* 47, 2: 309–40.

Pelto, P.J., and G.H. Pelto. 1997. 'Studying Knowledge, Culture, and Behaviour in Applied Medical Anthropology', *Medical Anthropology Quarterly* 11, 2:147–63.

Peritz, Ingrid. 2010. 'Despite Being Legal, Abortions Still Not Accessible for All Canadians', *The Globe and Mail* (18 Jun.), available at www.theglobeandmail.com/news/national/despite-being-legal-abortions-still-not-accessible-for-all-canadians/article1610254/.

Picard, André. 2011. 'Seven Health Risks That Could Lead to Alzheimer's', *The Globe and Mail* (19 July), available at www.theglobeandmail.com/life/health/new-health/health-news/seven-health-risks-that-could-lead-to-alzheimers/article2102783/.

Pickering, Andrew. 1995. *The Mangle of Practice: Time, Agency, and Science* (Chicago: University of Chicago Press).

Pieterse, Jan Nederveen. 1995. 'Globalization as Hybridization', in *Global Modernities*, eds Mike Featherstone and Scott Lash (London: Sage).

Pike, Kenneth L. 1943. *Phonetics, a Critical Analysis of Phonetic Theory and a Technique for the Practical Description of Sounds* (Ann Arbor: University of Michigan Press).

———. 1967. *Language in Relation to a Unified Theory of the Structure of Human Behaviour* (The Hague: Mouton).

Poewe, Karla. 1989. 'On the Metonymic Structure of Religious Experiences: The Example of Charismatic Christianity', *Cultural Dynamics* 2, 4: 361–80.

Poirier, Sylvie, and Lorraine Brooke. 2000. 'Inuit Perceptions of Contaminants and Environmental Knowledge in Salluit, Nunavik', *Arctic Anthropology* 37, 2: 78–91.

Polgar, S. 'Health and Human Behavior: Areas of Interest Common to the Social and Medical Sciences', *Current Anthropology* 3, 2: 159–205.

Popper, K.R. 1979. *The Logic of Scientific Discovery* (London: Unwin Hyman).

Potts, Richard. 1996. *Humanity's Descent* (New York: Morrow).

Press, Irwin. 1978. 'Urban Folk Medicine: A Functional Overview', *American Anthropologist* 80, 1: 71–84.

Price, David. 2002. 'Past Wars, Present Dangers, Future Anthropologies', *Anthropology Today* 18, 1 (Feb.): 3–5. *Anthropology Today* by Royal Anthropological Institute of Great Britain and Ireland. Reproduced with permission of Blackwell Publishing Ltd.

Rabinow, Paul. 1977. *Reflections on Fieldwork in Morocco* (Berkeley: University of California Press).

Rainforest Foundation US. 2003. 'The Panará', *Rainforest Foundation US Online*, available at www.rainforestfoundation.org/1panara.html.

Rasmussen, Susan. 1999. 'The Slave Narrative in Life History and Myth, and Problems of Enthnographic Representation of the Tuareg Cultrual Predicament', *Ethnohistory*, 46,1: 67–108. The American Society for Ethnohistory. All rights reserved. Reprinted by permission of the publisher, Duke University Press.

Ray, A.J. 1976. 'Diffusion of Disease in the Western Interior of Canada, 1830–1950', *Geographical Review* 66, 2: 139–57.

Redfield, Robert, Ralph Linton, and Melville Herskovits. 1936. 'Memorandum for the Study of Acculturation', *American Anthropologist* 38: 149–52.

Reeves, Edward, Billie DeWalt, and Kathleen DeWalt. 1987. 'The International Sorghum/Millet Research Project', in *Anthropological Praxis*, eds Robert M. Wulff and Shirley J. Fiske (Boulder, CO: Westview Press), 72–83.

Reeves-Ellington, Richard H. 1993. 'Using Cultural Skills for Co-operative Advantage in Japan', *Human Organization* 52, 2: 203–16. *Human organization: Journal of the Society for Applied Anthropology* by Society For Applied Anthropology. Copyright 1993 Reproduced with permission of Society For Applied Anthropology via Copyright Clearance Center.

Rezende, Claudia Barcellos. 1999. 'Building Affinity through Friendship', in *The Anthropology of Friendship*, eds Sandra Bell and Simon Coleman (Oxford: Berg), 79–97.

Ribeiro, Gustavo Lins. 1998. 'Cybercultural Politics: Political Activism at a Distance in a Transnational World', in *Cultures of Politics, Politics of Cultures: Re-visioning Latin American Social Movements*, eds Sonia E. Alvarez, Evelina Dagnino, and Arturo Escobar (Boulder, CO: Westview Press), 325–52.

Rich, E.E. 1961. *The Hudson's Bay Company, 1670–1870: Vol. I, 1670–1763* (New York: Macmillan).

Richards, Audrey. 1954. *Chisungu* (London: Methuen).

Riddington, Robin. 1982. 'Technology, World View, and Adaptive Strategy in a Northern Hunting Society', *Canadian Review of Sociology and Anthropology* 19, 4: 469–81.

———. 1998. 'Coyote's Canon: Sharing Stories with Thomas King', *American Indian Quarterly* 22, 3: 343–62.

Ringrose, Kathryn M. 1994. 'Living in the Shadows: Eunuchs and Gender in Byzantium', in *Third Sex, Third Gender*, ed. Gilbert Herdt (New York: Zone Books), 85–109.

Rogers, E.S., and M.B. Black. 1976. 'Subsistence Strategy in the Fish and Hare Period, Northern Ontario: The Weagomow Ojibwa, 1880–1920', *Journal of Anthropological Research* (SWJA) 32, 1: 1–43.

Ronan, Colin A., and Joseph Needham. 1978. *Shorter Science and Civilisation in China* (Cambridge: Cambridge University Press).

Rosaldo, Renato. 2008. 'Of Headhunters and Soldiers: Separating Cultural and Ethical Relativism', *Markkula Center for Applied Ethics*, available at www.scu.edu/ethics/publications/iie/v11n1/relativism.html.

Roscoe, Will. 1994. 'How to Become a Berdache: Toward a Unified Analysis of Gender Diversity', in *Third Sex, Third Gender*, ed. Gilbert Herdt (New York: Zone Books), 329–72.

Rosen, Lawrence. 1984. *Bargaining for Reality: The Constructions of Social Relations in a Muslim Community* (Chicago: University of Chicago Press).

Ross, Kaz A. 2010. 'An "Army of Bachelors"? China's Male Population as a World Threat', *Journal of Asia Pacific Studies* 1, 2: 338–63.

Rubin, Jeffrey W. 1997. *Decentering the Regime: Ethnicity, Radicalism, and Democracy in Juchitán, Mexico* (Durham, NC: Duke University Press).

Rylko-Bauer, Barbara, and Paul Farmer. 2002. 'Managed Care or Managed Inequality? A Call for Critiques of Market-Based Medication', *Medical Anthropology Quarterly* 16, 4: 476–502.

———, Linda Whiteford, and Paul Farmer, eds. 2009. *Global Health in Times of Violence* (Santa Fe, NM: School for Advanced Research Press).

Sabloff, Jeremy A. 2008. *Archaeology Matters: Action Archaeology in the Modern World* (Walnut Creek, CA: Left Coast Press, Inc.).

Sacks, Karen. 1979. *Sisters and Wives* (Urbana: University of Illinois Press).

Sahlins, Marshall. 1972. *Stone Age Economics* (Chicago: Aldine).

———. 1976a. *The Use and Abuse of Biology* (Ann Arbor: University of Michigan Press).

———. 1976b. *Culture and Practical Reason* (Chicago: University of Chicago Press).

———. 1995. *How 'Natives' Think: About Captain Cook for Example* (Chicago: University of Chicago Press).

Salzman, Philip Carl. 2002. 'On Reflexivity', *American Anthropologist* 104, 3: 805–13.

Sanjek, Roger. 1994. 'The Enduring Inequalities of Race', in *Race*, eds Steven Gregory and Roger Sanjek (New Brunswick, NJ: Rutgers University Press), 1–17.

Sapir, Edward. 1966 [1933]. *Culture, Language, and Personality*, ed. David Mandelbaum (Berkeley: University of California Press).

Sargent, Carolyn, and Grace Bascope. 1996. 'Ways of Knowing about Birth in Three Cultures', *Medical Anthropology Quarterly* 10, 2: 213–36.

Schiffauer, Werner. 1997. 'Islam as a Civil Religion: Political Culture and the Organization of Diversity in Germany', in *The Politics of Multiculturalism in the New Europe: Racism, Identity, and Community*, eds Tariq Modood and Pnina Werbner (London: Zed Books), 147–66.

Schiller, Nina Glick, and Georges Fouron. 2002. 'Long-distance Nationalism Defined', in *The Anthropology of Politics*, ed. Joan Vincent (Malden, MA: Blackwell), 356–65.

Schlegel, Alice. 1990. 'Gender Meanings: General and Specific', in *Beyond the Second Sex: Essays in the Anthropology of Gender*, eds P. Sanday and R. Goodenough (Philadelphia: University of Pennsylvania Press), 21–42.

Schneider, David. 1968. *American Kinship: A Cultural Account* (Englewood Cliffs, NJ: Prentice-Hall).

Schultz, Emily. 1984. 'From Pagan to Pullo: Ethnic Identity Change in Northern Cameroon', *Africa* 54, 1: 46–64.

———. 1990. *Dialogue at the Margins: Whorf, Bakhtin, and Linguistic Relativity* (Madison: University of Wisconsin Press).

Schwartzman, Helen. 1978. *Transformations: The Anthropology of Children's Play* (New York: Plenum).

Schwartzman, Steven. 1998. 'Success Story in Brazil: The Return of the Panará', *The Aisling Magazine*, available at www.aislingmagazine.com/Anu/articles/TAM23/Success.html.

Scotch, Norman A. 1963. 'Medical Anthropology', *Biennial Review of Anthropology* 3: 30–68.

Scott, James C. 1985. *Weapons of the Weak* (New Haven: Yale University Press).

———. 1990. *Domination and the Arts of Resistance: Hidden Transcripts* (New Haven: Yale University Press).

Segalen, Martine. 1986. *Historical Anthropology of the Family* (Cambridge: Cambridge University Press).

Sellen, Daniel W. 2003. 'Nutritional Consequences of Wealth Differentials in East African Pastoralists: The Case of the Datoga of Northern Tanzania', *Human Ecology* 31, 4: 529–70.

Sered, Susan, and Ephraim Tabory. 1999. '"You Are a Number, Not a Human Being": Israeli Breast Cancer Patients' Experiences with the Medical Establishment', *Medical Anthropology Quarterly* 13, 2: 223–52.

Service, Elman R. 1975. *Origins of the State and Civilization: The Process of Cultural Evolution* (New York: Norton).

Sewid-Smith, Daisy. 1979. *Prosecution or Persecution* (Cape Mudge, BC: Nu-yum-baleess Society).

Shahar, Shulamith. 1990. *Childhood in the Middle Ages* (New York: Routledge).

Shahid, Shaouli, Ryan Bleam, Dawn Bessarab, and Sandra C. Thompson. 2010. '"If You Don't Believe It, It Won't Help You": Use of Bush Medicine in Treating Cancer among Aboriginal People in Western Australia', *Journal of Ethnobiological Medicine*, 6: 18.

Shand, Peter. 2000. 'Can Copyright Be Reconciled with First Nations' Interests in Visual Arts?', paper presented at Protecting Knowledge: Traditional Resource Rights in the New Millennium (University of British Columbia), available at www.ubcic.bc.ca/files/PDF/shand.pdf.

Shapiro, Robert. 2007. 'A Simpler Origin for Life', *Scientific American* 296: 46–53.

Sharma, Ursula. 1999. *Caste* (Buckingham: Open University Press).

Shepherd, Gill. 1987. 'Rank, Gender, and Homosexuality: Mombasa as a Key to Understanding Sexual Options', in *The Cultural Construction of Sexuality*, ed. Pat Caplan (London: Tavistock), 240–70.

Shetty, Priya. 2011. 'Rani and Abhay Bang—Pioneers of Health Care in Rural India', *The Lancet* 377, 9761, doi: 10.1016/S0140-6736(11)60034-2.

Shostak, Marjorie. 1981. *Nisa: The Life and Words of a !Kung Woman* (New York: Vintage Books).

Sigerist, H.E. 1943. *Civilization and Disease* (Ithaca, NY: Cornell University Press).

Silverman, Eric K. 2004. 'Anthropology and Circumcision', *Annual Review of Anthropology* 33: 419–45.

Silverstein, Michael. 1976. 'Shifters, Linguistic Categories, and Cultural Description', in *Meaning in Anthropology*, eds Keith Basso and Henry Selby (Albuquerque: University of New Mexico Press), 11–55.

———. 1985. 'The Functional Stratification of Language and Ontogenesis', in *Culture, Communication, and Cognition: Vygotskian Perspectives*, ed. James Wertsch (Cambridge: Cambridge University Press), 205–35.

Singer, Merrill. 1995. 'Beyond the Ivory Tower: Critical Praxis in Medical Anthropology', *Medical Anthropology Quarterly* 9, 1: 80–106.

Smart, Alan. 1999. 'Expressions of Interest: Friendship and *Guanzi* in Chinese Societies', in *The Anthropology of Friendship*, eds Sandra Bell and Simon Coleman (Oxford: Berg), 119–36.

Smedley, Audrey. 1993. *Race in North America: Origin and Evolution of a Worldview* (Boulder, CO: Westview Press).

———. 1998. '"Race" and the Construction of Human Identity', *American Anthropologist* 100, 3: 690–702.

Smith, Mary F. 1981 [1954]. *Baba of Karo* (New Haven: Yale University Press).

Smith, Wilfred Cantwell. 1982. *Towards a World Theology* (Philadelphia: Westminster).

Sobo, Elisa J. 2004. 'Theoretical and Applied Issues in Cross-cultural Health Research', in *Encyclopedia of Medical Anthropology*, eds Carol R. Ember and Melvin Ember (New York: Kluwer Academic/Plenum Publishers), 3–11.

Solway, Jacqueline, and Richard Lee. 1990. 'Foragers, Genuine or Spurious: Situating the Kalahari San in History', *Current Anthropology* 31: 109–46.

Sontag, Susan. 2003. *Regarding the Pain of Others* (New York: Picador).

Speck, Frank G. 1918. 'Kinship Terms and the Family Band among the Northeastern Algonkian', *American Anthropologist* 20, 2: 143–61.

Spencer, Jonathan. 2000. 'On Not Becoming a "Terrorist": Problems of Memory, Agency, and Community in the Sri Lankan Conflict', in *Violence and Subjectivity*, eds Veena Das, Arthur Kleinman, Mamphela Ramphele, and Pamela Reynolds (Berkeley: University of California Press), 120–40.

Spiro, Melford. 1977. *Kinship and Marriage in Burma: A Cultural and Psychodynamic Account* (Berkeley: University of California Press).

Stephenson, Peter H. 2001. 'Expanding Notions of Culture and Ethics in Health and Medicine to Include Marginalized Groups: A Critical Perspective', *Anthropologica* 43, 1: 3–17.

Starn, Orin. 1992. '"I Dreamed of Foxes and Hawks": Reflections on Peasant Protest, New Social Movements, and the *Rondas Campesinas* of Northern Peru', in *The Making of Social Movements in Latin America: Identity, Strategy, and Democracy*, eds Arturo Escobar and Sonia E. Alvarez, Series in Political Economy and Economic Development in Latin America (Boulder, CO: Westview Press), 89–111.

Statistics Canada. 2005a. 'Family Violence in Canada: A Statistical Profile', *The Daily* (14 July), available at www.statcan.gc.ca/daily-quotidien/050714/tdq050714-eng.htm.

———. 2005b. 'Divorces', *The Daily* (9 Mar.), available at www.statcan.gc.ca Daily/English/050309/d050309b.htm.

Steward, Julian H. 1972. *Theory of Culture Change: The Methodology of Multilinear Evolution*. (Urbana: University of Illinois Press).

Stewart, Charles, and Rosalind Shaw. 1994. *Syncretism/Anti-syncretism* (London: Routledge).

Stone, Linda. 2000. *Kinship and Gender*, 2nd edn (Boulder, CO: Westview).

Strathern, Marilyn. 1972. *Women in Between* (London: Academic Press).

———. 1992. *Reproducing the Future: Anthropology, Kinship, and the New Reproductive Technologies* (New York: Routledge).

Suárez-Orozco, Marcelo M., and Antonius C.G.M. Robben, eds. 2000. 'Interdisciplinary Perspectives on Violence and Trauma', in *Cultures under Siege: Collective Violence and Trauma* (Cambridge: Cambridge University Press), 1–41.

Sutton-Smith, Brian. 1992. 'Notes Towards a Critique of Twentieth-Century Psychological Play Theory', in *Homo ludens: Der spielende Mensch*, vol. 2, ed. Günther G. Bauer (München-Salzburg: Musikverlag Emil Katzbichler), 95–108.

Sylvain, Renée. 2002. '"Land, Water, and Truth": San Identity and Global Indigenism', *American Anthropologist* 104, 4: 1074–85.

———. 2003. 'Class, Culture, and Recognition: San Farm Workers and Indigenous Identities', *Anthropologica* 45, 1: 105–13.

———. 2005. 'Disorderly Development Globalization and the Idea of Culture in the Kalahari', *American Ethnologist* 32, 3: 354–70.

Tannen, Deborah. 1990. *You Just Don't Understand: Women and Men in Conversation* (New York: Ballantine).

Tanner, Adrian. 1979. *Bringing Home Animals: Religious Ideology and Mode of Production of the Mistassini Cree* (New York: St Martin's Press).

Tcherkézoff, Serge. 1998. 'Is Aristocracy Good for Democracy? A Contemporary Debate in Western Samoa', in *Pacific Answers to Western Hegemony: Cultural Practices of Identity Construction*, ed. Jürg Wassmann (Oxford: Berg), 417–34.

Tedlock, Barbara. 2005. *The Woman in the Shaman's Body: Reclaiming the Feminine in Religion and Medicine* (New York: Random House).

Thomas, Nicholas. 1991. *Entangled Objects* (Cambridge, MA: Harvard University Press).

———. 1996. 'Cold Fusion', *American Anthropologist* 98: 9–25.

Thomsen, C.J. 1936 [1836]. *Ledetraad til Nordisk Oldkyndighed [A Guide to Northern Antiquities]* (Copenhagen).

Tollefson, Kenneth D. 1995. 'Potlatching and Political Organization among the Northwest Coast Indians', *Ethnology* 34, 1: 53–73.

Tonkinson, Robert. 1998. 'National Identity: Australia after Mabo', in *Pacific Answers to Western Hegemony: Cultural Practices of Identity Construction*, ed. Jürg Wassmann (Oxford: Berg), 287–310.

Tooker, Elisabeth. 1992. 'Lewis H. Morgan and His Contemporaries', *American Anthropologist* 94, 2: 357–75.

Trigger, B.G. 1975. 'Review of Culture and Nationality by A.G. Bailey', *American Anthropologist* 77, 3: 636–7.

———. 1981. 'Ontario People and the Epidemics of 1634–1640', in *Indians, Animals, and the Fur Trade*, ed. S. Krech III (Athens: University of Georgia Press), 21–38.

Trostle, James A., and Johannes Sommerfeld. 1996. 'Medical Anthropology and Epidemiology', *Annual Review of Anthropology* 25: 253–74.

Trouillot, Michel-Rolph. 1991. 'Anthropology and the Savage Slot: The Poetics and Politics of Otherness', in *Recapturing Anthropology*, ed. Richard Fox (Santa Fe, NM: SAR Press), 17–44.

———. 1994. 'Culture, Color and Politics in Haiti', in *Race*, eds Steven Gregory and Roger Sanjek (New Brunswick, NJ: Rutgers University Press), 149–74.

Turnbull, Colin. 1961. *The Forest People* (New York: Simon & Schuster).

Turner, Terence. 1989. 'Amazonian Indians Fight to Save Their Forest', *Anthropology Newsletter* 30, 3: 21–2.

Turner, Victor. 1969. *The Ritual Process* (Chicago: Aldine).

Tylor, E.B. 1958 [1871]. *Primitive Culture* (New York: Harper & Row).

UN (United Nations). 2007. *World Population Prospects: The 2006 Revision*, available at www.un.org/esa/population/publications/wpp2006/WPP2006_Highlights_rev.pdf.

———. 2011. *The Universal Declaration of Human Rights*, available at www.un.org/en/documents/udhr/.

Union of BC Indian Chiefs. 2008. 'First Nations Pressure Canada to Endorse the UN Declaration on the Rights of Indigenous Peoples' (12 Sept.), available at www.ubcic.bc.ca/News_Releases/UBCICNews09120801.htm. © Union of B.C. Indian Chiefs

Valentine, Bettylou. 1978. *Hustling and Other Hard Work: Life Styles in the Ghetto*. New York: Free Press.

Van Blerkom, Linda Miller. 1995. 'Clown Doctors: Shaman Healers of Western Medicine', *Medical Anthropology Quarterly*, New Series, 94, 4: 462–75. Reproduced by permission of the American Anthropological Association from *Medical Anthropology Quarterly* 9,4: 463–4, December 1995. Not for sale or further reproduction.

van den Berghe, Pierre. 1970. 'Race, Class, and Ethnicity in South Africa', in *Social Stratification in Africa*, eds Arthur Tuden and Leonard Plotnicov (New York: Free Press), 345–71.

van der Veer, Peter. 1997. '"The Enigma of Arrival": Hybridity and Authenticity in the Global Space', in *Debating Cultural Hybridity: Multicultural Identities and the Politics of Anti-racism*, eds Pnina Werbner and Tariq Modood (London: Zed Books), 90–195.

Van Esterik, Penny. 2002. 'Contemporary Trends in Infant Feeding Research', *Annual Review of Anthropology* 31: 257–78.

Van Gennep, Arnold. 1960. *The Rites of Passage* (Chicago: University of Chicago Press).

van Willigen, John. 1991. *Anthropology in Use: A Source Book on Anthropological Practice* (Boulder, CO: Westview Press).

——, and V.C. Channa. 1991. 'Law, Custom, and Crimes against Women', *Human Organization* 50, 4: 369–77.

Vecsey, Christopher. 1987. 'Grassy Narrows Reserve: Mercury Pollution, Social Disruption, and Natural Resources: A Question of Autonomy', *American Indian Quarterly* 11, 4: 287–314.

VeneKlasen, Lisa, and Valerie Miller. 2002. *A New Weave of Power, People, & Politics: The Action Guide for Advocacy and Citizen Participation* (Oklahoma: World Neighbors), available at www.justassociates.org/ActionGuide.htm.

Vincent, Joan, ed. 2002. 'Introduction', in *The Anthropology of Politics* (Malden, MA: Blackwell), 1–13.

Vogel, Susan M. 1997. *Baule: African Art, Western Eyes* (New Haven: Yale University Press). © Susan M. Vogel.

Voloshinov, V.N. 1986 [1929]. *Marxism and the Philosophy of Language*, trans. Ladislav Matejka and I.R. Titunik (Cambridge, MA: Harvard University Press).

——. 1987 [1926]. 'Discourse in Life and Discourse in Art', in *Freudianism*, trans. and ed. I.R. Titunik in collaboration with Neil H. Bruss (Bloomington: Indiana University Press), 93–116.

Von Maltzahn, K.E. 1994. *Nature as Landscape: Dwelling and Understanding* (Montreal and Kingston: McGill-Queen's University Press).

Vonnegut Jr, Kurt. 1976. *Slapstick, or Lonesome No More!* (New York: Dell Publishing).

Vygotsky, Lev. 1978. *Mind in Society: The Development of Higher Psychological Processes* (Cambridge, MA: Harvard University Press).

Walker, Marilyn. 2003. 'Music as Knowledge in Shamanism and Other Healing Traditions of Siberia', *Arctic Anthropology* 40, 2: 40–8.

Wallace, A.F.C. 1966. *Religion: An Anthropological View* (New York: Random House).

——. 1972. *The Death and Rebirth of the Seneca* (New York: Vintage).

Wallerstein, Immanuel. 1974. *The Modern World System* (New York: Academic Press).

Wardlow, Holly. 2007. 'Men's Extramarital Sexuality in Rural Papua New Guinea', *American Journal of Public Health* 97, 6: 1006–14.

Warner, W. Lloyd. 1936. 'American Caste and Class', *American Sociological Review* 42, 2: 234–7.

Waubageshig, ed. 1970. *The Only Good Indian: Essays by Canadian Indians* (Toronto: New Press).

Weiner, Annette. 1976. *Women of Value, Men of Renown* (Austin: University of Texas Press).

——. 1980. 'Stability in Banana Leaves: Colonization and Women in Kiriwina, Trobriand Islands', in *Women and Colonization: Anthropological Perspectives*, eds Mona Etienne and Eleanor Leacock (New York: Praeger), 270–93.

——. 1988. *The Trobrianders of Papua New Guinea* (New York: Holt, Rinehart, & Winston).

Weinker, Curtis. 1995. 'Biological Anthropology: The Current State of the Discipline', in *Biological Anthropology: The State of the Science*, eds Noel T. Boaz and Linda Wolfe (Bend, OR: International Institute for Human Evolutionary Research).

Werbner, Pnina. 1997. 'Afterword: Writing Multiculturalism and Politics in the New Europe', in *The Politics of Multiculturalism in the New Europe: Racism, Identity, and Community*, eds Tariq Modood and Pnina Werbner (London: Zed Books), 261–7.

Weston, Kath. 1991. *Families We Choose* (New York: Columbia University Press).

——. 1995. 'Forever Is a Long Time: Romancing the Real in Gay Kinship Ideologies', in *Naturalizing Power*, eds Sylvia Yanagisako and Carol Delaney (New York: Routledge), 87–110.

Whiteford, Linda. 2009. 'Failure to Protect, Failure to Provide: Refugee Reproduction Rights', in *Global Health in Times of Violence*, eds Barbara Rylko-Bauer, Linda Whiteford, and Paul Farmer (Santa Fe, NM: School for Advanced Research Press), 89–112.

WHO (World Health Organization). 2003. 'Summary Table of SARS Cases by Country, 1 November 2002–7 August 2003', available at www.who.int/csr/sars/country/2003_08_15/en/index.html.

——. 2010. 'Malaria', available at www.who.int/mediacentre/factsheets/fs094/en/.

Whorf, Benjamin. 1956. *Language, Thought, and Reality*, ed. John B. Carroll (Cambridge, MA: MIT Press).

Wilk, Richard. 1996. *Economies and Cultures* (Boulder, CO: Westview Press).

Williams, Brackette. 1989. 'A Class Act: Anthropology and the Race to Nation across Ethnic Terrain', *Annual Review of Anthropology* 18: 401–44.

Wilmsen, Edwin. 1989. *Land Filled with Flies: A Political Economy of the Kalahari* (Chicago: University of Chicago Press).

——. 1991. 'Pastoro-foragers to "Bushmen": Transformation in Kalahari Relations of Property, Production, and Labor', in *Herders, Warriors, and Traders: Pastoralism in Africa*, eds John G. Galaty and Pierre Bonte (Boulder, CO: Westview Press), 248–63.

Wilson, Monica. 1951. 'Witch Beliefs and Social Structure', *American Journal of Sociology* LVI, 4: 307–13. (Oxford: Oxford University Press).

Winn, Peter. 1992. *Americas* (New York: Pantheon).

Wissler, C. 1914. 'Material Cultures of the North American Indians', *American Anthropologist* 16: 447–505.

Witherspoon, Gary. 1975. *Navajo Kinship and Marriage* (Chicago: University of Chicago Press).

Wolcott, Harry F. 1999. *Ethnography: A Way of Seeing* (Walnut Creek, CA: AltaMira Press).

Wolf, Eric. 1969. *Peasant Wars of the Twentieth Century* (New York: Harper & Row).

——. 1982. *Europe and the People without History* (Berkeley: University of California Press).

——. 1994. 'Facing Power: Old Insights, New Questions', in *Assessing Cultural Anthropology*, ed. Robert Borofsky (New York: McGraw-Hill), 218–28.

——. 1999. *Envisioning Power: Ideologies of Dominance and Crisis* (Berkeley: University of California Press).

Wolfe, Linda. 1995. 'Current Research in Field Primatology', in *Biological Anthropology: The State of the Science*, eds Noel T. Boaz and Linda Wolfe (Bend, OR: International Institute for Human Evolutionary Research), 149–67.

Woolard, Kathryn A. 1998. 'Introduction: Language Ideology as a Field of Inquiry', in *Language Ideologies: Practice and Theory*, eds Bambi Schieffelin, Kathryn Woolard, and Paul V. Kroskrity (New York: Oxford University Press), 3–47.

Woost, M.D. 1993. 'Nationalizing the Local Past in Sri Lanka: Histories of Nation and Development in a Sinhalese Village', *American Ethnologist* 20, 3: 502–21.

Yengoyan, A. 1986. 'Theory in Anthropology: The Demise of the Concept of Culture', *Comparative Studies in Society and History* 28, 2: 368–74.

Young, Allan. 1976. 'Some Implications of Medical Beliefs and Practices for Social Anthropology', *American Anthropologist* 78, 1: 5–24.

——. 1986. 'Internalizing and Externalizing Medical Belief Systems: An Ethiopian Example', in *Concepts of Health, Illness, and Disease*, eds Caroline Currer and Meg Stacey (Oxford: Berg), 139–60.

Young, Meredith E., Geoffrey R. Norman, and Karin R. Humphreys. 2008. 'The Role of Medical Language in Changing Public Perception of Illness', *PLoS One*, doi: 10.1371/journal.pone.0003875.

Yuval-Davis, Nira. 1997. 'Ethnicity, Gender Relations, and Multiculturalism', in *Debating Cultural Hybridity: Multicultural Identities and the Politics of Anti-racism*, eds Pnina Werbner and Tariq Modood (London: Zed Books), 193–208.

Zhou, Yingying. 2005. 'Uncovering Children in Marginalization: Explaining Unregistered Children in China', paper prepared for the International Union for the Scientific Study of Population's General Conference (Tours, France), available at http://iussp2005.princeton.edu/download.aspx?submissionId=50479.

# CREDITS

Page 1: The Canadian Press/Bayne Stanley; page 2: © Matthieu Paley/Corbis; page 4: Library and Archives Canada, 'Sometimes A Great Nation: A Photo Album of Canada 1850–1925', by Edward Cavell. Plate 72, NPC-024. PA-024499; page 6: © Remi Benali/Corbis; page 9: © EdStock/iStockphoto.com; page 10: Picture taken by Rick Goulden, 1981; page 13: National Anthropological Archives, Smithsonian Institution, OPPS NEG MNH 8298; page 14: Danox /Dreamstime.com; page 20: © US Holocaust Memorial Museum, USHMM 14337 (The views or opinions expressed in this book, and the context in which the images are used, do not necessarily reflect the views or policy of, nor imply approval or endorsement by, the United States Holocaust Memorial Museum.); page 22: CP Photo/STREVT; page 23: CP Photo/Tom Hanson; page 27: Photo by James L. Stanfield/National Geographic/Getty Images; page 28: © Gary Cook /Alamy; page 32 (right): © Naomi McPherson; page 37: © Jack Fields/Corbis; page 40: (top) © Jeremy Edwards/iStockphoto.com, (bottom) Davewebbphoto /Dreamstime.com; page 45: © John Woodworth/iStockphoto.com; page 46: © Karel Gallas/iStockphoto.com; page 47: © Hans Martens/iStockphoto.com; page 53: Oland Magunia/AFP/Getty Images; page 54: Library and Archives Canada, PA-123653; page 55: Library and Archives Canada, PA-066645; page 56: Library and Archives Canada, Bud Glunz/National Film Board of Canada, PA-161446; page 59: © Bettmann/Corbis; page 61: Archives of Manitoba, Birtle - Indian School 1 (N10264); page 65: The Canadian Press/Fred Chartrand; page 67: © Bettmann/Corbis; page 69: © Peabody Essex Museum, Image # 21117; page 72: © Lieutenant-Governor of Zuni/Corbis; page 73: © Arjun Guneratne; page 77: © Joel Carillet/iStockphoto.com; page 78: © Gao Jing/Xinhua Press/Corbis; page 79: The Canadian Press Images/Francis Vachon; page 83: Speedo101/Dreamstime.com; page 84: © Megapress /Alamy; page 87: Canadian Press Images; page 89: Don Smetzer, TravelUSA Stock

Photos; page 92: The Canadian Press/Toronto Star-Colin McConnell; page 97: © Hugh Sitton/Corbis; page 99: The Canadian Press/Sean Kilpatrick; page 100: Valariej /Dreamstime.com; page 103: © Wendy Stone/Corbis; page 110: Lukasztymszan /Dreamstime.com; page 113: ©ImreCikajlo/iStockphoto.com;page116: © Karan Kapoor/Corbis; page 120: Gilles Peress/Magnum Photos; page 122: Library and Archives Canada, PA-001024; page 129: Cristina Mittermeier/National Geographic/Getty Images; page 131: ©Stringer/India/Reuters/Corbis;page133: CP Picture Archive/Toronto Star; page 140: © Victor Englebert; page 145: © Anthony Bannister/Gallo Images/Corbis; page 154: © Barry Lewis/In Pictures/Corbis; page 157: © Vanni Archive/Corbis; page 163: Photo by Yawar Nazir/Getty Images; page 164: Irven Devore/Anthro-Photo; page 166: Pg-images/Dreamstime.com; page 169: © Charles & Josette Lenars/Corbis; page 170: Image #411791, American Museum of Natural History, Library; page 172: © Bartosz Hadyniak/iStockphoto.com; page 177: © Wolfgang Kaehler/Corbis; page 180: © WoodyStock /Alamy; page 181: © Anthony Bannister/Gallo Images/Corbis; page 186: Sean Drakes/LatinContent/Getty Images; page 191: © fstockfoto/Dreamstime.com; page 193: (left) © Brian Brockman/iStockphoto.com, (right) © Bimarto sasri/iStockphoto.com; page 195: © Andy Clark/Reuters/Corbis; page 196: © Michelle Bigenho; page 197: Petitgolo /Dreamstime.com; page 199: © Susan Vogel; page 202: © Justin Kerr, K555; page 207: © Lawrence Karn/iStockphoto.com; page 213: Eric Lafforgue/Gamma-Rapho via Getty Images; page 214: Francois-Xavier Filteau/Library and Archives Canada/PA-173023; page 219: © George Steinmetz/Corbis; page 223: Glenbow Archives NA-504-1; page 224: © Howard Sayer /Alamy; page 226: © Keren Chernizon/Demotix/Corbis; page 229: © William Campbell/Corbis; page 234: © Imaginechina/Corbis; page 235: CP Photo/Kevin Frayer; page 236: © Philimon Bulawayo/Reuters/Corbis;

page 240: Sam Panthaky/AFP/Getty Images; page 246: Zanskar /Dreamstime.com; page 247: © Robert Churchill/iStockphoto.com; page 248: (top) I359702 / Dreamstime.com, (bottom) Cageun2005 /Dreamstime.com; page 249: Nyiragongo70 /Dreamstime.com; page 250: Reprinted from Barbara Myerhoff, Peyote Hunt. Copyright © 1974 by Cornell University. Used by permission of the publisher, Cornell University Press; page 253: Archive GetStock.com; page 257: © Daniel Lainé/Corbis; page 258: © Albrecht G. Schaefer/Corbis; page 265: National Geographic/Getty Images; page 266: Christopher Furlong/Getty Images; page 268: © Luis Galdamez/Reuters/Corbis; page 273: Snyderdf /Dreamstime.com; page 274: Courtesy Kelowna Public Archives: Photo No. TFL #160; page 277: © Str/Sri Lanka/Reuters/Corbis; page 279: Source: Statistics Canada, http://www19.statcan.gc.ca/12/12_004-eng.htm, accessed 13 Jan 2012; page 282: © Jeremy Horner/Corbis; page 284: © Chen How Sia/iStockphoto.com; page 291: Oli Scarff/Getty Images; page 293: © Alberto Pomares/iStockphoto.com; page 295: © Shawn Baldwin/Corbis; page 297: © Gideon Mendel/Corbis; page 299: © Dave G. Houser/Corbis; page 301: Schalkwijk /Art Resource, NY; page 309: © Matthew McKee/Eye Ubiquitous/Corbis; page 312: © David Gray/Reuters/Corbis; page 313: © Reuters/Corbis; page 318: zubin li/iStockphoto.com; page 320: © Rick Maiman/Sygma/Corbis; page 323: © Wendy Stone/Corbis; page 325: Cascoly /Dreamstime.com /GetStock.com; page 328: © Andy Rain/epa/Corbis; page 331: © Luke Macgregor/Reuters/Corbis; page 338: © Reuters/Corbis; page 340: © Micheline Pelletier/Sygma/Corbis; page 342: © Lynn Meisch; page 344: The Canadian Press/Waterloo Region Record-David Bebee; page 350: © Daniel Loiselle/iStockphoto.com; page 351: © Jim Sugar/Corbis; page 352: (bottom) © nadla/iStockphoto; page 355: Image Source/cpimages.com; page 359: © Nik Wheeler/Corbis; page 361: © Reuters/Corbis; page 364: © Orlando Sierra/Getty.

# INDEX

# Biology
*of* Spiders

Precolumbian gold pectoral showing five spiders, probably a fertility symbol.
Vicus culture, Peru.